MEDIEVAL WOMEN'S VISIONARY LITERATURE

Medieval Women's
VISIONARY
LITERATURE

ELIZABETH ALVILDA PETROFF

New York   Oxford
OXFORD UNIVERSITY PRESS
1986

Oxford University Press

Oxford   New York   Toronto
Delhi   Bombay   Calcutta   Madras   Karachi
Petaling Jaya   Singapore   Hong Kong   Tokyo
Nairobi   Dar es Salaam   Cape Town
Melbourne   Auckland

and associated companies in
Beirut   Berlin   Ibadan   Nicosia

Library of Congress Cataloging-in-Publication Data
Petroff, Elizabeth Alvilda
Medieval women's visionary literature.
Bibliography: p.
1. Christian literature, English—Europe—Addresses,
essays, lectures.   2. Christian biography—Europe—
Addresses, essays, lectures.   3. Women—Europe—Biography
—Addresses, essays, lectures.   4. Spiritual life—
Middle Ages, 600–1500—Addresses, essays, lectures.
I. Title.
BR53.P44   1985   270   85-13717
ISBN 0-19-503711-1
ISBN 0-19-503712-X (pbk.)

Printing (last digit): 9 8 7 6 5 4 3 2 1

Printed in the United States of America

For my father,
MERLIN O. PETROFF, Sr.

Acknowledgments

I am grateful to many people for their help in compiling this anthology, but most of all to Richard J. Pioli, who first suggested this project and then always did his best to keep me on the right track. The assistance of the Interlibrary Loan Office at the University of Massachusetts was crucial; without the efforts of Ms. Edla Holm and Ms. Ute Bargman, it would have been impossible to locate many of these texts. Ms. Karen Strickholm was my research assistant; she prepared the bibliography and volunteered many hours of typing and word processing. Dr. Joyce Vann and Ms. Karla Borecky of the university's Computing Center patiently assisted me with using Word-Star.

I would also like to thank the students in my classes on medieval women at the university and at Mt. Holyoke College for their discussions, and Professor Harold Garrett-Goodyear of the Mt. Holyoke history department, who arranged for my teaching at that institution. My friend and colleague professor Don Eric Levine gave me ready encouragement and suggestions and was a patient reader of the bibliography. Ms. Judy Pratt and Ms. Allie Wilder-Heaphy helped me develop my thoughts on women's spirituality. Ms. Chris Boucher and Ms. Linda Papirio, the secretaries of the Department of Comparative Literature, assisted me whenever I asked. Dr. Karen Greenspan graciously shared many ideas with me in our discussions on devotional literature and gave me concrete suggestions for writings to be included. Finally, my thanks to those who contributed translations for this anthology; because of their work, many texts can now be read by a new audience.

Amherst   E.P.
1985

Contents

IV. New Styles of Feminine Spirituality—The Beguine Movement: Marie d'Oignies, Christina Mirabilis, Hadewijch of Brabant, and Beatrijs of Nazareth   171

V. Beguine Spirituality and the Convent of Helfta: Mechthild of Magdeburg and St. Gertrude the Great   207

VI. Women and Spirituality in Medieval Italy: St. Clare of Assisi, St. Agnes of Assisi, St. Umiltà of Faenza, Blessed Angela of Foligno, and St. Catherine of Siena   231

VII. Women, Heresy, and Holiness in Early Fourteenth-Century France: Na Prous Boneta, Marguerite d'Oingt, and Marguerite Porete   276

VIII. Women Writers of the Late Fourteenth Century—Seeking Models: Julian of Norwich, Margery Kempe, Doña Leonor López de Córdoba, and Christine de Pizan, 299

MEDIEVAL WOMEN'S
VISIONARY LITERATURE

Introduction

The Visionary Tradition in Women's Writings: Dialogue and Autobiography

*W*OMEN WERE NOT THE ONLY writers of devotional and didactic literature, but they did write some of the best. I speculate on a number of reasons for this fact later, but perhaps the most important thing to remember in accounting for women's success in this area is that they were writing the literature they knew was needed by them and by large numbers of the faithful. That does not mean that this literature is easy to read in the twentieth century. If it is to have meaning for us, we need some preparation to be able to read it intelligently and learn from it. The purpose of this introduction is to provide that preparation. First I will explore the nature and significance of these devotional narratives by developing a few of the themes common to them and by analyzing some of the issues involved in their production. Then I will introduce the historical and social background of the writers whose works are included.

This anthology is intended to illustrate the wide variety of spiritual teachings and lifestyles recorded by and about women, as well as to suggest what they had in common. Devotional literature in the Christian tradition may be defined as literature written for the faithful and intended to develop or heighten feelings of devotion toward God or the saints. It takes for granted a basic knowledge of Christian belief and is not concerned with defining points of doctrine in a systematic way. The writers of devotional literature assumed that their readers and auditors already had some knowledge of the life of prayer as it was practiced in monasteries and convents and that they were interested in furthering their devotional practices. Moreover, devotional literature, though not specifically intended to present theological issues, is didactic in that it speaks about the proper Christian life and about the proper relationship between the individual soul and the divine.

But why should we study devotional literature written by women in the Middle Ages after all? Since most of the surviving texts written by women in the Middle Ages were devotional in intent, to ask why they should be studied is like asking why women writers in this period should be studied and also why women chose to write this kind of literature. One answer is that we study writers for what they tell us of the human condition, for what they reveal of human creativity and the uses of language; and we study women writers for the same reasons. But we are also aware that the gender of a writer shapes what a writer does or can do with language and that sex roles, along with other factors such as age, class, and occupation, affect the choices a

3

writer makes in creating a literary text. Sex roles and gender distinctions also shape an audience's response to a text, and it is likely that much of the literature written by women was also written for an audience composed primarily of women or for laypeople who, like women, were excluded from officiating in the central moments of Christian ritual.

The creation of literary texts does not just happen. Certain conditions must be met for writing to take place. As Katharina Wilson puts it,

> For medieval women as well as men, literary productivity goes hand in hand with the opportunity for education, as least a modicum of scholarly idleness, access to materials needed for her work, some financial independence, patronage in social, religious, or financial form, and (sometimes in lieu of all the above) religious or political zeal. With women writers, an added pre-requisite often entails the freedom from repeated pregnancies and childbearing. The combination of prerequisites was most likely to occur in the convents of the early and central middle ages.[1]

Thus, it is not surprising that most medieval women writers were single, whether virgins or widows, and that most of them were associated with some religious order or movement. Women who were destined to marry and bear children did not ordinarily receive a literary education: ability to read and write and access to literary texts were considered irrelevant, if not dangerous, for all but consecrated religious women until the thirteenth century.[2] From the thirteenth century on, laywomen were often taught to read and write in the vernacular languages, so that they might be more effective in running large households or more useful in the family business, but not for the sake of writing literature.[3]

Access to books and literacy, though it may create a group of readers, is not enough to create a class of writers, and there is evidence that even in convents women were not consistently encouraged to write.[4] In the face of pervasive institutional misogyny, something more is necessary—zeal, conviction, a belief that one's voice is important, a drive to communicate one's experience and ideas to others. In fact, it is this attitude that, according to Dronke, characterizes women's writings in the medieval period; the writing process is initiated more often by personal desires than literary ones.

> The women's motivation for writing at all, for instance, seems rarely to be predominantly literary: it is more often urgently serious than is common among men writers; it is a response springing from inner needs, more than from an artistic, or didactic, inclination. . . . Hence the women . . . show excellingly a quality (literary, but also "metaliterary") of immediacy: they look at themselves more concretely and more searchingly than many of the highly accomplished men writers who were their contemporaries.[5]

The drive to communicate one's experience must establish or be met by a comparable receptivity in one's audience, and for this to take place, the audience must be prepared to believe in the authority of the writer. For women writers, this clearly posed a problem. To understand why so many women writers chose to compose devotional literature, it may be helpful briefly to consider another kind of successful writing by women: secular love literature. In reading the poems of the women troubadours or the lais of Marie de France[6] we note a number of remarkable female voices, confident in expressing their ideas and fully competent in a literary language that shapes words to these ends. It is likely that this confident tone, this sense of the authority to write, was related to the current interest in the subjective experience of love expressed by the male troubadours and the male romance writers such as Chrétien de Troyes.[7] There was no intrinsic reason why women's skill in the poetic handling of the vernacular could not be as developed as that of men, for a traditional scholastic education acquired in Latin was not thought to be essential for the writing of love poetry. In those geographical areas where love lyric and romance flourished,[8] it seems that both men and women were exposed to an orally delivered (if not orally composed) literature, concerned with private emotions and addressed to an aristocratic public.[9] In this context, access to literature was provided, and once given that access, women found poetic voices to articulate their own, often quite different perceptions of the experience of love.[10]

There are analogies here with women's success in the area of devotional literature. Women in convents, even though their formal education may not have equaled that provided for male monastics, could and did write devotional literature based on their own experience: biographies of saints, treatises on the life of prayer, letters of spiritual encouragement, dramas illustrating the spiritual forces at work in a life of religious commitment. Examples of all these types are included in this anthology. But it was in the exploration of the subjective experience of divine love, however erotically experienced and expressed, that the creative energy behind women's devotional literature found its chief focus, and women especially excelled in mystical visionary literature. "It is to women that we owe some of the highest flights of mystical poetry in the Middle Ages," according to Dronke,[11] and the same could be said of women's achievements in prose. Wilson outlines some of the reasons why women's visionary literature was acceptable to the medieval world although it was not quite acceptable for women to be writers:

> Mystics considered orthodox and belonging to a monastic order, however, were respected and highly acclaimed; their gifts of prophecy and clairvoyance were generously acknowledged; and the church made abundant use of their visions. . . . [The female visionary] is depicted (and frequently describes herself) as a vessel of divine inspiration, not as a creative genius, and the scriptural injunction that God often elects the weak to confound the strong is frequently invoked to explain the phenomenon of lay and female mystical inspiration . . . the beliefs in women's mystical, prophetic, and oracular powers as well as in the female predilection for religious enthusiasm are as old as the record of human history.[12]

Women and Visions

The female visionary was celibate; her vocation—her commitment to virginity or to chaste widowhood—exempted her from the charge of female weakness or corruption, allowing her, as St. Jerome said, to become like a man.[13] Celibacy altered her status, moving her upward toward a position of potential authority.[14] Visions set the seal on that authority and for a number of reasons, the two most important being that visions gave an individual woman a voice and a belief in herself as chosen to speak and also gave her an experience of inner transformation that she felt compelled to communicate to others.[15]

Visions led women to the acquisition of power in the world while affirming their knowledge of themselves as women. Visions were a socially sanctioned activity that freed a woman from conventional female roles by identifying her as a genuine religious figure. They brought her to the attention of others, giving her a public language she could use to teach and learn. Her visions gave her the strength to grow internally and to change the world, to build convents, found hospitals, preach, attack injustice and greed, even within the church. Visions also provided her with the content for teaching although education had been denied her. She could be an exemplar for other women, and out of her own experience she could lead them to fuller self-development. Finally, visions allowed the medieval woman to be an artist, composing and refining her most profound experiences into a form that she could create and recreate for herself throughout her entire life.[16]

The texts of visions point to seven distinct stages, each dominated by a specific content and attitude: purgative, psychic, doctrinal, devotional, participatory, unitive or erotic, and cosmic ordering.[17] These stages are an inevitable outgrowth of the conditions of the religious life for women and of the kind of spiritual exercises they were given. There was a self-fulfilling element in the common medieval assumption that the natural bent of women's religious impulses was contemplative and visionary; for the environment recommended for women, a relatively closed community devoted to daily prayer, composed almost entirely of women, is exactly the environment in which religious impulses will surface in psychic phenomena and ecstatic states of consciousness.[18] In addition to the seven canonical hours of daily prayer that followed the cycle of the liturgical year, with specific prayers for special saints' days and major feasts, women (and men) were expected to perform two sorts of penitential acts: acts of contrition, such as self-flagellation, fasting, and vigils; and acts of mercy toward others, such as tending the sick and assisting the poor.[19] Mantric or repetitive prayer, consisting of countless numbers of Hail Mary's and Our Father's, was practiced daily, even by the totally illiterate.[20] Those who wished a more advanced form of spiritual exercise might be given devotional meditation and visualization exercises, which consisted of imaginings of the life of Mary and of Christ;[21] most of the visual imagery for these mental pilgrimages was provided by the pictorial cycles in the churches and by privately commissioned panel paintings. Even more immediate objects for pious meditation were life-size wooden figures of the infant Jesus, which could be held in the arms of the devout worshipper.[22]

The first stage in the visionary life, that of purgation, is the least appealing, and the descriptions of the spiritual attacks by demons during this period of penitence are nightmarish. Probably the most objective account is that given by Angela of Foligno in her *Liber de vere fidelium experientia* (*The Book of the Experience of the Truly Faithful* or *Divine Consolations*). The external violence of this first stage of the life of prayer is equaled by the violence and pain of the visionary's inner life. Her desire for true contrition expresses itself in fantasies of self-punishment, degradation, and public humiliation:

I did not blush to recite before the whole world all the sins that I ever committed. But I enjoyed imagining some way in which I could reveal those deceptions and iniquities and sins. I wanted to go through the squares and the towns naked, with fish and meat hanging about my neck, saying, "Here is that disgusting woman, full of malice and deception, the sewer of all vices and evils, . . . behold the devil in my soul and the malice of my heart. Hear how I am . . . the very daughter of pride . . . an abomination of God. For I displayed myself as a daughter of prayer, and I was a daughter of wrath and pride and devils. And I showed myself as having God in my soul and divine consolations in my cell, and I had the devil in my soul and in my cell."[23]

Images of humiliation alternate with vividly imagined attacks by Satan, who appears in various disguises, some banal, some terrifying. There is often an aggressively sexual component to these attacks, whether Satan is said to have taken the form of a snake or of a human male.[24] Or the visionary may have so internalized her feelings of guilt and shame that she actually harms herself. Thus Jacques de Vitry, in his *Life of Marie d'Oignies*, recalls:

From the horror she felt at her previous carnal pleasure, she began to afflict herself and she found no rest in spirit until, by means of extraordinary bodily chastisements, she had made up for all the pleasures she had experienced in the past. In vehemence of spirit, almost as if she were inebriated, she began to loathe her body when she compared it to the sweetness of the Paschal Lamb and, with a knife, in error she cut out a large piece of her flesh which, from embarrassment, she buried in the earth.[25]

In the second stage of visionary activity, the psychic, the visionary begins to look outside herself, becoming more concerned with the spiritual welfare of others. Her visionary activity is largely psychic and intuitive now; voices and figures tell her what she has to do; she has premonitions of the deaths and births of others; she foresees political events and their spiritual consequences; she has revelations of the spiritual states of others and how she may help them resolve their spiritual dilemmas. Delivering these messages often requires much tact and delicacy, for the mystic is privy to information people would rather she did not know, and her ability to read minds is disturbing even for those who trust her.

The life of St. Umiltà of Faenza illustrates the variety of psychic intuitions received by saintly women. She once drew aside the priest who was coming to celebrate mass, warning him not to consecrate the host until he had confessed his mortal sin; the stunned priest admitted his crime immediately. Another time she became aware that a recently admitted sister had a very serious sin on her conscience, something so frightful that she could not bring herself to put it into words. Umiltà herself went to the priest after assuring her sister that she knew the exact nature of her sin; since Umiltà had named the hidden crime, the guilty sister was then able to confess it herself and was freed from a burden she had carried for many years.[26] The *Life of Christina Mirabilis* provides similar examples and also details psychic intuitions on a larger and more public scale:

> When that unfortunate meeting at Stpes occurred in October 1213 between the duke of Brabant and his enemies where so many hundreds of men were killed, on that very day this blessed woman cried out as if in childbirth, "Alas! Alas! I see the air full of swords and blood! Hurry, sisters, hurry! Pray to the Lord! Shed tears lest from His wrath He repress His mercy!" And she said to a nun at the monastery of St. Catherine's in St. Trond, "Run, sister, quickly run to prayer! Beg the Lord for your father because he is in great danger!"[27]

An episode early in the *Life of St. Leoba* demonstrates the social significance the prophetic element in such psychic experiences might have.

> . . . she had a dream in which one night she saw a purple thread issuing from her mouth. It seemed to her that when she took hold of it with her hand and tried to draw it out there was no end to it; and as if it were coming from her very bowels, it extended little by little until it was of enormous length. When her hand was full of thread and it still issued from her mouth she rolled it round and round and made a ball of it. The labour of doing this was so tiresome that . . . she woke from her sleep and began to wonder what the meaning of the dream might be.[28]

Leoba, believing a mystery was hidden here, decided to consult an older nun who had a reputation for the "spirit of prophecy." Leoba, who was apparently diffident about confiding her experience, sent one of her disciples to report the dream as her own personal experience. The old nun saw through the ruse immediately and knew the dream was Leoba's.

> "Why do you lie to me in saying such things happened to you? These matters are no concern of yours; they apply to the beloved chosen by God." In giving this name, she referred to the virgin Leoba. "These things," she went on, "were revealed to the person whose holiness and wisdom make her a worthy recipient, because by her teaching and good example she will confer benefits on many people. The thread which came from her bowels and issued from her mouth, signifies the wise counsels that she will speak from the heart. . . . By these signs God shows that your mistress will profit many by her words and example, and the effect of them will be felt in other lands afar off whither she will go." That this interpretation of the dream was true later events were to prove.[29]

In fact, Leoba was one of the remarkable English women chosen by St. Boniface for his mission to Christianize Germany in the eighth century.

Having such insights about the spiritual welfare of others marks the visionary as a spiritual authority, and the urgency of the messages she receives provides her with the strength and confidence to act outside the stereotypes of proper female behavior. It is clear to us how these experiences were preparing women for an influential role in the lives of other Christians, but it is doubtful whether the visionaries themselves recognized this. At this point, their strongest felt need may well have been for more knowledge of Christian doctrine. The average medieval individual's knowledge of doctrine was dangerously inadequate, and women's conscious understanding of theology was often minimal. Yet women were exposed to doctrine in daily prayers, in sermons, and through the art in the churches. Those who lived in communities and had access to books directly or indirectly were able to learn more, and they probably also profited by discussions among the sisters although such discussions were not formally encouraged. All this absorption of doctrine bore fruit in the third stage of visionary activity, doctrinal visions. Even though confessors were reluctant to teach doctrine to women, they were bound to correct doctrinal errors or inconsistencies in women's visions. Doctrinal visions thus set in motion a dialogue between the visionary and her confessor. Women's doctrinal visions are not abstract theological speculation although they may comprise relatively abstract visual images, such as are found in St. Hildegard's vision of the Trinity.

> Then I saw a most splendid light, and in that light, the whole of which burnt in a most beautiful, shining colour, was the figure of a man of a sapphire colour, and that most splendid light poured over the whole of that shining fire, and the shining fire over all that splendid light, and that most splendid light and shining fire over the whole figure of the man, appearing one light in one virtue and power. And again I heard that living Light saying to me: "This is the meaning of the mysteries of God, that it may be discerned and understood discreetly what that fulness may be, which is without beginning and to which nothing is wanting, who by the most powerful strength planted all the rivers of the strong [places] . . . thou seest this most splendid Light, which is without beginning and to Whom nothing can be wanting: this means the Father, and in that figure of a man of a sapphire colour, without any spot of the imperfection of envy and iniquity, is declared the Son, born of the Father, according to the Divinity before all time, but afterwards incarnate according to the humanity, in the world, in time. The whole of which burns in a most beautiful, shining fire, which fire without a touch of any dark mortality shows the Holy Spirit, by whom the same only-begotten Son of God was conceived according to the flesh, and born in time of the Virgin, and poured forth the light of true brightness upon the world."[30]

Such visions often come in answer to a spiritual dilemma, solving that problem in the most comprehensive way possible. They are parables in visual form and are used as teaching devices by the saint or mystic in her guidance to others.

The fourth stage of visionary activity, devotional visions, arose from the meditations or directed imaginings of the life of Christ and the Virgin. Although such meditations had no doubt been practiced informally by many of the devout earlier, they were first taught formally in the thirteenth century by the Franciscan and Dominican friars, illustrated in churches and convents, and narrated in pious versions of apocryphal gospel stories.[31] To a great extent, devotional meditation was the only form of meditative exercise apart from repetitive prayer that was taught to laypeople and nuns, to tertiaries or beguines unable to read Latin. Devotional meditations based on the images in the prayers of the liturgical calendar are clearly behind the devotional visions that Marie d'Oignies shared with her biographer, Jacques de Vitry.

> Sometimes it seemed to her that for three or more days she held Him close to her so that He nestled between her breasts like a baby, and she hid Him there lest He be seen by others. Sometimes she kissed him as though He were a little child and sometimes she held Him on her lap as if He were a gentle lamb. At other times the Holy Son of the Virgin manifested Himself in the form of a dove . . . or He would walk around the church as if He were a ram with a bright star in

the middle of his forehead. . . . He manifested Himself to Marie in a form which was in keeping with the feast. Thus He showed Himself at the Nativity as though he were a baby sucking at the breasts of the Virgin Mary or crying in his cradle, and then she was drawn to Him in love just as if He had been her own baby. In this way the various feasts took on new interest according to how He manifested himself and each caused a different emotional state.[32]

It would be erroneous to assume that such meditations were not also practiced by more literate and theologically sophisticated religious women, however. At the convent in Helfta, St. Gertrude the Great practiced (and taught to others) such devotional meditations, as one of her visions on Christmas Eve reveals:

It was on that most sacred night in which the sweet dew of Divine grace fell on all the world, and the heavens dropped sweetness, that my soul, exposed like a mystic fleece in the court of the monastery, having received in meditation this celestial rain, was prepared to assist at this Divine Birth, in which a Virgin brought forth a Son, true God and Man, even as a star produces its ray. In this night, I say, my soul beheld before it suddenly a delicate Child, but just born, in whom were concealed the greatest gifts of perfection. I imagined that I received this precious deposit in my bosom with the tenderest affection. As I possessed it within me, it seemed to me that all at once I was changed into the colour of this Divine Infant, if we may be permitted to call that colour which cannot be compared to anything visible.

Then I understood the meaning contained in those sweet and ineffable words: "God will be all in all" [1 Cor. xv. 28]; and my soul, which was enriched by the presence of my Beloved, soon knew, by its transports to joy, that it possessed the presence of its Spouse.[33]

Angela of Foligno also has left us a remarkable account of this gradual movement from devotional meditation to visionary experience. At the seventh step (she distinguishes a total of twenty-six steps) of her visionary path, she began to meditate on the crucifixion. What she describes as her mental process is discursive, with little visual detail:

It was given to me to look on the cross, on which I saw Christ dead for us. But this was still a flavorless vision, although I felt great pain from it.[34]

With the next step, her understanding becomes both more personal and more immediate:

In gazing on the cross I was given a greater understanding of how the Son of God was dead for our sins. And then I recognized all my sins with the greatest grief, and I felt that I was crucifying him. But I did not understand then what a great benefit this was, nor that it had led me away from sin and from hell, and had turned me toward repentance, nor that for this he was crucified for me. But in this understanding of the cross there was given to me such a great fire that standing next to the cross I stripped myself of all my clothing, and I offered myself to him completely. And although fearfully, still I promised him to preserve perpetual chastity. . . . I could do nothing else.[35]

As she begins to identify more fully with Christ, the visions become more detailed and more visceral:

> Another time I was meditating on the great pain which Christ endured on the cross, and imagining those nails, which I had heard said drove the flesh of his hands and feet deep into the wood. I wanted to see at least that little bit of Christ's flesh that those nails forced so deeply into the wood. Then I felt such pain at that punishment of Christ that I couldn't stand on my feet. But I bent down my head and sat on the ground. And I leaned my head on my arm which I stretched out on the ground. And then Christ showed me his throat and his arms; suddenly my previous bitter sorrow was transformed in joy so great that I could not show anything of it. And it was a new joy unlike all other joys. And I neither saw nor heard nor felt anything except that.[36]

Angela's emotions and sensations spontaneously mirror Christ's experience and prepare her for participating in it. Her heart is now open to the fifth stage in the visionary life, participation in the passion of Christ, but the intensity of the pain involved makes this a very difficult next step—and the most dangerous for the sanity of the visionary. The introduction to participatory visions comes first through the exploration of female grief: the grief of the women at the foot of the cross, of Mary Magdalene when the risen Christ forbids her to touch him, of the Virgin when she loses the child Jesus in the temple. Here the visionary so fully identifies with the archetypal experience of grief that she is incapable of observing her vision or of reflecting on what she has seen until the vision is over.

Although it was a common medieval belief that, while on the cross, Christ surrendered to absolute love as well as to absolute pain, often love needed to be explored by the visionary separately from pain. All women visionaries lived through periods of intense suffering, but they did not all have periods in their lives when they had felt love. For those visionaries who had been deprived of love as children and as young women, meditation on the childhood of Christ and the visions that came from this meditation had the effect of healing the lonely visionary by making her part of the divine family. The initial stages in the visionary's exploration of human and divine love are generally mediated by Mary, and visions of the Virgin create a profound bond between the apprentice mystic and her Lady. Often this bond is visualized as a type of feudal ceremony in which the devotee takes Mary as her feudal Lord and is received into her protection as vassal. It is Mary who, as wise guardian and affectionate mother, brings together the saint and her son. She presents her child to the visionary, allowing her to cuddle and caress him, and later she is present at the mystical marriage of her son with her devoted daughter. By allowing her daughters to participate in her experience, she leads them to a mature and compassionate ability to love.

Ideally, participatory visions of love and suffering create a dialectic in which the two experiences interpenetrate. But the danger was that dualism might develop instead. Some episodes in the life of Blessed Margarita, St. Umiltà's disciple, show how visions might resolve the tendency to dualism. For a time, Margarita's chief spiritual exercise concerned devotional meditations on the infancy of Christ; her visions at this time gave her such marvelous sweetness that she was not interested in meditating on "higher things."

> Christ spoke to her, saying, "It is not a balanced thing to taste only my honey, and not the gall. If you wish perfectly to unite yourself with me, with an intent

mind you must experience those illusions, shames, flagellations, death, and torments which I bore for you."[37]

From then on, Margarita did her best to visualize all the details of the passion. After a vision of the crucifixion, when she again meditated on the infancy of Christ, she could move from it to the passion:

> Christ flooded her being with such sweetness, that she was unable to explain it to me in words, and so drunk was she with the sweetness of his nativity, that as if inebriated she made this supplication to Christ, saying, "Lord Jesus Christ, who has given me the gracious comfort of your honey-sweet infancy, flood my eyes with tears and my heart with grief, so that I may be strong enough to scrutinize the wounds of your passion . . ."[38]

Her prayer is granted by a participatory vision in which pain is inseparable from love:

> And then she was rapt in spirit before the Crucified, and looking on him, she immediately began to weep, sensing as a result of this sight extraordinary comfort and sweetnes.[39]

At this point, although her unconscious development is, of course, toward love, in her conscious development pain is the absolute toward which the visionary sees herself to be striving. All her spiritual exercises seem directed to the end of making her capable of experiencing totally the pain of the crucifixion. She desires not merely to bring her own suffering to Christ as she shares his suffering; she wants to lose herself in that pain, hoping that in this way her suffering may have some redemptive value for herself and others. This use of suffering drives a wedge between the visionary's self and the pain experienced, and the self may then surrender to the pain. Of course, a true loss of self in Christ's pain cannot be brought about by willing alone. If one has not attained true identification with Christ, the self becomes inflated with its own pain. The surrender to pain cannot become transcendent unless the visionary sees that Christ's pain is of a totally different order than normal human pain, for it is not so much physical pain, grief, or loss, as it is love and salvation.

Participatory visions reveal two distinct movements in the identification with Christ. The first is the understanding that comes about through identifying with female grief; here the visionary comes to accept her own suffering and loss as the archetype of the experience of being a woman: passive suffering. The second step is to see the suffering that links one to Christ as participation in the archetype of atonement; to see passive suffering leading onward to active, creative suffering, to suffering undergone to cure the pain of the human condition. Thus, for women visionaries, these visions of the crucifixion redefined passive suffering; the visionaries saw a new and powerful meaning in the active nature of Christ's surrender to the cross. If loss and passive suffering can be distinguished and separated as experience, then the image of Christ on the cross could (and did) provide women with the experience of a different order of suffering.

The figure of the crucified Christ is passive; he is violated by the violence of other men. I quote from Angela of Foligno again:

there appeared to me the image of the blessed God and Man crucified, as if newly taken down from the cross; his blood appeared so fresh and bright red and flowing as if it were right now pouring forth from his recent wounds. Then there also appeared in all the joints of the blessed body such a dissolution of the tendons and union of the limbs from the horrible stretching of those virgin limbs at the homicidal hands of those traitors above the suffering cross, that the nerves and junctures of the bones of that most holy body seemed all loosened from their proper harmonious union . . . but there was no break in the skin.[40]

Seeing the violence done to Christ, the saint feels it in her own body:

at this sight all my inner organs were transfixed with so much compassion that I truly seemed wholly transformed into the pain of the Crucified. And I was transfixed more profoundly, with a sharper blade, at the sight of the awful dissolution of his joints and the stretching of the limbs, from which all the nerves seemed to be slackened and undone and the bones displaced, and also transfixed at the sight of the open wounds, for in them was intimated to the soul seeing this a great secret of the passion and of the dire cruelty bringing death. The sight of the thus crucified body of the good and beloved Jesus was truly of such compassion to me that all of me, not just my inner parts but bones and joints seemed to feel fresh pain, and to provoke new lament, and I was transfixed as much in mind as in body by the sensing of terrible pain.[41]

There are two central metaphors here, dissolution and penetration; the image of penetration does not enter the vision until Angela experiences the crucifixion in her own body, for in her first sight of the crucifixion, "there was no break in the skin." In another, more abstract and clearly erotic vision, she utilizes the same metaphors to present her experience of union.

And then the eyes of her soul were opened, and she saw Love, which was coming gently towards her, and she saw its head and not the end, but only its continuation. She didn't know how to give any comparison with its color. And suddenly, when love came to her, it seemed that she saw with the eyes of her soul open, more clearly than anything could be seen with the eyes of the body; and love made toward her as if in the likeness of a sickle. This is not to say that there is to be understood any measurable similarity, for in the beginning love retracted itself, not giving its self as much as it gave her to understand and as much as she then understood him. On account of this it made her very faint, and now there is no measurable or sensible similarity, for the understanding is ineffable according to the operation of divine grace.[42]

Margery Kempe, who was no saint, although she knew enough about hagiography to model her life on the examples she had heard, tells of two similar episodes:

Thus she had a very contemplation in the sight of her soul, as if Christ had hung before her bodily eye in his manhood. And when . . . it was granted to this creature to behold so verily his precious tender body, all rent and torn with scourges, fuller of wounds than ever was a dove-cote full of holes, hanging on the cross with the crown of thorns upon his head, his beautiful hands, his tender feet nailed to the hard tree, the rivers of blood flowing out plenteously from every member, the grisly and grievous wound in his precious side shedding blood and water for her love and salvation, then she fell down and cried with a loud voice, wonderfully turning and wresting her body on every side, spreading her arms abroad as if she would have died, and could not keep herself from crying, and from these bodily movements, for the fire of love that burnt so fervently in her soul with pure pity and compassion.[43]

Later she is granted the experience of union—or as close to it as she ever comes:

Then, as she lay still in the choir, weeping and mourning for her sins, suddenly she was in a kind of sleep. And anon, she saw with her ghostly eye, our Lord's body lying before her, and his head, so she thought, close by her, with his blessed face upwards, the seemliest man that ever might be seen or thought of.

And then came one with a dagger knife to her sight, and cut that precious body all along the breast. And anon she wept wondrous sore, having more memory, pity, and compassion of the passion of our Lord Jesus Christ than she had had before. . . .

And anon, in the sight of her soul, she saw our Lord standing right up over her, so near that she thought she took his toes in her hand and felt them, and to her feeling it was as if they had been very flesh and bone.[44]

Similar experience and similar imagery govern St. Gertrude's description of the "wound of divine love." The background to the vision, as she presents it to us, is that she had requested a certain person, very probably Mechthild of Hackeborn, to pray for her before a crucifix, that she would be "pierced by the arrow of divine love" as Christ's heart was pierced. She then added her own urgent petition to that of her friend.

"I beseech Thee, by the merits and prayers of all here present, to pierce my heart with the arrow of thy love." I soon perceived that my words had reached Thy Divine Heart, both by an interior effusion of grace, and by a remarkable prodigy which Thou didst show me in the image of Thy crucifixion.

After I had received the Sacrament of life, and had retired to the place where I pray, it seemed to me that I saw a ray of light like an arrow coming forth from the wound of the right side of the crucifix, which was in an elevated place, and it continued, as it were, to advance and retire for some time, sweetly attracting my cold affections.[45]

These visions are representative, and on the basis of them I think we can say that the violence of the crucifixion becomes erotic and Christ's transfixed body becomes the body of the visionary, possessed by her divine lover. For women who were sensitive to the emotional content of traditional images of masculine and feminine, the participation in the crucifixion became enormously liberating, for the opposites of passive and active, female and male, were reconciled in this single act.

It is at this point in their visionary careers that women mystics break out of the traditional restrictions on female religious by beginning to work in the world and to write down their experiences. Through the image of Christ's passivity, the saintly women seem to discover their own activity. Often quite by accident, they find that their touch or their prayers have healed someone or that scarce food seems to multiply in their hands. Word gets around of their power, and they cannot ignore the outstretched hands of those who need healing. The movement toward a mature and compassionate love for others, the ability to heal spiritually, which brought women back into the world, is developed further through unitive visions, in which we find the fullest expression of erotic love. Hadewijch, in her account of a eucharistic vision, is very clear on this point:

> I desired to have full fruition of my Beloved, and to understand and taste him to the full ... I wished that he might content me interiorly with his Godhead, in one spirit, and that for me he should be all that he is, without withholding anything from me. For above all the gifts that I ever longed for, I chose this gift: that I should give satisfaction in all great sufferings. For that is the most perfect satisfaction: *to grow up in order to be God with God.*[46] [italics mine]

Christ first sends an eagle to her as a messenger of his coming and then appears in several forms himself.

> With that he came in the form and clothing of a Man, as he was on the day when he gave us his Body for the first time, looking like a Human Being and a Man, wonderful, and beautiful, and with glorious face, he came to me as humbly as anyone who wholly belongs to another. Then he gave himself to me in the shape of the Sacrament, in its outward form, as the custom is; and then he gave me to drink from the chalice, in form and taste, as the custom is. After that he came himself to me, took me entirely in his arms, and pressed me to him; and all my members felt his in full felicity, in accordance with the desire of my heart and my humanity. So I was outwardly satisfied and fully transported. Also then, for a short while, I had the strength to bear this; but soon, after a short time, I lost that manly beauty outwardly in the sight of his form. I saw him completely come to nought and so fade and all at once dissolve that I could no longer perceive him outside me, and I could no longer distinguish him within me. Then it was to me as if we were one without difference. ... After that I remained in a passing away in my Beloved, so that I wholly melted away in him and nothing any longer remained to me of myself; and I was changed and taken up in the spirit ...[47]

Beatrijs of Nazareth, in her *Seven Manners of Loving*, shows the kind of energy that takes over the visionary at the fifth stage or manner:

> In the fifth manner, it also sometimes happens that love is powerfully strengthened in the soul and rises violently up, as if it would break the heart with its assault and drag the soul out of itself in the exercise and the delight of love. ... When the soul is in this state, it is so strong in spirit, so open in heart to receive all things, so stronger in bodily power to do all things, more able to accomplish its works, achieving so much, that it seems to the soul itself that there is nothing which it cannot do and perform, even though in the body it were to remain idle.[48]

Although Beatrijs rarely speaks of the specific content of visions, her choice of imagery in this passage makes it clear that the experience she is describing is related to meditation on the Passion:

> it seems to the soul that the heart is wounded again and again, and that these wounds increase every day in bitter pain and in fresh intensity. It seems to the soul that the veins are bursting, the blood spilling, the marrow withering, the bones softening, the heart burning, the throat parching, so that the body in its every part feels this inward heat, and this is the fever of love . . . for what most afflicts and torments the soul is that which most heals and assuages it; what gives the soul its deepest wounds brings to it best relief.[49]

The experience of union with the divine is one for which the visionary has been yearning since the beginning of her spiritual path; in her earlier devotional visions, it was often she who was the more desirous partner, longing for a personal and erotic relationship with Christ the bridegroom and yearning equally for a tender relationship with the Virgin. In the sixth stage, unitive or erotic visions, the divine figures woo the visionary. I will give just two examples, the first from Mechthild of Magdeburg, who uses a number of dramatized voices to depict the wooing of the soul.

> *The Youth:*
> I hear a voice
> Which speaks somewhat of love.
> Many days have I wooed her
> But never heard her voice.
> Now I am moved.
> I must go to meet her.
> She it is who bears
> Grief and love together.
> In the morning, in the dew
> Is the intimate rapture
> Which first penetrates the soul.
>
> *The Five Senses, Her Waiting Maids:*
> Lady!
> Thou must adorn thyself!
>
> *The Soul:*
> Ah! Love! Whither shall I go?
>
> *The Senses:*
> We have heard a whisper,
> The Prince comes to greet thee,
> In the dew and song of the birds!
> Tarry not, Lady!

The Youth comes to greet the Soul in the woods where nightingales sing and invites her to dance.

The Soul:
I cannot dance, O Lord, unless
   Thou lead me.
If Thou wilt that I leap joyfully,
Then must Thou Thyself first
   dance and sing!
   Then will I leap for love,
From love to knowledge,
From knowledge to fruition,
From fruition to beyond all human sense.
There will I remain
And circle evermore.

The Youth:
Thy dance of praise is well done.
Now shalt thou have thy will
Of the Virgin's Son.[50]

Angela of Foligno had a similar experience, one that took place as she was walking to Assisi on a pilgrimage to the shrine of St. Francis. It is the Holy Spirit who is courting her:

> And he began to speak the following words, to challenge me to love of him. "My daughter sweet to me, my daughter my temple, my daughter my delight, love me, for you are much beloved by me, much more than you love me." And very often he called me, "Daughter and my sweet bride," adding, "I love you more than any other woman in the valley of Spoleto. Therefore, since I have entered you and rested in you, you may now enter me and rest in me. I was with the Apostles, and they saw with the eyes of the body, and they did not feel me as you feel me. . . . My beloved, my bride, love me, for your whole life, your eating and drinking and your sleeping and all your living pleases me, if you will love me." Again he said to me, "I shall do great things in you in the sight of the people, and . . . my name shall be praised in you by many people."[51]

The vision of union might take other, equally sensual forms. A vision in which the soul drinks of the blood of Christ was one that the women found to be highly significant for their spiritual growth; for the imagery points again to the profound interplay of masculine and feminine, governing and nurturing roles that was first discovered in the participatory visions of the crucifixion. Christ becomes the visionary's mother in his nurturing, life-sustaining aspect and her lover in his delight at her spiritual beauty and in his eagerness to bestow his potency on her. There are hints that the fusion of masculine and feminine roles may also be supplemented by a similar fusion of parental and child roles, so that the visionary also identifies with the Virgin Mary as parent. For instance, when Blessed Aldobrandesca of Siena experienced a series of visions on the passion, we are told this:

> While she was feeding her soul again and again with the recollection of this vision, she felt a great desire to taste the divine blood which she had seen welling up out of his right side. And while she kept her attention fixed on this and on the image of the crucified, begging for this grace from Jesus and Mary, she beheld

one drop of blood burst forth from the side of his image; gathering it up with her tongue, she felt an indescribable sweetness and deliciousness in her mouth. In memory of this benefit, she had the Virgin Mary painted, holding in her arms the body of her son which had been taken down from the cross, and applying her mouth to that wound in his side.[52]

The process of visions taught women not to sacrifice their desire but to transform it, to strengthen it by purifying it, so that finally all their most conscious desire might be directed toward union with the divine. They learned how to remain open to their desire, their yearning; through their experience of suffering on a divine scale they acquired a way of measuring and validating whatever pain there was in their unsatisfied yearning, which helped them to remain open to it. These visions of the loving encounter with the divine often are accompanied by a burst of activity in the outside world, for it is at this time that visionaries may leave their enclosures to do works of mercy, provide spiritual counseling, administer charitable foundations, and begin to write down their experiences. All these activities required determination, assertiveness, and inspiration in the face of ambivalence and hostility toward women. Beatrijs of Nazareth draws on two different types of metaphors to illustrate the connection between organized activity and the power of union with the divine. In her description of the sixth manner of loving, she first compares the soul's activity to that of a housewife:

And you may see that the soul is like a housewife who has put all her household in good order and prudently arranged it and well disposed it: she has taken good care that nothing will damage it, her provision for the future is wise, she knows exactly what she is doing, she acquires and discards, she does what is proper, she avoids mistakes, and always she knows how everything should be.[53]

To show the power of love that makes this possible, Beatrijs turns to natural images:

And like the fish, swimming in the vast sea and resting in its deeps, and like the bird, boldly mounting high in the sky, so the soul feels its spirit moving through the vastness and the depth and the unutterable richnesses of love . . . and then love makes the soul so bold that it no longers fears man nor friend, angel or saint or God himself in all that it does or abandons, in all its working or resting.[54]

At this stage of visionary activity, then, we can see a number of creative insights about the relationship between the divine and the human. Erotic or unitive visions, based as they are on meditations on the crucifixion yet leading to bridal images, are meditations on the dialectics of desire, the interplay of aggression and surrender. Both attributes were sex-typed in the medieval world, and it is obvious that the women who became spiritual leaders possessed much "masculine" aggressiveness, which they had to learn to control and direct. It is equally clear that these women did not find surrender easy, at least in the human realm, no matter how much their society valued it as the ideal feminine trait. There is a highly significant validation of the feminine that is being worked through in these visions, and it is this that accounts for the activity of women visionaries in the world. Their visions have reinterpreted the image of the male bleeding Christ in such a way that the hierarchy of male dominance is subverted; and the feminine, the all-nurturing blood, is discovered to be the origin of the efficacy of the sacrifice of Christ. In the process of discovering the femininity of Christ, the female visionary gets in touch with her own masculine activity and is provided with the inner strength to act in the world. The goal of the visionary—and the purpose of devotional literature written by her—was a continually deepening relationship with the divine, and the corollary of that was ever-deepening self-knowledge. Only from this foundation could she practice enlightened charity. Love and knowledge become one in the union with the divine.

If we properly understand this goal, we are not surprised to learn that the visionary experience does not end at the stage of unitive visions. For the medieval visionary, with her deep need for introspection, there is a final experience still to come: the vision of divine or cosmic order. And this ultimate experience presents the feminine as the operative principle in the cosmos. To be sure, the women have long had hints of the power of Mary in heaven; because of their devout meditations on the life of the Virgin, many, like Elisabeth of Schönau, had been granted detailed revelations concerning the bodily assumption of Mary into heaven and had witnessed her being crowned by her son. But now when they see that event again, they may be made aware of the absolute equality in heaven of male and female, mother and son. They see this in a much larger context, for now they see the whole of heaven, all neatly and hierarchically arranged, with two equal thrones in the most important position, and they witness the crowning of the Virgin over her triple kingdom of heaven, hell, and earth. Within this scheme, they often see the church, and they discover that there, too, the Virgin has a more central role than even they had thought. One often finds that the last recorded vision of a female mystic is of Mary, and she is seen with attributes that relate her to more ancient Great Mother divinities and that symbolize her cosmic ordering function. Such a vision may be quite remarkable in its simplicity and directness:

> She saw the Mother of God, dressed in the most glowing white linen and adorned with the most precious jewels, with a gold crown of marvelous beauty. And the Sunday after this, she saw her in a golden robe, having on her head a crown of twelve stars, with the moon beneath her feet, and a tablet in her hand, on which was written: "Daughters, be obedient to the law of the Mother."[55]

The preceding quotation records the last known vision of Aldobrandesca of Siena. But such a vision of order and reconciliation need not come at the close of one's earthly life; it might also signal a resolution to earthly difficulties, a harmonizing of the spiritual forces at work in one's life. For Christina of Markyate, this is the vision that came when she was finally freed to live a public religious life:

> She was suddenly rapt above the clouds even to heaven, where she saw the queen of heaven sitting on a throne and angels in brightness seated above her . . . as she gazed first at the angels and then at the mistress of the angels . . . she saw her countenance more clearly . . . and as she gazed upon her beauty the more fixedly and was the more filled with delight as she gazed, the queen turned to one of the angels standing by and said, "Ask Christina what she wants, because I will give her whatever she asks."
> Now Christina was standing quite close to the queen and clearly heard her speaking to the angel. And falling downwards to the ground, she saw in one flash

the whole wide world. But above all else she turned her eyes towards Roger's cell and chapel [where she had been in hiding for several years] which she saw beneath her, shining brilliantly, and she said, "I wish to have that place to dwell in."[56]

Although this typology of visionary experience is not intended to be exhaustive, it does provide us with a basic outline of the spiritual movement comprehended in women's devotional writings even when those writings are not explicitly visionary. The passages quoted in the preceding pages give us an initial sense of the originality of women's thinking about their own spiritual lives, of the intimate experience of the personal and the transpersonal expressed in their writings. But the success of medieval women in communicating their experiences should not blind us to the fact that the medieval world, especially the institutional church, was mistrustful of women who claimed spiritual authority. The difficulties that this mistrust or opposition caused for women are evident in their writings. Visions gave them authority, as we have seen; in their visions women were told that they must write, but each individual woman had to discover for herself how to write, how to express her insights within the framework of the teachings of the church and in response to the pervasive misogyny of the medieval world. The solitary pain of this endeavor is expressed in one of St. Umiltà's sermons, written while she was struggling to found a new convent on the outskirts of Florence and was meeting much criticism of her mission. She is addressing Mary and all the saints:

> The garden in which the color of the rose was predominant now is all a dark bramble. For this I went to the Virgin Mary and put myself under her standard—but now look at me, far from that path, and lost in the forest.
>
> I was planted in charity, but now I have been pulled out of that ground, and my roots are dried up, and every fruit has been made impossible for me. O unhappy me, and more than desolate! Abandoned to the waves of the sea, my grief is greater than the sea itself. If I could have the grace to lift my eyes on high, if I could see myself, my heart would leap like those waves. I think back on what I have lost, I recall with great pain that for which I was destined, and my heart shatters, thinking that I am plunged in error. I am far from my homeland, and I find myself among foreigners.[57]

Women and the Composition of Devotional Literature

Most of the women writers in this collection supported the basic beliefs of the church, for they were practicing Christians who were continually examined in their faith by their confessors. (A few of them were judged to be heretics by their contemporaries and by the institutional church, but they believed themselves to be truer Christians than those who were persecuting them.[58]) Several of these writers supported the Inquisition in the sense that they were very troubled by the existence of heresies, which they felt it was the responsibility of the church to suppress.[59] Others among them actively argued for Crusades on the grounds that fighting an external enemy would unify Christian Europe.[60] Most of them observed the church's restrictions of women's clerical functions—they did not preach on doctrinal issues, they did not celebrate Mass, and they did not give absolution.

Nevertheless, in their writings these women were very critical of church practices, quick to point out hypocrisy and crime in the clergy, sharply observant of the lack of spirituality in religious leaders, and indignant at the wealth of the church. They challenged very deeply the ideology concerning gender, and if they did not preach on doctrine, they certainly taught and gave sermons, often to large crowds (St. Umiltà, St. Hildegarde, St. Catherine of Siena).[61] Though they did not officiate at Mass nor give absolution, they did have visions of Mary bringing the chalice to communicants, and they listened to confessions.[62] As spiritual leaders, they offered an alternative to the corrupt clergy they saw all about them. In actuality, they were thinkers on the cutting edge of new developments in the church; even the most contemplative women were often active reformers in their own communities. In their meditations and visions, they were regularly developing new values for the feminine, for Christ, for human experience, and in their writings they developed new uses of language to speak of all this.[63]

Two points should be stressed here. First, if we read carefully what these writings have to say about the spiritual life, we come away with a very different understanding of the Middle Ages, one in which creative fulfillment through writing might be found in the religious as well as the secular world and one in which women were the active agents in the transformation of their society.[64] Second, if we read these texts with an eye to how they were produced, we can gain new insights about the creation of literary texts at the historical moment when oral composition is being replaced by written literature.[65] If we look at the languages in which these works were originally written,[66] we can learn about the relationship between Latin culture and early vernacular literature.

The literary significance of these texts may be approached by examining a number of factors that make them unusual in medieval literature: (1) the impulse toward autobiography, with the dominance of dialogue as a rhetorical strategy in presenting the self; (2) the method of composition, which combines oral composition with techniques of visual memory and writing, often involving two languages or a bilingual author; and (3) the attitude toward writing revealed by the author whether she is dictating an orally composed narrative or writing it down herself.

AUTOBIOGRAPHY AND THE DISCOVERY OF THE SELF

We do not ordinarily think of autobiography as a genre practiced in the Middle Ages, and if pressed to name autobiographies written after St. Augustine's *Confessions* and prior to the Renaissance, most scholars would point only to Guibert of Nogent's *Memoirs*, Abelard's *Story of My Calamities* and *The Book of Margery Kempe*, the first vernacular autobiography.[67] Yet none of these writers claims to be writing an autobiography. Guibert called his three-volume work *Monodiae* "Songs for One Voice"; Abelard cast his autobiographical reflections in the form of a letter of consolation; and Margery Kempe, who dictated her work in Middle English to two different scribes, modeled her story on saints' lives and vision collections. Clearly, we will have to modify our expectations about autobiography if we are to be alert to what is going on in these medieval writings about the self.

Rather than engage in debate over definitions of autobiography, we will find it more useful to view these narratives as exemplifying an autobiographical impulse, that is, a desire to put into words the search for what we would call a self—to express not just a formed and discovered self but to put into language the process of discovering and locating that self in relation to God, to the world, to others. We can clarify this notion further if we examine what it was that people in the late eleventh and early twelfth century saw as the self:

> The Middle Ages did not have our twentieth-century concepts of the "individual" or the "personality" . . . what they thought they were discovering when they turned within was what they called the "soul" (*anima*), or "self" (*seipsum*), or the "inner man" (*homo interior*). And this self, this inner landscape on which they laid fresh and creative emphasis, was not what we mean by "the individual." . . . the twelfth century regarded the discovery of *homo interior*, or *seipsum*, as the discovery within oneself of human nature made in the image of God—an *imago Dei* that is the same for all human beings. Moreover, the twelfth-century thinker explored himself in a direction and for a purpose. The development of the self was toward God.[68]

But this kind of self, like any modern self, comes into existence through language and the use of imagery. What the visionary autobiographies of medieval women present is quite similar to what Downing describes in the autobiographies of Freud and Jung:

> Both *Interpretation* and *Memories* are self-consciously formal innovations; Freud and Jung were conscious that there was no given form appropriate to their projects. Each recognized that in discovering the form for his telling he was at the same time discovering himself. . . . Both were well aware of the poetic or mythic dimensions of these works. . . . Scholes suggests that the mythic patterning is an inevitable correlate of the focus on the inner life; mimesis dissolves into mythos when the narrator penetrates the labyrinth of the psyche.[69]

Downing then suggests that "the recognition that our dreams create us as much as we create them suggests autobiography as a dream series";[70] this formulation is clearly parallel to the function of visions in medieval autobiographical narratives. The self that medieval women writers reveal is one that came into existence through language and before their very eyes in the course of visionary experience. The texts reproduce an experience that has already taken place (a vision in the past) and that takes place again as it is described. This primary visionary experience first occurred in an altered state of consciousness, characterized by enigmatic visual images and by heard language (what students of religion term "locutions"), and it involved the visionary directly—not just as viewer but as participant—so that both in the course of the vision and in her later reflections on it, the visionary felt herself to be transformed.

Thus, the autobiographical impulse in these texts cannot be separated from the visions; visions constitute a vehicle for the transformation of the self as we have just seen in the discussion of the seven stages of visionary activity. Visions are also responses to real-life situations: they may be compensatory or offer creative solutions to difficulties or provide images for identity, but they always come in response to something, and they always set in motion a new relationship to the original event that called them forth. (This responsive aspect of visionary activity is discussed more fully later.)

Dialogue in Autobiography

Women's mystical writings are often characterized by a peculiar and rather troubling double voice. For example, on the first page of Mechthild of Magdeburg's *Flowing Light of the Godhead*, we read the following:

> This book is to be joyfully welcomed, for God Himself speaks in it. . . . . The book proclaims Me alone and shows forth My holiness with praise. . . . This book is called The Flowing Light of the Godhead. Ah! Lord God! Who has written this book? I in my weakness have written it, because I dared not hide the gift that is in it.[71]

This relationship of two voices, of two first-person speakers, is defined for us a few pages later by Mechthild's description of the union of the soul with God, in which state the two are one as "water with wine."

> Then is she overcome and beside herself for weakness and can no more. And He is overpowered with love for her, as He ever was, He neither gives nor takes. Then she says, "Lord, Thou art my beloved! My desire! My flowing stream! My sun! and I am thy reflection!"[72]

In the second part of her book, Mechthild speaks of her doubts as a writer and of the resolution of those doubts. I repeat her thinking, for it is typical of women mystical writers.

> I was warned about this book and told by many that it should not be preserved, but rather thrown to the flames. Then I did what from childhood I have done when trouble overcame me: I betook myself to prayer. . . . "Lord, now I am troubled: Must I walk uncomforted for Thy Glory? Thou hast misled me for Thou Thyself commandest me to write!"[73]

God reassures her in several ways. He asserts the power of the truth to which her book witnesses: "The Truth may no man burn. Those who would take this book out of My hand must be stronger than I." The very physical nature of the book represents God, for the parchment itself deals with His humanity; the words with His divinity, "which flows . . . into thy soul from my Divine mouth." Furthermore, "the voice of the words denotes my Living Spirit."[74]

Although Mechthild remains concerned that doubt will be cast on a "golden house" built on "unworthy soil," God assures her that He consistently acts thus: "Whenever I gave special grace I sought for the lowest and smallest and most hidden." He and Holy Church are honored "that unlearned lips should teach the learned tongues of My Holy Spirit."[75]

What I would like to underscore here is that Mechthild's (and women mystics') writing is notable for its dialogue form, a colloquial exchange between a human and a divine voice and that this dialogue is mediated by two qualities or experiences common to both voices: an empowering and self-sacrificing love and an equally empowering yet sacrificial poverty or humility. Both voices express a love that is overpowering, both persons surrender to it, and both voices—God's and the women's—characterize themselves with claims of humility or poverty. But it is no accident that one of these voices, the female, expresses doubts about her right to speak; and the other of these voices, the more powerful, God's voice, the male voice, gives approval and encouragement to speak.

None of these elements is new to Christian mysticism. Face-to-face with God, the human speaks its humility. Prayer is by nature a reaching for dialogue, and in interior prayer, the individual often engages in dialogue with God. That people should love God as He loves people is an essential part of Christian doctrine, not the property of mystics alone. That God humbled himself in being born of the Virgin Mary is an equally basic tenet of Christianity. It is the combination of these elements that is new and, to my eyes, very important for an understanding of both the psychology and theology of women mystics. As an illustration of this point, it will be useful to remind ourselves how earlier writers such as St. Augustine and St. Anselm expressed these factors.

Augustine's *Confessions* is a search for dialogue, a search for a definition of God that will allow for a dialogue. This search for the rightful object of praise and love is in itself a transforming process, but in Augustine it is also a rational process and one in which the most distinctive voice throughout is Augustine's own. God's voice, when it is finally heard, is silence, a flash of intuition that floods the soul with answers, and then *Tolle et lege*, "take and read." Ultimately the dialogue with God is written, not heard. (But then, Augustine could read, and many women mystics could not.)

> To whom shall I turn for the gift of your coming into my heart and filling it to the brim, so that I may forget all the wrong I have done and embrace you alone, my only source of Good? . . . Why do I mean so much to you, that you should command me to love you? . . . Whisper in my heart, I am here to save you . . . I shall hear your voice and make haste to clasp you to myself. . . . But dust and ashes though I am, let me appeal to your pity, since it is to you in your mercy that I speak, not to a man, who would simply laugh at me.[76]

This is paragraph five of the *Confessions*. It is immediately followed by Augustine's account of his birth and his sinful childhood. "I do this, my God, not because I love those sins, but so that I may love you. For love of your love I shall retrace my wicked ways." The "I" of Augustine is defined through this love: "I cared for nothing but to love and be loved." But this is not love viewed as a mediator, a bridge. Rather it is love that defines the abyss that stretches between human beings, and their creator.

Augustine, educated in classical rhetoric, knew that it was necessary for the orator to use his exordium to put his hearers in the right state of mind. Cicero had said that it was expedient for the orator to demonstrate submissiveness and humility, and this rhetorical technique passed over into Christian literature. In medieval literature, secular as well as religious, formulas of submission and protestations of incapacity are found side by side and are often reinforced by a statement that one dares write only because a friend or patron or superior has expressly commanded it.[77]

When we turn to Anselm's *Prayers and Meditations*, we can see how this rhetorical technique has become a formula of abasement, the necessary state for beginning a prayer. In the "Prayer to St. John the Baptist," we read as follows:

> To you, sir, who are so great, holy and blessed,
>   comes a guilty, creeping thing,
>   a wretched little man
>   whose senses are almost dead with grief,
>   . . . a sinner with a dead soul . . .
>   very fearful, doubtful of his salvation,
>   because he is sure of the greatness of his
>   guilt,
>   but hoping in your greater grace.[78]

The prayer by a bishop or an abbot to the patron saint of his church illustrates the feeling of inadequacy in one who is called to be a spiritual leader:

> this sinner, this needy one, this one of yours,
> although unworthy, although incapable,
> although so unsuitable a substitute,
> again and again comes back to you,
> doubtful, ignorant, anxious about your people,
> your congregation, and about his own peril.
> Obviously, I am a useless person,
> adorned by no good works,
> but darkened by a profound ignorance,
> deformed by countless vices, burdened by huge sins . . .
> I beg to consult you, I pray you to listen,
> and I expect you through all to work on my behalf.[79]

In this and in other of Anselm's prayers, the distance between the human and the divine is slowly bridged by a developing understanding of the readiness of divine love to respond to human need. This process is detailed by the voice of the sinner, whose image of divine aid becomes clearer as his or her self-knowledge increases. Anselm's prayers are not yet dialogues, but each is a monologue that weaves together human need and divine succor.

Although the humble stance of the praying human being appears similar in all these examples, something quite different is going on in women's uses of the modesty topos combined with dialogue. The particular use women such as Mechthild make of dialogue is one of the identifying formal characteristics of women's autobiographical writings. This particular narrative strategy accomplishes a number of ends. First, the use of dialogue points to the orality of these texts. As Ong puts it:

> Suppose a person in an oral culture would undertake to think through a particular complex problem and would finally manage to articulate a solution which itself is relatively complex. . . . How does he or she retain for later recall

the verbalization so painstakingly elaborated? In the total absence of any writing, there is nothing outside the thinker, no text, to enable him or her to produce the same line of thought again or even to verify whether he or she has done so or not. . . . How, in fact, could a lengthy, analytic solution ever be assembled in the first place? An interlocutor is virtually essential: it is hard to talk to yourself for hours on end. Sustained thought in an oral culture is tied to communication.[80]

If we look at the content of dialogue in women's writings, we can see that these verbal exchanges meet two other goals: dialogue serves to hasten self-definition, and it provides a justification for women to write. It can meet these goals because the participants in the dialogue are God and a human soul. As the excerpts from Mechthild suggest, much of the dialogue in women's visions is amatory as well as didactic. And it is from these amatory dialogues that the female writing self emerges, taught by God what she must say and that she must say it. Poverty of spirit allows the woman visionary to be receptive to this dialogue and, at the same time, constitutes her identity with Christ. As Angela of Foligno explains:

> I experienced all these things in myself, and I would not have known how to discern such things well except that my soul came into a certain truth, for when love is pure, it . . . sees itself to be nothing. That which does not permit the soul to be deceived in such feelings is poverty of spirit. For in a divine locution made to me by God I heard poverty commended with so much proof as such a great good that it completely exceeds our understanding . . . for pride can only exist in those who think they possess something or believe themselves to have something.[81]

Hildegarde of Bingen begins similarly, so that we hear God speaking to her as directly as she speaks to us:

> It was in my forty-third year, when I was trembling in fearful anticipation of a celestial vision, that I beheld a great brightness through which a voice from heaven addressed me: "O fragile child of earth, ash of ashes, dust of dust, express and write that which thou seest and hearest. Thou art timid, timid in speech, artless in explaining, unlearned in writing, but express and write not according to art but according to natural ability, not under the guidance of human composition, but under the guidance of that which thou seest and hearest in God's heaven above."[82]

Julian of Norwich also finds through visions and dialogue a voice that is uniquely her own, yet divinely inspired:

> I write as the repesentative of my fellow Christians—and the more I love in this way whilst I am here, the more I am like the joy that I shall have in heaven without end, that joy which is the God who out of his endless love willed to become our brother and suffer for us. And I am sure that anyone who sees it so will be taught the truth and be greatly comforted, if he have need of comfort. But God forbid that you should say or assume that I am a teacher, for that is not and never was my intention; for I am a woman, ignorant, weak, and frail. But I

know very well that what I am saying I have received at the revelation of him who is the sovereign teacher. . . . But because I am a woman, ought I therefore to believe that I should not tell you of the Goodness of God, when I saw at the same time that it is his will that it be known?[83]

St. Umiltà, in claiming divine inspiration, also indicates the process of dialogue behind her sermons and other writings:

I am amazed and fearful and ashamed concerning these things, which I dare to write and dictate, for I have not read them in other books, nor have I ever applied myself to learning human knowledge; but only the Spirit of God has spoken in me, who fills my mouth with words that I ought to speak. . . . The divine words that I speak are not mine, but come from the Father and God most high. . . . He himself teaches me to ask and to answer, and speaks with me while in hiding. I however speak to you openly and publicly. He himself teaches me in the silence of the spirit, and I pronounce out loud to you the divine words which I hear.[84]

All these quotations—and many more that could be provided from each text from the twelfth century on—indicate that the self that comes into existence in the course of visionary experience is a writing self, a voice meant to be read as well as heard. (God tells Hildegard to "speak and write" what she hears.) But the discomfort with which each writer introduces her writing self also indicates that writing was a gender-determined activity, that writing could be considered as a usurpation of a male prerogative, and that the writing voice had to be assimilated to the male voice of God if it was to be heard. At the same time, most of the women writers distinguish their voices from what they consider to be typical male writing voices, that is, the voices of men educated in Latin and speaking in Latin—for their thinking process was based on how scholastic Latin perceives experience.

In distinguishing their voices from those of educated men, the women writers assert that they have not studied how to express themselves; they are ignorant of rhetoric; they have not read any of their ideas in books. They claim that their words are a direct representation of their experience—that they are translating what they have heard and seen. It is difficult to know just how literally we should take these assertions—Hildegard, for all her protestations of inadequacy, seems to have been familiar with much of the theology of her time and seems to have been influenced by the ideas in circulation at the school of Chartres. I interpret her remarks as a realistic disclaimer about not having received the equivalent of a university education.

Women writers seem to have been disadvantaged in terms of acquiring a systematic education in Latin.[85] In assessing what education they did have, we can assume that all the women writers from the twelfth century on were bilingual to some extent; that is, they received their education from both Latin and vernacular texts. Although many of the characteristics of their writing seem related to oral tradition, they certainly knew what to do with books, and they had enough access to the literate world that even if they could not read themselves, they were able to understand the reading aloud of Latin books. Nevertheless, their preparation for writing, and the act of composition were evidently not the same as those of literate men. (This twelfth-century situation is markedly different from that in the time of St. Leoba, for instance, when it is evident that the technology of book production was almost entirely in the hands of women in convents.)

Each woman's level of education was different, and it is difficult to generalize for all the countries covered in this anthology. For the sake of examples we can look at the situation in Italy. Four different kinds of experience with literary texts can be seen in the lives of four Italian women whose works are included here: St. Clare, St. Umiltà, Blessed Angela, and St. Catherine of Siena. St. Clare was a member of the nobility in the area of Assisi and could read and write Latin when she made her profession to St. Francis at the age of eighteen. A number of letters written by her in Latin are extant, as are her *Testament* (included here) and her *Rule of Life*. She did not think literacy was very important for the spiritual life, and she expressly says in her *Rule* that sisters who enter the convent unable to read should not ask to learn to read.[86] Her comments about St. Francis' early poetry in French suggest that she could also understand and read that language. St. Clare died in 1253, two years before St. Umiltà entered a Vallombrosan convent in Faenza at the age of twenty-five.[87] Umiltà evidently did not know how to read Latin at the time and perhaps did not know how to read Italian either. She acquired literacy as a miracle, when, as a joke, some of the older nuns asked her to read during the meal. By the time she was abbess, she could compose and dictate in Latin; her sermons are in prose, and her *Lauds to the Virgin Mary* are in verse. She put a high value on literacy, saw to it that the nuns were trained as scribes, and hired a woman teacher (a *magistra*) for her friend St. Margaret. (Margaret grumbled that she wanted to be literate only if it could happen by a miracle and insisted that she could understand spoken Latin well enough.[88]) Angela of Foligno evidently never learned to write in Latin or Italian; she dictated her works in Italian. The major collection of her writings, the *Liber de vere fidelium experientia*, was dictated in Italian and written down in Latin by her uncle, Fra Arnaldo. In the preface to the *Liber*, Fra Arnaldo writes of the difficulties of getting her account recorded correctly. Angela often found it impossible to put into words just what she had experienced, and when she had expressed herself as clearly as possible, she often complained that when this was put into Latin it sounded blasphemous or foolish.[89]

Catherine of Siena, the most prolific writer among these four women, tried to teach herself letters after she became a Dominican tertiary, but she gave up in frustration and prayed to the Virgin Mary for a miracle. The miracle was granted.[90] Catherine dictated her numerous letters and her *Dialogue* or *Book of Divine Doctrine* in Italian to a number of secretaries; the model she provided in the use of the vernacular became extremely important for the development of Italian prose style.

It should be stressed here that, for three out of these four women (St. Clare is the one exception), writing was essential for a public teaching career, and each woman found her own way of ensuring that her experiences and insights were recorded and distributed.

COMPOSITION AND STYLE IN WOMEN'S WRITINGS

The style of women's devotional writing may be characterized as emotional (concerned with affective responses), repetitive, proverbial, nonanalytical; the language is concrete rather than abstract, subjective, timeless, ahistorical; thoughts are connected by *and* or *then* rather than being subordinated to each other. Ong gives a checklist of the characteristics of oral thought and expression that is helpful in understanding why women's writing shows these traits. Oral expression tends to be[91] additive rather than subordinate; aggregative rather than analytic (preferring formulaic phrases such as "the brave soldier" or "the beautiful princess" to the words *soldier* and *princess*); redundant or copious ("Redundancy, repetition of the just-said, keeps both speaker and hearer surely on the track"); conservative or traditionalist ("formulas and themes are reshuffled rather than supplanted with new materials"); close to the human life world ("In the absence of elaborate analytic categories that depend on writing to structure knowledge at a distance from lived experience, oral cultures must conceptualize and verbalize all their knowledge with more or less close reference to the human lifeworld"); agonistically or violently toned; empathetic and participatory rather than objectively distanced; homeostatic ("oral societies live very much in a present which keeps in equilibrium or homeostasis by sloughing of memories which no longer have present relevance"); situational rather than abstract.[92]

Of course, the women writers of devotional literature did not continue to live in a timeless world of oral communication while the male elite had internalized the new psychodynamics that went with literacy, especially the greater emphasis on abstract thinking. Women were aware of the demands that writing imposed on thinking, especially the need for precision of meaning, and they took great care to get their ideas recorded properly, knowing that their words often would be read privately without the tonal and gestural context that oral delivery provides. By the fifteenth century there were some women, such as Magdalena Beutler, who preferred the written to the spoken word. What I am suggesting is that oral methods of composition, oral stylistic traits (exactly those traits that scholars are currently exploring in secular epic and romance)[93] were utilized more extensively in women's religious writing than in men's and that this was particularly important when women were composing in the vernacular rather than in Latin. Ong's observations on "Learned Latin" are useful here:

> For well over a thousand years, it was sex-linked, a language written and spoken only by males, learned outside the home in a tribal setting which was in effect a male puberty rite, complete with physical punishment and other kinds of deliberately imposed hardships. It had no direct connection with anyone's unconscious of the sort that mother tongues, learned in infancy, always have. . . . Of the millions who spoke it over the next 400 years, every one was also able to write it. . . . Learned Latin was a striking exemplification of the power of writing for isolating discourse and of the unparalleled productivity of such isolation. . . . Learned Latin effects even greater objectivity by establishing knowledge in a medium isolated from the emotion-charged depths of one's mother tongue, thus reducing interference from the human lifeworld and making possible the exquisitely abstract world of medieval scholasticism.[94]

I do not think that the preceding comments are completely true. As we have just seen, there were women who could understand Latin but could not read it or speak it, and there were certainly also women who *could* read it and write it. But the Latin that women knew best was ecclesiastical Latin, the Latin of the liturgy, the Psalter, and the daily canonical hours, not the more abstract Latin of scholasticism. To this extent Ong is correct when he says that learned Latin was a sex-linked language, and I think this accounts for the discomfort women felt using it even when they did not feel that, in so doing, they were violating the prohibition against women's preaching. Even Hrotsvit and Hugeberc found it necessary to justify their act of writing although they were living at a time when more women were writing.[95]

There is another reason for the survival of oral characteristics in women's writings, and that is related to the nature of their visions. The most obvious single narrative unit of women's writing is the retelling of a vision, and that vision has two mnemonic structural elements: visual iconography and dialogue. Visions are creative acts, and they seem to have been experienced by medieval women as direct seeing and hearing, not as reading. To have a vision was more like seeing a film than it was like writing or reading.

Visionary Composition

Visions were images, texts, and glosses on a woman's spiritual growth; there spiritual insights found visible form, which could be further explored and meditated on. A positive experience could be reexperienced and developed by unrolling it before the mind's eye; a negative one could be explored and dealt with in the same way, so that one could solve the problem it presented and thus grow beyond it. The writings of Hildegard of Bingen and Julian of Norwich exemplify the kind of composition and mental recreation of visionary experience that seems to be shared by most women visionaries. Taylor notes that "in some of Hildegard's voluminous writings, visions were apparently a form of composition; again, more veritable visions, deemed by her and by her friends to have been divinely given, made the nucleus of the work at length produced by the labour of her mind."[96] She described her visions as being projected on a brilliant light:

> From infancy, even to the present time when I am more than seventy years old, my soul has always beheld this *visio*, and in it my soul, as God may will, soars to the summit of the firmament, and into a different air, and diffuses itself among divers peoples, however remote they may be. Therefore I perceive these matters in my soul, as if I saw them through dissolving views of clouds and other objects. . . .
>
> The brightness which I see is not limited in space, and is more brilliant than the luminous air around the sun, nor can I estimate its height or length or breadth. . . . Just as sun, moon, or stars appear reflected in the water, I see Scripture, discourses, virtues and human actions shining in it.
>
> Whatever I see or learn in this vision, I retain in my memory; and as I may have seen or heard it, I recall it to mind, and at once see, hear, know; in an instant I learn whatever I know. On the other hand, what I do not see, that I do not know, because I am unlearned; but I have had some simple instruction in letters. I write whatever I see and hear in the vision, nor do I set down any other words, but tell my message in the rude Latin words which I read in the vision. For I am not instructed in the vision to write as the learned write; and the words

in the vision are not as words sounding from a human mouth, but as flashing flame and as a cloud moving in clear air.[97]

A similar process of reliving and exploring visionary experience is found in the longer account of Julian of Norwich's *Showings*, Chapter 51, where she presents the allegory of the lord and his servant. We possess two texts of these visions of Christ's passion, one written twenty years before the other. Most scholars are now in agreement that the shorter account is the original one made by Julian soon after she received the visions and that the longer version is built on it, enriched by twenty years of meditation on the contents.

Just what is this process of enrichment? When we study the development of a specific "showing" experienced by Julian[98] or compare an account of a meditative image given by St. Catherine of Siena's biographer with that presented by Catherine herself in her *Dialogues*, we can see that the original image is observed carefully in all its sensual detail; that then the feelings, associations and locutions that accompanied it are related; and finally that it is read as an allegory in which various details of the central image correspond to certain spiritual facts. Following this we may be given the meaning of the vision as a whole, as a spiritual truth to live by. For instance, this is how Julian describes the first appearance of a vision:

> I saw two persons in bodily likeness, that is to say a lord and a servant; and with that God gave me spiritual understanding. The lord sits in state, in rest and in peace. The servant stands before his lord, respectfully, ready to do his lord's will. The lord looks on his servant very lovingly and sweetly and mildly. He sends him off to a certain place to do his will. Not only does the servant go, but he dashes off and runs at great speed, loving to do his lord's will. And soon he falls into a dell and is greatly injured; and then he groans and moans and tosses about and writhes, but he cannot rise or help himself in any way. And of all this, the greatest hurt which I saw him in was lack of consolation, for he could not turn his face to look on his loving lord, who was very close to him, in whom is all consolation; but like a man who was for the time extremely feeble and foolish, he paid heed to his feelings and his continuing distress. . . .[99]

Julian's analysis begins immediately—"in which distress he suffered seven great pains." In the manner of medieval sermons and allegorical exegesis, she lists the seven aspects of his pain: bruising, clumsiness, weakness, unreason, inability to get up, isolation, and the hardness of the place where he had fallen. Then she looks inward to see the correspondence between his physical-emotional situation and his spiritual state, and here she is surprised: "I looked carefully to know if I could detect any fault in him, or if the lord would impute to him any kind of blame; and truly none was seen. . . ."[100] In response to her unspoken question, she hears the Lord's voice:

> See my beloved servant, what harm and injuries he has had and accepted in my service for my love, yes, and for his good will. Is it not reasonable that I should reward him for his fright and his fear, his hurt and his injuries and all his woe? And furthermore, is it not proper for me to give him a gift, better for him and more honorable than his own health could have been? Otherwise, it seems to me that I should be ungracious.[101]

It is typical of Julian's mental toughness that she wants to explore this issue further rather than rest with the insight she now possesses concerning the Fall. She knows that the servant is Adam, and yet "I saw many different characteristics which could in no way be attributed to Adam, that one man."[102] Her understanding of this vision progressed through three stages—her initial understanding at the time it came to her, then the "inward instruction which I have understood from it since," and finally, "the whole revelation from the beginning to the end, which our Lord God of his goodness freely and often brings before the eyes of my understanding."[103] Over the twenty years in which she explored this vision, she repeatedly heard this injunction: "You ought to take heed to all the attributes, divine and human, which were revealed in the example, though this may seem to you mysterious and ambiguous."[104] By isolating details of the vision, such as the blue color of the Lord's robe, she is able to explore first the literal and then the moral, tropological, and anagogical meaning of her visualized "scripture."

> A similar "ascent of the mind" through the three spiritual senses is equally evident in her progressive consideration of the place where the lord sits and of the ravine where the servant lay after his fall. The ravine was "narrow and comfortless and distressful" . . . The place where the lord was seated was "unadorned, on the ground, barren and waste, alone in the wilderness." Later this landscape becomes the scene of the servant's toil as a gardener, "digging and ditching and sweating and turning the soil over and over," the place where is the treasure which the lord loved; and finally becomes the City of God, the city of rest and peace which is at once man's world, redeemed and perfected, and the New Jerusalem, the bride of Christ. . . .[105]

With the purpose of interpretation in mind, Julian has constructed the narrative of her vision with great care; she clearly intends her readers to learn not just the content of her revelation but also her method of reading and interpreting as well. For these purposes, she has given primacy to neither the visual nor the auditory; both senses are initially engaged simultaneously, as in film, but, on reflection, they can be analyzed and understood separately.

Themes of Women's Devotional Writing

VIRGINITY, VISIONS, AND AUTHORITY

Several of the themes found in women's devotional writings reflect the connections proposed at the beginning of this essay between celibacy, visions, and authority. We can begin to explore these interrelationships by looking at the importance of the theme of chastity or virginity. St. Gregory of Nyssa identifies Macrina's choice of the virginal life as the key to her power and leadership, according to Wilson-Kastner:

> Macrina is the model of the virgin life. She is introduced to us as "the virgin," persuading her mother and her brother Basil to take up the virginal-philosophi-

cal life, and joining together others on the family estate to lead the virginal life in a community characterized by a common life and shared goods. Her virginal life in this community was "for her mother a guide to the immaterial and philosophical life," and the power of her example was such that the whole community rose toward the heights of this sort of life. . . . Virginity, in both its physical and spiritual manifestations, its most perfect form, is the highest form of the deifying life, and both men and women can engage in this kind of life. . . .

In terms of Gregory's theology, Macrina is a human being who has made progress in the virginal or philosophical life. She is judged as an individual human being recreated by Christ; she is the one who has gained mastery of spirituality, i.e., of reality. Therefore, she can teach and lead others on that same quest.[106]

The ideal of virginity-celibacy, to be practiced equally by women and men, is further illustrated in the two selections by Hrotsvit. *Pelagius* is the story of a male virgin martyr, who is killed for resisting the lecherous advances of a tyrannical Moslem ruler. Virginity is no passive virtue, for Pelagius earns his martyrdom by smashing the king in the mouth when he attempts to kiss him. (This contrasts with the story of St. Agnes, also told by Hrotsvit; the virgin martyr Agnes is the passive victim of a sadistic ruler, hostile to Christians and virgins.) The drama *Abraham* also rings changes on a traditional legend associated with celibacy; here the point of comparison is the legend of St. Mary the Egyptian, a famous courtesan of Alexandria who recognizes the power of a celibate life and spends many years as a hermit in the desert, devoted to ascetic practices and transcending the needs of the body in visions.[107] In Hrotsvit's *Abraham*,[108] Mary is a young girl entrusted to the care of her uncle Abraham and his friend Efrem, both hermits and ascetics. Mary is seduced by a young monk and runs away in shame to become a prostitute; her uncle has to disguise himself as a prospective client in order to bring her back to a celibate life. Abraham, it seems, had become absorbed in a vision—one concerning Mary—and failed to keep watch over the earthly girl. Visions, Hrotsvit may be implying, are perhaps the reward for the virginal life, but they do not obviate the necessity to keep careful watch on temptation.

Another view of the relationship between virginity and visions is exemplified in the *Life of Christina of Markyate*.[109] Christina's struggle with her family begins when her parents insist on her marrying a young man named Burthred although she has already vowed her virginity to Christ and his mother. She is forced to consent to the betrothal but refuses to consummate the marriage. During her family's persecution of her for this, her visions comfort her for her sufferings and promise her that she will escape the threats on her virginity and be permitted to live a contemplative life. Her identity as Christina, rather than her given name, Theodora, rests on her being able to act out her vocation; and she demonstrates great ingenuity and physical courage in avoiding rape and running away to a hermitage, where she may practice her chosen life.

St. Leoba is identified as a consecrated virgin by visions when she is still in her mother's womb, and a later vision (of a purple thread issuing from her mouth) locates her specific authority in speech as the Beloved (*Leoba* in Old English) of God.[110] Her choice of the virgin life allows her to acquire great learning under Mother Tetta, and it is this learning, along with her other charismatic gifts, that causes her to be selected by St. Boniface for his mission to Germany and accounts for her great success there. Virginity and visions are also associated with great learning in Hildegarde of Bingen's *Scivias*.[111] Again, virginity is not seen as linked to sex, but rather as a means to achieve freedom from gender, so that in the dialogue with God that begins the *Scivias*, Hildegarde is addressed by the neutral *homo* (man)[112] although feminine-inflected adjectives are used to describe her fragile human status.

For the mystics of the thirteenth century, virginity is important in a new way, for many of these writers, in their visions of a mystical union with Christ, suggest the paradox that virginity in this world is rewarded by marriage to the divine. Of the ten thirteenth-century women in whose lives erotic or nuptial imagery figures prominently, three were married, and five were probably associated with Beguine groups at some time in their lives; only four lived all their adult lives in the cloister;[113] and it is likely that one of them, St. Clare, in choosing to follow St. Francis, did not initially intend to live a cloistered life but wanted a life of voluntary celibacy and poverty similar to the ideals of the Beguines.[114] My point is that virginity is not seen as a woman's status in respect to males, that is, nonmarried, but has the older connotations of independence and self-sufficiency. One of the stranger episodes in the "Life of Christina Mirabilis," two different versions of which are recounted, suggests associations between virginity, nurturing, and self-sufficiency:

> The people thought she was possessed by demons and finally, with great effort, managed to capture her and bind her with iron chains. . . . One night, with the help of God, her chains and fetters fell off and she escaped and fled into remote desert forests. . . . Even when she needed food . . . and was tortured by a most terrible hunger, she did not at all wish to return home. . . . She therefore uttered a prayer to the Lord . . . without delay, turning her eyes to herself, she saw that her dry virginal breasts were dripping sweet milk against all the laws of nature. . . . Using the dripping liquid as food, she was nourished for nine weeks with the virginal milk from her own breasts.[115]

In these thirteenth-century writings, virginity is not as directly linked to the acquisition of wisdom and authority and leadership as it was for earlier women; authority for them is provided by visionary experience, particularly the conviction of divine approval that comes to them with the experience of union with Christ. Virginity is important because it signals a commitment to the kind of life that makes visions possible. Virginity is an inner spiritual state, and thus union with the divine is possible even for those women who had been married.

It is more difficult to generalize about the significance of the theme of virginity in the writers of the fourteenth and fifteenth centuries. Two of the fourteenth-century writers in this collection, Na Prous Boneta and Marguerite Porete, were identified as heretics and Beguines although the precise nature of Marguerite Porete's heresy is still debated, and she is now thought to have been a Beguine who wrote one of the earliest texts associated with the Free Spirit movement.[116] Na Prous Boneta was a disciple of the Spiritual Franciscan Peter John Olivi;[117] for her, virginity, like poverty, was essential to the spiritual life, as preparation for the new age that was about to begin. Both women were visionaries. Na Prous was not a writer as far as we know, yet she seems to have taken advantage of the opportunity provided by the

Inquisition to record her beliefs and the visions on which they were based. As she dictates to the court notary, she seems very conscious of forming her responses to questions into a final written testament to her discovery of herself as a prophet. Her virginity assimilates her to the figure of Mary, whose role she believes she will fulfill in the new age to come.

Margery Kempe was born several generations after Na Prous was burned at the stake. She regretted her loss of virginity very deeply even though in most respects she seems to have had a good relationship with her husband. Christ continually reassured her that he loved wives as well as virgins.[118] She experienced visions of union with the manhood of Christ, but only after she had finally convinced her husband to take a vow of celibacy with her. For all of these writers, virginity or celibacy was essential to true spiritual growth, but the real evidence of growth and transformation was not virginity, but visions.

ISOLATION AND ALIENATION

Another major theme found in most of these writings is that of isolation; isolation may be a physical fact, a period of time spent as a hermit or a recluse, or it may be a form of alienation, a sense of painful apartness, that convinces the woman of her call to a more spiritual life. Isolation may take the form of spiritual dryness, a frightening awareness of being alienated from God, or of an anguished yearning for God without any satisfaction. Two essential types of isolation may be discerned. The first is alienation from God because of the world's attractions, a feeling of being drawn away from God by material or sexual temptation or of being distracted through responsibilities for others. The second is spiritual isolation, a feeling of abandonment, a distance or separation from God in spite of one's commitment to a consecrated life. The first type is cured by leaving the world and making a fuller commitment to a religious life, a commitment that may reinforce one's sense of otherness in relation to ordinary life but that actually leads one to a greater sense of inclusion and community. The second can only be cured by God, and sometimes the mystic must simply wait for divine grace. Human isolation and divine community are often juxtaposed; thus, Perpetua (in the *Passion of Saints Perpetua and Felicity*) can comment on her fear at being isolated in an unfamiliar, dark prison, but at the same time she senses a completeness and a joy in herself that she never felt before.[119]

The *Life of Christina of Markyate* illustrates several types of isolation: Christina is almost tragically alienated from her family by their plans for her to marry and their ostracism of her when she refuses; after running away to a hermitage, she is physically isolated by having to spend her days in an enclosed angle of Roger the Hermit's cell, a space only a span and a half wide and too small for her to stand up. She cannot let herself be seen by anyone lest she be returned to her family as a runaway wife, and her health is ruined by her privations, but her visionary life is neither isolating nor enclosing.[120] Hadewijch, in her *Letters to a Young Beguine*, speaks of her isolation and of what seems to be ostracism by a community in which she had formerly been a respected spiritual leader.[121] Gertrude the Great begins her autobiography by describing her sense of alienation from her community and from God; she images her distance from Christ by a hedge of thorns, over which she is miraculously lifted.[122] Christine de Pizan is isolated within the court environment by her widowhood, her nonaristocratic rank, her occupation, and her Italian birth, as well as by her gender. Angela of Foligno and Margery Kempe are shunned or ridiculed by others for their uncontrollable weeping and screaming and by the intensity of their spiritual gifts.

BODY AND SENSE OF SELF

We have come to expect that the self presented in an autobiography will be an embodied self and that an autobiography will be concerned at least as much with the physical world in which that person lives and with which he or she interacts as with the inner self. But when we look for language about the body in these medieval devotional texts, we find something different. Bodies are talked about as opponents in a struggle, as objects of often fierce asceticism. Women's bodies are flagellated, forced to kneel for long hours in churches; they wear hair shirts. The interest in ascetic practices underscores a kind of body-soul duality, in which the body is seen as the enemy, as something external to the soul that must be defeated or somehow reduced.[123] But bodies also bear the imprint of the spiritual—it is Christ's body on the cross that is contemplated, and it is the mystic's body that gives visible evidence of her ecstatic experiences. Dissatisfaction with traditional body-soul stereotypes can be seen in a section of "The Life of Christina Mirabilis":

> she threw herself before the altar as if she were a sack filled with dry bones. Then wailing bitterly she began to beat her breast and her body ... "O miserable and wretched body! How long will you torment me ...? Why do you delay me from seeing the face of Christ? When will you abandon me so that my soul can return freely to its Creator?" ... then, taking the part of the body, she said ... "O miserable soul! Why are you tormenting me in this way? What is keeping you in me and what is it that you love in me? Why do you not allow me to return to the earth from where I was taken and why do you not let me be at rest until I am restored to you on the Last Day of Judgement?" ... She sighed and gasped and wept ... [then] she dissolved into a most sweet smile.... Taking her feet with both hands, she kissed the soles with the greatest affection and said, "O most beloved body! Why have I beaten you? Why have I reviled you? Did you not obey me in every good deed I undertook to do with God's help? You have endured the torment and hardships most generously and most patiently which the spirit placed on you."[124]

The body and soul dualism implicit in these generalizations is not found in the earliest visionary autobiography, the *Passion of St. Perpetua*. In that narrative, her body is very definitely a woman's body, and her awareness of needing to nurse her baby brings that fact home to us very clearly. She meets death in a body, too, but the narrative of the *Passion* gives us two versions of that event. Perpetua's vision of her struggle in the arena gives her a man's body; in the historical event, told by a witness, Perpetua is again definitely female and is even attacked by a female animal. She pins up her hair to show she is not a woman in mourning, and she modestly covers herself with her clothing after she has been tossed to the ground by the enraged cow. But this attitude toward the body is not found in the later medieval texts, nor even in the story of St. Macrina.

WOMEN'S BODIES: ILLNESS, VISIONS AND VIRGINITY

The two central images for women's bodies in these devotional texts are virginity and illness. Virginity, as we have seen, is above all a spiritual fact although the physical fact of virginity and the freedom gained by remaining physically intact are very important to women's sense of themselves. Yet in the narratives included here, this virginity, which is a sign of the consecration to a religious life, is most typically associated with illness. Illness is presented in devotional narratives in a number of ways; a few are more conventional Christian modes of thought, but most seem to be associated specifically with gender and with ecstasy.

Illness as a Test

In those narratives that depict illness as a test, it is not so much the experience of illness and pain that is commented on as it is the individual woman's response to that suffering. Thus, Macrina's nobility of spirit and her philosophical strength of mind shine through her illness. We have already been told by Gregory of Nyssa that she is a great soul, but when we come to read of her meeting with him, when we see her lying in pain on a board, struggling to bow to her brother, and we hear her reprimand him for his grief, we are expected truly to experience her nobility. A woman's saintliness is often validated by her heroic ability to put up with illness, illness that may be attributed to her earlier austerities. For instance, Christina of Markyate's health was permanently ruined by the privations she had to endure in hiding as a runaway:

> O what trials she had to bear of cold and heat, hunger and thirst, daily fasting! The confined space would not allow her to wear even the necessary clothing when she was cold. The airless little enclosure became stifling when she was hot. Through long fasting, her bowels became contracted and dried up. There was a time when her burning thirst caused little clots of blood to bubble up from her nostrils. But what was more unbearable than all this was that she could not go out until the evening to satisfy the demands of nature. Even when she was in dire need, she could not open the door for herself.[125]

Illness as a Call to a Different Life

A number of biographies and autobiographies in this collection begin with illness, but *The Book of Margery Kempe* is probably the most noteworthy in this regard. Margery tells of her collapse after the birth of her first child and attributes her madness to her internal conflict between the fear of death and hell and to her inability to confess a sin. She assigns her cure to the miraculous appearance of Christ at her bedside.

> When this creature was twenty years old or somewhat more, she was married to an honorable townsman, and she conceived a child. . . . She was troubled by severe illness until the child was born, and then, on account of the trouble she had in childbirth and the illness before, she despaired of her life. . . . And then she sent for her confessor for she had something on her conscience which she had never revealed before in her life. . . . Just when she came to the point of saying the thing that she had concealed for so long, her confessor was a little too hasty and began to reprove her sharply before she had finished saying what she had intended, and then she would say no more, no matter what he did. And between the dread she had, of damnation on one side and of her confessor's reproof on the other, this creature went out of her mind and was incredibly vexed and troubled by spirits for half a year, eight weeks, and some odd days.[126]

The return to health was sudden:

> And after she had been troubled . . . so long that men thought she would never recover or live, when she was lying all alone and her keepers were away, our merciful Lord Jesus Christ . . . appeared to this creature who had forsaken him. In the likeness of a man, the most handsome and beautiful and amiable that might ever be seen, wearing a purple cloak, sitting on her bedside, looking upon her with such a blessed expression that she felt strengthened in her spirits, he said . . . "Daughter, why have you forsaken me and I never forsook you?" . . . And immediately this creature was as sound in her wits and her reason as she had ever been before.[127]

A less dramatic example is that of Christine de Pizan. After describing her other misfortunes, her loss of her father and her husband, and her economic difficulties, she adds, "I came upon the culmination of my adversities when I was stricken like Job by a lengthy illness." At this point she decides she must write to support her family.

Illness as Abnormal or Uncontrollable Behavior

Christina Mirabilis came from St. Trond; she is called "Mirabilis" for her amazing behavior; when in trance states, she would spin around or roll into a ball or sing softly to herself. Sometimes she produced a kind of inhuman hum somewhere between her throat and her heart. Her behavior when she was young was so violent and unusual that many thought she was possessed:

> When she prayed and the divine grace of contemplation descended upon her, all her limbs were gathered together into a ball as if they were hot wax, and all that could be perceived of her was a round mass. After her spiritual inebriation was finished and her active physical senses had restored her limbs to their proper place, like a hedgehog her rolled up body returned to its proper shape and her limbs which had been bent formlessly once again were spread out.[128]

Other women wept uncontrollably, among them Marie d'Oignies, Angela of Foligno, and Margery Kempe. In Marie d'Oignies' case, the surprising element seems to have been the quantity of tears shed:

> When a constant outburst of tears gushed forth from her eyes both day and night and ran down her cheeks and made the church floor all muddy, she could catch the tears in the linen cloth with which she had covered her head. She went through many veils in this way since she had to change them frequently and put a dry one on in place of the wet one she had discarded.[129]

Jacques de Vitry, who was telling her story, asked her whether she felt pain with the tears:

> "These tears," she said, "are my refreshment. Night and day they are my bread. They do not impair my head but rather feed my mind. They do not torment me with pain but, on the contrary, they rejoice my soul with a kind of serenity. They do not empty the brain but fill the soul to satiety and soften it with a sweet anointing. They are not violently wrenched out but are freely given by the Lord."[130]

For Angela of Foligno and Margery Kempe, tears were accompanied by loud sobbing and much thrashing about, resulting in embarrassment for them and their supporters.[131] In both cases, the gift of tears was initiated with meditations on the Passion (in Margery's case in the Holy Land) and intensified when the women were exposed to certain physical reminders. Angela, for instance, recognized her lack of control but could do nothing about it:

> Still later, I came to so much greater a fire of love that I screamed if I heard someone speak about God. Even if someone had stood over me with an axe ready to kill me, I could not have stopped myself. Moreover, when people said to me that I was demonically possessed in that I couldn't stop myself, I was very ashamed, and I too said the same, that I was ill and possessed, and I could not satisfy those who were maligning me. And when I saw the passion of Christ depicted, I could scarcely endure it, but fever seized me and I became ill.[132]

It is important to remember that these unusual states, which troubled and annoyed others, were interpreted as teachings for others, as reminders of Christ's sacrifice. But it also seems that the violent crying of Margery Kempe, Marie d'Oignies, and Angela of Foligno is the inarticulate cry of one needing a voice, needing to have words, in a world that would deny that voice. All three were married women—which made them unlikely candidates as images of purity and sanctity. All three had unusual vocations that caused them to live on the periphery of religious society: Marie d'Oignies began a new movement by withdrawing to work in a leprosarium rather than joining a monastic order; Angela was a Franciscan tertiary; Margery never joined any religious order although, in a way, the white robes she wore constituted her an order unto herself. All three chose—had to choose—men to write their words for them. A number of other women in this collection also dictated their works to men (Hildegard of Bingen, Mechthild of Magdeburg, Christina of Markyate); but for Margery, Angela, and Marie, perhaps because they lived outside traditional boundaries, the choice of a scribe seems to have been difficult. Marie d'Oignies quite consciously chose Jacques de Vitry as her voice, and she chose someone very effective, but she was silenced. Angela of Foligno chose her uncle after St. Francis led her to him. Although he had been her confessor and spiritual director for five years, she had not told him all about her visions until after her experience at Assisi. When she collapsed screaming in the doorway of the Church of St. Francis after her first vision of love, he at first tried to get away; then, afraid of his brothers' criticisms, he angrily told her to leave town and never return to Assisi. Yet he is a sympathetic figure—he felt called to record her life, but because he had learned to write only as an adult, he was tormented by his deficiences as a scribe. He was harassed and criticized by his brothers for taking down her words.

Margery Kempe faced the same difficulty in trying to find a voice, a language to express her experiences. Her first amanuensis wrote such an incomprehensible Germanized English that it took her quite some time to convince her second scribe to read it and transcribe it. All three women were in part crying in humiliation at their helplessness to communicate, at their dependence on others, their desire to handle and control words.

They are also crying at the crucifixion, and this is what saves them from being lost in their own pain and frustration. They use their pain not to isolate themselves further but to link themselves to the crucified, and through him to all Christians. Their own humiliation is reflected, valued, transcended in the humiliation of the cross. This is why Marie d'Oignies can say that her tears are not painful, that they nourish her instead. Even the shame of crying uncontrollably in public that Angela and Margery experience finds its reflection in the crucifixion; in the reviling of Christ they find an image for their own passion.

Illness and Mystical Death

A surprising number of biographies and autobiographies tell of an apparent dying, often when a teenager, of being taken for dead and perhaps even put in a coffin, but then miraculously coming back to life, often with an explicit visionary message for the world. This happened to Christina Mirabilis, Catherine of Siena, Magdalena Beutler, St. Teresa of Avila, Julian of Norwich. One of the most detailed accounts of this state is given by Julian of Norwich, for it was while she was apparently dying or dead that she received her sixteen showings or revelations.

> And when I was thirty and a half years old, God sent me a bodily sickness in which I lay for three days and three nights; and on the fourth night I received all the rites of Holy Church ... but ... I suffered on for two days and two nights ... and on the third night ... my reasoning and my suffering told me that I should die; ... so I lasted until day, and by then my body was dead from the middle downwards.... After this my sight began to fail, and it was dark all around me in the room, dark as night.... After that I felt as if the upper part of my body were beginning to die. My hands fell down on either side, and I was so weak that my head lolled to one side. The greatest pain that I felt was my shortness of breath and the ebbing of my life. Then truly I believed that I was at the point of death. And suddenly in that moment all my pain left me, and I was as sound, particularly in the upper part of my body, as ever I was before or have been since.[133]

The first major event told in the Life of Christina of St. Trond, as narrated by Thomas of Cantimpré, is her mystical death, which occurs after she has been visited with spiritual graces while tending her family's herds as they went to pasture. The mythologizing of the event is evident:

> It happened that after these events she grew sick in body by reason of the exertions of inward contemplation and she died. Her dead body was laid out in the midst of her friends and her sisters and they wept copiously over it. The next day it was borne to the church but while Mass was being said for her, suddenly the body stirred in the coffin and immediately was raised up like a bird and ascended to the rafters of the church. All those present fled and only her elder sister remained behind fearfully. Christina stayed up there immoveable until Mass was finished. . . .[134]

Magdalena Beutler experienced a public mystical death very similar to Christine's and seems to have received the stigmata at the close of her ordeal. (Magdalena's experience is discussed more fully later.)

Ecstasy as a Type of Illness, or Illness as the Visible Sign of Ecstasy

The descriptions of ecstasy as a form of illness are sometimes related to accounts of mystical death, for certain trance states involve a similar kind of rigidity and insensibility of the body. But more frequently physical descriptions indicate that those women who are experiencing ecstasy are physically weak, unable to walk or to communicate, and incapable of performing the tasks they are accustomed to doing.[135] Illness of this type isolates women, making them feel more separated from others. Even when the members of their communities rally around them, they are embarrassed at being caught having visions and don't like having to be dependent on others in their weakened state. Descriptions of physical pain and weakness associated with ecstatic states, accompanied by statements of shame or embarrassment, are frequent, found in Christina Mirabilis, Gertrude the Great, Hadewijch, Angela of Foligno, and Margery Kempe, among others. Here I will provide just two illustrations: the first from Hildegard of Bingen; the second, from Elisabeth of Schönau. Hildegard's moving account reveals her sense of being unlike other people, at once more exalted and more vulnerable. She speaks in the third person.

> But from the day of her birth, she was as it were entangled in a net of suffering and illnesses, so that she was vexed with continual pains in all her veins and flesh to the very marrow, nor did it please God that she should be dissolved, because in the interior of her rational soul she saw spiritually certain things of God. But this vision so pierced through all the veins of this woman [*hominis . . . ipsa*] that she was often agitated with great weariness, sometimes struggling against this fatigue in depression, sometimes in consolation.
>
> From this she had manners different from those of other men, like an infant who is not yet able to distinguish the behaviour of men. For she appears a servant, with the inspiration of the Holy Spirit . . . and was so susceptible to this same air . . . that she never had any confidence in herself, nor any sense of security, otherwise the inspiration of the Holy Spirit would not have dwelt in her so powerfully.[136]

In Elisabeth of Schönau we see a physical struggle to reach the peace of ecstasy:

> during the night before . . . such an extreme faintness afflicted all my senses that the sisters who were attending me with the greatest concern, were waiting for me to die. But the angel of the Lord stood by me the whole night, and the prince of the apostles appeared to me in the great brilliance of his beauty. And I experienced such great delight in gazing upon him that I was compelled to forget the violent seizures that racked my whole body. . . . And I remained in that state of violent bodily agitation until about the sixth hour of the following day . . . finally I went into ecstasy and thus I was able to be at peace.[137]

Most ecstatics must have believed that such physical suffering was worth the reward of visionary experience, "consolation," and yet one wonders if there is not something defensive or apologetic in the frequent requests from divine figures for an affirmation that it was all worth it. As Elisabeth continues her account of this particular vision, we see an instance of this kind of affirmation.

> And in this ecstatic trance I saw the blessed apostles Peter and Paul, most gloriously crowned, cloaked in inconceivable brilliance, and bearing palm branches in their hands. Looking at me, the prince of the apostles said, "What is more pleasing to you, to be tormented thus and delight in gazing upon us, or to do without both the pain and the vision?" And I said to him, "My Lord, if it can be, with God's grace and yours, I desire to endure these sufferings rather than to be deprived of your sweet consolation." "You have spoken well," he said, "and therefore, from this time forth, you will suffer less pain in your visions."[138]

Illness as the Manifestation of a Conflict Related to Writing

Many women mystics speak of a period of illness that precedes their decision to write down their experiences. They are fearful about what they expect to be negative responses to their writing, yet inwardly compelled to speak publicly of what they have experienced. The resolution to their dilemma comes only when a divine voice tells them they must write. Once they begin, they find that it is a healing process and that they gain strength from articulating what they know about the spiritual life. Hildegard becomes ill when she cannot write and when she is not allowed to establish a new convent; she is cured when she is allowed to act on her desires, and the miracle of health helps convince her critics and detractors, too. Margery Kempe ignores suggestions to write down her experiences when she is still a young woman, but during an illness in her old age she responds to a divine command to write in spite of terrific difficulties in finding an amanuensis. She has to motivate both herself and her reluctant scribes, but she is rewarded by better health each time she dictates her story.

Gertrude the Great also resists the command to write her autobiography although she has translated the works of others. She first must be convinced rationally by God of the appropriateness of writing down her own experiences, and then she must have her writing time divinely budgeted for her so that she is not overwhelmed by the totality of what she has to say. Here is a highly educated woman, knowledgeable in the Church Fathers, gifted in writing in Latin and in the vernacular, with access to all types of spiritual literature and living in an almost ideally supportive environment in the convent at Helfta; and yet she seems to feel doubts and vulnerability similar to those of that uneducated maverick lay woman Margery Kempe. This is how she describes her beginning to write:

> I considered it so unsuitable for me to publish these writings, that my conscience would not consent to do so . . . the Lord conquered the repugnance of my reason by these words: "Be assured that you will not be released from the prison of the flesh until you have paid this debt which still binds you." And as I reflected that I had already employed the gifts of God for the advancement of my neighbor—if not by my writing, at least by my words—He brought forward these words which I had heard used at the preceding Matins, "If the Lord had willed to teach his doctrine only to those who were present, He would have taught by word only, not by writing. But now they are written for the salvation of many." He added further: "I desire your writings to be an indisputable evidence of my Divine goodness in these latter times, in which I purpose to do good to many."
>
> These words having depressed me, I began to consider within myself how difficult, and even impossible it would be to find thoughts and words capable of explaining these things to the human intellect without scandal.[139]

At this point she is overwhelmed with too many ideas, too much divine inspiration, and she cannot retain anything useful from the experience. Even more depressed, she turns again to prayer, wishing more reassurance about the value of her writing for others. God promises to deal with her more gently.

> And for four days, at a convenient hour each morning, Thou didst suggest with so much clearness and sweetness what I composed, that I have been able to write it without difficulty and without reflection, even as if I had learned it by heart long before; with this limitation, that when I had written a sufficient quantity each day, it has not been possible for me, although I applied my whole mind to it, to find a single word to express the things which on the following day I could write freely. . . .[140]

Marguerite d'Oingt seems to have had a more literal and physiological understanding of the imperative to write down her mystical experiences. For her, the knowledge and experience acquired from her visions became a kind of metaphysical congestion, so that she was unable to do anything except think about her visions obsessively; and the act of writing channeled that congested energy, led it away from her body and onto the page, where it could help others. In a letter (perhaps to her spiritual director) she says:

> My sweet father, I don't know if what is written in the book is in Holy Scripture, but I know that she who put these things into writing was so ravished in our Lord one night that it seemed to her that she saw all these things. And when she returned to herself, he had them all written in her heart in such a way that she could not think about anything else, but her heart was so full that she could not eat, nor drink, nor sleep, to the degree that she fell into such a great weakness that the doctors believed her close to death.

> She thought that if she were to put these things in writing, as Our Lord had sent them to her in her heart, her heart would be more relieved for it. She began to write everything that is in this book, all in order as she had it in her heart; and as soon as she put a word in the book, it left her heart. And when she had written everything, she was completely cured. I firmly believe that if she had not put it in writing she would have died or become crazy. . . . And this is why I believe that this was written by the will of Our Lord.[141]

We can see that illness was a crucial aspect of the lives of women mystics, the writers of devotional and didactic literature, because of its associations with asceticism, with ecstasy, and with the very act of writing. For these women, there were basically two motivations for writing—to tell one's own spiritual history and to teach others about God. These were not really separable motivations for medieval women, for one's own spiritual history was the discovery of the self made in the image of God, and to tell one's history was to teach about God. The God about whom they wrote was also made in their image and likeness; that is, they discovered in their explorations the feminine of God, the motherhood of Christ. That the self, made in the image of God, is the same for all persons, regardless of gender, accounts in part for the liberating effect of the discovery of self for women; and this fact has an important corollary, that autobiography can be seen as exemplary or representative: What happened to one woman can happen to any person, male or female. Thus, it was the discovery of the imprint of the divine in the innermost human soul that allowed for the narration of human history. The divinity of the individual soul, the god within each person that is subsumed in God—this is a dangerous idea, and it is no wonder that medieval women writers felt cautious about expressing themselves on this topic. The danger of sounding like heretics was a very real problem for writers of the thirteenth to fifteenth centuries, and women writers had to invent a very precise language to express accurately the deepest truths of their existence without being misunderstood.

The telling of one's own history up to the point of the discovery of the self and the identification of the self with the divine were the teachings that women had to impart. The self they encountered was not gender identified although it had both "masculine" and "feminine" qualities. They wanted to share with others God's gifts to them, so that others could experience the same thing. Because they drew from their own experience to teach, women as autobiographers cannot really be separated from women as teachers, and women as teachers are almost inevitably visionaries. It is in visions that the encounter between the self and the divine takes place. It is also in visions that conflicts are mediated—not just conflicts about writing, but about living, about expressing one's true nature in one's dealings with the world. And that is the topic to which I'd like to turn now. As a conclusion to this survey of themes in women's devotional and didactic writings, I want to explore the creative and healing relationship between vision and reality expressed in these texts.

On Symmetry in Vision Narratives: Creative Envisioning of Conflict Situations

The sections of the *Passion of Saints Perpetua and Felicity* written by Perpetua herself seem to be a kind of prison notebook in which she recorded the experiences leading up to her martyrdom.[142] Close examination of her writing reveals a very conscious structuring of the relationships between vision and reality, between human confrontation and divine resolution. The four visions of Perpetua are balanced by four confrontations with secular authority (her father figures in three of these confrontations) in which her identity as a Christian demands she put aside her pity for her father. She identifies her true self with her nature as a Christian—she can no more be called anything but Christian than a water jug can be called by any other name. The visions themselves are balanced in other ways. The first and last, which concern the fate of Perpetua and her fellow Christians in the arena, show Perpetua being helped or rewarded by benevolent fatherly figures. In the first, she ascends a narrow and dangerous ladder to a garden of the good shepherd, where she is given cheese by a venerable old man; she interprets this as a clear prophecy of death in the arena. In the final vision she is led to the arena and given instructions by another helpful male figure; then she is revealed to be a man at the moment of battle.[143] She fights and defeats an "Egyptian" and is rewarded for her victory. This she understands as her victory over Satan and the reward of eternal life through death in the arena. The threat posed by her father is that, torn by her love for him, she will be unable to meet death in her new identity as a Christian. The transformed father figures in the first and last visions mediate this internal conflict. As Dronke points out,

> The figure of the father returns transformed, I would suggest, in several of Perpetua's dream images. He who begs "have pity on my white hairs" (*canis meis*, V 2; cf. *canis patris tui*, VI 3) is echoed in dream in the huge white-haired shepherd (*hominem canum*, IV 8), who nurtured her with his delicious cheese, and again in the fencing master, also gigantic in size, who rewards her with golden apples and a kiss: "Daughter, peace be with you" (*Filia, pax tecum*, X 13). It is a serene father figure—not tormented and tormenting, but solacing—who appears to Perpetua in her first and last visions.[144]

These two visions frame the two middle dreams concerning her younger brother, Dinocrates. In the first she sees him as he was when he died of a tumor on his face; he is disfigured and dirty, comes from a confused dark place, and moves toward a basin of water that is too high for him to reach. In the second dream, after Perpetua has realized that she has the power to pray for other souls and has prayed fervently that Dinocrates be released from his suffering, she sees Dinocrates clean and happy, with a healed scar rather than an open wound; he is now able to drink from the basin. The center of Perpetua's narrative is her realization of her own charisma, her ability to pray for others; and this in turn is related to her relationship with her baby, who was taken from her when she was first imprisoned, then restored to her (easing her physical and mental anguish), and finally taken away again, but miraculously cared for, so that he no longer needs his mother's milk and her breasts are no longer painful.

Perpetua's short narrative reveals a number of the patterns to be developed by other writings in this anthology. The focus of interest in the narrative is on the visions, but each vision is carefully placed in a personal and historical context. The nonvisionary episodes are dramatic presentations of confrontations with the non-Christian world, where words and gestures count heavily in the total picture provided for us. Auerbach speaks of this text as the beginning of a new Christian style:

> In its beginnings it disclosed the full force of the crude reality in which these plain people who chanced to be called to martyrdom celebrated their triumph of suffering; everything—the persecutors, the scene of martyrdom, the happenings in the wholly or partly pagan families of the martyrs—is treated with unadorned realism. Yet this humble everyday reality is transfigured, it takes on a new *gravitas*.[145]

The blending of two realms, as Auerbach terms it, the sublime and the lowly, is presented by means of the dramatic symmetry between the visions in prison and the realistic, dramatic confrontations with the uncomprehending secular world.

The relationship between inner and outer worlds, between visions and conflict situations, is not one of simple opposition. The visions that come to a mystic apparently in response to some painful or conflicted situation in the day-to-day world are not only compensatory visions, for the process at work is not a matter of opposing negative life experiences with images of positive events. There is a transformation involved in visions, a transformation not yet of events, but of the self, in response to external events.

> In the dream Perpetua wins her conflict, wins the apples of immortality. The conclusion of the ladder dream, of the Dinocrates dreams, and of this combat dream, are all serene. In her dreaming, that is, Perpetua always triumphs in the *agon* she has set herself: to be brave enough to face death, despite all that life holds out—a young son, a family, the joy of earthly existence ("in carne hilaris," XII 7). There is a crescendo in the inner conquests portrayed in these visions, and in the rewards—the cheese, the water that never fails, the golden apples. As von Franz aptly observed, "The closer destruction comes in the outer sphere, the more do the consoling images in dreams become heightened."[146]

A vision in such circumstances thus becomes a way of strengthening, of firming the self; the vision provides the experience of an inner "I" against the crippling and maiming that the external world seems bent on inflicting. The vision is a response to something known to be negative, hostile to the self, and the visionary response forms and defines the self further. I would stress that the vision is a response to, not a rejection of, that outer world. (For example, Perpetua's father accuses her of not caring about her family and not providing for her little son; Perpetua's vision shows her discovering the ability to care for her dead brother, to rescue him from his suffering; and she would not have acquired this ability if she had not affirmed that she was a Christian in spite of her father's pleas.) The vision provides a creative way of relating genuinely to that world, preserving the self while crediting the world outside with power and intention. Ultimately, the developing inner life becomes a way of engaging or transforming the outer world. Not only is the external world included in the mirroring or symmetry of the response and transformed into something rich and strange that is the product of that imaginative engagement; but the self, which now embraces both the outer world and its visionary response, can envision new possibilities for action that will, in turn, elicit new responses from the external world and which may eventually transform that world.

A second example, which, while illustrating the same process, allows us to see the richness and complexity of these texts in general, is taken from the *Life of Christina of Markyate*.[147] Christina's inner experiences while she is still a young girl lead her to vow her virginity to Christ; she makes her vow in a chapel dedicated to the Virgin Mary, but tells no one. In the external world, her parents force her to exchange marriage vows with a young man named Burthred, but they cannot force her to consummate the marriage. Her mother beats her and even hires some old women to work magic on her so she will change her mind or go crazy. Her mother humiliates her by beating her in front of guests at a banquet, and she bears the scars of this beating for the rest of her life. In her inner life, she has a vision of Mary. She is given a flowering branch and told to present it to Mary, who gives her back a spray of it. In response to Mary's questions, Christina tells her how much she is suffering and that she cannot stop crying. Mary promises her deliverance. As Christina leaves her presence, she steps over the body of her betrothed husband, who is unable to touch her. She then sees Mary in an upper room and is helped to climb up to her. When Mary puts her head in Christina's lap, Christina wants to look at her, and Mary promises she will have more than that in the future. When Christina awakens from this dream vision, she finds her pillow wet with tears, which convinces her of the truth of the vision. She becomes cheerful again and invents a detailed and successful plan of escape, which involves both disguise and admitting her purpose.

Christina's vision does not deny the reality of her persecution. In fact, her telling Mary that she cries constantly shows us how painfully trapped she feels, more trapped than her brave demeanor before her mother would suggest. Her vision, instead, in allowing her to express her grief to a sympathetic listener, analyzes her parents' and Burthred's opposition to her, so that she can figure out possibilities for escape. There is one telling realistic detail about Burthred that reveals a great deal about his character and probably indicates to Christina that he will be ineffective in pursuing her:

> there lay Burthred prostrate on the ground swathed in a black cape with his face turned downwards. And as soon as he saw her passing by he stretched out his hand to seize her and hold her fast. But she, gathering her garments about her and clasping them close to her side, for they were white and flowing, passed him untouched. And as she escaped from him, he followed her with staring eyes, groaning horribly, and struck his head with repeated blows on the pavement to show his rage.[148]

In the vision she escapes from Burthred; in real life, she is able to escape from her parents and from the demands of the secular world, as well as from Burthred.

There are two symbolic oppositions at work in the imagery of this dream: horizontal-vertical and black-white. Burthred is horizontal, clothed in black; Christina is dressed in white, carrying a spray of white flowers, standing upright or climbing upward to Mary, first where she sits on a chair near the altar, then up a stair or ladder to an upper room. The white clothing clearly confirms her virginity and associates her with Mary, for later Christina has a vision of Mary clothed in white robes and crowned with a white bishop's miter. But there is another realistic detail here that finds a later echo in Christina's real escape. Christina has to wrap her clothing around her closely, or she will be grabbed by Burthred. She seems to expect that something similar will happen when she makes her escape, and she is fully prepared for it.

> And secretly taking masculine garb which she had got ready beforehand in order to disguise herself as a man, she went out swathed in a long cloak that reached to her heels. But when her sister Matilda saw her hastening out, for she recognized her from her clothes, she followed behind her. Christina, noticing this, pretended that she was going to the church of Our Blessed Lady. But, as she walked, one of the sleeves of the man's garment which she was hiding beneath her cloak slipped to the ground whether through carelessness or by design I do not know. And when Matilda saw it, she said, "What is this, Theodora, that you are trailing on the ground?" But she replied with an innocent look: "Sister dear, take it with you when you go back to the house for it is getting in my way." And she handed over to her a veil and her father's keys. . . .[149]

To make her escape, she hands over the two symbols of her female role—her veil and the household keys—and leaves dressed as a man. Several centuries later, Christine de Pizan uses the same kind of creative revisioning of conflict situations in her writings. As the *City of Ladies* begins, the protagonist Christine is in despair at reading an antifeminist tract; she has a vision in which Lady Reason helps her to build the foundation for her city. In her *Lavision* it is Philosophy who appears to her and helps her to find solutions for her difficulties.

Purpose and Scope of This Anthology

The foregoing has been intended as an introduction to, and a defense of, medieval women's devotional literature. I have attempted to contextualize these writings by examining what they reveal about the process of writing for medieval women, the attitudes of these women toward Latin and the vernacular languages, their doubts about being women and writers, and their use of certain strategies such as vision and dialogue to provide justification for their authority and to transcend their gender. I stress a few themes found in their works that seem directly related to the issue of writing and authority—virginity, illness, and creative envisioning of conflict situations. I suggest that a deeper understanding of the parallels between women's visionary writing and oral narrative is useful for a more sympathetic reading of texts characterized as subjective, repetitive, proverbial, nonanalytical, ahistorical, preferring the concrete to the abstract, and the formulaic to the self-consciously literary style. I believe that an awareness of the bilingualism of most of the writers from the twelfth century on can give the reader more insight into peculiar or unusual expressions, as when a woman's experience presents itself to her in two languages, one associated with her daily life and with the unconscious (as Ong suggests) and the other associated with her ritualized religious life, the language of the liturgy.

It is a commonplace among Latin scholars that medieval Latin isn't very good Latin, and by the standards of the classical period that is true. But I hope I have demonstrated that there is no reason to expect that medieval women would write good classical Latin—nor would their audience have been expected to understand it readily. The women writers of devotional literature don't write the Latin of the School of Chartres either—but it is probably only habit that causes us to see scholastic Latin as a standard against which to judge these writings. If we compare the writings in this anthology with comparable productions by male writers—chronicles, saints' lives, sermons, guides to meditation—I think we find that women are as skilled, by and large, as their male counterparts. Comparative studies of syntax, size of vocabulary, use of neologisms, and so on, have yet to be done; and it remains questionable whether such quantified studies could really address the issue of literary success. The question of relative skill in the use of the vernacular languages is also still to be decided, but it does seem significant that women, in writing devotional literature, are among the first to use the vernacular languages to express complex subjective states directly, forthrightly (by medieval standards), and precisely.

A few comments about translation are in order here. All the texts included in this collection were originally written in languages currently inaccessible to all but scholars. Naturally, all the poetic or literary characteristics cannot be reproduced in modern English; we lose the complex rhyme schemes, the alliteration, the puns and wordplays. But what can be reproduced are the flexibility of language to express complex states of mind, the unerring selection of a telling gesture in a portrait of someone, the use of metaphor and simile in order to stretch the understanding to make new connections in experience, and the ear for dialogue and colloquial speech.

Before I turn to the presentation of the historical background of these writers, I would like to say something about my choice of texts. Any anthology represents a personal selection of favorite authors, and this book is no exception. In planning this collection I decided to include as many previously untranslated writings as possible; in making decisions about authors who may be unknown to readers, I have sought to include whole works or self-contained chapters that represent the tone, style, and concerns of that writer. With two exceptions, I decided to omit the works of those writers that have been translated recently in readily available editions.[150] Instead, I chose to introduce a number of little-known authors in this anthology in the hopes that these selections will inspire other scholars to undertake complete translations in the future.[151]

Twenty-eight different women are represented, ten of them for the first time in English translation. Twelve of the works included here may be classed as visionary autobiography; six of those twelve were composed orally and then dictated, with the final written text supervised by the author.[152] Seven works of spiritual guidance are included, in the form of letters, sermons, or short treatises; three of these were dictated.[153] Of the remaining works, there are three plays, a number of poems, some prose narratives of visions, several personal letters, and one epic account of a pilgrimage. There is much variety in the languages employed in these selections.

One account is written in Greek; nine are in Latin. Almost all the European vernacular languages are represented: German, Old French, Dutch, Italian, Middle English, Spanish, Provençal and Franco-Provençal.[154] There are three instances, all of them biographies, where we do not know what language each woman used in speaking with her biographer; the surviving texts are in Latin, and we know that each of these women (Marie d'Oignies, Christina Mirabilis of St. Trond, Christina of Markyate) was literate in Latin.

Most of the women represented here led consecrated religious lives, but the ways in which they chose to devote their lives to God differed markedly. St. Perpetua, Margery Kempe, Doña Leonor López, and Christine de Pizan were married and belonged to no order; Angela of Foligno was also married and a Franciscan tertiary. Hrotsvit was a canoness. Five women— Hugeberc, St. Leoba, St. Gertrude the Great, Christina of Markyate, and Hildegard—were Benedictines. Beatrijs was Cistercian; and St. Umiltà, Vallombrosan; Marguerite d'Oingt, Carthusian—all three were orders that observed a stricter Benedictine rule. Five of the women visionaries were associated with Beguine groups in some way; and another five, with the Franciscan order either as nuns, tertiaries, or Spiritual Franciscans. Only one was a Dominican; St. Catherine of Siena was a Dominican tertiary. Many of these women visionaries lived for an extended period of time as hermits or recluses and then later lived in communities. Ten of the women included here held positions of authority within the groups to which they belonged, but the majority provided leadership to a sizable community of the faithful without taking on institutional roles such as abbess or prioress.

The historical periods in which the women lived also influenced the kinds of works they wrote and which languages they employed. The greatest variety is found in the early period of Christianity, from the third to the tenth century; from the five writers representing that period, we have four different types of narrative: a martyr's prison autobiography, two biographies utilizing first-person recollections, two plays, and a pilgrimage adventure story. In the writings from the twelfth century, there are more emphasis on personal visionary experience and a new tendency toward autobiography. As the same time, a number of new devotional themes become important: the humanity of Christ, the intercession of the Virgin Mary, and the importance of material poverty and humility. These themes are all developed further in the thirteenth and fourteenth centuries as the autobiographical and visionary elements become more dominant; and the sense of isolation, even persecution, of the woman visionary is often stressed. The writings are painfully personal and individualized in most cases, but the audience for whom the women are writing seems much larger, and a more public teaching role for female mystics is implied. Some of the theological issues touched on in women's devotional writing of the thirteenth and fourteenth centuries—the motherhood of Christ, the devotion to the Eucharist, the frequent occurrence of erotic imagery in contemplating the wounds of Christ—suggest that women were feeling very strongly their exclusion from the priesthood.

I should point out that although this collection is intended to represent writings by and for women over a twelve-hundred year period, not all the writings included are by women. This fact merits some explanation.

I have included writings by men when there are no extant writings by women for the same period, when the writings portray women who were the originators of new movements, and when the historical period involved is crucial for an overview of the roles of women as religious leaders and devotional writers over the long period covered by the term *medieval*. (In all cases, as I point out in discussing individual texts, the writings by men are based on first-person accounts by women or on accounts by female witnesses.) Thus, I have included St. Gregory of Nyssa's life of his sister, St. Macrina, for several reasons: aside from Jerome's letters, St. Gregory's biography is the best demonstration of the leadership role provided by women in early monasticism because it gives an excellent example of the inherent democracy and high intellectual standards of those early communities, because it comes from a time when the Greek and the Latin churches were not yet divided, and because I am inclined to believe that St. Macrina herself, in her last interview with her brother, suggested most of the structure and provided the essential details to be included in the biography.

Another historically significant moment is in the eighth century, when St. Boniface led a handpicked group of English religious persons in the mission to Christianize Germany. To do justice to the importance of Anglo-Saxon women in this mission I thought it necessary to include two quite different texts, one a heroic poem by a woman, Huneberc's *Hodoeporicon of St. Willibald*, and the other a biography written by a man, Rudolf of Fulda's *Life of St. Leoba*. Huneberc's heroic poem is a fascinating account of St. Willibald's epic pilgrimages and adventures, but it can tell us little of the roles and personalities of women in St. Boniface's mission except for what we can infer from the existence of a community in which a nun with Huneberc's interests and abilities flourished. This, to me, is only part of the story. The other side of this venture—the heroism, stamina, leadership, and charisma of the women involved in the mission—is better exemplified in the figure of St. Leoba herself. The entire *Life* proved to be too long to include, so in selecting passages from the biography, I have chosen to emphasize those parts of the *Life* that we know by internal evidence to have been provided by the testimony of three women disciples of St. Leoba, who knew her in England and who accompanied her to Germany.

The third historical moment is the period of the first Beguines in the Low Countries. Although some remarkable compositions by Beguines are extant and are included in this collection, none come from the first generation of Beguines at the end of the twelfth and the beginning of the thirteenth century. Our best witnesses to this first period of activity are Cardinal Jacques de Vitry's *Life of Marie d'Oignies* (the women who is generally credited with being the originator of the Beguine movement in the area around Liège) and Thomas de Cantimpré's *Life of Christina Mirabilis* or Christina of St. Trond. We know that Marie quite consciously chose Jacques de Vitry as her mouthpiece and that at least at the time that he was writing her life, Jacques de Vitry saw himself as a protector of holy women. He wanted to define their new mode of life—not so much for the women themselves, but for the church hierarchy that was disturbed at this new movement of feminine piety and apostolic fervor—and to write about these women in such a way that their insights and practices could be a source of renewal for the church as a whole. These two biographies tell us much about the lives holy women were leading and the influences they had on their society. They do not, of course, reveal much about women as writers (although Thomas de Cantimpré does say that Christina composed very elegant songs in Latin, which she sang to herself while meditating). Only a generation later, however, women like Beatrijs of Nazareth (born around 1200, twenty-three years after the birth of Marie de Oignies) and Hadewijch were writing remarkable books of introspection and spiritual guidance for the Beguine and Cistercian groups described by Jacques de Vitry and Thomas de Cantimpré.

The majority of these writings by women are about women, and in those cases where the chief figure in a narrative is male (as in Huneberc's *Hodoeporion of St. Willibald* or in Hrotsvit's *Pelagius* and *Abraham*), his experiences are relevant to women's as well as men's concerns, and his actions are meant to reflect on women's as well as men's actions or to provide models for both women and men. Because in God there are no gender distinctions, on earth, too, women writers tend to see gender distinctions as something man-made, not permanent. A woman may escape the human limitations of her gender, and many of these texts are intended to show women—and men as well—just how to make that escape. When the women identify the particular group for whom they are writing, it is often those who are oppressed, and I believe most of the writers in this anthology were aware that many men would identify with their experiences of exclusion and disenfranchisement.

And this leads me to my justification for another text that is included here. One may question the appropriateness of Christine de Pizan's works in this collection of devotional and didactic texts by and about medieval women. I feel she belongs here for a number of reasons. Although not a devotional writer, she did compose both didactic and autobiographical works. Although she is primarily a secular writer—and the first professional female writer in France—she retired to a religious community (evidently the Dominican convent at Poissy, where her daughter was a nun) for the last decade of her life. There are two primary reasons for including her works. First, she utilizes all the narrative techniques developed by her predecessors, especially the use of vision and dialogue; and she presents the same kind of conflicts over role models. Second, she addresses directly the antifeminism of the medieval world, the hostility to women, especially to women who want to have voices and who want to write. I see her autobiography (in *Lavision Christine*) and her role in the Romance of the Rose debate as fulfilling the same function that Virginia Woolf's *A Room of One's Own* had for our period. I thought for some time about writing a section of this introduction on what female devotional writers do not talk about directly—the oppression they encountered as women. But it seemed to me wiser to include a medieval woman's own words on that topic; it also seemed inevitable that for a secular woman to get any distance on the antifeminism of her society, she probably would not deal with oppression the way mystics had, which was to transcend it by becoming, in a sense, both Christ and Mary.

What Christine de Pizan exposes in her didactic works (*City of Ladies*, *Romance of the Rose debate*, *The Book of the Three Virtues*, and *Lavision*) is women's awareness that in the eyes of the world they have no business writing, yet they feel compelled to do so as part of their moral and spiritual growth. Christine shows us why women have come to believe they should not write; she shows how women are disadvantaged in terms of education, how difficult it is for the disenfranchised to learn to function in the economic and legal systems. She knows how the literary tradition creates an image of women that makes women hate themselves, and she insists that women have to create and discover their own tradition to gain the strength to counter the oppression of official tradition. She provides the theory and the analysis that can help explain why medieval women wrote the kind of literature collected here. Christine de Pizan speaks about the unspoken experience of those who wrote before her, and it is for them that she erects her City of Ladies.

NOTES

1. Katharina M. Wilson, *Medieval Women Writers* (Athens, Ga.: University of Georgia Press, 1984), p. ix.

2. For a recent assessment of female literacy, see Joan M. Ferrante, "The Education of Women in Theory, Fact, and Fantasy," in *Beyond their Sex: Learned Women of the European Past*, ed. Patricia Labalme (New York: New York University Press, 1980), pp. 9–42. Early but still valuable studies are Lina Eckenstein, *Women Under Monasticism* (Cambridge: Cambridge University Press, 1896); Emily James Putnam, *The Lady: Studies of Certain Significant Phases of her History* (Chicago: University of Chicago Press, 1969; reprint of 1910 ed.; and Eileen Power, *Medieval English Nunneries 1275–1535* (Cambridge: Cambridge University Press, 1922). For general observations, see Carolly Erickson, "The Vision of Women," in her *The Medieval Vision* (New York: Oxford University Press, 1976), pp. 181–212. On the education of the Beguines, see Ernest W. McDonnell, *The Beguines and Beghards in Medieval Culture* (New York: Octagon Books, 1969).

3. On literacy among laywomen, especially in Italy, see David Herlihy, "The Natural History of Medieval Women," in *Natural History* 87 (March 1978), pp. 56–67; "Family Solidarity in Medieval Italian History," in *Economy, Society, and Government: Essays in Honor of Robert J. Reynolds*, ed. Herlihy, Lopez, and Slessarev (Kent, Ohio: Kent State University Press, 1969), pp. 173–84; Lauro Martines, "A Way of Looking at Women in Renaissance Florence" in *Journal of Medieval and Renaissance Studies* 4 (Spring 1974), pp. 15–28; Iris Origo, *The Merchant of Prato* (London: J. Cape, 1957), and Eileen Power, *Medieval Women*, ed. M. M. Postan (Cambridge: Cambridge University Press, 1975), esp. "The Education of Women," pp. 76–88.

4. See Power, "Education of Women" and *Medieval English Nunneries* cited earlier; McDonnell, *The Beguines and Beghards*, and R. W. Southern, *Western Society and the Church in the Middle Ages* (Baltimore, M.: Penguin, 1970), pp. 309–31.

5. Peter Dronke, *Women Writers of the Middle Ages* (Cambridge: Cambridge University Press, 1984), p. x.

6. For English translations and a brief study of the women troubadours, see Meg Bogin, *The Women Troubadours* (New York: W. W. Norton, 1980; first pub. 1976); original texts in Oskar Schultz-Gora, *Die Proven-*zalischen Dichterinnen (Leipzig: G. Fock, 1888), and see notes in Bogin and in Dronke, *Women Writers*. For another study by Dronke, see the chapter by him on the trobairitz Castelloza in Wilson, *Medieval Women Writers*, pp. 131–52. On Marie de France, see the translations by Joan Ferrante and Robert Hanning, *The Lais of Marie de France* (Durham, N.C.: The Labyrinth Press, 1982, first published 1978) and the chapter on Marie by Ferrante in Wilson, *Medieval Women Writers*, pp. 64–89. For original texts, see Alfred Ewert, ed., *Lais* (Oxford: B. Blackwell, 1963, reprint of 1944 ed.); Jean Rychner, ed. *Les lais de Marie de France* (Paris: 1969); and Karl Warnke, *Die Lais der Marie de France* (Halle: 1925).

7. The question is, of course, more complicated than this. See Peter Dronke, *Medieval Latin and the Rise of European Love-Lyric* (Oxford: Clarendon Press, 1968), and *The Medieval Lyric* (New York: Harper & Row, 1969). There are some tantalizing suggestions about women's role regarding courtly literature in Amy Kelly's *Eleanor of Aquitaine and the Four Kings* (New York: Vintage Books, 1958), but her ideas have been challenged by several critics. See also Rita Lejeune, "Rôle littéraire d'Alienor d'Aquitaine et de sa famille," *Cultura Neolatina*, XIV (1954), pp. 1–53, and "Le rôle littéraire de la famille d'Alienor d'Aquitaine," *Cahiers de civilisation médiévale*, I (1958), pp. 319–37. For various views on courtly love, see the papers collected in Francis X. Newman, ed., *The Meaning of Courtly Love* (Albany: SUNY Press, 1972).

8. See Bogin's introduction, p. 36, and Dronke, *Women Writers*, pp. 202–15.

9. See Franz Bauml, "Transformations of the Heroine: From Epic Heard to Epic Read," in *The Role of Woman in the Middle Ages*, ed. Rosmarie Thee Morewedge (Albany: SUNY Press, 1975), pp. 23–40, and "Varieties and Consequences of Medieval Literacy and Illiteracy, "*Speculum* 55 (April 1980), pp. 237–65; M. T. Clanchy, *From Memory to Written Record: England 1066–1307* (Cambridge, Mass.: Harvard University Press, 1979); Ruth Crosby, "Oral Delivery in the Middle Ages," *Speculum* 11 (January 1936), pp. 88–110; Michael Curschman, "Oral Poetry in Medieval English, French and German Literature: Some Notes on Recent Research," *Speculum* 42 (January 1967), pp. 36–52. Joseph Duggan has collected a number of papers that speak to

this question in *Oral Literature* (New York: Barnes & Noble, 1975). See, too, James W. Thompson, *The Literacy of the Laity in the Middle Ages* (Berkeley and Los Angeles: University of California Press, 1939); Walter J. Ong, *Orality and Literacy: The Technologizing of the Word* (London and New York: Methuen, 1982).

10. Peter Dronke, "The Provençal *Trobairitz*: Castelloza," in Wilson, *Medieval Women Writers*, pp. 131–52; Bogin, Introduction to *The Women Troubadours*, pp. 8–76; Pierre Bec, "'Trobairitz' et chansons de femme," *Cahiers de civilisation medievale* XXII (1979), pp. 235–62; Marianne Shapiro, "The Provençal *Trobairitz* and the Limits of Courtly Love," *Signs* 3 (1977–78), pp. 560–71; D. Rieger, "Die Trobairitzin in Italien," *Cultural Neolatina* 31 (1971), pp. 205–23.

11. Peter Dronke, *The Medieval Lyric*, p. 81.

12. Katharina Wilson, *Medieval Women Writers*, p. xvii.

13. For a translation of Jerome's letter on the education of virgins (Letter to Marcella about her daughter, Paula), see Susan Groag Bell, ed., *Women from the Greeks to the French Revolution* (Belmont, Calif.: Wadsworth, 1973), pp. 90–5. For his defense of virginity (Letter 22 to Eustochium: The Virgin's Profession), see Elizabeth Clark and Herbert Richardson, eds., *Women and Religion: A Feminist Sourcebook of Christian Thought* (New York: Harper & Row, 1977), pp. 56–68.

14. On the authority provided by celibacy, see Elisabeth Schussler Fiorenza, "Word, Spirit and Power: Women in Early Christian Communities," and Rosemary Reuther, "Mothers of the Church: Ascetic Women in the Late Patristic Age," both in *Women of Spirit: Female Leadership in the Jewish and Christian Traditions*, ed. Rosemary Reuther and Eleanor McLaughlin (New York: Simon & Schuster, 1979).

15. On women and visions, see Elizabeth Petroff, *The Consolation of the Blessed* (New York: Alta Gaia, 1979). For the importance of visions in the early church, see Elaine Pagels, "Visions, Appearances and Apostolic Authority: Gnostic and Orthodox Traditions," in *Gnosis: Festschrift für Hans Jonas*, ed. B. Aland (Göttingen: 1978), pp. 415–30.

16. Petroff, pp. 39–82.

17. Petroff, pp. 194–9 for a comparison of these terms with the traditional division of the mystical life into three stages, purgative, illuminative and unitive, with bibliography.

18. On the conditions of religious life for women, see Elizabeth Petroff, "Women and Religion in Thirteenth Century Italy," in *Consolation of the Blessed*, pp. 14–38, and bibliography, pp. 183–93; Jean Leclerq, "Feminine Monasticism in the Twelfth and Thirteenth Centuries," in *The Continuing Quest for God*, ed. William Skudlarek

(Collegeville, Minn.: The Liturgical Press, 1982), pp. 114–26.

19. On penitential acts, see *Medieval Handbooks of Penance* ed. and trans. Helena M. Gamer and John T. McNeill (New York: Columbia Univ. Press, 1938).

20. See the prayers in the Rule for Franciscan Tertiaries, for example; Maurice Powicke, *The Christian Life in the Middle Ages* (Oxford: Clarendon Press, 1935).

21. For a representative text, see *Meditations on the Life of Christ: An Illustrated Manuscript of the Fourteenth Century*, ed. Isa Ragusa and Rosalie B. Green (Princeton: Princeton University Press, 1977, reprinted from 1961 ed.).

22. On her pilgrimage to Rome, Margery Kempe meets a woman returning from Jerusalem who has an image of Christ in a chest. "The woman who had this image ... took [it] out of the chest, and set it in worshipful wives' laps; and they would put shirts thereon, and kiss it as if it had been God Himself" (*The Book of Margery Kempe*, trans. W. Butler-Bowden [New York: Devin Adair, 1944], pp. 66–7).

23. Angela of Foligno, *Le Livre de l'expérience des vrais fidéles*, ed. and trans. by M. J. Ferré and L. Baudry (Paris: E. Droz, 1927). Letter 3, pp. 494–6. Vita B. Angelae de Fulginio, *AASS* 4 Januarii, par. 40.

24. For some examples of such attacks, see Petroff, *Consolation of the Blessed*, pp. 45–8, and "Transforming the World: The Serpent Dragon and the Virgin Saint," in *Arché, Notes and Papers on Archaic Studies* 6 (1981) pp. 53–70.

25. Vita B. Mariae Ogniacensis, *AASS* 23 Junii, Bk. I, ch. 22, transl. Margot H. King.

26. "Life of St. Umiltà, abbess of the Vallombrosan Order in Florence," in Petroff, *Consolation of the Blessed*, pp. 121–37. These incidents are found on pp. 127–8.

27. Vita Christinae Mirabilis, *AASS* 24 Julii, Ch. III, par. 29, transl. Margot H. King.

28. "The Life of St. Leoba by Rudolf, Monk of Fulda," in *The Anglo-Saxon Missionaries in Germany*, ed. and trans. C. H. Talbot (New York: Sheed & Ward, 1954), pp. 205–26. This vision is found on p. 212.

29. "Life of St. Leoba," pp. 212–13.

30. St. Hildegard's vision is found in Francesca Maria Steele, *The Life and Visions of St. Hildegarde* (London: Heath, Cranton and Ousely, Ltd., 1914), pp. 153–5.

31. See *Meditations on the Life of Christ*, ed. Ragusa and Green, and Jacopo da Voragine's *The Golden Legend*, English trans. and ed. Granger Ryan and Helmut Ripperger (New York: Arno, 1969); for the Latin text *Jacobi Voragine, Legenda aurea vulgati storia Lombardica dicta*, ed. Th Graesse (Leipzig: Arnold Lib., 1850, reprinted 1969).

32. Vita B. Mariae Ogniacensis, *AASS* 24 Junii, Bk. II, ch. 88, trans. Margot H. King.

33. *The Life and Revelations of Saint Gertrude* (Westminster, M.: The Newman Press, 1949), Part II, "The Revelations of Saint Gertrude," pp. 85–6.

34. Angela of Foligno, *Le Livre*, par. 10, p. 8. Cf. Vita B. Angelae de Fulginio, *AASS* 4 Januarii, par. 20 (authors transl.).

35. *Le Livre*, par. 11, pp. 8–9. Cf. Vita B. Angelae, par. 21.

36. *Le Livre*, par. 40, p. 62. Cf. Vita B. Angelae, par. 96.

37. "Concerning the Blessed Margarita of Faenza, Virgin and Abbess of the Vallombrosan Order," in Petroff, *Consolation of the Blessed*, p. 155.

38. "Revelations and Miracles of Blessed Margarita of Faenza," in Petroff, *Consolation of the Blessed*, p. 161.

39. "Margarita," p. 162.

40. *Le Livre*, par. 135, pp. 192–4. Cf. Vita B. Angelae, par. 100.

41. *Le Livre*, par. 135, p. 292. Cf. Vita B. Angelae, par. 101.

42. *Le Livre*, par. 75, p. 156. Cf. Vita B. Angelae, par. 68.

43. *The Book of Margery Kempe*, trans. Butler-Bowden, p. 59.

44. *The Book of Margery Kempe*, p. 190.

45. *The Life and Revelations of Saint Gertrude*, Part II, pp. 82 ff.

46. Letters of Hadewijch of Antwerp, in *Mediaeval Netherlands Religious Literature*, trans. E. Colledge (New York: London House and Maxwell, 1965), pp. 31–88.

47. *Hadewijch: The Complete Works*, trans. Mother Columba Hart (New York: Paulist Press, 1980), Vision Seven, pp. 280–2.

48. "There Are Seven Manners of Loving," Beatrijs [Beatrice] of Nazareth, in *Mediaeval Netherlands Religious Literature*, trans. E. Colledge, pp. 17–30. This is on p. 23.

49. Beatrijs, "Seven Manners of Loving," pp. 23–4.

50. *The Revelations of Mechthild of Magdeburg, or the Flowing Light of the Godhead*, trans. Lucy Menzies (London: Longmans, Green and Co., 1953), pp. 20–1.

51. Vita B. Angelae, pars. 49, 50. This is the Bollandist Acta Sanctorum text, which combines two sections of the earlier Assisi manuscript. See *Le Livre*, par. 35 and pars. 46–58. Angela evidently narrated the event to Fra Arnaldo twice, giving more details the second time.

52. "Life of the Blessed Aldobrandesca of Siena, Widowed Tertiary of the Umiliati (1245–1310)" in Petroff, *Consolation of the Blessed*, p. 172.

53. Beatrijs of Nazareth, "Seven Manners of Loving," p. 25.

54. Beatrijs, "Seven Manners of Loving," p. 25.

55. "Life of the Blessed Aldobrandesca of Siena," p. 173.

56. *The Life of Christina of Markyate, A Twelfth Century Recluse*, ed. and trans. C. H. Talbot (Oxford: Clarendon Press, 1959), pp. 109–11.

57. Pietro Zama, *Santa Umiltà: La Vita e i "Sermones"* (Faenza: Fratelli Lega Editori, 1974), Sermon 5, p. 146.

58. On the writings of Marguerite Porete, see Peter Dronke, *Women Writers of the Middle Ages*, pp. 207–28 and 275–8. On Prous Boneta, see William Harold May, "The Confession of Prous Boneta, Heretic and Heresiarch," in *Essays in Medieval Life and Thought*, ed. John Mundy et al. (New York: Columbia University Press, 1955), pp. 3–30.

59. Hildegard was thoroughly in favor of the Inquisition on the Cathars, and Marie d'Oignies encouraged Jacques de Vitry to preach the Albigensian Crusade, but Elisabeth of Schönau had doubts because the Cathars seemed so upstanding. See Eckenstein, *Woman Under Monasticism*, p. 281.

60. Catherine of Siena publicly preached a new Crusade, which she thought would provide a common focus for the bellicose energies that were disrupting Europe and would direct that aggression to a common enemy. See her letters on this topic in *Catherine of Siena as Seen in her Letters*, trans. Vida Scudder (London: J. M. Dent, 1927).

61. Lina Eckenstein and Francesca Maria Steele discuss Hildegard's preaching, as does Joan Ferrante; for St. Margarita's defense of her preaching, see her biography cited earlier. St. Umiltà, St. Angela of Foligno, and St. Catherine all preached publicly in Italy.

62. For two examples of hearing confessions, see "The Life of Christina Mirabilis," included here, and "The Life of St. Umiltà," cited earlier.

63. See Donald Weinstein and Rudolf M. Bell, *Saints and Society: The Two Worlds of Western Christendom 1000–1700* (Chicago and London: University of Chicago Press, 1982).

64. One example, on a rather large scale, of women effecting change is the successful campaign by Saint Birgitta of Sweden and Saint Catherine of Siena to move the Papacy back to Rome from Avignon. Not only did Catherine get Pope Gregory to Rome; "she persuaded him to share in her sense of sin by walking to the Vatican through the streets of Rome barefoot, an act of papal penitence never done before or repeated since" (E. McLaughlin, "Women, Power and the Pursuit of Holiness," in *Women of Spirit*, p. 117). But the changes felt by the most people were probably those improvements provided by women in the care of the poor and the

diseased. The contribution of women to medieval welfare systems has yet to be assessed, but it was significant.

65. See the references to oral tradition in note 9 earlier, especially Walter J. Ong, *Orality and Literacy: The Technologizing of the Word*.

66. This is another area of research where much work remains to be done. Nine of the writers included here composed in Latin, but for all except the first, Perpetua, and perhaps even for her, Latin was a second language. Two women (Angela of Foligno and Catherine of Siena) wrote in Italian but understood spoken Latin; two (Mechthild and Magdalena Beutler) wrote in German but understood Latin. Na Prous Boneta evidently could not read Latin, and she dictated her confession in Provençal, but she probably understood Latin and Italian. When God speaks to her, it is definitely in Provençal whereas when God speaks to Hildegard or Gertrude, he does so in Latin. Marguerite d'Oingt wrote in Latin, French, and Franco-Provençal; Marguerite Porete wrote in French and was well educated in Latin; the same is true of Christine de Pizan. The three Netherlands writers evidently could write Flemish or Dutch, French, and Latin. Even Margery Kempe, who knew only English, has a developed sense of levels of diction; when God speaks to her, it is in alliterative phrases.

67. For Guibert, see John F. Benton, *Self and Society in Medieval France: The Memoirs of Abbot Guibert of Nogent* (New York: Harper & Row, 1970).

68. Caroline Walker Bynum, *Jesus as Mother: Studies in the Spirituality of the High Middle Ages* (Berkeley: University of California Press, 1982), p. 87.

69. Christine Downing, "Revisioning Autobiography: The Bequest of Freud and Jung," in *Soundings* 60 (Summer 1977), pp. 210–28. This passage is from pp. 211–12.

70. Downing, "Revisioning Autobiography," p. 213.

71. *The Revelations of Mechthild of Magdeburg, or The Flowing Light of the Godhead*, p. 3.

72. *Revelations of Mechthild*, p. 9.

73. *Revelations of Mechthild*, Bk. 2, p. 58.

74. *Revelations of Mechthild*, p. 58.

75. *Revelations of Mechthild*, p. 59.

76. *St. Augustine Confessions*, trans. R. S. Pine Coffin (New York and Baltimore: Penguin, 1961), p. 24. The Latin text (*St. Augustine's Confessions*, 2 vols., with an English translation by William Watts, 1631 [Cambridge, Mass.: Harvard University Press, 1912: Loeb Classical Library]) is as follows:

quis dabit mihi, ut venias in cor meum et inebries illud, ut obliviscar mala mea et unum bonum amplectar, te? quid mihi es? miserere, ut loquar. quid tibi sum ipse, ut amari te iubeas a me et, nisi, faciam, irascaris mihi et mineris ingentes miserias? parvane ipsa est, si non amem te? ei mihi! dic mihi

per miserationes tuas, domine deus meus, quid sis mihi. dic animae meae: salus tua ego sum. sic dic, audiam ... curram post vocem hanc et adprehendam te. noli abscondere a me faciem tuam: moriar, ne moriar, ut eam videam.

Angusta est domus animae meae, quo venias ad eam: dilatetur abs te. ruinosa est: refice eam.

77. Ernst Robert Curtius, *European Literature and the Latin Middle Ages* (New York: Harper & Row, 1973; first pub. 1953). On classical and medieval use of humility topos, see pp. 83–5.

78. *The Prayers and Meditations of St. Anselm*, trans. Sister Benedicta Ward, SLG (New York and Baltimore: Penguin, 1973), p. 127, lines 14–22. Latin text: *S. Anselmi Cantuariensis Archiepiscopi, Opera Omnia*, vol. II, ed. F. S. Schmitt (Stuttgart-Bad Cannstatt: Friedrich Frommann Verlag, 1968), Prayer 8, pp. 26–9.

Ad te, domine, tam magnum, tam sanctum, tam beatum, ad te venit scelerosus vermis, aerumnosus homuncio, iam emortuo sensu vix se dolens, sed mortua anima sibi nimis dolendus peccator. Ad te, tam magne, amice dei, valde timens venit dubius de salute sua, quia certus de magna culpa sua, sed sperans de maiori gratia tua.

79. *Prayers and Meditations of St. Anselm*, Prayer 17, "Prayer by a Bishop or Abbot to the Patron Saint of his Church," pp. 207–11. This excerpt is on p. 207, lines 4–13, 19–20. The Latin text is in Schmitt, pp. 68–70.

iste peccator, iste indigens, iste tuus licet indignus, licet ineptus, licet nimis inconveniens vicarius, iterum et iterum redit ad te, dubius, nescius, sollicitus de populo tuo, de congregatione tua et de periculo suo. Ego scilicet inutilis persona, nullis bonis ornata, sed profunda ignorantia tenebrata, innumeris vitiis deformata, immensis peccatis onerata ... te rogo consultorem, te precor adiutorem, te expecto per omnia pro me operatorem.

80. Ong, *Orality and Literacy*, pp. 34–5.

81. Vita B. Angelae de Fulginio, par. 52. There is a longer version of this in the earlier Assisi ms. See *Le Livre*, p. 186.

82. These are the opening lines of Hildegard's *Scivias*, trans. Steele, p. 123. See *Sanctae Hildegardis Scivias*, col. 383 (*PL* 93).

83. *Julian of Norwich Showings*, trans. Edmund Colledge and James Walsh (New York: Paulist Press, 1978), pp. 134–5, short text.

84. St. Umiltà, from Latin text of Sermons, in Petroff, *Consolation of the Blessed*, p. 138.

85. "Disadvantaged" is obviously a relative term, and I am thinking here of women's education after the great cathedral schools and later the universities came into existence. I would not say that Hrotsvit or Leoba was disadvantaged educationally—in fact, their erudition

probably surpassed that of most of their male contemporaries. See Wilson, "The Saxon Canoness: Hrotsvit of Gandersheim," in Wilson, *Medieval Women Writers*, pp. 30–63, and the bibliography cited there. On Leoba's learning, see Eleanor McLaughlin, "Women, Power and the Pursuit of Holiness in Medieval Christianity," esp. pp. 103–108. "Lioba was a skilled classicist, read widely not only in Holy Scripture, but in the works of the Church Fathers, in canon law, and in the decisions of all the councils. In the world of the eighth century, such erudition gave her an almost magical authority ..." (p. 105). On learning in female monastic communities, see Lina Eckenstein, *Women Under Monasticism* (New York: Russell and Russell, 1963; reprint of 1896 ed.). When we look at the situation in the thirteenth century, we see some apparent exceptions: the convent at Helfta under the rule of the Abbess Gertrude, the Cistercian convents and communities of Beguines in Belgium, such as La Ramée, where Beatrijs was sent to perfect herself in the copying of manuscripts. Nevertheless, it would seem that when and if systematic education in the liberal arts and in theology was available to women, it was only intended for noblewomen who were identified as religious from childhood. Secondly, the new centers of learning, the cathedral schools and the universities, were closed to women. The area of women's education that needs exploration is their education in the vernacular. Susan Groag Bell's recent article in *Signs* is an important step in this direction: "Medieval Women Book Owners: Arbiters of Lay Piety and Ambassadors of Culture," *Signs* 7:4 (Summer 1982), pp. 742–69.

86. "The Rule of St. Clare," in *The Legend and Writings of St. Clare of Assisi* (New York: The Franciscan Institute, St. Bonaventure, 1953), pp. 65–81. For example, "Those who do not know letters shall say . . . Pater Nosters . . ." (p. 69) and "those who do not know how to read, should not be anxious to learn" (p. 79).

87. "Life of St. Umiltà, Abbess of the Vallombrosan Order in Florence," in *Consolation of the Blessed*, pp. 121–50, and Pietro Zama, *Santa Umiltà: La Vita e i "sermones"* (Faenza, Italy, 1974).

88. "The Blessed Margarita of Faenza. . . . Revelations and Miracles" by John of Faenza, Margarita's nephew, in *Consolation of the Blessed*, pp. 160–1: "When the most holy Umiltà, the said abbess, had given Margarita a woman teacher, to teach her letters, that remarkable nun said to her, 'Study, learn how to read, for you shall be abbess.' Yet Margarita soon abandoned her teacher, believing firmly that the omnipotent Lord would open her senses to the deep understanding of scripture in her mind. Once when I, the said John, was reading to her, I asked her if she wanted me to read it in the vernacular. She said, 'Not at all. I understand very clearly.'"

89. ". . . for, as she said to me many times, she didn't seem to herself to be saying anything at all when she was revealing something to me: rather she seemed to herself to be blaspheming on account of the highness of the revelation and the impossibility of expression, for nothing can be expressed in human words except only those things which are told to us or are done bodily or imaginatively. Divine things, and those which the mind undergoes under divine influence, are immeasurable for us in all respects ... and frequently she could not explain, although she might give me to understand something through what she was saying, and she would be disturbed and saddened, for she couldn't show me what she knew" (Second Prologue to the Vita by Fra Arnaldo, *AASS* 4 Januarii).

90. Raymond of Capua, *The Life of St. Catherine of Siena*, trans. Conleath Kearns (Wilmington, Delaware: Michael Glazier, 1980), p. 35. Latin text is in *AASS* 30 Aprilis.

91. Characteristics here from Ong, *Orality and Literacy*, pp. 37–61.

92. Ong, *Orality and Literacy*, p. 61.

93. See the works cited in note 9 earlier, especially the volume edited by Joseph Duggan, *Oral Literature*.

94. Ong, *Orality and Literary*, pp. 113–14.

95. Dronke, *Women Writers of the Middle Ages*, pp. 73 ff., has a very convincing analysis of the ironies involved in Hrotsvit's claims of inadequacy and humility. On Hugeberc's apologies, see p. 34 of the same text.

96. Henry Osborne Taylor, "Mystic Visions of Ascetic Women," in *The Medieval Mind*, vol. 2 (New York: Macmillan, 1919), pp. 458–86. This passage is from p. 465.

97. This is Taylor's translation of Hildegard's letter to Guibert of Gembloux, pp. 465–6 in 'Mystic Visions of Ascetic Women.'

98. *Julian of Norwich Showings*, Introduction, pp. 71–8.

99. *Showings*, long text, p. 267.

100. *Showings*, p. 268.

101. *Showings*, pp. 268–9.

102. *Showings*, p. 269.

103. *Showings*, p. 269–70.

104. *Showings*, p. 270.

105. *Showings*, Introduction, p. 76.

106. Patricia Wilson-Kastner, "Macrina: Virgin and Teacher," *Andrews University Seminary Studies* I (Spring 1979), pp. 105–17. This passage is from p. 108.

107. For the story of St. Mary the Egyptian, see Jacope da Voragine, *The Golden Legend*, and the brief discussion in Elise Boulding, *The Underside of History*, pp. 104. For versions of her story in Old French hagiography, see Peter Dembrowski, "St. Mary of Egypt and Problems of Hagiography in Old French," paper

presented at the Modern Language Association Annual Convention in 1978, at San Francisco.

108. Dronke (*Women Writers of the Middle Ages*, pp. 60, 79) says the play was originally entitled "Mary the Niece of Abraham."

109. *The Life of Christina of Markyate*, p. 72ff.

110. "*The Life of St. Leoba*," p. 210.

111. Hildegard's *Scivias* text: *Sanctae Hildegardis Scivias sive visionum ac revelationum, Patrologia Latina*, vol. 93. This is the text on which Francesca Maria Steele based her translation, *The Life and Visions of St. Hildegarde* (London: 1914). There is now a modern edition: *Hildegardis Scivias*, ed. Angela Carlevaris and Adelgundis Fuhrkotter (Turnhout: Brepols, 1978).

112. Hildegard's Latin text reads: "o homo fragilis, et cinis cineris et putredo putredinis, dic et scribe quae vides et audis. Sed quia timida es ad loquendum, et simplex ad exponendum, et indocta ad scribendum . . ." (*Patrologia Latina*, vol. 93, col. 383.)

113. Those who had been married were Marie d'Oignies, St. Umiltà, Blessed Angela of Foligno; those associated with Beguine groups: Marie d'Oignies, Christina Mirabilis of St. Trond, Hadewijch, Beatrijs, and Mechthild of Magdeburg. Of the four who lived all their adult lives in the cloister—St. Clare, St. Agnes, Beatrijs, St. Gertrude—only Gertrude entered as a child oblate with no memory of the outside world.

114. "St. Clare" by Christopher N. L. Brooke and Rosalind Brooke, in *Medieval Women*, ed. Baker, pp. 285 ff.; John Moorman, *A History of the Franciscan Order* (Oxford: Clarendon Press, 1968), pp. 205–08.

115. Vita Christinae Mirabilis, par. 9.

116. Marguerite Porete was a Beguine from Hainaut associated with the Free Spirit movement; her book, *The Mirror of Simple Souls* (full title: *Le Mirouer des simples âmes anienties et qui seulement demourent en vouloir et désir d'amour*) was condemned as heretical, and she was burned at the stake in Paris in 1310. Dronke devotes a chapter to her in his *Women Writers*; historical information is provided by Robert E. Lerner, *The Heresy of the Free Spirit in the Later Middle Ages* (Berkeley: University of California Press, 1972), pp. 68–78, 200–08. The Old French text of *Le Miroir* was only discovered and attributed to her in this century; it is published, with a lengthy introduction on the Free Spirit movement, in Romana Guarnieri, "Il Movimento del Libero Spirito," in *Archivio Italiano per la storia della pietà* 4 (1965), pp. 351–708.

117. The text of Na Prous Boneta's confession (ed. William Harold May) is printed in *Essays in Medieval Life and Thought*, ed. John Mundy et al., pp. 3–30. Na Prous was mentioned briefly by Henry Charles Lea, *A History of the Inquisition of the Middle Ages* (New York:

Harper, 1887) vol. 3, pp. 80–3. Pierre Péano, "Les Béguines du Languedoc ou la crise du T.O.F. dans la France Méridionale (xii–xivᵉ siècles), in *I Frati Penitenti di San Francesco*, ed. Mariano d'Alatri (Rome: Istituto Storico dei Cappuccini, 1977), pp. 139–58, makes reference to her and to the other Spiritual Franciscans and Beguines burned at the same time.

118. *The Book of Margery Kempe*, pp. 39–40, 41.

119. "The Martyrdom of Saints Perpetua and Felicity" in *The Acts of the Christian Martyrs*, trans H. R. Musurillo (Oxford: Oxford University Press, 1972), pp. 106–31. Perpetua speaks about her joy in prison on p. 111.

120. *The Life of Christina of Markyate, A Twelfth Century Recluse*, trans. C. H. Talbot, pp. 103 ff.

121. "Letters of Hadewijch of Antwerp," in *Mediaeval Netherlands Religious Literature*, trans. E. Colledge, pp. 31–88.

122. *The Life and Revelations of Saint Gertrude*, Part II, The Revelations of Saint Gertrude," pp. 71–3.

123. See Petroff, *Consolation of the Blessed*, pp. 40–8. It seems likely that women's ascetic practices were fueled by the medieval misogyny and that the attitudes toward the female body were inherited from the patristic period. For the basic attitudes, see *Religion and Sexism*, ed. Rosemary Reuthen (New York: Simon & Schuster, 1974), "Misogynism and Virginal Feminism in the Fathers of the Church," pp. 150–83.

124. Vita Christinae Mirabilis, pars. 47 and 48, trans. Margot H. King.

125. *Life of Christina of Markyate*, p. 103.

126. *The Book of Margery Kempe*, p. 1 of an unpublished translation by Susan Dickman.

127. *The Book of Margery Kempe*, trans. Dickman, p. 2.

128. Vita Christinae Mirabilis, par. 16, trans. Margot H. King.

129. Vita B. Mariae Ognaciensis, Ch. 18, trans. Margot H. King.

130. Vita B. Mariae Ognaciensis, Ch. 18.

131. For Margery's description of the physical agony associated with her crying, see *Book of Margery Kempe*, trans. Butler-Bowden, p. 58.

132. Angela of Foligno, *Le Livre*, par. 21, p. 24; cf. Vita Angelae de Fulginio, par. 34.

133. *Julian of Norwich Showings*, trans. Colledge and Walsh, pp. 127–8, short text.

134. Vita Christinae Mirabilis, par. 5, trans. Margot H. King.

135. See the passage by Jacques de Vitry from the "Life of Marie d'Oignies" in *Not in God's Image: Women in History from the Greeks to the Victorians*, ed. Julia O'Faolain and Lauro Marines (New York: Harper &

Row, 1973), pp. 140–1. The exception in this, as in many areas, was Catherine of Siena, who seemed to become stronger as she ate less and increased her austerites.

136. Hildegard of Bingen, in Steele trans., pp. 240–1.

137. The Life of Elisabeth of Schönau, trans. Thalia Pandiri, Bk. II, ix.

138. Life of Elisabeth of Schönau, Book II, ix.

139. "Revelations of Saint Gertrude," pp. 92–3.

140. "Revelations of Saint Gertrude," p. 94.

141. *Marguerite d'Oingt: édition critique de ses oeuvres*, ed. A. Duraffour, P. Durdilly, and P. Gardette (Paris: Les Belles Lettres, 1965). This is letter 137–8, p. 143.

142. "The Martyrdom of Saints Perpetua and Felicity," trans. Musurillo, pp. 106–31.

143. "Martyrdom of Saint Perpetua," p. 119.

144. Dronke, *Women Writers*, p. 5.

145. Erich Auerbach, *Literary Language and Its Public in Late Latin Antiquity and in the Middle Ages*, trans. Ralph Manheim (New York: Bollingen Foundation, 1965), p. 64.

146. Dronke, *Women Writers*, p. 15.

147. *The Life of Christina of Markyate*, trans. C. H. Talbot, pp. 73–7.

148. *The Life of Christina of Markyate*, p. 77.

149. *The Life of Christina of Markyate*, p. 91.

150. I have included Hadewijch and Julian of Norwich, both available in the Classics of Western Spirituality series by the Paulist Press.

151. Full translations are needed of Marguerite d'Oingt and Marguerite Porete. New translations are needed of Hildegard of Bingen, Mechthild of Magdeburg, Angela of Foligno, and Gertrude the Great. Authors and works not included here who deserve to be translated are Mechthild of Hackeborn, Sisters of Unterlinden, Life of St. Douceline, Life of Ida of Nivelles, and the autobiography of Beatrijs of Nazareth. (For these texts, see list of sources.)

152. The ten new translations are of Elisabeth of Schönau, Marie d'Oignies, Christina of St. Trond, Marguerite d'Oingt, St. Umiltà of Faenza, Na Prous Boneta, Christine de Pizan, Magdalena Beutler, Marguerite Porete, and Doña Leonor López de Córdoba. The visionary autobiographies are of St. Perpetua, Hildegard of Bingen, Elisabeth of Schönau, Hadewijch, Beatrijs of Nazareth, Mechthild of Magdeburg, St. Gertrude the Great, Angela of Foligno, Marguerite Porete, Na Prous Boneta, Margery Kempe, and Julian of Norwich. Although they are not included here, there are autobiographical works by Catherine of Siena (parts of the *Dialogue*) and Marguerite d'Oingt (*Pagina Meditationum*).

153. Works of spiritual guidance are by Hadewijch, Beatrijs, St. Umiltà, Angela of Foligno, Marguerite d'Oingt, St. Catherine of Siena, and Anna Bijn's *Mary of Nijmeghen*.

154. Latin writers include St. Perpetua, Hugeberc, Hrotsvit, Hildegard, Elisabeth of Schönau, Marguerite d'Oingt, St. Umiltà, St. Gertrude, St. Clare, and St. Agnes. Mechthild of Magdeburg and Magdalena Beutler wrote in German; Marguerite Porete and Christine de Pizan, in French; Angela of Foligno and Catherine of Siena dictated in Italian; Doña Leonor López, in Spanish; Na Prous Boneta, in Provençal; and Margery Kempe, in English. Julian of Norwich wrote in English; Hadewijch, Beatrijs, and Anna Bijns wrote in Dutch or Flemish.

I

Women in the Early Church

St. Perpetua and St. Macrina

*A*MONG THE FIRST HISTORICAL women in Christianity identified as writers or teachers are St. Perpetua (d. A.D. 203) and St. Macrina (d. A.D. 379). The story of holy women in Christianity begins earlier, however, with the images of three women in the Gospels: Mary, the mother of Christ; Mary Magdalene; and her sister, Martha. During the time of persecution in the early centuries of Christianity, the images of the holy martyrs were added: virgins walking gravely to their deaths in the arena. Then with the legalization of Christianity in the Roman Empire and the cessation of persecution, a new move into the deserts of Egypt and North Africa took place, and the image of another kind of woman appeared—St. Mary the Egyptian, the Alexandrian dancing girl turned ascetic.[1] Especially in the East, women began to be seen as leaders: St. Thecla, who disguised herself as a man in order to follow St. Paul in converting the Gentiles is one model;[2] another is St. Macrina, the sister of St. Basil and St. Gregory of Nyssa, mother and philosopher for a new community of women.[3]

These are the legends that influence women's consciousness of themselves, of the possibilities open to them, of the female role in salvation history. The images of the Virgin, of Mary Magdalene, and of Martha become part of the psychohistory of individual women as we shall see in many of the works in this anthology, but they are not really historical. The next images of women in Christianity are those of the early martyrs, the virgin saints who died during the persecution of the early church. Here we find both mythical and historical figures. St. Agnes, St. Catherine of Alexandria, St. Margaret of Alexandria, and St. Agatha may not actually have existed as historical persons, but their cults and legends influenced women throughout the Middle Ages.[4] All were said to have been tortured and martyred in early adolescence. The crime that brought them to the attention of the magistrates was a dual one: refusal to marry a pagan prince and insistence on their identity as Christians, which they felt permitted them to remain virgins. The cults of the early virgin martyrs often exhibit fantastic interweavings of pagan and Christian beliefs, and they retained their popularity well into the Reformation period as stories of these women were told, written, envisioned, dreamed about by holy women. As images of the feminine and as specific role models,[5] the virgin-saints are probably most significant for their near-fanatic defence of virginity and their highly articulate attacks on hypocrisy and immorality. In these legends, there is an idealization and an affirmation of the female commitment to a spiritual life, but this commitment entails virginity, and virginity invites attack and elicits rape and violence.[6]

Along with these legendary figures, there are two very real women of this era whose images have come down to us in the *Passion of Saints Perpetua and Felicity*.[7] Both were martyred, but neither was a virgin. In fact, Perpetua was a married women still nursing her infant son; and Felicity, her servant, was pregnant when arrested and gave birth prematurely in prison. Like the legendary virgin martyrs, they were delivered to violent deaths. When they were brought into the arena naked, even the bloodthirsty crowd was horrified "when they saw that one was a delicate young girl and the other was a woman fresh from childbirth with the milk still dripping from her breasts."[8]

Vibia Perpetua was a member of the illustrious family of the Vibii; the few facts we know about her are swiftly told by the anonymous editor of the text. She was "honeste nata, liberaliter instituta, matronaliter nupta, habens patrem et matrem et fratres duos, alterum aeque catechuminum, et filium infantem ad ubera; erat autem ipsa annorum circiter viginti et duorum" (She was nobly born, well educated, respectably married, with a father, mother, and two brothers, one of whom was a catechumen, and an infant son at the breast. She was about twenty-two years old.) Arrested at the same time were two slaves, Revocatus and Felicity, and two other catechumens, Saturninus and Secundulus. Saturus, who appears in Perpetua's first vision and who had converted all of them to Christianity, was not arrested with them, but he subsequently acted so aggressively toward the authorities that he was imprisoned with them and shared their fate.

Of this group, Perpetua was clearly the highest ranking socially, and she may well have been singled out by the Roman authorities as an example to others of her class who were attracted to Christianity. All were arrested under a recent (A.D. 202) decree of Septimus Severus aimed at identifying new converts; they died in the arena in Carthage on 7 March A.D. 203.

The text of the *Passio* as we have it in Latin (there is also a Greek translation of a somewhat later date) is divided into twenty-one short, numbered chapters. The two opening chapters, which stress the "power of the spirit" and "new prophecies," to some scholars suggest that this is a proto-Montanist document, perhaps from the circle of Tertullian or by Tertullian himself, several years prior to his conversion to the Montanist heresy, a sect in which prophetesses were revered as leaders.[9] Of particular interest to us is that Chapters III through X were written by Perpetua herself, her prison diary, "sicut conscriptum manu sua et suo sensu" (written by her own hand and according to her perceptions). Chapters XI through XIII were written by Saturus; and the concluding chapters, XIV to XXI, by the contemporary editor. Three styles of Latin may be distinguished quite clearly, and Perpetua's language is further characterized by her use of transliterated Greek words, some quite unusual and not associated with religious matters.

In this autobiographical narrative, Perpetua utilizes a number of rhetorical strategies to create a vivid persona: her dialogues with her father, mostly confrontational, in which she asserts her identity as a Christian, her visions and her interpretations of them, and her remarks about her emotional and physical responses to her family and her new surroundings. The self-image that she has created is then confirmed by Saturus' vision and by the editor's account of her behavior in the arena. The framing narrative of the *Passio*, by stressing prophecy and visions as being alive in the present, prepares us for a martyrdom tale that is more than an account of bravery under persecution or torment.

With the third chapter we hear Perpetua's own voice, and she opens with the first of several confrontations with her father: "My father, out of love for me, was trying to persuade me and shake my resolution." The scene is presented dramatically, utilizing dialogue, expressive gestures, and stage props. Perpetua points to a waterpot and asks her father if it can be called by any other name. When he agrees that it cannot, she drives her point home—"well, so too I cannot be called anything other than what I am, a Christian." Her father gestures violently toward her, but leaves without harming her; she adds that she is grateful to be separated from him. When she is baptized, she asks only for perseverance of the flesh; and when thrown into prison a few days later, she admits to being terrified by the darkness and the crowding and to being "tortured with worry for my baby." Bribery gains them better conditions for a few hours, so that she can nurse her fainting baby, whom she gives to her mother and brother. She tells of her pain as she sees the suffering they feel for her; when she receives permission for her baby to stay with her, she notes that "my prison had suddenly become a palace, so that I wanted to be there rather than anywhere else." All these details reveal someone who has many reasons for staying alive, who loves her family and grieves at being separated from them.

Yet Perpetua also demonstrates charismatic gifts to her companions, and her brother recognizes her unique relationship to God. He is confident that she has only to ask, and God will reveal to her the future. Perpetua agrees: "I knew that I could speak with the Lord. . . . And so I said, 'I shall tell you tomorrow.'" In this, her first vision, she is shown a bronze ladder reaching to heaven, with weapons associated with the games in the arena hanging from it; a dragon is crouched at the foot. Saturus climbs up first, then Perpetua, who uses the dragon's head as her first step. At the top is a garden occupied by a tall, white-haired man dressed as a shepherd and milking sheep, and by thousands of white-clad people. The old man gives her cheese to eat, and she awakens with the taste still in her mouth. As she tells the vision to her brother, she understands that it foretells their martyrdom. After this, she has two more scenes with her father, and pained as she is at his "unhappy old age," she knows she cannot make the sacrifice to the emperor that could free her. Her child is taken away from her, but her breasts are no longer painful, and the boy has been miraculously weaned.

Perpetua has lost her child, but in her inner life she encounters another child (perhaps an aspect of herself) whom she can help. A few days later in prayer she suddenly voices the name Dinocrates, her brother who had died at age seven. In her vision she sees him in a dark place of suffering, unable to reach the rim of a pool of water to drink and disfigured by the facial cancer of which he had died. She devotes all her efforts to praying for him, and shortly after she is told the date on which they are to die she is given a second vision of Dinocrates, whose face is now healed and who can now drink the water he needs. Perpetua's final vision comes the night before they are to fight with the beasts. Again she is aided by benevolent father figures: first Pomponius the deacon, who escorts her to the arena, and then a man of gigantic stature, a trainer of athletes. She is readied to fight, and as her body is rubbed with oil she sees that she is a man. When she defeats her opponent, an enormous Egyptian, the trainer rewards her with a green branch bearing golden apples. As she awakens, she realizes that she will die and that her real opponent is the Devil, over whom her victory is assured.

Saturus' vision shows us Perpetua already in paradise, speaking with the elders there in Greek. She tells Saturus, "as I was joyful in life, I'm even more joyful here now." The editor who completes the story also recognizes Perpetua's stature. He shows her protecting and leading her companions, confronting the prison authorities to assert their rights as prisoners of the state. Her behavior in the arena is of course impeccable. She enters singing a psalm; and even when she has been thrown to the ground by a mad heifer, she maintains her dignity and modestly covers her bare thighs. More significant is her asking for a hairpin to put up her loosened hair. Dronke sees this "fit of prudery" as "almost certainly fictitious"[10] but the request—which must have seemed startling and imperious from one condemned to death—and the accompanying gesture are typical of that flair for the dramatic that Perpetua demonstrated in her first confrontation with her father. To a world in which a married woman with loosened hair and torn clothing was the image of grief, where females were the ritual mourners for the dead, Perpetua's gesture denies both grief and death. Her own hand guiding the sword of the unskilled executioner is consonant with this reading and, for the crowd observing her, reaffirms the notion that her end is not death, but life.

Of all the authentic accounts of martyrdoms in the early years of Christianity, *The Passion of Saints Perpetua and Felicity* may be the most moving and impressive. Rader finds it to be unique as an early Christian account of protest that "represents a woman's response to elements of society which she considers restrictive to people's freedom in thought and action."[11] Von Franz reads Perpetua's account of her visions as a revelation of the unconscious spiritual situation of a time when the "*Weltanschauung* of antiquity was dissolving and the Christian conception of the world was breaking through."[12] Auerbach praises the text as a new kind of realistic style fostered by the spread of Christianity, the *sermo humilis*.[13] Dronke, too, sees in Perpetua's diary a new style:

> Her Latin is colloquial and homely . . . no emotion, no fantasy of Perpetua's appears disguised by stylistic ornaments. Nothing masks her tender—and determined—perceptions or her troubled dreams.[14]

Nevertheless, Dronke's primary concern is to interpret the outer narrative of events in conjunction with the inner activity of Perpetua's dreaming in order to illustrate the nature and quality of her self-awareness. In her use of visionary imagination to work through, comprehend, and transcend the grief and violence of the outer world, Perpetua is the foremother of all the later women mystics; and in her active leadership and sensitivity to others' pain, she also anticipates the famous abbesses and Beguine writers to follow.

During the third and fourth centuries—the same time that the martyrs' legends are circulating in written form—a historical movement of women and men out of the major cities of the Greek and Roman world is taking place, a profound surge of spiritual energy based on the hope of a new way of life and new freedom for women within this new religion, Christianity. Within the Christian community, the emphasis on the imminent second coming of Christ meant that procreation was no longer the highest ideal for women—it was spiritual prepared-ness that counted.[15] This belief allowed for the creation of a new female role outside the structure and needs of the family. It was no longer necessary for independent or single women to be identified as prostitutes; the celibate identification liberated women for more creative, active lives. These women evidently were seeking a complete transformation, not only of themselves but of society.[16] They went to the deserts of Egypt or Syria to live either as solitaries or in communities, supporting themselves at a subsistence level by weaving baskets or reed mats and practicing a life of abstinence, prayer, and charity.[17] As has been true in many reform movements in Christianity, those people who voluntarily chose a new life of hardship and scarcity were leaving behind a life of ease and affluence; there was a strongly utopian element in their repudiation of Roman or Greek society and in their attempt to reconstruct the social order around different values. But although they thought to leave the world behind, troubled individuals belonging to that world were still in contact with them. There are many stories of people journeying from the cities to the desert to ask the spiritual advice of the holy women and men who lived there.

It is in this context that we must place the *Life of St. Macrina*. The text is an important source of our knowledge of the regimen of an early community of Christian women in the East; it also details the childhood and spiritual development of St. Macrina, the eldest of nine children in a famous family that included St. Gregory and St. Basil. In fact, it is to Macrina's influence that Gregory attributes Basil's conversion from the worldly life of the rhetorician to the asceticism of the priesthood. Reuther sees Macrina's influence as seminal for her own time and for Greek monasticism in general:

> She was the originator of the ascetic life for the family circle and perhaps should be credited with being the immediate source of the plan of life that came to be called the "Basilian rule.". . . She is described as having been the true "father, teacher, paedagogue and counselor" of her brother Peter, born after their father's death. She brought her mother into the ascetic life and turned the family estates into a monastic community of prayer and charitable service.[18]

Ascetic did not mean uncultured; Macrina slept on a board, but even on her deathbed she argued philosophy with her brother, and the grief at her death was moderated by music although women were forbidden to sing in the church at large.[19] *The Life of Macrina* is our second text.[20]

To create a portrait of his sister Macrina and to demonstrate her importance as a role model in the Christian tradition, for she had "raised herself to the highest peak of human virtue through philosophy," St. Gregory draws on an image of female heroism and evangelistic activity from the past, St. Thecla, the disciple of St. Paul. This image Gregory combines with a presentation of Macrina's contemporary role in the creation of new women's houses and the establishment of double communities, her response to the spiritual currents of the fourth century. Recent scholarship[21] holds that Gregory's description of Macrina as virgin teacher is modeled on two depictions of St. Thecla, the apocryphal *Acts of Paul and Thecla* (first century A.D) and the *Symposion* of Methodius of Olympus (second half of the third century A.D.). In the *Acts*, Thecla is an "evangelist, a confessor who faced martyrdom, and a model and teacher in the virginal life."[22] When she first hears Paul preach, she is so drawn to him and his teaching about celibacy that she repudiates her fiancé and follows Paul to prison. She is sentenced to death by burning, but flames cannot touch her, and a cloudburst extinguishes the pyre. She catches up with Paul and insists on traveling with him although Paul still will not baptize her, but her rejection of another would-be suitor causes her to be arrested again and sentenced to execution in the arena. The first beast sent against her, a lioness, licks her feet and defends her from the other beasts; other attempted means to kill her also fail because she is surrounded by flame. Finally, she baptizes herself by diving into a tank where seals (sharks?) are kept. Her confession of faith converts many, and she is freed by the authorities "lest the city also perish with her." When she rejoins Paul, she is dressed as a man to avoid the advances that endangered her earlier. She reports her baptism and is sent to teach the word of God.

In the *Symposion*,[23] St. Thecla is the intellectual leader of a group of virgins. In this adaptation of Plato's *Symposium*, in which virginity rather than eros is the topic under discussion, Thecla reveals herself to be a master of scriptural interpretation and of rhetoric; she knows enough pagan philosophy to refute it for the benefit of Christianity. Virginity is here seen not as a rejection of the flesh as evil but as a state of freedom that prepares one for the kingdom of God.

How intimate the connection between St. Thecla and St. Macrina is appears in the following story.

> Macrina, Gregory writes, was only her public name; she had a true, secret name, revealed in a vision. For when her mother was giving birth to her, she dreamed three times that she was holding her child while a majestic figure, the virgin martyr Thecla, gave her the name of Thecla. The dream was crucial for Macrina's mother, a young woman, who had married unwillingly, merely to gain the protection of her husband when her parents had died, and for whom this was the first experience of childbirth; the labor became easy, and Macrina was born with her identity secured.[24]

The heavens named her Thecla, but Emmelia, Macrina's mother, also named her daughter after her mother-in-law, St. Macrina the Elder, who had heroically survived the persecutions of Christians under Galerius and Maximianus. She died about A.D. 340, close to the time when her younger namesake was betrothed. Emmelia and her husband, Basil, had also lived through such persecutions. In a turn-of-the-century handbook on holy women, Dunbar writes:

> Basil and Emily are represented walking off to the desert, where they took refuge during the persecution of Galerius, accompanied by a bear carrying bread on his back.[25]

Perhaps it was at this time that Emmelia first learned of other women who had formed communities in the desert.

It is in the context of this double perspective—the figural one of St. Thecla and the historical situation of the time—that Gregory gives us the facts about Macrina's education, her decision not to marry, and her creation of a new community, first for women and then for men. Seeing that the little girl responded to learning, her mother, St. Emmelia, took responsibility for her education and deliberately avoided teaching her secular literature, not because it was immoral but because of the negative or trivializing views of women found there.

> For she thought it was shameful and altogether unfitting to teach the soft and pliable nature either the passionate themes of tragedy (which are based on the stories of women and give the poets their ideas and plots), or on the unseemly antics of comedy, or on the shameful activities of the immoral characters in the *Iliad*, defiling the child's nature with the undignified tales about women.[26]

Instead Macrina is taught Scripture, particularly the Wisdom of Solomon and the Psalms. Though she is betrothed when she is twelve, the young man chosen for her dies, and Macrina considers herself a widow. She can then take control over her own life and begins to have an influential voice in family decisions. As the eldest of her mother's four sons and five daughters, with her father and paternal grandmother recently dead, she begins to plan for the future.

All of Gregory's examples of his sister's behavior illustrate her leadership, her ability to take charge of a situation and to see possibilities for action that others do not see. She sees from the beginning that her mother will be able to make some new choices when the other children are grown, and she lifts the burden of many responsibilities from her mother's shoulders until that time. She then puts into motion her plan for a women's religious community, in which Macrina, her mother, and their former servants will all hold property in common.

Macrina's ability to take control by understanding how to view a situation of pain (such as the loss of her fiancé, of her father, of a favorite brother, Naucratius) is essentially philosophical. It is philosophy that has trained her in controlling her emotions, in focusing on higher goals, and in bringing comfort to others. So before we actually meet Macrina in Gregory's narrative, we have created a mental image of her as a thinker and an organizer. When we return to Macrina, it is with Gregory, who has not seen her for eight years, who recently lost his beloved brother, Basil, and who has been divinely forewarned that more grief is coming. As Gregory draws physically nearer the community, he speaks of his sister as the Superior; yet when he sees her she is supine, lying on a board on the ground. She is too feeble to rise but attempts to bow to Gregory nevertheless. He is, after all, a bishop as well as being her younger brother. The scene is suffused with dignity and tact—she bows; she thanks God for this opportunity for servant and handmaiden to meet; she hides her pain and directs the conversation away from grief. When Gregory cries at the memory of Basil, Macrina uses the situation to lift her hearers' thoughts to heaven. We believe in her leadership, her ability as a teacher, because it so obviously works for Gregory and because, in the background to this meeting of brother and sister is a well-organized double community, a community whose very existence testifies to her imagination and leadership.

Macrina's control over the very story Gregory is writing is illustrated by one of their final conversations. Macrina, having called Gregory and his companion to her, "took up the story of her life from infancy as if she were putting it all into a monograph." What she notes as a family pattern is divine intervention in their lives; the material prosperity of the family is irrelevant except as a sign of divine favor. The family has been Christian for four generations: the great-grandparents on their mother's side (their great-grandfather was killed and had his property confiscated for being Christian) and both sets of grandparents, parents, and nine children. In spite of the fact that their paternal grandparents were also deprived of property as Christians, the wealth of their immediate family continued to multiply, so that in Macrina's generation each of the nine children inherited more than the parents had possessed initially. Macrina gave her share away—and never had to look for benefactors for her community. In Gregory's recollections I think we can hear Macrina's own voice, pleased with her self-sufficiency and that of her community:

> By divine dispensation, her existence was such that she never stopped using her hands in the service of God, nor did she look to men for help or any opportunity for living a life of comfort. She never turned away anyone who asked for something, nor did she look for benefactors, but God, in His blessings, secretly made her little resources of activity grow as seeds, as it were, into a full-flowering harvest.[27]

Macrina's deathbed teachings were recorded by Gregory in the *Dialogue on the Soul and the Resurrection*, evidently intended to accompany and fill out the *Life* by showing Macrina's Socratic method in action. The *Dialogue* is clearly modeled on Plato's *Phaedo*, with which it shares the themes of the death of the teacher, the nature of virtue, the life of philosophy, and the fate of the soul after death. As Macrina and Gregory mourn together over the death of Basil, Macrina refutes Gregory's fear of death by showing that the soul is one and indestructible; this proved, the discussion turns to individual resurrection and the final resurrection. Macrina uses two methods to prove her truths—syllogism and Scripture. Her familiarity with both is essential to her teaching mission. She is, according to Gregory's perceptions, a virgin-sage who has transcended the limits of the body, first through her choice of virginity, which freed her from the physical demands of marriage and childbearing and from the social demands of a traditional female role, and then through her attitude toward her final illness, in which, like Job, she chose to focus her attention on the divine rather than on the earthly aspects of her existence. While still alive, she is almost pure soul, and this confirms her authority in teaching about the nature of the soul and the resurrection of the body.

NOTES

1. For more information on women as hermits, see Margot H. King, *The Desert Mothers: A Survey of the Female Anchoretical Tradition*, and *The Desert Mothers: A Bibliography*, (Saskatoon: Peregrina Publishing, 1983). For details on the story and influence of St. Mary the Egyptian, see Peter F. Dembowski, "St. Mary of Egypt and Problems of Development of Hagiography in Old French," paper delivered at the Modern Language Association Annual Convention in 1978, San Francisco; Lina Eckenstein, *Woman Under Monasticism* (Cambridge: Cambridge University Press, 1896), and Donald Attwater, ed., *The Penguin Dictionary of Saints* (New York and Baltimore: Penguin, 1965).

2. St. Thecla is the central focus of an article by John Anson, "The Female Transvestite in Early Monasticism," *Viator*, 5 (1974), pp. 1–32. Her influence as a model for the female conversion to Christianity is discussed by Ross S. Kraemer in "The Conversion of Women to Ascetic Forms of Christianity," *Signs*, 6: 2 (Winter 1980), pp. 298–307. For more on the so-called transvestite saints, see Vern Bullough, "Transvestites in the Middle Ages," in *American Journal of Sociology* 79 (1973), pp. 1381–94, and Marie Delcourt, "Female Saints in Masculine Clothing," in *Hermaphrodite: Myths and Rites of the Bisexual Figure in Classical Antiquity*, trans. Jennifer Nicholson (London: Studio Books, 1961).

Two chapters in *Women of Spirit: Female Leadership in the Jewish and Christian Traditions*, ed. Rosemary Reuther and Eleanor McLaughlin (New York: Simon & Schuster, 1979), discuss the leadership of women like Thecla in the early church: "Word, Spirit and Power: Women in Early Christian Communities" by Elisabeth Schussler Fiorenza (pp. 29–70) and "Mothers of the Church: Ascetic Women in the Late Patristic Age" by Rosemary Reuther (pp. 71–96). For an excellent introduction and texts written by women of this period, including St. Perpetua, see Patricia Wilson-Kastner et al., *A Lost Tradition: Women Writers of the Early Church* (Washington, D.C.: University Press of America, 1981).

3. For the text of her biography, see *The Life of Saint Macrina* in *Saint Gregory of Nyssa, Ascetical Works*, trans. V. W. Callahan (Washington, D.C.: Catholic University of American Press, 1967). This is the translation I have edited for this anthology. For Macrina's importance as a teacher of music, see *Women in Music: An Anthology of Source Readings from the Middle Ages to the Present*, ed. Carol Neuls-Bates (New York: Harper & Row, 1982), pp. 6–10. For further discussion, see the Reuther article in *Women of Spirit* cited in note 2 and Peter Brown, *The Cult of the Saints, Its Rise and Function in Latin Christianity* (Chicago: University of Chicago Press, 1981), pp. 57–8 and passim.

4. Compare, for instance, the entries in the *Catholic Encyclopedia* for these figures with the vitae given in *The Golden Legend* by Jacopo da Varagine. St. Agnes was probably a real martyr in Rome about A.D. 304; and her relics, venerated since A.D. 354, may be genuine; but the other details of her legend cannot be verified. It is likely that she was quite young, twelve or thirteen, when she was martyred by being stabbed in the throat. St. Agatha may have lived in Sicily in the third century, and she was certainly venerated in Catania from early times, but her cult bears more similarities to great goddess cults than it does to typical martyrs' cults. See Eckenstein, *Woman Under Monasticism*, Ch. 1, for an account of the cult of St. Agatha in the nineteenth century. St. Catherine of Alexandria is the intellectual among the virgin martyrs; she is said to have defeated fifty Greek philosophers in a debate on the true faith. The wheel on which she was supposed to die shattered when she was tied to it; and when she was finally beheaded, milk, not blood, flowed from her body. St. Margaret is also known as St. Marina and St. Pelagia; the central event of one of her legends is her being swallowed by a dragon, who then burst asunder. In another legend, she disguises herself as a man in order to live an ascetic life. Accused of having fathered a child, she takes responsibility for it, and her true sex is only discovered at her death. For more on her cult, see the references to the transvestite saints in note 2.

5. St. Margaret and St. Catherine were models and inspirers of Joan of Arc, for instance; they told her how to dress and behave, how to speak in her own defense. See Petroff, "Transforming the World: The Serpent Dragon and the Virgin Saint," in *Arché, Notes and Papers on Archaic Studies* 6 (1981), pp. 53–70.

6. In all of these stories of the virgin martyrs, the martyrs are young, just entering puberty. Their Christianity is revealed when they refuse to marry pagan nobles as is their commitment to a life consecrated to God. All are violently tortured, and attempts are made to rape them except for St. Catherine.

7. There are two early texts of the martyrdom, a Latin original and a later Greek translation. There have been a number of English translations; the most recent are by Herbert Musurillo, *The Acts of the Christian Martyrs* (Oxford: Clarendon Press, 1972), and Patricia Wilson-Kastner et al., *A Lost Tradition: Women Writers of the Early Church* (Washington, D.C.: University Press of America, 1981). In addition to the comments provided by these two editors, one may also consult the stylistic analysis of Erich Auerbach in *Literary Language and Its Public*, trans. Ralph Manheim (London: Routledge and Kegan Paul, 1965) pp. 60–6; the Jungian psychoanalytical reading by Marie-Louise von Franz in *The Passion of Perpetua* (Irving, Tex.: Spring Publications, 1980). Peter Dronke's *Women Writers of the Middle Ages: A Critical Study of Texts from Perpetua (+203) to Marguerite Porete (+1310)* (Cambridge: Cambridge University Press, 1984) devotes a chapter to Perpetua's writing.

8. This is in contrast to the sadism of the virgin martyr legends, where the young women are publicly stripped naked, whipped, exposed to various tortures at the hands of men, or turned over to the beasts. For more on this issue of domination-humiliation in the legend of St. Margaret, see Petroff, "Transforming the World: The Serpent Dragon and the Virgin Saint," cited in Note 5.

9. In addition to the chapters cited in note 2 from *Women of Spirit*, see also Anne Yarborough, "Christianization in the Fourth Century: The Example of Roman Women," in *Church History* 45 (1976), pp. 149–65; Frederick C. Klawiter, "The Role of Martyrdom and Persecution in Developing the Priestly Authority of Women in Early Christianity: A Case Study of Montanism," in *Church History* 49 (1980), pp. 251–61; Jo Ann McNamara and Suzanne F. Wemple, "Sanctity and Power: The Dual Pursuit of Medieval Women," in *Becoming Visible: Women in European History*, ed. Renate Bridenthal and Claudia Koonz (Boston: Houghton Mifflin, 1977); and Patricia Wilson-Kastner, *A Lost Tradition*, cited earlier.

10. Peter Dronke, *Women Writers of the Middle Ages*, p. 15.

11. Rosemary Rader, "*The Martyrdom of Perpetua*: A

Protest Account of Third-Century Christianity," in Patricia Wilson-Kastner et al., *A Lost Tradition*, p. 1.

12. Marie-Louise von Franz, *The Passion of Perpetua*, pp. 8–9.

13. Erich Auerbach, *Literary Language and Its Public*, p. 60.

14. Dronke, *Women Writers*, p. 1.

15. See especially Rosemary Reuther, "Mothers of the Church," in *Women of Spirit* (cited in note 2); *The Desert Mothers: A Survey of the Female Anchoretical Tradition* (Saskatoon: Peregrina Publishing, 1984); George A. Tavard, *Woman in Christian Tradition* (Notre Dame, Ind.: University of Notre Dame Press, 1973); and Rosemary Rader, "Early Christian Forms of Communal Spirituality: Women's Communities," in *The Continuing Quest for God*, ed. William Skudlarek (Collegeville, Minn.: Liturgical Press, 1982), pp. 88–99.

16. For an exploration of the utopian element in this movement to the desert, see Elise Boulding, *The Underside of History: A View of Women Through Time* (Boulder, Colo.: Westview Press, 1976), pp. 354–74.

17. On the movement as a whole, see Derwas Chitty, *The Desert a City* (Oxford: Basil Blackwell, 1966), especially Chs. 1–3; and E. A. Wallis Budge, *Paradise of the Fathers*, 2 vols. (London: Chatto and Windus, 1970). The texts translated here may be supplemented by those in Helen Waddell's *The Desert Fathers* (Ann Arbor, Mich.: University of Michigan Press, 1957), and see the bibliography in King, "Women Hermits." Palladius' *Lausiac History*, written about A.D. 420, details a number of women's communities in Egypt, ranging in size from 50 to 400 members.

18. Rosemary Reuther, "Mothers of the Church," pp. 73–4.

19. See Patricia Wilson-Kastner, "Macrina, Virgin and Teacher," in *Andrews University Seminary Studies*, 17:1 (Spring 1979), pp. 105–18; and Carol Neuls-Bates, ed., *Women in Music*, pp. 6–10.

20. *The Life of Saint Macrina* and *The Dialogue on the Soul and the Resurrection* in *Ascetical Works of St. Gregory of Nyssa*, trans. V. W. Callahan (Washington, D.C.: Catholic University of America, 1957).

21. Wilson-Kastner, "Macrina, Virgin and Teacher," pp. 106 and passim.

22. For the Greek texts, see the introduction in E. Hennecke, *New Testament Apocrypha*, ed. W. Schneemelcher, 2 vols. (Philadelphia: Westminster Press, 1965). Montague R. James, *The Apocryphal New Testament* (Oxford: Clarendon Press, 1924), includes translations of many texts from Latin, Greek, Coptic, and Syriac.

23. Greek text in G. N. Bonwetsch, *Die griechischen christlichen Schriftsteller der ersten drei Jahrhunderte* (Leipzig, 1917), vol. 27, pp. 1–141; an English translation in *Ante-Nicene Fathers*, ed. Roberts and Donaldson, vol. VI (1885–97), pp. 309–55; and *Ancient Christian Writers*, trans. Robert Meyer, vol. XXVII (Westminster, Md.: Newman Press, 1965).

24. Peter Brown, *The Cult of the Saints*, p. 58.

25. Agnes Bell Dunbar, *A Dictionary of Saintly Women* (London: George Bell and Sons, 1904), vol. I, p. 269.

26. *Life of St. Macrina*, trans. Callahan, p. 165.

27. *Life of St. Macrina*, trans. Callahan, p. 178.

ST. PERPETUA   (died Carthage, c. A.D. 203)

The Passion of Ss. Perpetua and Felcitas

Translated by H. R. Musurillo

I. If the ancient examples of faith, such as both testified to the grace of God, and wrought the edification of man, have for this cause been set out in writing that the reading of them may revive the past, and so both God be glorified and man strengthened, why should not new examples be set out equally suitable to both those ends? For these in like manner will some day be old and needful for posterity, though in their own time because of the veneration secured to antiquity they are held in less esteem. But let them see to this who determine the one power of the one Spirit by times and seasons: since the more recent things should rather be deemed the greater, as being "later than the last." This follows from the pre-eminence of grace promised at the last lap of the world's race. For "In the last days, saith the Lord, I will pour forth of My Spirit upon all flesh, and their sons and their daughters shall prophesy: and on my servants and on my handmaidens will I pour forth of My Spirit: and their young men shall see visions, and their old men shall dream dreams." And so we who recognize and hold in honour not new prophecies only but new visions as alike promised, and count all the rest of the powers of the Holy Spirit as intended for the equipment of the Church, to which the same Spirit was sent bestowing all gifts upon all as the Lord dealt to each man, we cannot but set these out and make them famous by recital to the glory of God. So shall no weak or despairing faith suppose that supernatural grace, in excellency of martyrdoms or revelations, was found among the ancients only; for God ever works what He has promised, to unbelievers a witness, to believers a blessing. And so "what we have heard and handled declare we unto you also," brothers and little children, "that ye also" who were their eyewitnesses may be reminded of the glory of the Lord, and you who now learn by the ear "may have fellowship with" the holy martyrs, and through them with the Lord Jesus Christ, to whom belong splendour and honour for ever and ever. Amen.

II. Certain young catechumens were arrested, Revocatus and his fellow-slave Felicitas, Saturninus, and Secundulus, Among these also Vibia Perpetua, well-born, liberally educated, honourably married, having father and mother, and two brothers, one like herself a catechumen, and an infant son at the breast. She was about twenty-two years of age. The whole story of her martyrdom is from this point onwards told by herself, as she left it written, hand and conception being alike her own.

III. "When I was still, she says, with my companions, and my father in his affection for me was endeavouring to upset me by arguments and overthrow my resolution, 'Father,' I said, 'Do you see this vessel for instance lying here, waterpot or whatever it may be?' 'I see it,' he said. And I said to him, 'Can it be called by any other name than what it is?' And he answered, 'No.' 'So also I cannot call myself anything else than what I am, a Christian.'

Then my father, furious at the word 'Christian,' threw himself upon me as though to pluck out my eyes; but he was satisfied with annoying me; he was in fact vanquished, he

H. R. Musurillo, *The Acts of the Christian Martyrs* (Oxford: Clarendon Press, 1972).

and his devil's arguments. Then I thanked the Lord for being parted for a few days from my father, and was refreshed by his absence. During those few days we were baptized, and the Holy Spirit bade me make no other petition after the holy water save for bodily endurance. A few days after we were lodged in prison; and I was in great fear, because I had never known such darkness. What a day of horror! Terrible heat, thanks to the crowds! Rough handling by the soldiers! To crown all I was tormented there by anxiety for my baby. Then Tertius and Pomponius, those blessed deacons who were ministering to us, paid for us to be removed for a few hours to a better part of the prison and refresh ourselves. Then all went out of the prison and were left to themselves. [My baby was brought to me], and I suckled him, for he was already faint for want of food. I spoke anxiously to my mother on his behalf, and strengthened my brother, and commended my son to their charge. I was pining because I saw them pine on my account. Such anxieties I suffered for many days; and I obtained leave for my baby to remain in the prison with me; and I at once recovered my health, and was relieved of my trouble and anxiety for my baby; and my prison suddenly became a palace to me, and I would rather have been there than anywhere else.

IV. Then my brother said to me: 'Lady sister, you are now in great honour, so great indeed that you may well pray for a vision and may well be shown whether suffering or release be in store for you.' And I who knew myself to have speech of the Lord, for whose sake I had gone through so much, gave confident promise in return, saying: 'To-morrow I will bring you word.' And I made request, and this was shown me. I saw a brazen ladder of wondrous length reaching up to heaven, but so narrow that only one could ascend at once; and on the sides of the ladder were fastened all kinds of iron weapons. There were swords,

lances, hooks, daggers, so that if any one went up carelessly or without looking upwards he was mangled and his flesh caught on the weapons. And just beneath the ladder was a dragon couching of wondrous size who lay in wait for those going up and sought to frighten them from going up. Now Saturus went up first, who had given himself up for our sakes of his own accord, because our faith had been of his own building, and he had not been present when we were seized. And he reached the top of the ladder, and turned, and said to me: 'Perpetua, I await you; but see that the dragon bite you not.' And I said: 'In the name of Jesus Christ he will not hurt me.' And he put out his head gently, as if afraid of me, just at the foot of the ladder; and as though I were treading on the first step, I trod on his head. And I went up, and saw a vast expanse of garden, and in the midst a man sitting with white hair, in the dress of a shepherd, a tall man, milking sheep; and round about were many thousands clad in white. And he raised his head, and looked upon me, and said: 'You have well come, my child.' And he called me, and gave me a morsel of the milk which he was milking and I received it in my joined hands, and ate; and all they that stood around said: 'Amen.' And at the sound of the word I woke, still eating something sweet. And at once I told my brother, and we understood that we must suffer, and henceforward began to have no hope in this world.

V. After a few days a rumour ran that we were to be examined. Moreover, my father arrived from the city, worn with trouble, and came up the hill to see me, that he might overthrow my resolution, saying: 'Daughter, pity my white hairs! Pity your father, if I am worthy to be called father by you; if with these hands I have brought you up to this your prime of life, if I have preferred you to all your brothers! Give me not over to the reproach of men! Look upon your brothers, look upon your mother and your mother's sister, look upon your son who cannot live after you are gone! Lay aside your pride, do not ruin all of us, for none of us will ever speak freely again, if anything happen to you!' So spoke my father in his love for me, kissing my hands, and casting himself at my feet; and with tears called me by the name not of daughter but of lady. And I grieved for my father's sake, because he alone of all my kindred would not have joy in my suffering. And I comforted him, saying: 'It shall happen on that platform as God shall choose; for know well that we lie not in our own power but in the power of God.' And full of sorrow he left me.

VI. On another day when we were having our midday meal, we were suddenly hurried off to be examined; and we came to the market-place. Forthwith a rumour ran through the neighbouring parts of the market-place, and a vast crowd gathered. We went up on to the platform. The others on being questioned confessed their faith. So it came to my turn. And there was my father with my child, and he drew me down from the step, beseeching me: 'Have pity on your baby.' And the procurator Hilarian, who had then received the power of life and death in the room of the late proconsul Minucius Timinianus, said to me: 'Spare your father's white hairs; spare the tender years of your child. Offer a sacrifice for the safety of the Emperors.' And I answered: 'No.' 'Are you a Christian!' said Hilarian. And I answered: 'I am.' And when my father persisted in trying to overthrow my resolution, he was ordered by Hilarian to be thrown down, and the judge struck him with his rod. And I was grieved for my father's plight, as if I had been struck myself, so did I grieve for the sorrow that had come on his old age. Then he passed sentence on the whole of us, and condemned us to the beasts; and in great joy we went down into the prison. Then because my baby was accustomed to take the breast from me, and stay with me in prison, I sent at once the deacon Pomponius to my father to

ask for my baby. But my father refused to give him. And as God willed, neither had he any further wish for my breasts, nor did they become inflamed; that I might not be tortured by anxiety for the baby and pain in my breasts.

VII. After a few days, while we were all praying, suddenly in the middle of the prayer I spoke, and uttered the name of Dinocrates; and I was astonished that he had never come into mind till then; and I grieved thinking of what had befallen him. And I saw at once that I was entitled, and ought, to make request for him. And I began to pray much for him, and make lamentation to the Lord. At once on this very night this was shown me. I saw Dinocrates coming forth from a dark place, where there were many other dark places, very hot and thirsty, his countenance pale and squalid; and the wound which he had when he died was in his face still. This Dinocrates had been my brother according to the flesh, seven years old, who had died miserably of a gangrene in the face, so that his death moved all to loathing. For him then I had prayed; and there was a great gulf between me and him, so that neither of us could approach the other. There was besides in the very place where Dinocrates was a font full of water, the rim of which was above the head of the child; and Dinocrates stood on tiptoe to drink. I grieved that the font should have water in it and that nevertheless he could not drink because of the height of the rim. And I woke and recognized that my brother was in trouble. But I trusted that I could relieve his trouble, and I prayed for him every day until we were transferred to the garrison prison, for we were to fight with the beasts at the garrison games on the Caesar Geta's birthday. And I prayed for him day and night with lamentations and tears that he might be given me.

VIII. During the daytime, while we stayed in the stocks, this was shown me. I saw that same place which I had seen before, and Dinocrates clean in body, well-clothed and refreshed; and where there had been a wound, I saw a scar; and the font which I had seen before had its rim lowered to the child's waist; and there poured water from it unceasingly; and on the rim a golden bowl full of water. And Dinocrates came forward and began to drink from it, and the bowl failed not. And when he had drunk enough of the water, he came forward being glad to play as children will. And I awoke. Then I knew that he had been released from punishment.

IX. Then after a few days Pudens the adjutant, who was in charge of the prison, who began to show us honour perceiving that there was some great power within us, began to admit many to see us, that both we and they might be refreshed by one another's company. Now when the day of the games approached, my father came in to me worn with trouble, and began to pluck out his beard and cast it on the ground, and to throw himself on his face, and to curse his years, and to say such words as might have turned the world upside down. I sorrowed for the unhappiness of his old age.

X. On the day before we were to fight, I saw in a vision Pomponius the deacon come hither to the door of the prison and knock loudly. And I went out to him, and opened to him. Now he was clad in a white robe without a girdle, wearing shoes curiously wrought. And he said to me: 'Perpetua, we are waiting for you; come.' And he took hold of my hand, and we began to pass through rough and broken country. Painfully and panting did we arrive at last at an amphitheatre, and he led me into the middle of the arena. And he said to me: 'Fear not; I am here with you, and I suffer with you.' And he departed. And I saw a huge crowd watching eagerly. And because I knew that I was condemned to the beasts, I marvelled that there were no beasts let loose on me. And there came out an Egyptian, foul of look, with his attendants to fight against me. And to me also there came goodly young men to be my attendants and supporters. And I was

stripped and was changed into a man. And my supporters began to rub me down with oil, as they are wont to do before a combat; and I saw the Egyptian opposite rolling in the sand. And there came forth a man wondrously tall so that he rose above the top of the amphitheatre, clad in a purple robe without a girdle with two stripes, one on either side, running down the middle of the breast, and wearing shoes curiously wrought made of gold and silver; carrying a wand, like a trainer, and a green bough on which were golden apples. And he asked for silence, and said: 'This Egyptian, if he prevail over her, shall kill her with a sword; and, if she prevail over him, she shall receive this bough.' And he retired. And we came near to one another and began to use our fists. My adversary wished to catch hold of my feet, but I kept on striking his face with my heels. And I was lifted up into the air, and began to strike him in such fashion as would one that no longer trod on earth. But when I saw that the fight lagged, I joined my two hands, linking the fingers of the one with the fingers of the other. And I caught hold of his head, and he fell on his face; and I trod upon his head. And the people began to shout, and my supporters to sing psalms. And I came forward to the trainer, and received the bough. And he kissed me, and said to me: 'Peace be with thee, my daughter.' And I began to go in triumph to the Gate of Life. And I awoke. And I perceived that I should not fight with beasts but with the Devil; but I knew the victory to be mine. Such were my doings up to the day before the games. Of what was done in the games themselves let him write who will.''

XI. But the blessed Saturus also has made known this vision of his own, which he has written out with his own hand. ''Methought we had suffered, and put off the flesh, and began to be borne toward the east by four angels whose hands touched us not. Now we moved not on our backs looking upward, but as though we were climbing a gentle slope.

And when we were clear of the world below we saw a great light, and I said to Perpetua, for she was by my side: 'This is what the Lord promised us, we have received His promise.' And while we were carried by those four angels, we came upon a great open space, which was like as it might be a garden, having rose-trees and all kinds of flowers. The height of the trees was like the height of a cypress, whose leaves sang without ceasing. Now there in the garden were certain four angels, more glorious than the others, who when they saw us, gave us honour, and said to the other angels: 'Lo! they are come; lo! they are come,' being full of wonder. And those four angels which bare us trembled and set us down, and we crossed on foot a place strewn with violets, where we found Jucundus and Saturninus and Artaxius, who were burned alive in the same persecution, and Quintus who, being also a martyr, had died in the prison, and we asked of them where they were. The other angels said unto us: 'Come first and enter and greet the Lord.'

XII. And we came near to a place whose walls were built like as it might be of light, and before the gate of that place were four angels standing, who as we entered clothed us in white robes. And we entered, and heard a sound as of one voice saying: 'Holy, holy, holy,' without ceasing. And we saw sitting in the same place one like unto a man white-haired, having hair as white as snow, and with the face of a youth; whose feet we saw not. And on the right and on the left four elders; and behind them were many other elders standing. And entering we stood in wonder before the throne; and the four angels lifted us up, and we kissed Him, and He stroked our faces with His hand. And the other elders said to us: 'Let us stand.' And we stood and gave the Kiss of Peace. And the elders said to us: 'Go and play.' And I said to Perpetua: 'You have your wish.' And she said to me: 'Thanks be to God, that as I was merry in the flesh, so am I now still merrier here.'

XIII. And we went forth, and saw before the doors Optatus the bishop on the right, and Aspasius the priest-teacher on the left, severed and sad. And they cast themselves at our feet, and said: 'Make peace between us, for you have gone forth, and left us thus.' And we said to them: 'Are not you our father, and you our priest? Why should ye fall before our feet?' And we were moved, and embraced them. And Perpetua began to talk Greek with them, and we drew them aside into the garden under a rose-tree. And while we talked with them, the angels said to them: 'Let them refresh themselves; and if ye have any quarrels among yourselves, forgive one another.' And they put these to shame, and said to Optatus: 'Reform your people, for they come to you like men returning from the circus and contending about its factions.' And it seemed to us as though they wished to shut the gates. And we began to recognize many brethren there, martyrs too amongst them. We were all fed on a fragrance beyond telling, which contented us. Then in my joy I awoke."

XIV. Such are the famous visions of the blessed martyrs themselves, Saturus and Perpetua, which they wrote with their own hands. As for Secundulus, God called him to an earlier departure from this world while still in prison, not without grace, that he might escape the beasts. Nevertheless his body, if not his soul, made acquaintance with the sword.

XV. As for Felicitas indeed, she also was visited by the grace of God in this wise. Being eight months gone with child (for she was pregnant at the time of her arrest), as the day for the spectacle drew near she was in great sorrow for fear lest because of her pregnancy her martyrdom should be delayed, since it is against the law for women with child to be exposed for punishment, and lest she should shed her sacred and innocent blood among others afterwards who were malefactors. Her fellow-martyrs too were deeply grieved at the thought of leaving so good a comrade and fellow-traveller behind alone on the way to the same hope. So in one flood of common lamentation they poured forth a prayer to the Lord two days before the games. Immediately after the prayer her pains came upon her. And since from the natural difficulty of an eight-months' labour she suffered much in child-birth, one of the warders said to her: "You who so suffer now, what will you do when you are flung to the beasts which, when you refused to sacrifice, you despised?" And she answered: "Now I suffer what I suffer: but then Another will be in me who will suffer for me, because I too am to suffer for Him." So she gave birth to a girl, whom one of the sisters brought up as her own daughter.

XVI. Since, therefore, the Holy Spirit has permitted, and by permitting willed, the story of the games themselves to be written, we cannot chose but carry out, however unworthy to supplement so glorious a history, the injunction, or rather sacred bequest, of the most holy Perpetua, adding at the same time one example of her steadfastness and loftiness of soul. When they were treated with unusual rigour by the commanding officer because his fears were aroused through the warnings of certain foolish people that they might be carried off from prison by some magic spells, she challenged him to his face: "Why do you not at least suffer us to refresh ourselves, 'the most noble' among the condemned, belonging as we do to Caesar and chosen to fight on his birthday? Or is it not to your credit that we should appear thereon in better trim?" The commanding officer trembled and blushed; and so ordered them to be used more kindly, giving her brothers and other persons leave to visit, that they might refresh themselves in their company. By this time the governor of the prison was himself a believer.

XVII. Moreover, on the day before the games when they celebrated that last supper, called "the free festivity," not as a "festivity," but, so far as they could make it so, a "love-feast," with the same steadfastness they flung

words here and there among the people, threatening them with the judgement of God, calling to witness the happiness of their own passion, laughing at the inquisitiveness of the crowd. Said Saturus: "To-morrow does not satisfy you, for what you hate you love to see. Friends to-day, foes to-morrow. Yet mark our faces well, that when the day comes you may know us again." So all left the place amazed, and many of them became believers.

XVIII. The day of their victory dawned, and they proceeded from the prison to the amphitheatre, as if they were on their way to heaven, with gay and gracious looks; trembling, if at all, not with fear but joy. Perpetua followed with shining steps, as the true wife of Christ, as the darling of God, abashing with the high spirit in her eyes the gaze of all; Felicitas also, rejoicing that she had brought forth in safety that so she might fight the beasts, from blood to blood, from midwife to gladiator, to find in her Second Baptism her child-birth washing. And when they were led within the gate, and were on the point of being forced to put on the dress, the men of the priests of Saturn, the women of those dedicated to Ceres, the noble Perpetua resisted steadfastly to the last. For she said: "Therefore we came to this issue of our own free will, that our liberty might not be violated; therefore we pledged our lives, that we might do no such thing: this was our pact with you." Injustice acknowledged justice; the commanding officer gave permission that they should enter the arena in their ordinary dress as they were. Perpetua was singing a psalm of triumph, as already treading on the head of the Egyptian. Revocatus, Saturninus, and Saturus were threatening the onlookers with retribution; when they came within sight of Hilarian, they began to signify to him by nods and gestures: "Thou art judging us, but God shall judge thee." The people infuriated thereat demanded that they should be punished with scourging before a line of beast-fighters. And they for this at least gave one another joy, that they had moreover won some share in the sufferings of their Lord.

XIX. But He who had said: "Ask and ye shall receive" had granted to those who asked Him that death which each had craved. For, whenever they talked amongst themselves about their hopes of martyrdom, Saturninus declared that he wished to be cast to all the beasts; so indeed would he wear a more glorious crown. Accordingly at the outset of the show he was matched with the leopard and recalled from him; he was also (later) mauled on the platform by the bear. Saturus on the other hand had a peculiar dread of the bear, but counted beforehand on being dispatched by one bite of the leopard. And so when he was offered to the wild boar, the fighter with beasts, who had bound him to the boar, was gored from beneath by the same beast, and died after the days of the games were over, whereas Saturus was only dragged. And when he was tied up on the bridge before the bear, the bear refused to come out of his den. So Saturus for the second time was recalled unhurt.

XX. For the young women the Devil made ready a mad heifer, an unusual animal selected for this reason, that he wished to match their sex with that of the beast. And so after being stripped and enclosed in nets they were brought into the arena. The people were horrified, beholding in the one a tender girl, in the other a woman fresh from child-birth, with milk dripping from her breasts. So they were recalled and dressed in tunics without girdles. Perpetua was tossed first, and fell on her loins. Sitting down she drew back her torn tunic from her side to cover her thighs, more mindful of her modesty than of her suffering. Then having asked for a pin she further fastened her disordered hair. For it was not seemly that a martyr should suffer with her hair dishevelled, lest she should seem to mourn in the hour of her glory. Then she rose, and seeing that Felicitas was bruised, approached, gave a

hand to her, and lifted her up. And the two stood side by side, and the cruelty of the people being now appeased, they were recalled to the Gate of Life. There Perpetua was supported by a certain Rusticus, then a catechumen, who kept close to her; and being roused from what seemed like sleep, so completely had she been in the Spirit and in ecstasy, began to look about her, and said to the amazement of all: "When we are to be thrown to that heifer, I cannot tell." When she heard what had already taken place, she refused to believe it till she had observed certain marks of ill-usage on her body and dress. Then she summoned her brother and spoke to him and the catechumen, saying: "Stand ye all fast in the faith, and love one another; and be not offended by our sufferings."

XXI. Saturus also at another gate was encouraging the soldier Pudens: "In a word," said he, "what I counted on and foretold has come to pass, not a beast so far has touched me. And now, that you may trust me wholeheartedly, see, I go forth yonder, and with one bite of the leopard all is over." And forthwith, as the show was ending, the leopard was let loose, and with one bite Saturus was so drenched in blood that the people as he came back shouted in attestation of his Second Baptism, "Bless you, well bathed! Bless you, well bathed!" Blessed indeed was he who had bathed after this fashion. Then he said to the soldier Pudens: "Farewell! Keep my faith and me in mind! And let these things not confound, but confirm you." And with that he asked for the ring from Pudens's finger, plunged it in his own wound, and gave it back as a legacy, bequeathing it for a pledge and memorial of his blood. Then by this time lifeless he was flung with the rest on to the place allotted to the throat-cutting. And when the people asked for them to be brought into the open, that, when the sword pierced their bodies, these might lend their eyes for partners in the murder, they rose unbidden and made their way whither the people willed, after first kissing one another, that they might perfect their martyrdom with the rite of the Pax. The rest without a movement in silence received the sword, Saturus in deeper silence, who, as he had been the first to climb the ladder, was the first to give up the ghost; for now as then he awaited Perpetua. Perpetua, however, that she might taste something of the pain, was struck on the bone and cried out, and herself guided to her throat the wavering hand of the young untried gladiator. Perhaps so great a woman, who was feared by the unclean spirit, could not otherwise be slain except she willed.

O valiant and blessed martyrs! O truly called and chosen to the glory of Jesus Christ our Lord! He who magnifies, honours, and adores that glory should recite to the edification of the Church these examples also, not less precious at least than those of old; that so new instances of virtue may testify that one and the self-same Spirit is working to this day with the Father, God Almighty, and with His Son Jesus Christ our Lord, to whom belong splendour and power immeasurable for ever and ever. Amen.

ST. MACRINA   (c. A.D. 327–379, Cappadocia, Greece)
The Life of St. Macrina, by St. Gregory of Nyssa

Translated by V. W. Callahan

Gregory, Bishop of Nyssa,
to Olympius

... you suggested that a history of her good deeds ought to be written because you thought such a life should not be lost sight of in time and, that having raised herself to the highest peak of human virtue through philosophy, she should not be passed over in silence and her life rendered ineffective. Accordingly, I thought it right to obey you and to write her life story as briefly as I could in an artless and simple narrative.

The maiden's name was Macrina. She had been given this name by her parents in memory of a remarkable Macrina earlier in the family, our father's mother, who had distinguished herself in the confession of Christ at the time of the persecutions. This was her official name which her acquaintances used, but she had been given another secretly in connection with a vision which occurred before she came into the light at birth. Her mother was extremely virtuous, following the will of God in all things and embracing an exceptionally pure and spotless way of life, so that she had chosen not to marry. However, since she was an orphan and flowering in the springtime of her beauty, and the fame of her loveliness had attracted many suitors, there was danger that, if she were not joined to someone by choice, she might suffer some unwished-for violence, because some of the

Gregory of Nyssa, *Ascetical Works*, Vol. 58 of the Fathers of the Church series. Copyright © 1967 by The Catholic University of America Press.

suitors maddened by her beauty were preparing to carry her off. For this reason, she chose a man well known and recommended for the dignity of his life, and thus she acquired a guardian for her own life. In her first pregnancy, she became Macrina's mother. When the time came in which she was to be freed from her pain by giving birth to the child, she fell asleep and seemed to be holding in her hands the child still in her womb, and a person of greater than human shape and form appeared to be addressing the infant by the name of Thecla. (There was a Thecla of much fame among virgins.) After doing this and invoking her as a witness three times, he disappeared from sight and gave ease to her pain so that as she awoke from her sleep she saw the dream realized. This, then, was her secret name. It seems to me that the one who appeared was not so much indicating how the child should be named, but foretelling the life of the child and intimating that she would choose a life similar to that of her namesake.

So the child grew, nursed chiefly by her mother although she had a nurse of her own. Upon leaving infancy, she was quick to learn what children learn, and to whatever learning the judgment of her parents directed her, the little one's nature responded brilliantly. Her mother was eager to have the child given instruction, but not in the secular curriculum, which meant, for the most part, teaching the youngsters through poetry. For she thought that it was shameful and altogether unfitting to teach the soft and pliable nature either the passionate themes of tragedy (which are based on the stories of women and give the poets their ideas and plots), or the unseemly antics of comedy, or the shameful activities of the immoral characters in the *Iliad*, defiling the child's nature with the undignified tales about women. Instead of this, whatever of inspired Scripture was adaptable to the early years, this was the child's subject matter, especially the Wisdom of Solomon and beyond this what-

ever leads us to a moral life. She was especially well versed in the Psalms, going through each part of the Psalter at the proper times. . . .

Growing up with these and similar pursuits and becoming extraordinarily skilled in the working of wool, she came to her twelfth year in which the flowering of youth begins especially to shine forth. Here, it is worth marveling at how the young girl's beauty did not escape notice, although it had been concealed. . . .

Consequently, a great stream of suitors for her hand crowded round her parents. Her father (he was wise and considered outstanding in his judgment of what was good) singled out from the rest a young man in the family known for his moderation, who had recently finished school, and he decided to give his daughter to him when she came of age. During this period, the young man showed great promise and brought to the girl's father (as a cherished bridal gift as it were) his reputation as an orator, displaying his rhetorical skill in lawsuits in defense of the wronged. But envy cut short this bright promise by snatching him from life in his piteous youth.

The girl was not unaware of what her father had decided, and when the young man's death broke off what had been planned for her, she called her father's decision a marriage on the grounds that what had been decided had actually taken place and she determined to spend the rest of her life by herself; and her decision was more firmly fixed than her age would have warranted.

Thrusting aside the arguments of those trying to persuade her, she settled upon a safeguard for her noble decision, namely, a resolve never to be separated for a moment from her mother, so that her mother often used to say to her that the rest of her childen she had carried in her womb for a fixed time, but this daughter she always bore, encompassing her in her womb at all times and under all circumstances. . . . She shared her mother's worries.

Her mother had four sons and five daughters and was paying taxes to three governors because her property was scattered over that many provinces.

In a variety of ways, therefore, her mother was distracted by worries. (By this time her father had left this life.) In all of these affairs, Macrina was a sharer of her mother's toils, taking on part of her cares and lightening the heaviness of her griefs. In addition, under her mother's direction, she kept her life blameless and witnessed in everything by her, and, at the same time, because of her own life, she provided her mother with an impressive leadership to the same goal; I speak of the goal of philosophy, drawing her on little by little to the immaterial and simpler life. After the mother had skilfully arranged what seemed best for each of Macrina's sisters, her brother, the distinguished Basil, came home from school where he had had practice in rhetoric for a long time. He was excessively puffed up by his rhetorical abilities and disdainful of all great reputations, and considered himself better than the leading men in the district, but Macrina took him over and lured him so quickly to the goal of philosophy that he withdrew from the worldly show and began to look down upon acclaim through oratory and went over to this life full of labors for one's own hand to perform, providing for himself, through his complete poverty, a mode of living that would, without impediment, lead to virtue. . . .

When there was no longer any necessity for them to continue their rather worldly way of life, Macrina persuaded her mother to give up her customary mode of living and her more ostentatious existence and the services of her maids, to which she had long been accustomed, and to put herself on a level with the many by entering into a common life with her maids, making them her sisters and equals rather than her slaves and underlings. . . .

The arrangement of their life, the high level of their philosophy, and lofty regimen of their activities night and day was such that it transcends description. Just as by death souls are freed from the body and released from the cares of this life, so their life was separated from these things, divorced from all mortal vanity and attuned to an imitation of the existence of the angels. Among them was seen no anger, no envy, no hatred, no arrogance, or any such thing; neither was there in them longing for foolish things like honor and fame and vanity, nor a contempt for others; all such qualities had been put aside. Continence was their luxury and not being known their fame; their wealth consisted in their poverty and the shaking off of all worldly abundance like dust from the body. They were not occupied with the concerns of this life; that is, they were not preoccupied. Rather, their one concern was the Divine; there was constant prayer and an unceasing singing of hymns distributed throughout the entire day and night, so that this was for them both their work and their rest from work. . . .

When I had almost finished the journey and was about one day away from my destination, a vision, appearing in my sleep, aroused fearful forebodings about the future. I seemed to be carrying the relics of martyrs in my hand and a light seemed to come from them, as happens when the sun is reflected on a bright mirror so that the eye is dazzled by the brilliance of the beam. That same night, the vision occurred three times. I was not able to interpret its meaning clearly, but I foresaw some grief for my soul and I was waiting for the outcome to clarify the dream. When I came near the outskirts of the place where that lady was leading her angelic celestial life, I asked one of the workmen, first, if my brother happened to be there. He replied that he had gone out to meet us about four days earlier, and this was true, but he had taken a different road. Then, I inquired about the Superior and, when he said that she was ill, I was more eager than ever to complete the trip, for a certain fear, an omen of the future, was disturbing me. As I made my way (rumor had announced my presence beforehand to the community), a line of men streamed toward us. It was customary for them to welcome guests by coming out to meet them. However, a group of women from the convent waited modestly at the entrance of the church for us.

When the prayer and blessing were finished and the women had responded to the blessing by bowing their heads, they removed themselves from our presence and went off to their own quarters. Since not one of them remained with me, I correctly surmised that their Superior was not among them. An attendant led me to the house where the Superior was and opened the door, and I entered that sacred place. She was already very ill, but she was not resting on a couch or bed, but upon the ground; there was a board covered with a coarse cloth, and another board supported her head, designed to be used instead of a pillow, supporting the sinews of her neck slantwise and conveniently supporting the neck. When she saw me standing at the door, she raised herself on her elbow; her strength was already so wasted by fever that she was not able to come towards me, but she fixed her hands on the floor and, stretching as far forward as she could, she paid me the honor of a bow. I ran to her and, lifting her bowed head, I put her back in her accustomed reclining position. But she stretched out her hand to God and said: "You have granted me this favor, O God, and have not deprived me of my desire, since you have impelled your servant to visit your handmaid." And in order not to disturb me, she tried to cover up her groans and to conceal somehow the difficulty she had in breathing, and, through it all, she adjusted herself to the brighter side. She initiated suitable topics of conversation and gave me an opportunity to speak by asking me questions. As we spoke, we recalled the memory of the great Basil and

my soul was afflicted and my face fell and tears poured from my eyes. But she was so far from being downcast by our sorrow that she made the mentioning of the saint a starting point towards the higher philosophy. She rehearsed such arguments, explaining the human situation through natural principles and disclosing the divine plan hidden in misfortune, and she spoke of certain aspects of the future life as if she was inspired by the Holy Spirit, so that my soul almost seemed to be lifted up out of its human sphere by what she said and, under the direction of her discourse, take its stand in the heavenly sanctuaries.

And just as we hear in the story of Job,[1] that when the man was wasting away and his whole body was covered with erupting and putrefying sores, he did not direct attention to his pain but kept the pain inside his body, neither blessing his own activity nor cutting off the conversation when it embarked upon higher matters. Such a thing as this I was seeing in the case of this Superior also; although the fever was burning up all her energy and leading her to death, she was refreshing her body as if by a kind of dew, she kept her mind free in the contemplation of higher things and unimpeded by the disease. . . .

Guessing, I know not how, that we were dejected by the grief that was to come, Macrina sent a message bidding us to cheer up and to be more hopeful about her condition for she perceived a turn for the better. This was not said to deceive us, but was actually the truth, although we did not recognize it at the time. . . .

When we returned to her presence (for she did not allow us to idle away the time by ourselves), she took up the story of her life from infancy as if she were putting it all into a monograph. She told what she remembered of our parents' life, both what happened before my birth and afterwards. What she concentrated on in her story was thanksgiving to God, for what she stressed in the life of our parents was not so much their being outstanding among their contemporaries because of their prosperity, but their having been enhanced by divine favor. Our father's parents had been deprived of their possessions because of the confession of Christ; our mother's grandfather was killed by the anger of the emperor and all his property handed over to other masters. Nevertheless, their life was so exalted on account of their faith that no one had a greater reputation among the men of that time. Later, when their property was divided nine ways in accordance with the number of the children, the share of each had been so bountifully increased that the children lived more prosperously than their parents. Macrina did not accept the amount that was assigned to her in the equal distribution, but gave it all into the hands of the priest in accordance with the divine command. By divine dispensation, her existence was such that she never stopped using her hands in the service of God, nor did she look to men for help or any opportunity for living a life of comfort. She never turned away anyone who asked for something, nor did she look for benefactors, but God, in His blessings, secretly made her little resources of activity grow as seeds, as it were, into a full-flowering harvest.

As she went on this way, I kept wishing that the day might be lengthened so that we could continue to enjoy the sweetness of her words. But the sound of the choir was calling us to vespers and, having sent me off to the church, the Superior withdrew to God in prayer and the night was devoted to it. When dawn came, it was clear to me that this day was to be the last for her in the life of the flesh, for the fever had consumed all her natural strength. When she saw our concern about her weakness, she tried to rouse us from our downcast hopes by dispersing again with her beautiful words the grief of our souls with her last slight and labored breathing. At this point, especially, my soul was in conflict because of what it was confronted by. My disposition was naturally made gloomy by the anticipation of never again hearing such a voice, but actually I had not yet accepted the idea that she was going to leave this mortal life, and my soul was so exalted by appearances that I secretly thought that she had transcended the common nature. For the fact was that, in her last breath, she experienced nothing strange in the expectation of the change and displayed no cowardice towards the departure from life. Instead, she philosophized with high intelligence on what had been decided upon by her about this life from the beginning up to her last breath, and this made her appear to belong no longer to the world of men. It was as if an angel had by some providence taken on human form, an angel who had no relation with or similarity to the life of the flesh and for whom it was not at all unreasonable to remain detached since the flesh was not part of her experience. For this reason, she seemed to me to be making clear to those present the divine and pure love of the unseen Bridegroom which she had secretly nourished in the depths of her soul, and she seemed to be communicating the disposition in her heart to go to the One she was longing for, so that, once loosed from the chains of the body, she might quickly be with Him. Truly, her race was towards the Beloved and nothing of the pleasure of life diverted her attention.

The day was almost over and the sun was beginning to set, but the zeal in her did not decline. Indeed, as she neared her end and saw the beauty of the Bridegroom more clearly, she rushed with greater impulse towards the One she desired, no longer speaking to those of us who were present, but to that very One toward whom she looked with steadfast eyes. Her couch was turned to the East and, stopping her conversation with us, for the rest of the time she addressed herself to God in prayer, beseeching Him with her hands and speaking in a low soft voice so that we barely heard what she said. This was her prayer and there is no doubt that it made its way to God and that it was heard by Him.

She said: "O Lord, You have freed us from the fear of death;[2] You have made the end of life here the beginning of a true life for us. For a time, You give rest to our bodies in sleep and You awaken us again with the last trumpet.[3] The dust from which You fashioned us with Your hands You give back to the dust of the earth for safekeeping, and You who have relinquished it will recall it after reshaping with incorruptibility and grace our mortal and graceless substance. You redeemed us from the curse[4] and from sin, having taken both upon Yourself; You crushed the heads of the serpent[5] who had seized us with his jaws in the abyss of disobedience. Breaking down the gates of hell[6] and overcoming the one who had the empire of death,[7] You opened up for us a path to the resurrection. For those who fear You, You gave as a token the sign of the holy cross for the destruction of the Adversary and the salvation of our life. O God everlasting, towards whom I have directed myself from my mother's womb, whom my soul has loved[8] with all its strength, to whom I have dedicated my body and my soul from my infancy up to now, prepare for me a shining angel to lead me to the place of refreshment where is the water of relaxation[9] near the bosom of the holy Fathers.[10] You who broke the flaming sword[11] and compassionately gave Paradise back to the man crucified with You,[12] remember me also in Your kingdom, for I, too, have been crucified with You, having nailed my flesh through fear of You and having feared Your judgments. Let the terrible abyss[13] not separate me from Your chosen ones; let the Slanderer not stand in my way or my sins be discovered before Your eyes if I have fallen and sinned in word or deed or thought because of the weak-

ness of our nature. Do You who have power on earth to forgive sins[14] forgive me so that I may be refreshed and may be found before You once I have put off my body, having no fault in the form of my soul, but blameless and spotless may my soul be taken into Your hands as an offering before Your face." As she said this, she made the sign of the cross upon her eyes and mouth and heart, and little by little, as the fever dried up her tongue, she was no longer able to speak clearly; her voice gave out and only from the trembling of her lips and the motion of her hands did we know that she was continuing to pray.

Then, evening came on and the lamp was brought in. Macrina directed her eye toward the beam of light and made it clear that she was eager to say the nocturnal prayer and, although her voice failed her, with her heart and the movement of her hands, she fulfilled her desire and moved her lips in keeping with the impulse within her. When she had completed the thanksgiving and indicated that the prayer was over by making the sign of the cross, she breathed a deep breath and with the prayer her life came to an end.

NOTES

1. Cf. Job 2.8; 7.5.
2. Cf. Heb. 2.15.
3. Cf. 1 Cor. 15.52.
4. Cf. Gal. 3.13.
5. Cf. Ps. 7.3. 13–14.
6. Cf. Matt. 16, 18.
7. Cf. Heb. 2.14.
8. Cf. Cant. 1.7.
9. Cf. Ps. 22.2.
10. Cf. Luke 16, 22.
11. Cf. Gen. 3, 24.
12. Cf. Luke 23, 42.
13. Cf. Luke 16, 26.
14. Cf. Matt. 9.6; Mark 2.10.

II

Holy Women and the Christianizing of Europe

Hugeberc of Hildesheim, St. Leoba, and Hrotsvit of Gandersheim

JUST AT THE TIME that Eastern monasticism ceased to be an alternative for women, about the year A.D. 500, in Western Europe other conditions were developing that reinforced the appeal of a collective spiritual life for women. Although Christianity was officially the religion of the Roman Empire after A.D. 313 (except for a few years under pagan emperors, when persecution was resumed), in some areas its triumph over pagan forms of worship did not occur until the ninth century A.D. Rome fell to Alaric in A.D. 410, and repeated barbarian invasions made life in cities less and less possible. In such times of widespread violence and periodic famine, a new form of community life was essential. The idea of community that had been evolving over the past centuries was codified in the monastic rule of St. Benedict in A.D. 529:

> It was in a world that owned no civil authority and which had no principle on which such an authority could be based that Benedict worked out his conception of an ordered life based not on the power of law but on voluntary obedience in a family-like setting. The abbey which he founded at Monte Cassino was destined to be sacked within sixty years of its foundation, and twice more within the next five hundred years; but the life that was worked out there was to supply the principle of order no longer supplied by the state, and indeed was to keep an ordered civilization alive during the centuries of chaos that were to come.[1]

The force of the Benedictine ideal gave needed shape to early medieval Europe in its material as well as in its spiritual dimension. Life for monks and nuns in a Benedictine house was essentially the same and was based on "an organized and disciplined corporate life which should by its common nature be a means of sanctification to the individuals involved, and which would incidentally provide a principle of order in a disordered Europe."[2] The concepts of obedience and stability were fundamental: The Rule was binding on all members, from novice to abbot or abbess.[3] All members shared prayer seven times daily and once at night; waking hours were divided equally among prayer, manual labor, and study. Work included farming, housekeeping tasks, caring for the sick in the infirmary, and providing shelter for visitors and pilgrims. More intellectual members of the community might be involved in scholarly projects such as the study of theology, the composition of music, the copying of manuscripts, and the teaching of those children and young adults who lived in the house.

The appeal of convent life for women who manifold, as St. Benedict's sister, St. Scholastica, no doubt foresaw when she urged that the Rule be written for women too. A woman's convent provided an escape from male domination and from the polygamy that was still being practiced by many chieftains and nobles.[4] It gave women personal power and prestige; offered a political role as abbess or prioress; and provided the possibility for education, intellectual development, and training in the arts. Physical safety was not guaranteed by the monastic life, for even monasteries were pillaged and burned, but the only inhabited stone buildings in Europe until well after Charlemagne were monastic ones, and they must have given a very real feeling of protection to their inhabitants. And in a warlike society, where family feuds and the necessity for revenge seem to have dominated, a monastery might be a haven of peace, where personal tensions were harmonized by the law of silence and the repetition of prayer throughout the liturgical year.

The number of influential holy women in the so-called Dark Ages—women whose names and lives, if not writings, are still known to us—is quite remarkable.[5] Many had been queens or members of the higher nobility while they lived in the secular world; and when they retired to found women's houses, they brought with them their great administrative abilities, their habits of command, and their high level of culture and education. The lives of three Anglo-Saxon women illustrate the role of heroic women in the Christianizing of northern Europe: Hild of Whitby (A.D. 614–680), St. Leoba (c. A.D. 700–780), and Hugeberc (c. A.D. 740–c. A.D. 790?).

England was just beginning to convert to Christianity when Hild was a child (Pope Gregory had sent St. Augustine to England to convert the populace at the end of the sixth century A.D.). She was the grandniece of King Edwin of Northumbria and was baptized with him and other members of the royal court when she was thirteen. Twenty years later she became a nun, and another decade later, when she was forty-three, she was made abbess of the double monastery at Whitby. She was evidently a prodigious educator and administrator; five of the men who studied under her became bishops, and the first Christian religious poetry in Old English, written by Caedmon in A.D. 664, was encouraged by her. Her friend and contemporary, the historian Bede, says that "So great was her prudence that not only ordinary folk, but kings and princes used to come and ask her advice in their difficulties and take it."[6]

In the second decade of the seventh century, when St. Boniface began his missionary efforts in Germany, there was already a strong tradition of women religious leaders in England, and it was to the nuns and abbesses of these women's houses that Boniface turned. One such woman was St. Leoba, and another was Hugeberc. For Leoba we possess a complete biography (written after her death but based on written and oral accounts by those who knew her, especially on evidence provided by four of her disciples who had left England for Germany with her), and a letter by her to St. Boniface.[7] Her reputation for learning and for sanctity are remarkable in any age. She was a nun in Wessex and had been sent as a child to study the sacred sciences at Wimborne under Mother Tetta. (In secular life Tetta was Cuthberga, sister of Ine, king of Wessex, and wife of Aldfrith, king of Northumbria.) She became the spiritual friend of her kinsman St. Boniface, who called her and a group of other women from the abbey at Wimborne to come to Saxony to aid him in the conversion of the Germans.

> What Lioba did amid the wilderness, violence, and moral chaos of eighth century Europe is inextricably tangled with who she was—her doing cannot be separated from her being. The reasons for her call to Germany, learning and holiness, were elaborated in that new context ... Lioba ... was a skilled classicist. She sent Latin verses to Boniface. She was never without a book to read ... learned not only in Holy Scripture, but in the works of the Church Fathers, in canon law and in the decisions of all the councils. In the world of the eighth century, such erudition gave her an almost magical authority, and in addition afforded practical power in the vast administrative task of bringing order to the raw new church of Germany.[8]

At first glance, one would expect that this life of St. Leoba would be dominated by a male perspective, for the narrative was composed by Rudolf of Fulda at the request of Hrabanus Maurus (probably the most learned man of his age) and was based on the notes of several men, especially those taken by Mago just before he died. But this expectation is not met, for the vital role of women in the Christianization of Europe is everywhere acknowledged. As soon as we begin to read, we see that "explicit is the wholly female context of Lioba's education."[9] The narrative takes us back a century in time, before Leoba was born and before Boniface organized his mission. There was in Britain a place named Wimborne, Rudolf says, and here there was a double monastery, well ordered and famous. Here the sister of the king, Mother Tetta, became abbess and ruled over both houses. Leoba's reminiscences were rich with stories about Tetta, we are told. Leoba herself was the daughter of noble English parents who had remained childless until their old age. Leoba's mother dreamed of a church bell in her bosom, which rang merrily when she drew it out with her hand. Her old nurse knew this dream prophesied a child who must be consecrated to God; the child was named Thrutgeba and nicknamed Leoba or Lioba ("beloved"). When Leoba was grown, her mother turned her over to Mother Tetta to be taught and freed the old nurse who had announced her birth. Leoba loved the monastic life with its opportunity to read and hear the Word of God. She was moderate in eating and was either praying or working with her hands all the time, for she knew that "who will not work should not eat." The excellence of her memory is stressed repeatedly: "whatever she heard or read she commited to memory;" "she took great care not to forget what she had heard or read." She had learned to read as a child, and it seems she read almost constantly; even when she was napping, she had the younger nuns read to her.

We can identify the sources of two anecdotes about her in Rudolf's account. The story of the crippled girl who drowns her newborn baby in the convent water supply must be told by the nun Agatha, who was accused of the deed herself because she was the only one absent from the convent when the crime occurred. The story of Leoba calming the storm must be told by Thecla, her kinswoman, for in the story it is she who urges Leoba to take control of the situation and calm the terrified villagers. This latter anecdote must be typical of those legends in circulation that acknowledged the spiritual power of the new religion. As the *Life of St. Leoba* tells us, a terrible storm came up, so dark that day was turned into night. The flocks were driven into the houses for shelter, but when the storm worsened, the terrified people fled to the church. When the church filled with their anguished cries—for they thought it was the Day of Judgment—Leoba tried to calm them and asked them to pray with her. Finally, the crowd rushed Leoba, prostrate at the altar, and Thecla asked her to pray for divine intercession.

> Leoba arose from prayer and, as if she had been challenged to a contest, flung off the cloak which she was wearing and boldly opened the doors of the church. Standing on the threshold, she made a sign of the cross, opposing to the fury of the storm the name of the High God. . . . Suddenly God came to their aid. The sound of thunder died away, the winds changed direction and dispersed the heavy clouds, the darkness rolled back and the sun shone, bringing calm and peace.

After demonstrations like this, it is no wonder that "the people's faith was stimulated by such tokens of holiness."

Two different styles are being combined here, as Rudolf weaves together the anecdotes he has been given concerning St. Leoba. Those anecdotes provided by Leoba's disciples emphasize the miraculous and the dramatic, utilizing remembered dialogue and phrases treasured over the years. Like the stories about Mother Tetta, these anecdotes focus on the collective power of holiness and the collective responsibility for sins. The connecting narrative by Rudolf tries to summarize Leoba's virtues, her organizational ability, and her prodigious learning. He catalogs rather than quotes speech, generalizes rather than specifies isolated instances. At the close of the *Life*, he brings in several anecdotes that illustrate the respect in which Leoba was held by those in power—specifically St. Boniface and Queen Hiltigard the wife of Charlemagne. Boniface obviously sees her as his comissionary, his equal who must be treated with respect and deference by all the monks:

> He commended her to Lull and to the senior monks of the monastery who were present, admonishing them to care for her with reverence and respect and reaffirming his wish that after his death her bones should be placed next to his in the tomb, so that they who had served God during their lifetime with equal sincerity and zeal should await together the day of resurrection.

Leoba's no-nonsense attitude appears in her exchange with Queen Hiltigard: "Queen Hiltigard also revered her with a chaste affection and loved her as her own soul. . . . But Leoba detested the life at court like poison . . . her deepest concern was the work she had set on foot."

Boniface said goodbye to Leoba in A.D. 754, only six years after she had become abbess of Tauberbischofsheim; she survived him by twenty-eight years, maintaining a unique relationship with the monks of Fulda until she died in A.D. 782. Four years before her death, on the summer solstice, A.D. 778, Hugeberc, another member of Boniface's group, began to write.

In the double monastery over which she was abbess, the Saxon Hugeberc wrote down the words of her kinsman Bishop Willibald as he told her about his adventures. The book she wrote on the basis of these facts constitutes a guide for pilgrims to the Holy Land—including all the shrines along the way—but it is also a history of Willibald's role in the Christianization of Germany, and Hugeberc's analysis of Willibald's character[10]. In her preface to this epic account, Hugeberc identifies herself only as an "unworthy sister of Saxon origin." (Her name was hidden in a cryptogram that was only deciphered in this century.) She writes for the sake of posterity, for it doesn't seem right to her to allow these things to pass into oblivion. She has three purposes in mind: to give an account of St. Willibald's early life, to provide a nosegay of his virtues, and to transmit a description of those "scenes where the marvels of the incarnate Word were enacted." She is, in fact, inventing a new genre, a new literary form, the first travel book written by an Anglo-Saxon, in order to record a new spiritual movement, the conversion of Germans and Franks. Talbot sees Hugeberc's contribution as symptomatic of the central role played by women in this missionary effort:

> It is no coincidence that of all the companions who surrounded Willibald in his bishopric of Eichstatt it was a nun who undertook the task of recording . . . his journeys and the founding of his diocese. The degree of freedom and independence which these nuns enjoyed, the influence they were able to exert and the confidence they inspired in such men as Boniface, Lull and Willibald, is no small tribute. . . . Never, perhaps, has there been an age in which religious women exercised such great power . . . we must conclude that the production of books, on which [Boniface] largely depended for personal study and for the training of others, was their particular province.[11]

It is a disservice to Hugeberc to think of her as simply recording Willibald's reminiscences. She frames and orders them, placing his lengthy pilgrimage in the context of his childhood on the one hand and of his mature role as bishop on the other; in writing, she is seeking the personality that motivated the actions. She is asking what made Willibald the leader he was, what traits might be identified in his life that could account for his prodigious activity and for the spiritual impact he had on others. She often presents pairs of traits; for instance, in describing his early childhood, she underlines the love he evokes in others ("a loveable little creature . . . cherished fondly" by parents who "lavished their affection on him") and the spiritual understanding he manifests at an early age. Another pair of traits seems to determine his pilgrimage: the appeal of asceticism and his curiosity about the world. These two traits are not seen in the opposition; rather, they complement each other, especially because the difficulties of travel in this period made deprivation the rule rather than the exception. Both motives sustain Willibald as he travels down Europe toward the Mediterranean, going from shrine to shrine, and stand him in good stead during his four visits to Jerusalem. The theme of ascetic discipline occurs frequently; even when ill, Willibald and his brother Winnebald keep up the strictest monastic observances; and when Willibald finally reaches Monte Cassino, he is able to teach the monks there a thing or two about what it means to observe the Benedictine Rule.

The theme of curiosity is developed in a number of anecdotes: Willibald's observations on the unusual behavior of red cattle; his desire to look inside a volcano, the "Hell of Theodoric" near Sicily; his cleverness in smuggling balsam out of the Holy Land in a gourd. Hugeberc also suggests that Willibald and his companions may have been the objects of curiosity themselves. For instance, when she tells of the brothers' imprisonment by the Saracens, she notes that "the citizens of the town, who are inquisitive people, used to come regularly to look at them, because they were young and handsome and clothed in beautiful garments."

Stillness and movement are another pair of traits in Willibald. Both are extraordinarily pronounced, but they complement rather than oppose each other. Thus, Willibald remains for two years in Constantinople at the church in which the bodies of Saints Andrew, Timothy, Luke, and John Chrysostom were buried. He "had an alcove in the church so that every day he could sit and gaze upon the place where the saints lay at rest." The same ability to be still, combined with his "great self-discipline and natural aptitude for obedience," makes him an exemplary observer of the Rule. But the movement is always there, too—the text is full of verbs of motion.

Hugeberc's familiarity with heroic poetry is evident in the epithets she applies to her saintly bishop. He is "the soldier of Christ," "the illustrious athlete of God," "celebrated bearer of Christ's cross," and a "restless battler." He is "our bishop the active servant of Christ," the "venerable high priest." The pope is the "Glorious Ruler of the People," the "Shepherd of the People." Other passages that may derive from heroic poetry (although they might also have come through Latin reading) are her descriptions of the "perils of the pathless sea" and "swift-sailing ships." She uses what is evidently a conventional description of the movement of the seasons to bring in summer as the time of pestilence:

> whilst the cold and bare winter was passing and spring with its flowers was beginning to appear and Eastertide was shedding its sunny radiance over the whole earth, the two brothers had been leading a life of monastic discipline. . . . Then with the passing of the days and the increasing heat of the summer, which is usually a sign of future fever, they were struck down with sickness. . . . They had caught the black plague.

All these themes associated with Willibald's personality and much of Hugeberc's own reading and experience come together in her concluding description of his success in Germany.

> Soon after the energetic champion of our good God had begun to dwell in the monastery men flocked to him from all sides . . . to hear his salutary teaching and wisdom. Willibald and Mother Church, like a hen that cherishes her offspring beneath her wings, won over many adoptive sons to the Lord, protecting them continually with the shield of his kindliness. These he trained with gentleness and sympathy, detaching them from their imperfections until they reached perfect maturity. . . . Far and wide through the vast province of Bavaria he drove his plough, sowing the seed and reaping the harvest with the help of many fellow-labourers.

All Europe became Christianized in the course of the next few centuries, and the activities of women like Hild, Leoba, and Hugeberc were crucial to that transformation. Particularly in the northern European context, Christianity may have seemed a "feminine" religion, and women were gradually seen to be innately suited to manifesting the Christian virtues of faith, hope, and charity. The center of culture was to be found in the cloister, for as Eckenstein points out, "The monotony of life in the castles or burghs of this period can hardly be exaggerated."[12] The women of northern Europe were fully as energetic as the men, and the same "impulse toward leadership which kept the men in the world sent the women out of it."[13] Consequently, it was the women of the noble families who promoted and endowed religious houses:

> Settlements such as Herford, Gandersheim, Essen, and Quedlinburg offered the companionship of equals, and gave a domestic and intellectual training which was the best of its kind. Later ages were wont to look upon the standard of education attained . . . as exemplary. The word college (collegium), which early writers often apply to these settlements in its modern sense of a learning and a teaching body, aptly designates their character. For the religious settlement was an endowed college where girls were received to be trained, and where women who wished to devote themselves to learning and the arts permanently resided.[14]

The writings of Hrotsvit of Gandersheim (c. A.D. 932–1000) demonstrate the possibilities for a woman in such an environment. The earliest poet known in Germany and the first dramatist since classical times, she wrote eight sacred legends in verse, six dramas in rhymed prose, two historical poems or epics, three lengthy prose prefaces, and a number of shorter works.[15] Her knowledge of classical and religious literature is evidence that Gandersheim had a rich collection of manuscripts, and the library must have been the center of intellectual life in the cloister. Two of her works are included in this collection: the verse legend *Pelagius* and the play *Abraham*. Pelagius was a recent martyr, a Spanish youth who fell victim to a lecherous Moorish despot. One of the unusual aspects of this legend is that Hrotsvit says she bases her version on the account of an eyewitness to the execution of Pelagius, someone who must have traveled far to tell this tale to a young canoness in Germany.[16]

The presence of a good library at Gandersheim is not enough to account for Hrotsvit's genius in the writing of *Pelagius*. Her narrative plays with certain conventions of a martyrdom tale. The events ought to take place in a time of trials for Christians; the chief protagonist ought to be a virgin who attracts the notice of a ruler, who is sexually excited by her. The virgin's Christian identity is revealed in her commitment to virginity, and the lecherous ruler can be expected to apply tortures to get her to make the obligatory sacrifices to the emperor's statue. When torture fails, mass conversions ought to result, and the legend will end with the exemplary death of the virgin. Some of these expectations are met, for Hrotsvit identifies the Spain of her tale as a time of persecution for Christians, who are expected to sacrifice to idols associated with the Moslem emperor. The lecherous ruler is sexually attracted to the virgin saint—but the virgin is male, and the lecherous ruler is homosexual. But the Christian martyrs in this story are active; the Spanish Christians prior to Pelagius have actively insulted the idols and the emperor; and Pelagius himself, although he tries to be tactful when brought before the caliph, aggressively protects his virginity by smacking the caliph in the mouth when he tries to kiss him. The sadism of some of the early virgin-martyr legends is completely absent here; there is no emphasis on the vulnerability or the passivity of the saint, and there is no interest in tortures that are inflicted. The attempt to violate Pelagius' body by hurling it from a catapult fails, so he is undramatically beheaded, and his body is given to the waves.

It is impossible to say what the focus of this legend was as Hrotsvit heard it. In the legend she has created, initial emphasis falls on the political history of Spain, on placing this martyr's death historically and politically. In contrast to this rather "realistic" concern, her portrait of Pelagius is unabashedly idealized. He is gorgeous, verbally skilled, intensely loyal to his father, fearless in facing the consequences of his repudiation of Abderrahman, the caliph. The poem moves quickly, with rapid shifts in narrative viewpoint and the location of the observer. Of the 412 lines of the poem, 143 are devoted to giving the background of the political history of Spain and of Abderrahman's motives; the central third of the poem introduces Pelagius with his father and shows his imprisonment as a hostage for his father, his presentation to the caliph, and their confrontation. Pelagius' death and the testing of his body occupy the final third. As a saint's legend *Pelagius* is remarkable for its interest in ascertaining historical, not just spiritual, truth. The cast of characters is not divided into good guys and bad guys; we meet a specific villain, who has very specific reasons for putting Pelagius to death. All Arabs are not perceived as evil; although the members of the court recognize and condone the caliph's homosexuality, they are troubled by seeing Pelagius in prison and are motivated to use any means possible to get him freed. Pelagius is perfect, but his is not a stereotyped perfection.

Hrotsvit wrote her plays somewhat later, sometime after the year A.D. 962, when she was already well known as a poet. In choosing to write plays, she was attempting something new in a number of important respects:

> in her six dramas, Hroswitha's fundamental purpose is to celebrate in dramatic form a symbolic representation of the spiritual wrestlings of her female *dramatis personae*, virgins, martyrs, and sinners, who find moving dignity and religious fulfillment in the conflicting demands of sin and salvation, the dramatic context within which the drama of human salvation is articulated ... Hroswitha, transcending the narrow limits imposed by spiritual abstractions, utilized women as visible and vibrant figures to transmute, with unexampled immediacy into drama, the deep spiritual experience of the human drama of salvation.[17]

Abraham, Hrotsvit's fourth and probably most interesting play, centers on the young virgin Maria, raised in a chaste and ascetic life by her uncle Abraham. Seduced by a monk who pretends a spiritual friendship, she runs away in shame and becomes a prostitute. Abraham determines to find her even though it takes him two years; in the end he can only see her by disguising himself as a prospective client. As in the legends of Mary Magdalene and Mary the Egyptian, there are two competing forces within Maria, the sacred and the profane, the divine and the sensual. The resolution of the drama is the harmony of these forces under love, which is why Abraham must visit her at the inn disguised as her lover.

NOTES

1. Sister Edna Mary, *The Religious Life* (Harmondsworth, England: Penguin, 1968), p. 37. For more on the Benedictines in early medieval Europe, see David Knowles, *From Pachomius to Ignatius: A Study in the Constitutional History of the Religious Orders*, Sarum Lectures 1964–65 (Oxford: Clarendon Press, 1966), pp.

75 ff.; R. W. Southern, *The Making of the Middle Ages* (New Haven and London: Yale University Press, 1965), and *Western Society and the Church in the Middle Ages* (Baltimore: Penguin, 1970).

2. Lina Eckenstein, *Woman Under Monasticism* (Cambridge: Cambridge University Press, 1896), p. 65. See

also Emily James Putnam, *The Lady: Studies of Certain Significant Phases of Her History* (Chicago: University of Chicago Press, 1969; first pub. in 1910).

3. Herbert B. Workman, *The Evolution of the Monastic Ideal* (Boston: Beacon Press, 1962; first pub. in 1913), pp. 139–60.

4. Eckenstein, *Women Under Monasticism*, pp. 90 ff.; Putnam, *The Lady*, p. 21; and see Suzanne Wemple, *Women in the Frankish Kingdom* (Philadelphia: University of Pennsylvania Press, 1980). Wemple believes that church-enforced monogamy was probably worse for women than polygamy had been; this is contrary to the earlier view, that monogamy enhanced the status of wives.

5. Elizabeth Judd, *Women Before the Conquest: A Study of Women in Anglo-Saxon England*, Papers in Women's Studies, 1: 1 (February 1974) (Ann Arbor: University of Michigan Press), pp. 127–49; Angela M. Lucas, *Women in the Middle Ages: Religion, Marriage, and Letters* (New York: St. Martin's Press, 1983); Joan Nicholson, "Feminae Gloriosae: Women in the Age of Bede," in *Medieval Women*, ed. Derek Baker (Oxford: Basil Blackwell, 1978), pp. 15–29; Suzanne Wemple, *Women in the Frankish Kingdom*, cited earlier, note 4; Richard P. Lyman, Jr., "Barbarism and Religion: Late Roman and Early Medieval Childhood," in *The History of Childhood*, ed. Lloyd de Mause (New York: Harper & Row, 1974), pp. 75–100; and, in the same volume, Mary Martin McLaughlin, "Survivors and Surrogates: Children and Parents from the Ninth to the Thirteenth Centuries," pp. 101–82, especially 129–32; on Hild or Hilda, see Christine E. Fell, "Hild, Abbess of Streonaeshalch," in *Hagiography and Medieval Literature* (Odense: Odense University Press, 1981), pp. 76–99; Jane Campbell, "Women Scholars of the Middle Ages," *American Catholic Quarterly Review* 43 (April 1918), pp. 237–48; Elise Boulding, *The Underside of History, A View of Women through Time* (Boulder: Westview Press, 1976), pp. 218–19, 376, 423–25. On Leoba or Lioba, see McLaughlin, "Women, Power, and the Pursuit of Holiness," in *Women of Spirit*, pp. 103–07, and in *Religion and Sexism*, p. 237; Francis and Joseph Gies, *Women in the Middle Ages* (New York: Crowell, 1978), pp. 66–67; JoAnn McNamara and Suzanne Wemple, "Sanctity and Power," in *Becoming Visible*, pp. 100–01.

6. Bede, *A History of the English Church and People*, trans. Leo Sherley-Price (Baltimore: Penguin, 1968), p. 247. "The Life and Death of Abbess Hilda" occupies Ch. 23, pp. 245–50; Caedmon is found in Ch. 23, pp. 250–53.

7. Texts in C. H. Talbot, *The Anglo-Saxon Missionaries in Germany* (New York: Sheed & Ward, 1954). See Judd, *Women Before the Conquest*, pp. 132 ff., and Eleanor McLaughlin, "Women, Power, and the Pursuit of Holiness," pp. 103–08 in *Women of Spirit*, ed. Rosemary Reuther and Eleanor McLaughlin (New York: Simon & Schuster, 1979).

8. McLaughlin, "Women, Power, and the Pursuit of Holiness," p. 105.

9. McLaughlin, "Women, Power, and the Pursuit of Holiness," p. 104.

10. Text in Talbot, *The Anglo-Saxon Missionaries in Germany*. On Hugeberc as a writer, see Peter Dronke, *Women Writers of the Middle Ages*, pp. 33–35.

11. Talbot, *Anglo-Saxon Missionaries*, pp. xii–xiii.

12. Eckenstein, *Women Under Monasticism*, p. 149.

13. Putnam, *The Lady*, p. 78.

14. Eckenstein, *Women Under Monasticism*, p. 149.

15. For the bibliography of Hrotsvit (Hroswitha), see Anne L. Haight, ed., *Hroswitha of Gandersheim* (New York: Hroswitha Club, 1965). Texts are found in *Hroswitha Opera*, ed. Karl Strecker (Leipzig: Biblioteca Teubneriana, 1906, 1930); Helena Homeyer, *Hroswithae Opera* (Munich: Schonigh, 1970). For a summary of recent scholarship, see Katharina M. Wilson, "The Saxon Canoness: Hrotsvit of Gandersheim," in *Medieval Women Writers* (Athens, Ga: University of Georgia Press 1983), and Peter Dronke, *Women Writers of the Middle Ages*, pp. 55–83.

16. See the notes to the translation of *Pelagius* by Katharina Wilson, which follows.

17. Sandro Sticca, "Sin and Salvation: The Dramatic Context of Hroswitha's Women," in *The Roles and Images of Women in the Middle Ages and Renaissance*, ed. Douglas Radcliff-Umstead, University of Pittsburgh Publications on the Middle Ages and Renaissance, vol. 3 (Pittsburgh: University of Pittsburgh Press, 1978), pp. 3–22. This passage is found on pp. 8–9.

HUGEBERC OF HILDESHEIM

(8th century A.D; born Wessex; died Germany)

The Hodoeporicon of St. Willibald

Translated by C. H. Talbot

PREFACE

To the venerable priests, deacons, abbots and brethren beloved in Christ, whom our holy bishop, as a good leader and tender father, has appointed throughout his diocese to be priests, chaste levites, monks and novices, to all these who live under religious observance, I, an unworthy sister of Saxon origin, last and least in life and manners, venture to write for the sake of posterity and present to you who are religious and preachers of the Gospel a brief account of the early life of the venerable Willibald. Although I lack the necessary experience and knowledge because I am but a weak woman, yet I would like, as far as lies in my power, to gather together a kind of nosegay of his virtues and give you something by which you may remember them. And here I repeat that I am not urged on through presumption to attempt a task for which I am so ill fitted. It is your authority and kindness and God's grace which has prompted me to describe the scenes where the marvels of the Incarnate Word were enacted, for Willibald visited and saw these places with his own eyes and trod with his feet in the footsteps of Him who was born into this world, suffered and rose again for our sake. Of all these places Willibald has given us a faithful description. For this reason, it did not seem right to allow these things to pass into oblivion, nor to be silent about the things God has shown to His servant in these our days. We heard them from his own lips in the presence of two deacons who will vouch for their truth: it was on the 20th of June, the day before the summer solstice.

I know that it may seem very bold on my part to write this book when there are so many holy priests capable of doing better, but as a humble relative I would like to record something of their deeds and travels for future ages.

In the hope, then, that you will excuse me and kindly grant me your indulgence, relying also on the grace of God, I present to you this narrative, traced in letters of ink and dedicated to the glory of God, the Giver of all good.

First of all, I will tell of the early life of the venerable high priest of God, Willibald: how he submitted to the discipline of monastic life, how he followed the examples of the saints and how he imitated and observed their way of life. Then I will speak of his early manhood, the time of his maturity and of his old age, even till he became decrepit, combining and putting into order the new facts that there are and weaving them into a continuous narrative.

When he was a baby in the cradle, a lovable little creature, he was cherished fondly by those who nursed him, especially by his parents, who lavished their affection on him and brought him up with great solicitude until he reached the age of three. At that age, when his limbs were still weak and delicate, he was suddenly attacked by a severe illness: the contraction of his limbs made it impossible for him to breathe and threatened to end his life. When his father and mother saw that he was at the doors of death they were full of fear and

The Anglo-Saxon Missionaries in Germany (New York: Sheed & Ward, 1954).

grief, and their suspense grew as they saw him, gripped by the disease, hovering between life and death. It seemed that the child, whom they had hoped would be their survivor and heir, would soon be carried to an untimely grave. But God Almighty, Creator of heaven and earth, did not intend that His servant be released from the prison of his body and depart unknown to the rest of the world, for he was destined to preach the Gospel to the ends of the earth and to bring a multitude of neophytes to the faith of Christ.

But let us return to the early infancy of the blessed man. When his parents, in great anxiety of mind, were still uncertain about the fate of their son, they took him and offered him up before the holy Cross of our Lord and Saviour. And this they did, not in the church but at the foot of the Cross, for on the estates of the nobles and good men of the Saxon race it is a custom to have a cross, which is dedicated to our Lord and held in great reverence, erected on some prominent spot for the convenience of those who wish to pray daily before it. There before the cross they laid him. Then they began earnestly to implore God, the Maker of all things, to bring them consolation and to save their son's life. And in their prayers they made a solemn promise that in return for the health of their child they would at once have him tonsured as the first step to Sacred Orders and would dedicate him to the service of Christ under the discipline of monastic life.

No sooner had they made these vows than they put their words into deeds. They enlisted their son in the service of the heavenly King; their favour was granted by the Lord, and the former health of the child was restored.

When this remarkable boy had reached the age of five he began to show the first signs of spiritual understanding. His parents hastened to carry out the promises they had made, and as soon as they had taken council with their noble friends and kinsfolk they lost no time in instructing him in the sacred obligations of monastic life. Without delay they entrusted him to the care of Theodred, a man both venerable and trustworthy, and begged him to be responsible for taking the child to the monastery, where he should make suitable arrangements and dispositions on his behalf. So they set out and took him to the monastery which is called Waldheim [Bishops Waltham]. There they handed him over to the venerable Abbot Egwald, offering him as a novice, because of his age, to be obedient in all things. In accordance with the rules of monastic life the abbot immediately laid the case before the community and asked them if they would advise and allow this to be done. The response of the monks was immediate, and by their unanimous consent he was accepted and received by them into the community to share in their life.

Afterwards this boy of unassuming manners was initiated and perfectly trained in sacred studies. He gave careful and assiduous attention to the learning of the psalms and applied his mind to the examination of the other books of Holy Writ. Young though he was in age, he was advanced in wisdom, so that in him through the divine mercy the words of the prophet were fulfilled: "Out of the mouths of babes and sucklings thou hast perfected praise." Then, as his age increased and his mental powers developed, and more so as the growth of divine grace kept pace with his increasing strength and stature, he devoted his energies to the pursuit of divine love. Long and earnest meditation filled his days. Night and day he pondered anxiously on the means of monastic perfection and the importance of community life, wondering how he might become a member of that chaste fellowship and share in the joys of their common discipline.

Next he began to inquire how he could put these ideas into effect so that he could despise and renounce the fleeting pleasures of this world and forsake not merely the temporal riches of his earthly inheritance but also his country, parents and relatives. He began also to devise means of setting out on pilgrimage and travelling to foreign countries that were unknown to him. After some time had elapsed, when he had outgrown the foolish pranks of childhood, the unsteadiness of youth and the disturbing period of adolescence, through the ineffable dispensation of divine grace he came to manhood. By that time he was greatly beloved by the community because of his obedience and his meekness. All held him in the deepest affection and respect. By assiduous application to his daily duties and continual attention to his studies he disciplined his mind with such vigour and firmness that he made unbroken progress in the way of monastic perfection.

The young servant of Christ, as we have already mentioned, was eager to go on pilgrimage and travel to distant foreign lands and find out all about them. When he had decided to brave the perils of the pathless sea he went immediately to his father and opened his heart to him, telling him the secrets he had concealed from others. He begged him earnestly to advise him on the project and to give his permission; but not content with that, he asked his father to go with him. He invited him to share in this hazardous enterprise and to undertake this difficult mode of life, eager to detach him from the pleasures of the world, from the delights of earth and from the false prosperity of wealth. He asked him to enter, with the help of God, into the divine service and to enroll in the heavenly army, to abandon his native country and to accompany him as a pilgrim to foreign parts. Using all his powers of persuasion, he coaxed him to join his sons on a visit to the sacred shrine of St. Peter, Prince of the Apostles. At first his father declined, excusing himself from the journey on the plea that he could not leave his wife and small children. It would be cruel, and unchris-

tian, he said, to deprive them of his protection and to leave them at the mercy of others. Then the soldier of Christ repeated his solemn exhortations and his long and urgent entreaties, beseeching him, now with fearful threats of damnation, now with bland promises of eternal life, to consent, softening his heart by describing the beauty of paradise and the sweetness of the love of Christ. In this way, employing every means of persuasion and speaking to him heart to heart, he strove to extort from him his agreement to the plan. At last, by the help of Almighty God, his insistence prevailed. His father and his brother Wynnebald gave their promise that they would embark on the enterprise he had in mind and in which he had persuaded them to join.

Following this discussion, a certain time elapsed. At the change of the seasons, towards the end of summer, his father and unmarried brother set out on the journey to which they had agreed. At a suitable time in the summer they were ready and prepared. Taking with them the necessary money for the journey and accompanied by a band of friends, they came to a place, which was known by the ancient name of Hamblemouth, near the port of Hamwih. Shortly afterwards they embarked on a ship. When the captain of the swift-sailing ship had taken their fares, they sailed, with the west wind blowing and a high sea running, amidst the shouting of sailors and the creaking of oars. When they had braved the dangers at sea and the perils of the mountainous waves, a swift course brought them with full sails and following winds safely to dry land. At once they gave thanks and disembarked, and, pitching their tents on the banks of the river Seine, they encamped near the city which is called Rouen, where there is a market.

For some days they rested there and then continued their journey, visiting the shrines of the saints that were on their way and praying there. And so going by degrees from place to place they came to Gorthonicum.[1] Pursuing their journey, they came to Lucca. Hitherto Willibald and Wynnebald had taken their father along with them on their journey. But at Lucca he was struck down almost at once by a severe bodily sickness and after a few days it seemed that his end was near. As the sickness increased, his weary limbs grew cold and stiff, and in this way he breathed his last. As soon as the two brothers saw that their father was dead they wrapped his body in a fine shroud and with filial piety buried it in the Church of Saint Frigidian at Lucca, where it still rests.[2] Immediately afterwards they set out on their way, going steadily on foot through the vast land of Italy, through the deep valleys, over the craggy mountains, across the level plains, climbing upwards towards the peaks of the Apennines. And after they had gazed on the peaks covered with snow and wreathed in banks of cloud, with the help of God and the support of His saints they passed safely through the ambushes of the fierce and arrogant soldiery[3] and came with all their relatives and company to the shrine of St. Peter, Prince of the Apostles. There they besought his protection and gave many thanks to God, because they had escaped unscathed from the previous perils of the sea and the manifold difficulties of travel in a foreign land, and been accounted worthy to climb the Scala Santa and reach the famous basilica of St. Peter.

The two brothers remained there from the feast of St. Martin until Easter of the following year. During that time, whilst the cold and bare winter was passing and spring with its flowers was beginning to appear and Eastertide was shedding its sunny radiance over the whole earth, the two brothers had been leading a life of monastic discipline under the prescriptions of the Holy Rule. Then with the passing of the days and the increasing heat of the summer, which is usually a sign of future fever, they were struck down with sickness. They found it difficult to breathe, fever set in,

and at one moment they were shivering with cold, the next burning with heat. They had caught the black plague. So great a hold had it got on them that, scarcely able to move, worn out with fever and almost at the point of death, the breath of life had practically left their bodies. But God in His never-failing providence and fatherly love deigned to listen to their prayers and come to their aid, so that each of them rested in turn for one week whilst they attended to each other's needs. In spite of this, they never failed to observe the normal monastic Rule as far as their bodily weakness would allow; they persevered all the more zealously in their study and sacred reading, following the words of Truth, who said: "He who perseveres unto the end shall be saved."

After this celebrated bearer of Christ's Cross had continued to pursue the life of perfection with great steadfastness of mind and inward contemplation, he grew more eager to follow a stricter mode of life. A more austere and rigorous observance of the monastic Rule, not an easier one, was what he most desired. He longed to go on pilgrimage to a more remote and less well-known place than the one in which he was now staying. So, energetic as ever, he sought the advice of his friends and asked permission from his kinsmen to go. He begged them to follow him on his wanderings with their prayers, so that throughout the course of his journey their prayers would keep him from harm and enable him reach the city of Jerusalem and gaze upon its pleasant and hallowed walls.

So after the solemnities of Easter Sunday were over this restless battler set off on his journey with two companions. On their way they came to a town east of Terracina [Fondi] and stayed there two days. Then, leaving it behind, they reached Gaeta, which stands at the edge of the sea. At this point they went on board a ship and crossed over the sea to Naples, where they left the ship in which they had sailed and stayed for two weeks. These cities belong to the Romans: they are in the territory of Benevento, but owe allegiance to the Romans. And at once, as is usual when the mercy of God is at work, their fondest hopes were fulfilled, for they chanced upon a ship that had come from Egypt, so they embarked on it and set sail for a town called Reggio in Calabria. At this place they stayed two days; then they departed and betook themselves to the island of Sicily, that is to say, to Catania, where the body of St. Agatha, the virgin, rests. Mount Etna is there. Whenever the volcanic fire erupts there and begins to spread and threaten the whole region the people of the city take the body of St. Agatha and place it in front of the oncoming flames and they stop immediately.[4] They stayed there three weeks. Thence they sailed for Syracuse, a city in the same country. Sailing from Syracuse, they crossed the Adriatic and reached the city of Monembasia,[5] in the land of Slavinia, and from there they sailed to Chios, leaving Corinth on the port side. Sailing on from there, they passed Samos and sped on towards Asia, to the city of Ephesus, which stands about a mile from the sea. Then they went on foot to the spot where the Seven Sleepers lie at rest.[6] From there they walked to the tomb of St. John, the Evangelist, which is situated in a beautiful spot near Ephesus, and thence two miles farther on along the sea coast to a great city called Phygela, where they stayed a day. At this place they begged some bread and went to a fountain in the middle of the city, and, sitting on the edge of it, they dipped their bread in the water and so ate. They pursued their journey on foot along the sea shore to the town of Hierapolis, which stands on a high mountain; and thence they went to a place called Patara, where they remained until the bitter and icy winter had passed. Afterwards they sailed from there and reached a city called Miletus,[7] which was formerly threatened with destruction from the waters. At this place there were two solitaries living on "stylites,"

that is, columns built up and strengthened by a great stone wall of immense height, to protect them from the water. Thence they crossed over by sea to Mount Chelidonium and traversed the whole of it. At this point they suffered very much from hunger, because the country was wild and desolate, and they grew so weak through lack of food that they feared their last day had come. But the Almighty Shepherd of His people deigned to provide food for His poor servants.

Sailing from there, they reached the island of Cyprus, which lies between the Greeks and the Saracens, and went to the city of Paphos, where they stayed three weeks. It was then Eastertime, a year after their setting out. Thence they went to Constantia,[8] where the body of St. Epiphanius rests, and they remained there until after the feast of St. John the Baptist.

Once more they set sail and reached the town of Antarados,[9] which lies near the sea in the territory of the Saracens. Then they went on foot for about nine or twelve miles to a fort called Arche,[10] where they had a Greek bishop. There they sang a litany according to the Greek rite.[11] Leaving this place, they set out on foot for the town named Emesa,[12] about twelve miles distant, where there is a large church built by St. Helena in honour of St. John the Baptist[13] and where his head was for a long time preserved. This is in Syria now.

At that time there were seven companions with Willibald and he made the eighth. Almost at once they were arrested by the pagan Saracens, and because they were strangers and came without credentials they were taken prisoner and held as captives. They knew not to which nation they belonged, and, thinking they were spies, they took them bound to a certain rich old man to find out where they came from. The old man put questions to them asking where they were from and on what errand they were employed. Then they told him everything from the beginning and acquainted him with the reason for their journey. And the old man said: "I have often seen men coming from those parts of the world, fellow-countrymen of theirs; they cause no mischief and are merely anxious to fulfil their law." Then they left him and went to the court, to ask permission to pass over to Jerusalem. But when they arrived there, the governor said at once that they were spies and ordered them to be thrust into prison until such time as he should hear from the king what was to be done with them. Whilst they were in prison they had an unexpected experience of the wonderful dispensation of Almighty God, who mercifully deigns to protect his servants everywhere, amidst weapons of war and tortures, barbarians, and soldiers, prisons and bands of aggressors, preserving and shielding them from all harm. A man was there, a merchant, who wished to redeem them and release them from captivity, so that they should be free to continue their journey as they wished. He did this by way of alms and for the salvation of his own soul. But he was unable to release them. Every day, therefore, he sent them dinner and supper, and on Wednesday and Saturday he sent his son to the prison and took them out for a bath and then took them back again. Every Sunday he took them to church through the market place, so that if they saw anything on sale for which they had a mind he could buy it for them and so give them pleasure. The citizens of the town, who are inquisitive people, used to come regularly to look at them, because they were young and handsome and clothed in beautiful garments. Then whilst they were still languishing in prison a man from Spain came and spoke with them inside the prison itself and made careful inquiries about their nationality and homeland. And they told him everything about their journey from first to last. This Spaniard had a brother at the king's court, who was the chamberlain of the King of the Saracens. And when the

governor who had sent them to prison came to court, both the Spaniard who had spoken to them in prison and the captain of the ship in which they had sailed from Cyprus came together in the presence of the Saracens' king, whose name was Emir-al-Mummenin. And when the conversation turned on their case, the Spaniard told his brother all that he had learned about them whilst speaking to them in the prison, and he asked his brother to pass this information on to the king and to help them. So when, afterwards, all these three came to the king and mentioned their case, telling him all the details from first to last, the king asked whence they came; and they answered: "These men come from the West where the sun sets; we know nothing of their country except that beyond it lies nothing but water." Then the king asked them, saying: "Why should we punish them? They have done us no harm. Allow them to depart and go on their way." The other prisoners who were in captivity had to pay a fine of three measures of corn, but they were let off scot-free.

With this permission they at once set out and travelled a hundred miles to Damascus, in Syria, where the body of St. Ananias rests. They stayed there a week. About two miles distant stands a church on the spot where St. Paul was first converted and where our Lord said to him: "Saul, Saul, why persecutest thou me," etc. After praying in the church, they went on foot to Galilee, to the place where Gabriel first came to our Lady and said: "Hail Mary." There is a church there now, and the village where the church is is called Nazareth. The Christians have often had to come to terms with the pagan Saracens about this church, because they wished to destroy it. After commending themselves to the Lord there, they set out on foot and came to the town of Chana, where our Lord changed water into wine. A vast church stands there, and in the church one of the altars has on it one of the six waterpots which our Lord ordered to be filled with water and then changed into wine; from it they drank some wine. They stayed for one day there. Departing thence, they reached Mount Thabor, where our Lord was transfigured. At the moment there is a monastery of monks there, and the church is dedicated to our Lord, Moses and Elias, and the place is called by those who live there Holy Mount. There they prayed.

Then they made for the town called Tiberias. It stands at the edge of the sea on which our Lord walked dry-shod and where Peter sank when walking on the waters towards Him. Many churches and synagogues of the Jews are built there, and great honour is paid to our Lord. They remained there for several days. At that point the Jordan flows into the lake. Thence they set off round the lake and went to the village of Magdalene and came to the village of Capharnaum, where our Lord raised to life the ruler's daughter. Here there was a house and a great wall, and the people said that Zebedee used to live there with his sons John and James. Then they went to Bethsaida, the native place of Peter and Andrew. A church now occupies the site where their home once stood. They passed the night there, and on the following morning set off for Corazain, where our Lord cured the man possessed of the devil and drove the demons into a herd of swine. A church stands there now.

After praying there, they departed and came to the spot where two fountains, Jor and Dan, spring from the earth and then pour down the mountainside to form the river Jordan. There, between the two fountains, they passed the night and the shepherds gave us[14] sour milk to drink. At this spot there are wonderful herds of cattle, long in the back and short in the leg, bearing enormous horns; they are all of one colour, dark red. Deep marshes lie there, and in the summer-time, when the great heat of the sun scorches the earth, the herds betake themselves to the marshes and, plunging

themselves up to their necks in the water, leave only their heads showing.

Departing thence, they came to Caesarea, where there was a church and a great number of Christians. They rested there for a short time and set out for the monastery of St. John the Baptist, where about twenty monks were living. They stayed the night and then went forward about a mile to the Jordan, where our Lord was baptized. At this spot there is now a church built high up on columns of stone; beneath the church, however, the ground is dry. On the very place where Christ was baptized and where they now baptize there stands a little wooden cross: a little stream of water is led off and a rope is stretched over the Jordan and tied at each end. Then on the Feast of the Epiphany the sick and infirm come there and, holding on to the rope, plunge themselves in the water. Barren women also come there. Our Bishop Willibald bathed himself there in the Jordan. They passed the day there and then departed.

Thence they came to Galgala, which is about five miles away. In the church there, which is small and made of wood, there are twelve stones. These are the twelve stones which the children of Israel took from the Jordan and carried more than five miles to Galgala and set up as witnesses of their passage. After saying prayers there, they went on towards Jericho, which is more than seven miles distant from the Jordan. The fountain which bubbled up there on the brow of the hill was barren and quite useless to man before the prophet Eliseus came and blessed it and made it flow. Afterwards the people of the city drew it off into their fields and gardens and other places that needed it, and now wherever this fountain flows, the crops increase and promote health, all by reasons of the blessing given by Eliseus the prophet. They went on from there to the monastery of St. Eustochium, which stands in the middle of the plain between Jericho and Jerusalem.

Then they came to Jerusalem, to the very spot where the holy cross of our Lord was found. On the site of the place called Calvary now stands a church. Formerly this was outside Jerusalem, but when Helena discovered the cross she placed the spot within the walls of Jerusalem. There now stand three crosses outside the church near the wall of the eastern end, as a memorial to the cross of our Lord and those who were crucified with Him. At present they are not inside the church, but outside beneath a pent roof. Nearby is the garden in which the tomb of our Saviour was placed. This tomb was cut from the rock and the rock stands above ground: it is squared at the bottom and tapers towards a point at the top. On the highest point of it stands a cross, and a wonderful house has been constructed over it. At the eastern end a door has been cut in the rock of the sepulchre, through which people can enter into the tomb to pray. Inside there is the slab on which the body of our Lord lay, and on this slab fifteen lamps of gold burn day and night; it is situated on the north side of the interior of the tomb and lies at one's right hand as one enters the tomb to pray. In front of the door of the sepulchre lies a great square stone, a replica of that first stone which the angel rolled away from the mouth of the sepulchre.

On the Feast of St. Martin our bishop came there, and as soon as he reached the spot he began to feel sick and was confined to his bed until a week before Christmas. Then when he recovered and began to feel a little better he got up and went to the church called Holy Sion, which stands in the centre of Jerusalem. He prayed there and then went to Solomon's Porch, where there is a pool at which the sick used to lie waiting for the angel to move the waters, after which the first who went down into them was cured: this is where our Lord said to the paralytic: "Arise, take up thy bed and walk."

Willibald himself said that in front of the gate of the city stood a tall pillar, on top of which rose a cross, as a sign and memorial of the place where the Jews attempted to take away the body of our Lady. For when the eleven Apostles were bearing the body of Holy Mary away from Jerusalem the Jews tried to snatch it away as soon as they reached the gate of the city. But as soon as they stretched out their hands towards the bier and endeavoured to take her their arms became fixed, stuck as it were to the bier, and they were unable to move until, by the grace of God and the prayers of the Apostles, they were released, and then they let them go. Our Lady passed from this world in that very spot in the centre of Jerusalem which is called Holy Sion. And then the eleven Apostles bore her, as I have already said, and finally the angels came and took her away from the hands of the Apostles and carried her to paradise.

Bishop Willibald came down from the mount and went to the valley of Josaphat: it is situated to the east of the city of Jerusalem. In the valley there is a church of our Lady and in the church is her tomb (not that her body lies at rest there, but as a memorial to her). After praying there, he climbed Mount Olivet, which is near to the valley at its eastern end— the valley lies between Jerusalem and Mount Olivet. On Mount Olivet there is now a church on the spot where our Lord prayed before His passion and said to his Disciples: "Watch and pray that ye enter not into temptation." Then he came to the very hill whence our Lord ascended into heaven. In the centre of the church is a beautiful candlestick sculptured in bronze: it is square and stands in the middle of the church where our Lord ascended into heaven. In the middle of the bronze candlestick is a square vessel of glass, and in the glass is a small lamp, and round about the lamp, closed on all sides, is the glass. The reason why it is closed on all sides is that the lamp may burn both in good weather and bad. The church has no roof and is open to the sky, and two pillars stand there inside the church, one against the northern wall, the other against the southern wall. They are placed there in remembrance of the two men who said: "Men of Galilee, why stand ye looking up into heaven?" Any man who can squeeze his body between the pillars and the wall is freed from his sins.

Then he came to the place where the angel appeared to the shepherds and said: "I announce to you tidings of great joy." Thence he came to Bethlehem, where our Lord was born, about six miles distant from Jerusalem. The place where our Lord was born was formerly a cave underneath the ground and is now a square chamber cut out of the rock; the earth has been dug away on all sides and thrown aside, and now the church has been built above it. There our Lord was born. An altar has been raised above it also, but another small [portable] altar has been made, so that when they wish to celebrate Mass within the cave they can take up the small altar whilst Mass is being said and afterwards can take it out again. The church which stands over the spot where our Lord was born is built in the form of a cross, a house of great beauty.

After praying there, they departed and came to a large town called Thecua: this is the place where the Holy Innocents were slaughtered by Herod. A church stands there now. In it rests the body of one of the prophets. Then they came to the Laura in the valley: it is a great monastery and there resides the abbot and the doorkeeper who keeps the keys of the church. Many are the monks who belong to that monastery, and they dwell scattered round the valley on the summits of the hills where they have little cells cut out for them from the stony rock of the hills. The mountain surrounds the valley in which the monastery is built: there lies the body of St. Saba.[15]

Thence they came to the spot where Philip baptized the eunuch. A small church stands there in the wide valley between Bethlehem

and Gaza. From there they made towards Gaza,[16] where there is a holy place, and after praying there they went to St. Mathias, where there is a large temple to the Lord. And whilst solemn High Mass was being celebrated there, our Bishop Willibald, standing and listening, lost his sight and was blind for two months. Thence they went to St. Zacharias, the prophet, not the father of St. John the Baptist, but the other prophet. Thence they went to the town of Hebron, where lie the bodies of the three patriarchs Abraham, Isaac and Jacob with their wives.

Then he returned to Jerusalem, and, going into the church where the holy Cross of Christ was found, his eyes were opened and he received his sight. He stayed there for a little while and then set out for a place called Lydda, to the Church of St. George,[17] which lies about ten miles distant from Jerusalem. Thence he came to another village [Joppe], where stands a church to St. Peter, the Apostle: this was where St. Peter raised up the widow Dorcas to life. He prayed there and set out once more and came to the Adriatic sea at a great distance from Jerusalem, to the cities of Tyre and Sidon. These two cities are six miles apart and stand on the edge of the sea. Thence he went to Tripoli on the seashore, and crossed over Mount Libanus to Damascus. From there he went to Caesarea and back once more, for the third time, to Jerusalem, where he spent the whole winter.

He then travelled over three hundred miles to the town of Emesa in Syria, and thence he came to Salamias[18] which is on the farther borders of Syria. He spent the whole season of Lent there because he was ill and unable to travel. His companions, who were in his party, went forward to the King of the Saracens, named Murmumni, to ask him to give them a letter of safe conduct, but they could not meet him because he himself had withdrawn from that region on account of the sickness and pestilence that infested the country. And when they could not find the king they returned and stayed together in Salamias until a week before Easter. Then they came again to Emesa and asked the governor there to give them a letter of safe conduct, and he gave them a letter for every two persons. They could not travel there in company but only two by two, because in this way it was easier for them to provide food for themselves. Then they came to Damascus.

From Damascus they came for the fourth time to Jerusalem, and after spending some time there they went to the town of Sebaste, which was formerly called Samaria; but after it was destroyed they built another town there and called it Sebaste. At the present time the bodies of St. John the Baptist, Abdias and Eliseus the prophet rest there. Near the town is the well where our Lord asked the Samaritan woman to give Him water to drink. Over that well there now stands a church, and there is the Mount on which the Samaritans worshipped and of which the woman said to our Lord: "Our forbears worshipped on this mount, but Thou sayest that Jerusalem is the place where men ought to worship." Then, after praying there, they passed through the country of the Samaritans to a large town on the far borders of their land and spent one night there.

Then they travelled across a wide plain covered with olive trees, and with them travelled an Ethiopian and his two camels, who led a woman on a mule through the woods. And as they went on their way, a lion with gaping jaws came out upon them, growling and roaring, ready to seize and devour them; it terrified them greatly. But the Ethiopian said: "Have no fear—let us go forward." So without hesitation they proceeded on their way and as they approached the lion it turned aside and, through the help of Almighty God, left the way open for them to continue their journey. And they said that a short time after they had left that place they heard the same lion

roaring, as if in his fury he would devour many of the men who went there to gather olives. When they came to the town which is called Ptolomaeis, which stands by the edge of the sea, they continued their journey and reached the summit of Libanus, where that mountain juts out into the sea and forms a promontory. There stands the tower of Libanus. Anyone who lands there without having a safe conduct cannot pass through the place because it is guarded and closed; and if anyone comes without a pass the citizens arrest him immediately and send him back to Tyre. The mount is between Tyre and Ptolomaeis. Then the bishop came to Tyre for the second time.

When Bishop Willibald was in Jerusalem on the previous occasion he bought himself some balsam and filled a calabash with it; then he took a hollow reed which had a bottom to it and filled it with petroleum and put it inside the calabash. Afterwards he cut the reed equal in length to the calabash so that the surfaces of both were even and then closed the mouth of the calabash. When they reached the city of Tyre the citizens arrested them, put them in chains and examined all their baggage to find out if they had hidden any contraband. If they had found anything they would certainly have punished them and put them to death. But when they had thoroughly scrutinized everything and could find nothing but one calabash which Willibald had, they opened it and snuffed at it to find out what was inside. And when they smelt petroleum, which was inside the reed at the top, they did not find the balsam which was inside the calabash underneath the petroleum, and so let them go.

They were there for a long time waiting for a ship to get ready. Afterwards they sailed during the whole of the winter, from the feast of St. Andrew [30 November] until a week before Easter. Then they landed at the city of Constantinople, where the bodies of three saints, Andrew, Timothy and Luke the Evangelist, lie beneath one altar, whilst the body of

St. John Chrysostom lies before another. His tomb is there where, as a priest, he stood to celebrate Mass. Our bishop stayed there for two years and had an alcove in the church so that every day he could sit and gaze upon the place where the saints lay at rest. Thence he went to Nicea, where formerly the Emperor Constantine held a council at which three hundred and eighteen bishops were present, all taking an active part. The church there resembles the one at Mount Olivet, where our Lord ascended into heaven; and in the church are all the portraits of the bishops who took part in the Council. Willibald went there from Constantinople to see how the church was built, and then returned by water to Constantinople.

After two years they set sail from there with the envoys of the Pope and the Emperor[19] and went to the city of Syracuse in the island of Sicily. Thence they came to Catania and then to Reggio, a city of Calabria. They embarked again for Volcano, where the Hell of Theodoric is.[20] When they arrived there they disembarked to see what this inferno was like. Willibald, who was inquisitive and eager to see without delay what this Hell was like inside, wanted to climb to the top of the mountain underneath which the crater lay: but he was unable to do so because the ashes of black tartar, which had risen to the edge of the crater, lay there in heaps: and like the snow which, when it drops from heaven with its falling masses of flakes, heaps them up into mounts, the ashes lay piled in heaps on the top of the mountain and prevented Willibald from going any farther. All the same, he saw the black and terrible and fearful flame belching forth from the crater with a noise like rolling thunder: he gazed with awe on the enormous flames, and the mountainous clouds of smoke rising from below into the sky. And that pumice stone which writers speak of he saw issuing from the crater, thrown out with flames and cast into the sea, then washed up again on the seashore by the tide, where men were collecting it and carting it away. After they had satisfied their curiosity with the sight of the fearsome and terrible burning fire, its fumes, its stinking smoke and its shooting flames, they weighed anchor and sailed to the church of St. Bartholomew the Apostle [at Lipari], which stands on the seashore, and they came to the mountains which are called Didyme, and after praying there they spent one night. Embarking once more, they came to a city called Naples and remained there several days. It is the seat of an archbishop whose dignity is great there. Not far away is the small town of Lucullanum, where the body of St. Severinus is preserved. Then he came to the city of Capua, and the archbishop there sent him to the bishop of another town; that bishop sent him to the Bishop of Teano, and he in turn sent him to St. Benedict's [at Monte Cassino]. It was autumn when he reached Monte Cassino, and it was seven years since he first began his journey from Rome and ten years in all since he had left his native country.

And when the venerable man Willibald and Tidbercht, who had travelled everywhere with him, came to St. Benedict's, they found only a few monks there under Abbot Petronax. Without delay he joined the community, for which he was so well fitted both by his great self-discipline and his natural aptitude for obedience. He learned much from their careful teaching, but he in turn taught them more by his outward bearing; he showed them not so much by words as by the beauty of his character what was the real spirit of their institute; and by providing himself to be a model of monastic virtue he compelled the admiration, love and respect of all.

In the first year that he spent there he was sacristan of the church, in the second a dean of the monastery, and for eight years afterwards he was porter in two monasteries, four years as porter in the monastery which is perched on a very high hill, and four years more in the other monastery which stands lower down near the river Rapido, about two miles away. So for ten years the venerable man Willibald tried to observe, as far as possible, every detail of the monastic observance as laid down by the Rule of St. Benedict. And he not only observed it himself but led the others, whom he had brought over long distances by foot and by sea, to follow him in the traditional path of regular life.

After this, a priest who came from Spain to St. Benedict's and stayed there asked permission of Abbot Petronax to go to Rome. When the permission was asked Petronax without hesitation begged Willibald to accompany him and take him to St. Peter's. He gave his consent at once and promised to fulfil the mission. So they set out, and when they came to Rome and entered the basilica of St. Peter they asked the protection of the heavenly keeper of the keys and commended themselves to his kindly patronage. Then the sacred Pontiff of the Apostolic See, Gregory III, hearing that the venerable man Willibald was there, sent for him to come into his presence. And when he came to the Supreme Pontiff he fell down at once on his face to the ground and greeted him. And immediately that pious Shepherd of the People began to question him about the details of his journey and asked him earnestly how he had spent seven years travelling to the ends of the earth and how he had contrived to escape for so long a time the wickedness of the pagans. . . .

After they had discussed these matters during a pleasant and intimate conversation, the sacred and holy Pontiff intimated to Willibald in a serious and unmistakable tone that St. Boniface had asked him to arrange for Willibald to leave St. Benedict's and come to him without delay in the country of the Franks. And after the Apostolic Lord, Pope Gregory III, had made known to him the desires of St. Boniface, he tried to persuade him, now with

peaceable words of exhortation, now pleading, now commanding, to go to St. Boniface. Then the illustrious athlete of God, Willibald, promised that he would carry into immediate effect the request and command of the Pontiff provided he could ask permission, according to the prescriptions of the Rule, from his abbot. The Supreme Pontiff, in whom is vested the highest authority, at once replied that his command was sufficient permission, and he ordered him to set out obediently without any qualm of conscience, saying: "If I am free to transfer the abbot Petronax himself to any other place, then certainly he has no permission or power to oppose my wishes." And so Willibald replied on the spot that he would willingly carry out his wishes and commands, not only there but anywhere in the world, wherever he had a mind to send him. He then pledged himself to go in accordance with his wishes without any further delay. After this, the discussion being ended, Willibald departed at Easter-time, reaching his journey's end on the Feast of St. Andrew. Tidbercht, however, remained behind at St. Benedict's.

He went to Lucca, where his father was buried, and thence to the city of Pavia, from there to Brescia and thence to a place which is called Garda. Then he came to Duke Odilo and stayed a week with him, and thence to Suitgar, with whom he also stayed a week. Suitgar and Willibald left there for Linthard, where St. Boniface was, and St. Boniface sent them to Eichstatt to see how they liked the place. Suitgar handed over the territory there to St. Boniface for the redemption of his soul, and St. Boniface passed it on to our bishop Willibald. At that time it was all waste land— there was not a single house there and the only building was the church of St. Mary, which still stands, smaller than the other church which Willibald afterwards built on the site.

When Willibald and Suitgar had remained together at Eichstatt for some little time, they explored and surveyed the ground and eventually chose a site suitable for a house. After that they went to St. Boniface at Freising and stayed with him until all of them returned once more to Eichstatt. There St. Boniface ordained Willibald to the priestly dignity. The day on which Willibald was ordained was 22 July, the Feast of St. Apollinaris and St. Mary Magdalen.

After a whole year had passed, St. Boniface commanded him to come to him at once in Thuringia. And the venerable man of God, Willibald, set off at once for Thuringia and dwelt as a guest in the house of his brother St. Wynnebald, who had not seen him for the past eight and a half years since he had parted from him in Rome. And they were glad to see each other and congratulated each other on their meeting. It was then the season of autumn when Willibald came to Thuringia.

Soon after he came there, the archbishop St. Boniface, Burchard and Wizo consecrated him and invested him with the sacred authority of the episcopate. He remained there for a week after he was consecrated bishop and then returned once more to the place which had been allotted him. At the time of his consecration Willibald was forty-one years old; he was consecrated at Salzburg in the autumn, about three weeks before the Feast of St. Martin.

The long course of Willibald's travels and sightseeing on which he had spent seven long years was now over and gone. We have tried to set down and make known all the facts which have been ascertained and thoroughly investigated. These facts were not learned from anyone else but heard from Willibald himself; and having received them from his own lips, we have taken them down and written them in the Monastery of Heidenheim, as his deacons and other subordinates can testify. I say this so that no one may afterwards say that it was an idle tale.

At the time that he came to the province from Rome with three of his fellow-countrymen he was forty-one years old, already mature and middle-aged; then he was consecrated bishop. Afterwards he began to build a monastery in the place called Eichstatt, and he shortly afterwards practised the monastic life there according to the observance which he had seen at St. Benedict's [Monte Cassino], and not merely there, but also in many other monastic houses, which he had examined with his experienced eye as he travelled through various lands. This observance he taught to others by the example of his own life. With a few fellow-labourers he tilled the wide and spacious fields for the divine seed, sowing and cultivating them until harvest-time. And so like a busy bee that flits through the meadows, purple with violets, aromatic with scented herbs and through the tree branches yellow with blossom, drinking the sweet nectar but avoiding bitter poison, and returns to the hive bearing honey on its thighs and body, so the blessed man chose out the best from all that he had seen abroad with his own eyes, adopted it, and, having adopted it, submitted it to his disciples for acceptance, showing them good example by word and deed, in zeal for observance, avoidance of evil, piety, forbearance and temperance.

Soon after the energetic champion of our good God had begun to dwell in the monastery men flocked to him from all sides, not only from the neighbouring provinces but even from distant countries, to hear his salutary teaching and wisdom. Willibald and Mother Church, like a hen that cherishes her offspring beneath her wings, won over many adoptive sons to the Lord, protecting them continually with the shield of his kindliness. These he trained with gentleness and sympathy, detaching them from their imperfections until they reached perfect maturity. These, having followed in the steps of their master and absorbed his teaching, have now become famous for the training they give to others.

This, then, was Willibald, who at first began to practise a holy life with the support of but a few helpers, but who at last, after struggling in many ways against the opposition of numerous chieftains and courtiers, gained possession of a people worthy of the Lord. Far and wide through the vast province of Bavaria he drove his plough, sowing the seed and reaping the harvest with the help of many fellow-labourers. And all through the land of Bavaria, now dotted about with churches, priests' houses and the relics of the saints, he amassed treasures worthy of our Lord. From these places antiphons now resound, sacred lessons are chanted, a noble throng of believers shout aloud the miracles of Christ and with joyful hearts echo from mouth to mouth triumphant praises of their Creator.

What shall I now say of Willibald, my master and your devoted brother? Who was more outstanding than he in piety, more perfect in humility? Who more forbearing in patience, more strict in temperance, greater in meekness? When was he ever backward in consoling the downcast? Who was more eager to assist the poor or more anxious to clothe the naked? These things are said not for the sake of boasting but for the sake of recounting what I have seen and heard, things done not by the power of man but by the grace of God, in order that, according to the words of the Apostle: "He who glories may glory in the Lord." Amen.

NOTES

1. Possibly Dertonicum or the neighbourhood of the chief town in Liguria, called Chortina in the ancient Life of Charlemagne.

2. On the legend created by Reginald of Eichstatt about St. Richard, the father of Willibald, see M. Coens, "Légende et Miracles du Roi S. Richard," *Analecta Bollandiana*, xlix, 1231, pp. 353–97.

3. In [A.D.] 721 the Saracen conquerors of Spain had been defeated by Duke Eudes beneath the walls of Toulouse. Liudprand, King of the Lombards, held armed possession of the greater part of Italy, while the Exarchs of Ravenna represented the tyranny of the Eastern Empire, ruled at that time by Leo, the Isaurian. The reigning Pope was Gregory II.

4. This is reported in her *Acta* to have taken place for the first time in A.D. 252, when the pagans took her veil. See *Acta Sanctorum* for 5 February.

5. Monembasia is a small town near the south of Morea. The Slavonic Bulgarians were all-powerful at Constantinople, where they had placed Leo III on the imperial throne. It is not surprising, then, that Morea should have been occupied by them.

6. See Bollandists, *Acta Sanctorum*, 27 July. These seven martyrs suffered under the Emperor Decius about A.D. 250. He stopped up the mouth of the cave where they had taken refuge and so starved them to death. The names are: John, Constantine, Maximinian, Malchus, Martinian, Denys and Serapion.

7. If Miletus is meant, the pilgrims must have landed there before reaching Patara. The only place between Patara and Chelidonia is a town, now a village, called Myra, mentioned in the Acts of the Apostles xxvii. 27 in the Greek version. The Vulgate calls it Lystra.

8. Costanza near Famagosta, anciently called Salamis. St. Epiphanius was Bishop of Salamis for thirty-six years and died in A.D. 403.

9. Called Antaradus by the Greeks and Tortosa in the Middle Ages. The ruins of a magnificent Gothic cathedral can still be seen. The modern name is Tartus.

10. Akkar on Jebel Akkar? It has a ruined Saracenic castle, but is quite off the road. The place corresponding to Willibald's description may be Husn el-Akrad, or the Kurds' castle, which is fifteen miles from Antaradus.

11. The Greek liturgy with its constant repetition of the *Kyrie* would naturally strike the pilgrims as a litany, and this is the word they use here.

12. The modern name is Hums, with extensive ruins dating from the first century. It was captured by the Saracens in A.D. 636.

13. The church which is mentioned by Eusebius as among those built by the Empress Helena; but he says (*Vita Constantini*, iii, 47) that at the same time that Helena was building churches in Jerusalem and

Bethlehem Constantine was building them "in all the other provinces."

14. It will be noticed that the writer seems to be reporting the very words of Willibald as she introduces the pronoun *us*.

15. St. Saba founded the monastery in A.D. 483 and was made by the Patriarch of Jerusalem archimandrite over all the monasteries of Palestine.

16. The pilgrims seem to have gone back on their tracks. The ruins of the church built by Constantine at Gaza may still be seen.

17. The remains of the church of St. George, who was said to have been born there, are still to be seen: they have been restored as a Greek Church. Arculf gives the first account of St. George known to have been circulated in Britain. It is worthy of notice that the north of England, where his narrative was well known, had a great devotion to St. George, a place being assigned to him in the Anglo-Saxon ritual of Durham, which is probably of the early ninth century A.D. A "Passion of St. George" was written by Aelfric, Archbishop of York, A.D. 1021–51. Arculf describes the marble column to which St. George was bound whilst being scourged.

18. Now 'Salámeyeh.

19. The return of the legates to Rome was occasioned by the excommunication of Leo the Isaurian in 728, who had threatened Pope Gregory II.

20. See the *Dialogues* of Gregory the Great, iv. c. 30. Theodoric was supposed to have been cast into hell for having imprisoned and caused the death of Pope John V and for having killed Symmachus, the Senator. Arculf's narrative, written by Adamnan, also describes the volcano. This island, the ancient Hiera, known as *Volcani Insula* from its volcanic phenomena, is the southernmost of the Lipari islands. It lies twelve miles from Sicily.

ST. LEOBA (c. A.D. 700–779; born Wessex; died Germany)

The Life of St. Leoba, by Rudolf, Monk of Fulda

Translated by C. H. Talbot

The small book which I have written about the life and virtues of the holy and revered virgin Leoba has been dedicated to you, O Hadamout, virgin of Christ, in order that you may have something to read with pleasure and imitate with profit. Thus by the help of Christ's grace you may eventually enjoy the blissful reward of him whose spouse you now are.

PROLOGUE

Before I begin to write the life of the blessed and venerable virgin Leoba, I invoke her spouse, Christ, our Lord and Saviour, who gave her the courage to overcome the powers of evil, to inspire me with eloquence sufficient to describe her outstanding merits. I have been unable to discover all the facts of her life. I shall therefore recount the few that I have learned from the writings of others, venerable men who heard them from four of her disciples, Agatha, Thecla, Nana and Eoloba. Each one copied them down according to his ability and left them as a memorial to posterity. . . .

But before I begin the narration of her remarkable life and virtues, it may not be out of place if I mention a few of the many things I

The Anglo-Saxon Missionaries in Germany (New York: Sheed & Ward, 1954).

have heard about her spiritual mistress and mother, who first introduced her to the spiritual life and fostered in her a desire for heaven. In this way the reader who is made aware of the qualities of this great woman may give credence to the achievements of the disciple more easily the more clearly he sees that she learned the elements of the spiritual life from so noble a mistress.

In the island of Britain, which is inhabited by the English nation, there is a place called Wimbourne, an ancient name which may be translated "Winestream." It received this name from the clearness and sweetness of the water there, which was better than any other in that land. In olden times the kings of that nation had built two monasteries in the place, one for men, the other for women, both surrounded by strong and lofty walls and provided with all the necessities that prudence could devise. From the beginning of the foundation the rule firmly laid down for both was that no entrance should be allowed to a person of the other sex. No woman was permitted to go into the men's community, nor was any man allowed into the women's, except in the case of priests who had to celebrate Mass in their churches; even so, immediately after the function was ended the priest had to withdraw. Any woman who wished to renounce the world and enter the cloister did so on the understanding that she would never leave it. She could only come out if there was a reasonable cause and some great advantage accrued to the monastery. Furthermore, when it was necessary to conduct the business of the monastery and to send for something outside, the superior of the community spoke through a window and only from there did she make decisions and arrange what was needed.

It was over this monastery, in succession to several other abbesses and spiritual mistresses, that a holy virgin named Tetta was placed in authority, a woman of noble family (for she was a sister of the king), but more noble in her conduct and good qualities. Over both the monasteries she ruled with consummate prudence and discretion. She gave instruction by deed rather than by words, and whenever she said that a certain course of action was harmful to the salvation of souls she showed by her own conduct that it was to be shunned. She maintained discipline with such circumspection (and the discipline there was much stricter than anywhere else) that she would never allow her nuns to approach clerics. She was so anxious that the nuns, in whose company she always remained, should be cut off from the company of men that she denied entrance into the community not merely to laymen and clerics but even to bishops. There are many instances of the virtues of this woman which the virgin Leoba, her disciple, used to recall with pleasure when she told her reminiscences.

We will now pursue our purpose of describing the life of her spiritual daughter, Leoba the virgin.

As we have already said, her parents were English, of noble family and full of zeal for religion and the observance of God's commandments. Her father was called Dynno, her mother Aebba. But as they were barren, they remained together for a long time without children. After many years had passed and the onset of old age had deprived them of all hope of offspring her mother had a dream in which she saw herself bearing in her bosom a church bell, which on being drawn out with her hand rang merrily. When she woke up she called her old nurse to her and told her what she had dreamt. The nurse said to her: "We shall yet see a daughter from your womb and it is your duty to consecrate her straightway to God. And as Anna offered Samuel to serve God all the days of his life in the temple, so you must offer her, when she has been taught the Scripture from her infancy, to serve Him in holy virginity as long as she shall live." Shortly after the woman had made this vow she conceived and bore a daughter, whom she called Thrutgeba, surnamed Leoba because she was beloved, for this is what Leoba means. And when the child had grown up her mother consecrated her and handed her over to Mother Tetta to be taught the sacred sciences. And because the nurse had foretold that she should have such happiness, she gave her her freedom.

The girl, therefore, grew up and was taught with such care by the abbess and all the nuns that she had no interest other than the monastery and the pursuit of sacred knowledge. She took no pleasure in aimless jests and wasted no time on girlish romances, but, fired by the love of Christ, fixed her mind always on reading or hearing the Word of God. Whatever she heard or read she committed to memory, and put all that she learned into practice. She exercised such moderation in her use of food and drink that she eschewed dainty dishes and the allurements of sumptuous fare, and was satisfied with whatever was placed before her. She prayed continually, knowing that in the Epistles the faithful are counselled to pray without ceasing. When she was not praying she worked with her hands at whatever was commanded her, for she had learned that he who will not work should not eat. However, she spent more time in reading and listening to Sacred Scripture than she gave to manual labour. She took great care not to forget what she had heard or read, observing the commandments of the Lord and putting into practice what she remembered of them. In this way she so arranged her conduct that she was loved by all the sisters. She learned from all and obeyed them all, and by imitating the good qualities of each one she modelled herself on the continence of one, the cheerfulness of another, copying here a sister's mildness, there a sister's patience. One she tried to equal in attention to prayer, another in devotion to reading. Above all, she was intent on practis-

ing charity, without which, as she knew, all other virtues are void.

When she had succeeded in fixing her attention on heavenly things by these and other practices in the pursuit of virtue she had a dream in which one night she saw a purple thread issuing from her mouth. It seemed to her that when she took hold of it with her hand and tried to draw it out there was no end to it; and as if it were coming from her very bowels, it extended little by little until it was of enormous length. When her hand was full of thread and it still issued from her mouth she rolled it round and round and made a ball of it. The labour of doing this was so tiresome that eventually, through sheer fatigue, she woke from her sleep and began to wonder what the meaning of the dream might be. She understood quite clearly that there was some reason for the dream, and it seemed that there was some mystery hidden in it. Now there was in the same monastery an aged nun who was known to possess the spirit of prophecy, because other things that she had foretold had always been fulfilled. As Leoba was diffident about revealing the dream to her, she told it to one of her disciples just as it had occurred and asked her to go to the old nun and describe it to her as a personal experience and learn from her the meaning of it. When the sister had repeated the details of the dream as if it had happened to her, the nun, who could foresee the future, angrily replied: "This is indeed a true vision and presages that good will come. But why do you lie to me in saying that such things happened to you? These matters are no concern of yours: they apply to the beloved chosen by God." In giving this name, she referred to the virgin Leoba. "These things," she went on, "were revealed to the person whose holiness and wisdom make her a worthy recipient, because by her teaching and good example she will confer benefits on many people. The thread which came from her bowels and issued from her mouth, signifies the wise counsels that she will speak from the heart. The fact that it filled her hand means that she will carry out in her actions whatever she expresses in her words. Furthermore, the ball which she made by rolling it round and round signifies the mystery of the divine teaching, which is set in motion by the words and deeds of those who give instruction and which turns earthwards through active works and heavenwards through contemplation, at one time swinging downwards through compassion for one's neighbour, again swinging upwards through the love of God. By these signs God shows that your mistress will profit many by her words and example, and the effect of them will be felt in other lands afar off whither she will go." That this interpretation of the dream was true later events were to prove.

At the time when the blessed virgin Leoba was pursuing her quest for perfection in the monastery the holy martyr Boniface was being ordained by Gregory, Bishop of Rome and successor to Constantine, in the Apostolic See. His mission was to preach the Word of God to the people in Germany. When Boniface found that the people were ready to receive the faith and that, though the harvest was great, the labourers who worked with him were few, he sent messengers and letters to England, his native land, summoning from different ranks of the clergy many who were learned in the divine law and fitted both by their character and good works to preach the Word of God.

Likewise, he sent messengers with letters to the abbess Tetta, of whom we have already spoken, asking her to send Leoba to accompany him on this journey and to take part in this embassy: for Leoba's reputation for learning and holiness had spread far and wide and her praise was on everyone's lips. The abbess Tetta was exceedingly displeased at her departure, but because she could not gainsay the dispositions of divine providence she agreed to his request and sent Leoba to the blessed man. Thus it was that the interpretation of the dream which she had previously received was fulfilled. When she came, the man of God received her with the deepest reverence, holding her in great affection, not so much because she was related to him on his mother's side as because he knew that by her holiness and wisdom she would confer many benefits by her word and example.

In furtherance of his aims he appointed persons in authority over the monasteries and established the observance of the Rule: he placed Sturm as abbot over the monks and Leoba as abbess over the nuns. He gave her the monastery at a place called Bischofsheim, where there was a large community of nuns. These were trained according to her principles in the discipline of monastic life and made such progress in her teaching that many of them afterwards became superiors of others, so that there was hardly a convent of nuns in that part which had not one of her disciples as abbess. She was a woman of great virtue and was so strongly attached to the way of life she had vowed that she never gave thought to her native country or her relatives. She expended all her energies on the work she had undertaken in order to appear blameless before God and to become a pattern of perfection to those who obeyed her in word and action. She was ever on her guard not to teach others what she did not carry out herself. In her conduct there was no arrogance or pride; she was no distinguisher of persons, but showed herself affable and kindly to all. In appearance she was angelic, in word pleasant, clear in mind, great in prudence, Catholic in faith, most patient in hope, universal in her charity. But though she was always cheerful, she never broke out into laughter through excessive hilarity. No one ever heard a bad word from her lips; the sun never went down upon her anger. In the matter of food and drink she always showed the utmost understanding for others but was most sparing in her own use of them. She had a small cup from which she used to drink and which, because of the meagre quantity it would hold, was called by the sisters "the Beloved's little one." So great was her zeal for reading that she discontinued it only for prayer or for the refreshment of her body with food or sleep: the Scriptures were never out of her hands. For, since she had been trained from infancy in the rudiments of grammar and the study of the other liberal arts, she tried by constant reflection to attain a perfect knowledge of divine things so that through the combination of her reading with her quick intelligence, by natural gifts and hard work, she became extremely learned. She read with attention all the books of the Old and New Testaments and learned by heart all the commandments of God. To these she added by way of completion the writings of the church Fathers, the decrees of the Councils and the whole of ecclesiastical law. She observed great moderation in all her acts and arrangements and always kept the practical end in view, so that she would never have to repent of her actions through having been guided by impulse. She was deeply aware of the necessity for concentration of mind in prayer and study, and for this reason took care not to go to excess either in watching or in other spiritual exercises. Throughout the summer both she and all the sisters under her rule went to rest after the midday meal, and she would never give permission to any of them to stay up late, for she said that lack of sleep dulled the mind, especially for study. When she lay down to rest, whether at night or in the afternoon, she used to have the Sacred Scriptures read out at her bedside, a duty which the younger nuns carried out in turn without grumbling. It seems difficult to believe, but even when she seemed to be asleep they could not skip over any word or syllable whilst they were reading without her immediately correcting them. Those on whom this duty fell used afterwards to confess that often when they saw her becoming drowsy they made a mistake on purpose to see if she noticed it, but they were never able to escape undetected.

Whilst the virgin of Christ was acting in this way and attracting to herself everyone's affection, the devil, who is the foe of all Christians, viewed with impatience her own great virtue and the progress made by her disciples. He therefore attacked them constantly with evil thoughts and temptations of the flesh, trying to turn some of them aside from the path they had chosen. But when he saw that all his efforts were brought to nought by their prayers, fasting and chaste lives, the wily tempter turned his attention to other means, hoping at least to destroy their good reputation, even if he could not break down their integrity by his foul suggestions.

There was a certain poor little crippled girl, who sat near the gate of the monastery begging alms. Every day she received her food from the abbess's table, her clothing from the nuns and all other necessities from them; these were given to her from divine charity. It happened that after some time, deceived by the suggestions of the devil, she committed fornication, and when her appearance made it impossible for her to conceal that she had conceived a child she covered up her guilt by pretending to be ill. When her time came, she wrapped the child in swaddling clothes and cast it at night into a pool by the river which flowed through that place. In this way she added crime to crime, for she not only followed fleshly sin by murder, but also combined murder with the poisoning of the water. When day dawned, another woman came to draw water and, seeing the corpse of the child, was struck with horror. Burning with womanly rage, she filled the whole village with her uncontrollable cries and reproached the holy nuns with these indignant words: "Oh, what a chaste community! How admirable is the life of nuns, who beneath their veils give birth to children and exercise at one and the same time the function of mothers and priests, baptising those to whom they have given birth. For, fellow-citizens, you have drawn off this water to make a pool, not merely for the purpose of grinding corn, but unwittingly for a new and unheard-of-kind of Baptism. Now go and ask those women, whom you compliment by calling them virgins, to remove this corpse from the river and make it fit for us to use again. Look for the one who is missing from the monastery and then you will find out who is responsible for this crime." At these words all the crowd was set in uproar and everybody, of whatever age or sex, ran in one great mass to see what had happened. As soon as they saw the corpse they denounced the crime and reviled the nuns. When the abbess heard the uproar and learned what was afoot she called the nuns together, told them the reason, and discovered that no one was absent except Agatha, who a few days before had been summoned to her parents' house on urgent business: but she had gone with full permission. A messenger was sent to her without delay to recall her to the monastery, as Leoba could not endure the accusation of so great a crime to hang over them. When Agatha returned and heard of the deed that was charged against her she fell on her knees and gazed up to heaven, crying: "Almighty God, who knowest all things before they come to pass, from whom nothing is hid and who hast delivered Susanna from false accusations when she trusted in Thee, show Thy mercy to this community gathered together in Thy name and let it not be besmirched by filthy rumours on account of my sins; but do Thou deign to unmask and make known for the praise and glory of Thy name the person who has committed this misdeed."

On hearing this, the venerable superior, being assured of her innocence, ordered them all to go to the chapel and to stand with their arms extended in the form of a cross until each

one of them had sung through the whole psalter, then three times each day, at Tierce, Sext and None, to go round the monastic buildings in procession with the crucifix at their head, calling upon God to free them, in His mercy, from this accusation. When they had done this and they were going into the church at None, having completed two rounds, the blessed Leoba went straight to the altar and, standing before the cross, which was being prepared for the third procession, stretched out her hands towards heaven, and with tears and groans prayed, saying: "O Lord Jesus Christ, King of virgins, Lover of chastity, unconquerable God, manifest Thy power and deliver us from this charge, because the reproaches of those who reproached Thee have fallen upon us." Immediately after she had said this, that wretched little woman, the dupe and the tool of the devil, seemed to be surrounded by flames, and, calling out the name of the abbess, confessed to the crime she had committed. Then a great shout rose to heaven: the vast crowd was astounded at the miracle, the nuns began to weep with joy, and all of them with one voice gave expression to the merits of Leoba and of Christ our Saviour.

So it came about that the reputation of the nuns, which the devil had tried to ruin by his sinister rumour, was greatly enhanced, and praise was showered on them in every place. But the wretched woman did not deserve to escape scot-free and for the rest of her life she remained in the power of the devil. Even before this God had performed many miracles through Leoba, but they had been kept secret. This one was her first in Germany and, because it was done in public, it came to the ears of everyone.

I think it should be counted amongst her virtues also that one day, when a wild storm arose and the whole sky was obscured by such dark clouds that day seemed turned into night, terrible lightning and falling thunderbolts struck terror into the stoutest hearts and everyone was shaking with fear. At first the people drove their flocks into the houses for shelter so that they should not perish; then, when the danger increased and threatened them all with death, they took refuge with their wives and children in the church, despairing of their lives. They locked all the doors and waited there trembling, thinking that the last judgment was at hand. In this state of panic they filled the air with the din of their mingled cries. Then the holy virgin went out to them and urged them all to have patience. She promised them that no harm would come to them; and after exhorting them to join with her in prayer, she fell prostrate at the foot of the altar. In the meantime the storm raged, the roofs of the houses were torn off by the violence of the wind, the ground shook with the repeated shocks of the thunderbolts, and the thick darkness, intensified by the incessant flicker of lightning which flashed through the windows, redoubled their terror. Then the mob, unable to endure the suspense any longer, rushed to the altar to rouse her from prayer and seek her protection. Thecla, her kinswoman, spoke to her first, saying: "Beloved, all the hopes of these people lie in you: you are their only support. Arise, then, and pray to the Mother of God, your mistress, for us, that by her intercession we may be delivered from this fearful storm." At these words Leoba rose up from prayer and, as if she had been challenged to a contest, flung off the cloak which she was wearing and boldly opened the doors of the church. Standing on the threshold, she made a sign of the cross, opposing to the fury of the storm the name of the High God. Then she stretched out her hands towards heaven and three times invoked the mercy of Christ, praying that through the intercession of Holy Mary, the Virgin, He would quickly come to the help of His people. Suddenly God came to their aid. The sound of thunder died away, the winds changed direction and dispersed the heavy clouds, the dark-

ness rolled back and the sun shone, bringing calm and peace. Thus did divine power make manifest the merits of His handmaid. Unexpected peace came to His people and fear was banished.

The people's faith was stimulated by such tokens of holiness, and as religious feeling increased so did contempt of the world. Many nobles and influential men gave their daughters to God to live in the monastery in perpetual chastity; many widows also forsook their homes, made vows of chastity and took the veil in the cloister. To all of these the holy virgin pointed out both by word and example how to reach the heights of perfection.

In the meantime, blessed Boniface, the archbishop, was preparing to go to Frisia, having decided to preach the Gospel to this people riddled with superstition and unbelief. . . . After giving . . . other instructions, he summoned Leoba to him and exhorted her not to abandon the country of her adoption and not to grow weary of the life she had undertaken, but rather to extend the scope of the good work she had begun. He said that no consideration should be paid to her weakness and that she must not count the long years that lay ahead of her; she must not count the spiritual life to be hard nor the end difficult to attain, for the years of this life are short compared to eternity, and the sufferings of this world are as nothing in comparison with the glory that will be made manifest in the saints. He commended her to Lull and to the senior monks of the monastery who were present, admonishing them to care for her with reverence and respect and reaffirming his wish that after his death her bones should be placed next to his in the tomb, so that they who had served God during their lifetime with equal sincerity and zeal should await together the day of resurrection.

After these words he gave her his cowl and begged and pleaded with her not to leave her adopted land. And so, when all necessary preparations had been made for the journey, he set out for Frisia, where he won over a multitude of people to the faith of Christ and ended his labours with a glorious martyrdom. His remains were transported to Fulda and there, according to his previous wishes, he was laid to rest with worthy tokens of respect.

The blessed virgin, however, persevered unwaveringly in the work of God. She had no desire to gain earthly possessions but only those of heaven, and she spent all her energies on fulfilling her vows. Her wonderful reputation spread abroad and the fragrance of her holiness and wisdom drew to her the affections of all. She was held in veneration by all who knew her, even by kings. Pippin, King of the Franks, and his sons Charles and Carloman treated her with profound respect, particularly Charles, who, after the death of his father and brother, with whom he had shared the throne for some years, took over the reins of government. He was a man of truly Christian life, worthy of the power he wielded and by far the bravest and wisest king that the Franks had produced. His love for the Catholic faith was so sincere that, though he governed all, he treated the servants and handmaids of God with touching humility. Many times he summoned the holy virgin to his court, received her with every mark of respect and loaded her with gifts suitable to her station. Queen Hiltigard also revered her with a chaste affection and loved her as her own soul. She would have liked her to remain continually at her side so that she might progress in the spiritual life and profit by her words and example. But Leoba detested the life at court like poison. The princes loved her, the nobles received her, the bishops welcomed her with joy. And because of her wide knowledge of the Scriptures and her prudence in counsel they often discussed spiritual matters and ecclesiastical discipline with her. But her deepest concern was the work she had set on foot. She visited the various convents of nuns

and, like a mistress of novices, stimulated them to vie with one another in reaching perfection.

Sometimes she came to the Monastery of Fulda to say her prayers, a privilege never granted to any woman either before or since, because from the day that monks began to dwell there entrance was always forbidden to women. Permission was only granted to her, for the simple reason that the holy martyr St. Boniface had commended her to the seniors of the monastery and because he had ordered her remains to be buried there. The following regulations, however, were observed when she came there. Her disciples and companions were left behind in a nearby cell and she entered the monastery always in daylight, with one nun older than the rest; and after she had finished her prayers and held a conversation with the brethren, she returned towards nightfall to her disciples whom she had left behind in the cell. When she was an old woman and became decrepit through age she put all the convents under her care on a sound footing and then, on Bishop Lull's advice, went to a place called Scoranesheim, four miles south of Mainz. There she took up residence with some of her nuns and served God night and day in fasting and prayer.

In the meantime, whilst King Charles was staying in the palace at Aachen, Queen Hiltigard sent a message to her begging her to come and visit her, if it were not too difficult, because she longed to see her before she passed from this life. And although Leoba was not at all pleased, she agreed to go for the sake of their long-standing friendship. Accordingly she went and was received by the queen with her usual warm welcome. But as soon as Leoba heard the reason for the invitation she asked permission to return home. And when the queen importuned her to stay a few days longer she refused; but, embracing her friend rather more affectionately than usual, she kissed her on the mouth, the forehead and the eyes and took leave of her with these words: "Farewell for evermore, my dearly beloved lady and sister; farewell, most precious half of my soul. May Christ our Creator and Redeemer grant that we shall meet again without shame on the day of judgment. Never more on this earth shall we enjoy each other's presence."

So she returned to the convent, and after a few days she was stricken down by sickness and was confined to her bed. When she saw that her ailment was growing worse and that the hour of her death was near she sent for a saintly English priest named Torhthat, who had always been at her side and ministered to her with respect and love, and received from him the viaticum of the body and blood of Christ. Then she put off this earthly garment and gave back her soul joyfully to her Creator, clean and undefiled as she had received it from Him. She died in the month of September, the fourth of the kalends of October. Her body, followed by a long cortège of noble persons, was carried by the monks of Fulda to their monastery with every mark of respect. Thus the seniors there remembered what St. Boniface had said, namely, that it was his last wish that her remains should be placed next to his bones. But because they were afraid to open the tomb of the blessed martyr, they discussed the matter and decided to bury her on the north side of the altar which the martyr St. Boniface had himself erected and consecrated in honour of our Saviour and the twelve Apostles. . . .

HROTSVIT OF GANDERSHEIM

(c. A.D. 932–c. A.D. 1000; Germany)

Pelagius[1]

Translated by Katharina M. Wilson

Peerless Pelagius,
   thou fearless martyr of Christ!
Soldier, loyal and strong,
   of Him who's eternally Lord.
Look with gracious regard,
   on her who's thy humble, poor servant.
Devoted to thee in her heart
   and cherishing thee in her mind.
Be mindful of Hrotsvit thy maid
   and to her song, too, lend thy kind aid.[2]
Grant thou, I pray, that my mind's
   dark and unlit recesses
Sprinkled with dew from above,
   be moistened gently with love,

That I may so worthily sing
   and the tale of thy marvels depict,
And that my pen may acclaim
   thy triumphs and also thy fame,
Tell how in death thou hast conquered,
   the blood-thirsty world in the end
And how with your precious sweet blood,
   You purchased the glorious palm.

In the Western part of the world
   there glowed an ornament bright,
A city famous in lore,
   proud of its new might at war

It throve under the reign
  of colonists from Spain.
Cordoba was its name;
  wealthy it was and of fame;[3]
Well known for its pleasures
  and for its splendid treasures
Held, too, in great esteem,
  for the seven-forked stream
Of learning. Also in the fore
  for its great triumphs at war.
Once this famous town
  to Christ in faith was bound
And gave its sons to God,
  cleansed in the baptismal font
But suddenly a martial force
  changed the well-established course
And laws of holy faith,
  by spreading through the state
Errors of false dogma,
  harming the faithful folk.
For the faithless tribe
  of unrestrained Saracens
Fell upon the stout
  people of this town.
They seized by force
  the reign of this glorious domain,
And murdered the good king,
  who cleansed by holy baptism
Held the royal scepter
  by right and with might;
And ruled his men for long
  with just restraints and laws.
Vanquished now he lay,
  by hostile swords, and they
Who survived the carnage,
  were now a conquered folk.
The leader of the barbaric tribe,
  the author of the strife
A person quite perverse,
  in life and customs cursed,
Seized for himself the entire
  glorious and splendid Empire.
He settled his wicked allies
  in the wasted country
And filled the mourning city

with many a foe
Polluting thus this place
  of pure and ancient faith
Through barbarian customs
  —it is sad to say,—
By mixing his pagans
  with the faithful natives
So they may urge the Christians
  to give up the old customs
And stain themselves, like he,
  through cults of pagan worship.
But the gentle crowd,
  whom Christ the shepherd ruled,
Scorned the doleful orders
  of the sinful tyrant,
Saying they'd rather die
  and with Christ's law comply
Than survive, and serve
  his foolish cult absurd.
The king having learned this,
  realized in full
That it would bring him harm
  if he did not change his mind
And put all wealthy people
  to death in this rich town
Which he had just now captured
  in valiant fighting.
Therefore he decided
  to change the first decree
And issued a pronouncement
  to such a new effect,
That whoever so desired
  to serve the eternal King
And desired to honor
  the customs of his sires,
Might do so without fear
  of any retribution.
Only a single condition,
  he set to be observed,
Namely that no dweller
  of the aforesaid city
Should presume to blaspheme
  the golden idol's name
Whom this prince adored
  or whoever else was King.

Or else, it was so willed,
  this man was promptly to be killed,
And had to bear the sentence
  of punishment by death.
Following these decrees,
  calm in apparent peace,
The faithful city was weighed
  down with a thousand evils.
But those whom their desire
  for Christ's love set on fire,
And whom the thirst for martyrdom
  urged to insult and scorn
Those images of marble
  which, with jewels adorned,
The prince with prostrate body,
  adored with frankincense,
These men's bodies perished
  at the prince's orders,
But their souls, purified,
  heavenwards repaired.

Many years so passed,
  and amidst vicissitudes
Cordoba since that time
  was subject to pagan kings.
Then in our own days
  an offspring of that race
Assumed in succession,
  the reign of his fathers.
He was worse than they,
  and stained with wantonness,
And called Abderrahman,
  haughty with his kingship's glory.[4]
He treated the Christians,
  in his fathers' manner
And kept enforced the law
  concerning their faith.
He did not abolish
  through kindness the harsh edict
Which the author of woe,
  the city's cruel foe
Once had ordained
  as he vanquished the town.
But mindful of the law
  and in his heart aglow

He drenched with guiltless blood,
  frequently the land
Ending the holy lives,
  thus, of those just men,
Who were burning to chant
  the sweet praise of Christ
And were eager to denounce
  the King's own foolish idols.
This sacrilegious King
  showed such pride at court,
(earning great punishments,
  well deserved, for later)
That he even boasted
  to be the King of Kings
And boasted that all nations
  were subject to his rule
And that no tribe was ever
  filled so with strength and valor
That they would dare to smite
  his army in a fight.
As he was, more than lawful,
  puffed up in arrogance
He heard of a nation
  living in the region
Of far-away Galicia,
  quite excellent in war,
Worshipping the true Christ
  and making war on idols
Who freely dared to spurn
  his decrees and laws
And refused to be serving
  masters so clearly undeserving.
Hearing this, set afire,
  the king burned with demonic ire.
And in his heart, awake,
  was the bile of the ancient snake.
In his mind he wondered,
  and craftily he pondered
How he would deal a blow,
  and destroy such a foe.
He disclosed at length
  to all his ill intent
And addressed the nobles
  of that wealthy city
Barking such evil words

from his pestiferous maw:[5]
"It is not a secret
　　that kings have submitted to us
And that all the nations
　　that the deep sea surrounds
Live in accordance
　　and submission to our laws.
But what bold confidence
　　drives the subject Galicians
That they would have foresworn
　　and our treaties scorn,
Ungrateful for past kindness,
　　I simply do not know.
What we'll have to do,
　　thus, is to attack Galicia
Harassing with armed forces
　　those insurgent foes,
Until before our weapons,
　　prostrate, against their will
They submit their necks
　　forever to our chains."
After he had boasted,
　　and his evil intent revealed,
He ordered that, in time,
　　arranged in rank and file
The folk should gather
　　provided with arms and banners
So that, joined with him,
　　they should destroy that tribe.
He displayed his face
　　under his bejeweled helmet,
Iron armor decking
　　his wanton and lewd limbs.
He engaged the Galicians
　　in a first encounter,
And promptly he chanced to gain
　　and such a triumph obtain
That he trapped twelve nobles
　　and captured their lord,
Seizing all these men
　　and putting them in chains.
With their nobles taken,
　　the faithful nation, shaken,
After much fierce fighting
　　surrendered to the foe,

And submitted to the fold
　　of the perverse Lord.
Then, the treaty, too,
　　was restored anew,
And twelve captive nobles
　　set forth in their chains
With their fellow captive,
　　the leader of that nation.
The nobles were set free
　　quite soon from their fetters
Ransomed at high prizes
　　drawn on their wealth,
But on the king's command,
　　the duke's ransom was doubled,
To a sum exceeding
　　what he could pay just then:
And when he bore as ransom
　　to the greedy ruler
Whatever of treasures
　　he could find at home,
By some mishap it was
　　less than the demanded sum.
This the king declined,
　　fostering fraud in mind,
And refused to return
　　the sweet duke to his people
Until, in full, he was told,
　　he'd pay the required gold.
The king acted thus,
　　not just in his greed
But in his desire strong,
　　to kill the nation's lord.

The duke had an only son,
　　of illustrious descent,
Endowed with every charm
　　of body and of shape.
Pelagius by name,
　　elegant and lustrous;
Prudent in council,
　　replete with all the virtues.
He barely had completed
　　the years of his boyhood
And had just now reached
　　the first blossoms of youth.

When he learned the king's
  treatment of his father
He coaxed his grieving sire
  with such caressing words
"Oh my dear father,
  hear my speech with kindness
And, to what I implore thee,
  please be well disposed.
I am quite aware that
  thy years are now declining,
And that thy strength now lacks
  its accustomed vigor.
Thou can't bear any labor,
  however slight it be;
I on the other hand,
  can cope with all demand
And can with limbs still strong
  submit to a cruel lord.
Therefore I entreat thee
  and with prayers beseech thee
That as a pledge thou bring
  me to the pagan king,
Until thou can furnish
  the ransom gold in full,
Or thou may die, gray haired,
  in narrow fetters snared."

But the old man pled
  and with stern voice this said:
"Cease such speech sweet son,
  cease such speech my dear,
Or your gray-haired father
  may promptly die for grief.
My very life's dependent
  wholly on your welfare,
And without you, my dear,
  I couldn't live a day.
You are all my glory,
  splendor of our fathers,
You the only hope, too,
  for our conquered nation.
Therefore it is better
  if I leave our country
And enter proud Spain
  as a captive in chains,

Than that you go instead up,
  turning my hope to dread."
Pelagius, however,
  heeded not his father
But with honeyed words
  he coaxed his sire's mind
And forced him so at length
  to yield to intent pleas.
The venerable father
  finally agreed
And delivered as hostage
  his son, the wretched boy.
The king then gave the order
  that Pelagius cross the border
And returned rejoicing,
  as victor to his land.
No one, though, should credit
  this to the King's own merit,[6]
That he should have succeeded
  in such a splendid way,
But rather the reason lies,
  and with God the judge resides
Whose secret plan was either
  that this tribe, so chastized,
Should beweep the sins
  of which they all stood charged,
Or that Pelagius
  be killed for faith in Christ,
and might so reach the spot,
  where to die was his lot,
and pour forth the flow there
  of his blood for Christ,
Giving his soul to God,
  made holy by his death.[7]

When this savage King
  had entered his rich city
Bearing the victory
  over the faithful tribe,
He instantly ordered
  that Christ's illustrious friend
Be bound and then thrown
  into a dark prison
And be fed but little food
  he who was used to plentitude.

Cordoba has a place,
  foul and under vaults
Oblivious to light,
  consigned to deep darkness,
Source of great suffering,
  they say, to poor wretches.
Hereto Pelagius,
  distinguished son of peace
Was confined by the King's
  strict and wicked orders.
Hereto came eagerly
  the foremost men of town
Moved by care humane,
  to soften the youth's grave pain.
As they beheld the grace
  of the captive's lovely face
And as they had tasted, each,
  of the sweetness of his speech
And heard words embellished,
  with the honey of rhetoric
Then they all desired
  to free him from his bondage.
They wished to be kind
  and change the ruler's mind.
As they knew for sure
  of the great allure
And the burning passion,
  that the city's lord
Stained by pederasty,
  felt for handsome youths,
With whom to join he longed
  in friendship's tender bond,
They felt encouraged to hope
  for the boy's salvation.
With pity in their hearts, they pleaded with
  the King:
"Bravest prince, it is not proper
  nor becoming for you to order
That such a handsome youth
  be punished so harshly,
And that the tender arms
  of this guiltless boy be fettered.
If you would ever deign
  to behold his splendid beauty
And would taste the flow

of his honeyed speech
You would then desire
  to join him to yourself
And to have him take on
  the rank of officer,
So in his dazzling beauty,
  he might serve at court.
The king, much mollified
  and roused by this speech
Ordered that Pelagius
  be freed from his bonds
And his body be cleansed
  with pure and clean water
And his body be decked
  with rich and purple garments
And his neck adorned
  with a jeweled necklace
So he may consort
  in that well-wrought court.
Following the King's
  arrogant command
The martyr was released
  promptly from black prison
And dressed in splendid garb
  was presented at court.

Now as he was placed
  in the midst of courtiers,
He surpassed them all
  in beauty of countenance.
At him they all marveled,
  at him they all gazed
Admiring now his face,
  now his sweet speech.
The King, too, was drawn
  to him at first sight,
Enflamed with love
  by the royal offspring's beauty.
Finally he ordered
  that the ardently beloved
Pelagius be placed
  on the throne with him,
Fervently desiring
  the youth's proximity.
As he bent his head,

he tried to steal kisses
From the desired youth,
  embracing his sweet neck
But Christ's valiant soldier
  would clearly disavow
Such love from a pagan
  so stained by lechery
So playfully he turned
  his ear to the King's lips
Denying him thus,
  amidst much mirth, his mouth.
While, with his lovely lips,
  he spoke these fearless words:
"It is not fit for a man
  cleansed by Christian baptism
To submit his chaste neck
  to barbarous embrace,
Neither is it meet
  for a one with chrism anointed
To entice the kiss
  of an idol's lewd servant
Therefore embrace those fools
  with your uncurbed heart
Who, like you, appease
  those foolish earthen gods.
Those men be your friends,
  who serve the stupid idols."
But the King responded,
  not moved to any anger,
Softly he tried to calm
  the beloved youth;
"Oh you foolish boy,
  you boast that you can toy
and scorn, without punishment
  the kindness of our law
And dare to make such sport
  with our gods at court.
Are you not moved to bend,
  knowing your young life must end
And that you will make childless
  your grieving parents?
We kill those who assault
  and blaspheme our cult,
We subject them to death
  and pierce their throats with swords

Unless they cease their chant
  and their blasphemies recant.
I urge you, thus, insisting,
  with kind paternal pleading,
That you forbear and limit
  such words of savage spirit
And that you join with me
  in lasting affection
And from now on not dare
  to go against our laws,
But rather with eagerness
  obey my royal words
For you alone I cherish
  and you I desire to honor
With great magnificence
  before all others at court.
You'll be second only
  to me in this great kingdom."
Thus he spoke and with his right
  he held the martyr's face,
Embracing with his left
  the martyr's sacred neck,
So that thus he may place
  at last a single kiss.
But the martyr thwarted
  the King's shrewd playful act
And swung at the King's lips
  promptly with his fist.
He dealt such a blow
  to the King's face below
That the blood gushing forth
  from the inflicted wound
Stained the King's beard
  and wetted all his garments.
Then the King was moved
  and to great anger provoked,
And ordered that Pelagius,
  child of heaven's king,
Be thrown over the walls
  and hurled from an engine
Which, when used in war,
  threw rocks at the foe,
So that the noble martyr,
  dashed on the river's shore
(Which with its mighty waves

surrounded the city)
Be broken in all members
  and so meet his death.[8]
The King's haughty servants
  obeyed his cruel words
And promptly they performed
  this unheard-of punishment,
Throwing from a sling
  Pelagius to be martyred
Across the very tall
  ramparts of that town.
But even though large masses
  of rocks stood in the way
Obstructing much the fall
  of the martyr's glorious body,
Nevertheless Christ's friend
  stayed totally unharmed.
Promptly, of course, the news
  was brought to the royal ears
That the body of the martyr
  could not, as he had ordered,
Be torn to pieces and rent
  by rocks on the river's bank.
Even more furious
  because he had been foiled,
The King then gave the order
  that the martyr be beheaded
And that so, as he willed,
  the punishment be fulfilled.
Promptly the King's henchmen,
  trembling at his orders
Killed the faithful youth,
  witness of Christ's law
And gave his lifeless body
  to the waves to hold.

The soldier of the Heavenly King
  destroyed in body by death
Flew swiftly as victor
  through the stars to heaven
Borne by heavenly angels
  singing hymns and songs.
Then seated above the stars,
  at the right hand of the father
He duly received the palm

from the equitable Judge
For his martyrdom achieved
  through laudable death.
He was also granted,
  a reward for the love
Which led him to assume
  his father's chains for life
And caused him to abandon
  his land and his people.
No tongue, indeed, can aspire
  to depict with affectionate desire
That beauteous laurel bright,
  sparkling with celestial light,
With which he is crowned
  for his virginity renowned.
Joined to the chosen throng
  of the Heavenly kingdom,
He sings perpetually
  the praise of the Lamb. Amen.

After the executioners
  had followed the king's orders,
And had duly committed
  the martyr's noble remains
To the bosom of the waters
  and placed them among rocks
So the sacred remains
  would stay without a tomb,
Christ, who suffers not
  that even the tiniest spot
Of hair be harmed of those
  who bear witness to His cause
Did not allow His witness
  to remain in the stream
But duly He provided
  for him a worthy place
Which was to preserve
  his holy limbs in a tomb.

It happened that some fishermen,
  pounding the waves
With their oars and catching
  the wandering fishes
Saw the martyr's limbs
  at a distant spot,

Tossing to and fro
  amidst the loud waves.
Discerning it from afar
  with their careful eyes,
They quickly set sail
  and lifted up the body.
They did not recognize
  who the person was
Because the limbs despoiled,
  with purple blood were soiled,
And his noble head
  lay farther down the stream.
Yet they sensed this much
  and believed it to be such
That whoever he be,
  this man perished for Christ,
Because only those
  were condemned to beheading
Who, sprinkled with the waters
  of Christian baptism
Did not fear to insult
  the King's pagan cult.
When they found the head
  and placed it on the shoulders,
They recognized the handsome
  face of Pelagius.
Pity in their hearts,
  they poured forth these words:
"Alas here lies dead
  the sole hope of his nation
And the glory of his land
  lies here without a tomb.
Don't we also know
  that the remains of those
Whose decapitations
  prove them to be Christians,
Can easily be sold
  for large amounts of gold?
And who would doubt this
  to be the body of a martyr
Since the body lies,
  bereft of the head's glory?"
As they were thus talking,
  they placed the saint's remains
In their boat's tail.

And quickly they turned sail
And traveled to the port
  of that famous city.
Here, after having docked
  and their vessel locked,
They sought out in secret
  a sacred monastery
Which lay within the walls
  surrounding the city.
They carried, hoping for gains,
  the blessed martyr's remains
Honored now by all,
  to be sold for gold.
The throng of the faithful
  received them rejoicing,
And with sweet hymns performed
  the sacred funeral rites
They paid generously
  a high price to the shipmen
Eager to buy the remains
  of the beloved saint.
After they have won
  the body for no small sum,
They chose a worthy spot
  in which to keep the body.
Here after the service
  has been splendidly performed,
The sacred relics lay
  buried under a mound of clay.
Soon the Almighty Lord
  of the star bearing court
Made the grave illustrious
  through signs miraculous,
So that as the martyr's soul,
  that now reigned in heaven,
So, on earth his body
  may also reign in glory.

At length the citizens
  of the city noticed
That a sizable throng
  of men afflicted for long
With diverse diseases,
  was here freely healed
Their loathsome limbs

were cured, without payment.
They were quite perplexed
    that this unknown saint
Could be of such merit
    as to cause such marvels.
Finally the abbot
    and pastor of the people
Pondering the best counsel
    in well advised council
Felt that the Lord Most High
    must be asked to comply
And be begged sincerely
    to reveal to all clearly
The secret of the case
    and, thus, remove all doubt.[9]
This plan all people admired
    and both men and women desired.
Thus through self-imposed fasting
    for three whole days lasting
They solicited the Lord
    with hymns and sacred prayers.
With devout hearts
    those prayers were performed
And the people thought
    that the heavenly King has been brought
By their effusive prayers
    and their eager pleadings
To where he was not opposed
    to settle their doubts.
So promptly they prepared
    a threatening hot furnace
By heaping up much wood
    with united efforts.
When the fire raged
    in the stove's huge lap
They took the severed head
    of the true servant, of Christ,
Gently speaking such words
    of persuasive speech
"Kind King and noble Lord,
    ruling the stellar court,
Thou Who knowest to settle
    all things in just manner
Cause the merit, Sire,
    of the saint be proved by fire.

If he is indeed
    of such virtue and honor
That because of his grace
    these gifts of healing take place,
Then cause thou that the fire
    not burn his facial skin
And also that his hair
    be totally unharmed.
But, perchance, if he
    of lesser merit might be
Then make thou that be known
    by that his skin alone
Be harmed as would be proper
    for frail and perishable flesh.
Speaking thus they cast
    the glorious head, at last,
For testing, to the waves
    of the high surging flames.
And after the full measure
    of an hour had passed,
They finally then retrieved
    the head from the flames,
Inspecting whether the heat
    had harmed the martyr's head.
But the head just glowed
    more splendidly than gold
Unharmed and entire,
    in spite of the raging fire.
Then the faithful flock
    praised with upturned faces
And with sweet melodies
    Christ enthroned on high
Who has made resplendent
    with many and frequent signs
The mortal relics of those
    who died for His cause.
Pelagius' relics, as meet,
    were placed in a worthy tomb
Where they are venerated
    with humble and due respect.
And ever since that day
    all doubts were cast away
And the folk rejoiced
    in the patron granted them by God.

NOTES

1. *Pelagius,* unlike Hrotsvit's other legends, is not based on a written source but on eyewitness reports. It has been suggested that perhaps a member of Emperor Otto's embassy to Abderrahman provided Hrotsvit with the details of the new martyr. The legend is composed in leonine hexameters (that is, dactylic hexameters with internal rhyme or, more frequently, homoeoteleuton) and ornamented with the frequent use of hyperbaton, alliteration, antonomasia, and litotes. I have used the edition of Helena Homeyer, *Hrotsvithae Opera* (Munich: Schönigh, 1970), for the translation.

2. Hrotsvit records her name six times in her works (Epistola; Preface to the epics; "Maria," line 18; "Ascensio," line 148; "Gongolf," line 3; "Pelagius," line 3. She herself translates her Old Saxon name as *"Ego Clamor Validus"*—the "Forceful Voice."

3. Hrotsvit spells the city's name "Corduba."

4. Abd-ar-Rahman, caliph of Cordoba.

5. The animal imagery is quite pronounced in these lines. Usually applied to the Devil and his cohorts, animal imagery is also frequently associated with the infidels in Hrotsvit's works.

6. Hrotsvit's authorial intervention makes sure that the reader does not wonder about divine injustice.

7. Pelagius, thus, becomes both a martyr of faith and of virginity as well as a paradigm of self-sacrifice. His rewards in heaven, are also threefold: He is rewarded as witness of the faith, as a virgin, and as a loving son.

8. It is curious that Pelagius is first hurled from a war machine rather than beheaded as prescribed by the edict. Perhaps Abderrahman wishes to destroy his beauty as well.

9. Pelagius, being a brand-new saint, must be tested. No other legend of Hrotsvit's contains the description of such a test, for all other legends deal with well-established cults of saints.

HROTSVIT OF GANDERSHEIM
Abraham[1]

Translated by Katharina M. Wilson

The Fall and repentance of Mary, Abraham the hermit's niece/ who, after she had lived twenty years in anchoretic peace,/ having lost her virginity,/ returned to the world's vanity,/ and did not even fear to live in a brothel with prostitutes./ But after two years, admonished by the aforementioned Abraham who sought her out disguised as a lover, she returned and purged herself from the stains of her sins for a period twenty years lasting,/ through effusive tears, vigils, and prayers and the constant exercise of fasting.[2]

I.1

Abraham:
Do you, brother and cohermit Effrem find it convenient to allow/ that I speak with you now,/ or do you wish for me to wait until you have finished your divine praises?

Effrem:
Our conversations should always be in His praise,/ who promised to be in the midst of those who have gathered in His name.

The Dramas of Hrotsvit of Gandersheim, translated and with an introduction by Katharina M. Wilson (Saskatoon: Peregrina Press, 1985).

Abraham:

I have come to speak of nothing else except of what I know is in concordance to God's will.

Effrem:

Then I shall not keep myself from you another moment but turn/ and give myself entirely to your concern.

Abraham:

A certain impending task has upset my mind/ concerning which I hope that you will be inclined/ to concur with my judgment.

Effrem:

As we are to be of one heart and one soul, we ought to want the same/ and not want the same.

Abraham:

I have a young niece bereaved of the solace of both parents, for whom I bear great affection and for whom I feel sorry/ and on whose account I tire myself with constant worry.

Effrem:

And what are the cares of this world to you, you who have triumphed over the world?

Abraham:

This is my care: that the immense radiance of her beauty should wane/ and be dimmed by some pollution's stain.

Effrem:

Such concern no blame will earn.

Abraham:

I hope that so it'll be.

Effrem:

How old is she?

Abraham:

When the course of this year is completed, She will have breathed the breath of life for two Olympiads.[3]

Effrem:

An immature girl.

Abraham:

That's the reason for my concern.

Effrem:

Where does she dwell?

Abraham:

In my own cell. When, asked by her relatives, I undertook to raise her, but decided to bequeath her wealth to the poor.

Effrem:

Contempt for worldly things befits the soul intent on heaven.

Abraham:

I desire passionately that to Christ she be espoused and that for His service she be trained.

Effrem:

An aim worthy to be praised.

Abraham:

I am forced to do so by her name.

Effrem:

What is she called?

Abraham:

Mary.

Effrem:

Is that so? The excellence of such an exalted name/ deserves virginity's garland and acclaim.

Abraham:

I am convinced that, if she is kindly urged by our exhortations and aid,/ she will prove easy to persuade.

Effrem:

Let us go to her and let us instill in her mind/ the desirable security of the virginal life.

II.1

Abraham:

Oh my adopted daughter, oh, part of my soul, Mary, heed my fatherly admonitions/ and the beneficial instructions/ of my companion Effrem. Strive to imitate in your chastity/ her who is the fount of virginity and whose name you bear.

Effrem:
It would be most unfitting, daughter, if you, who are joined to Mary, the mother of God through your name's secret mystery/ and have been, thereby, raised to the axis of the sky among the stars that never set, if you wished to debase yourself in your actions/ and sink to the lowest realms of the world.

Mary:
I am ignorant of the secret of my name:/ therefore, I do not grasp the meaning of what you say in such a roundabout way.

Effrem:
Mary means *stella maris*, the "star of the sea," around which, as you may learn, the earth is borne and the poles turn.[4]

Mary:
Why is it called the "star of the sea"?

Effrem:
Because it never sets but is the source/ that guides sailors on the path of the right course.

Mary:
But how could it ever happen that I, such a little thing and made of clay,/ could, through my own merits, attain to that glorious place/ where the mysterious symbol of my name resides in grace?

Effrem:
Through the unimpaired wholeness of your body and the pure holiness of your mind.

Mary:
Great is the honor for a mortal to equal the rays of stars.

Effrem:
For if you remain uncorrupt and a virgin you will become the equal of God's angels; Surrounded by them, when you have cast off the burden of your heavy body, you will traverse the sky,/ rising above the ether high,/ and journey through the circle of the zodiac, not slowing down or delaying your flight/ until you have reached the Virgin's Son's arms' delight,/ and are embraced by Him in the luminous wedding chamber of His mother.

Mary:
Whoever undervalues this is an ass. Therefore I renounce the world and deny myself so that I may deserve to be bequeathed the joys of such great felicity.

Effrem:
Behold, the child's breast brings forth the maturity of age.

Abraham:
It is by the grace of God on High.

Effrem:
This no one can deny.

Abraham:
Yet even though God's grace has been made manifest, it would not be prudent to leave such a young child to her own counsel.

Effrem:
True.

Abraham:
Therefore, I shall build her a little cell, narrow of entrance and adjacent to my own dwelling. I will visit her often and through the window/ instruct her in the Psalms and other pages of God's law.

Effrem:
Rightly so.

Mary:
I commit myself, father Effrem, to your guidance.

Effrem:
May the Heavenly Bridegroom, to whose affections you have pledged yourself at such a tender age,/ succour you, daughter, from all the guiles of Satan.

III.1

Abraham:
Brother Effrem, whenever anything happens to me;/ either good fortune or misery,/ to you I come, you alone I consult; so do not turn away from the laments I utter/ but help me in the pain I suffer.

Effrem:
Abraham, Abraham, what a heartrending sight./ Why are you more dejected than is meet and is right?/ A hermit should never be perturbed in the manner of men in the world.

Abraham:
My distress is incomparable,/ my grief is intolerable!

Effrem:
Don't keep me in suspense with your roundabout words,/ but explain what occurred.

Abraham:
Mary, my adopted daughter whom for twice ten years, I brought up to the best of my ability, whom I instructed to the best of my skill . . .

Effrem:
What happened to her whom you so clearly cherished?

Abraham:
Woe to me, she has perished.

Effrem:
How?

Abraham:
In great wretchedness; then she stole away, secretly.

Effrem:
With what tricks did the guile of the ancient serpent beset her?

Abraham:
Through the forbidden passion of a certain deceiver/ who, disguised as a monk, often came to see her/ under the pretence of instructive visits,/ until he ignited the undisciplined instincts of her youthful heart to burn in love for him, so much so that she jumped from her window to perform that awful deed.

Effrem:
Ah, I shudder to hear it.

Abraham:
And when the wretched girl, so beguiled,/ found herself lapsed and defiled,/ she beat her breast,/ lacerated her face and her hands,/ tore her clothes amidst sighs,/ pulled out her hair, and raised her voice in lamentations to the skies.

Effrem:
Not without reason, for her ruin must be mourned/ and with great outpouring of tears deplored.

Abraham:
She bewailed not to be what she was.

Effrem:
Poor girl, alas.

Abraham:
She mourned that she had acted against our admonitions.

Effrem:
Rightly so.

Abraham:
She lamented that she had rendered void the toils of her vigils, prayers and fastings.

Effrem:
If she had persevered in such great remorse, she would have been saved.

Abraham:
She did not persevere for long/ but added worse to prior wrong.

Effrem:
In fear my stomach is turned; my limbs are all unnerved.

Abraham:
For after she has punished herself with these laments, defeated by the immenseness of her grief, she was carried headlong, into the lap of desperation.

Effrem:
Alas, alas, what grave perdition!

Abraham:
And because she despaired of ever attaining forgiveness, she chose to return to the world and to serve its vanities.

Effrem:
Well, up until now, the spirits of iniquity had been unaccustomed to gain/ such victory in the abode where hermits stay.

Abraham:

But now we are the demons' prey.

Effrem:

I wonder how it could have happened that she escaped you unnoticed.

Abraham:

For some days I was very much troubled by the horror of a revelation,/ a vision, which, if my mind had not been careless, would have foretold me of her perdition.

Effrem:

I would like to know the nature of this vision.

Abraham:

I thought I stood before the entrance of my cell,/ when, behold, a dragon of miraculous size and of foul smell,/ came, rushing with great speed towards a little white dove near me. He snatched the dove, devoured it and then suddenly vanished.

Effrem:

A vision with clear meaning.

Abraham:

But, I, when I roused myself from the vision, thought about what I had seen and was gripped with terror/ that a persecution threatened the church which might lead some of the faithful into error.

Effrem:

That was to be feared.

Abraham:

Therefore, prostrate in prayer, I beseeched Him who has foreknowledge of future events to unveil for me the meaning of the sight.

Effrem:

You did all right.

Abraham:

Then on the third night,/ when I gave my exhausted body to sleep,/ I thought I saw the very same dragon, wallowing deep,/ crushed under my feet and I saw the same white dove, dart forth unhurt.

Effrem:

I am delighted to hear this because without

doubt, your daughter Mary will someday return.

Abraham:

When I awoke, I smoothed my prior grief with the solace of this new vision, and collected myself to remember my pupil; then I also recalled, not without sadness that I have not heard her recite her customary prayers for the last two days.

Effrem:

You remembered too late.

Abraham:

I confess it. Then I approached her cell, knocked on her window and repeatedly called my daughter by name.

Effrem:

Alas, you called in vain.

Abraham:

I did not realize that yet, but asked her why she was neglecting her prayers and to my concern,/ I received not the slightest sound of response in turn.

Effrem:

What did you do then.

Abraham:

When I understood, at last, that she whom I sought had left I was aghast with fear, my innermost parts trembled,/ and in terror quaked all my members.

Effrem:

No wonder! Indeed, even now, listening to you I feel the same sensation.

Abraham:

Then I filled the air with doleful sounds wild,/ asking what wolf has snatched away my lamb, what thief has stolen my child?

Effrem:

You were right to bewail the loss of her whom you have raised.

Abraham:

Then people came who knew for sure/ that what I have now told you is actually true/ and they said that she has given herself over to sin.

Effrem:
Where is she gone?

Abraham:
It is not known.

Effrem:
What will you do next?

Abraham:
I have a loyal friend who, without rest, is traveling through villages and towns and will not stop/ until he finds the very spot/ whereto she is bound.

Effrem:
What if she is found?

Abraham:
I will change my habit and will go to her disguised as a lover. Perchance, admonished by me after her awful shipwreck, she may return to the safe port of earlier tranquillity.

Effrem:
And what will you do if meat to eat and wine to drink is placed before you?

Abraham:
I will not refuse so that I won't be recognized.

Effrem:
Indeed it is praiseworthy that you should use correct discretion in saving the erring girl for Christ even if it means that you will have to relax the strict rules of our monastic practice.

Abraham:
I am all the more eager to undertake this daring deed now that I know that you agree with me.

Effrem:
He who knows the secrets of our hearts, and knows the intents that underlie our actions, does not disapprove that one of us relaxes temporarily the rigor of our strict rules and behaves like our weaker brethren, if it is done so that he may all the more efficiently win/ and regain a soul that has strayed into sin.

Abraham:
Meanwhile, it will be your task to assist me

with prayers so that I will not be impeded by the devil's guiles.

Effrem:
May that greatest of all goods, without which no other good may be, bring your intent to good ends.

IV

Abraham:
Is this my friend whom I sent out two years ago to find Mary? It is he, indeed!

Friend:
Greetings, venerable father.

Abraham:
Greetings, dear friend. Long I have waited/ and I even abated/ and lost hope for your return.

Friend:
The reason I took so long was that I did not wish to agitate you with unconfirmed news; but when I could investigate and the truth learn,/ I promptly hurried to return.

Abraham:
Did you see Mary?

Friend:
I have.

Abraham:
Where?

Friend:
In a city, close by.

Abraham:
With whom does she reside,/ on whom does she rely?

Friend:
It hurts me to reply.

Abraham:
Why?

Friend:
It is too awful to say.

Abraham:
But tell me, I pray.

Friend:

She has chosen as her abode the house of a certain procurer who treats her with tender love. And not without profit I may say, for every day he receives large sums of money from her lovers.

Abraham:

From Mary's lovers?

Friend:

Yes, from them.

Abraham:

Who are her lovers?

Friend:

There are many.

Abraham:

Woe is me. Oh, good Jesus, what misfortune is this I hear, that she, whom I raised to be Your bride/ has strange lovers at her side?

Friend:

This has been the custom of whores in all ages/ that they delight in the love of strangers.

Abraham:

Bring me a soldier's clothes and a good steed/ so that, after I lay aside my religious habit, disguised as a lover to her I may speed.

Friend:

Here is all you need.

Abraham:

Give me a hat, too, with which to cover my tonsure I pray.

Friend:

This too is very necessary so as not to give your identity away.

Abraham:

Should I take this coin that I have to pay the innkeeper?

Friend:

Otherwise you won't be able to meet with Mary.

V

Abraham:

Greetings good host!

Innkeeper:

Who is it that calls? Greetings!

Abraham:

Do you have a nice place for a traveler to stay overnight?

Innkeeper:

Indeed we do; our hospitality is for all who alight.

Abraham:

Good!

Innkeeper:

Come in, so that dinner can be prepared for you.

Abraham:

I owe you much for this merry welcome, but I ask for even more from you.

Innkeeper:

Tell me what you desire,/ so that I can attain to what you aspire.

Abraham:

Here, take this little gold that I brought and arrange that that most beautiful girl who, as I hear, stays with you, shares our meal.

Innkeeper:

Why do you wish to see her?

Abraham:

I would delight in getting to know her whose beauty I have heard praised by so many and so often.

Innkeeper:

Whoever praised her beauty, did not tell a lie, for in the loveliness of her face she outshines all other women.

Abraham:

That is why I burn/ and for her love so yearn.

Innkeeper:

I wonder that in your decrepit old age you aspire/ and the love of a young woman desire.

Abraham:

For sure, I come for no other purpose but to see her.

VI

Innkeeper:

Come, Mary, come along. Show your beauty to our newcomer.

Mary:

Here I come.

Abraham:

What boldness, what constancy of mind I must muster as I see her whom I raised in my hidden hermitage decked out in a harlot's garb./ But this is not the time to show in my face what is in my heart;/ I must be on guard:/ like a man I will bravely suppress my tears gushing forth. With feigned cheerfulness of countenance I will veil the bitterness of my internal grief.

Innkeeper:

Lucky Mary, be merry; because now not only men your age flock to you, as before, but even men ripe of age seek your favors.

Mary:

Those who seek me in love, receive equal love from me in return.

Abraham:

Come on, Mary, give me a kiss.

Mary:

I will not only give you a taste of sweet kisses/ but will caress your ancient neck with close embraces.

Abraham:

That is what I am after.

Mary:

What is it I feel? What is this spell?/ What is this rare and wonderful odor I smell?/ Oh, the smell of this fragrance reminds me of the fragrance of chastity I once practiced.

Abraham:

Now, now I must pretend, now I must persist and be lustful in the manner of lewd young men and play the game/ so that I am not recognized by my seriousness or else she might leave and hide for shame.

Mary:

Woe me, wretched woman! How I sunk, how I fell into perdition's ravine!

Abraham:

This is not a fit place for complaints, where the band of jolly guests convene.

Innkeeper:

Lady Mary, why do you sigh?/ Why do you cry?/ In the two years you have lived here, never such groans and complaints bursting forth did I hear; never such grieving words!

Mary:

Oh, I wish I could have died three years ago,/ then I would not have sunk into such disgrace and woe.

Abraham:

I didn't come all this way/ to join you in lamenting your sins but to be joined to you making love and being gay.

Mary:

I was moved by a slight regret to utter such words; but let us now dine and be merry because, as you admonished me,/ this is certainly not the time to bewail one's sins.

Abraham:

Abundantly we have wined,/ abundantly we have dined/ and are now tipsy, good host, with the generous portions you served. Give us now leave to rise from the table/ so that I might be able/ to lay down and refresh my weary body by sweet rest.

Innkeeper:

I'm at your behest.

Mary:

Rise, my lord, rise up. I shall accompany you to your bedroom.

Abraham:

That pleases me. In fact, I could not have been forced to go, were I not to go with you.

VII

Mary:
Here is a bedroom for us to stay in. Here is the bed, decked with rich and lovely covers. Sit down, so that I may take off your shoes so you won't have to tire yourself removing them.

Abraham:
First, lock the door so no one may enter.

Mary:
Don't worry on that account,/ I will make sure that the bolt is secure/ and that no one finds easy access to disturb us.

Abraham:
Now the time has come to remove my hat and reveal who I am. Oh my adoptive daughter, oh part of my soul, Mary,/ don't you recognize me,/ the old man who raised you like a father and who pledged you with a ring/ to the only begotten Son of the Heavenly King?

Mary:
Woe is me! It is my father and teacher Abraham who speaks!

Abraham:
What happened to you, daughter?

Mary:
Tremendous misery.

Abraham:
Who deceived you! Who seduced you?

Mary:
He who overthrew our first parents.

Abraham:
Where is that angelic life that already here on earth you led?

Mary:
Destroyed, it fled.

Abraham:
Where is the modesty of your virginity? Where your admirable continence?

Mary:
Lost and gone from hence.

Abraham:
What reward for the efforts of your fasting, prayers, and vigils can you hope for unless you return to your senses, you who fell,/ from the height of heaven and have sunk in the depth of hell?

Mary:
Woe is me, alas!

Abraham:
Why did you disdain me?/ Why did you desert me?/ Why did you not tell me of your wretched sin; so that I and my beloved friend Effrem could perform worthy penance for you?

Mary:
After I first sinned, and sunk into perfidy/ I did not dare, polluted as I was, to even approach your sanctity.

Abraham:
Who ever has lived free from sin/ except for the Son of the virgin?

Mary:
No one.

Abraham:
It is human to err but evil to persist in sin; he who fell suddenly is not the one to be blamed/ but he who fails to rise promptly again.

Mary:
Woe is me, wretched woman.

Abraham:
Why did you fall down?/ Why do you stay unmoving, lying on the ground? Arise and hear what I have to say!

Mary:
I fell, shaken with fear because I could not bear the force of your fatherly admonitions.

Abraham:
Consider my love for you and put aside your fears.

Mary:
I cannot.

Abraham:
Did I not relinquish my accustomed hermitage on your behalf/ and did I not leave aside/ all observance of our regular rule,/ so much so,

that I who am an old hermit, have turned into a pleasure-seeking lewd fool,/ and I who for so long practiced silence, made jokes and spoke merry words so that I wouldn't be recognized? Why do you still stare at the ground with lowered face? Why do you refuse to speak with me?

Mary:
I am troubled by my grave offence; this is why I don't dare to presume to lift my eyes to heaven or have the confidence to speak with you.

Abraham:
Don't lose faith, my daughter, don't despair,/ but from the abyss of dejection repair/ and place your hope in God.

Mary:
The enormity of my sins has cast me into the depth of despair.

Abraham:
Your sins are grave, I admit,/ but heavenly pity is greater than anything we can commit./ Therefore cast off your despair/ and beware/ to leave unused this short time given to you for penitence because of laziness, that divine grace abounds even where the abomination of sins prevails.

Mary:
If I had any hope of receiving forgiveness, my eagerness to do penance would burst forth.

Abraham:
Have mercy on my exhaustion which I had to bear on your account, and cast off this dangerous and sinful despair which we know to be a graver offense than all other sins. For whoever despairs,/ thinking that God forbears/ to come to the aid of sinners, that person sins irremediably. Because just as the spark from a flintstone cannot set the sea on fire,/ so the bitter taste of our sins cannot likewise aspire/ to change the sweetness of divine goodwill.

Mary:
It is not the magnificence of heavenly grace which I doubt,/ but when I consider my own

sin, so profound,/ then I fear that the performance of even a worthy penance will not suffice.

Abraham:
I take your sins upon myself; Only come back to the place which you deserted/ and take up again the life which you subverted.

Mary:
I will never go against any of your wishes but will embrace obediently all your commandments.

Abraham:
Now I believe, you are my child whom I raised, indeed; now I feel you are the one to be loved above all others.

Mary:
I possess some clothes and a little gold;/ I wait to be told/ how to dispose of them.

Abraham:
What you acquired through sin,/ must be cast off together with the sins.

Mary:
I thought, perhaps, they could be given to the poor, or offered to the sacred altars.

Abraham:
It is neither sanctioned nor acceptable that gifts be given to God which were acquired through sin.

Mary:
Beyond this, I have no concern.

Abraham:
Dawn arrives; the day breaks, Let us return.

Mary:
You, beloved father, must lead the way/ as the good shepherd leads the sheep gone astray;/ and I, advancing in your footsteps, will follow your lead.

Abraham:
Not so; on foot, I will proceed/ but on my horse, you will have a seat/ so that the sharp rocks of the road will not harm your tender little feet.

Mary:
What shall I say? How shall I ever compensate your kindness? You do not force me, miserable wretch, with threats, but exhort me to do penance with kind benevolence.

Abraham:
I ask nothing of you, except that you remain intent upon spending the rest of your life in God's service.

Mary:
Out of my own free will I shall remain contrite,/ I shall persist in my penance with all my might,/ and even if I lose the ability to perform the act,/ the will, though, shall never lack.

Abraham:
It is important that you serve the divine will as eagerly/ as you served the worldly vanities.

Mary:
The Lord's will be done in me, because of your merits.

Abraham:
Let us return and hurry our way.

Mary:
Let us hurry, I am weary of delay.

VIII

Mary:
With what speed we have traveled over this difficult and rugged road.

Abraham:
Whatever is done with devotion, is accomplished with ease. Behold, here is your deserted little cell.

Mary:
Woe me, this cell is witness to my sin,/ therefore I fear to go in.

Abraham:
And understandably. Any place where the ancient enemy has won a triumph is to be avoided.

Mary:
And where do you intend me to devote myself to my penance?

Abraham:
Go into the small interior room/ so that the ancient serpent will not find an opportunity to deceive you anew.

Mary:
I will not contradict you but embrace eagerly what you command.

Abraham:
I shall go to Effrem, my friend, so that he who alone mourned with me over your loss may rejoice with me over your return.

Mary:
A worthy concern!

IX

Effrem:
Are you bringing me joyous news?

Abraham:
Most joyous news.

Effrem:
I am glad. Doubtless you have found Mary.

Abraham:
Indeed I found her and led her back, rejoicing, to the fold.

Effrem:
I believe this was done by the grace of God.

Abraham:
I doubt it not.

Effrem:
I would like to know how from this day on she will conduct her life and her penance fulfill.

Abraham:
Entirely according to my will.

Effrem:
That will be of great advantage to her.

Abraham:
Whatever I have suggested for her to do,

however difficult, however harsh, she has not refused to perform.

Effrem:
Very praiseworthy.

Abraham:
She put on a hair shirt and is weakened by the constant exercise of vigils and fastings, but still she forces her tender body to follow her soul's mandate/ and observes the strictest rules, bearing penance's weight.

Effrem:
It is only right that the filth of her sinful delight/ be purged by the bitter severity of her plight.

Abraham:
Whoever hears her lamentations is wounded in his heart by its force;/ whoever feels the pangs of her remorse,/ himself feels remorse.

Effrem:
It usually happens so.

Abraham:
She works with all her strength to become an example of conversion/ for those for whom she was the cause of perdition.

Effrem:
That is proper.

Abraham:
She strives, to appear as brightly radiant as she was once foul.

Effrem:
I rejoice in hearing this; I am happy with heartfelt joy.

Abraham:
And justifiably, for even the angelic choirs rejoice and praise the Lord when a sinner repents.

Effrem:
No wonder, for the steadfast perservance of the just man delights Him no more than the penance of a sinner.

Abraham:
So that He should be all the more praised for this gain,/ as there was no hope for her to become herself again.

Effrem:
Rejoicing let us praise and by praising let us glorify the only begotten son of God, honored, kind and cherished,/ who does not wish that those whom he redeemed with his precious blood should ever perish.

Abraham:
His be all honor, and glory, praise and jubilation, for time everlasting, Amen.

NOTES

1. *Abraham* is based on a legend ascribed to the Syrian Ephrem (fourth century A.D.); Hrotsvit's source, the Latin translation of the vita, originated in the sixth century A.D. Cf. Homeyer, *Opera*, pp. 288–302. *Abraham*, like all of Hrotsvit's plays, is composed in rhymed rhythmic prose, whereby homoeoteleuton usually suffices. It is ornamented with the sophisticated and frequent use of stichomythia, anaphora, interjectio, and aposiopeses.

2. The drama like all of Hrotsvit's plays, is preceded by a narrative epitome, highlighting the theme and the moral of the play.

3. That is, she is in her eighth year.

4. Hrotsvit's source does not contain this "etymology lesson." It gives only the name.

III

Visionaries of the Early Twelfth Century

Christina of Markyate, Hildegard of Bingen, and
St. Elisabeth of Schönau

*T*HE NEXT THREE WOMEN whose works will be considered here were all visionaries alive in the first half of the twelfth century. Christina of Markyate and Hildegard of Bingen were born within two years of each other, and Elisabeth of Schönau was born a little more than a generation later, but was old enough to have been strongly influenced by her compatriot Hildegard. All were Benedictines, all lived in communities, and the first two lived as recluses in their youth. All were participants in the renaissance of the twelfth century and responded to that intellectual and political ferment in varying ways.

Christina of Markyate (1096-98–1160) was born into an influential Anglo-Saxon family in Norman England.[1] The part of her life story that we possess does not go beyond about 1142, by which time she was a professed nun in the community of St. Alban's. What we do have is a rich account of her childhood, the marriage forced on her by her parents but never consummated, her flight to the cell of a nearby hermit where she lived in secrecy for a number of years, and her assumption of a more regularized life in a small community after her husband, Burthred, publicly released her from her betrothal. The portion included here opens with her mother's mistreatment of her because she will not marry, and it ends with a vision of the Virgin Mary in which she learns that she can now be secure in her own hermit's cell. We do not know who wrote down the life, but it is clear that he knew Christina well (or Theodora as she was called before her profession) and that he often transcribed her own first-person accounts of her adventures. The only other literary document associated with her is the St. Alban's Psalter, presumably commissioned by her.[2] The Psalter contains texts in both Latin and Old French, with numerous glosses in Old English.[3]

Our selection begins with Christina isolated in a world of archetypally evil women; Christina's mother, Beatrix, is the equal of any wicked stepmother in fairly tales, and she is determined to break her daughter's will and get her to submit to the marriage arranged for her with Burthred. She wastes money hiring old crones (*annosas vetulas*) to mix potions that will make Christina mad with desire, and when they fail, she hires a Jewess who comes to the house to see Christina. She seems to have genuine spiritual perception, and she sees two white-dressed phantoms accompanying Christina and protecting her at all times. In spite of this woman's advice to give up, Beatrix continues to torment her daughter, including one time when she pulls her out of a banquet, secretly beats her, then brings her back into the banquet to be exhibited as an object of derision. The scars of the beating—physical and perhaps emotional as well—remained throughout her life.

As one reads this passage, one is struck by the rage in it, the depth of the conflict of wills between this mother and daughter. The intervening years have not erased the pain, but this narrative of conflict with a bad mother is immediately followed by a vision of a good mother. Christina dreams that she is in a church where a priest gives her a flowering branch, which she is to bring to a lady "like an empress sitting on a dais not far from the altar." The lady questions her, offers comfort, and promises deliverance. As Christina leaves, she walks past Burthred, who is lying on the floor, beating his head against the pavement in rage. He is unable to touch Christina, and she climbs to an upper chamber, where the lady-queen is. The queen puts her head in Christina's lap but averts her face, and Christina is disturbed until the "empress" tells her she shall have her fill of looking on her when she and the Biblical Judith are brought to her chamber. When Christina awakes to find her pillow wet with tears, the reality of her dream is proved. "From that moment you could see that she was completely changed, and the immense joy which filled her at the thought of her freedom was displayed for all to see in the cheerfulness of her countenance."

This reads like a first-person narrative. Not only are we given information, such as this paragraph, which only Christina knows, but the very order in which we are given this information is privileged. The account of Beatrix's persecution and of the rescue promised by the lady is so psychologically accurate in its mirroring effect that one comes to perceive it as dictated autobiographical material that had been meditated on for years. Furthermore, this mirroring is supported by the pivotal figure of Burthred, who is inserted between the first and second appearances of the lady and who will reappear similarly in the later narrative.

Visions are one of the central structural units of this autobiography-biography. As units of narration, visions are positioned symmetrically opposite to historical recitals of Christina's persecutions or uncertainties. It is in the visions that we often understand her real doubts; the historical narrative shows her planning, proceeding rationally to protect herself; but in the visions we see how great an effort this is, how much pain it costs her.

For example, we are told of how she is shut up in a tiny closet a span and a half wide. (A span is nine inches.) The board that covers the opening is held in place by a log, and she's sitting on a stone, with no air to breathe and not enough room to wear warm clothes in the winter. She must remain hidden, or her protectors will be killed. On the day of the Annunciation, "the fairest of the children of men came to her through the locked door, bearing in his right hand a cross of gold." This iconography combines two traditional illustrations, of the Annunciation and of the Harrowing of Hell. When the angel Gabriel comes to Mary to announce her pregnancy, he enters through a locked door; and when Christ enters hell to release its inhabitants, he bears a cross in his hand. But this is not a static image for Christina, and "at his appearance the maiden was terrified." Christ reassures her, saying he has come to increase her confidence; she must take the cross and hold it steadily upright. As he leaves, he promises to take it back again after a short time. When Christina tells this to Roger, the hermit who is protecting her and giving her spiritual instruction, he begins to weep for joy and speaks the only words in English in the entire book: "Rejoice with me, myn sunendaege dohter" (my Sunday daughter).[4] He recognizes that her trials will soon be at an end and her cross will be taken from her.

Two days later, March 27, Easter Sunday ("the day of the Resurrection"), Burthred, with two of his brothers, comes to Roger's cell, confesses to having sinned against "God's handmaid Theodora," and says that he's willing to release her from her marriage vows and to accept the guidance of Roger. Roger gives no indication that he knows Christina's whereabouts and demonstrates extreme caution although Burthred reveals he has been convinced to release Christina by a terrifying vision two nights earlier, in which Mary reproached him for his treatment of the "sacred maiden." Roger's caution is reasonable, for he knows that Burthred's two brothers have little standing as witnesses. We have already seen how much prestige Christina's family possesses, for when Burthred released her from her vows once before, they bribed the judges and the witnesses to reverse the decision. Now Roger asks for time to consider the proposal while Burthred rounds up better witnesses: the Burthred who married them: Robert, the dean of Huntington; and Ralph of Flamstead. These three are matched by the five hermits who live with Roger, and in the presence of all Burthred puts his hand in Roger's and releases Christina.

Roger is so relieved at this event that he discusses with Christina his idea of leaving his hermitage to her when he dies. This initiates another vision. She is in heaven, where she sees the Queen enthroned, with angels in brightness all about her. As Christina gazes, able to see more and more in that brilliance, she focuses closely on the lovely face of Mary. When Mary promises to give her whatever she wants, she sees in a flash the whole world and locates Roger's cell and chapel, shining brightly. This is what she wants, and the Queen promises her she shall surely have it.

There are two circular movements encoded here: first, the cycle from the Annunciation to Easter, the complete circle of Christ's life; and second, a circle closed in Burthred's relationship with Christina. Her choice of virginity over marriage is finally acknowledged, and she is legally released from marriage, which means that she can come out of the cramped space where she has been for four years. Burthred is no longer the person he was seven years ago, when in her vision Christina saw him beating his head on the pavement; and she is no longer the young girl with her pillow wet with tears. Her enclosure was miraculously entered by Christ in her Annunciation vision, fused with the release suggested by the Harrowing of Hell iconography; and on Easter, as Christ transcended the confinement of the tomb, so Burthred gives Christina freedom to leave her enclosure. The final vision of this section concerns Christina's choosing her future home, and she is led to do this by gazing on the lovely face of the Queen of heaven, just as she had wanted to do in her first vision.

The seer Hildegard of Bingen (1098–1179) composed most of her works for the world outside the walls of her convent. Her writings—letters, visions, prophecies, songs, a morality play, even a handbook on medicine—fill an entire volume of the *Patrologia Latina*.[5] Her religious life began at seven or eight, when she joined her aunt, who was a recluse; later their walled-up retreat was opened and turned into a convent, and she made her profession as a nun when she was fourteen. She was unable to write German, and she was diffident about the correctness of her Latin, but her dictated compositions exhibit wide learning.

Although she claimed that all her knowledge came from a mystical source, it is obvious that she was familiar with the Scriptures, natural science, classical Latin literature, and Neoplatonic philosophy. Joan Ferrante, in referring to her letters, many of them to ordinary people but including as well all the important figures of her age, says Hildegard was a sort of Dear Abby of the twelfth century.[6] She was taken seriously as a prophet by everyone, it would seem, from St. Bernard of Clairvaux and the pope down to the humblest laborers. Throughout her period of prolific writing she was a forceful administrator of her convent, often traveling great distances to represent the interests of her house when they were threatened. She began the *Scivias*, her major visionary and autobiographical work, when she was forty-two. Its introduction reveals her particular gifts, but it is also typical of most women visionaries in its mingling of self-confidence and humility:

> I had been conscious from earliest girlhood of a power of insight, and visions of hidden and wonderful things, ever since the age of five years.... But I did not mention it save to a few religious persons ... I kept it hidden by silence until God in his grace willed to have it made manifest.... It was in my forty-third year, when I was trembling in fearful anticipation of a celestial vision, that I beheld a great brightness through which a voice from heaven addressed me: O fragile child of earth, ash of ashes, dust of dust, express and write that which thou seest and hearest. Thou art timid, timid in speech, artless in explaining, unlearned in writing, but express and write not according to art but according to natural ability, not under the guidance of human composition, but under the guidance of that which thou seest and hearest in God's heaven above....[7]

After this beginning, Hildegard tells us more of her history. Although she began to have mystical experiences when still a child, she told very few people, and in general she "repressed ... in quiet silence" the contents of her visions. She insists she sees them in spiritual and psychological wholeness; they are not dreams, not frenzy; they are not given to her physical senses; they take place not when she is in "hidden places" but when she is "looking carefully in an innocent mind, with the eyes and ears of the interior man, in open places."[8] This defense is followed by a remarkable description of the interior life of a woman mystic as seen by God:

> For in the marrow of her bones and in the veins of her flesh she was aching, having her mind and judgment bound, so that no security dwelt in her and she judged herself culpable in all things.[9]

She has been protected from pride and vainglory by these feelings of fear and grief. But she knows enough or is pressured enough by her visions and doubts that she consciously searches for an amanuensis who must be "like to herself in that part of his work which concerned me."[10] This person, although he is a man, the monk Volmar, in fact a learned theologian, does not take his expected place above her, but reverses the roles and yields to her in his humility and goodwill. With support from him and from a young nun, Richardis von Stade, Hildegard can write what she sees and hears.

This Hildegard, with her conflicts and doubts, is also one of the most gifted of medieval writers, and her astute autobiographical observations must not be allowed to overshadow the controlled brilliance of her work. Consider what has been said of her contribution to medieval lyric in her hymn sequences:

> Hildegard of Bingen, prodigiously gifted in many directions, scientific, mystical, and poetic, composed a cycle of Latin liturgical lyric—hymns and sequences, antiphons and responses—in which such fusion of images is taken to an unparalleled visionary extreme. In its forms and melodies, as in its poetic techniques, this "symphony of the harmony of heavenly revelations," as she called it, stands apart from all other religious lyric, Latin or vernacular, of its time.[11]

The Trinity vision from Book II of the *Scivias* demonstrates that combination of scientific learning and spiritual insight that informs all of Hildegard's work. Here she begins with a visionary image of light and fire, in the center of which is the figure of a man of glowing sapphire. This image cluster develops into a meditation on the interrelationships of the three persons of the Trinity and on the necessity of the Incarnation. Having analyzed three discrete aspects of the initial vision—gemstone, fire, breath or word—as revelatory of divine stability, she then explores these three aspects as natural images, each a trinity of three forces or virtues. Thus, for instance, the three essential characteristics of a gemstone are moisture, palpability, and fire; it is the unity of these three qualities that creates the wholeness of a stone, its resistance to change. Here the moisture teaches about the Father, who is never dried up or exhausted; the palpability is the Son, incarnate in palpable flesh; and the power of fire is the holy spirit as the kindler (*accensor*) of the hearts of humans. As she works through the characteristics of her vision, she steadily moves from the physical to the spiritual, which for her is another parable, that of the life in humanity striving to be perfected. That she intended her readers to visualize her visions is brought home by the illustrations she supervised for the *Scivias*. There are thirty-five miniatures for the entire book; this one is illustrated

> by a silver circle enclosing a circle of gold, representing the Father and the Holy Spirit, and both circles surrounding the human form of Christ. His arms are uplifted in supplication and blessing, and the whole figure is painted a brilliant sapphire, thus depicting his redemptive and intercessory powers and his glorified body, now imbedded in the Trinity.[12]

Elisabeth of Schönau, the next figure in this anthology, occupies a transitional position;[13] her life has ties to that world of Benedictine monasticism represented by Christina and Hildegard, but in many respects her visionary life more closely resembles that of the women mystics of the end of the twelfth century. She was born in 1129, thirty-one years after Hildegard's birth, and died in 1165 at age thirty-six, fourteen years before Hildegard died. She joined the nunnery attached to the monastery at Schönau when she was twelve; her first recorded visions began in 1152 (when she was twenty-three) and continued until 1160. In 1157 she became *magistra* of the nuns. As far as we know, she was not a child prodigy like Hildegard, nor was she persecuted in her choice of a religious life as was Christina of Markyate. Nevertheless, "as a result of her prophetic pronouncements against moral corruption in the Church and secular society, Elisabeth suffered ridicule, disbelief, and calumny, especially on the part of the clergy."[14] Though she did not travel and preach as Hildegard did, her works were widely distributed and well known, and she clearly had extraordinary gifts as a visionary. Her visions, dictated to her brother Eckbert, a priest in Cologne, are unusual in several respects. The first book gives a careful chronological account of the beginnings of visionary experience while she tells of her feelings over a period of time when struggling with temptation. Illness was a central fact in her life, and in her written works it always precedes visionary attacks; she describes extreme pain, along with a sense of strangulation or suffocation. (Illness does not inhibit her activities in the monastic community, however—another indication that illness is directly related to her visions.) She describes the combination of illness and visionary experience as martyrdom, and her language echoes that of Perpetua. It would seem that this conviction about herself as a martyr allows her—in visions—to bypass the limitations on women's roles in the institutional church. No priestly mediation is necessary for her communion with the divine, for just as the experience of martyrdom gave women in the early church a status like that of priests,[15] the visionary martyrdom gives her a priestly kind of authority. Many of her visions come when she is prevented from taking communion; she then sees the host, the pyx, a dove plunging its beak into the chalice, the wine turning to blood. In the course of her first long illness, during which she experienced many visions (18 May to 5 June 1152), she saw the Virgin Mary standing by the altar and wearing the vestments of a priest.

Book 2 of the *Visions*, included here, develops these themes further. Elisabeth places herself in the Old Testament tradition of female prophets like Deborah, Jael, and Judith. The narration of one vision (which she dates 14 May 1155) is similar to a vision of Hildegard's: Elisabeth describes the central visual images that came to her in a bright light; then she hears an angelic voice telling her to contemplate all that she observes. At her request, this voice then provides an allegorical exegesis of the details of the image: the colors are related to the three persons of the Trinity, the ten rays represent the Ten Commandments, and so on. The angel then asks, "Why, tell me, do you not entrust your visions to writing, as you used to do?"

A community of supportive women always seems to surround her; she has her visions for them, and they in turn help her through her suffering and eagerly perform any prayers requested in her visions. In her identification with her sisters, she uses the pronoun *we* as often as *I*. For example, in one vision the figure of Mary keeps her face averted from Elisabeth, as if she were angry, and St. Peter explains that Mary feels her devotees have become lukewarm in serving her. All the sisters and the abbot are concerned:

> We had, in fact, begun to ask in communal prayer for this very thing, that our Lady not deny me her accustomed favor; for while in the past she had very frequently shown me her glorious countenance even without my undergoing physical suffering, she had now for many days withheld her countenance from me, and we feared that we had by our communal negligence offended her benevolence.[16]

Elisabeth's sense of herself as a vessel was no doubt reinforced by her correspondence with St. Hildegard, who wrote to her:

> I, a poor earthen vessel, say these things, not of myself but through the Living Light. . . . Those who desire to do the works of God should always remember that they are fragile, earthen vessels. They should put on the breast-plate of Faith and be humble and poor, living as He did, the Lamb Whose trumpet-sound they are . . . O daughter! May God make thee a mirror of Life![17]

What do these three women of the early twelfth century have in common? All three demonstrate a kind of heroic individuality that allows them to deal with adversity and potential tragedy in creative ways and also a physical resourcefulness that permits them to develop their intellectual and spiritual gifts. All three women knew severe limits to their aspirations; Christina had to hang by her fingernails behind a curtain to escape Burthred's drunken attempt to rape her and then to live for four years in a kind of closet, unable to stand up or lie down. Hildegard struggled with self-doubt until she became seriously ill, and only then was she able to dictate the prophetic visions that were possessing her. Yet in their maturity all three became important public figures, givers of wise counsel to others and gifted with unusual self-knowledge. All were learned—perhaps more learned in both classical and religious literature than women would be again until the Renaissance. All three women were aware of the intellectual and philosophical questions of their day, and they were educated in or near communities where they knew other learned women. (Christina was educated by a holy anchoress named Aelfwen for two years before she joined Roger in his hermitage.) In all three women, however, we see a painful sense of isolation and awareness of an unusual and demanding vocation that has removed them from ordinary human comfort. These latter qualities they share with almost all the women mystical writers who follow them.

NOTES

1. See Christopher J. Holdsworth, "Christina of Markyate," in *Medieval Women*, ed. Derek Baker, pp. 185–204. The text of *The Life of Christina of Markyate, A Twelfth Century Recluse*, trans. C. H. Talbot (Oxford: Clarendon Press, 1959), is the one utilized in this anthology. Eleanor McLaughlin discusses her at length (*Women of Spirit: Female Leadership in the Jewish and Christian Traditions*, ed. Eleanor McLaughlin and Rosemary Reuther (New York: Simon & Schuster, 1979), pp. 108–14), and Mary Martin McLaughlin sees her as an unusual instance of successful resistance to parental authority (*The History of Childhood*, ed. Lloyd de Mause (New York: Harper & Row, 1974), pp. 126–27). Caroline Walker Bynum offers an important analysis of Christina's adventures and her dressing as a man in "Women's Stories, Women's Symbols: A Critique of Victor Turner's Theory of Liminality," in *Anthropology and The Study of Religions*, ed. Frank E. Reynolds and Robert Moore, Chicago: Center for the Study of Religion, 1984.

2. On the connection between Christina and the St. Alban's Psalter see Talbot's introduction to the *Life*, and Holdsworth, "Christina of Markyate," pp. 189–95.

3. *The St. Alban's Psalter*, ed. Otto Pächt, C. R. Dodwell, and Francis Wormald (London: Warburg and Courtauld Institute, 1960).

4. Christina's world was largely populated by Anglo-Saxons. Until she entered St. Albans and became friends with the Norman abbot Geoffrey, she seems to have avoided Normans.

5. *Patrologia Latina*, ed. Migne, vol. 197. A modern edition is Hildegard of Bingen, *Scivias*, ed. Adelgundis Fuhrkotter and Angela Carlevaris, *Corpus Christianorum Continuatio Medievalis* 43–43A (Thornholt: Brepols, 1978). The modern edition of the lyric poetry is *Lieder*, ed. and trans. P. Barth, M. I. Ritscher, J. Schmidt-Gorg (Salzburg: O. Muller, 1969).

6. Joan Ferrante, "The Education of Women in the Middle Ages in Theory, Fact, and Fantasy," in *Beyond Their Sex: Learned Women of the European Past*, ed.

Patricia LaBalme (New York: New York University Press, 1980), pp. 9–42. This comment is on p. 25.

7. This passage is quoted in Eckenstein, *Women Under Monasticism*, p. 264. For another translation, see *The Life and Visions of St. Hildegarde*, trans. Francesca Maria Steele (London: Heath, Cranton and Ousely, n.d.), p. 123. This passage begins the first book of the *Scivias*. For discussions of Hildegard, see Frances and Joseph Gies, "Hildegard of Bingen," in *Women of the Middle Ages* (New York: Crowell, 1978), pp. 63–96; Eckenstein, *Women Under Monasticism*, pp. 270 ff.; H. O. Taylor, "Mystic Visions of Ascetic Women," in *The Medieval Mind* (New York: Macmillan, 1919), pp. 458–86; Peter Dronke, "Hildegard of Bingen as Poetess and Dramatist," in *Poetic Individuality in the Middle Ages: New Departures in Poetry* (Oxford: Clarendon Press, 1970), pp. 150–92, and *Women Writers of the Middle Ages* (Cambridge: Cambridge University Press, 1984), pp. 144–201; Kent Kraft, "The German Visionary: Hildegard of Bingen," in Katharina Wilson, ed., *Medieval Women Writers* (Athens, Ga.: Univ. of Georgia Press, 1984), pp. 109–30; Barbara L. Grant, "Five Liturgical Songs by Hildegard von Bingen," in *Signs* 5:3 (Spring 1980), pp. 560–67, and "An Interview with the Sybil of the Rhine: Hildegard von Bingen (1098–1179)," in *Heresies* 3:2 (Summer 1980), pp. 7 ff.; Bruce W. Hozeski, "Ordo Virtutem: Hildegard of Bingen's Liturgical Morality Play," in *Annuale Medievale* 13 (1978), pp. 45–69, and "The Parallel Patterns in Hrotsvitha of Gandersheim and in Hildegard of Bingen ...," in *Annuale Medievale* 12 (1977), pp. 42–53.

8. Steele, *Life*, pp. 125–26.

9. Steele, *Life*, p. 127.

10. Steele, *Life*, p. 127.

11. Peter Dronke, *The Medieval Lyric* (New York: Harper & Row, 1969), p. 75.

12. Valerie M. Lagorio, "The Medieval Continental Women Mystics," in *An Introduction to the Medieval Mystics of Europe*, ed. Paul Szarmach (Albany: SUNY Press, 1984), p. 165.

13. For the texts of Elisabeth's visions, see F. W. E. Roth, *Die Visionen von der heil. Elisabeth und die Schriften der Aebte Ekbert und Emecho von Schönau* (Brunn: Studien aus dem Benedictiner und Cistercienser Orden, 1884). On her influence, see *Poem on the Assumption*, ed. J. D. Strachey (*Cambridge Anglo-Norman Texts* (Cambridge: Cambridge University Press, 1924); and Ruth J. Dean, "Elisabeth, Prioress of Schönau, and Roger of Ford," in *Modern Philology* XLI (May 1944), pp. 209–20. For general discussions, see Eckenstein, *Women Under Monasticism*, pp. 227 ff.; Taylor, "Mystic Visions of Ascetic Women," pp. 458–86, and Lagorio, "The Medieval Continental Women Mystics," pp. 166 ff.

14. Lagorio, "The Medieval Continental Women Mystics," p. 166.

15. Frederick C. Klawiter, "The Role of Martyrdom in Developing the Priestly Authority of Women in Early Christianity," in *Church History* 49 (1980), pp. 251–61.

16. *The Life of Elisabeth of Schönau*, trans. Thalia Pandiri, par. xi.

17. Quoted in Lagorio, "Medieval Women Mystics," p. 165.

CHRISTINA OF MARKYATE (1096–8–1160; England)

Of S. Theodora, a Virgin, Who Is Also Called Christina

Translated by C. H. Talbot

From that day forward her mother, Beatrix, with God's permission but at the instigation of the devil, loosed all her fury on her own daughter, neglecting no sort of wicked artifice which might, in her opinion, destroy her integrity. . . .

In the end she swore that she would not care who deflowered her daughter, provided that some way of deflowering her could be found. Henceforward she wasted a great deal of money on old crones who tried with their love potions and charms to drive her out of her mind with impure desires. But their most elaborate potions had no effect. One Jewess wanted to harm Christina with tricks which were more powerful than the rest. She therefore entered Autti's house. As she saw the maiden walking by, she said to her mother Beatrix: "Our trouble has been all for nothing: I can see two phantoms, two persons, as it were, dressed in white, who accompany her at all times and protect her from assaults at all points. It is better for you to give up now rather than to waste time in vain." But Beatrix, in her obstinacy, would put no term to her malice, and as she could not break her daughter's will, tried to gain satisfaction from the shameful sufferings she inflicted on her. There was one time when on impulse she took her out from a banquet and, out of sight of the guests, pulled her hair out and beat her until she was weary of it. Then she brought her back, lacerated as she was, into the presence of the revellers as an object of derision, leaving on her back such weals from the blows as could never be removed as long as she lived.

Amidst all these trials Christ, wishing to comfort His spouse, gave her consolation through His holy Mother. It happened in this way. One night whilst she was sleeping, it seemed to her that she was brought with some other women into a most beautiful church. At the altar stood a man clothed in priestly vestments, as if ready to celebrate Mass. Looking over his shoulder, he beckoned to Christina to come to him. And when she approached with trembling, he held out to her a branch of most beautiful leaves and flowers saying: "Receive this, my dear, and offer it to the lady." At the same time he pointed out to her a lady like an empress sitting on a dais not far from the altar. Curtsying to her, she held out the branch which she had received. And the lady, taking the branch from Christina's hand, gave back to her a twig and said, "Take care of it for me"; and then added as a question: "How is it with you?" She said: "Ill, my lady: they all hold me up to ridicule[1] and straiten me from all sides.[2] Among those that suffer there is none like me. Hence I cannot stop crying and sobbing from morning till night." "Fear not," she said. "Go now, since I will deliver you from their hands[3] and bring you to the brightness of day." So she withdrew, full of joy as it seemed to her, carrying in her right hand the little branch of blossoms. And where she had to go down, there lay Burthred prostrate on the ground swathed in a black cape with his face turned downwards. And as soon as he saw her passing by he stretched out his hand to seize her and hold her fast. But she, gathering her garments about her and clasping them close to her side, for they were white and flowing, passed him untouched. And as she

The Life of Christina of Markyate, A Twelfth Century Recluse (Oxford: Clarendon Press, 1959).

escaped from him, he followed her with star-ing eyes, groaning horribly, and struck his head with repeated blows on the pavement to show his rage.

Meanwhile, the maiden looked closely in front of her, and saw an upper chamber, lofty and quiet, which could be reached only by a series of steps, steep and difficult for anyone wishing to climb. Christina had a great desire to climb up, but as she hesitated on account of its difficulty, the queen whom she had seen just a short time before helped her, and so she mounted to the upper chamber. And as she sat there enjoying the beauty of the place, behold, the aforesaid queen came and laid her head in her lap as if she wished to rest, with her face turned away. This turning away of her face was a source of disquiet to Christina, and not daring to speak, she said inwardly: "O, if only I were allowed to gaze upon your face." Straightway the empress tuned her face to-wards her and said to her with winning kind-ness: "You may look now; and afterwards when I shall bring both you and Judith also into my chamber, you can gaze to your full content." After this vision she awoke and found her pillow wet with tears, so that she was convinced that as the tears she dreamed she had shed were real, so were the rest of the things which she had dreamed. From that moment you could see she was completely changed, and the immense joy which filled her at the thought of her freedom was displayed for all to see in the cheerfulness of her coun-tenance.

Meantime she sought and found an oppor-tunity of talking with Sueno, the sharer of her secrets, being unable to withhold from him this new source of gladness. . . .

As the obstinacy of the aforesaid people could not be remedied, Sueno prayed to Christ day and night for the afflicted maiden's deliverance. And at last his prayers and tears were heard.[4] For one day whilst he was stand-ing at the altar to say Mass, a voice was heard

saying to him: "Fear not, Sueno: the woman for whom you have prayed I will make free. And with your own eyes you shall see her and with your lips you shall speak to her when she is free, and your heart shall rejoice." After this the voice was silent. In the meantime, how-ever, the maiden was not spared any suffering, nay every day increasingly stringent steps were taken to prevent her from gaining her liberty. But the time was not far off when the divine promise would be fulfilled, and in this one can see how great was her prudence and fortitude. [. . .]

The longed-for day arrived: after her par-ents had gone to the country, Christina went out towards the river, carefully scanning the meadow to see if her accomplice was there. As he was nowhere to be seen, she put it down to his laziness and set off for the church of Our Lady the Virgin to receive Sueno's permission to depart. But not finding him, she did all the other things for which she had come, that is, she prayed to God that her companion would come quickly and that the journey on which she was embarking would be successful. Then she went to her aunt's house, whose affection for her, gained by giving presents, was such that far from betraying her niece, she would expedite her escape. Hence it was that under her eye, so to speak, she wandered that day where she liked, free from the vigilance of the others. When she complained about the late coming of her companion, she was soothed by the sympathy of her aunt. And with her eyes fixed all the time on the meadow beyond the river, fearing the return of her parents at any minute, she went out again to the church of Blessed Mary. On her way she met the reeve of the town accompanied by some citizens. And he took her by the mantle and entreated her to tell him whether she intended to run away. And she smiled and said: "Yes." "When?" said he. "Today," she replied. So when he let her go, she entered the church. And, falling on her face, she prayed with great sorrow in her heart: "O Lord my God, my only hope, the searcher-out of hearts and feelings,[5] whom alone I wish to please, is it Thy pleasure that I should be deprived of my wish?[6] If Thou deliver me not this day, I shall be left in the world, anxious about worldly things and how to please my husband.[7] My one desire, as Thou knowest, is to please Thee alone and to be united to Thee for all time without end. But whether this be Thy decision will become clear if today Thou drive me from my father's house and from my relatives,[8] nevermore to return. For it is better for me never to leave it than to return like a dog to its vomit.[9] But Thou seest what is more profitable for me: I wish not my will, but Thine to come to pass for ever. Blessed be Thy name for evermore.[10] When she had said this, she rose and left the church.

And, scanning the meadow beyond the river once more and not seeing the man she longed for, she turned her steps homeward and sat down amongst her mother's servants, sad at heart and worn out with disappointment. She was already beginning to lose hope, when suddenly something inside her, like a small bird full of life and joy, struck her inward parts with its fluttering. And she felt it flying upwards towards her throat and forming these words: "Theodora, arise. Why are you so slow? Behold, Loric is here" (for this was the boy's name). Astonished at the unusual voice, she trembled and glanced round to see if those sitting with her had heard it. And when she saw them all busy about their tasks, she jumped up immediately, full of trust in the Lord. And secretly taking masculine garb which she had got ready beforehand in order to disguise herself as a man, she went out swathed in a long cloak that reached to her heels. But when her sister Matilda saw her hasting out, for she recognized her from her clothes, she followed behind her. Christina, noticing this, pretended that she was going to the church of Our Blessed Lady. But, as she walked, one of the sleeves of the man's garment which she was hiding beneath her cloak slipped to the ground whether through carelessness or by design I do not know. And when Matilda saw it, she said. "What is this, Theodora, that you are trailing on the ground?" But she replied with an innocent look: "Sister dear, take it with you when you go back to the house for it is getting in my way." And she handed over to her a veil and her father's keys, adding: "And these too, sweetheart, so that if our father returns in the meantime and wishes to take something from the chest, he will not get angry because the keys are missing." And when she had allayed Matilda's suspicions with these words, she sallied forth as if she were going towards the monastery, and then turned her steps towards the meadow.

And making herself known by raising her finger to her forehead, she got both her companion and the horses. And seizing hold of one of them, she paused, covered with embarrassment. Why delay, fugitive? Why do you respect your feminine sex? Put on manly courage and mount the horse like a man. At this she put aside her fears and, jumping on the horse as if she were a youth and setting spurs to his flanks, she said to the servant: "Follow me at a distance: for I fear that if you ride with me and we are caught, they will kill you." It was about nine in the morning; and about three in the afternoon they reached Flamstead, having covered over thirty miles in that time. There[11] she was welcomed with joy by Alfwen the venerable anchoress, and on the same day she put on the religious habit, and she who had been accustomed to wearing silk dresses and luxurious furs in her father's house was now covered with a rough garment. Hidden out of sight in a very dark chamber hardly large enough, on account of its size, to house her, she remained carefully concealed there for a long time, finding great joy in Christ. And on that very day she took for her reading five verses from the thirty-seventh psalm, of which the first runs: "Lord, all my desire is before thee."[12]. . . In the meantime her parents had returned from the hermitage, and when they could find their daughter neither at home nor among the recluses of Huntingdon nor at the monastery of Our Lady, they came to the conclusion that she had run away. But where she had gone passed their comprehension. So they swiftly despatched search parties along all the roads that led to Huntingdon with orders to pursue and catch her and to bring her home in disgrace, killing anyone whom they might find in her company. Whilst some of them went raging in one direction, others in another, her husband Burthred, suspecting that she had taken refuge with Roger the hermit, went thither and, making careful inquiries from one of his disciples whether he knew of any woman there, offered him two shillings to disclose where she was. With indignation the man replied to him: "Who do you think you are, expecting to find a woman here at this hour? It is with the greatest difficulty that a woman is allowed here even in broad daylight and accompanied. And you look for a girl here before daybreak?" Hearing this, he hurried off to Flamstead to speak with the venerable Alfwen and got this answer. "Stop, my son, stop imagining that she is here with us. It is not our custom to give shelter to wives who are running away from their husbands." The man, deluded in this way, departed, resolved never to go on such an errand again.

That very day, whilst Roger was sitting at his table to take his meal, about three in the afternoon his servant said to him: "That fellow who came here today before dawn looking for a girl did not know you very well." "Who was it?" he asked. "I don't know," the servant replied, "but he came from Huntingdon and was looking for some girl of noble family who, so he told me, had run away from her father and her husband." Then Roger gave a sigh and ordered the table to be cleared, and went fasting into his chapel, where day and night, giving himself up to laments and tears, he neither ate nor drank until, worn out with sorrow, he sank on his couch and said: "I know, O Lord almighty and most rigorous judge, that Thou wilt claim her soul at my hands.[13] For I knew that she had a good will, but I was unwilling to give her my help when she asked for it: and now some fellow, at the instigation of the devil, having cunningly gained her confidence, has abducted and ruined her whilst she was off her guard." And as he could find no rest as long as he was ignorant of what had happened to Christina, he prayed without ceasing to the Lord to give him a sign.

After some days, one of the servants of his house, named Ulfwine, set out, as was his custom, to take counsel with the venerable Alfwen: and hearing from her about the arrival and concealment of Christina, returned to tell the whole story to his master Roger. When Roger heard it, he broke out into joyful thanks to the Lord and said to Ulfwine: "This day you have called me back from the grave. May the Lord who made heaven and earth be blessed out of Syon."[14] . . .

After Christina had spent two years at Flamstead, it was necessary for her to go elsewhere. And whilst her departure was being prepared, the sound of virgins singing was heard by Roger's two companions, Leofric and Acio his friend, as they were rendering their due praises to God. They wondered what it was and, being enchanted by the melody, they did not sing alternately, as was their custom, but sang the same verse in unison. At the end of the verse they kept silent and listened to the following verse being sung to a sweet melody by the opposite choir. Quite often a whole psalm would be sung completely by the men and the maidens in this way. They spent much time trying to find out the meaning of this, and finally it was partially revealed to Roger in prayer. He called Acio and Leofric to him immediately and said to them: "Get yourselves ready and make certain that you are found worthy of the visitation of God. For I am certain that God will soon visit this place, sending hither something which He much loves. What it is I cannot tell. All I know is, that it is something dearer to Him perhaps than us sinners." A few days later, whilst Roger was recalling the discomfort that Christina suffered at Flamstead, not only with patience but with joy, and judging from these and her other qualities that she was deeply rooted and grounded in the love of God,[15] he decided that he would no longer deny her his assistance. And so he had her cell brought near his in spite of Alfwen's opposition. All the same he would not consent to see her or to speak with her, but only indirectly through Acio, in order that there might be no excuse for Alfwen to accuse him before the bishop of being a cause of dissension. Nevertheless they saw each other the same day; and it happened in this way. The virgin of God lay prostrate in the old man's chapel, with her face turned to the ground. The man of God stepped over her with his face averted in order not to see her. But as he passed by he looked over his shoulder to see how modestly the handmaid of Christ had composed herself for prayer, as this was one of the things which he thought those who pray ought to observe. Yet she, at the same instant, glanced upwards to appraise the bearing and deportment of the old man, for in these she considered that some trace of his great holiness was apparent. And so they saw each other, not by design and yet not by chance, but, as afterwards became clear, by the divine will. For if they had not had a glimpse of each other, neither would have presumed to live with the other in the confined space of that cell: they would not have dwelt together: they would not have been stimulated by such heavenly desire, nor would they have attained such a lofty place in heaven.

The fire, namely, which had been kindled by the spirit of God and burned in each one of them cast its sparks into their hearts by the grace of that mutual glance; and so made one in heart and soul[16] in chastity and charity in Christ, they were not afraid to dwell together under the same roof. . . . Yet they acted with circumspection in not letting this become known, for they feared scandal to their inferiors and the fury of those who were persecuting the handmaid of Christ. Near the chapel of the old man and joined to his cell was a room which made an angle where it joined. This had a plank of wood placed before it and was so concealed that to anyone looking from outside it would seem that no one was present within, since the space was not bigger than a span and a half. In this prison, therefore, Roger placed his happy companion. In front of the door he rolled a heavy log of wood, the weight of which was actually so great that it could not be put in its place or taken away by the recluse. And so, thus confined, the handmaid of Christ sat on a hard stone until Roger's death, that is, four years and more, concealed even from those who dwelt together with Roger. O what trials she had to bear of cold and heat, hunger and thirst, daily fasting! The confined space would not allow her to wear even the necessary clothing when she was cold. The airless little enclosure became stifling when she was hot. Through long fasting, her bowels became contracted and dried up. There was a time when her burning thirst caused little clots of blood to bubble up from her nostrils. But what was more unbearable than all this was that she could not go out until the evening to satisfy the demands of nature. Even when she was in dire need, she could not open the door for herself, and Roger usually did not come till late. So it was necessary for her to sit quite still in the place, to suffer torments, and to keep quiet,[17] because if she wished Roger to come to her, she had to summon him either by calling or knocking. But how could she do this from her hiding-place when she dared hardly breathe? For she was afraid that someone else besides Roger might be near and, hearing her breathing, would discover her hiding-place. And she would rather die in the cell than make her presence known to anyone at that time. . . .

She bore all these daily anxieties and troubles with the calm sweetness of divine love; she prayed earnestly in those moments at night when she was free to devote herself to prayer and contemplative meditation, just as her friend Roger had trained her, first by word, then by example. . . . No day passed without his taking her into his chapel for this purpose. O how many tears of heavenly desire did they shed: on what rare delicacies of inward joy were they feasted!

At first they were haunted by the fear, and a deep one at that (which spoilt their joy), that if by chance Christina were found in his company she might be snatched away on the orders of the bishop and handed over to her husband to do as he liked: for the old enemy did not stop importuning these two, and any others he could associate with them, to discover where she was. Therefore she prayed much for Christ's mercy on this matter. And not without effect. For on the day of Our Lord's annunciation, whilst Christina was sitting on her stone and giving anxious thought to the senseless behaviour of her persecutors, the fairest of the children of men[18] came to her through the locked door, bearing in His right hand a cross of gold. At His appearance the maiden was terrified, but He put her fears at rest with this comforting assurance: "Fear not," He said: "for I have not come to increase your fears, but to give you confidence. Take this cross, therefore, and hold it firmly, slanting it neither to right nor left. Always hold it straight, pointing upwards: and remember that I was the first to bear the same cross. All who wish to travel to Jerusalem must carry this cross." Having said this, He held out the cross to her, promising that after a short time

He would take it back again from her. And then He vanished. When Christina recounted this experience to Roger, the man of God, he understood its meaning and began to weep for joy, saying: "Blessed be God, who succours His lowly ones at all times." And he said to the maiden in English: "Rejoice with me, myn sunendaege dohter," that is, my Sunday daughter, because just as much as Sunday excels the other days of the week in dignity so he loved Christina more than all the others whom he had begotten or nursed in Christ. "Rejoice with me," he said, "for by the grace of God your trials will soon be at an end. For the meaning is this: the cross which you have received as a token will shortly be taken from you." And it happened as the man of God had foretold.

Two days later, that is, on the 27th of March, the day on which the Redeemer of the world rose from the dead,[19] Burthred came to Roger's cell with his two brothers, one a canon, the other a layman, humbly asking to be granted pardon. For he was aware, and he admitted it, that he had gravely sinned against him, and especially against Christ's handmaid Theodora. And now he came, he said, to release her from her marriage vows and to submit himself to the guidance of the old man. So, he declared, had it been enjoined upon him by the queen of the world, Mary mother of God, who two nights before had appeared to him in a terrifying vision, harshly reproaching him for his needless persecution of the sacred maiden. Roger, considering that the two persons who accompanied him had little public standing, wisely offered and obtained a few days' respite whilst he himself thought over the matter and whilst Burthred produced other witnesses. At the end of the period Burthred returned and according to the injunction which he had received, released his wife, placing his right hand in the right hand of Roger and promising and confirming her release in the presence of the following priests, namely Burthred who had married them, Robert, dean of Huntingdon,[20] and Ralph of Flamstead, and before five hermits who lived with Roger. After this the man of God felt more safe: and taking heart from the manifold virtues which he had proved Christina possessed, he conceived the idea of leaving her as successor to his hermitage. On this point he sometimes spoke with her. And though she feared that this would be beyond her capacities, she did not at once refuse, nor did she give her consent: she acted in her usual manner and placed both this and the charge of herself in the hands of the Lord[21] and the Virgin Mary. Wherefore a wonderful thing, more wonderful than any wonder, happened. For once when she was at prayer and was shedding tears through her longing for heaven, she was suddenly rapt above the clouds even to heaven, where she saw the queen of heaven sitting on a throne and angels in brightness seated about her. Their brightness exceeded that of the sun by as much as the radiance of the sun exceeds that of the stars. Yet the light of the angels could not be compared to the light which surrounded her who was the mother of the Most High. What think you then was the brightness of her countenance which outshone all the rest? Yet as she gazed first at the angels and then at the mistress of the angels, by some marvellous power she was better able to see through the splendour that encompassed the mistress than through that which shone about the angels, though the weakness of human sight finds brighter things harder to bear. She saw her countenance therefore more clearly than that of the angels; and as she gazed upon her beauty the more fixedly and was the more filled with delight as she gazed, the queen turned to one of the angels standing by and said: "Ask Christina what she wants, because I will give her whatever she asks."

Now Christina was standing quite close to the queen and clearly heard her speaking to the angel. And falling downwards to the ground, she saw in one flash the whole wide world. But above all else she turned her eyes towards Roger's cell and chapel which she saw beneath her, shining brilliantly, and she said: "I wish to have that place to dwell in." "She shall certainly have it," replied the queen, "and even more would gladly be given if she wanted it." From then on, therefore, she knew that she would follow Roger as the tenant of that place.

NOTES

1. Cf. Apoc. 2.23.
2. Cf. Ps. 77.30
3. 1 Cor. 7.34.
4. Ps. 6.9.
5. Cf. Apoc. 2.23.
6. Cf. Ps. 77.30.
7. 1 Cor. 7.34.
8. Gen. 24.40.
9. Prov. 26.11
10. Ps. 71.17.
11. The hermitage of Alfwen should not be coupled with the Priory of Nuns "St. Giles of the Wood," founded there in the time of King Stephen by Roger de Toney (Dugdale, iv. 299–302).
12. Ps. 37.10.
13. Cf. Gen. 9.5.
14. Ps. 133.3.
15. Eph. 3.17.
16. Acts 4.32.
17. Cf. *Verba Seniorum*, i. 190 (*PL* 73, 801): 'Tu sede, tu tace, tu sustine.'
18. Ps. 44.3.
19. i.e. 27 March, the date usually assigned in medieval calendars for the resurrection.
20. A Robert, priest of Huntingdon, witnessed the agreement between Autti [Christina's father] and the abbot of Ramsey about the church of Shillington between 1114 and 1123; *Cast. de Ramesia*, i. 138 and 139. He also appears on pp. 135–6.
21. Ps. 54.23.

HILDEGARD OF BINGEN   (1098–1179; Germany)

The Visions of St. Hildegarde: Extracts from the SCIVIAS

Translated by Francesca Maria Steele

PREFACE[1]

Behold in the forty-third year of my age, while with a trembling effort and in great fear I fixed my gaze upon a celestial vision, I saw a very great splendour, from which a voice from Heaven came to me saying: "O fragile man, ashes of ashes and dust of dust, say and write that thou seest and hearest.

"But because thou art timid in speaking, and simple in expounding, and unlearned in writing these things, say and write them not according to the speech of man, nor according to the human intellect and will, but according to that which thou seest and hearest in celestial matters from above, in the wonderful things of God.

"In declaring these things, act even as one who hears the words of his preceptor, and in receiving and publishing them, (he being willing) gives them out according to the purport of his speech.

"Thus, oh man! do thou therefore speak what thou hearest and seest, and write these things not according to thyself, nor according to another man, but according to the desire of seeing, knowing, and setting down all things according to the secrets of their mysteries."

And again I heard a voice from Heaven, saying to me: "Tell these wonderful things and write them, taught in this manner, and say:

"'It happened in the year 1141 of the Incarnation of the Son of God, Jesus Christ, when I was forty-two years and seven months old,

that a fiery light of the greatest brilliancy coming from the opened heavens, poured into all my brain, and kindled in my heart and my breast a flame, that warms but does not burn, as the sun heats anything over which he casts his rays.'"

And suddenly I knew and understood the explanation of the Psalter, the Gospels and other Catholic books of the Old and the New Testaments, but not the interpretation of the text of the words, nor the division of the syllables, nor did I understand the cases and the tenses.

But from my girlhood, that is to say from the fifteenth year, I felt in myself in a wonderful way the power of the mysteries of secret and wonderful visions. Nevertheless I showed these things to no one except a few religious people, living in the same way as I was. In the meantime, till God wished His favours to be manifested, I repressed them in quiet silence.

But I saw these visions not in dreams, nor sleeping, nor in frenzy, nor with the eyes of my body, neither did I hear them with my exterior ears, nor in hidden places did I perceive them, but watching them, and looking carefully in an innocent mind, with the eyes and ears of the interior man, in open places, did I perceive them according to the Will of God.

In what way this may be, it is difficult to explain to the carnal man. But when my girlhood was passed, when I had arrived at the

Francesca Maria Steele, *The Life and Visions of St. Hildegarde* (London: Heath, Cranton and Ousely, 1914).

aforesaid age of perfect strength, I heard a voice from Heaven saying: "I am the living and obscure Light, illuminating one[2] whom I desired, and whom I sought out according to what pleased me in her wonderful gifts, beyond those of the ancients who saw many secrets in Me, but I humbled her to the dust lest she should be elated.

"The world had no joy nor pleasure in her, nor recreation in the things that pertained to her, and I delivered her, fearing and trembling in her labours, from obstinate presumption. For in the marrow of her bones and in the veins of her flesh, she was aching, having her mind and judgment bound, so that no security dwelt in her and she judged herself culpable in all things. For I guarded her heart from danger lest her mind should be elated by pride and vain-glory, but rather that she should feel fear and grief than joy or wanton pleasure in all these things.

"Then she considered in her mind, where she could find some one in My love who would run in the way of salvation. And she found such an one[3] and loved him, recognizing what a faithful man he was, like to herself in that part of his work which concerned Me. And holding fast to him, she laboured together with him in all these matters, in the high and earnest endeavour that My hidden miracles should be revealed.

"And this man did not exalt himself above her, but yielded to her with many sighs in the height of that humility which he obtained, and in the intention of a good will. Thou, therefore, oh man, who receivest these things not in the inquietude of deception, but in the straightforward purity of simplicity, for the manifestation of hidden things, write what thou seest and hearest."

But I, although I had seen and heard these things, nevertheless because of the doubt and bad opinion and divers remarks of men, refused for a long time the duty of writing, not in obstinacy but in humility, until I fell on a bed of sickness, cast down by the scourge of God, until at length I was compelled to write by many infirmities.

By the evidence of a certain noble girl[4] of good morals, and of that man[5] whom as beforesaid I had secretly sought and found, I applied my hand to write. While I did this, feeling the deep profundity of the explanation of the books as I said above, and the strength I received raising me from my sick-bed, at the end of ten years I had with difficulty finished this work. But in the days of Henry, Archbishop of Mainz, and Conrad, the Roman Emperor, and Kuno, Abbot of Mount St. Disibode, under Pope, Eugenius III, these visions and words were completed. And I said and wrote them not according to the curious invention of my heart, nor of any man, but as I saw, heard, and perceived them in a heavenly way, though the secret mysteries of God. And again I heard a voice from Heaven saying to me, "Cry aloud therefore, and write thus."

NOTES

1. Migne, *Pat. Lat.* vol. cxcvii, p. 383 et seq.
2. St. Hildegard herself. See *Acta Sanctae Hildegardis*, p. 15 (Migne).
3. The Monk Volmar.
4. The nun Richarda, daughter of the Margrave of Stada.
5. He was her director. See Migne, *Acta*, p. 16.

VISION II (from Book II)[1]

Of the Blessed Trinity

Then I saw a most splendid light, and in that light, the whole of which burnt in a most beautiful, shining fire, was the figure of a man of a sapphire colour, and that most splendid light poured over the whole of that shining fire, and the shining fire over all that splendid light, and that most splendid light and shining fire over the whole figure of the man, appearing one light in one virtue and power. And again I heard that living Light saying to me: This is the meaning of the mysteries of God, that it may be discerned and understood discreetly what that fulness may be, which is without beginning and to which nothing is wanting, who by the most powerful strength planted all the rivers of the strong (places). For if the Lord is wanting in His own strength, what then would His work be?

Certainly vain, and so in a perfect work is seen who was its maker. On which account thou seest this most splendid Light, which is without beginning and to Whom nothing can be wanting: this means the Father, and in that figure of a man of a sapphire colour, without any spot of the imperfection of envy and iniquity, is declared the Son, born of the Father, according to the Divinity before all time, but afterwards incarnate according to the humanity, in the world, in time. The whole of which burns in a most beautiful, shining fire, which fire without a touch of any dark mortality shows the Holy Spirit, by Whom the same only-begotten Son of God was conceived according to the flesh, and born in time of the Virgin, and poured forth the light of true brightness upon the world.

But that splendid Light pours forth all that shining fire, and that shining fire all that splendid Light, and the splendid shining light of the fire, the whole of the figure of the man, making one Light existing in one strength and power: this is because the Father, Who is the highest equity, but not without the Son nor the Holy Spirit, and the Holy Spirit who is the kindler of the hearts of the faithful, but not without the Father and the Son, and the Son who is the fulness of virtue, but not without the Father and the Holy Spirit, are inseparable in the majesty of the Divinity; because the Father is not without the Son, neither the Son without the Father, nor the Father and the Son without the Holy Spirit, neither the Holy

Spirit without them, and these three Persons exist one God in one whole divinity of majesty: and the unity of the Divinity lives inseparable in the three Persons, because the Trinity is not able to be divided, but remains always inviolable without any change, for the Father is declared through the Son, and the Son through the birth of creatures, and the Holy Spirit through the same Son, Incarnate.

How? It is the Father Who before all ages begat the Son, the Son, through Whom all things were made in the beginning of creatures, by the Father, and the Holy Spirit Who appeared in the form of a dove, in the baptism of the Son of God in the end of the ages.[2]

Whence never let man forget to invoke Me as One God in three Persons, because these things are shown to man, that he may burn more ardently in My love, when for love of him I sent My own Son into the world, as My beloved John testified, saying: "In this appeared the Love of God to us, because He sent His only begotten Son into the world that we might live through Him. In this is love, not as if we had loved God, but because He first loved us, and sent His Son as a propitiation for our sins" (1 *John iv.*).

Why so? Because in this way God loved us; another salvation has sprung up, than that which we had in the creation, when we were heirs of innocence and of sanctity, because the Father above showed His love, when we in our peril were placed in punishment, sending His Word, Who alone among the sons of men was perfect in holiness, into the darkness of this world, where that same Word, doing all good works, led them back to life through His meekness, who were cast out by the malice of transgression, nor were they able to return to that holiness which they had lost.

Why so? Because through that fountain of life came the paternal love of the embrace of God, which educated us to life, and in our dangers was our help, and is the most deep and beautiful light teaching us repentance.

In what way? God mercifully remembered His great work and His most precious pearl, man, I say, whom He formed from the dust of the earth, and into whom He breathed the breath of life. In what manner? He taught (us) how to live in repentance whose efficacy will never perish, because the crafty serpent deceived man by tempting him through pride, but God cast him down into repentance which brings forth humility, which the devil neither knew nor made, because he was ignorant of how to rise to a just life.

Thence this salvation of love did not spring from us, because we did not know, neither were we able to love God unto salvation, but because He the Creator and Lord of all so loved the world, that He sent His Son for its salvation, the Prince and Saviour of the faithful, Who washed and dried our wounds, and from Him also came that most sweet medicine, from which all the good things of salvation flow.

Wherefore, O man, do thou understand that no shadow (*instabilitas*) of change touches God. For the Father is the Father, the Son is the Son, and the Holy Spirit is the Holy Spirit, three Persons living inseparably in the unity of the Divinity.

In what manner? There are three virtues in a stone, three in a flame and three in a word. How? In the stone is the virtue of moisture, the virtue of palpability, and the power of fire, for it has the virtue of moisture lest it should be dissolved and broken in pieces, but it shows its palpable comprehension when used as a habitation and a defence, and it has the virtue of fire so that it may be heated and consolidated to its hardness. And this virtue of moisture signifies the Father, Whose power is never dried up nor finished; and the palpable comprehension means the Son, Who being born of the Virgin is able to be touched and comprehended, and the fiery power signifies the Holy Spirit Who is the kindler and the illuminator of the hearts of faithful men.

How is this? As man frequently attracts into his body the damp power of the stone, and falling ill is weakened, so man who through the instability of his thoughts will fear to look up to the Father, loses his faith: and in the palpable comprehension of the stone is shown that men make a habitation with it for themselves, as a defence against their enemies, thus the Son of God, Who is the true Corner-stone, is the habitation of the faithful, protecting them from evil spirits.

But as the shining fire illuminates darkness, burning those things upon which it had been lying, thus the Holy Spirit drives away infidelity, taking away all the foulness of iniquity. And in the same way that these three powers are in one stone, so the true Trinity is in one Deity.

Again, as the flame in one fire has three powers, so the One God is in Three Persons. In what manner? For in the flame abides splendid light, innate vigour, and fiery heat, but it has splendid light that it may shine, innate vigour that it may flourish, and fiery heat that it may burn. Thence consider in the splendid light, the Father Who in His paternal love sheds His light upon the faithful, and in that innate vigour of the splendid flame in which that same flame shows its power, understand the Son, Who took flesh from the Virgin, in which the Divinity declared His wonders, and in the fiery heat, behold the Holy Spirit, Who gently kindles the hearts and minds of the faithful.

But where there is neither a splendid light, nor innate vigour, nor fiery heat, there no flame is discerned: thus where neither the Father, nor the Son, nor the Holy Spirit is worshipped, there neither is He worthily venerated.

Therefore as in one flame these three powers are discerned; thus in the unity of the Divinity, three Persons are to be understood.

So also as three powers are to be noted in a word, thus the Trinity in the Unity of the

Divinity is to be considered. In what way? In a word there is sound, power and breath. For it has sound that it may be heard, power that it may be understood, breath that it may be perfected.

In the sound, note the Father, Who with unerring power makes manifest all things. In the power, note the Son, Who is wonderfully begotten of the Father; and in the breath, note the Holy Spirit, Who breathes where He will and all things are accomplished.

But where no sound is heard, there neither power works, nor breath is raised, thence neither there is the Word to be understood; so also the Father, the Son, and the Holy Spirit are not to be divided from themselves, but their work is performed unanimously.

Then as these three things are in one word, so also the supernal Trinity is in the supernal Unity: and as in a stone there is neither the virtue of moisture, without palpable comprehension, nor fiery power, nor palpable comprehension without the power of moisture, and the fiery vigour of a shining fire; neither the vigour of the shining fire, without the power of moisture and palpable comprehension; and as in a flame there is not, neither can there be caused, a splendid light without innate vigour and fiery heat, neither innate vigour without splendid light and fiery heat, neither fiery heat without splendid light and innate vigour, so in a word there neither is nor can be made a sound without power and breath, neither power without sound and breath, neither breath without sound and power, but these in their work are indivisibly inherent in each other, so also these three Persons of the supernal Trinity exist inseparably in the majesty of Divinity, neither are they divided from each other.

Thus understand, O man, One God in three Persons. But thou in the foolishness of thy mind thinkest God to be so impotent, that it is not possible to Him to subsist truly in three Persons, but to be able only to consist of One, when neither dost thou see a voice to consist without three. Why so? God is certainly in three Persons, one true God first and last.

But the Father is not without the Son, neither the Son without the Father, nor the Father nor the Son without the Holy Spirit, nor the Holy Spirit without them, because these three Persons are inseparable in the Unity of the Divinity. As a word sounds from the mouth of a man, but not the mouth without the word, nor the word without life. And where remains the word? In the man. Whence does it go out? From the man. In what way? From the living man.

Thus is the Son in the Father, Whom the Father for the salvation of men sitting in darkness, sent to earth, conceived in the Virgin by the Holy Spirit. Which Son as He was only begotten in His divinity, so He was only begotten in virginity, and as He is the only Son of the Father, so He is the only Son of His mother, because as the Father begat Him before all time, so His Virgin Mother bore Him only in time, because she remained a Virgin after His birth.

Thence, O man, understand in these three Persons Thy God, Who created thee in the power of His divinity, and Who redeemed thee from perdition. Be unwilling therefore to forget thy Creator as Solomon says, "Remember thy Creator in the days of thy youth, before the time of thy affliction shall come, and the years draw nigh of which thou sayest: They do not please me" (*Eccles. xii*). What does this mean? To remember in thy intellect Him Who made thee, when, for example, in the days of thy foolish confidence, thou thoughtest it possible that thou shouldst ascend on high, casting thyself into the depths, and when standing in prosperity falling into extreme afflictions.

For the life which is in thee strives always that it may be perfected, until that time when it shall appear perfect.

In what way? An infant advances from its first birth until (it attains) its perfect stature, forsaking the petulancy of manners of foolish youth, only when providing solicitously with great care, that which may be used for himself in his business, which he never did when swayed by the inconstancy of foolish youth.

Thus does the faithful man, he leaves the manners of infancy, and he mounts up to the height of the virtues, persevering in their strength, forsaking the exaltation of his covetousness, which in the madness of vices increased, and he meditates carefully in poverty what may be useful to him after he has forsaken the manners of youth.

Thence, O man! thus embrace thy God in the courage of thy strength, before the Judge of thy works shall come, when all things shall be manifested, lest anything hidden should be left, when those times come which in their duration shall not fail.

Concerning which things, but murmuring thou sayest in thy human thought: "They do not please me, neither do I understand whether they are meritorious or not, because in this my human mind is always doubtful, for when a man does good works he is anxious whether they please God or not. And when he does evil he fears concerning the remission which is of salvation." But he who sees with watchful eyes, and hears with attentive ears, offers an embrace to these mystic words of mine which emanate from me, living.

XXXVIII[3]

And again I heard a voice from Heaven teaching me these words: Now praise be to God in His work, that is man, for whose reparation He fought an exceeding great battle, and whom He deigned to raise to Heaven, that together with the angels, he may praise His face, Who is true God and man. But this omnipotent God in His mercy deigned to anoint with oil the poor little woman through

whom this writing is published, because she lived without any confidence in herself, nor had she any knowledge of the composition of the writings, which the Holy Spirit proposed for the instruction of the Church, and which seemed as it were the walls of a great city.

But from the day of her birth, she was as it were entangled in a net of suffering and illnesses, so that she was vexed with continual pains in all her veins and flesh to the very marrow, nor did it please God that she should be dissolved, because in the interior of her rational soul she saw spiritually certain mystical things of God. But this vision so pierced through all the veins of this woman, that she was often agitated with great weariness, sometimes struggling against this fatigue in depression, sometimes in consolation.

From this she had manners different from those of other men, like an infant who is not yet able to distinguish the behaviour of men. For she appears a servant, with the inspiration of the Holy Spirit, and has an affinity with the air, and so she was so susceptible to this same air, and to the wind, and to rain, and to every kind of tempest, that she never had any confidence in herself, nor any sense of security, otherwise the inspiration of the Holy Spirit would not have dwelt in her so powerfully.

But the Spirit of God in the great strength of His love, sometimes raised her up by this infirmity from death, as by a refreshing dew, so that she was able to live in the world as a servant of God with the inspiration of the Holy Spirit. But Almighty God, Who knew truly all the weariness of the suffering of this woman, deigned to perfect His grace in her, that His love might be glorified in her, and that when her soul should migrate from this world to eternal glory, it should rejoice to be mercifully received and crowned by Him.

But He breathed out the book of life, which is the writing of the Word of God, by Whom every creature appeared, and He gave out this book by no teaching of human knowledge, but through a simple and unlearned woman, as it pleased Him in a wonderful way to do.

Thence, let no man be so audacious as to add anything to this writing, or to take anything away from it, lest he be blotted out from the book of life, and from all happiness under the sun, for these things were brought forth by the inspiration of the Holy Spirit simply. And who should presume otherwise, he sins against the Holy Spirit. And then neither here nor in the future world shall it be forgiven him.

Now again praise be to Almighty God in all His works for ever and ever, because He is the first and the last. But let the faithful receive these words with a devout affection of the heart, because through Him Who is the first and the last, they are brought forth for the usefulness of the faithful.

NOTES

1. *Scivias*, Migne, 450–54.
2. *In fine temporum.*
3. The Book of the Divine Works of a Simple Man, *Liber Divinorum Operum Simplicis Hominis*, pp. 1037–38, ed. Migne, *Patrologia Latina*.

HILDEGARD OF BINGEN

Liturgical Songs

Translated by Barbara L. Grant

ANTIPHON 5: *About the Blessed Virgin Mary*

O most radiant jewel,
Resplendent glory of the sun;
The fountain from the heart of the Father
Has streamed into you:
His own unique Word
Through which he created the primordial
   matter of the world
Which Eve overturned like a whirlwind
The Word fashioned humanity for your sake
   Father
And thus you Mary are that lucid matter
Through whom the Word breathed forth
   everything of value,
Just as it led all creatures into being out of
   primordial matter.

ANTIPHON 6: *About the Blessed Virgin Mary*

Today
He has appeared to us
Through the gate that was hidden and locked,
Because the serpent has suffocated in a woman.
Thus the flower of the Virgin Mary
Radiates illuminated in the first red of daybreak.

ANTIPHON 7: *About the Blessed Virgin Mary*

Because a woman instituted death;
The clear Virgin has abolished it;

Therefore the consummate benediction is
In womanly form,
Beyond all creation
Since God was made human
In a Virgin most sweet and blessed.

ANTIPHON 8: *About the Blessed Virgin Mary*

O budded, greening branch!
You stand as firmly rooted in your nobility
As the dawn advances.
Now rejoice and be glad;
Consider us frail ones worthy
To free us from our destructive ways:
Put forth your hand and
Raise us up.

ANTIPHON 11: *About the Blessed Virgin Mary*

What a great wonder it is
That into the humble form of a woman
The King entered.
God did this,
Because humility rises above everything.
And what great fortune is contained
In this feminine form,
Because the malice that flowed from one
    woman,
This woman has wiped away hereafter;
She has established the sweetest odor of vir-
tues,
And she has honored and adorned heaven
Far more than she earlier disordered the earth.

HYMN 12: *About the Blessed Virgin Mary*

Greetings, noble, glorious and chaste beloved.
You image of purity,
You ground of sanctity,
Pleasing to God.

Certainly a heavenly infusion
Poured into you,
Because the highest Word
In you took on flesh.

You are the radiant white lily
Whom God perceived
Prior to all creation.

You the most beautiful and loveliest;
God so delighted in you that he pressed within
    you
The passionate embrace of his own heat,
So that his own son was suckled by you.

Truly has your body contained joy,
Since out of you every heavenly harmony
    sounded,
Because, Virgin, you carried the son of God,
When your own purity became illuminated in
    God.

Your womb contained joy
Just as the grass was infused with
Greenness, when the dew sank into it;
Therefore Mother everything joyful has been
Created through you.

Now let the whole Church, dawning rose-red,
    break the day in joy
And sound in harmony because of the loveliest
    Virgin
And most praiseworthy Mary, Mother of
    God. Amen.

ANTIPHON 16: *Love Overflows*

Love overflows into all things,
From out of the depths to above the highest
    stars;
And so Love overflows into all best beloved,
    most loving things,
Because She has given to the highest King
The Kiss of Peace.

ST. ELISABETH OF SCHÖNAU (1129–1165; Germany)

Visions—Book Two

Translated by Thalia A. Pandiri

I. Kind is the mercy of our God and richly does he heap his grace on those who love Him. In the abundance of His goodness He has multiplied His consolations upon His handmaid, as the preceding book shows, and behold! His hand is still no less stretched out to console her. For it is not held in check by the muttering of those who think themselves great and disdain all that appears weaker, and who fear not to sneer at the richness of His goodness in her. And yet they should fear that they may hear the rebuke of their master, as did that man who murmured against the master of the house and was told "is thine eye evil, because I am good?"[1] Because in these times the Lord deigns to show His mercy most gloriously in the weak sex, such men are offended and led into sin. But why do they not remember that something similar happened in the days of our fathers? While the men were given over to sluggishness, holy women were filled with the spirit of God, that they might prophesy, govern God's people forcefully, and indeed triumph gloriously over the foes of Israel: so it happened with Olda, Deborah, Judith, Jahel, and other women of this sort. And now, hoping that the account of what the Lord deigned to work in his handmaid after the completion of the first book of Visions will bring some edification to the minds of the humble, we set forth her words, as she related them.[2]

II. But perhaps the reader may be puzzled, because in the first book it was written that the angel said to her[3] she would not again, until the day of her death, see the holy visions she was seeing; yet, in fact, even after the angel had spoken thus, she did see visions similar to the earlier ones. In my judgment, when the angel said holy visions, he meant specifically those glimpses into the secrets of heaven which she had been accustomed to see as if through an open door in the sky, on high holy days and especially on Sundays. For from that time when he spoke those words to her, she ceased altogether to have visions of this particular kind. But in that spot where what seemed like a door had appeared, there continued to be revealed to her an exceeding bright light, in accordance with the words of the angel, who said to her: "Watch steadily and behold a holy light, a celestial light; this is given to you until the end of your life."

III. The vision which the Lord's handmaid saw on the vigil of Pentecost in the beginning of the fourth year of her visitation by the Lord (14 May 1155) she related in the following words:

IV. I was transported in the spirit to what seemed a green and very pleasant meadow, and with me was the angel of the Lord. And I saw something like a marble column that appeared to rise up out of an abyss, up to the high heavens, and it was triangular in shape. One angle was white as snow, the other red, the third was the color of marble. And alongside the lower parts of the column were ten rays of the utmost brilliance, forming a circle, and descending at an angle from the column to the earth. And each of these rays seemed in turn to be resting on a great many white and red rays. And as I was marveling at this vision, the angel spoke to me: "Contemplate carefully what you see." And I said to him, "My lord, tell me, I beg you, what these things signify." And he said, "This column that you see extends down from the throne of God into the abyss, and the three angels represent the Holy Trinity. You see three colors: white, red, and marble. White is the color of Christ's humanity, red represents the Holy Spirit, and the marble color signifies the divinity of the Father. The ten rays that you see are the ten commandments. And, as you see, innumerable rays extend in turn from these, some white, others red. These represent those who observe God's law: the white rays those who have kept themselves chaste and immaculate for the sake of God's law, the red rays those who preferred to shed their own blood for Christ rather than to transgress against God's law. Look up!" And I saw around the top of the column other innumerable rays, half-white and half-red, extending out from it on all sides, and to these rays clung a multitude of others. And as I marvelled in silence at these things, the angel said to me: "These are my companions and fellow-citizens, white in their purity, red in their ardent love for God which burns continually in them. And those who cleave unto them are saints, who enjoy their blessed company." And afterwards he added, "Pay careful heed to these things. For behold, you are already beginning to think these visions of little account. Why, tell me, do you not entrust your visions to writing, as you used to do?" And when I came out of my ecstatic trance and began to return to myself, immediately, as soon as I could draw breath, I said, "Thy mercy, O Lord, reacheth unto heaven; and thy faithfulness reacheth unto the clouds. Thy righteousness is like the great mountains; thy judgments are a great deep. They shall be intoxicated with the bounteousness of thy house; and thou shalt make them drink of the torrent of thy delight. For with thee is the fountain of life: in thy light shall we see light."[4] And I added these words: "Thanks be to you, Jesus Christ, that you have shown me, your unworthy servant, a great and marvelous thing full of mysteries."

V. After these events, on the feast of the blessed precursor of the Lord (John the Baptist) did not neglect to show me his usual kindness. For on the vigil of his nativity, around nones, after most painful suffering of my flesh, he appeared to me in that glory in which I had been accustomed to see him, and I entreated him strenuously that he might help me see the countenance of our Lady, which had been hidden from me longer than usual. And immediately after I uttered this prayer he disappeared; returning to myself, I burst out in his praise: "He is the one of all the powerful and sublime in heaven whom the hand of the Lord blessed in the womb of his mother, by whose virtues we pray as suppliants to be helped." And again I began to struggle more painfully than before, and I heard the angel, who was by my side helping me, respond: "You will remain longer in this crucifixion of pain unless you receive indulgence from your spiritual father." But I was in no way strong enough to make known these words to my sisters, who were around me. So they, thinking that my death was imminent, used their own judgment and sent word to the Lord abbot and he came and recited litanies and prayers over me. But finally, with great difficulty, I formed these words, "Forgive me, father." And when I had received indulgence from him, I immediately felt at peace and entered into ecstasy. And lo, our most glorious Lady with that blessed Precursor appeared walking forth from on high, and she deigned to turn her lovely countenance towards her handmaid. And indeed they conversed with me for quite some time, but their words have fallen from my memory, driven out by my faults.

VI. Again, on St. John's day, after the reading of the Gospel, the man of God deigned to show himself to me. And when I scrupulously commended myself and the whole congregation of brothers and sisters to him, he answered me thus: "Persuade them of this, that through those things that the Lord has worked in you, they may be warned and they may zealously attempt to correct themselves in all things; for the Lord has taken pity on them and will be even more merciful, and in this matter I will be their ready helper." And when he had uttered these words, he removed himself from my sight.

VII. And immediately the angel of the Lord carried me away and we came to a green and pleasant meadow. There I saw three fair maidens, strolling by a stream. They wore dresses that were soiled and no longer white, and their feet were bare and very reddened. And while I was thinking to myself who they might be, and what they might be doing there, all by themselves, they said to me: "Do not be amazed, we are souls, and we were placed under monastic rule, one of us as a child, the other as an adolescent, the third at a more advanced age. And because we seemed among men to be of some merit, we were helped less by the prayers of the faithful after we departed life, than would have been necessary. And so, although we could have been set free in the space of a single year, had the help owed us been given us, now we have been detained here for thirty years. Indeed, we suffer no other punishments, except the terror inspired by three monstrous dogs, who seem to threaten constantly to bite us. But, if you would be willing to ask your abbot to offer the divine sacrifice for the deliverance of our souls and those of all the faithful departed, we hope that we will be set free more quickly and be able to pass over to the joys that have been prepared for us." And when I communicated these things to our sisters, they themselves devotedly gathering together undertook as a group to do bodily penance in their behalf. They also divided up the psalter among them and prayed

to the Lord with the utmost zeal for the deliverance of those souls.

VIII. Enjoined by me, the Lord abbot also came on the next day when the office of the vigil was said, and zealously celebrated the divine office for the faithful departed. Again, at the moment of the sacrifice I was carried to that same meadow and again those same maidens appeared, walking up in a great hurry against the course of that stream. I joined them and asked them eagerly from where they had come and what their names were. One of them answered for all three: "Our story would take long to relate, but briefly, we are from Saxony; my name is Adelheid, she who is next to me is Mechthild, my sister in the flesh as well as in the spirit, and the other is Libista, our spiritual sister." Seeing that they wished no delay, I was unwilling to detain them longer, but I commended myself and our entire congregation to them emphatically, and asked them to remember us when they were received in the company of the saints. As soon as they had benevolently promised to do so, they began to press forward more swiftly. And as they went on their way, an angel of the Lord appeared before them in the guise of a comely youth; leading them, he rushed along before them. And as they drew near to a certain edifice in which I often see the souls of the blessed received, there stepped forth out of that edifice three vēnerable men, each holding a gold thurible in his hand, and each offered incense to each of the maidens. And soon the faces of the maidens and their robes were made whiter than snow by the incense, and thus they were led joyously into that edifice.

IX. After this vision, I remained exhausted with illness until the feast of the apostles. But during the night before the sacred vigil, such an extreme faintness afflicted all my senses that the sisters who were attending me with the greatest concern were waiting for me to die. But the angel of the Lord stood by me the whole night, and the prince of the apostles appeared to me in the great brilliance of his beauty. And I experienced such great delight in gazing upon him that I was compelled to forget the violent seizures that racked my whole body, while the sisters who stood around me could not look upon me without feeling heavy grief. And I remained in that state of violent bodily agitation until about the sixth hour of the following day. A messenger was sent to the lord abbot to tell him about my anguish, and he came to visit me. While he was calling on the Lord in my behalf, and blessing me, finally I went into ecstasy and thus I was able to be at peace. And in this ecstatic trance I saw the blessed apostles Peter and Paul, most gloriously crowned, cloaked in inconceivable brilliance, and bearing palm-branches in their hands. Looking at me, the prince of the apostles said, "What is more pleasing to you, to be tormented thus and delight in gazing upon us, or to do without both the pain and the vision?" And I said to him, "My Lord, if it can be, with God's grace and yours, I desire to endure these sufferings rather than to be deprived of your sweet consolation." "You have spoken well," he said, "and therefore, from this time forth, you will suffer less pain in your visions." I then questioned him, saying "Lord, why, for what reason, have I just experienced such great suffering?" And he replied, "For no other reason have you been made so ill, but that the miracle of your sudden recovery might glorify God all the more. Rise up, therefore, and be healed. Speak, and guard your tongue from idle boasting, and the Lord will give you wisdom and understanding." And immediately, as soon as he said this, I drew breath and said, "Peter, if God commands, loose the chains, you who open the kingdom of heaven to the blessed. St. Paul, apostle, preacher of truth, intercede for us with God, who chose you." And I added, "the Lord put forth his hand and touched my mouth and filled it with the spirit of wisdom and understanding."[5]

And immediately I rose up from my bed and went off, healed, with all my strength completely restored.

X. On the feast day, at mass, with less physical pain than usual I saw again the apostles of Christ, and while the lord abbot was blessing the holy sacrament, I saw it become transformed into the true likeness of flesh and blood. And when we had all received communion and the celebration of the mass was over, one of the two angels whom I had seen assisting at the altar, holding a gold thurible in his hand, rose up to where I saw the apostles, up above. And looking at blessed Peter, I said, "Lord, give us some sign, that we may understand if you deign to care at all for us." And immediately he raised his right hand and made the sign of the cross over us, and then disappeared.

XI. Again on the octave of the apostles, just at the time of the sacred mystery, those same princes appeared to me in their glory and along with them the blessed mother of our savior, but not in her accustomed way. For she kept her face turned away from me as if she were angry, and I felt sad and soon spoke to the blessed Peter, saying, "My lord, what fault have I committed, that I do not deserve to see the countenance of our Lady? And he said, "Because you have become lukewarm in serving her, and do not perform the duty you owe her as you used to do. Now therefore, fulfill that vow you made to her, as devoutly as you can, and ask your abbot to commemorate her in the divine office as he did on the preceding Saturday so as to obtain that which you prayed for with your sisters. He should do this for a second and a third time before the feast of the Assumption, and so you will placate her countenance." We had, in fact, begun to ask in communal prayer for this very thing, that our Lady not deny me her accustomed favor; for, while in the past she had very frequently shown me her glorious countenance even without my undergoing physical suffering, she had now for many days withheld her countenance from me, and we feared that we had by our communal negligence offended her benevolence. On this occasion I vowed to read the psalter seven times in her honor. After this conversation was over and the apostles had disappeared, I began to see in my usual manner and to watch closely the signs the abbot was making over the host, during the canon of the mass. I was waiting to see the transformation of the host. But the angel of the lord said to me, "That which you desire, you cannot see right now, but confess your error and you will see it." He said this because of the vanity of my nocturnal vision.

XII. After this, on the feast of the Translation of St. Benedict, when high mass was beginning in the church of the brothers, I went into ecstasy and saw again in the region of light our Lady with her face averted, as before, and with her was the venerable father of our order. Gazing upon him, I besought him devoutly to deign to intercede and reconcile my Lady to me. But he gave me no response. Yet the angel of the Lord stood by me and consoled me tenderly, saying. "Look, do not be sorrowful about these matters, for very soon you will be consoled by the Lord. Ask your abbot that he not desist from what he has begun, for it will benefit not only you but himself as well; soon, when he celebrates the mass for Mary, you will receive holy communion from the abbot himself." Saying these things, he left, and I came back to myself.

XIII. On the following Saturday while the lord abbot was celebrating the divine office in our chapel, at the beginning of the mass I was led into ecstasy after painful striving. And lo, my Lady deigned to gaze at her handmaid from on high with a serene and most agreeable countenance. And I greeted her, saying, "Hail Mary full of grace, the Lord is with you." And I added, "Most holy Lady, most merciful Lady, queen of heaven, may you deign to show me, a sinner, in what I offended your

grace. For I am ready to correct my error with the greatest goodwill, and to give every satisfaction to regain your mercy." And she answered, "Too much have you neglected me in your heart, nor do you zealously serve me with that devotion you ought to show, and you have been quick to set aside the small measure of the special service you used to render me." And I replied, "Most merciful Lady, if you care at all about that, how gladly would I render you that service!" And I added further, "Most pious Lady, have you any concern about the celebration of this mass?" And she replied, "Truly I say to you, that today there is a very sweet odor in the sight of the Lord." While she was conversing with me, the servers at the altar were singing most devoutly that melody "Hail O radiant one" and when they came to the verse "Pray Virgin that we be made worthy of that celestial bread," she turned to the east and knelt in prayer until the reading of the gospel. Afterwards, turning again toward me she said, "This is my chosen servant, and for the service he has rendered me in your behalf he will be rewarded along with you; in whatever need he may find himself, if he calls to me with all his heart he will find my help, because he has served me today with a contrite and humbled heart."

XIV. On August 1st, on the feast of St. Peter, during the divine office I was transported in the spirit to that abode of the blessed which I am accustomed to see often, and there came to meet me the three sisters I spoke of earlier; along with them was a youth, radiant and most venerable. They gazed upon me with a pleasing and joyous countenance, as if rejoicing in my arrival, and they kept turning to their companion as if asking his permission to address me. And he nodded assent benignly to them and said, "Speak with her and give thanks to her because she has transacted your business well with her abbot." And they said to me, "May the Lord God repay you because you carried out our request well, delivering it to your abbot, and may the Lord thank him, because he helped us much. Now it seems to us that we never suffered grievous toil." And I said to them, "Now therefore repay the sisters, in turn, who are with us, and by whose intercession you have been helped, so that they will deserve to come to a place of spiritual refreshment and repose when they die." And they said, "Most willingly will we pray to our Lord ceaselessly, that this may be accomplished."

XV. Immediately thereafter, the angel of the Lord bore me up into another place of a most charming pleasantness, and he placed me under a tree that was decked all over with the fairest flowers. And I said to him, "Milord, let us rest for a little while in this spot." And he replied, "It is pleasing to me, that you rest." Immediately I sat down on the grass, and I gathered up a handful of the flowers that lay strewn about me on all sides, and pressing them to me I breathed in their marvelously sweet fragrance. And as I desired to linger there longer, I saw coming towards us from afar a most venerable man, and with him were two most beautiful maidens. And my lord, who was standing at my side, said to me, "Look! Our Lord the blessed Peter is approaching." And without delay I stood up and rushed to meet him, and falling to my knees before him as a suppliant I placed myself and my loved ones under his protection. He received my plea kindly and said, "Tell your abbot that blessed Laurence expects a service of him," And I said to him, "And what, my Lord, can he hope for from you?" He replied, "He can hope to receive good from me and my fellow apostles because it is his custom to render us devout obedience." And when St. Peter had withdrawn from my sight, the angel said to me, "Come and I will show you one of the brothers of your monastery." And so he showed me, in the place of refreshment, a certain monk, called Erminricus. He said also that another of our

brothers, Gerardus by name, would soon come to that same place.

XVI. Again, however, the angel bore me to a spot between two mountains and said to me, "Up to this point you have seen the joys and the abodes of the just; now look down at the place and the punishment of the impious." And I saw a great abyss, where the darkness was so thick that because of its density I could not recognize any of those present there. But this I did note, that their punishments surpassed anything one can imagine. And when I asked him, who they were and whether they could ever be set free from that place, he answered that they were the ones who had brought death upon themselves, and that they could never be set free. But around the mountain I saw what seemed to be the most hideous men, and I learned that these were souls to whom it had been granted to go out of that abyss from time to time and rest there for a little while. When I asked about them, what must happen to them, the angel answered me: "This is for the Lord alone to know, what He wishes to do with them on the Day of Judgment."

XVIII. Afterwards he bore me up to a towering mountain and placed me on the mountainside. And as I looked up to the summit, a light so great and brilliant appeared there that I could scarcely bear to look at it. "This is the mountain," the angel said, "that you began to climb three years ago, and this is how far you have come. You will climb the rest of the way, and when you reach the top, you will not regret all your toil."

XVIII. On the feast day of blessed Laurence, I was led to an indescribable height and I heard a great and terrible voice speaking to me out of the heavens: "I have visited you with my spirit, desiring in you to bring my will to fulfillment. I have undertaken this and I will accomplish it, fear not, for I the Lord recognize from the beginning those in whom I delight to dwell. I have chosen you because you were little in your own eyes since you are frail, and I have established you as a sign to those who are stronger than you, and I have worked in you a great miracle. And no one has recognized that I show my goodness not in acknowledging worldly position; rather, he who seeks me with all his heart and loves me, him I love and to him will I show myself. Alas, what will become of those who slander the ones in whom I would dwell? That ancient deceiver has inspired certain men to envy and calumniate those whom I love, that he might deceive and destroy them. Truly I say to you, those who have toiled the most, they will be the most splendid in my sight. No one can grasp the words I speak and have spoken except he who is of me. I the Lord have created man in my image and likeness and I have made him know me, that he might be wiser than all other creatures. But he did not wish to remain in this state; rather he was puffed up by the counsel of the venomous serpent to do his bidding. Thinking he saw that what the serpent proposed was good, man agreed. And he taught him to rise while he fell. And what then? That which man lost through disobeying, Man gained by obeying His father. O man,⁶ listen carefully and understand the words that you hear, and rejoice with me that I have found you and set you up to be my houseservant, and I have blessed you and filled you with light and opened your eyes that you might see, not through ordinary sight but through knowledge of God, what I revealed to you. Now therefore, listen carefully what you must pay back to me, since you have received from me grace untold. You have seen, I say. How have you seen? You have gazed on my secrets, with a more than human sight. And what have I hidden from you? Nothing. In your vision you have seen what seemed to be three figures in a single essence, seated on a divine throne, sharing a single substance and power. And in the center of the throne and around it you beheld the mysteries of God, God's holy ministers rejoicing and uttering benedictions in perfect praise of the Lord. Seeing, you saw in that same vision that I speak of, on the right of that same throne, the renowned queen of heaven crowned with the purest gold and cloaked in bright colors. On the left you saw the holy rood, your redemption, and twenty-four elders seated and falling to worship before the throne of Him who lives forever. And you saw also the holy apostles, the martyrs, the confessors and the virgins, monks and widows, and you were terror-stricken at the sight of all, and you were distressed. Now doubt no more, but trust in the Lord your God, for everything is possible for those who trust in God. These visions and many others you saw in these wicked times, for no other reason but because of the unbelief of many, and to confirm the faith. For this same reason the visions appeared to you at the time of the holy sacrament also. It is proper and necessary to reveal such visions, which come opportunely to confirm the faith of Christendom. For many are called Christians, but few are true Christians desirous of following Him whose name they have taken."

XIX. Then the angel bore me to that great and delightful edifice which I often see, and there among many venerable bishops he pointed one out to me and said, "This is the Lord bishop Ekbert,⁷ your mother's paternal uncle, who has recently arrived here." On another day, when I was in ecstasy, he showed me some places of punishment, and I saw among other things what seemed like an underground cave full of fire and horrible smoke. And as I was looking, there stepped forth from the cave a form that resembled a man; he stood at the mouth of the cave, and a flame that burst forth from within burned him violently. And when I said, "Lord, who is this?" he replied, "This is Theodoric your mother's brother." And I said, terrified, "Oh my Lord, can he never be freed?" And he replied, "He can be set free from the punishments he suffers now, if in his memory and that of all the faithful departed thirty masses and as many vigils are celebrated, and alms are given as many times." And I asked, if he would ever be wholly delivered, and he nodded assent. He showed me further the maternal uncle of my father, the Lord Helid undergoing a grievous torment in his mouth; he said that he was being tortured in this way because of his unbridled utterances. For, although he was a God-fearing man, he used to joke a great deal. And when I was mournful about my kinsmen, the angel said to me, "Why do you wonder that they are tortured thus? They have no one who would offer them a drink." "What drink do they need?" I asked. "They must quench their thirst with hot tears."

XX. It came to pass that seven months after I saw this vision the angel showed me these same kinsmen, freed from the torments in which I had seen them, and my Lord Helid was now fair in form, and in a pleasant place, but not in that perfect consolation of blessed souls; my other kinsman, however, he did not show me thus. And after many days, the angel showed me once more my uncle Theoderic, lying on an arid plain as if he were resting after exhausting toil. And I recognized his form and asked my lord for permission to speak with him; he granted me leave. "O sweetest soul," I said, "I pray you, speak to me, tell me what punishments you now endure." And he answered me, "My torment consists in extreme hunger and thirst." And I questioned him again, "Tell me, I beg you, how can this torment be lifted from you?" And he answered, using both Latin and German words together, "If someone could offer me for forty days the bread of life and the chalice of salvation, he would free me from this torment and I could bear it better." And again I said, "Do not the prayers offered for you, without the divine office, come to your aid?" And he said, "Whatever is offered me besides the bread of life and the chalice of salvation gives me that

nourishment which a famished man derives when he is deprived of bread and wine, but given other things."

XXI. On the day before the feast of blessed Michael, the angel carried me up to a pleasant isle, which seemed to be surrounded by burning water. And I saw a numberless throng of souls walking on the island. I questioned the angel, and he said, "They are souls, and all this night through the intercession of the blessed Michael they rest here." And then I heard a great lamentation around the island, and an exceeding wretched wailing. And when I asked about the soul of Count Rupert, where it was, my guide answered me, "In a place where he endures the most heavy punishments." And when I asked about his deliverance, he gave me no answer. But I heard a resounding voice, coming from I know not where, beside me: "Frequent prayer speeds the deliverance of souls. Ask for prayers, and give alms." And I turned again to my lord and said, "Won't you tell me anything, my lord, that I might bear a message to his wife, who is concerned about him?" And he answered, "Tell her what you have heard."

XXII. Again one day, when my guide was with me, I asked him, "Lord, may it please you to tell me where a certain young cleric is, Gerard, who was a colleague of my brother's in Bonn? What is happening to him?" And he immediately said to me, "He has been freed. Do you wish to see him?" And when I nodded yes, he suddenly lifted me up and led me to the blessed abodes of saintly souls, and there he showed him to me with a radiant and joyful face. And he also showed me that famous master Adam among the souls of the blessed, full of glory and rejoicing; he said that Adam had been set free within five years and that he had been delivered at the time when one of his close associates was ordained to the priesthood.[8]

XXIII. On the feast of All Saints, when after I had suffered violent seizures my angel bore me up at the silent of the Mass and showed me some secrets in his accustomed way, I spoke to him in my trance and said, "Lord, why have I experienced such great suffering now, more than usual?" And he answered, "Because you do not intend today to receive communion." And I said, "Lord! I feared to take communion, because I have not prepared myself sufficiently to merit it. Besides, I recently took communion on the feast of the apostles Simon and Jude." Again he said, "And how could you ever do so much good, that you would make yourself worthy of such a gift? It can happen only by the grace of God. Now therefore we will make haste to return, and you will approach with the sisters to receive communion." And immediately I came back to myself just at the moment of communion when the priest had taken the water, and I rose and did as the angel had commanded me.

XXIV. One day during Lent, the angel carried me to a towering mountain and placed me on the mountainside. When I looked up, I saw an immense precipice, with what looked like dark water underneath. And he said to me, "Here you see the abyss." And when we had made our way up the mountain, we came to a very handsome gate; passing through it, we came upon another, more magnificent, and a third even more beautiful than the first two. And when we passed through that third gate we found a large multitude of most beautiful people, rejoicing and praising God fervently, with a clear and joyous voice. And they all bowed their heads to my guide as he entered. But of the song they were singing, only these words have remained in my memory: Praise and glory to the God of fame. And I said to my guide, "Lord, who are these men we see?" And he, "These are the holy desert fathers, who lived in ancient times." And when I asked where blessed Paul, the first eremite was, he pointed him out to me, preeminent among all the others in his glory. And blessed

Antony too he pointed out to me, and he bore witness that they had all gazed on God face-to-face.

XXV. I will relate a matter that troubled us with heavy grief but which, by God's mercy, had an outcome full of consolation. During Easter, when we had come together to celebrate the sacramental Easter meal and were already about to approach and receive communion, it happened by accident that the priest who was assisting at the altar carelessly jostled the chalice so that some of the Lord's blood spilled onto the corporal cloth. And at that time I had fallen into ecstasy and I saw how it all happened. For there were two angels assisting him, one on the right and one on the left. And when the priest dissolved in most bitter tears as he stood there, waiting for the lord abbot to come, the angel on his right looked at me and spoke, "Console this brother, because this has happened not on account of any sin of his but through the sins of another." But the priest, unwilling to be consoled, continued to weep most bitterly for three days, and drew away from those who would console him. But on the morning of the third day, just as it was growing light before dawn, with great physical suffering I came into ecstasy and there appeared to me in celestial light our Lady, the mother of mercy. And when I prayed to her devoutly for this brother, she said, "His sobs and tears have risen to my ears. Console him and tell him that he should raise himself up, for he has bowed himself down too much. He is my servant, I know, because he loves me and I love him, and I will be his helper whenever he is in need and calls on me from his heart." And I said, "Lady, what is to be done about the corporal, which is stained with the Lord's blood?" And she said, "It should be placed among the relics." This had already been done, in accordance with the terms of our usage, as they are written. And I added, "But what if, at some future time, someone steals the reliquary and, not knowing that the cloth is steeped in the Lord's blood, defiles that linen cloth?" And she answered, "The Lord will protect it, since it is his."

XXVI. It happened, however, that after many prayers to the Lord on account of this careless accident, when a year had gone by and Easter was approaching, on Palm Sunday, at the time of the divine office I saw what appeared to be a cloth spread out in the air above the altar, in the form of a corporal. It was very white, but in one spot it had a red stain about the size of a man's thumbnail. And this vision I saw on each day of that week, during the celebration of mass, but from one day to the next I saw the stain grow smaller and smaller, until on Easter Sunday the corporal appeared whiter than snow, sparkling as cloth does when it has been adorned with glass and the sun shines on it. And I saw that no trace of the earlier stain remained. And so I asked the angel, who was at my side at that moment, what that vision meant. And he said, "Just as this cloth you see appears beautiful and clean, so also in the sight of the Lord is that man's fault of carelessness cleansed, which happened in this place last year."

XXVII. On that same Easter Sunday, during the divine office, I went into ecstasy and I was led in the spirit to a place where three men of immense radiance and divine beauty came face to face with me. One of them was cloaked in the whitest of robes, and he addressed me, saying: "Do you believe that on this day I rose from the dead, truly God and truly man?" And I answered him, "I believe, Lord, but if I believe imperfectly, help me, that my faith may be more perfect." And again, repeating the same words, he said, "Do you believe that on this day I rose from the dead, truly God and truly man?" And a second time I answered, "I believe, Lord, but if I believe imperfectly, help me, that my faith may be more perfect." And when he asked me the same question a third time, and I made the same

answer once more, he said, "Because you truly believe, know that you will have a share in my resurrection."

XXIX. On the feast day of the blessed apostles Peter and Paul (29 June) I saw, in a vision of the spirit, the passion of blessed Peter; I saw how he was crucified with his feet above and his head down below, and the angel of the Lord said to me: "Lo, you have seen what he suffered for Christ, and now you will see with what reward he received in payment." And immediately he showed Peter to me in the heavens, in miraculous glory. And I turned to him in my heart and began to pray and supplicate, remembering two of my kinsmen to whom God had given the grace of weeping in their prayers. And I said, among other things, "Help them, Lord, that their tears may be as efficacious as yours were in the sight of the savior." And immediately he answered, "I will show you by means of a likeness what their tears have done and will do for them." And without delay I saw a handsome bird. It was white, but its wings were sprinkled with dust. It was flying about, here and there, near a river. And when it had done this for a while, plunging into the water it submerged itself and washed with great care. And once it had become white as snow, finally it flew up into a beautiful tree that grew by the stream, and perched there.

XXVIII. On the feast day of the blessed martyrs John and Paul (26 June), a certain brother, who was celebrating the divine office in our monastery, among the other collects recited one about blessed John the Evangelist, because in the calendar his dormition was noted on that day. And so, during the secret of the mass, John the Evangelist appeared to me with the two martyrs John and Paul. Instructed in advance by this brother, I asked John the Evangelist eagerly what it meant that his Dormition was announced on that day. And he answered me, "This is the day on which I entered the sepulcher by myself, and it was a great miracle." And he said no more. But let no one think, because of these words, that the church errs in observing his feast in winter; for perhaps the feast was moved to honor the day of the Lord's birth.

XXX. On the day of the Division of the Apostles, all the apostles together appeared to me in accordance with their customary kindness. But the blessed Peter and Paul seemed to be standing above the others. So I asked the angel, who at that moment was standing in my sight, what it meant that those two were standing apart. And he said, "On this day their bones were divided and this feast is especially for them." And I said, "So why is it, Lord, that all the apostles have shown themselves to me?" And he said, "This they have done for you out of kindness, because today the divine office is celebrated for all of them in common."

XXXI. THE VISION OF ELISABETH ABOUT THE RESURRECTION OF THE BLESSED VIRGIN, THE MOTHER OF GOD In the year in which through the angel of the Lord the *Book of the Ways of God* was dictated to me, on the day when the church observes the octave of the Assumption of our Lady, at the time of the holy sacrifice I was in ecstasy and my consoler, my Lady of the heavens, appeared to me as is her custom. As I had been instructed in advance by one of our elders, I asked her, "My Lady, may it please your kindness to deign to give us certain information about whether you were assumed into the heavens in the spirit only, or in the flesh as well?" I was asking about this because, as they say, this is not set forth clearly in the books of the fathers. And she said to me, "What you ask, you cannot yet know, but it will come to pass that this will be revealed through you." And so for the entire year that followed I did not dare to ask anything about this matter either of the angel, who is my especial friend, or of our Lady herself when she showed herself to me. But that brother who kept urging me to make this inquiry charged me with certain prayers, by means of which I might seek from our Lady the revelation she had promised me. When a year had elapsed and it was once again the feast of the Assumption, I lay faint in illness for many days, and as I lay on my cot during the time of the divine sacrifice I came into ecstasy with violent suffering. And I saw in a very distant place a sepulcher bathed in a strong light, and in it what seemed the form of a woman, and all about stood a large throng of angels. And after a little while, she rose up out of the sepulcher and together with that throng of angels she was lifted up into the heavens. And while I was gazing at her, there rushed to meet her from on high a man, glorious beyond description, holding in his right hand the crucifix and a standard, and I understood that this was our Lord and Savior Himself, and with Him were countless thousands of angels. And so, taking her up they bore her rapidly up to the highest heavens, with mighty and harmonious singing. And when I had seen these things clearly, my Lady soon went forth to that doorway in the light in which I have been accustomed to see her, and standing there she showed herself to me in her glory. And at the same time the angel of the Lord was at my side, for he had come to dictate to me the tenth discourse of the *Book of the Ways of God*. And I said to him, "Milord, what does this great vision that I saw mean?" And he said, "In this vision it has been revealed to you how Our Lady was assumed into the heavens in the flesh as well as in the spirit." Afterwards, on the octave day, I asked again of the angel who was visiting me then also and finishing the book, on which day, counting from the day of her Dormition, that assumption of Our Lady in the flesh had taken place. And again he kindly gave me certain information, saying "Since on that day, on which her assumption is now celebrated, she departed this life, she was resurrected on the fortieth day after this one, that is on September 23rd." And he added further, "The holy fathers, who have established the day of the feast of the Assumption had no certain knowledge of her assumption in the body, and so they made the day of her dormition a feast day, and called it also the assumption, because they believed without a doubt that she had been taken up in the flesh as well. Afterwards, I hesitated to make public the text of this revelation, fearing that I would be accused of inventing new doctrines. After two years had passed, however, and it was again the feast day of her Assumption, my Lady appeared to me and I questioned her, "Lady, should we not make known that word which was revealed to me about your resurrection?" And she replied, "This must not be made public among the masses, because the world is an evil place and those who hear you will entrap themselves and not know how to extricate themselves." And again I said, "Do you wish, therefore, that we erase altogether what has been written about this revelation?" And she said, "These things have not been revealed to you in order that they be erased and consigned to oblivion, but so that my praises may be magnified among those who love me especially. These things must be made known by you to those dear to me, and they will be shown openly to them who open their hearts to me, that they may offer me special praise and receive special rewards from me. For there are many who will receive this word with great exultation and veneration." Because of these conversations, we have celebrated that day I spoke of above as a feast day in private and in secret devoutly singing the praises of our venerable Lady. And when the mystery of the divine office was being celebrated, she showed herself to me in her accustomed way and while she was conversing with me at length, I asked her, "My Lady, for how long did you live on this earth after the ascension of the Savior? Were you not assumed into the heavens during that same year of his ascension?" And she responded mildly,

"After the ascension of the Lord I remained on earth, in mortal life, for an entire year, and for as many days as there are between the feast of the Ascension and the day on which my assumption is observed." And I added, "And were not the apostles of the Lord present at your burial?" She said, "They were all present, and they entrusted my body to the earth with great veneration."

XXXII. Once when we were celebrating the feast of the Assumption, when once again my Lady showed me her glorious countenance, I dared to ask this also of her, how old she was, when she conceived the word of God that the angel announced, in the virginal temple of her womb. And to this question too she deigned to answer, "I was fifteen years old then, and in addition as many days as there are between the celebration of my birth and that of the annunciation."

NOTES

1. Matt. 20, 15, the parable of the laborers in the vineyard.

2. The *Visions* were set down in Latin from written notes and dictation by Elisabeth's brother Ekbert, who joined her at the Benedictine double monastery at Schönau in 1155 and was made abbot after her death. It is his voice we hear in the first three chapters of this book. He insists elsewhere that he was not altered her words, dictated in Latin and German, but faithfully recorded them, translating when necessary.

3. Cf. *Visions*, I. 79. The angel of the Lord is a comely youth, Elisabeth's particular guide, consoler, chastiser. She calls him a close friend (*familiaris*) and addresses him as her lord rather as a wife might speak to her husband.

4. Ps. 36, 5; 6; 8; 9.

5. Cf. Isa. 6, 7; 11, 2; Jer. 1, 9. The context is significant, particularly Isa. 11, 1–4, and Jer. 1, 4–10.

6. The Latin *homo*, human being, is used to refer to Adam, to Christ's humanity, and to Elisabeth.

7. Ekbert, bishop of Muenster (d. 1132), after whom his grand-nephew and godson Ekbert of Schönau was named.

8. The close associate is Ekbert of Schönau, who, along with Rainald of Dassel (archbishop of Cologne 1159–67), studied with Adam.

IV

New Styles of Feminine Spirituality— The Beguine Movement

Marie d'Oignies, Christina Mirabilis, Hadewijch of Brabant, and Beatrijs of Nazareth

*A*T *THE CLOSE* of the twelfth century, women all over Europe were striving to lead more perfect religious lives; and by the opening years of the thirteenth century, conditions for female spirituality, for deepening the devotional life of women, had changed enormously. The older Benedictine houses and even the reform movements of the late twelfth century, which had made specific accommodations for women (the Order of Fontevrault, the Premonstratensians, the Gilbertines), could not accept all the women who wanted to embrace a religious life.[1] Furthermore, women wanted a new kind of religious life, and this made the institutional church very uneasy.

It is clear that there was a women's movement of the thirteenth century and that this movement posed two different dilemmas for the church. Women who could not be accommodated by existing communities within the church were often attracted to the heretical groups that were on the rise all over Europe, and the life women were trying to create for themselves was active as well as contemplative, something the church had not supported for many centuries. Women of this century wanted a life of evangelical poverty; they wanted the opportunity to work, to a self-sufficiency not based on the income from property but on the work of their hands; they wanted a daily religious practice and the education to pursue that practice intelligently and the opportunity to discuss spiritual ideas among themselves. They desired flexibility of commitment and life-style, so that there would be the possibility for active charity in the world as well as for a solitary contemplative existence when the need arose. They were eager to live chaste lives in completely female communities, but they preferred not to take permanent vows of chastity, and they resisted strict enclosure.[2]

The positive demands and needs that we have just described are essentially the program of the Beguines in northern Europe and of the Umiliati and early followers of St. Francis and St. Dominic in Italy. To many churchmen, this program seemed too unstructured, too radical, dangerously close to heresy. Both the Beguine movement and that of the Umiliati are first evidenced in documents dating from around the year 1200; contemporary observers saw them as parallel outpourings of lay piety that demanded orthodox leadership if they were not to threaten the church.

The term *Beguine* probably originated as a derogatory label for a female heretic, perhaps associated with the Albigensians, perhaps referring to the color of the robes worn by beguines. The movement as a whole—never codified by its members and never identified with individual leaders—lasted in northern Europe (especially in the area around Liège) until the French Revolution. It is thought to have been characterized by four stages. In the first stage, individual ecstatic women lived scattered about the city, leading strict religious lives while remaining in the world. It was a spontaneous movement with no founder and no legislator, and the women were simply called "holy women," *mulieres sanctae*. Only at the beginning of the thirteenth century did these women begin to organize themselves into congregations centered on spiritual discipline and common tasks.

> The women submitted to a grand mistress, aided by a council of other mistresses, each with a specific function. In organization and daily practices they often emulated the nunnery. They held meetings, followed common exercises, performed acts of charity, and recommended compulsory prayers. But ordinary religious practices remained parochial as before. To foster piety, practical or contemplative, to hold aloof from the dangers of the world without stopping ordinary work, such was their aim.[3]

It was at this second stage of growth that the church intervened. If the women were going to build communities, those communities ought to be under the control of one of the existing orders. But the existing orders were not interested in poor women without dowries, and they made no allowance for women working. At this point Jacques de Vitry (we will see more of him later) became their spokesman, and the women received papal consent to form their own self-regulated communities.[4]

The third stage was that of enclosure; communities, at first quite small, grew around infirmaries and hospices in which the "holy women" worked. But other women who identified themselves as Beguines continued to live at home or as solitaries, meeting occasionally with other like-minded women. Spiritual guidance for these communities was generally provided by the friars, Franciscan or Dominican, who were supposed to preach and hear confession regularly. The fourth stage organized the beguine enclosure into a parish:

> The full-blown beguinage comprised a church, cemetery, hospital, public square, and streets and walks lined with convents for the younger sisters and pupils and individual houses for the older and well-to-do inhabitants. In the Great Beguinage at Ghent, with its walls and moats, there were at the beginning of the fourteenth century two churches, eighteen convents, over a hundred houses, a brewery, and an infirmary.[5]

Male writers defended these holy women on the grounds of the exemplary simplicity and purity of their life-style, the importance of their economic self-sufficiency, and the profound emotionality of their spiritual life. The emotional fulfillment that may have been lacking in the medieval notion of marriage and motherhood was found by Beguine women in their relationship with the divine and, no doubt, was reinforced by their living and working together to create a supportive environment. As R. W. Southern summarized

> In many ways it is an idyllic picture—women escaping from the sordid frustrations of the world into the liberty of an unpretentious spiritual life: enjoying vivid experiences of a loving God, and occupied in useful services ranging from the care of the sick to the embroidery of ecclesiastical vestments.[6]

Yet, he adds, "these women and their way of life raised up enemies, all in some degree afraid and not all unreasonably."[7]

Perhaps one of the reasons the new holy women elicited such varied responses was that their lives were so various—individual women or each small cluster of women might take quite different paths to the same goal of spiritual enlightenment. Bolton, speaking of the first movement of holy women around Liège, emphasizes the multiplicity of life-styles:

> These women are interesting because their lives bring us into contact with most of the possible forms of religious life available to women at the time in this area: a beguine, Mary of Oignies, a recluse Ivetta of Huy, a Dominican tertiary Margaret of Ypres, a Cistercian nun Lutgard of Aywieres and Christina of St. Trond, called *Mirabilis*, claimed by Benedictines, Cistercians and Premonstratensians alike but who in reality was not attached to any religious order nor to a beguine group. The very close spiritual currents which ran between Cistercians and beguines in Lotharingia and especially in Liège have now been shown to have parallels in the almost equally close relationship between the beguines and the Dominicans in the same area.[8]

Jacques de Vitry[9] observed and reported on the lives of those women gathered around Marie d'Oignies in Liège—women whose ideas he felt could transform the church—and he compared their activities to those of other groups, the Beguines in the Low Countries, the followers of St. Francis and St. Clare in Umbria, and the Umiliati in Lombardy. He might also have included the Pauvres Catholiques in the Midi, the Papelards in the north of France, the Bizocche in northern Italy, and the Coquenunnen in western Germany.[10] All these groups shared certain commitments and attitudes, and all were viewed with mistrust by the ecclesiastical establishment. But the most exciting center of activity seems to have been in the Low Countries:

> there, as nowhere else in Europe, the newly emancipated women religious were able to evolve a way of life hitherto unknown in the West, free from monastic enclosure, observing the rules which they themselves devised to meet the needs of individual communities, following lives of intense activity which might be devoted to prayer, to teaching and study, to charitable works, or to all three.[11]

Drawn by this world, Jacques de Vitry abandoned his life at the University of Paris to become a disciple of the woman visionary Marie. In many respects he was conservative theologically and deeply troubled by the success of Catharism, so much so that he would later— at Marie's urging—become one of the preachers of the Albigensian Crusade. In other ways, he was very advanced in his thinking; he immediately recognized the importance of the community forming around Marie and staunchly defended the orthodoxy of her ideas. In the course of his steady rise in the church, he had the opportunity to travel over the whole of Europe and the Middle East, and as he traveled, he investigated and reported on what he saw was a new movement of *mulieres sanctae* over the entire continent. Thanks to him we know much about these women: their visions, their emotional lives, the kinds of communities they created, the impact they had on the world around them.

What Marie d'Oignies and her associates had in common were the practice of evangelical poverty, a willingness to support themselves by the work of their hands, ascetic self-sacrifice in the service of others, and a tendency to have visions. They were mystics—and mystics of a new sort who focused their meditative effort on the suffering humanity of Christ, on dedication to the Eucharist, and finally on mystical marriage with Christ. Jacques de Vitry wrote at length in their defense.

> You ... saw ... some of these women dissolved with such a particular and marvelous love toward God that they languished with desire, and for years had rarely been able to rise from their cots. They had no other infirmity, save that their souls were melted with desire of Him, and sweetly resting with the Lord, as they were comforted in spirit they were weakened in body. ... The cheeks of one were seen to waste away, while her soul was melted with the greatness of her love. Another's flow of tears had made visible furrows down her face. Others were drawn with such intoxication of spirit that in sacred silence they would remain quiet a whole day, with no sense of feeling for things about them, so that they could not be roused by clamour or feel a blow. ... I saw another who sometimes was seized with ecstasy five-and-twenty times a day, in which state she was motionless, and on returning to herself she was so enraptured that she could not keep from displaying her inner joy with movements of the body, like David leaping before the ark.[12]

This is the language of the *Song of Songs* and of a certain kind of medieval love poetry, of *amour courtois* and *minnemystik*, of the writings of Hadewijch and Beatrijs of Nazareth a generation later. But de Vitry is utilizing this rhetoric for specific ends. In this passage he does not speak of the contents of the visions these women were experiencing; he is describing them as creditable ecstatics, primarily on the basis of their physical behavior. He is, in fact, protecting them by making them seem harmless, that is, by making them seem traditional or by assimilating them to a medieval stereotype, the holy nun. You would not expect, reading this passage, that such women were experiencing visions of violence and dismemberment as well as of erotic love. You would not think that such women could go out and change the world, yet that is exactly what they were doing.

This anthology includes the biographies of two women important in the first generation of this movement (*The Life of Marie d'Oignies*, by Jacques de Vitry, and *The Life of Christina Mirabilis*, by Thomas de Cantimpré). These are followed by the mystical writings of two women associated with Beguine spirituality in the Low Countries, Hadewijch of Brabant and Beatrijs of Nazareth.

The rapid expansion of associations of holy women was apparent even within Marie's lifetime. She was born in 1177 and married at age fourteen, in 1191. That same year she and her husband, agreeing on a vow of chastity, went to work in the leper colony at Willambrouk. When she decided she wanted to live a more austere and more spiritual life in 1207, she went to the Augustinian community of St. Nicholas of Oignies near Namur; this was a coenobium founded by secular priests for apostolic perfection. Not affiliated with any order and following the rule of St. Augustine, it admitted lay brothers and sisters. The focus of the group was a balance of contemplation and intensive pastoral care. Other women, who seem to have been immediately attracted to this life-style and to Marie's example, lived right next to the canons of St. Nicholas. But soon, perhaps by 1210 but certainly by the death of Marie in 1213, there were too many of them, and a new beguinage had to be built. Municipal records from the 1280s indicate that women had for some time been willing their houses to other single women so that they might live in the area of the new beguinage. Each sister occupied her own cottage, but the sisters spent most of their time in common and ate meals together.[13]

Details in the life of Ida of Nivelles (March 1199–12 December 1231), Marie's younger contemporary, give a further picture of how extensive and lively these new female communities were and how rapidly they were growing. St. Ida joined a group of seven pious women when she was nine (1208); the women were already calling themselves Beguines. She lived with them in a house in the parish of Saint-Sepulchre from 1208 to 1211; she left to join another Beguine house for a few more years and then, when about sixteen years old, joined the Cistercian convent of La Ramée, where she met Beatrijs of Nazareth. By the middle of the century, there were perhaps two thousand beguines living in the Nivelles community.[14]

It is in this world of new spiritual energies and apostolic service that we must imagine Christina of St. Trond. As one reads her biography, it is at once apparent how she acquired the epithet *mirabilis*, "amazing," for her activities as her biographer Thomas de Cantimpré recounts them "exceed all understanding of men."[15] The narrative begins like a folktale: Christina is the youngest of three orphaned sisters, all of whom wish to live a religious life. Christina is given the task of taking the herds to pasture, and it is while she is doing this that her visionary life begins. Soon she is exhausted by her contemplation and undergoes a mystical death, during which she is taken to purgatory and then heaven. Her mission is to undergo purgatory while on earth in order to liberate other suffering souls. But what strange forms her mission takes:

> Then Christina began to do those things for which she had been sent back by the Lord. She crept into fiery ovens where bread was baking and was tormented by fires just like any of us mortals so that her howls were terrible to hear. Nevertheless when she emerged, no mutilation of any sort appeared on her body. When no oven was at hand, she threw herself into roaring fire . . . or else . . . she jumped into cauldrons of boiling water. . . . Although she howled as if she were suffering the pangs of childbirth, when she climbed out again she was quite unharmed.[16]

These activities initiate her return to the human community from which she had been estranged by the violence of her inner life. They follow on a visit to Liège, where she had run to the Meuse river, entered the water "like a phantasm," and emerged untouched by it. Even after this second baptism, many people, her sisters among them, remained convinced she was possessed. Only when they had indisputable evidence of miracles being worked by God through Christina did they cease trying to contain her:

> Her sisters and friends never stopped their persecution, for . . . they bound her fast with a heavy wooden yoke and fed her like a dog. . . . The hardness of the wooden yoke which lay heavily on her neck rubbed her shoulders and caused festering wounds. . . . No one there had compassion on her wretchedness but the Lord marvelously had pity on her and wrought in her that miracle. . . . Her virginal breasts began to flow with a liquid of the clearest oil and she used that liquid as a flavouring for her bread and ate it as food and smeared it on the wounds of her festering limbs as ointment. And when her sisters and friends saw this, they began to weep and they struggled no more against the miracles of the Divine Will in Christina and they released her from her chains and knelt down begging for mercy for their injuries to her and let her go.[17]

Beatrijs of Nazareth was born around the turn of the thirteenth century, perhaps in 1202. She died 29 August 1268. Her mother taught her how to read, using the Latin Psalter, and instructed her in the rudiments of Latin grammar.[18] When she was eleven, she was sent to be educated by the Beguines at Léau (or Zoutleeuw) and was later sent to the Cistercian convent of La Ramée, famous for its instruction in calligraphy, so that she might gain more experience in the copying of manuscripts. She lived there only a year, making friends with Ida of Nivelles. At about the same time, possibly when she was still at Léau, she was assigned a *magister liberalium artibus*, a teacher university-educated in the liberal arts. She next entered the school for intending novices in the Cistercian abbey of Florival, where she spent two years at most, continuing her study of the liberal arts. She spent a brief time at the Cistercian house at Val-des-Vierges, but she is really associated with the convent at Nazareth, where she became prioress and lived the rest of her life. It was evidently there that she wrote *The Seven Manners of Loving*. That she wrote this speculative mystical text in the vernacular tells us a number of things, the most important being that she was addressing a mixed audience who did not read Latin but were quite advanced in speculative mystical thought. She came from a family that undoubtedly encouraged her religious gifts; her father, Barthelmy De Vleeschouwer, founded the houses at Florival, Val-des-Vierges, and Nazareth; and after his wife died, he became a lay brother and lived successively at each of them. Three sisters also became Cistercian nuns, her older brother was a Premonstratensian canon at Averbode, and her younger brother Wicbert lived with their father as a lay brother in each house founded by him.[19]

There exists an autobiography of Beatrijs, of which the *Seven Manners* is evidently an excerpt; it has never been translated into English.[20] For Hadewijch, no such document has been found. A Flemish Beguine of the thirteenth century, she achieved no particular fame in her own lifetime as far as we know. She and her work were known in the fourteenth century, especially in the houses of the Canons Regular of Windesheim and the Carthusians of Diest; and the manuscripts of her works, discovered in 1838, date from the same century.[21] Her name is not unusual; there are documents for 111 pious women named Hadewijch in the twelfth and thirteenth centuries. Her familiarity with the vocabulary of chivalry and courtly love suggests that, like Mechthild of Magdeburg, she was of the higher class. She probably attended schools as Beatrijs did, for she uses the metaphors of the curriculum and Schoolmen in her "school of love" poems. Her most recent translator, commenting on the range of her education, notes that she was familiar with the Latin language, rules of rhetoric, numerology, Ptolemaic astronomy, and the theory of music. She introduces a number of French words into her writings and knew many of the Church Fathers and most of the canonical twelfth-century writers. Hart also believes Hadewijch must have known a great deal of vernacular love poetry, as well as being familiar with the Latin verse of Alain of Lille and Peter Abelard.[22]

From her extensive writings (thirty-one letters, forty-five poems in stanzas, fourteen visions, sixteen poems in couplets), a sketchy outline of her life can be constructed. She either founded or joined a Beguine group and had become its mistress, and she was supervising the spiritual development of a number of young Beguines who she believed were specially called to mysticism, when she ran into opposition. Her authority was called into question by members of her group and by outsiders, and her closest companions were sent away from her. We do not know how her life ended, but it is possible to speculate, as Hart does:

> The general opinion of scholars at present seems to be that Hadewijch actually was evicted from her Beguine community and exiled; that she was made the talk of the town because of her doctrine that one must live Love. . . . It may perhaps be conjectured, considering how often Hadewijch urged her Beguines to care for the sick, that when she finally became homeless she offered her services to a leprosarium or hospital for the poor, where she could nurse those who suffered and sleep at least part of the night in some corner, with access to the church or chapel always attached to such establishments in her time.[23]

The writings of Hadewijch chosen for inclusion in this anthology come from her letters and visions; the poetic texts are all available in Hart's translation.[24] Hadewijch wrote thirty-one letters, many of which seem to be addressed specifically to those young Beguines for whom she felt spiritually responsible. Letter 6 is a kind of manifesto on the Beguine life, detailing what it means to live love in the world and in the context of a female community; Letter 11 is more autobiographical, defining the nature of Hadewijch's love: "in the end, I cannot believe that I have loved Him best, and yet I cannot believe that there is any living man who loves God as I love Him."

NOTES

1. There is now a large bibliography on these three founders, their careers, and their communities. One may begin by consulting the overview provided by Jean Leclercq in "Feminine Monasticism in the Twelfth and Thirteenth Centuries," in *The Continuing Quest for God*, ed. William Skudlarek (Collegeville, Minn.: The Liturgical Press, 1982), pp. 114–26. See the bibliography cited by M. M. McLaughlin in her "Abelard and the Dignity of Women," and the comments by Lester Little, "Intellectual Training and Reform," both found in the volume *Pierre Abélard—Pierre le Vénérable* (Paris: Éditions du Centre National de la recherche scientifique, 1975). Still one of the best studies is Lina Eckenstein, *Woman under Monasticism* (Cambridge: Cambridge Univ. Press, 1896); this can be updated by consulting Jacqueline Smith, "Robert of Arbrissel: Procurator Mulierum," in *Medieval Women*, ed. Derek Baker (Oxford: Basil Blackwell, 1978), pp. 175–84.

2. On the Beguines in general, see Ernest W. McDonnell, *The Beguines and Beghards in Medieval Culture* (New York: Octagon, 1969; reprint of 1953 ed.) and R. W. Southern, *Western Society and the Church in the Middle Ages*, especially pp. 309–31. On the Beguines as a women's movement and its economic goals, see Elise Boulding, *The Underside of History* (Boulder: Westview Press, 1976), pp. 415 ff.; Carolly Erickson, *The Medieval Vision* (Oxford: Oxford Univ. Press, 1976), pp. 210 ff.; JoAnn McNamara and Suzanne Wemple, "Sanctity and Power," pp. 110–16 in *Becoming Visible: Women in European History*, ed. Renate Bridenthal and Claudia Koony (Boston: Houghton Mifflin, 1977). On women as a problem, see John B. Freed, "Urban Development and the 'Cura Monialium' in Thirteenth Century Germany," in *Viator* 3 (1972), pp. 311–27; Brenda Bolton, "Mulieres Sanctae," in *Women in Medieval Society*, ed. Susan M. Stuard (Philadelphia: University of Pennsylvania Press, 1976), and "Vitae Matrum," in *Medieval Women*, ed. Baker, pp. 141–58, and "Tradition and Temerity: Papal Attitudes Toward Deviants," in *Schism, Heresy, and Religious Protest*, ed. Derek Baker (Cambridge: Cambridge Univ. Press, 1972). On feminine piety in the diocese of Liège in Belgium, see Simone Roisin, *l'Hagiographie cistercienne dans la diocèse de Liège au xiii᷄ siècle* (Louvain: Bibliothèque de l'université, 1947), and "L'efflorescence cistercienne et le courant feminin de piété au xiii᷄ siècle," in *Revue d'histoire ecclésiastique* 39 (1945), pp. 458–86. Further information will be found in Louis Bouyer, Jean Leclercq, and Francois Vandenbroucke, *The Spirituality of the Middle Ages* (London: Burns and Oates, 1968), and Giles Constable and Bernard Smith, ed. and trans., *Libellus de diversis ordinibus et professionibus qui sunt in ecclesia* (Oxford: Clarendon Press, 1972), and Giles Constable, "Twelfth Century Spirituality and the Late Middle Ages," in *Medieval and Renaissance Studies* 5 (1971), pp. 29 ff.

3. McDonnell, *Beguines*, p. 5.
4. Bolton, "Vitae Matrum," p. 256.
5. McDonnell, *Beguines*, p. 479.
6. Southern, *Western Society*, p. 32.
7. Southern, *Western Society*, p. 328.
8. Boulton, "Vitae Matrum," p. 260.
9. On Jacques de Vitry and the women associated with Marie d'Oignies, see Bolton, "Vitae Matrum"; Southern, *Western Society*, pp. 314 ff.; Boulding, *Underside of History*, pp. 449–51; Roisin, *L'Hagiographie Cistercienne*;

Benjamin de Troeyer, "Beguines et Tertiares en Belgique et aux Pays-Bas aux XII–XIV᷄ siècles," in *I Frati Penitenti di S. Francesco nella società del 2 e 300*, ed. Mariano d'Alatri (Rome: Istituto Storico dei Cappuccini, 1977) pp. 133–38.

10. On the Beguines, see Joseph M. H. Albanes, *La vie de Sainte Douceline, fondatrice des béguines de Marseille* (Marseille: E. Camoin, 1879); Brenda Bolton, "Vitae Matrum" and "Some Thirteenth Century Women in the Low Countries: A Special Case?" in *Nederlands Archief voor Kerkgeschiedenis* 61 (1981), pp. 7–29; De Troeyer, "Beguines et Tertaires . . ." and in the same volume, Pierre Peanò, "Les Béguines du Languedoc ou la crise du T.O.F. dans la France méridionale (XIII–XIV᷄ siècles)," pp. 139–58; Charles McCurry, "Religious Careers and Religious Devotion in 13th Century Metz," *Viator* 9 (1978), pp. 325–33; Dayton Phillips, *The Beguines in Medieval Strasburg* (Ann Arbor, Mich.: University of Michigan Press, 1941).

11. Eric Colledge, *Mediaeval Netherlands Religious Literature* (New York, 1965), p. 8.

12. Julia O'Faolain and Lauro Martines, eds., *Not in God's Image* (New York: Harper & Row, 1973), pp. 140–41. This is De Vitry's preface to the *Life of Marie d'Oignies*.

13. McDonnell, *Beguines*, pp. 71 ff.
14. Roisin, *L'Hagiographie*, pp. 126 ff.
15. "Vita Christinae Mirabilis," par. 5, trans. Margot H. King. The Latin text is "Vita Beatae Christinae Mirabilis Trudonopoli in Hasbania" by Thomas de Cantimpré, ed. J. Pinius. AASS Jul. t. 5 (Paris: Th. Graess, 1868), pp. 637–60.
16. Vitae Christinae, par. 11, trans. King.
17. Vita Christinae, par. 19, trans. King.
18. Roisin, *L'Hagiographie*, pp. 126 ff.; McDonnell, *Beguines*, pp. 71 ff.; Mother Columba Hart, *Hadewijch: The Complete Works* (New York: Paulist Press, 1980), p. 5.
19. Beatrijs of Nazareth. Roisin, *L'Hagiographie*, pp. 136 ff.; Colledge, *Medieval Netherlands*, pp. 8 ff.
20. L. Reypens, ed., *De autobiographie van de Z. Beatrijs van Tienen* (Antwerp, 1964).
21. Hart, *Hadewijch*, p. 5.
22. Hart, Introduction, *Hadewijch*, pp. 1–42.
23. Hart, Introduction, *Hadewijch*, p. 5.
24. Hart, Poems in Stanzas, *Hadewijch*, pp. 123 ff.; Poems in Couplets, *Hadewijch*, pp. 307 ff.

MARIE D'OIGNIES (1177–1213; Brabant-Flanders)

The Life of Marie d'Oignies, by Jacques de Vitry

Translated by Margot King

BOOK I, Chapter 16

The beginning of her conversion to you, O Lord, the first fruits of her love, was your Cross and Passion. She heard you hearing and was afraid (Hab. 3:2), she considered your works and feared. One day when she was reflecting on the blessings you had sent and visited upon her and which you had graciously shown forth in the flesh to mankind, and while she was considering your torment upon the Cross, she found such grace of compunction and wept so abundantly that the tears which flowed so copiously from her eyes fell on the floor of the church and plainly showed where she had been walking. For a long time after this visitation, she could not look at an image of the Cross, nor could she speak of the Passion of Christ, nor hear other people speaking of it without falling into ecstasy by reason of her enfeebled heart. She therefore would sometimes moderate her sorrow and restrain the flood of her tears and, leaving behind His humanity, would raise her mind so that she might find some consolation in His unchangeableness. The more, however, she tried to restrain the vehemence of the flood, the more wondrously did her ardor increase it. When she considered how great was He who had allowed Himself to be so humiliated for us her sorrow was redoubled and her soul renewed with sweet compunction and fresh tears.

BOOK I, Chapter 17

Once, just before Holy Thursday when the Passion of Christ was approaching, she began

to offer herself up as a sacrifice to the Lord with an even greater flood of tears, sighs, and sobs. One of the priests of the church exhorted her with honey-tongued rebukes to pray in silence and to restrain her tears. Although she had always been bashful and would, with dove-like simplicity, make an effort to obey in all things, yet she knew that she could not restrain these tears. She therefore slipped quietly out of the church and hid herself in a secret place far from everyone and she tearfully begged the Lord that he show this priest that it is not in man to restrain the impulse of tears when the waters flow with the vehemence of the blowing wind (cf Ps. 147:18; Ex. 14:21).

On that very day while the priest was celebrating Mass, it happened that "the Lord opened and none shut" (Isa. 22:22) and "He sent forth waters and they overturned the earth" (Job 12:15). His spirit was drowned with such a flood of tears that he almost suffocated. The harder he tried to restrain this force, the more drenched he became and the more soaked did the book and the altar become. What could he do, he who had been so lacking in foresight, he who had rebuked the handmaid of Christ? With shame and through personal experience he was taught what he previously had not learned through humility and compassion. Sobbing frequently and with disordered and broken speech, he barely avoided total collapse, which one of his acquaintances has testified. After Mass was finished, the handmaid of Christ returned to the church and told the priest everything that had happened, as if she herself had been present. "Now," she said, "you have learned through personal experience that man cannot restrain the impulse of the spirit 'when the south wind blows'" (cf. Acts 28:13).

BOOK I, Chapter 18

When a constant outburst of tears gushed forth from her eyes both day and night and ran down her cheeks and made the church floor all muddy, she would catch the tears in the linen cloth with which she covered her head. She went through many veils in this way since she had to change them frequently and put a dry one on in place of the wet one she had discarded.

In my love for her I suffered with her in her long fasts and frequent vigils and while she was enduring many such deluges of tears. I therefore asked her whether she felt any pain or discomfort as one is accustomed to experience in such a state of exhaustion. "These tears," she said, "are my refreshment. Night and day they are my bread. They do not impair my head but rather feed my mind. They do not torment me with pain but, on the contrary, they rejoice my soul with a kind of serenity. They do not empty the brain but fill the soul to satiety and soften it with a sweet anointing. They are not violently wrenched out but are freely given by the Lord."

BOOK I, Chapter 22

Having once tasted the spirit, she held as nothing all sensual delights until one day she remembered the time when she had been gravely ill and had been forced, from necessity, to eat meat and drink a little wine for a short time. From the horror she felt at her previous carnal pleasure, she began to afflict

herself and she found no rest in spirit until, by means of extraordinary bodily chastisements, she had made up for all the pleasures she had experienced in the past. In vehemence of spirit, almost as if she were inebriated, she began to loathe her body when she compared it to the sweetness of the Paschal Lamb and, with a knife, in error cut out a large piece of her flesh which, from embarrassment, she buried in the earth. Inflamed as she was, however, by the intense fire of love, she did not feel the pain of her wound and, in ecstasy of mind, she saw one of the seraphim standing close by her. Much later when women were washing her corpse, they were amazed when they found the places of the wounds but those to whom she had made her confession knew what they were. Why do those who marvel at the worms which swarmed from the wounds of Simeon [Stylites] and are awe-struck at the fire with which Antony burst his feet not wonder at such strength in the frail sex of a woman who, wounded by charity and invigorated by the wounds of Christ, neglected the wounds of her own body?

BOOK I, Chapter 35

Even her slumber was not without fruit for even while she slept her heart was vigilant and, clinging to Christ in her vigilance, she kept Him in her heart and dreamed only of Christ. Just as a person who is thirsty dreams while asleep that he is drinking from water fountains and just as one who is hungry imagines that a banquet has been placed before him, just so she had Him whom she desired always before her eyes in her dreams. For where love is, there is the eye; "where the treasure is, there also is the heart" (Matt. 6:21). In the same way Christ said of Himself, "Where I am, there also shall my minister be" (John 12:26). Often the Lord admonished her in her dreams just as He did Joseph and other saints and He visited His handmaid with many revelations lest her sleep pass by unprofitably. In the same way the Lord promised through the prophet "Your old men shall dream dreams and your young men shall see visions" (Joel 2:28).

Sometimes she was permitted to find rest in her cell and at other times, especially when great solemnities were approaching, she could find rest nowhere but under the church in the very presence of Christ. When this happened, she had to remain there day and night for it was not within her power or freedom of will either to rest in her cell or to remain in the church. She had to obey her familiar angel who had been given to watch over her just as if he had been her own abbot. Sometimes when she was exhausted by excessive vigils, he would admonish her to rest and after she had rested a very little time, he would lift her up and lead her back into the church.

BOOK I, Chapter 38

The prudent woman knew that after the sin of the first parents, the Lord enjoined penance through them to their sons, that is to say "you will earn your bread by the sweat of your brow" (Gen. 3:19). This is the reason why she worked with her own hands as often as she could. In this way she mortified her body with penance, furnished the necessities of life to the poor, and acquired food and clothing for herself—that is, all the things she had given up for Christ. The Lord bestowed on her such strength in labour that she far exceeded her companions and was able to obtain for herself and for one companion the fruit of her hands and she gave heed to the words of the Apostle "Whoever will not work, will not eat" (2 Thess. 3:10). She considered all exertion and labor sweet when she considered that the only begotten Son of the High King of heaven "who opens his hand and fills with blessing every living creature" (Ps. 144:16) was nourished by Joseph's manual labour and by the work of the poor little Virgin. In quiet and silence she followed the injunction of the Apostle and by the labor of her hands she ate her bread for her strength was in silence and hope. She so loved quiet and silence that she fled noisy crowds and once barely said a word from the Feast of the Holy Cross until Easter. The Holy Spirit revealed to her that the Lord had accepted this silence and that especially because of it she had obtained from the Lord that she would fly up to heaven without going to Purgatory.

BOOK II, Chapter 72

It frequently occurred that when the priest raised the Host, she saw between his hands the corporeal form of a beautiful boy and an army of the heavenly host descending with a great light. When the priest received the Host after the general confession, she saw in the spirit the Lord remain in the soul of the priest illuminating him with a wondrous brightness. If, on the other hand, he received it unworthily, she saw the Lord withdraw with displeasure and the soul of the wretched man would remain empty and dark. Even when she was not present in the church but remained in her cell, she prayed with her eyes covered with a white veil, as was her habit, and when Christ descended to the altar at the utterance of the sacred words, then, wondrously transformed, she felt His coming. If she was present at the reception of the sacrament of Extreme Unction by invalids, she felt the presence of Christ when, with a multitude of saints, He tenderly strengthened the sick person, expelled demons, and purged the soul and, as it were, transfused Himself in light throughout the whole body of the invalid while the different limbs were being anointed.

BOOK II, Chapter 88

Sometimes it seemed to her that for three or more days she held Him close to her so that He nestled between her breasts like a baby, and she hid Him there lest He be seen by others. Sometimes she kissed him as though He were a little child and sometimes she held Him on her lap as if He were a gentle lamb. At other times the Holy Son of the Virgin manifested Himself in the form of a dove for the consolation of His daughter or He would walk around the church as if He were a ram with a bright star in the middle of his forehead and, as it seemed to her, He would visit His faithful ones. And just as the Lord showed Himself to His doubting disciples in the form of a pilgrim and took the shape of a merchant when he sent St. Thomas to the Indies, just so He deigned to manifest Himself to His friends for their consolation under the form of a friend. Thus St. Jerome testified that when St. Paula came to Bethlehem, she saw Him as a baby lying in a crib. He manifested Himself to Marie in a form which was in keeping with the feast. Thus he showed Himself at the Nativity as though he were a baby sucking at the breasts of the Virgin Mary or crying in His cradle, and then she was drawn to Him in love just as if He had been her own baby. In this way the various feasts took on new interest according to how He manifested Himself and each caused a different emotional state. At the Feast of the Purification she saw the Blessed Virgin offering her Son in the temple and Simeon receiving Him in his arms. In this vision she exulted no less from joy than if she had been present herself when this happened in the temple. Sometimes during this same feast, after she had been walking in procession for a long time with her candle snuffed out, suddenly it burned with a most brilliant light which only God had kindled. Sometimes at the Passion the Lord appeared to her on the cross, but this happened rarely because she

could scarcely endure it. When any great solemnity approached she would sometimes feel joy for a full eight days before the feast. Thus was she transformed throughout the course of a whole year in different ways and was wondrously filled with love.

BOOK II, Chapter 107

When her last hour was approaching, the Lord showed His daughter the portion of her inheritance among the brothers and she saw the place in heaven prepared for her by the Lord (John 14:3). She saw and was glad (cf. John 8:56; Acts 11:23); Matt. 2:10; John 20:20; Tob. 11:8; Isa. 66:14). We could in some way judge the height of her place and the greatness of its glory if we could remember the precious stones and the virtues of those gems—indeed if we could even remember their names—she so wondrously described which the Lord had named when He showed them to her. We cannot, however, even understand, for it is written "Eye has not seen, O God, those things which you have prepared for those who love you" (Isa. 64:1). We can only understand how she who served God so devoutly and who loved Christ so ardently was worthy of such glory and whom especially the Lord honored with so many privileges while she lived on earth.

On the Thursday evening before she died she was lying outside her cell in the open air when we came to visit her. She could neither speak nor turn her eyes towards us and her gaze was fixed immoveably in heaven (Acts 7:55). Then her countenance began to glow with a kind of brightness and, smiling all the while, from her joy she started to sing I know not what in a low murmur, for at that time she could not raise her voice. When I approached her I could understand only a little of her song, only this: "How beautiful you are, Lord our God." After she had remained some time in such joy, singing, smiling, and sometimes clapping her hands, she returned to herself and she began to groan a little as if she had come back again to a sense of how sick she was which she had not experienced before. When we asked her what she had seen and if she was able or wished to tell us about it, she said, "I would tell marvels if I dared."

On Saturday evening when her wedding day was close at hand, the day of joy and gladness (cf Luke 1:14), "the day the Lord has made' (Ps. 117:24), the day the Lord had foreordained and promised His handmaid, the day of the Lord, the day of the Resurrection, the day of the Vigil of St. John the Baptist when it is said that the Apostle John left the world, although the Church usually celebrates his feast on another day—on that day, having eaten nothing for fifty-two days, the handmaid of Christ began to sing the Alleluia in a sweet voice and was in jubilation and gladness almost the whole night as though she had been invited to a banquet.

BOOK II, Chapter 108

On Sunday Satan appeared to her as if seated on her foot and, greatly disturbed, she began to fear for a short time and asked for help from those standing around her. She recovered confidence in the Lord, however, and crushing the head of the dragon (Ps. 73:14) and

fortifying herself with the Sign of the Cross, she said, "Get behind me, Filth and Foulness." (Note that she did not simply call him "foul" but "Foulness.") When he had departed she again began to sing the Alleluia and to give thanks to God. When it was almost time for the Vespers of the Feast of St. John, about the hour when Our Lord gave up the spirit (that is to say, about the ninth hour), she too went to the Lord. The ravages of death did not alter the cheerfulness of her expression nor the gladness of her countenance; indeed I do not remember her face even in health being so serene or inwardly glowing with such an eager expression. Her face was not pallid nor did it have that bluish cast typical of death but, with an angelic and dove-like expression and a countenance white and shining in its simplicity, she stirred many to devotion both during her death and after it. Not a few people, sweetly refreshed with an abundant flood of tears by her death, perceived that they had been visited by the Lord because of her merits. Just so had a certain holy woman foreseen in the Holy Spirit and predicted that those present at her passing would receive great consolation from the Lord.

When her sainted little body was washed after death, it was found to be so frail and shrivelled from illness and fasting that her spine touched her belly and the bones in her back seemed to be lying under her stomach as if under a thin linen cloth.

CHRISTINA MIRABILIS   (1150–1224; Brabant-Flanders)

The Life of Christina of St. Trond, Called Christina Mirabilis, by Thomas de Cantimpré

Translated by Margot King

CHAPTER I

4. Christina, the well-remembered virgin of Christ, was born of respectable parents in the town of St. Trond in Hasbania. After her parents had died, she was left with two older sisters who wished to arrange her life according to the religious state of life. They arranged that the oldest sister would occupy herself in prayer, the middle one to take care of the house and the youngest—that is, Christina—to take care of the herds as they went to pasture. Immediately Christ did not fail to the lower and more humble office and He gave her the grace of an inward sweetness and very often visited her with heavenly secrets. She remained unknown to all and the more hidden she was, the more she was known to God alone. This is why Isaiah boasted, when he said "My secret to myself, my secret to myself" (Isa. 24:16), for God is a bashful lover.

5. It happened that after these events she grew sick in body by reason of the exertions of inward contemplation and she died. Her dead body was laid out in the midst of her friends and her sisters and they wept copiously over it. The next day it was borne to the church but while Mass was being said for her, suddenly the body stirred in the coffin and immediately was raised up like a bird and ascended to the rafters of the church. All those present fled and only her older sister remained behind fearfully. Christina stayed up there immoveably until Mass was finished, kept in check by the ecclesiastical sacrament when she was

forced to descend. Some say that the subtlety of her spirit was revolted by the smell of human bodies. Finally she returned home with her sisters where she was reinvigorated by food. Her spiritual friends then hastened to her and asked what she had seen and they wanted her to explain what had happened. She said to them:

6. "As soon as I died, angels of God—the ministers of light—took my soul and led me into a dark and terrible spot which was filled with the souls of men. The torments which I saw in that place were so cruel that no tongue can tell of them and I saw many dead men whom I had previously known in the flesh. I had great compassion on those wretched souls and asked them what place it was. I thought it was hell, but my guides said to me, "This place is purgatory and it is here that repentant sinners atone for the sins they committed while they were alive." Then then led me to the torments of hell and there also I recognized some people whom I had known while I was alive.

7. Afterwards I was carried to Paradise, to the throne of the Divine Majesty. When I saw the Lord rejoicing with me and well satisfied, I rejoiced above all measure and thought that I would remain with the Lord forever after. At once the Lord answered my desire and said, "Certainly, my most beloved, you will be with me, but I am now proposing two options for you. Either remain with me now, or return to

184

your body and suffer the punishments of an immortal soul in a mortal body which, however, will remain unharmed. Thus by the pains you will suffer, you will deliver all those souls in purgatory whom you pitied. Indeed, by the example of your suffering and your way of life, you will incite living men to turn to me and to turn aside from their sins. When you will have done all these things, then you shall return to me and will have earned a reward of much profit." Without hesitation I answered that I wanted to return under the conditions which were proposed to me.

8. With no delay the Lord joyfully replied and commanded my soul to be led back to my body. See how quickly the angels obeyed the bidding of the Lord! My soul was standing before the throne of the Divine Majesty when the *Agnus Dei* was being sung during the Mass celebrated for me, but I was restored to my body by those swift angels by the time they sang the third *Agnus Dei*. This is how I returned and how I left and I am given back to life for the improvement of men."

"Now therefore do not be disturbed about the things you are going to see in me, because those things which God has ordained in me are above understanding. Indeed, such things have not been seen among men."

9. After this, Christina ran from the presence of men with wondrous horror and fled into the deserts and into trees and perched on the peaks of turrets or steeples and on other lofty places. The people thought she was possessed by demons and finally, with great effort, managed to capture her and bind her with iron chains. Thus bound, she endured many pains and great privation, yet she suffered most from the stench of men. One night, with the help of God, her chains and fetters fell off and she escaped and fled into remote desert forests and there lived in trees as though she were a bird. Even when she needed food—for despite the extreme sensitivity of her body, she could not live without food—

and was tortured by a most terrible hunger, she did not at all wish to return home but she remained alone with God in the secret deserts. She therefore uttered a prayer to the Lord and humbly begged that he gaze on her anguish with the eyes of His mercy. Without delay, turning her eyes to herself, she saw that her dry virginal breasts were dripping sweet milk against all the laws of nature. Wondrous thing! Unheard of in all the centuries since the incomparable Mother of God! Using the dripping liquid as food, she was nourished for nine weeks with the virginal milk from her own breasts.

While all this was happening, the people had been searching for her and she was found and captured and, as before, they bound her with chains, but in vain.

10. After she had been freed by the Lord, she came to the city of Liège. Thirsting for the most holy flesh of the spotless Paschal Lamb, she besought the priest of St. Christopher's to strengthen her with Holy Communion against the anguish she was suffering from so many things. The priest promised he would do so but he said that he could not give her Communion right then because he was busy. She was impatient at any delay, so she went to a priest at another church and asked for the Body of Christ. As soon as she had received communion, she was struck with emotion, she fled and left the city. The priest wondered greatly at this fleeing woman and he ran to the other priest at St. Christopher's and they both followed her as far as the rapidly flowing Meuse river. When they reached the river's edge, they rejoiced because they thought they could seize her but, stupified, they observed the woman in front of them enter the deep streams of the water and come out on the other side, untouched by the river. Although she was in the body, she appeared like a phantasm.

11. Then Christina began to do those things for which she had been sent back by the Lord. She crept into fiery ovens where bread was

baking and was tormented by fires just like any of us mortals so that her howls were terrible to hear. Nevertheless when she emerged, no mutilation of any sort appeared in her body. When no oven was at hand, she threw herself into roaring fires which she found in mens' houses or else she thrust her feet and hands into fires and held them there for so long that they would have been reduced to ashes had it not been a divine miracle. At other times she jumped into cauldrons of boiling water and stood there immersed either up to the breast or the waist, depending on the size of the cauldron, and poured scalding water over those parts of her body which were untouched by the water. Although she howled as if she were suffering the pangs of childbirth, when she climbed out again she was quite unharmed.

12. Often in cold weather she would remain for a long while under beneath the waters of the Meuse; indeed frequently she stayed there for six or more days at a time. The priest, however, who was attending to her came and stood on the river bank and adjured her, in the name of Christ, to come out. Thus forced, she came out. In the winter she would stand upright on a water-wheel throughout its entire revolution and the waters ran over head and limbs. At other times she would swim with the current and revolved with the wheel through the waters. Despite this, no hurt appeared on her body.

CHAPTER II

15. Her body was so subtle and light that she walked on dizzy heights and, like a sparrow, hung suspended from the topmost branches of the loftiest trees.

16. When she wanted to pray, she had to flee to tree-tops or towers or any lofty spot so that, remote from everyone, she might find rest for her spirit. And again when she prayed

and the divine grace of contemplation descended upon her, all her limbs were gathered together into a ball as if they were hot wax and all that could be perceived of her was a round mass. After her spiritual inebriation was finished and her active physical senses had restored limbs to their proper place, like a hedgehog her rolled-up body returned to its proper shape and her limbs which had been bent formlessly once again were spread out. Many many times she would stand erect on fence palings and in that position would chant all the Psalms, for it was very painful indeed for her to touch the ground while she was praying.

21. It happened one day that, violently stirred by the Spirit, she visited a church in the city of Wellen and coming upon a baptismal font, she completely immersed herself in it. It is said that after this event occurred her manner of life was more moderate with regard to society and she behaved more calmly and was more able to endure the smell of men and to live among them.

22. She frequently partook of the Sacrament of the Body and Blood of the Lord with holy devotion and on almost every Sunday, and she said that she received from it strength of body and a greatest joy of spirit. Consequently she who had given up everything of her own for Christ (as well as those things which belonged to her by right and which could have been used for food and drink) used to beg from door to door every day for the common alms of men, so that she might bear the sins of those people from whose alms she was fed. Indeed she said that she was driven by the Spirit of God to beg the alms of sinful men because they might thereby be called to a horror of their sins and to a penitent life. Furthermore she said that nothing made God weep more with mercy for sinners than when sinners are moved by mercy towards their neighbours, for mercy and pity never can result in anything but good at the last day.

And as these things show by example, so we confirm those things we are telling about Christina's behaviour.

CHAPTER III

29. She had insight into many things with the spirit of prophecy and forewarned many to salvation and privately reprimanded many of their secret sins and recalled them to penance. When that unfortunate meeting at Stpes occurred in October 1213 between the duke of Brabant and his enemies where so many hundreds of men were killed, on that very day this blessed woman cried out as if in childbirth, "Alas! Alas! I see the air full of swords and blood! Hurry, sisters, hurry! Pray to the Lord! Shed tears lest from His wrath He repress His mercy!" And she said to a nun at the monastery of St. Catherine's in St. Trond, "Run, sister, quickly run to prayer! Beg the Lord for your father because he is in great danger!"

35. She later became intimate with the nuns of St. Catherine's who lived outside the town of St. Trond. Sometimes while she was sitting with them, she would speak of Christ and suddenly and unexpectedly she would be ravished in the spirit and her body would roll and whirl around like a hoop. She whirled around with such extreme violence that the individual limbs of her body could not be distinguished. When she had whirled around for a long time in this manner, it seemed as if she became weakened by the violence of the rolling and all her limbs grew quiet. Then a wondrous harmony sounded between her throat and her breast which no mortal man could understand nor could it be imitated by any artificial instrument. Her song had not only the pliancy and tones of music but also the words—if thus I might call them—but if they could be called words they sounded together incomprehensibly. The voice or spiritual breath, however, did not come out of her mouth or nose, but a harmony of the angelic voice resounded only from between the breast and the throat.

36. While all this was happening, all her limbs were quiet and her eyes were closed as if she were sleeping. Then after a little time, restored to her former self, she rose up like one who was drunk—indeed she *was* drunk—and she cried aloud, "Bring the nuns to me that together we might praise Jesus for the great liberality of His miracles." Shortly thereafter the nuns of the convent came running from all sides and greatly rejoiced in Christina's solace and she began to sing the *Te Deum laudamus* and all the convent joined in and she finished her song. Afterwards when she was fully restored to herself, she knew what had happened from the tales of the others, and she fled for shame and embarrassment or if anyone forcibly detained her she languished with a great sorrow and thought herself stupid or foolish.

CHAPTER IV

41. When Louis, count of Looz and a most noble man, learned of her famous sanctity through hearsay, he began to love her in his heart and to follow sincerely her counsels and advice. Whenever he saw her, he would rise and run to her and call for his mother and when he did anything against justice or against the Church of Christ or against its ministers, she would weep for him like a mother weeping for her son. She would go to him in his palace and, trusting that she had the protection of a mother, would reprimand him and would obtain from him whatever was owing for the satisfaction of justice.

44. When Count Louis was near death he called Christina to him and most persistently begged her to stay with him until the hour of death. She very obligingly granted this and he

commanded all the counts who were with him to leave the bedchamber and kept Christina alone with him in the chamber. Without delay the Count pulled himself up with all the strength he could summon and lay fully prostrate before the feet of Christina and, with great lamentation, recited to her all his sins from his eleventh year right up to that very day. He did this not for absolution which she had no power to give but rather that she be moved by this atonement to pray for him. After this he called all his counts into the bedchamber and, following the advice of Christina, he disposed of his goods and then he died. She saw his soul being carried to purgatory and there tormented with the most bitter punishments.

45. The goodly woman was not a little compassionate towards him and obtained from the Lord that she suffer with him the exacted punishment in purgatory. When therefore he appeared to her after his death and asked for help, Christina said to him, "Well then, go hence and fulfill the punishments due your sins according to the Divine Judgment. As for me, I will accept in my own body a half part of your purgatorial torments which must be exacted." Having taken on these burdens, for a long time afterwards you might have seen Christina in the middle of the night being tormented with burning smoke and at other times with freezing cold. Indeed she suffered torments in turn according what the soul of the Count was suffering. She also watered with her tears the places where the Count had been accustomed to sin and she grieved in the places where he had been happy to no purpose.

46. In the last year of her life solitude and the desert place were frequently her home. She returned, although most rarely, when, in the spirit, she was driven either for the salvation of men or for the partaking of food. No mortal man could, at that time, restrain her when she wanted to go into the desert. When she returned no one dared greet her, no one dared ask her anything. Once she returned at Vespers and passed above the ground right through the middle of a house like a spirit and people could scarcely tell whether a spirit or a material body had passed by since she barely seemed to touch the ground. Indeed in the last year of her life, the spirit so controlled virtually all the parts of her animal body that scarcely could either human minds or eyes look at the shadow her body cast without horror or a trembling of the spirit. She then returned to the town of St. Trond and more frequently dwelt in the monastery of St. Catherine's.

CHAPTER V

51. When the time approached that she should be held fast in the languor of death, she was overtaken by such an unbroken grace of contemplation that she found it very difficult to direct the attention of her mind anywhere else. At the very end, resting in the spirit, she gently asked Beatrice who was a nun at St. Catherine's that a bed be prepared secretly for her in one of the rooms because her final sickness was close at hand. She quickly did what she was asked and Christina lay down and was overcome by an increasingly serious illness. After three days of this sickness, she asked for the Communion of the Body of the Lord and for the Holy Oils. When this was done, the Beatrice of whom I have spoken fell down on her knees and openly begged that she make known certain things before she died. When Christina did not answer, Beatrice thought that her attention was on other things and, postponing her question, left the room to do something else and left her alone for a time.

52. Some people say that Christina often prayed to the Lord while she was alive that He not honor her in death by any miracles but that He allow her to die the common death of

men. In this too the Lord heard her, for before the aforementioned Beatrice could return, Christina called on Christ and gave up her spirit. As soon as Beatrice returned with another nun she found the lifeless body stretched out on the ground after the manner of corpses and truly, I believe, in the care of the angels. Beatrice was fearsomely impatient at this and fell upon the body of the dead woman and began to wail violently. She often interrupted her shouts by asking the dead woman why she had gone to the Lord without her permission, without the leave of the sisters. Nevertheless in her vehement spirit, she still had trust and, putting her face to the mouth of the dead woman, she said, "O Christina! You were ever obedient to me in life! I now therefore beseech you and admonish you earnestly through the Lord Jesus Christ whom you loved with ardent desire while you lived, that you now obey me because you are powerful and, through Him with whom you are now joined, you can do what you want, that you return to life and tell me what I begged you to reveal to me with great desire while you were alive."

53. Wondrous event! As soon as Beatrice had cried out into the ears of the dead woman, Christina returned to her body and, heaving a great sigh, opened her haggard eyes like one roused from a profound sleep. Turning her grief-stricken face to the one who had called her back, she said, "O Beatrice! Why have you disturbed me? Why have you called me back? Just now I was being led to the face of Christ! But now, my sister, quickly ask me what you want and then, I beg you, allow me to return to the Lord for whom I have longed eagerly." Then Beatrice asked her question and received a reply from her. In the meantime the sisters of the monastery gathered together from all sides and Christina blessed them with the sign and the words of the Cross and in this way she who had experienced death three times and died three times passed to the immortal age of ages.

HADEWIJCH OF BRABANT (first half of thirteenth century; Antwerp)

Letters to a Young Beguine

Translated by Eric Colledge

LETTER 6

Now I want to warn you about one thing from which great harm can come. I assure you that this is one of the worst sicknesses which prevail today, and sickness there are in plenty. Nowadays everyone is constantly questioning the good faith of his friends, putting them to the test and complaining of their faithlessness; and people spend their time in this way who ought to be filled with an exalted love for our great God.

What does it matter to us, if our intention is good and we want to exalt our lives to God, who is so great and so exalted, whether people are faithful or unfaithful to us, kind or unkind, treat us ill or well? If we cannot show good faith and kindness to them, we are harming ourselves, and the worst of the harm is that we are ruining for ourselves the sweetness of true love.

If anyone keeps good faith with you and consoles you in your need with his help, you must show your gratitude and help him in his turn, but, more than this, we must serve and love God the more fervently because of this, and leave it to Him to reward others or not as He wills. For He in His being is just, and when He gives or takes away it is always justly done; for He is exalted in the delight of His own being, and we are here, infinitely beneath Him in all our shortcomings. And especially you and I, who have not yet attained what we are, not yet acquired what we have, fall so far short of what is ours, we must forgo everything if we are to be and to have everything, we must learn, in the unity and boldness of the spirit learn the perfect life of that love which has moved us both to its works.

Ah, dear child, above all I beg you to be on your guard against instability. For there is nothing so able and so quick to separate you from our Lord as instability. Whatever troubles may come to you, do not commit the folly of believing that you are set for any other goal than the great God Himself, in the fullness of His being and of His love; do not let folly or doubt deflect you from any good practice which can lead you to this goal. If you will confide yourself to His love, you will soon grow to your full stature, but if you persist in doubting, you will become sluggish and grudging, and everything which you ought to do will be a burden to you. Let nothing trouble you, do not believe that anything which you must do for Him whom you seek will be beyond your strength, that you cannot surmount it, that it will be beyond you. This is the fervour, this is the zeal which you must have, and all the time your strength must grow.

And when you find any man who hungers for God's love, who labours for it, who lives in exile wanting it and suffers many pains for it, do all you can to help such a one, hold nothing back from him: give him your heart in compassionate affection, your counsel in consolation, your labours in service and toil. Towards sinners show compassion, and pray many prayers for them to God. But beyond saying prayers for them, and fervently asking God to free them from their sins, have nothing to do with them: you would be wasting your time and achieving very little.

But those who do love God you must requite with love, helping to strengthen them so that their love for Him may grow. That you must do for them, and nothing more. And for those weaker ones, sinners separated from God, great labours and special prayers are not required from you: merely include them in your love for God. The more God's lovers love Him, the more are sinners set free from their sins, the more are His lovers confirmed in their love.

To live in perfect accord with the will of His love is to live so wholly in that will of that true love, longing always to be all that love asks of us, that even if we wished we would choose and ask nothing better than what pleases love, whether the world should curse us or bless us for it. Nor should we ever wish the peace and the blessedness of that love to fail in us, except only so that we may know that we are not yet grown to the perfect stature of love.

And knowing this we must always know that for us life must be a loving service and a longing exile, for so Jesus Christ lived as a man upon this earth. It is nowhere written that Christ in all His earthly life ever asked for any privilege from His Father or from His own omnipotent nature, so that He might here enjoy the blessedness of His divine being; He never granted Himself any respite, but lived in greater toil from day to day, from His first day until His last. It was His gracious will to live as we must live, to be what we should be, and He says to those who live now as He then did that where there is love there is great labour and much suffering. But to such men, their sufferings are sweet. *Qui amat non laborat*, 'Who loves does not labour.'

When Christ lived here as man, there was a time for all His works. When the proper time came, He did the proper work: His words and His deeds, His preaching and teaching, His admonitions, consolations, miracles, absolutions, His toils, His reproofs, His humiliations, His griefs, His sorrows until His Passion and death: in all these He waited patiently for the right time. And when the hour came for Him to work, He perfected it, valiant and mighty, and in these great and honest labours He paid the debt which every human being owes to the Father, who is God and who is truth. "Mercy and truth met one another, justice and peace embraced one another."

In union with God's humanity, you should live here in labour and exile; and in union with God's eternal omnipotence you should in your heart love and rejoice, gently laying all your trust in Him. In the truth which that humanity and that omnipotence share, God finds a single delight; and just as His humanity here on earth submitted to the will of His majesty, you too must submit in love to the will of Them both together. Humbly serve Them, in Their united might, and stand before Them as one standing ready to do all Their will. And let Them then do with you what They will.

Let this be your only concern, and nothing else. Serve God's majesty with ready hands, and with a great desire for every work of virtue. You should love God's divinity not merely with devotion but with unspeakable longings, standing always with renewed fervour before Him as He manifests Himself, dreadful in His glory, where His love reveals itself and consumes all works in itself. In this manifestation you shall read your judgment and the terms of all that you have to do in this life; and then throw off all the heaviness which weighs you down, abandon all the meannesses that oppress you, and choose for yourself rather to live all your life far off from God than to accept any satisfaction that is less than God. All your perfection depends upon this: forsake every delight which is less than God, forsake every suffering which is not suffered only for His sake.

And yet indeed in all things you must have great compassion, though this for me is very hard. With a true will turn towards the highest truth. We have a true will when we refuse every consolation in heaven or on earth, in body or in soul, except only that for which God has loved us and has chosen us.

And let this be for you the highest good, and never turn to anyone for encouragement or consolation. Stand always ready to do its bidding, never failing, never paying heed to others: let them mock, let them approve, let them rail, let them bless, let them do as they like.

Never abandon the true life of good works, whether this seem bad or good to others. We can be glad to suffer the contempt which we earn with the good we do, when we know that they are God's will; and we can gladly suffer praise which we gain with those works of virtue in which God is glorified. The pains which our dear God suffered, when He lived as man on earth, merited that we should gladly suffer every pain and every contempt, and that we should long for pain of every kind. And the everlasting nature of His sweet love merits indeed that we should perform, with a perfect will, every work of virtue in which God, our love, is glorified.

Therefore you must not avoid contempt or blame. For everything which we can endure or perform is welcome to God's love, which can never be sated, for that love is the consuming fire which devours all things, and which never will be quenched in all eternity.

And because you are still young, and

untried in all these things, you must strive greatly to grow up, as it were out of nothing, as one who has nothing and can become nothing but who yet labours to climb out of the depths. And you must always cast yourself deep into the abyss of humility, denying everything which you have to sacrifice to God. He asks this of you, that in all your dealings with all men you use a perfect humility. Raise yourself above everything which is inferior to God Himself, if you want to be what He wants of you: and in doing this you will find peace in your whole being.

If you would act according to the being in which God has created you, your nature would be so noble that there would be no pains which you would shun, it would be so valiant that you could not bear to leave anything undone, but you would reach out for that which is best of all, for that great oneness which is God, knowing that to be your only riches. And then in mercy you must give your riches to others, and make rich those who are poor; for those who love truly will never fail in their free gifts to those others who with all their heart and all their will have surrendered themselves to God's love. True love has always given what it had to give, always conquered what it had to conquer, always withheld what it had to withhold.

Oh, now I ask you, my dear child, always to perform all the works of virtue which you have to do, never complaining, with a settled disposition towards them all, the little works and the great works. And do not ask and beg from God for anything, not for your own needs or for your friends, and do not ask Him for any sort of rest or consolation, but let Him give you what He pleases. Let Him come, let Him go, according to His holy will, and let Him do as is needful for His glory with you and with those to whom you would teach a loving submission to Him.

You may pray that His will be done both for yourself and for them; but you should not pray for them to have those things which they choose and decide for themselves. Nowadays most people go astray, deceiving themselves that sanctity is what they long for, when in reality they are taking their ease in second-rate consolations, more is the pity.

That is why you must choose and love God's will alone in all things. His will for you, for your friends, for Himself, even though your own wish might be for Him to give you consolation, so that you might live your life here in peace and rest.

But today, instead of loving God's will, everyone loves himself: it is everyone's will to have peace and rest, to live with God in riches and might, and to be one with Him in His joy and glory. We all want to be God along with God; but God knows that there are few of us who want to be man with Him in His humanity, to carry His Cross with Him, to hang upon it with Him, to pay with Him the debt of human kind. If we look at ourselves we can see that this is true: we will not suffer anything, we will not endure. Just let our hearts be stabbed by the slightest grief, just let someone say a scornful or slanderous word about us, let anyone act against our reputation or our peace or our will, and at once we are mortally injured: we know exactly what we want and what we do not want, there are so many different things which give us pleasure or pain, now we want this and now we want that, our joy today is our sorrow tomorrow, we would like to be here, we would like to be there, we do not want something and then we want it, and in everything all we are thinking of is our own satisfaction and how we can best seek it.

This is why we are still unenlightened in our thinking, unstable in all our being, uncertain in our reasoning and understanding. This is why we suffer so, poor wretched exiled beggars, painfully travelling through a foreign land, and there would be no need for this, were it not that all our thinking is false; and how false it is we show plainly when we do not live with Christ as He lived, do not abandon all as He did, are not abandoned by all as He was. If we look at what we do, we can see that this is true: whenever we can, we strive for our own ease, where we can gain it we fight for advancement, we fight to get our own way, we know exactly what is going to please us, we seek our own advantage in everything, in spiritual matters as well as worldly, and whatever we achieve in these ways, that is our joy and our delight, and when we have it we think that now we are something. And just as we say that, we are in truth nothing. This is how we destroy ourselves in our whole way of life, and we do not live with Christ and we do not carry the Cross with the Son of God. We only carry it with Simon, who was hired to carry the Cross of our Lord.

It is the same when we suffer and endure. We demand God as the reward for our good deeds, we want to know Him in this present life, because it seems to us that we are very deserving and that it is only right that He should give us some of what we ask in return for what we do. We think that what we do or suffer for Him is a great matter, and there is no rest for us until we have our reward and feel that we are pleasing to God, and what we would choose would be to have our reward here and now, a reward of consolation and rest in Him. And there is yet another reward which we choose, the reward of our own self-satisfaction and complacency. And our third reward is when we know that we are pleasing to others, and receive their respect and praise and honour.

All this is carrying the Cross with Simon, who laboured under the Cross for a short while, but did not die upon it. People who live in this way, even though to other men their lives may seem exalted and their works fine and splendid, so that sometimes they seem to live in wisdom and sanctity, well ordered and virtuous, have little about them which is pleasing to God, for they are neither upright nor enduring. The virtues which they seem to possess are in truth their failings; the most trifling opposition, if they encounter it, can expose them for what they are. One moment they are all exaltation and consolation, the next moment they are plunged into bitterness; because their lives are not built upon truth, their foundations are false and infirm. However much men may esteem them, in their works and in their lives they remain unstable and untrue. They are not upright, they are not persevering, and they do not die with Christ. They may perform the works of virtue, but their intention is neither pure nor true. There is so much falsehood mingled with their virtues that they can have no power to guide or illumine others, nor to persevere in a settled and firm truth, in which their everlastingness should be established.

For we are obliged to perform virtuous works not to gain admiration or happiness, not for wealth or power, nor for any pleasure in heaven or on earth, but only so that we may be pleasing to God's greatest honour, who created human nature for this, making it to His honour and His praise, and for our joy in eternal glory.

This is the way that the Son of God walked before us, the way which He showed and made known to us when He lived as a man. For all the time that He was on earth, from His beginning until the end, He performed and perfected in knowledge the will of His Father, in all He did, in all His days, with all that He was, with every service which He could do, in words, in works, in joy, in sorrow, in great things and little things, in miracles, in contempt, in suffering, in labour, in sorrow, in the anguish of His bitter death. With all His heart, with all His soul, with all His strength He stood ready to endure all things at all times to make perfect that which we had undone; and with all His might as God, and with all His goodness as man, He carried us and He drew us up, back to our first honourable state, back to that freedom in which we were created by a loving Creator, back to what we are now called to and chosen for in His predestination, to what He has foreseen from all eternity that we should be.

The mark of grace is holy living. The mark of predestination in an inward and confident lifting-up of the heart, with a living trustfulness, and with an unspeakable longing to honour and to satisfy Him in His glory, which is majestic and incomprehensible and divine.

The cross which we must carry with the living Son of God is that sweet exile which men suffer for their true love, when in a longing trustfulness we await that great day on which Love shall reveal itself and manifest its noble powers and its great might on earth and in heaven. Then Love shall show itself so mighty to those who love that it will draw them out of themselves, it will rob them of heart and mind, it will make them die and make them live in the loving service of true Love.

But before Love shall show itself so greatly, before it calls men so utterly to come out of themselves to it, before it so touches them that they become one spirit and one life with Love in Love, men must pay to Love the tribute of honourable service and a life of longing exile: honourable service in all the works of virtue, and a life of longing exile in perfect obedience, always standing ready with fresh zeal and willing hands for every deed in which virtue is exercised, with a will submissive to every virtue which can pay honour to Love. And in all this there must be no other intention than that Love should be enthroned, as it should be, in men and in all creatures, according to Love's pleasure. This is to hang upon the Cross with Christ, this is to die with Him and with Him to rise again. May He help us always to do this; and for this help I entreat Him in whom is every perfect virtue.

LETTER 11

Ah, dear child, may God give you what my heart longs that you should have: and that would be for you to love God as He deserves. And yet, dear child, I have never been able to endure the thought that anyone before me could have loved Him so dearly as I. Yet of course I believe that there were many who have loved Him as much and as dearly, even though I could not suffer to think that anyone could have known Him or loved Him so greatly as I.

Since I was ten years old, I have been so possessed by a wholehearted love for God that in the first two years when I began to love Him so, I should have died, had He not given me greater strength than most people have, and given to my nature the power of His nature; and often He gave me counsel, which sometimes was illumined with many gracious shewings; and I received from Him many wonderful gifts in which I felt and I saw what He is. And in all these tokens of love which I felt between Him and me, according to the usages of love, just as lovers use between themselves, concealing little, giving much, finding most in their close communion one with another, each one as it were tasting all, eating all, drinking all, consuming all the other, in all these tokens which God my Love so plentifully gave to me at the beginning of my life, He gave me trust in Him, that from then on I generally felt that no one had loved Him with so whole a heart as I. But there were times when reason said indeed to me that I was not the one who loved Him best. But though I thought this, I could never feel it or believe it, so closely was I bound to Him in the bonds of true Love.

So this is how I am now: in the end, I cannot believe that I have loved Him best, and yet I cannot believe that there is any living man who loves God as I love Him. So sometimes Love illumines me so that I know how far short I fall, that I am not enough for my Love, that I do not love Him as He deserves; and at times the sweet nature of Love grants me so to taste and to feel Love that I am blinded, that that suffices me, that I am so rich in being together with Love that I confess to Love that Love alone suffices me.

HADEWIJCH OF BRABANT

Visions

Translated by Mother Columba Hart

Vision 7: Oneness in the Eucharist

On a certain Pentecost Sunday I had a vision at dawn. Matins were being sung in the church, and I was present. My heart and my veins and all my limbs trembled and quivered with eager desire and, as often occurred with me, such madness and fear beset my mind that it seemed to me I did not content my Beloved, and that my Beloved did not fulfill my desire,[1] so that dying I must go mad, and going mad I must die. On that day my mind was beset so fearfully and so painfully by desirous love that all my separate limbs threatened to break, and all my separate veins were in travail. The longing in which I then was cannot be expressed by any language or any person I know; and everything I could say about it would be unheard-of to all those who never apprehended Love as something to work for with desire, and whom Love had never acknowledged as hers. I can say this about it: I desired to have full fruition of my Beloved, and to understand and taste him to the full. I desired that his Humanity should to the fullest extent be one in fruition with my humanity, and that mine then should hold its stand and be strong enough to enter into perfection until I content him, who is perfection itself, by purity and unity, and in all things to content him fully in every virtue. To that end I wished he might content me interiorly with his Godhead, in one spirit, and that for me he should be all that he is, without withholding anything from me. For above all the gifts that I ever longed for, I chose this gift: that I should give satisfaction in all great sufferings. For that is the most perfect satisfaction: to grow up in order to be God with God.[2] For this demands suffering, pain, and misery, and living in great new grief of soul: but to let everything come and go without grief, and in this way to experience nothing else but sweet love, embraces, and kisses. In this sense I desired that God give himself to me, so that I might content him.

As my mind was thus beset with fear, I saw a great eagle flying toward me from the altar, and he said to me: "If you wish to attain oneness, make yourself ready!"

I fell on my knees and my heart beat fearfully, to worship the Beloved with oneness, according to his true dignity; that indeed was impossible for me, as I know well, and as God knows, always to my woe and to my grief.

But the eagle turned back and spoke: "Just

and mighty Lord, now show your great power to unite your oneness in the manner of union with full possession!"

Then the eagle turned round again and said to me: "He who has come, comes again; and to whatever place he never came, he comes not."

Then he came from the altar, showing himself as a Child; and that Child was in the same form as he was in his first three years. He turned toward me, in his right hand took from the ciborium his Body, and in his left hand took a chalice, which seemed to come from the altar, but I do not know where it came from.

With that he came in the form and clothing of a Man, as he was on the day when he gave us his Body for the first time; looking like a Human Being and a Man, wonderful, and beautiful, and with glorious face, he came to me as humbly as anyone who wholly belongs to another. Then he gave himself to me in the shape of the Sacrament, in its outward form, as the custom is; and then he gave me to drink from the chalice, in form and taste, as the custom is. After that he came himself to me, took me entirely in his arms, and pressed me to him; and all my members felt his in full felicity, in accordance with the desire of my heart and my humanity. So I was outwardly satisfied and fully transported. Also then, for a short while, I had the strength to bear this; but soon, after a short time, I lost that manly beauty outwardly in the sight of his form. I saw him completely come to nought and so fade and all at once dissolve that I could no longer recognize or perceive him outside me, and I could no longer distinguish him within me. Then it was to me as if we were one without difference. It was thus: outwardly, to see, taste, and feel, as one can outwardly taste, see, and feel in the reception of the outward Sacrament. So can the Beloved, with the loved one, each wholly receive the other in all full satisfaction of the sight, the hearing, and the passing away of the one in the other.

After that I remained in a passing away in my Beloved, so that I wholly melted away in him and nothing any longer remained to me of myself; and I was changed and taken up in the spirit, and there it was shown me concerning such hours.

Vision 10: The Bride in the City

I was taken up in the spirit on the feast of Saint John the Evangelist in the Christmas Octave. There I saw prepared a new city of the same name as Jerusalem and of the same appearance. It was being adorned with all sorts of new ornaments (cf. Apoc. 21:2) that were unspeakably beautiful. They who served in the city were the most beautiful of heaven, and all belonged among those called Auriolas and Eunustus. And all who had been sanctified by Love, together with all the living, adorned it and evoked all the new wonders that gave rise to new admiration. And in the midst of the high city flew an eagle crying with a loud voice: "All you lords and wielders of power, here shall you learn the eternity of your domain!" And he flew a second time through the city, crying: "The time is at hand! All you living, find joy in her who possesses the true life!"

And a third time he cried and said: "O you dead, come into the light and into the life! And all you who are unready, insofar as you are not too naked to attend our marriage (cf. Matt. 22:1–14), come to our abundance and contemplate the bride, who by love has experienced all needs, heavenly and earthly! She is so experienced with need in the alien land that I shall now show her how she has grown in the *land of darkness* (Job 10:33). And she shall be great, and she shall see her repose, and the voice of power shall be wholly hers."

After this an Evangelist came and said: "You are here, and you shall be shown the glory of your exile. The city you here see adorned is your free conscience; and the lofty beauty that is here is your manifold virtues with full suffering; and the adornment is your fiery ardor, which remains dominant in you in spite of all disasters. Your unknown virtues with new assiduity are the manifold ornaments that adorn the city. Your blessed soul is the bride in the city. Here is that highest society which wholly lives in love and in the spirit of the highest virtue. All those whom you see here, Eunustus and Auriolas, and the whole multitude who are highest in power, have come here to participate in your marriage. Moreover all the living, both of heaven and earth, shall renew their life in this marriage. The dead sinners—who have come without hope, and are enlightened by the knowledge of your union,[3] and desire grace or entrance into purgatory—cling somewhat to virtue and are not altogether naked. If only they believe in the oneness of you both, they will find full contentment through your marriage."

Then I heard a Voice loudly crying: "New peace be to all of you, and all new joy! Behold, this is my bride, who has passed through all your honors with perfect love, and whose love is so strong that, through it, all attain growth!" And he said: "Behold, Bride and Mother, you like no other have been able to live me as God and Man! What do you think they who are Eunustus to all earthly repose become? That is what you are for all of them collectively. You alone have never tasted earthly poison; you like no other have superhumanly suffered much among men. You shall suffer everything to the end with what I am, and we shall remain one. Now enjoy fruition of me, what I am, with the strength of your victory, and they shall live eternally contented through you."

The Voice embraced me with an unheard of wonder, and I swooned in it, and my spirit failed me to see or hear more. And I lay in this fruition half an hour; but then the night was over, and I came back, piteously lamenting my exile, as I have done all this winter. For truly the whole winter long I have been occupied with this kind of thing. I lay there a long time and possessed love, or revelations, or anything else in particular that Love gave me.

Vision 11: The Abyss of Omnipotence

I was in a very depressed frame of mind one Christmas night, when I was taken up in the spirit. There I saw a very deep whirlpool, wide and exceedingly dark; in this abyss all beings were included, crowded together, and compressed. The darkness illuminated and penetrated everything. The unfathomable depth of the abyss was so high that no one could reach it. I will not attempt now to describe how it was formed, for there is no time now to speak of it; and I cannot put it in words, since it is unspeakable. Second, this is not a convenient time for it, because much pertains to what I saw. It was the entire omnipotence of our Beloved. In it I saw the Lamb (cf. Apoc. 5:6) take possession of our Beloved. In the vast space I saw festivities, such as David playing the harp, and he struck the harp strings.[4] Then I perceived an Infant being born in the souls who love in secret, the souls hidden from their own eyes in the deep abyss of which I speak, and to whom nothing is lacking but that they should lose themselves in it.[5] I saw the forms of many different souls, according to what each one's life had been. Of those whom I saw, the ones whom I already knew remained known to me; and those I did not know became known to me; I received interior knowledge about some, and also exterior knowledge about many. And certain ones I knew interiorly, having never seen them exteriorly.

Then I saw coming as it were a bird, namely the one called phoenix.[6] It devoured a grey eagle that was young, and a yellow eagle with new feathers that was old.[7] These eagles kept flying about incessantly in the deep abyss.

Then I heard a voice like thunder (cf. Apoc. 6:1) that said: "Do you know who these different-colored eagles are?"

And I answered: "I should like to know this better."

And although I asked to know this, I nevertheless perceived the essence of all the things I saw. For all that is seen in the spirit when one is ravished by Love is understood, tasted, seen, and heard through and through. So was it also here. I wished, however, to hear the Voice that came to my hearing from the Beloved. And indeed the truth was told me concerning all this, in particular the natures and perfections comprised in my vision. All this would take too long; I pass over it. For a great book would be required if one were to write everything perfectly in full truth.[8]

One of the eagles who were swallowed was Saint Augustine, and the other myself. The old feathers that were grey, and the eaglet that was young—this was I, for I was attaining to perfection, beginning, and growing in love. The feathers that were yellow and old—this was the full-grownness of Saint Augustine, who was old and perfect in the love of our Beloved.[9] The old age I had was in the perfect nature of eternal being, even though I was youthful in created nature.[10] The young feathers of the old eagle were the renewed splendor he received from me in the new heavenly glory of my love, with which I loved him and so greatly desired with him to pour forth one single love in the Trinity, where he himself was burning so totally with an unquenchable love. The youth that the old feathers that were yellow had signified also the renewal of Love, which continually grows in heaven and on earth (cf. Ps. 102:5).[11] The phoenix that swallowed the eagles was the Unity in which the Trinity dwells, wherein both of us are lost.

When afterwards I returned to myself, where I found myself poor and miserable, I reflected on this union with Saint Augustine to which I had attained. I was not contented with what my dearly Beloved had just permitted, in spite of my consent and emotional attraction; it weighed on me now that this union with Saint Augustine had made me so perfectly happy, whereas previously I had possessed union far from saints and men, with God alone. From this I understood that neither in heaven nor in the spirit can one enjoy one's own will, except in accordance with the will of Love. And as I thought about this attitude, I asked my Beloved to deliver me from it. For I wished to remain in his deepest abyss, alone in fruition. And I understood that, since my childhood, God had drawn me to himself alone, far from all the other beings whom he welcomes to himself in other manners. But I well know that whatever was in him is, in highest measure, eternal glory and perfect enjoyment, but I likewise wished to remain in him alone. I understood this when I asked for it, and so greatly desired it, and suffered so much; then I remained free. No doubt I continued to belong to God alone while being united in Love to this creature. But my liberty I gained then was given me moreover for reasons of my own, which neither Augustine nor many others had.

I did not suggest this as a claim to be more privileged than Saint Augustine; but in the time when I knew the truth of Being, I did not want to receive any comfort from him insofar as he was a creature, or to accept any joy amid my pains, and so I would allow myself no satisfaction in the security that was given me in this union with Saint Augustine. For I am a free human creature, and also pure as to one part,[12] and I can desire freely with my will, and I can will as highly as I wish,[13] and seize and receive from God all that he is, without objection or anger on his part—what no saint can do. For the saints have their will perfectly according to their pleasure; and they can no longer will beyond what they have. I have hated many great wonderful deeds and experiences, because I wished to belong to Love alone, and because I could not believe that any human creature loved him so passionately as I—although I know it is a fact and indubitable, still I cannot believe it or feel it, so powerfully am I touched by Love.

In this wonderful way I belong to God alone in pure love, and to my saint in love, and then to all the saints, each one according to his dignity, and to men according to what each one loved and also according to what he was and still is. But in striving for this I have never experienced Love in any sort of way as repose; on the contrary, I found Love a heavy burden and disgrace. For I was a human creature, and Love is terrible and implacable, devouring and burning without regard for anything. The soul is contained in one little rivulet; her depth is quickly filled up; her dikes quickly burst. Thus with rapidity the Godhead has engulfed human nature wholly in itself.

I used to love the blessedness of the saints, but I never ceased to desire the repose in which God within them had fruition of himself; their quietude was many a time my inquietude; yes, truly, it was always forty pains against one single pleasure. I could not but know that they were smiled at, while I wept; that they boasted themselves fortunate, while I pitied myself; and that they were honored by God, and that God was honored because of them in every land, while I was an object of derision. All this, nevertheless, was my greatest repose, for he willed it—but this was such repose as comes to those who desire love and fruition, and who have in this desire such woe as I do.

Now for persons, my repose lay in loving each of them in what was proper to him, and wishing for each of them that only what he held desirable and good might happen to him; whether this good was that of their will or of the divine will was a question with which I did not meddle. But what they had in love, I loved for God, in order that he might strengthen it for himself and cause it to grow to perfection;

such was my desire. Because I loved God's being loved, I wished no pleasure from it but that.

As for persons who failed God and were strangers to him, they weighed heavy on me. For I was so laden with his love and captivated by it that I could scarcely endure that anyone should love him less than I. And charity for others wounded me cruelly, that he should let these souls[14] be such strangers to him and so deprived of all the good that he himself is in love. This was such an intolerable burden to me in many an hour that it happened to me as it did to Moses because of his love for his sister: I would have wished that he give his love to others or withdraw it from me. I would gladly have purchased love for them by accepting that he should love them and hate me. And sometimes, too, because he did not do this, I would willingly have turned away from him in love and would have loved them in spite of his wrath (cf. Rom. 9:3); seeing that these unfortunates could not know the sweet and ardent love that dwells in his holy Nature, I would most gladly have loved them, had I been able.

Also, charity has wounded me the most— except for actual Love. What is actual Love? It is the divine power that must have priority; and it does so in me. For the sovereign power that is actual Love spares no one, either in hate or in love; favor is never found in it. This power held me back once again when I had wished to free all men in the twinkling of an eye, otherwise than in accordance with how God had chosen them. When I could thus turn myself against him, it was a beautiful and free expression of life as a human being. Then I could desire what I wished. But when I did the opposite, I was more beautiful and taken up into a fuller participation in the Divine Nature.

Thus I have lived quietly as a human being, so that I have taken repose neither in saints nor in men on earth. And so I have lived in misery without love, in the love of God and of those who are his: and while I do not receive from him what is mine,[15] and what God does not yet give me—I have it nevertheless, and it shall remain mine! Hence I never felt love, unless as an ever-new death—until the time of my consolation came, and God granted me to know the perfect pride of love;[16] to know how we shall love the Humanity in order to come to the Divinity, and rightly know it in one single Nature.[17] This is the noblest life that can be lived *in the kingdom of God* (Col. 4:11). This rich repose God gave me,[18] and truly in a happy hour.

NOTES

1. This statement suggests the theme of paradoxical unfaith; cf. Letter 8: P. 27, last sentence, and Vision 13: P. 159, "[they] disavowed their love out of humility."

2. Theme "to be God with God."

3. Theme that they who love are a source of light in the intellectual sense. Cf. Letter 1: P. 33.

4. Beatrice of Nazareth, in her Christmas vision (A.D. 1216), also saw David playing the harp; cf. *Vita Beatricis*, 1.11.55; p. 46.

5. Theme of the soul as mother of Christ.

6. The symbolism of the phoenix is explained in P. 49, *Hadewijch The Complete Works*, trans. Hart.

7. The old-young antithesis, weaving in and out through this entire paragraph, mounts to an unexpected climax in the affirmation of eternal progress.

8. See Vision 13: P. 82. Probably a vague reminiscence of John 21:25.

9. The emphasis here on love in Saint Augustine certainly connects Hadewijch's conception of love with his. Van Mierlo affirms the connection but does not cite this proof (Cf. "Hadewijch une mystique," p. 277).

10. Cf. Introduction, p. 6.

11. Theme of eternal progress.

12. This may refer to the purity of Hadewijch's love, or to the part of each person that God reserves for himself. Cf. Porion, "La onzième vision de Hadewijch," *Nova et Vetera* 19 (1949): 47, note 2.

13. Van Mierlo regards this statement as *fierbeit* (good pride), expressing the wish to love God as perfectly as possible (*Visioenen*, vol. 1, p. 116).

14. "These souls" refers to Hadewijch's young Beguines; see Spaapen (1970): 38 and note 53.

15. This seems to mean the fruition of God to which she has a right.

16. Good pride.

17. Viz., Person.

18. By using the word *repose* in five different senses in the account of this vision, Hadewijch comes to this strong climax.

BEATRIJS OF NAZARETH   (c. 1200–1268; Antwerp)

There Are Seven Manners of Loving

Translated by Eric Colledge

There are seven manners of loving, which come down from the heights and go back again far above.

I

The first manner is an active longing, which proceeds from love, and must rule a long time

in the heart before it can conquer all opposition, and can work with its power and judgment, and grow within us in holiness.

This manner is a longing which without doubt comes from love: that is, the pious soul, which faithfully wants to serve our Lord and to follow Him in holiness and truly to love

Him, as it longs does everything in its power to attain and to keep the purity and the nobility and the freedom in which it was made by its Creator, in His image and likeness, which the soul must love greatly and zealously preserve. And the soul longs to lead its whole life so, and to act so and to grow and to climb to still greater heights of love and nearer knowledge of God, to that perfection for which it was made and is called by its Creator. This is all the soul's work, early and late, and to this the soul gives itself wholly. All the soul's seeking, all its teaching, all its petitions to God and all its meditations are for this: how it can approach and how it can attain to the presence and the likeness of love, adorned with all virtues and with that purity which is the sovereign excellence of love.

Always such a soul ponders what it is and what it ought to be, what it possesses and what it lacks; with its whole attention and with great longing and with all its powers it strives to preserve itself and to shun everything which could burden or hinder it as it works to this end. Its heart never ceases, its will never falters in seeking, entreating, learning, gaining and keeping everything which can help it and bring it to love.

This is the soul's greatest concern, when it is established in this way and can work so and labour greatly, until it is granted by God, through its zeal and its faith, that it may thenceforth be in the service of love, no longer hindered by its past misdeeds, its conscience free and its spirit pure and its understanding clear.

Longing of this kind, of so great a purity and excellence, undoubtedly comes from love and not from fear. Fear makes us work and suffer, act and be still out of dread of the anger of our Lord, of the judgment of our righteous Judge, of punishment in eternity or of chastizing in this life. But love, in all that it does, strives for the purity and the exaltation and the supreme excellence which is love's very nature and possession and delight; and it is

this striving which love teaches to those who serve love.

2

Yet the soul has a second manner of loving, when at times it offers itself to our Lord to serve Him for nothing, doing this only in love and asking for no answer, no reward of grace or of glory; but the soul is like a maiden who serves her master only for her great love of him, not for any payment, satisfied that she may serve him and that he suffers her to serve. So the soul longs to serve love with love, without measure, beyond measure, and beyond human sense and reason, faithfully performing every service.

When the soul attains this state, it becomes so ardent in longing, so ready to serve, so joyful labouring, so calm in sorrow, so gay in suffering; and with every quality which it possesses the soul longs to be pleasing to its love, and all that it asks is to act and to suffer for the use and the honour of love.

3

The third manner of loving is attained by the pious soul when it comes into a time of much suffering. This is when the soul longs to be sufficient for love, to perfect itself for the honour of love and to serve it in every way, in utter obedience and submission.

Sometimes this desire grows violent in the soul, and it is seized with great longings to perform all things and to achieve all virtues, to suffer and to endure everything, to make all its works perfect in love, withholding nothing and counting nothing. In this state the soul is ready to do anything, eager and unafraid in labours and in suffering; and yet in all that it does the soul remains unfulfilled and dissatisfied.

But it is above all else the greatest torment

to the soul that despite its great longings it cannot do enough for love, and that in loving it comes so short. Yet it knows well that it is above human ability and beyond its powers to do as it wishes, for what it longs to do is impossible and unnatural to created beings. For the soul longs single-handed to do as much as all the men upon earth, as all the spirits in heaven, as every creature that ever is, to do more beyond all telling than they do, serving, loving, glorifying love as is love's due. And because the soul comes so short in what it does, it wants with all its will and with great longing to do yet better. Yet this cannot satisfy the soul. It knows well that to achieve what it longs for is far above its powers, beyond human reason and all the senses; yet it cannot moderate or restrain or calm itself. It does everything that it can; it gives thanks and praises to love; it acts and it works for love, it surrenders its whole self for love, and all its works are perfected for love.

But none of this gives the soul any rest, and it is a great torment to long for what it cannot attain. And so the soul must stay in sorrow and longing, and it will seem that living, it dies, and dying, it feels the pains of hell, and its whole life is torment and rejection and refusal, racked as it is with these desires which it can never appease or quieten or satisfy. And the soul must remain in this anguish till the time when our Lord comforts it and establishes it in a different manner of loving and longing, when He gives it a closer knowledge of Himself; and then the soul can do as our Lord allows it.

4

In the fourth manner of loving, it is our Lord's custom to give sometimes great joy, sometimes great woe; and let us now speak of this.

Sometimes it happens that love is sweetly awakened in the soul and joyfully arises and stirs itself in the heart without any help from human acts. And then the heart is so tenderly touched in love, so powerfully assailed, so wholly encompassed and so lovingly embraced in love that the soul is altogether conquered by love. Then it feels a great closeness to God and a spiritual brightness and a wonderful richness and a noble freedom and a great compulsion of violent love, and an overflowing fullness of great delight. And then the soul feels that all its senses and its will have become love, that it has sunk down so deeply and been engulfed so completely in love, that it has itself entirely become love. Love's beauty has adorned the soul, love's power has consumed it, love's sweetness has submerged it, love's righteousness has engulfed it, love's excellence has embraced it, love's purity has enhanced it, love's exaltedness has drawn it up and enclosed it, so that the soul must be nothing else but love and do nothing else.

When the soul feels itself to be thus filled full of riches and in such fullness of heart, the spirit sinks away down into love, the body seems to pass away, the heart to melt, every faculty to fail; and the soul is so utterly conquered by love that often it cannot support itself, often the limbs and the senses lose their powers. And just as a vessel filled up to the brim will run over and spill if it is touched, so at times the soul is so touched and overpowered by this great fullness of the heart that in spite of itself it spills and overflows.

5

In the fifth manner, it also sometimes happens that love is powerfully strengthened in the soul and rises violently up, with great tumult and force, as if it would break the heart with its assault and drag the soul out of itself in the exercise and the delight of love. And then the soul is drawn in the longing of love to fulfill the great and pure deeds of love and the desires implanted by love's many promptings. Or sometimes the soul longs to rest in the sweet embrace of love, in that desirable state of richness and satisfaction which comes from the possession of love, so that the heart and all the senses long and seek eagerly and long wholly for this. When the soul is in this state, it is so strong in spirit, so open in heart to receive all things, so stronger in bodily power to do all things, more able to accomplish its works, achieving so much, that it seems to the soul itself that there is nothing which it cannot do and perform, even though in the body it were to remain idle. At the same time the soul feels itself so greatly stirred from within, such an utter dependence upon love, such an impatient desire for love and the countless sorrows of a deep dissatisfaction. And sometimes when the soul experiences love that brings it woe without it ever knowing why, or it may be because it is so stirred to long for love, or because it is filled with dissatisfaction that it cannot know love's full delight.

And at times love becomes so boundless and so overflowing in the soul, when it itself is so mightily and violently moved in the heart, that it seems to the soul that the heart is wounded again and again, and that these wounds increase every day in bitter pain and in fresh intensity. It seems to the soul that the veins are bursting, the blood spilling, the marrow withering, the bones softening, the heart burning, the throat parching, so that the body in its every part feels this inward heat, and this is the fever of love. Sometimes the soul feels that the whole body is transfixed, and it is as if every sense would fail; and like a devouring fire, seizing upon everything and consuming everything which it can master, love seems to be working violently in the soul, relentless, uncontrollable, drawing everything into it and devouring it.

All this torments and afflicts the soul, and the heart grows sick and the powers dwindle;

yet it is so that the soul is fed and love is fostered and the spirit is subjected to love.

For love is exalted so high above the soul's comprehension, above all that the soul can do or suffer, that even though at such times it may long to break the bond that unites it to love, that cannot harm love's singleness; and the soul is so fettered with the bond of love, so conquered by the boundlessness of love, that it cannot rule itself by reason, cannot reason through understanding, cannot spare itself this weariness, cannot hold fast to human wisdom.

For the more there is given from above to the soul, the more is demanded of it: the more is revealed to the soul, the more it is filled with longing to come close to the light of that truth, that purity, that excellence and that delight which are love's attributes. Always the soul will be driven and goaded on, never will it be satisfied and at rest. For what most afflicts and torments the soul is that which most heals and assuages it; what gives the soul its deepest wounds brings to it best relief.

6

In the sixth manner, as the bride of our Lord advances and climbs into greater holiness, she feels love to be of a different nature, and her knowledge of this love is closer and higher.

The soul feels that love has conquered its every shortcoming, and has mastered the senses and adorned its humanity, and increased and exalted its being, and has utterly overpowered it without any resistance, so that the heart is made steadfast in confidence, and can freely practise all the exercises of love and delight in love and take its rest. When the soul is in this state, there is nothing which it must perform or abandon, suffer and endure, which does not seem to it petty and easy, for this is one of love's noble qualities, and so it is easy for the soul to busy itself in the exercises of love.

Then the soul feels in itself a closeness to God which comes from Him, a radiant purity, a sweetness of the spirit, a loving freedom, a savouring wisdom, a gentle drawing near to our Lord and a close comprehension of God.

And you may see that now the soul is like a housewife who has put all her household in good order and prudently arranged it and well disposed it: she has taken good care that nothing will damage it, her provision for the future is wise, she knows exactly what she is doing, she acquires and discards, she does what is proper, she avoids mistakes, and always she knows how everything should be. So it is with the soul: the soul is all love, and love rules in the soul, mighty and powerful, working and resting, doing and not doing, and all which is in the soul and comes to the soul is according to love's will.

And like the fish, swimming in the vast sea and resting in its deeps, and like the bird, boldly mounting high in the sky, so the soul feels its spirit freely moving through the vastness and the depth and the unutterable richnesses of love.

It is love's power which has seized the soul and led it, sheltered and protected it, given it prudence and wisdom and the sweetness and the strength which belong to love. Yet still at this time love hides from the soul its own power, that it has mounted to yet greater heights and that it is master of itself and that it is love which reigns triumphantly in it. And then love makes the soul so bold that it no longer fears man nor friend, angel or saint or God Himself in all that it does or abandons, in all its working and resting. And now the soul feels indeed that love is within it, as mighty and as active when the body is at rest as when it performs many deeds.

The soul knows well and feels that love is not found in the labours and sufferings of those in whom it rules, but that all who want to attain to love must seek it in fear and pursue it in faith, exercising themselves in longing, not sparing themselves in great labours, in many sufferings, undergoing many sorrows and enduring much contempt. The soul must not despise these things: small though they be, they must seem great, until it attains to the state where love rules in it and performs its own mighty works, making great things small, labour easy, suffering sweet, and all debts paid.

This is freedom of conscience, sweetness of heart, subjection of the senses, the soul's excellence, the spirit's exaltation, and the beginning of everlasting life. This is to live the life of angels here in the flesh, that everlasting life which may God grant to us all. Amen.

7

Yet the blessed soul has a seventh manner of yet higher loving, in which it will experience little activity of itself. For it is drawn, above humanity, into love, and above human sense and reason and above all the works of the heart, and it is drawn along with love alone into eternity and incomprehensibility, into the vastness and the unattainable exaltation and into the limitless abyss of Divinity, which is all in all things, remaining incomprehensible in all things, immutable in all being, all-powerful, all-comprehending, all-doing in its might.

And in this the blessed soul sinks down so deeply and softly in love, it is so mightily led in desire, that the heart fails and is within full of disquiet, the soul flows away and liquefies in love, the spirit is possessed with the violence of great longing. All the senses prompt the soul to long for the delight of love. The soul begs and entreats this from God, it seeks it ardently in God, it cannot but long for it above all, for love will not allow the soul to dally or find rest or be at peace. Love draws it on, love thrusts it back, love gives it death and brings it life, love heals it and then wounds it again, love makes it sorry and then glad again: and so love draws the soul on up into a higher life.

So the soul has climbed in spirit above time into eternity, it is exalted above all that love can give into the eternity which is love itself, which is beyond time, which is set above all human modes of love, the soul has transcended its own nature in its longing for the life which is there.

Its life and its longing, its desires and its love are all there in that unshakeable truth and that pure brightness, that noble exaltation and that transfiguring beauty, in the sweet company of those highest spirits who all flow out in the superabundance of love, who have their being in the bright knowledge, the possession and the delight of their love. The will of the soul is set up there among those spirits: it is there that it longs to be, and most of all among the flaming seraphim; and whilst still here in the body it finds its rest and its dearest dwelling-place in the immense Divinity, in the exalted Trinity.

The soul seeks God in His majesty, it finds Him there and it beholds Him with heart and with spirit. It knows Him, it loves Him, it longs for Him, so much that it cannot heed saints or angels, men or created things, except in that common love which it has towards Him in whom it loves all. It is He alone whom the soul has chosen in love, above all, beneath all, in all, so that with all the longing of its heart and all the strength of its spirit it longs to see Him and to have Him and to delight in Him.

And now this earth is for the soul a cruel exile and a dire prison and a heavy torment: it despises the world, and earth revolts it, and here is nothing earthly which can console or satisfy it, and it is for the soul a great punishment that it can live in this estrangement and appear so alien. It cannot forget that it is in exile, its longings cannot be stilled, its desires torment it so cruelly and it is so martyred and

afflicted that it is beyond all measure and without any measure.

Therefore the soul is filled with great longing to be set free from this exile, to be loosed from this body; and sometimes it says with sorrowing heart, as the apostle said: *Cupio dissolvi et esse cum Christo*, that is "I long to be set free and to be with Christ." So it longs greatly and with a tormenting impatience for death to this world and for life with Christ; and this is not because the soul abhors this present time or fears the afflictions which time may bring, but because a holy and eternal love makes it to desire, in longing and languishing and great coveting, to attain to the land of eternity and into the glories of love's delight.

This longing is so great and violent in the soul, this present life is to it so hard and cruel, that the torments which it suffers in its longings cannot be described. Yet the soul must live in hope, and it is hope which makes it yearn and pine. Oh, holy longings of love, how mighty you are in the loving soul! This is a blessed martyrdom, a cruel suffering, a long torment, a murderous death and an expiring life. The soul cannot gain the heights above, nor can it rest or stay here below. To think of God is longing such as it cannot endure, to lack Him fills it with tormenting longing. And so the soul must go on living in great sorrow.

And therefore the soul cannot, will not be consoled, as the prophet says: *Renuit consolari anima mea*, "My soul refuses to be comforted." So the soul refuses every consolation, often from God Himself and from His creatures, for every consolation which could come to it only strengthens its love and draws it up towards a higher life; and this renews the soul's longing to live in love and to delight in love, its determination to live unconsoled in this present exile. And so there is no gift which can appease or comfort it, for the soul's one need is to be in the presence of its love.

This is a hard and laborious life, for the soul will take no consolation here, but longs only to achieve what it seeks so restlessly. Love has seized it and led it and taught it to walk love's ways, and the soul has followed them so faithfully, sometimes in great labour and in painful works, in great longings and in cruel desires, in much impatience and in woeful displeasure, in joy and in sorrow and in much suffering, in seeking and searching, in wanting and having, in climbing and in drawing back, in following and pursuing, in need and in pain, in fear and sorrow, in woe and desolation, in great faith and in much doubt. The soul is ready to suffer in well and in woe, in death and in life it wishes to belong to love, and in its heart it feels the suffering of cruel pain, and for the sake of love it longs to come to its true home. And when the soul has known all this, all it desires is to flee from earth to heaven; for all the works of love are ruled by the soul's longing to live close to love, its striving to ascend to love, where it can be nearest to love.

So the soul always wishes to follow after love, to see love, to delight in love; and this cannot come to the soul here in this exile. So it longs to leave this life and find its home, where already it has established its dwelling, where it directs its longings that it may in love find rest. For the soul knows well that there all hindrances will be removed, that there it will in love by its own true love be received.

For there the soul will look upon that which it has so sorrowfully longed for: it will have Him for its eternal reward whom it has so faithfully served, and find the delight of every consolation in Him whom so often it has in love embraced in the soul.

Then it will enter into the joy of its Lord, as St. Augustine says: "Who goes into the joy of the Lord goes into Him, and he shall not fear, for in Him who is perfect shall all perfection be had."

There the soul will be united with its Bridegroom, and will become with Him one spirit in an indivisible love and in everlasting faith. And the soul which has striven in the time of grace shall rejoice in Him in everlasting glory, where all our work will be to praise and love Him.

May God make speed to bring us all to this. Amen.

V

Beguine Spirituality
and the Convent of Helfta

Mechthild of Magdeburg and St. Gertrude the Great

*I*N GERMANY AS WELL AS in the Low Countries there was much Beguine activity in
urban areas, and as pressure increased to enclose Beguine communities and to regularize their
way of life, Dominican friars often took on responsibility for these holy women as the
Cistercians had done in Belgium. The Dominicans were not alone in this; in certain urban areas
Franciscans and Beguine groups inspired and protected each other, and in other places it was
the Cistercians and Benedictines who sheltered the Beguines. The best-known German
Beguine is Mechthild of Magdeburg,[1] born about 1207 to a family apparently of the minor
nobility. Near the end of her life she left the Beguine group with which she had been associated
and came to Helfta, perhaps advised to make such a retreat because of her outspoken criticism
of corruption in the church.

The Benedictine convent at Helfta, which provided a home for the aged Mechthild, had
already become famous under the enlightened rule of Abbess Gertrude of Hackeborn. The
house had initially been founded in 1229 at Mansfield in Saxony, with Cunegunde von
Halberstadt as its first abbess. Gertrude of Hackeborn was elected abbess in 1251, at the age of
nineteen; she governed the monastery for "forty years and eleven days." Although she was not a
writer herself, she was very learned, and she encouraged the development of intellectual and
spiritual gifts among her nuns: "This she approached by an insistence on rigorous study—
primarily of scripture and of the liberal arts. She was so successful that during her lifetime
Helfta became a center of mysticism in Germany and radiated influence in all directions."[2]

The lives of the four women associated with Helfta—Gertrude of Hackeborn, Mechthild of
Hackeborn, Mechthild of Magdeburg, and Gertrude the Great—reveal a number of themes
typical of the lives and writings of women religious in the late thirteenth century. Mechthild of
Magdeburg's work, *The Flowing Light of the Godhead*,[3] represents, in its blending of courtly and
religious language and literary form, exactly that combination of spiritual and secular that the
Beguines' way of life strove for—to be in the world but not of it. Mechthild probably grew up at

a small court, and it was not until she was twenty-two that she decided to devote her life to God although she had first received a call when she was twelve.[4] It is thought that she had finished the writings included in the first four books of *The Flowing Light* by 1250, when she was in her forties. The fifth and sixth books were composed during the next fifteen years; all six books were in circulation by the time she retired to Helfta, where she composed the seventh. We do not know to what extent Mechthild may have been involved in the ordering and arranging of each chapter. It seems likely that the book was put in its present form by Henry of Halle, her spiritual adviser, a Dominican theologian who had been a student of Albert the Great. Her original low German text no longer exists; there are two early translations, one into Latin, perhaps made as early as 1290, and a high German version done by the secular priest Henry of Nordlingen sometime in the fourteenth century.[5] Mechthild uses a variety of styles and techniques—poetry and prose, monologue and dialogue—to express her spiritual development. Dronke stresses the importance of her contribution to lyric poetry—the discovery of a new subjective mode—and compares her in this respect to Hadewijch.

> Where Hildegarde's *Symphonia* was, outwardly at least, in the objective liturgical mode, Hadewijch's and Mechthild's poetry is a poetry of meditation; it is their inner colloquy with divine Love ... Love (*Die Minne*) is a womanly figure, divinely beautiful and seductive; she is both relentless tyrant and sweet enchantress. Under her spell, these women know and recreate in themselves all the heights and all the abysses, the raptures and the torments of the beloved in the Song of Songs.[6]

When Mechthild moved to Helfta in 1270, the abbess Gertrude of Hackeborn, who was about twenty years her junior, had been abbess since 1251. The other Mechthild, Gertrude's younger sister, was about thirty-five, mistress of the novices and singing teacher. The future Gertrude the Great was fourteen. Abbess Gertrude died in 1291; Mechthild of Magdeburg probably died in 1282 though she may have lived until 1297.[7] Mechthild of Hackeborn, who entered the convent at age seven, may have died the following year (1298, aged fifty eight). Gertrude the Great also entered the convent as a small child. She wrote down her own spiritual journey (the *Legatus Divinae Pietatis* or *The Herald of Divine Love*) probably in 1289, and then two years later she wrote down Mechthild of Hackeborn's visionary experience, *The Book of Special Grace*, in 1291. She died about a decade later, in 1301 or 1302.[8]

For a little more than fifty years the convent of Helfta was a great center of feminine spiritual activity, and for forty of those years it was under the direction of one abbess. Without Gertrude's leadership and the high standard of excellence in education that she encouraged, it is difficult to imagine the development of mystical writers such as her sister Mechthild and her namesake Gertrude the Great. The novices were instructed in the trivium (grammar, rhetoric, and logic) and the quadrivium (arithmetic, geometry, astronomy, and music). These seven liberal arts, as in the new universities, were supplemented with study in theology, especially the works of St. Bernard. But the newer devotional education—the kind of education Mechthild of Magdeburg must have received as a Beguine—was also provided at Helfta, probably supervised by the Dominican friars who came to Helfta to give sermons, hear confessions, and provide spiritual guidance.

Mechthild of Magdeburg's life had been very different from that of the sisters in Helfta, but there was clearly mutual respect. One of the nuns told a story, recorded by St. Gertrude the Great, about Mechthild's preliminary visit to the convent:

> Having gone to the convent, . . . Mechthild prayed that God might direct her to someone there who could assist her spiritually. She was given to understand that a person who would come and take a place near her was a true and faithful spouse of Christ, preferred by him before all the others. Gertrude came, seated herself near Mechthild, and spoke to her, but the saint's manner was so humble that the visitor could not believe her to be the one designated by Christ. Returning to her prayer with many complaints, she was informed that Gertrude was indeed the true and faithful spouse whom he preferred. Subsequently, the beguine had a conversation with St. Mechthild, sister of the abbess, and was enchanted by her. Why, she wondered, had God exalted Gertrude above this admirable and holy nun? He answered, "I am working great things in Mechthild, but those which I am working and shall work in Gertrude are far greater."[9]

Gertrude was brought to Helfta as an oblate in 1261, aged four or five. Only her name, Gertrude, is known; and her birthday, 6 January, the Feast of the Epiphany; nothing is known of her parents or her birthplace. In her writings she calls herself an orphan, and her lack of a recorded surname means that she was surely not of the nobility and perhaps illegitimate. Although Gertrude was able to appreciate her good fortune in having been brought to Helfta, she was not always comfortable there. In her youth she found the convent a *regio disimilitudinis*, a "land of unlikeness," where she did not belong.[10] We possess both a biography and an autobiography for her. Books I, III, and IV of the *Legatus Divinae Pietatis* were written by another nun of Helfta as a memorial after her death, and the second book is her spiritual autobiography, written in the first person and addressed directly to God.[11] Both versions of her life imply that as a young woman she loved the life of the intellect far more than the life of the spirit. In fact, she says she paid no more attention to her interior life than to the interior of her feet. She loved to study and became noted for her eloquence both in speech and in writing. By her early twenties, she had become tense and melancholy. She said of herself, "If you [Christ] had not given me a natural aversion to evil and an attraction toward the good that I saw in my companions, I should have succumbed to every temptation without remorse as if I had been a pagan living among pagans."[12] She saw herself as a nun in appearance only, and she found her intellectual interests empty and unsatisfying. She was lonely, with a consciousness of her singularity that reminds one of Heloise. Then on 27 January 1281, just after her twenty-fifth birthday, Christ intervened. He seemed to her to be a handsome youth of about sixteen, and his words were from the Office for Advent: "Thy salvation is at hand; why art thou so consumed by grief? Hast thou no counselor, that thou art so changed by sadness?"

> When he had said these words, although she knew she was in the convent dormitory, yet it seemed to her that she was in her usual corner in the chapel where she was accustomed to say her half-hearted prayers. "I shall save you and deliver you. Do not be afraid," he said. After these words she saw the gentle

hand of Christ take her own right hand as if in solemn assurance. He spoke again: "You have licked the dust with my enemies and have sucked honey among thorns. Now return to me and I shall make you drink from the torrent of my delights."[13]

But even as Gertrude listens, she visualizes a barrier between them, a tremendous hedge set with thorns and too dangerous to surmount. Filled with the desire to be with Christ, yet convinced she cannot approach, she feels herself lifted over the hedge and placed beside him. Only then, as she looks at Christ's outstretched hand, does she see the wound.

This vision marks the beginning of a path toward wholeness, detaching her, as she says, "from an inordinate love of literature and from all my vanities." The relationship between herself and Christ adumbrated here becomes a central motif of the rest of her spiritual autobiography. Her desire and her isolation produce the figure of Christ, but her sense of inadequacy creates barriers to union with him, which can only be overcome by Christ's actively reaching toward her. Yet his reaching toward her is always accompanied by an image of his passion. Here the reminder is conveyed by Christ's wounded hand; this will culminate in Gertrude's visions of the sacred heart, a cult that was central to the devotional life of Helfta.

Although scholars have long recognized the poetic gifts of Mechthild of Magdeburg and acknowledged the important theological contributions of Gertrude the Great, it is only recently that the writings of these two women have been explored in the context of female mysticism. In her study of medieval mysticism, *Jesus as Mother*, Bynum analyzes the specific contributions of the spirituality of Helfta from several angles because she is convinced that, in studying this community and the works of these individual women, scholars can reach a better understanding of the prominence of women in mysticism and of the particular characteristics of female piety in the Middle Ages.[14] She sees five aspects of the religiosity of the Helfta nuns: The mystical union attained by these women gave them leadership roles, priestly roles denied to them by the church. The eucharistic piety, especially in the form of the cult of the sacred heart developed by Saint Gertrude, expressed the same need for an unmediated experience of God that authorized these women to act as mediators for others. At the same time, their spirituality did not undercut the power of the clergy, for they supported the bearers of the Eucharist. Fourth, the serenity with which these writers exercised their leadership was validated by Christ's authorization of them and by their image of Christ as judge and sweet comforter. Finally, comparing the "more anxious quality of the writing of Mechthild of Magdeburg" to the "positive sense of self found in Gertrude and Mechthild of Hackeborne," Bynum finds that women "who grew up in monasteries were less likely to be influenced by the contemporary stereotype of women as morally and intellectually inferior."[15]

These observations are well taken, and several of the characteristics associated with Helfta have been observed in other writers who were living in female communities that placed a high value on education—the world of Beatrijs of Nazareth, for instance. It is true that there is at times, in the voices of Gertrude and Mechthild of Hackeborn, a serenity rarely found in medieval women writers. But two qualifications are necessary. First, if we compare the fears expressed about writing autobiography by Mechthild of Magdeburg and Gertrude the Great, we find more similarity than Bynum suggests. Second, I think we may assume that Mechthild of Magdeburg's arrival at Helfta was a major stimulus for the writing that went on there. When Mechthild arrived there in 1270 (at sixty-three years of age if she had been born in 1207), Helfta was a place of learning, a bookish environment, but not yet a home of writers. Gertrude wrote her autobiography in 1289, beginning with her experience of spiritual rebirth in 1281; her earlier writings seem to have been translations, and she found the act of writing down her own subjective experiences quite threatening. Because she was only a teenager when Mechthild arrived, her identity as a writer could only have been acquired after the aged Beguine entered the community. Mechthild of Hackeborn confided her book to two nuns in 1291, basing it on visions dating from ten years earlier. Even if Mechthild died in 1282, we know that during her twelve years at Helfta she was working on the final part of *The Flowing Light*—just at the time that Gertrude and the younger Mechthild were beginning to have similar visionary experiences. It is not necessary to suppose that Mechthild of Magdeburg lived until 1297 to see her as a powerful model for the younger nuns around her. We know that Mechthild badly needed the serenity of Helfta, but it seems equally clear that Helfta was in need of her experience, too, in order to become a home, not just for learned women, but for women writers. This may be the point of God's reassurance to Mechthild when she was going blind: "Thou shalt enlighten and teach and stay here in great honor."

NOTES

1. For a bibliography on Mechthild of Magdeburg and the convent at Helfta, see Caroline Walker Bynum, *Jesus as Mother* (Berkeley and Los Angeles: University of California Press, 1982); John Howard, "The German Mystic, Mechthild of Magdeburg," in Katharina Wilson, *Medieval Women Writers* (Athens, Ga.: Univ. of Georgia Press, 1984), pp. 153–85; Hans Neumann, "Beiträge zur Textegeschichte des 'Fliessenden Lichts der Gottheit' und zur Lebensgeschichte Mechthilds von Magdeburg," *Nachrichten der Akademie der Wissenschaften in Göttingen* (1954) pp. 27–80; and Jeanne Ancelet-Hustache, *Mechthilde de Magdebourg: Etude de Psychologie religieuse* (Paris: H. Champion, 1926). The only English translation is that by Lucy Menzies, *The Revelations of Mechthild of Magdeburg* (New York: Longman, Green & Co., 1953). Brief discussions of Mechthild are found in Valerie M. Lagorio, "The Medieval Continental Women Mystics," in Paul Szarmach, ed., *An Introduction to the Medieval Mystics of Europe* (Albany: State Univ. of New York Press, 1984), pp. 167–72; Rufus M. Jones, *The Flowering of Mysticism: The Friends of God in the Fourteenth Century* (New York: Hafner, 1971; reprint of 1939, Macmillan ed.), pp. 47–50; Peter Dronke, *The Medieval Lyric* (New York: Harper & Row, 1969), pp. 81–85.

2. John Howard, "Mechthild of Magdeburg," in Wilson, p. 155.

3. The Latin text, "Lux divinitatis," is found in *Revelationes Gertrudianae ac Mechtildianae* (Paris: Ondin, 1877), II, pp. 437–707. The German text is Gall R. Morel, ed., *Offenbarungen oder Das fliessende Licht der Gottheit* (Regensburg: G. J. Manz, 1869; reprint Darmstadt, 1963).

4. Howard, "Mechthild of Magdeburg," p. 153.

5. See the history of text transmission in Howard, "Mechthild of Magdeburg," p. 157. There are five surviving manuscripts, three in German and two in Latin. The oldest German translation is Einsiedeln, Stiftsbibliothek 277, which forms the basis for the Morel edition.

6. Dronke, *Medieval Lyric*, p. 81.

7. Neumann, "Beiträge," arrives at this date after examining all the evidence; others, notably Lucy Menzies, have suggested 1297. Lagorio thinks Mechthild was still in Magdeburg in the 1270s as prioress of the Dominican convent of St. Agnes, was seriously ill in 1281, came to Helfta around 1285, and died in 1297. Bynum follows Ancelet-Hustache in accepting the 1282 date.

8. For texts of Mechthild of Hackeborn, see the edition by the monks of Solesmes, "Liber specialis gratiae" in *Revelationes Gertrudianae ac Mechtildianae* II (Paris: 1877). The Middle English translation was edited

by Theresa A. Halligan, *The Book of Gostlye Grace of Mechthild of Hackeborn* (Toronto: Pontifical Institute of Medieval Studies, 1979) Studies and Texts, No. 46. The French translation of Mechthild of Hackeborn by monks of Solesmes is *La Livre de la grâce speciale: Révélations de sainte Mechtild Vierge de l'ordre de saint Benoit* (1879; reprint Tours, 1920).

9. Sister Mary Jeremy, *Scholars and Mystics* (Chicago: Henry Regnery Co., 1962), pp. 20–21.

10. Jeremy, *Scholars and Mystics*, p. 21.

11. See Bynum, *Jesus as Mother*, pp. 180 ff. and Eckenstein, *Women Under Monasticism*, pp. 347 ff.

12. Jeremy, *Scholars and Mystics*, p. 114; Eckenstein, *Women Under Monasticism*, pp. 348–49.

13. Jeremy, *Scholars and Mystics*, pp. 75–6.

14. Bynum, *Jesus as Mother*, Ch. 5, "Women Mystics in the Thirteenth Century: The Case of the Nuns of Helfta," pp. 170 ff. This chapter summarizes earlier approaches and supplies a more inclusive perspective.

15. Bynum, *Jesus as Mother*, pp. 184–85.

MECHTHILD OF MAGDEBURG   (1207–1282; Germany)

The Flowing Light of the Godhead

Translated by Lucy Menzies

Of the Revelations to a loving soul

This is the first part of the book

In the year of our Lord, A.D. 1250, and for fifteen years thereafter, this book was revealed in German by God to a Sister who was holy both in body and spirit. She served God devoutly in humble simplicity, abject poverty and heavenly contemplation, suffering oppression and scorn for more than forty years. She followed the light and teaching of the Preaching Order steadfastly and absolutely, advancing steadily and improving herself from day to day.

But this book was copied and put together by a Brother of the same Order. Much good is in this book on many things, as is seen in the Table of its contents.

Thou shalt read it nine times, faithfully, humbly and devoutly.

This book is to be joyfully welcomed for God Himself speaks in it.

This book I now send forth as a messenger to all spiritual people both good and bad—for if the pillars fall,[1] the building cannot stand. The book proclaims Me alone and shows forth My holiness with praise. All who would understand this book should read it nine times.

This Book is called The Flowing Light of the Godhead.

Ah! Lord God! Who was written this book? I in my weakness have written it, because I dared not hide the gift that is in it. Ah! Lord! What shall this book be called to Thy Glory!

Lucy Menzies, *The Revelations of Mechthild of Magdeburg, or The Flowing Light of the Godhead* (London: Longman's Green and Co., 1953).

It shall be called *The Flowing Light of My Godhead* into all hearts which dwell therein without falseness.

1. *How Love and the Soul, who sits enthroned as Queen, speak together*[2]

Soul:
God greet thee Lady, thy name
Is known to me, it is Love!

Love:
God reward thee, O Queen!

Soul:
Love! I am happy to meet thee!

Love:
And I by the greeting, much honoured.

Soul:
Love, thou didst wrestle long years
With the Holy Trinity
Till the overflow fell once for all
In Mary's humble lap!

Love:
But, O Queen, these things were done
For thy honour and thy delight.

Soul:
Ah Love! thou hast taken from me
All I had won on earth!

Love:
A blessed exchange, O Queen!

Soul:
To deprive me of my childhood?

Love:
In exchange for heavenly freedom!

Soul:
Thou hast taken away my youth!

Love:
In exchange for many virtues.

Soul:
Thou hast taken my friends and relations!

Love:
Queen! that is a false charge!

Soul:
And taken from me the world,
Honour and all my possessions!

Love:
These all I shall, O Queen,
In one hour by as much as thou wilt
Of the Holy Spirit, make good to thee.

Soul:
Love, thou hast tried me so sore
Through suffering, that now my body
Can barely support its weight.

Love:
Against that loss, O Queen,
Thou hast gained great understanding.

Soul:
Ah Love! thou hast consumed
My very flesh and blood!

Love:
Thereby art thou enlightened
And raised up to God.

Soul:
But Love, thou art a robber,
Make thou that good to me!

Love:
That will I do, O Queen,
I pray thee—take myself!

Soul:
Now even here on earth
Thou'st paid me back again
A hundred-fold, O Love!

Love:
My Queen, now God and all
His heavenly realm, are thine.

2. *Of three persons and three gifts*[3]

The true greeting of God, which comes from the heavenly flood out of the spring of the flowing Trinity, has such power that it takes all strength from the body and lays the soul bare to itself. Thus it sees itself as one of the blessed and receives in itself divine glory. The soul is thus separated from the body with its power and love longing. Only the smallest part of life remains to the body which is as it were in a sweet sleep. The soul sees God as One and Undivided in Three Persons, and the Three Persons as one Undivided God. God greets the soul in the language of the Court of Heaven not understood in this kitchen (earthly world). And He clothes it with such garments as are worn in His Palace and girds it with strength. Then it may ask for what it will, it will be granted to it.

Should it not be granted, it is because the soul is taken further by God to a secret place where it must not ask nor pray for anyone, for God alone will play with it in a game of which the body knows nothing, any more than the peasant at the plough or the knight in the tourney; not even His loving mother Mary; she can do nothing here. Thus God and the soul soar further to a blissful place of which I neither can nor will say much. It is too great and I dare not speak of it for I am a sinful creature.

Moreover, when the Infinite God brings the unmoored soul up into the heights of contemplation, it loses touch with the earth in face of that wonder and forgets that it ever was upon the earth. When this flight is at its highest, the soul must leave it.

Then the All-Glorious God speaks: "Maiden! thou must humble thyself and descend again!"

She is affrighted and says: "Lord! Thou hast drawn me up so high, that I am out of myself and cannot praise Thee with any order in my body, for I suffer grievously and strive against my body!"

Then He speaks: "Ah! my dove! Thy voice is as music to my ears, thy words as savour to my mouth, thy longings as the gentleness of My gifts!"

And she replies: "Dear Lord! all must be as the Master ordains!"

And she sighs so deeply that her body is awakened and asks, "Lady! where hast thou been? Thou comest so lovingly back, so beautiful and strong, so free and full of spirit! But thy wanderings have taken from me all my zest, my peace, my colour, all my powers."

The soul exclaims, "Silence! Destroyer! Cease thy complaints! I will ever guard myself against thee. That my enemy should be wounded does not trouble me, I am glad of it!"

Such an encounter surges from the Flowing Godhead by many channels into the arid soul, ever bringing fresh knowledge and holier revelation.

O loving God, fiery within, radiant without, now that Thou has given this even to me, so undeserving, hunger wakes in me for that life Thou has given to Thy chosen ones. To that end I would gladly suffer longer here. For no soul can or may receive this greeting till it has utterly conquered self: but in this greeting will I, yet living, die.

3. *Of the handmaids of the soul and of the blow of Love*[4]

Soul:
Ah dearest Love, for how long
Hast thou lain in wait for me!
What, O what can I do?
I am hunted, captured, bound,
Wounded so terribly
That never can I be healed.
Cunning blows hast thou dealt,
Shall I ever recover from thee?
Would it not have been well
That I had never known thee?

Love:
I hunted thee for my pleasure,
I caught thee for my desire,
I bound thee for my joy,
Thy wounds have made us one,
My cunning blows, me thine.
I drove Almighty God
From Heaven and it was I

Who took His human life
And gave Him back again
With honour to His Father—
How couldst thou hope, poor worm,
To save thyself from me?

Soul:
But Queen, I fear I might
Through one small gift of God,
Through food and drink, escape thee?

Love:
That prisoners may not die
One gives them bread and water
And God has given thee these
Mere respites for a time.
But when thy death-blow falls,
And when thy Easter comes,
I shall be all around thee
I shall be through and through thee,
And I shall steal thy body
And give thee to thy Love.

Soul:
Love! I have been thy scribe,
Seal those words with thy sign.

Love:
Who loves God more than self
Knows where to find the seal
It lies between us twain.—
The seal is there, thine Easter come
And God, thy glorious grave, thy Home.

4. *Of the presence at Court of the soul to whom God shows Himself*

When the poor soul comes to Court, she is discreet and modest. She looks at her God with joyful eyes. Ah! how lovingly she is there received! She is silent but longs above everything to praise Him. And He, with great desire, shows her His Divine heart. It glows like red gold in a great fire. And God lays the soul in His glowing heart so that He, the great God, and she, the humble maid, embrace and are one as water with wine. Then she is overcome and beside herself for weakness and

can no more. And He is overpowered with love for her, as He ever was, He neither gives nor takes. Then she says, "Lord! Thou art my Beloved! My desire! My flowing stream! My Sun! And I am Thy reflection!"

Thus does the loving soul who cannot exist without God, come to Court.

5. *Of the torment and reward of Hell*

My body is in long torment, my soul in high delight, for she has seen and embraced her Beloved. Through Him, alas for her! she suffers torment. As He draws her to Himself, she gives herself to Him. She cannot hold back and so He takes her to Himself. Gladly would she speak but dares not. She is engulfed in the glorious Trinity in high union. He gives her a brief respite that she may long for Him. She would fain sing His praises but cannot. She would that He might send her to Hell, if only He might be loved above all measure by all creatures. She looks at Him and says, "Lord! Give me Thy blessing!" He looks at her and draws her to Him with a greeting the body may not know—

Thus the body speaks to the soul
"Where hast thou been? I can bear this no
    more!"
And the soul replies "Silence! Thou art a fool!
I will be with my Love
Even shouldst thou never recover!
I am His joy; He is my torment—"

This is her torment,
Never must she recover from it
But must ever endure it
And never escape from it.

21. *Of Knowledge and Revelation*

Love without Knowledge
Is darkness to the wise soul.
Knowledge without revelation

Is as the pain of Hell.
Revelation without death,
Cannot be endured.

22. *Of the mission of the Virgin Mary; how the soul was made in honour of the Trinity*

The sweet dew of the uncreated Trinity distilled from the spring of the eternal Godhead in the flower of the chosen Maid. And the fruit of the flower is an immortal God and a mortal man and a living comfort of everlasting love; our Redeemer is become our Bridegroom!

The bride is intoxicated by the sight of His glorious countenance. In her greatest strength she is overcome, in her blindness, she sees most clearly; in her greatest clearness, she is both dead and alive. The richer she becomes, the poorer she is. . . . The more she storms, the more loving God is to her. The higher she soars, the more brightly she shines from the reflection of the Godhead the nearer she comes to Him. The more she labours, the more sweetly she rests. The more she understands, the less she speaks. The louder she calls, the greater wonders she works with His power and her might. The more God loves her, the more glorious the course of love, the nearer the resting-place, the closer the embrace. The closer the embrace, the sweeter the kiss. The more lovingly they gaze at each other, the more difficult it is to part. The more He gives her, the more she spends, the more she has. The more humbly she takes leave, the sooner she returns. The more the fire burns, the more her light increases. The more love consumes her, the brighter she shines. The vaster God's praise, the vaster her desire for Him.

Ah! whither fares our Bridegroom and Redeemer in the Jubilation of the Holy Trinity? As God willed no longer to remain in Himself, alone, therefore created He the soul and gave Himself in great love to her alone. Whereof art thou made, O Soul, that thou soarest so high over all creatures and whilst mingling in the Holy Trinity, yet remainest complete in thyself?

Soul: Thou hast spoken of my beginning, I was created in love, therefore nothing can express or liberate my nobleness save Love alone. Blessed Mary! Thou art the mother of this Wonder. When did that happen to thee?

The Virgin Mary: When our Father's joy was darkened by Adam's fall, so that He was an-angered, the everlasting wisdom of Almighty God was provoked. Then the Father chose me as bride that He might have something to love, because His noble bride, the soul, was dead. Then the Son chose me as mother and the Holy Spirit received me as friend. Then was I alone the bride of the Holy Trinity and the mother of orphans whom I bore before the sight of God (that they might not quite disappear as some did). As I thus became the mother of many noble children, I was so full of the milk of compassion that I nurtured the wise men and prophets before the birth of the Son of God. After that, in my youth, I nurtured Jesus; later, as the bride of God, I nurtured holy Church at the foot of the Cross; but from that I became dry and wretched, for the sword of the human agony of Jesus spiritually pierced my soul. . . . But it was reborn of His life-giving wounds and lived again, young and child-like. But were it fully to recover, God's mother must be its mother and its nurse. Ah! God! it was so and it was just! God is the soul's rightful Father and the soul His rightful bride who resembles Him in all her sorrows.

Ah! blessed Mary! In thine old age thou didst nurture the holy Apostles with thy maternal wisdom and thy powerful prayer, so that God's honour and will should be fulfilled in them. Likewise didst thou then, as now, nurture the martyrs with strong faith in their hearts; the confessors by thy protection of their ears, the maidens by thy purity, the widows with constancy, the perfect with gentleness, sinners through thy intercession. Ah! Lady! thou must still nurture us ... till the Last Day. Then shalt thou see how God's children and thy children are weaned and grown up into everlasting life. Then shall we see and know in unspeakable joy, the milk and e'en the self-same breast, which Jesus oft as infant kissed.[5]

26. *In this way the soul leads the senses and is free and without grief*

It is a wondrous and lofty way in which the faithful soul walks, leading the senses after it as a man with sight might lead one who was blind. In this way the soul is free and travels without grief in its heart, seeing that it wills nothing but what its Lord wills Who does everything for the best.

27. *How thou art to become worthy of the Way, to walk in it and be perfected*

Three things make the soul worthy of this way so that it recognizes it and walks in it. Firstly, that it wills to come to God, renouncing all self-will, joyfully welcoming God's grace and willingly accepting all its demands against human desires. The second thing which keeps the soul in the way is that all things are welcome to it save sin alone. The third thing makes the creature perfect in the way, namely, that it does all things to the glory of God, so that even its smallest desire will be as highly prized by God as if it were in the highest state of contemplation possible to humanity.

For all is done in love to the glory of God. Therefore all is one.

But if I sin, then I am no longer in this way!

35. *The desert has twelve things*

Thou shalt love the naughting,
And flee the self.[6]
Thou shalt stand alone

Seeking help from none,
That thy being may be quiet,
Free from the bondage of all things
Thou shalt loose those who are bound,
And exhort the free.
Thou shalt care for the sick
Yet dwell alone.
Thou shalt drink the waters of sorrow,
And kindle the fire of love
With the faggot of virtue—
    Thus shalt thou dwell in the desert.

36. *Of malice, goodness and wonders*

With the malice of thine enemies thou shalt be
    adorned.
With the virtues of thy heart thou shalt be
    honoured.
With thy good works thou shalt be crowned.
With our mutual love thou shalt be raised up.
With My glorious wonders thou shalt be sanc-
    tified.

37. *The soul answers that she is not worthy of such graces*

Ah! Beloved! undeserved contempt delights
    me;
The virtues of the heart I desire,
Of good works alas! I have none,
I tarnish the beauty of our two-fold love,
Of Thy glorious wonders, I am alas!
    unworthy!

38. *God rejoices that the soul has overcome four sins*

Our Lord delights in Heaven
Because of the loving soul He has on earth,
And says, "Look how she who was wounded
    Me has risen!
She has cast from her the apes of worldliness;
Overcome the bear of impurity,
Trodden the lion of pride underfoot,
Torn the wolf of desire from his revenge,

And comes racing like a hunted deer
To the spring which is Myself.
She comes soaring like an eagle
Swinging herself from the depths
Up into the heights."

39–43. *God asks the soul what it brings*[7]

God:
Thou huntest sore for thy love,
What bring'st thou Me, my Queen?

Soul:
Lord! I bring Thee my treasure;
It is greater than the mountains,
Wider than the world,
Deeper than the sea,
Higher than the clouds,
More glorious than the sun,
More manifold than the stars,
It outweighs the whole earth!

God:
O thou! image of My Divine Godhead,
Enobled by My humanity,
Adorned by My Holy Spirit,—
What is thy treasure called?

Soul:
Lord! it is called my heart's desire!
I have withdrawn it from the world,
Denied it to myself and all creatures.
Now I can bear it no longer.
Where, O Lord, shall I lay it?

God:
Thy heart's desire shalt thou lay nowhere
But in mine own Divine Heart
And on My human breast.
There alone wilt thou find comfort
And be embraced by My Spirit.

44. *Of the way of love in seven things, of three bridal robes and of the dance*

God speaks:
Ah! loving soul! wouldst thou know where thy
    way lies?

Soul:
Yes! Holy Spirit! Show it me!

Holy Spirit:
Thou must overcome the need of remorse, the pain of penitence, the labour of confession, the love of the world, temptation of the devil, pride of the body, and annihilation of self-will which drags so many souls back that they never come to real love. Then, when thou hast conquered most of thine enemies, thou art so wearied, that thou criest out—Ah! beautiful Youth! where shall I find thee?

The Youth:
I hear a voice
Which speaks somewhat of love.
Many days have I wooed her
But never heard her voice.
Now I am moved
I must go to meet her,
She it is who bears grief and love together,
In the morning, in the dew is the intimate
    rapture
Which first penetrates the soul.

Her Waiting-Maids, The Five Senses Speak:
Lady! Thou must adorn thyself!

Soul:
Ah! Love! Whither shall I go?

The Senses:
We have heard a whisper,
The Prince comes to greet thee,
In the dew and the song of the birds!
Tarry not, Lady!

And so the soul puts on a shift of humility, so humble that nothing could be more humble. And over it a white robe of chastity, so pure that she cannot endure words or desires which might stain it. Next she wraps herself in a mantle of Holy Desire which she has woven out of all the virtues.

Thus she goes into the wood, that is the company of holy people. The sweetest nightingales sing there day and night and she hears also many pure notes of the birds of holy wisdom. But still the youth does not come. He sends her messengers, for she would dance. He sends her the faith of Abraham, the longings of the Prophets, the chaste modesty of our Lady St. Mary, the sacred perfection of our Lord Jesus Christ and the whole company of His elect. Thus there is prepared a noble Dance of Praise. Then the Youth comes and speaks to her—

Maiden! thou shalt dance merrily
Even as mine elect!

Soul:
I cannot dance O Lord, unless Thou lead me.
If Thou wilt that I leap joyfully
Then must Thou Thyself first dance and sing!
  Then will I leap for love
From love to knowledge,
From knowledge to fruition,
From fruition to beyond all human sense
There will I remain
And circle evermore.[8]

The Youth
Thy Dance of Praise is well done.
Now shalt thou have thy will
Of the Virgin's Son.

First Part (44):
For thou art weary! Come at midday
To the shade by the brook
To the resting-place of love.
There thou mayst cool thyself.

Soul:
Ah! Lord! that is too much
That Thou shouldst companion my love;
Where the heart has no love of itself,
It will ever be aroused thereto by Thee!

Then wearied by the dance, the soul says to the senses, "Leave me! I must cool myself!" The senses answer, "Lady! wilt thou be refreshed by the tears of Mary Magdalene? Can they suffice thee?"

Soul:
Hush! ye know not what I mean!

Hinder me not! I would drink of the unmingled wine![9]

Senses:
Lady! In virgin chastity
The love of God is ready for thee!

Soul:
That may be so. For me
It is not the highest.

Senses:
Thou mayst cool thyself
In the blood of the martyrs.

Soul:
I have been martyred so many a day
I can no longer go that way.

Senses:
Many pure souls abide
By the counsel of confessors.

Soul:
Their counsel will I obey
And yet—I cannot go that way!

Senses:
In the wisdom of the Apostles
Thou wilt find sure refuge?

Soul:
Their wisdom have I in my heart,
It bids me choose the better part.

Senses:
Lady! The angels are clear and bright
And full of Love;
If thou wouldst cool thyself,
Ascend to them above.

Soul:
The angels' joy is woe to me
Unless my Lord, my Love, I see.

Senses:
In holy austerity cool thyself and save
That which God to John Baptist gave.

Soul:
Pain and suffering do not appal,
Yet Love rules ever over all.

Senses:
Ah! Lady! wouldst thou be refreshed,

Bend thee down to the Virgin's knee
To the tiny Babe and taste and see
How the angels drink of Eternity,
In the milk of the joy of the Maid!

Soul:
That is a childish joy
To suckle and rock a Babe!
But I am a full-grown Bride
I must to my lover's side!

Senses:
Ah! Lady! Comest thou there
Then are we blinded,
So fiery is the glory of the Godhead
As thou well knowest—
That all the flame and all the glow
In Heaven above and earth below
Which burneth and shineth—
All doth flow from God Himself;
From His Divine breath,
Through His Divine lips
From the counsel of the Holy Spirit—
Who may abide it, even one hour?

Soul:
Fish cannot drown in the water,
Birds cannot sink in the air,
Gold cannot perish
In the refiner's fire.
This has God given to all creatures
To foster and seek their own nature,
How then can I withstand mine?
   I must to God—
My Father through nature,
My Brother through humanity,
My Bridegroom through love,
His am I for ever!
   Think ye that fire must utterly slay my soul?
Nay! Love can both fiercely scorch
And tenderly love and console.
Therefore be not troubled!
Ye shall still teach me.
When I return
I will need your teaching
For the earth is full of snares.

Then the beloved goes in to the Lover, into
the secret hiding place of the sinless Godhead. . . . And there, the soul being fashioned
in the very nature of God, no hindrance can
come between it and God.
Then our Lord said—

Stand, O Soul!

Soul:
What wilt thou Lord?

The Lord:
Thy SELF must go!

Soul:
But Lord, what shall happen to me then?

The Lord:
Thou art by nature already mine!
Nothing can come between Me and thee!
There is no angel so sublime
As to be granted for one hour
What is given thee for ever.
Therefore must thou put from thee
Fear and shame and all outward things.
Only of that of which thou art sensible by
   nature
Shalt thou wish to be sensible in Eternity.
That shall be thy noble longing,
Thine endless desire,
And that in My infinite mercy
I will evermore fulfil.

Soul:
Lord! now am I a naked soul
And Thou a God most Glorious!
Our two-fold intercourse is Love Eternal
Which can never die.
   Now comes a blessed stillness
   Welcome to both. He gives Himself to her
   And she to Him.
   What shall now befall her, the soul knows:
      Therefore am I comforted.
   Where two lovers come secretly together
   They must often part, without parting.

   Dear friend of God! I have written down
this, my way of love, for thee. May God give it
to thee in thy heart. AMEN.

NOTES

1. The clergy and rulers of the Church.

2. This Dialogue forms a Prologue to the whole work and brings us right into the atmosphere of the Middle Ages. Mechthild's language here is that of the Minnesingers, of Court Life. Love appears as a lady of rank at the Court of Heaven, wooing a Royal Bride for her Lord. Though the whole of this first part deals with a rich and living spirituality, its matter is also religious and philosophical. The philosophy is that of early German mysticism, pointing back to the Neo-Platonism of the fourth century. Here as in all Mechthild's writing "flashes of creative imagination evoke truths far deeper and more fruitful than the literal parallel they describe." Evelyn Underhill, *Essentials of Mysticism*, p. 69.

3. The reader will notice Mechthild's fondness for numbers. After the example of St. Bernard, she, too, liked to number and relate the degrees of love; how the soul praises God in five things; how God resembles the soul in four things and so on.

4. This theme, the "love chase," the spirit fleeing from the overpowering presence of God, is found in many mediaeval mystics. We are familiar with it in Francis Thompson's *Hound of Heaven*. See Underhill, *Mysticism*, p. 135.

This chapter was probably written soon after Mechthild had left her home, pursued by a mighty following love which would give her no rest.

5. In this mingling of philosophical symbolism with legend, we see the Pseudo-Dionysian teaching of Albertus Magnus, whose fame was then beginning. We come in this chapter to Mechthild's fundamental thought, "Why did God create the soul?" and her answer "From the necessity of love."

6. Here Mechthild seems to forestall Eckhart in treating the interchange between God and the soul according to the abstract terms of areopagite writings which came to her through Albertus Magnus.

7. In her *Essentials of Mysticism*, Evelyn Underhill gives this celebrated letter of Mechthild, "written to a fellow-pilgrim on that Love-path which she herself trod with so great a fortitude. It represents not only the rich variety of Mechthild's resources, but also those several forms of artistic expression which the great mystics have employed ... the imagery is double-edged, evoking moods as well as ideas.... It opens with a spiritual love scene ... this develops into a dramatic dialogue between soul and senses ... this leads again ... to the soul's acclamation of its destiny and the crowning announcement of the union of lover and beloved. The soul is described as a maiden, the Divine Lover as a fair Youth whom she desires. The very setting of the story is just such a fairy landscape as we find in the lays and romances of chivalry ... the dewy morning, the bird-haunted forest, the song, the dance. It is in fact a love story of the period adapted with extraordinary boldness to the purposes of mystical experience." Op. cit., pp. 79–85.

8. See Dante, *Paradiso*, xxiv, where he sees the saints as circling lights; and xxv, where they are seen "wheeling round ... as their burning love befitted."

9. "By this romantic method Mechthild has appealed to the fancy and emotion of the reader, and has enticed him into the heart of the spiritual situation. Next she passes to the intellectual appeal, the argument between the soul and the senses. From this she proceeds by a transition ... which is the outcome of consummate art, to the supreme declaration of the 'deified spirit at home with the Lord' as St. Paul said."—Underhill, *Essentials*, p. 82.

ST. GERTRUDE THE GREAT (1241–1298; Germany)

Part II of The Revelations of St. Gertrude

CHAPTER I. The Saint's thanksgiving to God for the first grace vouchsafed to her, by which her mind was withdrawn from earthly things and united to Him.

Let the Abyss of Uncreated Wisdom invoke the Abyss of Omnipotent Power to praise and extol the amazing charity which, by an excess of Thine infinite mercy, O most sweet God of my life and only Love of my soul, hast led Thee through a desert, pathless, and dry land—that is, through the many obstacles I have placed to Thy mercy—to descend into the valley of my miseries.

I was in the twenty-sixth year of my age when, on the Monday[1] before the Feast of the Purification of Thy most chaste Mother, in a happy hour, after Compline, at the close of day, Thou the true Light, who art clearer than any light, and yet deeper than any recess, having resolved to dissipate the obscurity of my darkness, didst sweetly and gently commence my conversion by appeasing the trouble which Thou hadst excited in my soul for more than a month. . . .

Being, then, in the middle of our dormitory, at the hour I have named, and having inclined to an ancient religious, according to our rule, on raising my head I beheld Thee, my most loving Love, and my Redeemer, surpassing in beauty the children of men, under the form of a youth of sixteen years, beautiful and amiable, and attracting my heart and my eyes by the infinite light of Thy glory, which Thou hadst the goodness to proportion to the weakness of my nature; and standing before me, Thou didst utter these words, full of tenderness and sweetness: "Thy salvation is at hand; why art thou consumed with grief? Hast thou no counsellor, that thou art so changed by sadness!" When Thou hadst spoken thus, although I knew that I stood corporally in the place I have mentioned, it seemed to me, nevertheless, that I was in our choir, in the corner[2] where I had been accustomed to offer up my tepid prayers, and that there I heard these words: "I will save thee, I will deliver thee; fear not;" and after I had heard them, I saw Thee place Thy right hand in mine, as if to ratify Thy promise.

Then I heard Thee speak thus: "You have licked the dust with My enemies, and you have sucked honey amidst thorns; but return now to Me—I will receive you, and inebriate you with the torrent of My celestial delights." When Thou hadst said these words, my soul melted within me; and as I desired to approach Thee, I beheld between Thee and me (I mean, from Thy right hand to my left hand) a hedge of such prodigious length that I could see no end to it either before or behind, and the top of it appeared so set with thorns that I could find no way to return to Thee, Thou only consolation of my soul. Then I paused to weep over my faults and crimes, which were doubtless figured by this hedge which divided us. In the ardour of the desires with which I desired Thee, and in my weakness, O charitable Father of the poor, "whose mercies are over all Thy works," Thou didst take me by the hand, and place me near Thee instantly, without difficulty, so that, casting my eyes upon the precious Hand which Thou hadst extended to me as a pledge of Thy promises, I recognised, O sweet Jesus, Thy radiant

Book Two of *The Life and Revelations of Saint Gertrude, Virgin and Abbess of the Order of St. Benedict* (Westminster, Md.: The Newman Press, 1949).

wounds, which have made of no effect the handwriting that was against us.[3]

By these and other illuminations Thou didst enlighten and soften my mind, detaching me powerfully, by an interior unction, from an inordinate love of literature and from all my vanities, so that I only despised those things which had formerly pleased me; and all that was not Thee, O God of my heart, appeared vile to me, and Thou alone wert pleasing to my soul. . . .

CHAPTER II. How the grace of God illuminated her interiorly.

Hail, Salvation and Light of my soul! may all that is in heaven, in earth, and in the abyss, return thanks to Thee for the extraordinary grace which has led my soul to know and consider what passes within my heart, of which I had no more care formerly than (if I may so speak) of what passes within my hands or feet. But after the infusion of Thy mos' sweet light, I saw many things in my hea which offended Thy purity, and I even perceived that all within me was in such disorder and confusion that Thou couldst not abide therein.

Nevertheless, my most loving Jesus, neither all these defects, nor all my unworthiness, prevented Thee from honouring me with Thy visible presence nearly every day that I received the life-giving nourishment of Thy Body and Thy Blood, although I only beheld Thee indistinctly, as one who sees at dawn: Thou didst endeavour by this sweet compliance to attract my soul, so that it might be entirely united to Thee, and that I might know Thee better and enjoy Thee more fully. And as I disposed myself to labour for the obtaining of these favours on the Feast of the Annunciation of Thy Mother, when Thou didst ally Thyself with our nature in her virginal womb,—Thou who saidest, "Here I am before I called Thee,"—Thou didst anticipate this day by pouring forth on me unworthy though I am, on the Vigil of the Feast, the sweetness of Thy benediction, at Chapter, which was held after Matins, on account of the Sunday following. . . .

Thou didst give me from henceforward a more clear knowledge of Thyself, which was such that the sweetness of Thy love led me to correct my faults far more than the fear of the punishments with which Thy just anger threatened me. But I do not remember ever to have enjoyed so great happiness at any other time as during these days of which I speak, in which Thou didst invite me to the delights of Thy royal table; and I know not for certain whether it is Thy wise Providence which has deprived me of them, or whether it is my negligence which has drawn on me this chastisement.

CHAPTER III. Of the pleasure which God took in making His abode in the soul of Gertrude.

Whilst Thou didst act so lovingly towards me, and didst not cease to draw my soul from vanity and to Thyself, it happened on a certain day, between the Festival of the Resurrection and Ascension, that I went into the court before Prime, and seated myself near the fountain,—and I began to consider the beauty of the place, which charmed me on account of the clear and flowing stream, the verdure of the trees which surrounded it, and the flight of the birds, and particularly of the doves,— above all, the sweet calm,—apart from all, and considering within myself what would make this place most useful to me, I thought that it would be the friendship of a wise and intimate companion, who would sweeten my solitude or render it useful to others, when Thou, my Lord and my God who are a torrent of inestimable pleasure, after having inspired me with the first impulse of this desire, Thou didst will to be also the end of it, inspiring me with the thought that if by continual gratitude I return Thy graces to Thee, as a stream returns to its source; if, increasing in the love of virtue, I put forth, like the trees, the flowers of good works; furthermore, if, despising the things of earth, I fly upwards, freely, like the birds, and thus free my senses from the distraction of exterior things,—my soul would then be empty, and my heart would be an agreeable abode for Thee.

As I was occupied with the recollection of these things during the same day, having knelt after Vespers for my evening prayer before retiring to rest, this passage of the Gospel came suddenly to my mind: "If any man love Me, he will keep My word, and My Father will love him, and We will come to him and will make Our abode with him" (John xiv. 23). At these words my worthless heart perceived Thee, O my most sweet God and my delight, present therein. Oh, that all the waters of the sea were changed into blood, that I might pass them over my head, and thus wash away my exceeding vileness, which Thou hast chosen for Thine abode! or that my heart might be torn this moment from my body and cast into a furnace, that it might be purified from its dross, and made at least less unworthy of Thy presence! for Thou my God, since that hour, hast treated me sometimes with sweetness and sometimes with severity, as I have amended or been negligent; although, to speak the truth, when the most perfect amendment which I could attain, even for a moment, should have lasted my whole life, it could not merit to obtain for me the most trifling or the least condescending of the graces which I have ever received from Thee, so great are my crimes and sins.

The excess of Thy goodness obliges me to believe that the sight of my faults rather moves Thee to fear Thou wilt see me perish than to excite Thine anger, making me know

that Thy patience is supporting my defects until now, with so much goodness, is greater than the sweetness with which Thou didst bear with the perfidious Judas during Thy mortal life; and although my mind takes pleasure in wandering after and in distracting itself with perishable things, yet, after some hours, after some days, and, alas! I must add, after whole weeks, when I return into my heart, I find Thee there; so that I cannot complain that Thou hast left me even for a moment, from that time until this year, which is the ninth since I received this grace, except once, when I perceived that Thou didst leave me for the space of eleven days, before the Feast of St. John Baptist,—and it appeared to me that this happened on account of a wordly conversation the Thursday preceding; and Thy absence lasted until the Vigil of St. John, when the Mass *Ne timeas, Zacharia,*[4] is said. Then Thy sweetest humanity and Thy stupendous charity moved Thee to seek me, when I had reached such a pitch of madness, that I thought no more of the greatness of the treasure I had lost, and for the loss of which I do not remember to have felt any grief at that time, nor even to have had the desire of recovering it. . . .

CHAPTER IV. Of the stigmata imprinted in the heart of Gertrude, and her exercises in honour of the Five Wounds.

I believe it was during the winter of the first or second year when I began to receive these favours, that I met the following prayer in a book of devotions:

"O Lord Jesus Christ, Son of the living God, grant that I may aspire towards Thee with my whole heart, with full desire and with thirsty soul, seeking only Thy sweetness and Thy delights, so that my whole mind and all that is within me may most ardently sigh to

Thee, who art our true Beatitude. O most merciful Lord, engrave Thy Wounds upon my heart with Thy most precious Blood, that I may read in them both Thy grief and Thy love; and that the memory of Thy Wounds may ever remain in my inmost heart, to excite my compassion for Thy sufferings and to increase in me Thy love. Grant me also to despise all creatures, and that my heart my delight in Thee alone. Amen."

Having learned this prayer with great satisfaction, I repeated it frequently, and Thou, who despisest not the prayer of the humble, heard my petitions; for soon after, during the same winter, being in the refectory after Vespers, for collation, I was seated near a person to whom I had made known my secret. I relate these things for the benefit of those who may read what I write, because I have often perceived that the fervour of my devotion is increased by this kind of communication; but I know not for certain, O Lord my God, whether it was Thy Spirit, or perhaps human affection, made me act thus, although I have heard from those experienced in such matters that it is always better to reveal these secrets—not indifferently to all, but chiefly to those who are not only our friends, but whom we are bound to reverence; yet, as I am doubtful, as I have said, I commit all to Thy faithful Providence, whose spirit is sweeter than honey. If this fervour arose from any human affection, I am even more bound to have a profound gratitude for it, since Thou hast deigned to unite the mire of my vileness to the precious gold of Thy charity, that so the precious stones of Thy grace might be encased in me.

Being seated in the refectory, as I said before, I thought attentively on these things, when I perceived that the grace which I had so long asked by the aforesaid prayer was granted to me, unworthy though I am; for I perceived in spirit that Thou hadst imprinted in the depth of my heart the adorable marks of Thy

sacred Wounds, even as they are on Thy Body; that Thou hadst cured my soul, in imprinting these Wounds on it; and that, to satisfy its thirst, Thou hadst given it the precious beverage of Thy love.

But my unworthiness had not yet exhausted the abyss of Thy mercy; for I received from Thine overflowing liberability this remarkable gift—that each time during the day in which I endeavoured to apply myself in spirit to those adorable Wounds, saying five verses of the Psalm *Benedic, anima mea, Domino* (Ps. cii.), I never failed to receive some new favour. At the first verse, "Bless the Lord, O my soul," I deposited all the rust of my sins and my voluptuousness at the Wounds of Thy blessed Feet; at the second verse, "Bless the Lord, and never forget all He hath done for thee," I washed away all the stains of carnal and perishable pleasures in the sweet bath of Blood and Water which Thou didst pour forth for me; at the third verse, "Who forgiveth all thine iniquities," I reposed my spirit in the Wound of Thy Left Hand, even as the dove makes its nest in the crevice of the rock; at the fourth verse, "Who redeemeth thy life from destruction," I approached Thy Right Hand, and took from thence all that I needed for my perfection in virtue; and being thus magnificently adorned, I passed to the fifth verse, "Who satisfieth thy desire with good things," that I might be purified from all the defilement of sin, and have the indigence of my wants supplied, so that I might become worthy of Thy presence—though of myself I am utterly unworthy,—and might merit the joy of Thy chaste embraces.

I declare also that Thou hast freely granted my other petition—namely, that I might read Thy grief and Thy love together. But, alas! this did not continue long, although I cannot accuse Thee of having withdrawn it from me; but I complain of having lost it myself by my own negligence. This Thine excessive goodness and infinite mercy has hidden from itself, and has procured to me, without any merit on my part, the greatest of Thy gifts—the impression of Thy Wounds; for which be praise, honour, glory, dominion, and thanksgiving to Thee for endless ages!

CHAPTER V. Of the Wound of Divine Love; and of the manner of bathing, anointing, and binding it up.

Seven years after, a little before Advent, by Thine ordinance, who art the Source of all good, I engaged a certain person to say this prayer every day for me before a crucifix, "O most loving Lord, by Thy pierced Heart, pierce her heart with the arrow of Thy love, so that nothing earthly may remain therein, and that it may be entirely filled with the strength of Thy Divinity." Being moved, as I believe, by these prayers, on the Sunday when they sang the Mass *Gaudete in Domino*,[5] Thy infinite liberality having permitted me, by an excess of mercy, to approach the Communion of Thy adorable Body and Blood, Thou didst infuse a desire in me when I approached It, which broke forth in these words: "Lord, I am not worthy to receive the least of Thy gifts; but I beseech Thee, by the merits and prayers of all here present, to pierce my heart with the arrow of Thy love." I soon perceived that my words had reached Thy Divine Heart, both by an interior effusion of grace, and by a remarkable prodigy which Thou didst show me in the image of Thy crucifixion.

After I had received the Sacrament of life, and had retired to the place where I pray, it seemed to me that I saw a ray of light like an arrow coming forth from the wound of the right side of the crucifix, which was in an elevated place, and it continued, as it were, to advance and retire for some time, sweetly attracting my cold affections. But my desire was not entirely satisfied with these things until the following Wednesday,[6] when, after

the Mass, the faithful meditated on Thy adorable Incarnation and Annunciation, in which I joined, however imperfectly. And behold, Thou camest suddenly before me, and didst imprint a wound in my heart, saying these words: "May the full tide of your affections flow hither, so that all your pleasure, your hope, your joy, your grief, your fear, and every other feeling may be sustained by My love!" And I immediately remembered that I had heard a wound should be bathed, anointed, and bandaged. But Thou didst not teach me then in what manner I should perform these things; for Thou didst defer it, to discover it to me more clearly in the end by means of another person, who had accustomed the ears of her soul to discern far more exactly and delicately than I do the sweet murmurs of Thy love.

She advised me to reflect devoutly upon the love of Thy Heart when hanging on the cross, and to draw from this fountain the waters of true devotion, to wash away all my offences; to take from the unction of mercy the oil of gratitude, which the sweetness of this inestimable love has produced as a remedy for all adversities, and to use this efficacious charity and the strength of this consummate love as a ligament of justification to unite all my thoughts, words, and works indissolubly and powerfully to Thee. May all the deprivation of those things which my malice and wickedness has caused be supplied through that love whose plentitude abides in Him who, being seated on Thy right hand, has become "bone of my bones, and flesh of my flesh!" As it is by Him, through the operation of the Holy Spirit, that Thou hast placed in me this noble virtue of compassion, humility, and reverence, to enable me to speak to Thee, it is also by Him that I present to Thee my complaint of the miseries I endure, which are so great in number, and which have caused me to offend Thy Divine goodness in so many ways by my thoughts, words, and actions, but principally by the bad use which I have made of the aforesaid graces, by my unfaithfulness, my negligence, and my irreverence. For if Thou hast given to one so unworthy even a thread of flax[7] as a remembrance of Thee, I should have been bound to respect it more than I have done all these favours.

Thou knowest, O my God, from whom nothing is hidden, that the reason why I have written these things, so much against my inclination, is, that I have profited so little by Thy liberality, that I cannot believe they were made known to me for myself alone, since thine eternal wisdom cannot be deceived. Grant, then, O Giver of gifts, who hast so freely and unreservedly bestowed them on me, that whoever reads these things may be touched with tenderness and compassion for Thee; and, knowing that the seal which Thou hast for the salvation of souls has induced Thee to leave such royal gems[8] so long in my defiled heart, they may praise, adore, and extol Thy mercy, saying with their lips, and with their hearts, "Praise, honour, glory, and benediction be to Thee, O God the Father, from whom all things proceed," thus to supply for my deficiencies.[9]

CHAPTER VI. Of the intimate union of the Infant Jesus with her heart.

... It was on that most sacred night in which the sweet dew of Divine grace fell on all the world, and the heavens dropped sweetness, that my sould, exposed like a mystic fleece in the court of the monastery, having received in meditation this celestial rain, was prepared to assist at this Divine Birth, in which a Virgin brought forth a Son, true God and Man, even as a star produces its ray. In this night, I say, my soul beheld before it suddenly a delicate Child, but just born, in whom were concealed the greatest gifts of perfection. I imagined that I received this precious deposit in my bosom

with the tenderest affection. As I possessed it within me, it seemed to me that all at once I was changed into the colour[10] of this Divine Infant, if we may be permitted to call that colour which cannot be compared to anything visible.

Then I understood the meaning contained in those sweet and ineffable words: "God will (*erit*) be all in all" (1 Cor. xv:28); and my soul, which was enriched by the presence of my Beloved, soon knew, by its transports of joy, that it possessed the presence of its Spouse. Then it received these words with exceeding avidity, which were presented as a delicious beverage to satisfy the ardour of its thirst: "As I am the figure of the substance of God, My Father, in His Divinity, so also you shall be the figure of My substance in My Humanity, receiving in your deified soul the infusions of My Divinity, as the air receives the brightness of the solar rays, that these rays may penetrate you so intimately as to prepare you for the closest union with Me."

O most noble balsam of the Divinity, pouring Thyself out like an ocean of charity, shooting forth and budding eternally, diffusing Thyself until the end of time! O invincible strength of the Hand of the most High, which causes so frail a vessel, and one which should be cast away in contempt, to receive within it so precious a liquor! O evident testimony of the exuberance of Divine goodness, not to withdraw from me when I wandered in the devious ways of sin, but rather to unite me to itself as far as my misery would permit!

CHAPTER VII. The Divinity is imprinted upon the soul of Gertrude as a seal upon wax.

The day of the most holy Purification, as I was confined to bed after a severe illness, and as I was troubled in my mind about daybreak, fearing that my corporal infirmity would deprive me of the Divine visit with which I had been so often consoled,—on the same day the august mediatrix, the Mother of God the true Mediator, consoled me by these words: "As you never remember to have endured more severe corporal sufferings than those caused by your illness, know also that you have never received from my Son more noble gifts than those which will now be given to you, and for which your sufferings have prepared you."

This consoled me exceedingly; and having received the Food which gives life immediately after the Procession, I thought only of God and myself; and I beheld my soul, under the similitude of wax softened by the fire, impressed like a seal upon the bosom of the Lord; and immediately I beheld it surrounding and partly drawn into this treasurehouse, where the ever-peaceful Trinity abides corporally in the plenitude of the Divinity, and resplendent with its glorious impression.

O ardent fire of my God, which contains, produces, and imprints those living ardours which attract the humid waters of my soul, and dry up the torrents of earthly delights, and afterwards soften my hard self-opinionatedness, which time has hardened so exceedingly! O consuming fire, which even amid ardent flames imparts sweetness and peace to the soul! in Thee, and in none other, do we receive this grace of being reformed to the image and likeness in which we were created. O burning furnace, in which we enjoy the true vision of peace, which tries and purifies the gold of the elect, and leads the soul to seek eagerly for its highest good, even Thyself, in Thy eternal truth.

CHAPTER VIII. Of the admirable union of her soul with God.

On the following Sunday, at the Mass *Esto mihi*,[11] Thou didst enkindle my spirit, and increase my desires to receive yet more noble gifts which Thou wert about to bestow on me; especially by these two words, which moved my soul deeply, namely, the versicle of the first response: "*Benedicens*[12] *benedicam tibi*"—"With blessings I will bless thee," and the versicle of the ninth response: "*Tibi enim et semini tuo dabo universa regiones has*"—"To thee and to thy posterity I will give all these countries" (Gen. xxvi.). For then Thou didst show me what were these countries which Thy boundless liberality had promised. O blessed country, where blessings flow upon blessings! O field of delights, whose least grain is capable of satisfying the hunger which any of the elect may have for those things which the human heart considers desirable, delightful, amiable, sweet, and joyful.... I saw (to express as far as I can that which is inexpressible) that the part of His blessed Heart where the Lord received my soul on the Feast of the Purification, under the form of wax softened by the fire, was, as it were, dropping a sweat, which came forth with violence, even as if the substance of the wax was melted by the excessive heat hidden in the depth of this Heart. This sacred reservoir attracted these drops to itself with surprising force, powerfully and inexpressibly, and even so inconceivably, that one saw evidently that love, which could not be hindered from communicating itself, had an absolute power in this place, where it discovered secrets which were so great, so hidden, and so impenetrable.

O eternal solstice! secure mansion, containing all that is desirable! Paradise of unchanging delights, continual fountain of inestimable pleasures, wherein there is eternal springtime, soothing by its sweet song, or rather by its delicious and intellectual melodies, rejoicing by the odour of its vivifying perfumes, inebriating by the soothing sweetness of its mystic liquors, and transforming by its secret caresses!...

CHAPTER IX. Of another admirable manner in which St. Gertrude was closely united to God.

Soon after, during the fast[13] when I was confined to bed for the second time by a severe sickness, and the other sisters were occupied elsewhere, so that I was left alone one morning, the Lord, who never abandons those who are deprived of human consolation, came to verify these words of the prophet: "I am with him in tribulation" (Ps. xc.). He turned His right Side towards me, and there came forth from His blessed and inmost Heart a pure and solid stream, like crystal; and on His Breast there was a precious ornament, like a necklace, which seemed to alternate between gold and rose-colour. Then our Lord said to me: "This sickness which you suffer will sanctify your soul; so that each time you go forth from Me, like the stream which I have shown you, for the good of your neighbour, either in thought, word, or act, even then, as the purity of the crystal renders the colour of the gold and the rose more brilliant, so the coöperation of the precious gold of My Divinity, and the rose of the perfect patience of My Humanity, will render your works always agreeable to Me by the purity of your intention." ...

CHAPTER X. How the Lord obliged her to write these things; and how He illuminated her.

I considered it so unsuitable for me to publish these writings, that my conscience would not consent to do so; therefore I deferred doing it until the Feast of the Exaltation of the Holy Cross.[14] On that day, having determined before Mass to apply myself to other occupations, the Lord conquered the repugnance of my reason by these words: "Be assured that you will not be released from the prison of the flesh until you have paid this debt which still binds you." And as I reflected that I had already employed the gifts of God for the advancement of my neighbour—if not of my writing, at least by my words—He brought forward these words which I had heard used at the preceding Matins: "If the Lord had willed to teach His doctrine only to those who were present, He would have taught by word only, not by writing. But now they are written for the salvation of many." He added further: "I desire your writings to be an indisputable evidence of My Divine goodness in these latter times, in which I purpose to do good to many."

These words having depressed me, I began to consider within myself how difficult and even impossible it would be to find thoughts and words capable of explaining these things to the human intellect without scandal. But the Lord delivered me from this pusillanimity by pouring out on my soul an abundant rain, the impetuous fall of which weighed me down like a young and tender plant—vile creature that I am!—instead of watering me gently, so as to make me increase in perfection; and I could find no profit from it, except from some weighty words, the sense of which I was unable perfectly to penetrate. Therefore, finding myself still more depressed, I inquired what would be the advantage of these writings; and Thy goodness, my God, solaced my trouble with Thy usual sweetness, refreshing my soul by this reply: "Since this deluge appears useless to you, behold, I will now approach you to My Divine Heart, that your words may be gentle and sweet, according to the capabilities of your mind." Which promise, my Lord and my God, Thou didst most faithfully fulfil. And for four days, at a convenient hour each morning, Thou didst suggest with so much clearness and sweetness what I composed, that I have been able to write it without difficulty and without reflection, even as if I had learned it by heart long before; with this limitation, that when I had written a sufficient quantity each day, it has not been possible for me, although I applied my whole mind to it, to find a single word to express the things which on the following day I could write freely: thus instructing and refraining my impetuosity, as the Scripture teaches:[15] "Let none so apply himself to action as to omit contemplation." Thus art Thou jealous for my welfare; and whilst Thou givest me leisure to enjoy the embraces of Rachel, Thou dost not permit me to be deprived of the glorious fruitfulness of Lia. May Thy wise love deign to accomplish in me these two things!

CHAPTER XXIV. Conclusion of this Book.

Behold, O loving Lord, I offer Thee the talent of Thy condescending intimacy, which Thou hast confided to me, vile creature that I am. I have traded with it for love of Thy love in that which I have written, or which I may yet write. And I can boldly declare, by Thy grace, that I have had no other motive in saying or writing these things, except that of obeying Thy will, of promoting Thy glory, and of zeal for the salvation of souls. I desire, therefore, that all should praise Thee and give Thee thanks, that my unworthiness has not caused Thee to withdraw Thy mercy from me. I desire also that Thou shouldst be praised for those who, reading these things, are charmed with the sweetness of Thy charity, and inwardly drawn to desire the same; and also for those who, studying them as students, commence with the alphabet, and attain to philosophy,—thus being led by the persual of these things, as by pictures and images, to search for the hidden manna, which increases the hunger of those who partake of it, and which is not found in corporal substances.

Therefore, since Thou, the Almighty Dispenser of all good things, dost vouchsafe to pasture us during our exile, until, "beholding the glory of the Lord with unveiled countenance, we are transformed into His image, and from glory to glory by the power of the spirit of love" (2 Cor. iii. 18); meanwhile, according to Thy faithful promises and the humble desire of my heart, grant, I beseech Thee, to all who read these writings with humility, the peace of Thy love, compassion for my miseries, and a salutary compunction for their furtherance in perfection; so that, elevating their hearts towards Thee with burning love, they may be like so many golden censers, whose sweet colours shall abundantly supply all my negligence and ingratitude. Amen.

NOTES

1. "Secunda feria ante, &c., quae fuit sexto kalendas Februarii." The French translation has: "Lundi vingt-cinquième janvier;" the Italian, "Che fu alli 27 di Genaio."
2. "In angulo."
3. An allusion to Col. ii. 14.
4. "Fear not, Zachary; thy prayer is heard," &c. (Introit for Mass, Vigil of St. John Baptist.)
5. Introit for Third Sunday in Advent.
6. *Feria quartum.* The Annunciation is specially commemorated on the Wednesday in the third week in Advent. Formerly, feasts which fell on this day were transferred; and in monasteries, the Abbot delivered a homily on the Gospel *Missus est.*
7. "Filum de stupá."
8. "Tam regalem gemmam."
9. The words, "*Hic distalit scribere usque in Octobrem,*" are at the end of chapter v. in the original, in italics.
10. "In eumdem colorem."
11. Introit of Mass for Quinquagesima Sunday.
12. Response, i. Nocturn.
13. Lent.
14. September 14. The words quoted in the following page are not in the present Office.
15. "Sicut Scriptura docet." The exact words are not in Scripture.

VI

Women and Spirituality in Medieval Italy

St. Clare of Assisi, St. Agnes of Assisi, St. Umiltà of Faenza, Blessed Angela of Foligno, and St. Catherine of Siena

*W*HEN WE TURN to southern Europe, the calm of Helfta seems very distant, both geographically and spiritually. Religious ferment and a drive for spiritual renewal and apostolic poverty were found here as well as in the north, and here, too, such new movements created fear in the ecclesiastical establishment. The immediate result of this fear, at base a terror concerning the possibility of uncontrolled popular emotion among the uneducated lay population, was to attempt to bring such movements into the already existing structures of the church. This was primarily the work of Pope Innocent III, who correctly assessed the great power that might be wielded by groups such as the Umiliati in Milan and by the followers of St. Francis and St. Clare in Umbria.[1] Rather than trying to suppress the Umiliati, a well-organized group of laypeople who had banded together to purify themselves and the church through penitence and self-mortification, he allowed them to become a new semimonastic order.

> The Umiliati of Lombardy consisted of men and women determined to live strict lives, with a rigorous ban on lying and swearing, and a thirst for moralistic rather than dogmatic teaching ... Pope Innocent III, who recognized the need to fight heresy by its own weapons and by allying with puritans and ascetics, formed a brotherhood of the Umiliati, which consisted first of a cloistered order, then of a second lay order of pious men and women living and working in their own segregated communities, and finally of a third order whose members did not live as a community, but led pious lives under supervision.[2]

The situation of the early years of the Franciscan movement was similar, and again Innocent III took care to find a way to include the followers of the Poverello, as Francis was called, within the church. But the conditions of Francis's life, his renunciation of all property in order to share the life of the poor and to minister to them, which were exactly what had attracted St. Clare and her disciples, were not acceptable as a life for women. Gradually, Clare had to accept increasing limitations on the heroic ideal of service she had initially chosen; finally the Rule she was given by the pope was, in all essentials, that of the Benedictines. Even the "privilege of poverty," the right to own no property individually or collectively, was granted only to the motherhouse in Assisi and only during Clare's lifetime. In the early years of the group

> the sisters lived by their own work or on alms collected by the friars or given to them by the people of Assisi. In 1216 Jacques de Vitry described the women as living "in various hospices near the towns. They will accept nothing and live entirely by the labours of their hands. They are greatly distressed and perturbed because, by both clergy and laity, they are honoured more than they would wish to be." They made a little money by spinning and by making altar linens, and grew a few vegetables in their garden, but they remained very poor.[3]

The Rule imposed by Pope Honorius, the successor to Innocent III, ended this mode of life for the Poor Clares. Its provisions required that

> no sister is to go out of the convent for any purpose whatsoever except to found a new community. Similarly, no one, religious or secular, is to be allowed to enter the monastery. Perpetual silence is imposed on all members of the community, and continuous fasting, often on bread and water. Strict rules were also laid down about the clothing of the sisters and about the divine office. . . . The strict claustration also finally brought to an end any hope which the sisters might have entertained of being allowed to minister to the poor.[4]

It is no wonder that St. Clare received this Rule with "amazement and affliction of soul." Yet, in spite of it, within her lifetime she is said to have gained ten thousand women followers, so hungry were women for an organized spiritual life. Women who admired her example but were themselves unable to leave the secular world because of family obligations joined the Franciscan third order, a penitential group devoted to a combination of spiritual discipline (private as well as shared) and practical works of mercy, caring for the poor, the ill, and the despairing. Both men and women were tertiaries; by and large, they were older married people or widows and widowers who still had secular responsibilities but who were ready to make a commitment to a spiritual life. By the mid-thirteenth century, houses had been created for "regular" tertiaries as well, who lived an enclosed life under a *regula* or rule. A parallel development could be seen in the Dominican order; the first house for women was established in Toulouse in 1206 as a refuge for women converted from the Albigensian heresy, and the first house for men was created in 1215, also a Toulouse. The Dominican third order was at first restricted to older widows; only in the late fourteenth century, when the Dominicans in Siena received St. Catherine as the first virgin tertiary, were younger unmarried women admitted to the association.[5]

The institution of the third orders provided women in southern Europe with something similar to the independence of the Beguine movement, for as a tertiary a woman could continue to live in the world and actively help others while being provided with (in theory at least) spiritual guidance and the support of a community for her spiritual practices.[6]

The story of St. Clare is familiar. A few months before her birth, a noblewoman of Assisi named Ortolana prayed for a safe delivery; a voice spoke from the crucifix in the church, saying, "Fear not, woman, for you shall bring forth without danger a light that shall greatly illumine the world." As soon as the baby girl was born, she was name Chiara ("bright" or "light" in Italian). When Clare was about twelve, another prophecy was spoken concerning her, but she did not learn about this one until much later. Around 1206, when St. Francis was rebuilding the walls of San Damiano in response to a divine command, he suddenly leaped onto the walls and began to cry out in French, "Here there will be an order of ladies whose fame and holy life will glorify the heavenly Father in his whole church." In the spring of 1212, St. Francis preached a cycle of sermons in Assisi, and Clare attended them. She must have heard of him as she was growing up, and she, too, had a reputation for piety and unusual grace. They met secretly several times after the sermons in the cathedral at Assisi, and on Palm Sunday of that year Clare made her secret flight to Francis and her new life. She and a companion went to St. Mary of the Porziuncula, where Francis cut her hair and received her into the order. She was then led to the church of San Paolo, where her kinsmen came to try to remove her. She clung to the altar and uncovered her head to reveal the tonsure, and they desisted. After a few days she moved to the Benedictine convent of San Angela di Panzo, where her sister Agnes joined her. This time twelve men descended on the convent and tried to drag Agnes down the mountain. Miraculously, her body became too heavy to carry, "as if," said one of her relatives, "she had been eating lead all night." St. Clare appeared, made peace with her relatives, and carried the half-dead Agnes back to the convent. Soon Clare, Agnes, her friend Pacifica (who had accompanied her on Palm Sunday), and a few other girlhood friends were installed in a more Franciscan environment at San Damiano. Initially, St. Francis seems to have thought that St. Clare would set out on a course parallel to his, that she would provide the same kind of leadership for a group of women that he was providing for men, serving the needs of the poor, the sick, and the troubled. But within four years (1216 or shortly thereafter), the small community at San Damiano was enclosed, and St. Clare did not leave it again.[7]

The *Testament* of St. Clare[8] reveals a great deal about her—the principles she stands for, her personality, her conception of the religious life, and her conviction about the importance of her mission and vocation. Clare announces the theme of her *Testament* in the opening lines: her vocation has been and is the greatest of God's gifts to her. It consists, first of all, in a commitment to the apostolic way of life—a direct and unmediated following of the Gospel ("The Son of God became for us the Way")—and secondly in an unbreakable bond between Clare and Francis that had existed even before Clare's conversion at eighteen. Finally, her vocation calls her to be a mirror for those sisters who share her vocation and for them, in turn, to be mirrors and examples to those living in the world. This role for herself and her sisters obliges them to observe the "commandments of God and of our Father," Father Francis, that is, whose word in this context is as important as that of God.

The reason for this stress on obligation and on obedience is made clear in the next few paragraphs. Francis converted Clare to a life of penance, humility, and poverty. His teaching on poverty was presented to her in three ways—in the example of his own life, in writings specifically composed for Clare and her sisters, and in the "form of life" he created for them. Clare sees this as a divine mandate. Just as Christ never departed from holy poverty, neither did Francis, and neither shall Clare or her daughters. It is this commitment to holy poverty that strengthens Clare after the death of St. Francis (she outlived him by twenty-seven years) and that she wishes all abbesses after her to observe. In the years after Francis's death, it was this issue of poverty that split the order. The Spiritual Franciscans, led by men like Ubertino da Casale, believed in the literal observance of poverty—no possessions, no property either collectively or individually—as the absolutely necessary precondition for true spirituality, true humility of spirit. The Conventual Franciscans, on the other hand, acknowledged that the world had changed since Francis's time and that the collective ownership of property was necessary for the continuance of the work of the friars. St. Clare obviously had closer ties with the Spiritual Franciscans. But there is more to her commitment to poverty than this; the issue is also tied to the existence of the second order, the Poor Clares, which was intended to be a new kind of order for women. Bolton is convinced that Pope Innocent III knew exactly what he was doing in his negotiations with Francis:

> One man alone grasped the significance of the feminine piety movement. In his treatment of Francis, Innocent III had taken a long step towards creating the possibility of an order for women. . . . It was logical that Innocent III should have been in favor of adding a woman's order to the church to strengthen it in its struggle with heresy and its current political difficulties.
>
> When in 1215 the Lateran Council imposed on all new movements the obligation to accept an approved rule, the community at San Damian had to apply for a privilege to enable it to maintain its renunciation of poverty and its profession of strict poverty. [Clare] received from Innocent III the *privilegium pauperitatis*, a privilege which allowed the sisters of San Damian to live without an assured income. . . . It seemed that Innocent had, therefore, helped her to create an entirely new form of convent community, which maintained itself on alms and the profits of manual labor in the same way as the Franciscans.[9]

Even with this support from Innocent, Clare and her sisters continued to be pressured to abandon their dual commitment to St. Francis and to poverty. A number of anecdotes in Thomas of Celano's *Legend of St. Clare* demonstrate just how fiercely Clare was willing to act on those two commitments. The first concerns the relationship between the Franciscans and the Poor Clares, the kind of responsibility Francis had promised regarding Clare.

> When at one time the Lord Pope Gregory had forbidden any Friar to go to the monasteries of the ladies without his permission, the loving Mother lamented that her daughters would receive less often the food of sound doctrine, and said with a sigh, "Let him take away all the Friars from us now that he has taken away those who furnished us the food of life." She "was unwilling to keep the questors who provided only material bread if the sisters could not have those who provided spiritual bread." When Pope Gregory heard this, he immediately mitigated his prohibition, leaving the matter in the hands of the Minister General.[10]

When Moorman says that Clare was "trained as a powerful and tenacious fighter," this is the kind of tactic he has in mind. The privilege of poverty for women's houses was tied to this question of the friars' responsibility for the sisters. "The Holy See was therefore prepared to use its influence and its power in various ways to compel the sisters to acquire enough property to make them self-supporting."[11] Many houses of Poor Clares were in great penury, and many of the sisters went hungry. At San Damiano, earlier conditions were very rigorous, not just from self-imposed discipline but from a real shortage of food. Yet Clare made it clear that she would not surrender the privilege of poverty even though they should all die of starvation. When Pope Gregory offered to release Clare from her vow of poverty, she would only reply, "Never do I wish, Holy Father, to be released in any way from following Christ."[12] In the summer of 1253, when Clare was on her deathbed, Pope Innocent IV visited her, "now a figure of great prestige, generally and widely admired. Two days before her death the pope at last confirmed her own version of her own rule."[13]

The remainder of the *Testament* is devoted to the sisters. Clare acknowledges that her order has become very widespread and proposes a bond of charity between all the sisters that will ensure further growth in charity and love of God. Her treatment of the role of abbess is remarkable—she does not even use the title abbess but speaks of "that sister who shall be entrusted with the care of the sisters," who is to govern through example, not through power, so that she will be obeyed out of love rather than duty. The model for behavior is the mother-daughter relationship; the mother is to provide for each daughter's needs and to be kind and approachable, so that her daughters will be confident about revealing their own needs or those of their sisters. The obedience of the daughters, freely given as to God, will make the burden of being abbess much easier to bear: "and what is painful and bitter will, by their holy living, be turned to sweetness for her."[14] St. Agnes, in her letter to her sister, seems to be finding the support of her new sisters in her new convent the best help for her loneliness and feeling of separation from St. Clare.[15]

As the life of Saint Clare may suggest, the thirteenth and fourteenth centuries in Italy were particularly fertile times for women religious leaders. Five of the women included in this anthology—St. Clare, St. Agnes, St. Umiltà, Blessed Angela of Foligno, St. Catherine—represent this era as saints. In their study of medieval saints, Weinstein and Bell[16] identify five characteristics of the holy or saintly life: supernatural grace, asceticism, good works, worldly power, and evangelical activity. The relative importance of each of these factors will vary with time and place, but what Weinstein and Bell stress is that in the thirteenth and fourteenth centuries, the emphasis was on those qualities of saintliness that could be expressed equally well by men or women, particularly supernatural grace (visions, prophecy, mind reading) and asceticism. And, in fact, supernatural grace is far more prominent in the lives of women saints (and, by extension, in the lives of religious women) than in the lives of male saints; women are also more known as helper or healer saints, and their acts of penitence and their asceticism are more visible and strenuous.[17]

The women whose voices were heard in thirteenth- and fourteenth-century Italy were saints and visionaries: Visions were the source of their power and their identity. In the *Sermons* of St. Umiltà, we hear the voice of a woman who claims to have acquired literacy through a miracle, who dictates her sermons in Latin to a large audience of both male and female followers, and who is confident that it is the voice of God that speaks through her. She is surrounded by supernatural protection all the time.[18] Umiltà was born in 1226 to a wealthy and noble family in Faenza and named Rosanese; although, as a child, Rosanese was precocious in her piety and unwilling to marry, when she was about fifteen her father died, and the changed financial circumstances in her family made it necessary for her to marry. She seems to have loved her husband, with whom she had several daughters, but the children died young, and her husband fell ill with an unnamed disease. When Rosanese was told by the doctors that her husband would have to live a celibate life from then on, her desire for a religious life immediately reasserted itself, and she convinced her husband that they should both take vows of celibacy and enter monasteries. They first entered the Benedictine double house of St. Perpetua in Faenza. As a nun, aged twenty-five, she was given the name Humility, or Umiltà in Italian; the name itself may be an indication that she, too, was part of the new movement among women and laypeople seeking a life of penance, poverty, and humility. Eagerly persevering in austerities, Umiltà did not find convent life appropriate at this time. What she yearned for was the solitary life, and she was soon guided by her invisible protector to make an escape from the convent and to find the necessary support to establish herself as a recluse. The order she chose and in which she later became an abbess was the Vallombrosan, a reform order in Tuscany (founded in 1036 by St. John Gualbert) with a rule based on the Benedictine but with greater stress on austerity and penance. The order was named after the rustic location of the motherhouse, a wooded or shady valley, where both the cenobitic and eremetic lives were pursued. Umiltà was enclosed in a cell attached to the church of St. Apollinaris for the next decade (from age twenty-eight to thirty-eight), and, even thus isolated, she attracted followers who began to build cells near hers. It was at this time that she began to write and deliver her sermons. At length she left her cell to found a number of new houses, first in Faenza (Santa Maria Novella in Malta, a suburb of Faenza), then in Florence. She came to Florence when she was fifty-five and died there in 1310, aged seventy-six. Her biography makes her life sound as if it was one of unqualified success,[19] but her own writings reveal the near-despair she felt after she left her enclosure, when she must have been severely criticized for her activities.

Nine sermons, or meditations in prose, have been preserved, along with a number of Lauds to the Virgin Mary in verse. Umiltà composed in Latin, and although she knew how to read and write herself, she preferred to dictate to one of her disciples, Sister Donnina. In her sermons she uses her personal experiences as the basis for teaching others, sometimes through a prayer-dialogue and other times through parable. The first three sermons in the collection of her works are primarily doctrinal and were probably written after she had come to Florence (between 1281 and 1310); the remaining six are closer in form to prayer and meditation, and they convey a sense of an overheard dialogue of the saint with God and various saints. These sermons may have been written or delivered during the ten years Umiltà was a recluse as she was beginning to gather a circle of disciples about her. The fifth sermon has been assigned to the period of time in which she was asked to leave her hermitage and found a new convent for women just outside Faenza. The responsibility of leading a community of women after having spent ten years as a recluse, in almost continuous meditation, must have been very difficult for her. The sixth sermon combines a number of erotic themes that are favorites of hers, her love for St. John the Evangelist particularly. In her "little lamb" meditation in the sixth sermon, Umiltà's motherhood and her desire to nurture become metaphors for the soul's relation to Christ.

Blessed Angela of Foligno[20] was born in 1248, a generation after Umiltà. Foligno, only a few miles from Assisi, was early a center of Franciscan spirituality, and it was not unusual for pious married women living there to become tertiaries. Angela confessed that she joined the third order for the prestige it would give her, for she wanted the reputation of being a virtuous married woman. But her mother, her husband, and all her children died suddenly; and her attachment to Saint Francis and his order became more profound. She had undergone a powerful conversion experience in 1285, and she has detailed for us the steps from that point to becoming a visionary when she was in her early forties. In 1291, when she was forty-three, she had a vision of God's love for her as she was walking on the path between Spello and Assisi, making a pilgrimage to the shrine of St. Francis. (This part of her autobiography is included here.) Between 1290 and 1296 she dictated her experiences to her uncle and confessor, Fra Arnaldo, a Franciscan and a priest; and the book, *Liber de Vere Fidelium Experientia* (often identified in English as the *Divine Consolations*) was read immediately and widely copied and circulated.[21]

Ubertino da Casale, one of the leaders of the Spiritual Franciscans in the controversy over poverty, became her disciple. As Underhill tells the story, Ubertino had been a "vain, brilliant, and self-indulgent young friar" whose spiritual life had "stopped short of real self-renouncement."[22] He preached brilliantly but lived comfortably, and his complete conversion was only effected when he came under the influence of Angela when he was about forty. As he put it

> She restored, even a thousand-fold, all the gifts of my soul that I had lost through my sinfulness, so that from henceforth I was not the same man as before. When I had experienced the splendour of her ardent virtue, she changed the whole face of my mind; and so drove out weakness and languor from my soul and body, and renewed my mind that was torn asunder with distractions, that no one who had known me before could doubt that the spirit of Christ was begotten anew within me through her.[23]

The first of the three treatises that compose Angela's book, "Of the Conversion and Penitence of Blessed Angela . . . and of her many and divers temptations" details her inner life from the time she first became a tertiary. She found penitence very rough going, especially the renunciation of material comforts.

> And then I began to put aside my better clothing, and food, and my headcoverings. But this was for me still shameful and burdensome, for at this point I was not feeling any love and I was living with my husband.[24]

Angela identifies nineteen steps in her penitential period. The one just quoted is the ninth. At the eleventh, she desired to commit herself fully to poverty although she had doubts that she would be able to withstand the temptations that might come to her if she were compelled to beg for subsistence. It was only when she had decided on full renunciation of property that Angela began to experience the joys as well as the difficulties of the spiritual life. Profoundly aware of her own limitations, she is still comforted by a deep and unceasing awareness of the goodness of God.

The second part of her book tells of her visions during the next seven stages of her illumination, including the one best known to students of mysticism — her wooing by the Holy

Spirit as she was on pilgrimage to Assisi. She successively beheld God inasmuch as he is all goodness, as he is beauty, as He is invincible omnipotence, humility, supreme wisdom, then supreme justice. The seventh vision of this series shows her God in three persons; in the eighth she beheld God as clearly as is possible in this life. After a number of confirmatory visions that reassured her about the contents of this experience, she received a series of visions on the passion of Christ, his poverty, bitter suffering mentally and physically, and the love contained within his death. After these visions, she was able to participate in the crucifixion with her own body.

The third part of the book, dictated to various unidentified scribes, is known as the treatise on evangelical doctrine; it is composed of letters and discourses based on further visions and addressed to her spiritual sons and daughters. Like St. Catherine of Siena, she believed that the beginning and end of true wisdom is to know God and ourselves. In these lectures to her students, Angela is genuinely helpful; her language is always clear, never obscurantist. She uses anecdotes from her own life to show how she came to resolve conflicts and doubts, and she manages to avoid both false humility and inflated self-satisfaction. She shows a sense of humor in revealing her own faults, as in the following:

> I was making it known that I did not want to accept anything except what was sufficient for me, and yet I had things saved for another day. I studied to seem poor externally and to lie down in a poor place; where I slept I had many sheets put down and in the morning I had them taken up again so no one would know.[25]

Caterina Benincasa, the future St. Catherine of Siena,[26] was born almost a century after Angela of Foligno, in 1347, the year the Black Death began its sweep over all Europe. Like Angela, she was a woman of great strength and personal magnetism, a leader who attracted many followers. But, unlike Angela, she discovered her visionary path when she was still a child. Her first recorded vision occurred as she was walking along a lonely road near Siena with one of her brothers:

> Raising her eyes toward heaven, she saw in the air, not very high above the ground, a loggia, rather small and full of light, in which Christ appeared clothed in a pure white garment like a bishop in his cope, with a crozier in his hand; and he smiled at the young girl, and there issued from him, as from the sun, a ray, which was directed at her; and behind Christ [there were] several men, all saints, among whom appeared St. Peter and St. Paul and St. John, just as she had seen them painted in the churches.[27]

Sometime after this and before she was fifteen, she had a vision of mystical marriage to Christ, in which she vowed her virginity to him.

> One day she suddenly went out of the house and out of Siena by the Porta di Sant' Ansano to a region where she thought there were certain dells and caves almost hidden from the eyes of men; there she entered into one, and finding herself in a place where she could neither be seen nor heard, she kneeled on the ground, and in a transport of overwhelming love called the mother

of Christ, and with a childlike simplicity asked her to give her in marriage to her son Jesus; and praying thus she felt herself raised somewhat from the ground into the air, and presently there appeared to her the Virgin Mary with her son in her arms, and giving the young girl a ring he took her as his spouse and then suddenly disappeared; and she found herself set back on earth and she returned to Siena and to her home.[28]

Catherine's ascetic practices—fasting, prayers, hours of flagellation daily—reflect tremendous strength of will. In spite of the limitations of her sex and her class, she did not allow herself to be deterred from her goals. She resisted her family's pressure to marry, and when as punishment she was reduced to a kind of servitude in her parents' home, she transformed the situation by visualizing family members as the holy apostles and her parents as the divine family. At about seventeen (1363–64), she was stricken with smallpox, and she used this opportunity to get her mother finally to arrange an interview with the Dominican sisters of the third order, the Mantellate. They had been unwilling to admit any women except mature widows in their group because they were not cloistered and could not protect a virgin. But Catherine seemed to be so disfigured by smallpox and so sober in her speech that she became the first virgin accepted as a Dominican tertiary.[29] The status of tertiary was congenial for her because she wanted to live outside any detailed fixed rule. During her years of silence in her parents' home, she had learned to build an internal cell to which she could go to meditate, and this was one of the teachings she passed on to her followers.

As a child, Catherine had wanted to disguise herself as a male so that she could travel about and preach. She had abandoned this fantasy by the time she reached adolescence, but God reminded her of it though she protested that she could not be a public preacher, that she would not be listened to because she was a woman. God reminded her that because "it is as easy for me to make an angel as an ant,"[30] she would certainly be able to preach if he wished it. And so she did, with the authority of her visions behind her, but she was not without enemies.

In 1374, when she was twenty-seven and a public figure, she was called to Santa Maria Novella in Florence to be questioned by the provincial chapter of the Dominican order. As a result of this interrogation, she was assigned a spiritual director who was her companion until her death and eventually became her biographer: Brother Raymond of Capua. From this point on, her career became more publicly active, reaching beyond Siena to Rome, Avignon, and the whole of Italy. As her letters reveal, she was

> opposed now to mere asceticism and contemplation, and preaching a militant Christianity, she advocated a crusade in the east, and attempted to persuade the condottiere John Hawkwood to abandon his free-booting for generalship of the Christian forces. She tried to end the war between Florence and the pope, and her persistent attempt to induce the latter to quit Avignon for Rome is a familiar chapter in European history.[31]

The letters of Catherine of Siena indicate that she was the right voice for her time and that she knew it. This youngest child of the Sienese dyer and his wife, Monna Lapa, reveals a clear awareness of who she is—her plebeian status; her female sex; her lack of traditional education; her self-knowledge; her devotion to God, to her church, and to Italy. She had only about ten years of active ministry. She joined the Dominican tertiaries in 1363–64, learned to read between 1364 and 1367, when she was living in isolation under a vow of silence at home. This period ended on the last day of carnival 1367, when she was mystically married to Christ. From 1367 to 1370 she gradually widened her circle of contacts, working to help the sick and the needy. In 1370 she suffered a mystical death and returned to life, having received the command to go abroad into the world to save souls. By 1374 she had attracted enough attention to be called to Florence by the Dominican chapter. On 1 April 1375, in Rome, she received the stigmata and prophesied the Great Schism that took place four years later. In 1376 she undertook to try to make peace between Florence and Pope Gregory XI, who had been feuding, and finally convinced the pope to return to Rome from Avignon. In 1378, after the death of Pope Gregory and the temporary peace established by Pope Urban, she turned to composing the *Dialogue*, her major visionary work. At the end of 1378 she was again living in Rome and acting as Urban's trusted adviser. During these last years of her life, she offered herself as an expiatory victim for the sins of the church. Shortly before her death, she had a vision of the weight of the ship of the church descending on her shoulders, and her physical sufferings increased. She died 3 April 1380 when thirty-three years old.[32]

The letter to Raymond of Capua included here concerns the death of a young man from Perugia, Niccoló Tuldo, who had been sentenced to death for criticizing the new Sienese government. Niccoló was not religious and had not even received communion in his entire life. His crime was in actuality a trivial one, a drunken slur against the government, not the beginning of a conspiracy. When Catherine first met him, he must have been enraged at what seemed like injustice and in despair of help. Catherine's letter, with its recurring imagery of blood, is perhaps the best and clearest instance of what the Blood of Christ meant to Catherine—her transcendent vision of the healing power of blood was constantly revealed to her in ordinary brutal life. The blood shed during the beheading of this youth, the blood that spatters over her clothes, has the smell of heaven to her, the smell of Christ's blood; and, in fact, she sees the wound in Christ's side open to receive the soul that has just left the bloody body. The other letters by her included in this collection are all to Blessed Daniella of Orvieto, a young Dominican nun. They are letters of great sophistication about the spiritual life— Catherine writes to Beata Daniella as she would write to herself, and she speaks to her about matters of importance to all mystics, but especially to women: how to view ascetic practices so that they do not replace the real goal of spiritual attention, which is God; how to understand and act on revelations and flashes of intuition concerning others for whom one has spiritual responsibility; and, finally, how to follow the call to leadership even when it goes against obedience and against accepted female roles.

NOTES

1. See Herbert Grundman, "Innocent III and the Heretics," in Jeffrey Burton Russell, ed., *Religious Dissent in the Middle Ages* (London: Wiley, 1971), pp. 131–33; and Brenda Bolton, "Tradition and Temerity . . ." in *Schism, Heresy, and Religious Protest*, ed. Derek Baker (Cambridge: Cambridge Univ. Press, 1972), pp. 79–92.

2. Brian Pullan, *A History of Early Renaissance Italy* (London: Penguin Books, 1973), pp. 65–66.

3. John Moorman, *A History of the Franciscan Order* (Oxford: Clarendon Press, 1968), p. 35.

4. Moorman, *History of the Franciscan Order*, p. 38.

5. Ernest W. McDonnell, *The Beguines and Beghards in Medieval Culture* (New York: Octagon Books, 1969;

reprint of 1954 edition, Rutgers Univ. Press, New Brunswick N.J.), pp. 55–60; Richard W. Southern, *Western Society and the Church in the Middle Ages* (Baltimore: Penguin, 1970), pp. 279 ff.; Freed, "Urban Development," pp. 311 ff.

6. Fausta Casolini, "I Penitenti in 'Leggende' e Cronache," in *I Frati Penitenti di San Francesco nella società del 2 e 300*, ed. Mariano D'Alatri (Rome: Istituto storico dei cappuccini, 1977), pp. 69–85.

7. All the passages quoted in the biography given here are from Thomas of Celano's biography (Thomas of Celano, *The Legend of St. Clare of Assisi*), in *The Legend and Writings of St. Clare of Assisi* (New York: St. Bonaventure Press, 1953), pp. 17–51.

8. Celano, *Legend*, pp. 82–87.

9. Brenda Bolton, "Mulieres Sanctae," in *Women in Medieval Society*, ed. Brenda Bolton et al. (Philadelphia: Univ. of Pennsylvania Press, 1976), p. 148.

10. Moorman, *Franciscan Order*, p. 205.

11. Moorman, *Franciscan Order*, p. 206.

12. Moorman, *Franciscan Order*, pp. 206–7.

13. Christopher N. L. Brooke and Rosalind B. Brooke, "St. Clare," in *Medieval Women*, ed. Derek Baker (Oxford: Basil Blackwell, 1978), p. 285.

14. See "Testament," p. 86, in *The Legend and Writings of St. Clare*.

15. "Letter of St. Agnes," in *The Legend and Writings of St. Clare*, pp. 113–14.

16. Donald Weinstein and Rudolph M. Bell, *Saints and Society: The Two Worlds of Western Christendom 1000–1700* (Chicago and London: University of Chicago Press, 1982), pp. 30–52.

17. Weinstein and Bell, *Saints and Society*, pp. 159 ff.

18. Elizabeth Petroff, *Consolation of the Blessed* (New York: Alta Gaia, 1979), pp. 139–41 on Umiltà's guardian angels.

19. Petroff, *Consolation*, pp. 121–37; Weinstein and Bell, *Saints and Society*, p. 91. For an Italian translation of the sermons, see the edition by Pietro Zama, *Santa Umiltà: La Vita e i 'sermones'* (Faenza: Fratelli Lega Editori, 1974).

20. *Le Livre de l'Experience des vrais fidèles par Sainte Angèle de Foligno*, ed. M.-J. Ferré (Paris: Éditions E. Droz, and trans. M.-J. Ferré and L. Baudry, 1927).

21. On the manuscript used for this edition and for the textual history of Angela's book, see the Preface to the Ferré edition, pp. xvi–xxxiii.

22. Evelyn Underhill, *Mystics of the Church* (Cambridge: James Clark and Co., Ltd., 1975; first pub. 1925), p. 100.

23. Underhill, *Mystics of the Church*, p. 100.

24. *Le Livre* of Angela of Foligno, par. 12, p. 10.

25. *Le Livre* of Angela of Foligno, Letter 3, pp. 494–96.

26. Basic sources for Catherine of Siena are the *Letters* and the *Dialogue* or *Book of Divine Doctrine*. The Italian text of the *Letters* is edited by Piero Misciatelli, *Le Lettere di Santa Caterina da Siena*, 6 vols. (Siena: Bentivoglio, 1913–22; reprinted 1970 by Marzocco, Florence); *Il Libro della divina dottrina*, ed. Matilde Fiorilli (Bari: G. Laterza, 1912, 1928). Some of the letters have been translated; see Vida Scudder, *Saint Catherine of Siena as Seen in her Letters* (London and New York: J. M. Dent, 1927); and Kenelm Foster and Mary John Ronayne, *I, Catherine: Selected Writings of Catherine of Siena* (London: Collins 1980). The *Dialogue* has recently been published in the Classics of Western Spirituality Series: *Catherine of Siena, The Dialogue*, trans. Suzanne Noffke (New York: Paulist Press, 1980). The biography of St. Catherine by Raymond of Capua is another important source; *The Life of Saint Catherine of Siena by Raymond of Capua*, trans. Conleath Kearns (Wilmington, Del.: Michael Glazier, 1980). The basic critical work on sources is Robert Fawtier, *Sainte Catherine de Sienne: Essai de critique des sources*, 2 vols. (Paris: E. de Boccard, 1921). There is a chapter devoted to Catherine in Katharina Wilson, ed., *Medieval Women Writers* (Athens Ga.: Univ. of Georgia Press, 1984), "The Tuscan Visionary, St. Catherine of Siena," by Joseph Berrigan, pp. 252–68.

27. Millard Meiss, *Painting in Florence and Siena After the Black Death* (New York: Harper & Row, 1964), p. 105.

28. Meiss, *Painting*, p. 111, quoting from the 1374 text of *Miracoli* (Miracles). *I Miracoli di Caterina di Iacopo da Siena . . .* ed. Francesco Valli. (Siena: R. Università, 1936).

29. For a discussion of Catherine's handling of her disfigurement, a tragedy for a female in a patriarchal society, see Elizabeth Petroff, "The Paradox of Sanctity: Lives of Italian Women Saints 1200–1400," in *Occasional Papers of the International Society for the Comparative Study of Civilization* 1: 1 (Fall 1977), pp. 4–24.

30. *Life of St. Catherine of Siena*, trans. Kearns, p. 15.

31. Meiss, *Painting*, p. 89.

32. Ethel Rolt-Wheeler, *Women of the Cell and Cloister* (London: Methuen and Co., 1913); Edith Deen, *Great Women of the Christian Faith* (Baltimore and London, 1959), pp. 50–60; Eleanor McLaughlin, "Women, Power, and the Pursuit of Holiness," in *Women of Spirit*, ed. Eleanor McLaughlin and Rosemary Reuther (New York: Simon & Schuster, 1979), pp. 115–22.

ST. CLARE OF ASSISI   (1196–1253; Italy)

The Testament of St. Clare

Translated by Ignatius Brady, O.F.M.

In the Name of the Lord, Amen.

1. Among the many graces which we have received and continue daily to receive from the liberality of the Father of mercies (II. 1:3), and for which we must give deepest thanks to our glorious God, our vocation holds first place. Indeed, because it is the more perfect and the greater among these graces, so much the more does it claim our gratitude. Therefore the Apostle says: "Know your vocation" (cf. I Cor. 1:26).

2. The Son of God became for us the Way (John 14:16); and that Way our Blessed Father Francis, His true lover and imitator, has shown and taught us by word and example.

3. Therefore, beloved Sisters, we must consider the immense benefits which God has conferred upon us, but especially those which He has deigned to work in us through His beloved servant, our Father the Blessed Francis, not only after our conversion but even while we yet dwelt among the vanities of the world.

4. For when the Saint as yet had neither Friars nor companions and, shortly after his conversion, was repairing the Church of San Damiano and there, filled completely with divine consolation, was led to abandon the world wholly and forever, in great joy and in the illumination of the Holy Spirit he prophesied concerning us what the Lord later fulfilled. For at that time he mounted the wall of the church and cried with a loud voice in the French tongue to certain poor folk of the neighborhood; "Come and help me in build-ing the Monastery of San Damiano; for here will dwell Ladies whose good name and holy life will glorify our Heavenly Father throughout His holy Church."

5. In this therefore we can behold the great kindness of God toward us, who of the abundance of His mercy and love deigned to speak thus through His Saint of our vocation and election. And it was not of us alone that our most blessed Father prophesied these things, but of all others likewise who were to enter the holy calling to which God has called us.

6. With what solicitude, therefore, and fervor of mind and body must we not observe the commandments of God and of our Father, that with the help of God we may return to Him with increase the talent He has given us! For the Lord has placed us as an example and mirror not only for other men, but also for our Sisters whom God has called to our way of life, that they in turn should be a mirror and an example to those living in the world.

Since therefore the Lord has called us to such heights of holiness that in us our other Sisters may behold themselves who are to be an example to mankind, we are truly bound to bless the Lord and praise Him and to be strengthened in Him more and more to do good. Wherefore if we live according to the pattern given us, we shall leave others a noble example and after life's short labor gain the prize of eternal happiness.

7. After the most high celestial Father had deigned to enlighten my heart by His mercy

and grace to do penance after the example and teaching of our most Blessed Father Francis shortly after his own conversion, I voluntarily promised him obedience with the few Sisters whom the Lord had given me soon after my conversion, according to the light of His grace which the Lord had given us by the holy life and teaching of His servant.

8. But when the Blessed Father saw that though we were weak and frail of body, we shirked neither privation nor poverty, hardship, tribulation, ignominy, nor the contempt of the world, but rather, as he and his Friars often saw for themselves, that after the example of the Saints and his Friars we accounted all these as great delight, he rejoiced in the Lord. And moved to love for us, he bound himself always to have, in his own person or through his Order, the same diligent care and special solicitude for us as for his own Friars.[1]

9. And thus by the will of God and of our most blessed Father Francis we came to dwell at the church of San Damiano. There in a short time the Lord by His mercy and grace increased our number that what He had prophesied through His Saint might come to pass. Before this we had dwelled in another place, but for a little while only.[2]

10. Afterwards he wrote for us a form of life, especially that we should persevere always in holy poverty. Nor was he content while living to exhort us by many words and examples to the love and observance of most holy poverty, but also gave us many writings[3] that after his death we would in no wise turn aside from it, even as the Son of God while He lived in this world wished never to desert this same holy poverty. And our most blessed Father Francis, following the footsteps of Christ, never while he lived departed in example or in teaching from His holy poverty, which he had chosen for himself and for his Friars.

11. And I, Clare, the unworthy handmaid of Christ and of the Poor Sisters of the Monastery of San Damiano, and the little plant of the holy Father, considered with my Sisters our most high calling and the command of so great a Father, and the frailty of the other Sisters, which we feared in ourselves after the death of our holy Father Francis, who was our pillar of strength, and after God our one consolation and our support. Therefore we have bound ourselves again and again to our Lady most holy Poverty, that after my death the Sisters present and to come may never in any way abandon her.

12. And as I have ever been zealous and careful to observe and have the others observe the holy poverty which we have promised the Lord and our holy Father Francis, so the other Abbesses who shall follow me in my office are bound always to observe holy poverty unto the end and to cause it to be observed by their Sisters.[4]

Indeed, for greater surety I took care to have our profession of holy Poverty, which we promised our Father, strengthened by the privileges granted us by the Lord Pope Innocent, in whose Pontificate we had our beginning, and by his sucessors,[5] that at no time or in any fashion we might ever depart from it.

13. Wherefore on bended knees and prostrate in body and soul I recommended all my Sisters present and to come to our holy Mother, the Roman Church, to the Supreme Pontiff, and especially to the Lord Cardinal who has been appointed for the religion of the Friars Minor and for us.[6] And for love of that Lord who was poor in the crib, who lived a poor life, and who hung naked upon the gibbet of the Cross, may the Lord Cardinal always cause his little flock to observe the holy poverty which we have promised God and our most blessed Father Francis, and may he always strengthen and preserve them in this poverty. For this is the little flock which the Lord and Father had begotten in His holy Church by the word and example of the blessed Father Francis, who followed the

poverty and humility of His beloved Son and of the glorious Virgin, His Mother.

14. The Lord gave us our most blessed Father Francis as Founder, Planter and Helper in the service of Christ and in those things which we have promised God and him our Father; and in his lifetime he was ever solicitous in word and in work to cherish and foster us, his little plants. Wherefore I also recommend and entrust my Sisters, present and to come, to the successor of our blessed Father Francis and to the whole Order, that they may always help us to advance to better things in the service of God and above all to observe most holy poverty in a more perfect way.

15. If it should ever happen that the aforesaid Sisters leave this place and go elsewhere, they are bound nevertheless, wherever they may be after my death, to observe the aforesaid manner of poverty which we have promised God and our most blessed Father Francis.

16. In such an event, let that Sister who fills my office and the other Sisters be ever careful and prudent not to acquire or receive more land around such a place than strict necessity demands for a garden wherein to grow vegetables. But if at any time it should be expedient for the proper solitude of the monastery to have more land beyond the limits of the garden, they may not permit more to be acquired than strict necessity demands. And this land shall not be cultivated nor sown but is to remain always untouched and uncultivated.[7]

17. I admonish and exhort in the Lord Jesus Christ all my Sisters present and to come that they strive always to follow the way of holy simplicity, humility and poverty and to live worthily and holily, as we have been taught by our blessed Father Francis from the beginning of our conversion to Christ. Thereby, though not by our own merits but only through the mercy and bounteous grace of the Father of mercies, they may always diffuse the fragrance of their good name to our other Sisters near and afar off.

18. Love one another with the charity of Christ, and let the love which you have in your hearts be shown outwardly by your deeds that, inspired by this example, the Sisters may always grow in the love of God and in mutual charity.[8]

19. And I beseech that Sister who shall be entrusted with the care of the Sisters to govern others more by her virtues and holy life than by her office, so that, encouraged by her example, they may obey her not only out of duty but rather out of love.[9] Let her be prudent and watchful toward her Sisters as a good Mother toward her daughters; and from the alms which the Lord shall give let her take care to provide for them according to the needs of each one. Let her also be so kind and approachable that they may reveal their necessities without fear and have recourse to her at any hour with all confidence as may seem good to them for themselves or for their Sisters.[10]

20. But the Sisters who are under her should remember that they have renounced their own wills for God's sake.[11] Therefore I will that they obey their Mother as they have of their own free will promised the Lord; and thus the Mother, seeing their charity and humility and the unity that exists among them, will carry more lightly the burdens of her office, and what is painful and bitter will, by their holy living, be turned to sweetness for her.

21. And because straight is the way and the path one walks, and narrow the gate by which one enters into life, so few there are that walk thereon and enter through it (Cf. Matt. 7, 13:14); and if there are some that walk that way for a time, how few indeed are those who persevere thereon. Happy those to whom it is given to walk that way and to persevere to the end! (Cf. Matt. 10:22).

22. Let us take care, therefore, if we have entered the way of the Lord, lest by our own fault or negligence or ignorance at any time and in any way we turn aside therefrom and so do injury to so great a Lord and His Virgin Mother, and to our blessed Father Francis and to the Church Triumphant and the Church Militant. For it is written: "Cursed are they who turn aside from Thy commandments!" (Ps. 118:21).

23. For this reason I bend my knees to the Father of our Lord Jesus Christ (Eph. 3:14), that through the prayers and merits of the glorious and holy Virgin Mary, His Mother, and of our most blessed Father Francis and all the Saints, the Lord Himself who has given us a good beginning will give also the increase (cf. I Cor. 3, 7), and likewise constant perseverance to the end. Amen.

24. This writing, that it may be better observed, I leave to you, my most beloved and dearest Sisters present and to come, as a sign of the blessing of the Lord and of our most blessed Father Francis, and of my blessing, who am your Mother and Handmaid.

NOTES

1. Cf. the Rule of St. Clare, VI, 1, and XII, 5.
2. Cf. the Legend, 8 and 10, pp. 23–24.
3. Besides the *Formula Vitae* and the *Ultima Voluntas* (found in the Rule of St. Clare VI, 2 and 3), none of these writings has survived. See the *Mirror of Perfection*, 90 and 108.
4. Cf. the Rule of St. Clare, VI, 4. The second half of this sentence, missing in the latin text of Wadding, is supplied from the ancient French and Italian versions.
5. That is, the Privilege of Poverty, pp. 103 ff.
6. Cf. the Rule of St. Clare, XII, 10.
7. Ibid., VI, 6.
8. Ibid., X, 5.
9. Ibid., IV, 7.
10. The Rule of St. Clare, X, 1 and 3.
11. Ibid., X, 2.

ST. AGNES OF ASSISI (1198–1254; Italy)

Letter to St. Clare

Translated by Ignatius Brady, O.F.M.

1. To her venerable Mother and excellent Mistress in Christ, the dearly beloved Lady Clare, and to her whole convent: Agnes, the humble and least servant of Christ, kneeling in all submission and devotion at her feet and petitioning for her whatever sweet and precious gifts the power of the Most High King can give.

2. Since the fate of every creature is such that it can never continue in the same state (Job 14:2), when anyone therefore thinks himself to be in good fortune then is he plunged into adversity. Know then, Mother, that in my body and soul there is great distress and overwhelming sorrow, and I am oppressed above measure and tormented and almost unable to speak, because I am separated in body from you and from my other Sisters with whom I had thought to live and to die in this world. This distress had indeed a beginning,

but it knows no end; never does it know surcease, but always gains increase; it has risen upon me recently, but gives no promise of decline; it is always near me and never desires to be apart from me. I used to believe that those who shared in one life and converse in heaven would share alike in death and life on earth, and that one sepulchre would enclose those who are one and equal by nature. But I see I am deceived; I am straitened, I am forlorn, I am in tribulation on every side.

My dearest Sisters, be with me in my grief, I implore you; mourn with me, lest at some time you suffer like things, and see that there is no sorrow like to my sorrow (Lam. 1:12). This sorrow torments me always, this homesickness ever plagues me, this fire ever burns within me. Because of this I am straitened on every side and I know not what to choose (cf. Dan. 13:22). Help me, I implore you, by your pious prayers, that this burden be made light and bearable for me. O sweetest Mother and Lady, what shall I do, what shall I say, for I have no hope of seeing you and my Sisters again in the body! Oh that I could express my thoughts as I would! Oh that I could convey to you by this letter the sorrow that stretches out before me which I must ever face. My soul burns within me, tormented by the fires of intense suffering. My heart groans within me, and my eyes cease not to pour forth rivers of tears. I am filled with grief, my spirit is gone, I waste away. I find no consolation, no matter where I seek; I feel grief upon grief, when I think in my heart that I can never expect to see you and my Sisters again; and so in my sorrow I have completely lost heart. There is none to comfort me among all that are dear to me (Lam. 1:2).

3. But on the other hand, I am greatly consoled and you will be able to rejoice with me in this, that I have here found great unity of mind without the least division, far beyond what I could believe. All have received me with great joy and gladness and promised obedience to me with the greatest devotion and reverence. All these Sisters recommend themselves to God and to you and your convent; and I recommend them and myself to you in all things and through all, that you may have in your heart a solicitous care for me and for them as your sisters and daughters, in the knowledge that they and myself desire to keep inviolate for the whole of our life your admonitions and precepts. In reference to these, you should know that the Lord Pope has agreed with me, as I said, and with you, in all things in accordance with your desire and mine, concerning the question of property as you fully know [i.e., the Privilege of Poverty]. I pray that you beg Brother Elias to take it upon himself to visit me often, very often, and console me in the Lord.

ST. UMILTÀ OF FAENZA   (1126–1310; Italy)

Sermons

Translated by Richard J. Pioli

SECOND SERMON: *The Angels, or Treatise of the Court of Paradise*

1. My two Angels

Whoever wishes to listen well to divine speech must enclose himself in great silence. This is the sermon in which the angels are spoken of; they are the joy of the saints. And here are described two noble creatures who have always faithfully remained near, and I have been moved by love of them to say how powerful is the greatness God gave them, marking in them an image of his own beauty, adorning them with every embellishment, placing them above the firmament. He gave them the knowledge of every science with which they might testify to the divine power. He gave wings to each one so that they might fly as merry announcers of the newest things, conquerors of grandeurs, capable of reaching every height.

They are in nine orders, and each order is named for its power, but they also have names among themselves, and each has a personal name of great beauty. The first of whom I will begin to speak are those I know well, who are no less than the others, who have a name of great significance.

I love all the angels of heaven, but two constitute my delight and my joy, for day and night they comfort me and overwhelm me with riches. The Lord has given them to me to watch over me and to protect me from every danger. They have observed well the commandment they were given, and have placed me as if in a fortress, and they sustain me on both sides so that it is impossible to fall except through my own weakmindedness. I know how to speak their names through the grace of John the Evangelist.

One comes from the choir of angels bestowed as guardians to men in this life. Mine is not among the lesser. I know this because they have told me. His appearance is most handsome; he is like a jewel, or a perfect pearl. I love him more than all the others who are with him. His name is rightfully proclaimed, for he explains divine wisdom. He is called the angel Sapiel. He came with me at my life's beginning as soon as I was born.

I accuse myself before him; I expressed grief to him. I led a sinful life. But he is good, and tolerated my sinning and my stupidity, and was always a most faithful advocate on my behalf before God. He is adorned with precious gems, and his garment is made of the most varied colors.

The other angel is one of the Cherubim who has six wings and dwells upon a throne of greater height, and is above every power, of the higher order. The splendor from which the divine love is kindled is always burning in him, and since he is very beautiful, he remains near the Trinity, and he must shine with the fire of beauty. He has been admirably named with a name solely his own, worthy of sublime heights. He is the angel Emmanuel. I know it from the mouth of John the Evangelist. It would be easier to count the drops in the great amplitude of the sea than to say, think, or hear a discourse on his great goodness. I cannot tell you. My mouth is that of a stuttering baby.

This angel full of every good was given to me by God after I had reached my thirtieth year, when I entered into thoughts of greater weight. The angels which I had received were wise, but they possessed neither the rod nor the potency that express his strength. The angel Emmanuel opened his wings and relieved me of the worry of a great labor, for he is in the glory of God, interpreter of the immensity, expression of the power of greater height. Being compassionate, he counselled me, and was always extremely generous with his many goods.

FIFTH SERMON: *Discourse on Weeping and Lamentation*

1. In the Abyss

O my unhappy and desolate soul, struck on every side! I wish to tell my misfortune to you beings who are on high, strong among the strong, so that you may pray to the sublime Savior for me.

You know and remember that by grace I was elevated almost to heaven, and now I feel myself precipitated into the abyss. From the highest mountains I descended into the dark shadowy valley. The great treasure that had been given to me as a precious vessel has fallen: I saw myself rich before and now I am poor. I no longer have anything for myself, I can give nothing to others, my friends have abandoned me, and I have remained among enemies. The heart from which I drew breath of life has been mortally transfixed by the sword: I lost the wealth that I was supposed to preserve, that made me capable of ascending to a throne of precious gems worth more than the entire world. Gold and silver have turned into tin that bends, my mind that penetrated the heavens with its rapid flight toward the throne of the queen now no longer knows how to fly and is tied to the low places of the earth. My eyes that were raised on high to contemplate God now are weighed down by sleep; the mouth that was closed to foul speech now pronounces vain words, and my tongue no longer celebrates those things that gave me such joy, nor does it repeat what was said by Christ and by Mary, but it is made frantic by quarrelling, or is sluggishly inactive. My ears which were intent on holy speech now listen to useless words. My breath, that was fed by perfume and with which I enjoyed that blossom that now I cannot see but I could find then, is offended by another smell that gives me nausea and pain.

My hands that were lifted on high invoking and blessing God, fall exhausted on earthly things. From my eyes there came one stream only, that was for me a sweet bath in which I continually delighted, overcoming all weakness. My face that was luminous is now dark. O unhappy me!

The garden in which the color of the rose was predominant now is all a dark bramble. For this I went to the Virgin Mary and put myself under her standard—but now look at me, far from that path, and lost in the forest.

I was planted in charity, but now I have been pulled out of that ground, and my roots are dried up, and every fruit has been made impossible for me. O unhappy me, and more than desolate! Abandoned to the waves of the sea, my grief is greater than the sea itself. If I could have the grace to lift my eyes on high, if I could see myself, my heart would leap like those waves. I think back on what I have lost, I recall with great pain that for which I was destined, and my heart shatters, thinking that

I am plunged in error. I am far from my homeland, and I find myself among foreigners.

2. The Tree in the Garden

I was a prisoner with my lady, and the prison was a garden full of roses and flowers. In that garden there was a plant that produced the sweetest fruit; it had green leaves in every season, and among the leaves were many apples. The plant was very tall, but it bent down to me whenever I wished. In whatever hour I might look at that tree, I was sated with every food. Its roots reached down deep to where the best source is, the source of the water of life. No matter what time I might wish to nourish myself, there were fruits and water for me, Christ held me in his arms, and in no way could I fall.

But now look at me, fallen to the bottom of the sea, and I do not see the port where I might take refuge. The waves of the sea injure me, and compel me to drown: from the abyss I invoke you, Lady of Paradise, highest created being. I have greatly offended you, but may you forgive me; my sins are so many that I would not know how to count them. I present myself before you, completely diseased, and I beg of you the supreme well-being. Pull me from the depths of the sea, don't leave me to perish down here; remember me, grant me pardon. Yes, I have denied you, and I have denied Christ, and my works have been base. I have wasted the favors that were granted me, I am spotted with sin, and I should be worthy of death. But free me instead from eternal death and give me some other suffering in its place. Lady, remember that you are the medicine of the sick, the mercy of sinners, the charity of the poor: give yourself no rest in sympathizing with me. I beg supreme pity from her who is the supreme mercy, who has such great mercy that it is impossible to think and speak it. The sores that are on me have become intolerable, I am ashamed to seek healing for them, and I consume myself in grief thinking that I must confess them.

3. As your Servant

Help me, O my blessed lady, you who sit on the high throne for the sake of sinners—I am then one of the reasons for which you are sitting there, therefore extend your hand to me. I know too that I am not worthy of this help, because my wounds came to me from enemies among whom I was placed for chastisement. But hope leads me to believe, and thus I invoke your aid, and I ask for the ointment for my wounds. Anoint my sores with that ointment; it was given to you so that you would preserve it for me. The ointment with which I must be healed was made then when Christ was bound to the column.

Moreover I invoke the drink that was given on the cross to my Lord; make me smell that scent and I shall be cured. Give me that precious perfume that was made for me in the burial; Mary Magdalene made it to anoint the highest Creature. Cause it to be that I may anoint all my wounds with it, and thus my stench will be transformed into fragrance, and then you will remain near me and hold out your medicines to me.

I know that I am not worthy to dwell in the house of the sons of the most high Father. But take me as your servant and in such garments keep me in your house. Accept me at your table as if I were your little dog, and give me the crumbs that fall from the hands of the sweet Christ; they will be strong to nourish me. The dogs collect the scraps that fall from the hands of the master, and those are what I beg of you, my mistress, and I beg them by your pity, not by my right.

I don't know how to make an end to my speaking with you. The more I talk, the more remains to be said. The more I reason the more remains to be reasoned. O poor abandoned me, o poor woman of Judaea! The Canaanite woman did not sin so gravely, nor did Mary Magdalene. You are the highest altitude, and me, I am the abyss of sins.

4. Petition

O sweet Christ, supreme love, have compassion for me and do not abandon me. I take refuge near you who are my assurance, for you have all my hope. To you alone do I find the possibility of addressing my petition. If you wish, you can indeed show me that in this life you have no obligation to me; but I know that by rights I should have nothing. Nevertheless, the wood of the cross sets me on fire. Those hands that were pierced to make visible their generosity give me hope of finding you, and those arms that remain open on the cross tell me that I can put my trust in becoming rich through that gesture. And the breast that was struck by the lance tells me how great is the divine love reserved for me. These stigmata, reminding me of your suffering, encourage me not to despair of my sins.

O Lord, you came for sinners, not for the saved. And you yourself, O Christ, said you would establish this pact. Forgive me my going astray, and hold me in your arms that are open for me on the cross.

I ask mercy of you who are in paradise; pray to Christ crucified for me. May the divine Trinity receive me, the Father, the Son, and the Holy Spirit, and may the Virgin Mary receive me. May my body and soul be in your custody. So may it be.

O Holy Spirit, you who are the consoler, who grant as a gift the love of Christ, give me again those gifts that I have lost. Rekindle in my heart the torch of the love of Christ my lord, by the love of the Virgin Mary, Mother of Christ, my singing mistress, who taught me a melody for your love. Give me grace that my soul may contemplate your Son in every moment. So may it be.

SIXTH SERMON: *In Honor of Jesus Christ*

1. Come unto Me!

O my sweetest Christ, who are my only hope, come to me, and do not delay. Visit my heart that has such need of divine love. Fill it with divine grace, and cause my mind and my soul to be joined and burn always in you who are flame without smoke, wholly resplendent. Draw near to me with your love, o most exquisite fire that makes fruitful, and draws forth the seeds from the dry ground; the earth that you fertilize may indeed be called blessed for its blessed fruit. Hear my voice, o good Sower; my heart asks of you only the seed of love, which immediately increases and gives the best fruit. I beg of you only love. Come then, O Jesus, sweet lover, and do not delay. Clasp me with a new friendship ornamented only with flowers of love, so that every man must sense the fragrance of them, and fulfill all his works in your name. O sweet resplendent Jesus, flame of charity, enflame me with your love and make me luminous like a torch that can cast brightness into any kind of darkness. From the overshadowing heaven descend into the valley, and create abundance of grain. . . .

O Lord who illumined Mary Magdalene, made by divine grace a light in a candlestand, you gave her then so much water from the living fount of your love—illuminate me also, O Christ, in abundance, so that I may join you in walking on the straight way that Magdalene travelled when she burned in your love and wept near the sepulchre.

O love, you are without doubt good to attempt; grant me a good portion of the fire of love, and make me strong and constant in every kind of combat. If you will deign to give yourself wholly to me, O Jesus gentle love, it will seem lovely to me to guard the cross, and sweet and precious and gentle to bear it for your love. Up now and come, hesitate no longer. And you who are the true and complete peace in every discord, bring peace and concord to every conflict. When you are with me and I feel your power, my heart is merry and leaps with joy, my mind adorns itself with flowers of great beauty, and my soul dreams in the sweetness of blessed love. Let my enemies come, who in the world are so numerous, but if I feel myself to be with you, I overthrow them all, and the world itself I overthrow, along with all its speeches. I am like a fish that rests in the sea; when the waves sweep over him and the great tempests assail him, he enjoys swimming, because he cannot be captured, and he leaps more nimbly. Thus do I in this world that is a troubled sea: the great currents arrive, and I sail below them, and I take shelter in your bosom, and let them pass by. Then my soul arms itself with two wings so noble and flying so high that no one can see me: I rush then into your arms, O Jesus, up, into your heavenly realms. Still I offer invocations to you, so that you may be always near me. Feeling myself with you I have no fear of the currents. I even conquer them in navigating, and I come forth from them unharmed. But if I do not possess you, I am like the whale that when the tide goes out sits on the sand and is condemned to death, because without the tide she no longer has the chance to escape.

2. The little Sheep

O sublime, eternal King, full of pity, humble and sweet, greatest in charity, hear the little sheep that bleats with hunger. O good shepherd of flocks, do not abandon me on this arid ground, but lead me to the pasture where there is new grown grass, where I may feed myself on flowers to cover myself with fat flesh and to give good milk. And after this, O Lord, give me the white lamb that sucks on the teats, and always is hungry and always is satisfied at my breasts, and never goes far from them. The lamb that I beg of you—you know who it is, O divine Love—and may he be taken away from those who don't understand.

Let's explain who the hungry lamb is. You are the Lamb of God that expiated sin on the wood of the cross and always healed sinners; you are the starving lamb that cannot be satisfied. And this sheep that bleats in hunger, who implores a pasturage capable of fattening her, is the faithful soul who wishes to remain with Christ who is her proper pasture. She wants to go where there is new grass, and just wants to gather the flowers, and contemplate the beauty of her delightful love, and with a great desire of her heart she wants to fill her breasts again with the milk of charity, and enter into the garden of her true love, and gather red roses, and pick white roses, and drink in the passion of that white lamb, pure in sacrifice, who for our sins was lifted up onto the cross. Behold then the sheep with the immaculate lamb, behold the faithful soul with Christ, who is glad of that love, who desires it so much that he is always famished and can never be sated by it, for too little does he find of that milk of love.

O king of eternal glory, do this great charity for me: cause the things that you teach me to become my actions. May what I say with words be demonstrated through my works— and this in praise of your name.

Give yourself wholly to me, and don't hide yourself from me if you want truly to console me. Cause all my inner organs to be made fertile by you and nourished by your love. I desire a fruitful progeny who will be capable of multiplying my inheritance in your honor. O sweet Jesus, glad love of lovers, glory of the angels, mirth of the saints, come into my soul completely, don't delay, O born from love, and look on me with those eyes of yours that even see what is occult, and from which nothing may be hidden; and if, O Lord, you have really decided to benefit me, don't delay an instant to work on me.

You are my creator who has formed me, my Redeemer who has ransomed me, my debtor who for love of me gave yourself on the cross. I am the little sheep made a pilgrim for your love; you know the grass that I pluck from the pasture where I find myself. You are my life, whether bitter or sweet. You should not wonder overmuch if I ask only love: consider those swords they have planted in my heart, what wounds I bear and how much poison brings me near death, at the time when I see assigned to sinners such a miserable fate for their works.

3. My Roots

O my sweetest Christ, I talk with you so that you may instruct me in what I should ask of you. Thus the grief of my heart is not unknown to you; put your hand on it. You know well my roots and how they were planted, how they grew and were propagated. These roots of mine took my heart and mind and bound my soul with a chain of love. O Jesus, son of the Virgin, who have been continually the cultivator of virtues, cause the root implanted in my heart not to dry out but to propagate. Indeed, you know how it may be valued or esteemed, and how it should fructify in honor of you and blessed John who together with the divine Mother represents regal love.

This sermon has expressed by means of similitudes what is an impediment to those who fail to understand. The root of which I speak is the intention of the heart: it increases through great desire and is led by love to do good. Now if my root is planted as is pleasing to you, O Lord, cause the branches to sprout, so that all may see the leaves and with them the flowers and fruit that come forth through praise of your name. The root is always

covered with earth, and can only be judged by the tree. Thus if good fruits come forth, the root is genuine. But my root was blighted by envy before its flowering was seen, and my enemies want to destroy it. Protect me, O Lord! Behold these axes being grasped for chopping; they strike me with such violence that I seem almost to die of it. Bring me the wine and the oil, and you who know how to heal, anoint poor me, and don't allow these blows.

May my deeply desired good intention lead to love, so that the pains that I suffer in the beginning may be transformed through me into consoling rest. You are the one who said of a woman that when she gives birth she suffers, but when the child is born, she no longer remembers her suffering because of her new responsibilities.

O Jesus Nazarene, who are the highest humility, grant me tonight a great charity, hear my prayers on this your glorious nativity. On your birthday may you distribute rich gifts, and incline your ear in compassion to listen to my voice. For the love of your blessed Mother who carried you in the bosom from which you were born, and nursed you with the milk on which you were nourished, and held you in her blessed hands, give me this generous gift. In memory of that holy land in which you were born, and of the manger in which you were placed and of the straw on which you lay in your condescension, don't stand aloof from my prayer. Weigh, O Lord, the sufferings that I have sustained, as you did with Susanna, when you permitted her to be brought to trial, and then set her free.

4. Against my Enemies

Twice have I given birth with pain. O Lord, be generous with your reward, and cause me to gather everything that will turn to your greater honor, my sweetest Christ. You know what my desire is—I shall be filled with joy if my sweet loving will give fruit that will prove to be in your honor. One thing only I ask of you with firm determination, and that is that you take away all power from my enemies, so that they can no more be opposed to my completing your works.

O cursed ones! O great indignation! They rip up the flower and the lily and throw them away. They despise the holy work that is done in honor of you and St. John the Evangelist. I implore you, O Lord, to drive them away from this blundering. You shall give counsel on what is to be done, now and later. You know the exile that was given to me, and the proofs are in your hands. Weigh whether I, unhappy as I am, have any rights, and grant me peace. Let a judgment come from you by which everyone may see that my enemies have no rights, and that their witnesses are false.

You who freed Daniel from the lion's den, because you held him so dear, may you return persuasion to me, free me from my enemies, so that they may wound me no further. Put me near your friends so that I may work to your honor. Finally, hear me, for the love of John the Evangelist, whom you loved so much, and who rested on your breast in the supper of great desire.

And you, O Evangelist, sweet bringer of love, on this day consecrated to you, hear your faithful ones. If ever you have seen me, if you still recognize me, be mindful of me, my mortal remains. If you cared for me when I was rich, don't abandon me in this misery. If I had come here (as I have come for you) not for you but for the Sultan, Emperor of the Turks, he would have been most generous with his regal aid. O blessed John, reflect that I have come in your name and under your protection, and that I have been covered with injuries inasmuch as I am your servant, and it is for your sake that I have entered this ocean of difficulties. When the raging waves came, I began to swim with both arms, and I remained strong in your love. Now drive the tempest far away from me, lead me to the toilsome port, let us fulfill your work with joy, so that your name be praised.

Recall now your continuous gift of those lovely things, lovely with the most exquisite beauty, and recall your expressions of the greatest sweetness which you gave me so that I would be the more eager. If I love you, O John, although I am a worthless leaf and you a lily-flower of fragrant whiteness, do not despise me. Be mindful of that lovely blade you have fashioned; it is love and not a scourge. You have plunged it into my heart and firmly held it there. My love for you can never be lost, for you have bound me with your chain, you have wed me with your ring, have welcomed me into your protection.

Delightful love, do not abandon me!

I could tell of so many other gifts received from you, but it is time to put an end, lest those who listen without a healthy mind gather thorns where I strew roses. I accuse myself of having preserved badly the gifts from you, of not having loved you as I should, but may you have pity. Let us recreate peace in holy love, so that I may revive in love, and can give better fruit, and that the desire I have in my heart may become work in your honor.

BLESSED ANGELA OF FOLIGNO   (1248–1309; Italy)

From the Liber de Vere Fidelium Experientia
(The Book of the Experience of the Truly Faithful)

Translated by Elizabeth Petroff

1. The experience of the truly faithful proves, sees, and touches the Incarnate Word of life. Just as Christ says in the Gospel, "If a man love me, he will keep my words, and my father will love him, and we will come unto him, and make our abode with him," "he that loveth me . . . I will manifest myself to him" (John 14:23 and 21). For God himself causes his faithful souls to prove very deeply their experience and the knowledge that comes from this experience. Recently he himself deigned to reveal something of this experience and this knowledge by means of one of his faithful souls, in order to increase the devotion of his followers. . . . Here begins a little piece concerning the experience of a truly faithful soul, in which may be found the treasure hidden in the field of the Gospels.

3. A certain person, a faithful follower of Christ, said that when telling a companion something about God she counted thirty steps or transformations which she discovered in herself that the soul makes as it proceeds on the path of penitence.

4. The first step is the recognition of sin, in which the soul is greatly afraid of being damned to hell; and in this stage she wept bitterly.

5. The second step is confession, in which she felt shame and bitter sadness; and so far she did not feel love, but only grief. Whence she recalled to me how many times she had received communion with unconfessed sins, for because of shame she could not confess fully, and day and night her conscience

rebuked her. And when she prayed Blessed Francis to find her a confessor who would understand sins thoroughly, so that she could confess to him, there appeared to her that same night an aged friar who said, "Sister, if you had asked me earlier, I would have done this more quickly. But what you have asked is already acomplished." And immediately in the morning I went to the Church of St. Francis and came back quickly, and on my return, I found a friar preaching in the cathedral, San Feliciano, and that friar was a chaplain of the bishop. And I decided immediately, God willing, to fully confess myself to him, if he had the authority of the bishop, or if he could get the bishop for me. And I confessed fully to him. He, after he had heard my confession, said that if I was not content with that, he would tell all my sins to the bishop. And he said that the penance which he imposed I will carry to you, although I can absolve you without the bishop. In this stage she still felt shame and bitter sadness, and she did not feel love but felt grief.

6. The third step is the penance she performed for satisfaction to God for her sins, and she was still in grief.

7. The fourth step is the recognition of divine mercy, which granted her the abovesaid mercy in pulling her back from hell. And here she began to be illuminated, and then she wept and grieved more than before, and urged herself to perform harsher acts of penance.

I, the friar writing this, say that in all these steps I did not wish to write down the remarkable penances which this faithful servant of Christ performed, for I learned them after I had written down the aforesaid steps; and then she had only told me as much as was necessary for her to say in order to distinguish each step, and I was not willing to write down a single word unless it was just as she had said it. Therefore I have omitted many things I could not write properly.

8. The fifth step is the understanding of her self; since she was now a little enlightened, she saw nothing in herself except defects, and she condemned herself before God, for she was most surely worthy of hell. And here she received bitter weeping.

And you should understand that at each of these steps there is a pause. For this reason it is a great pity and heart-break for the soul that it can only move so slowly, and experience so much pain, and it moves toward God so ponderously. It takes such tiny steps. And I know that for myself I stopped and wept at every step, and nothing additional was given to me, although it was a little consolation to me that I could weep at each stage. But it was a bitter consolation.

9. The sixth step is a certain illumination of grace whereby there was given to me a profound cognition of all my sins, and I saw in that illumination that I had offended all the created things made for me. And my sins came back to me in my memory very deeply, even in that confession which I made about them before God. And I asked all creatures whom I saw I had offended not to accuse me. And then it was given to me to pray with a great fire of love. And I invoked all the saints, and the Blessed Virgin, to intercede for me, and pray to that love who had done so many good things for me, so that they who knew me to be dead would cause me to live. And it seemed to me that all creatures had pity and compassion on me.

10. The seventh. It was given to me to look on the cross, on which I saw Christ dead for

us. But this was still a flavorless vision, although I felt great pain from it.

11. The eighth. In gazing on the cross I was given a greater understanding of how the Son of God was dead for our sins. And then I recognized all my sins with the greatest grief, and I felt that I was crucifying him. But I did not understand then what a great benefit this was, nor that it had led me away from sin and from hell, and had turned me toward repentance, nor that for this he was crucified for me. But in this understanding of the cross there was given to me such a great fire, that standing next to the cross I stripped myself of all my clothing, and I offered myself to him completely. And although fearfully, still I promised him to preserve perpetual chastity and not to offend him with any of my members, accusing all my members one by one. I prayed that he would cause me to observe the aforesaid, that is, that chastity of all members and senses, for on the one hand I was afraid to promise, and on the other that fire compelled me to promise, and I could do nothing else.

12. Ninth. It was given to me to seek the way of the cross, that I might stand at the foot of the cross where all sinners take refuge. And I was instructed and illuminated and shown the way of the cross in this fashion, for I was inspired with the thought that if I wanted to go to the cross I should strip myself so I would be lighter and naked I should go to the cross; that is, that I should forgive all who had offended me and strip myself of all earthly goods and of [attachments to] all men and women, of all friends and relatives and everyone else, and of my possessions and of my very self, and I should give my heart to Christ who had given me so many benefits, and I should walk on the path of thorns, that is, of tribulations. And then I began to put aside my better clothes, and food, and my headcoverings. But this was still shameful and burdensome for me, for at this point I was not feeling any love, and I was living with my husband. So it was

bitter for me when people spoke slanders about me, or did things to injure me, but I endured them as patiently as I could.

And as this time, God willing, it happened that my mother, who was a great impediment for me, died; and within a short time after this my husband and all my children were dead. And since I had embarked on the aforesaid path and had prayed God that they would die, I felt great consolation at their deaths. And I thought that from then on, after God had done these things for me, that my heart would always be within God's heart, and God's heart always within mine.

13. Tenth. When I asked God what I could do to please him more, in his pity he appeared to me many times, both while I was sleeping and while I was keeping vigil, crucified on the cross, and he told me I might look on his wounds. And in a marvelous fashion he showed me how he had endured all this for me—and he did this many times. And when he showed me individually, one by one, all that he had endured for me, he said to me, "What then can you do that would suffice for you?" Likewise he appeared to me many times while I was keeping vigil, that is, more pleasantly than when I was sleeping, although he always appeared to me in great suffering, and he spoke to me just as he had when I was sleeping, showing his pains from his feet up to his head. He even showed me the hairs plucked from his beard and his eyebrows and his head, and he enumerated all his flagellations, that is, pointing out each individual welt. And he said, "I endured all these things for you." And then all my sins were brought back amazingly to my memory, by which it was shown to me that when I recently wounded him afresh with my sins I should have felt the greatest pain. And then I felt greater grief for my sins than I had ever felt. Likewise with my seeing his passion he said to me, "What can you do for me that would suffice for you!" And then I wept very much and I cried so ardently that

my tears burned my flesh, and I had to put water on it afterward to cool it.

14. Eleventh. Because of these things I drove myself to performing harsher penances.

This is the longest and most remarkable step to write about, and difficult beyond human capacity, say I, the friar scribe who learned afterwards about her penances.

15. Twelfth. Since it did not seem to me that I could perform sufficient penance while possessing the things of this world and that I could come to the cross as I had been inspired to do by God, I decided to give up everything totally so that I could perform penance and come to the cross.

The aforesaid decision was granted to me miraculously by God in this way. While I was eagerly desiring to be made poor, I often thought with much zeal about poverty, afraid that by chance my death might come about before I could become poor; and on the other side, I would be beset by many temptations, for example, that since I was young, begging would be dangerous for me and shameful, and that it would be necessary for me to die of hunger and cold and nakedness, and since I was dissuaded from this [total renunciation] by everyone, one time, with God taking pity on me, a certain great illumination came to me in my heart, and with this illumination there came to me a certain firmness (that I did not then nor do I now believe I will lose for eternity): that is, that in that illumination I disposed myself and determined that even if it were necessary for me to die of hunger or nakedness or shame, as long as God were pleased by it or could be pleased, I would in no way omit doing this for these reasons, even if I were convinced that all these evils were to befall me. For even if all these evils happened to me, I would die happy in God. And then on this basis I truly made up my mind.

16. Thirteenth. I entered into the grief of the Mother of Christ and of St. John, and I prayed that they would obtain for me a certain

sign by which I might always and continually remember the passion of Christ. With this, it happened that in sleep I was shown the heart of Christ and it was said: "In this heart there is no falsehood, but all things are true." And it seemed to me that this happened because I had spoken some inappropriate pleasantries about a certain preacher.

17. Fourteenth. While I was in prayer, keeping vigil, Christ showed himself to me on the cross with such clarity—that is, that he gave me greater knowledge of him. And then he called me and said I should put my mouth to the wound in his side. And it seemed to me that I saw and drank his blood flowing freshly from his side. And I was given to understand that by this he would cleanse me. And at this I began to feel great joy, although when I thought about the passion I felt sadness. And I prayed the Lord that he would cause me to shed all my blood for his love, just as he had done for me. And I so disposed myself on account of his love that I wished that all my limbs might suffer a death unlike his passion, that is, a more vile death. And I was meditating and desiring that if I could find someone to kill me, in some way that it would be lawful to kill me, on account of his faith or his love, that I would beg him to do this favor for me, that is, that since Christ was crucified on the wood of the cross he should crucify me in a low place, or in some unsavory place or with a loathsome weapon. And I could not think of a death as vile as I desired, and I grieved deeply that I could not find a vile death that would in no way be like those of the saints, for I was totally unworthy.

18. The fifteenth. I fixed my attention on St. John and on the Mother of God, meditating on their grief and praying them to obtain this grace for me, that is, that I might always feel the pain of the passion, or at least their pain. And they came to me, and for this purpose. Thus one time St. John gave me so much [of his pain] that it was the greatest suffering I have ever felt. And I was given to understand that St. John endured so much pain at the passion and death of Christ and at the pain of the Mother of Christ, that I thought then, and still think, that he was more than a martyr.

From this there was then given to me the desire of disposing of everything with so much will that although I was much attacked so that I would not do this, and I was often tempted by these remarks, and although it was forbidden to me by the friars and by you, and by all from whom it was appropriate for me to ask advice, nevertheless I could in no way hold back, either for the good or for the evil they might do to me. And if I had not been able to give to the poor otherwise, I would give away all my goods completely, for it did not seem to me that I could hold anything back for myself without great sin. Nevertheless my soul was still feeling bitter sorrow for my sins, and I didn't know if what I was doing pleased God. So I cried out in the most sorrowful weeping, saying, "Lord, if I am damned, still I'm going to do this penance and I will give everything away and serve you." And up to that point I was feeling bitter sorrow for my sins and I did not yet feel divine sweetness. I was transformed from that state in the following way.

19. The sixteenth. Once I was going to church and I prayed God that he would give me some grace. And while I was praying, he placed the paternoster in my heart with such a clear understanding of the divine goodwill and of my unworthiness, and explained each individual word in my heart, and I was reciting that Pasternoster so slowly and with consciousness of myself, that, on the one hand, although I was weeping bitterly for my sins and my unworthiness that I recognized, nevertheless I also felt great consolation and I began to taste something of the divine sweetness, since I was recognizing better the divine goodwill in that Paternoster than in anything else, and now I have found even better. But

since in that Paternoster my unworthiness and my sins were pointed out to me, I began to be overcome by so much shame that I could scarcely raise my eyes. But I depicted to myself the Blessed Virgin, so that she would ask forgiveness of my sins for me. And I was feeling bitter sorrow for my sins.

And I remained for some time in each of the above steps, before I could move on to the next. But some steps I remained longer, and less in others. Thus that faithful servant of Christ marvelled: "O, nothing is here written of the great heaviness with which the soul goes forward, for it has such strong obstacles, that is, shackles, on its feet, in the world and the devil."

Note what follows concerning faith.

20. The seventeenth. And afterwards it was shown to me that the Blessed Virgin obtained this grace for me, that she gave me faith unlike what I had had before, for it seemed to me that up until that time my faith had been almost dead in comparison, and the tears which I had shed were as if forced out of me in comparison. But afterwards, I grieved for the passion of Christ and of the Mother of Christ more earnestly than I had before. And then whatever I did and however I did it it seemed to me a small thing to do, and I had the desire of doing greater penance. And then I enclosed myself in the passion of Christ. And hope was given to me that there I would be able to be freed.

Note what follows concerning hope.

And then I began to have consolation in dreams, and I had many lovely dreams, and much comfort was given to me in them, and there began to be given to me sweetness deep within my soul from God continually, both sleeping and waking. But since I still didn't feel any certainty, this was still mixed with sorrow and I wanted to have something else from God.

From her dreams and visions she brought forth one out of many, saying, "One time, while I was in prison where I had enclosed myself for the greater Lent, and was enjoying and meditating on a word in the Gospel, which was of great honor and extreme delight, there was a book next to me, a missal, and I thirsted to see that word, at least as it was written. I continued to do so, scarcely containing myself and restraining myself from opening the book in my hands, out of too great a thirst and love, because I feared pride, when overcome by sleep, I fell asleep in that desire. And at once I was led into a vision and I was told that the understanding of the Gospel is such a delectable thing that if one understood it well he would forget everything of this world. And he who was leading me asked, 'Do you want to experience this?' When I agreed to experience it, at once he led to it. And I understood the divine goodness with so much sweetness that I immediately forgot all worldly things. And he who was leading me said that now the understanding of the Gospel was something so very delectable that if one understood it he would forget not only everything of the world but he would also totally forget himself. And he led me to this and made me experience it. And immediately I understood with great delight the divine goodness so that I completely forgot not only everything of the world, but even myself. And I was in so much divine delectation that I sought of him who led me that I would never again have to leave that state. He replied to me that what I sought could not yet be. And he led me back at once, and I opened my eyes. And I felt the greatest happiness at what I saw, but I felt very sad to have lost it. And this still makes me happy when I remember. And from this so much certitude remained with me, so much light and ardor of the love of God, that I was affirming most certainly that nothing is preached about the delectation of God. Those who preach cannot preach about this, and what they do preach they don't understand. This is what he who led me in this vision said to me."

Note that in the preceding step, three things—faith, hope, charity—are perfectly granted to her at the same time.

21. The eighteenth. Afterwards I had feelings of God, and I felt such delight in prayer that I didn't remember to eat. And I wished that it were not necessary to eat, so that I might remain in prayer. But intermixed with this was a certain temptation, that is, that I shouldn't eat, or if I ate, that I would only eat a very small amount—but I recognized this as a temptation. And in my heart the fire of love was so great that I wasn't tired by genuflexions nor by any other penitential act. Still later I came to so much greater a fire of love that I screamed if I heard anyone talking about God. Even if someone had stood over me with an axe ready to kill me, I could not have prevented myself. This happened to me for the first time when I sold a piece of land so that I could give to the poor. I was the best land that I had. And before I used to make fun of Petrucchio, but afterwards I could not. Moreover, when people said to me that I was demonically possessed so that I couldn't stop myself, I was very ashamed, and I too said the same, that I was ill and possessed, and I could not satisfy those who were maligning me. And when I saw depicted the passion of Christ, I could hardly endure it, but fever took me and I fell ill. So my companion hid from me pictures of the Passion or tried to hide them.

22. The nineteenth. But during this period of screaming, after that illumination which I miraculously received during the *pater noster*, the first great consolation of the sweetness of God I sensed in this way, that is, as I was one time inspired and drawn to meditating on the delight there is in the contemplation of the divinity and humanity of Christ. And this was the greatest consolation I had experienced, in so much as for the major part of that day I stood on my feet in the cell where I was accustomed to praying, overwhelmed and alone. And my heart was in that delectation. After this I fell down and lost all speech. And my companion then came to me and thought that I was dying or might be dead. But it irritated me that she disturbed me in that greatest consolation.

Another time, she said before she had finished giving away all her possessions, although little enough remained to be distributed, one evening when she was in prayer, since it did not seem to her that she felt anything of God, she prayed to God and lamented in this way, saying, "Lord, what I am doing I do only so I may come to you. May I find you after I complete it!" And she said many other things in that prayer. She was given this response. "What do you wish?" And she answered saying, "I do not want gold or silver; even if you were to give me the whole world, I want only you." And then he responded thus: "Make haste, for as soon as you have finished what you are doing, the whole Trinity will come to you." And he promised many other things to me then, and removed me from every tribulation, and left me with much sweetness. And since then I have expected that it would be done as he had promised. I told all this to my companion, doubting because what was said and promised to me was much too great. But he left me with much divine enjoyment.

Note here that God fulfilled what he had promised her before she had fulfilled her vow of complete poverty.

23. Twentieth. Following this I went to the church of St. Francis in Assisi. And on the way there, the preceding promise happened to me and was fulfilled, just as I told you. And I don't recall if I had yet managed to give away everything—rather, I still hadn't finished giving everything to the poor. Nevertheless, little

remained to be done. A certain man had asked me to wait for him while he went quickly to the realm of Apulia to divide into parts his possessions to share them with his brother who lived in that kingdom. He would come back very soon, he said, in order to give his entire share of these possessions to the poor, to make himself poor like me. And since he wanted to dispose of everything completely, again like me, for he had been converted and encouraged by the grace of God through my admonitions, I waited for him there. But very soon afterwards it was reliably reported to me that he died on that journey, and that God performed miracles through him, and that his grave is held in reverence.

24. This step, which is here written as the twentieth, is the first writing which I, the friar taking this down, unworthy to write, had and heard from the mouth of this faithful servant of Christ. For this reason I did not finish and follow through on this step, which is very marvelous, containing great revelations of the divine, much longer, of much delectation and divine intimacy. But the twenty-first step is even more marvelous. I abandoned this after it was barely begun, or I put it aside until I had briefly told how, by the marvelous action of Christ, I came to the recognition of these things and was constrained to write them.

25. It should also be noted here that I, the friar writing this, with the help of God, urged myself to continue the material from the first step up to that place which is described in the twenty-first step, or in the end according to revelation, where it is written that God miraculously revealed to her that everything we were writing was true and without any falsehood, although these things were much fuller than what I wrote, which I shortened and wrote defectively.

[This is followed by a number of paragraphs in which Fra Arnaldo fills in more details of the first seven steps. Before he gives us the description of the powerful visitation that came to Angela at Assisi, he tells us, with some embarrassment, of his reaction to it. He was at that time living in the Franciscan house in Assisi.]

34. The real cause or reason for which I began to write, from my point of view, is this. One day, the aforesaid person, the faithful servant of Christ, came to the church of St. Francis in Assisi, where I was living as a conventual brother, and she screamed, sitting in the entrance to the portals of the church. I, because I am her confessor and her blood relative, her principal and special adviser, was very ashamed, particularly because of a number of brothers who had come to see her screaming or yelling, and they knew me and her, and although that holy man (whom we spoke of earlier, where it is noted in the twentieth step, where we mentioned that he wanted to divest himself of everything along with her), her companion on this journey, was sitting on the ground just inside the church, humbly on the pavement, not very far from her, and although he was looking at her with the greatest reverence and a certain sadness, and watching over her, and likewise other good men and women companions of hers were waiting for her and protecting her, nevertheless, my pride and my shame were so great that out of embarrassment and indignation I waited for her to finish screaming and kept myself at a distance. And after she stopped that strident clamor and got up from the entrance and came over to me, I could hardly speak to her calmly. I told her that never again in the future should she dare to come to Assisi where this evil overtook her. And I said to her companion that he should never have led her here. Later, after a short time, I left Assisi for the place from which she and I came.

[After his return to Foligno, Fra Arnaldo gets to know more about Angela's experiences; it seems that she had told him very little of her visionary life prior to this. As Fra

Arnaldo gains more and more respect for Angela, he becomes more critical of himself and more aware of his inadequacies as a scribe. She is equally critical of his failures in capturing what she has really said. Yet both felt compelled to get these revelations into written form, and their common sense of exclusion, even of persecution, from the Franciscan community bound them together.]

[The difficulty in writing] was doubtless my inadequacy—not that I would add anything, but that I honestly could not understand everything she said; and she said that what I wrote down was true, but it was truncated and reduced. And since I learned to write very late and since on account of fear of the brothers who grumbled because I was sitting with her in the church to write I was in a great hurry when I wrote, I consider that it was a divine miracle that what I wrote I could put in order.

35. . . . Here begins to be told the marvelous step which is begun as the twentieth above. And among other things she asked Blessed Francis to pray to God for her that she might feel something of Christ and that Blessed Francis might acquire for her from God the grace of observing well the Rule of St. Francis, which she had recently vowed, and particularly to pray for this, that he would cause her to be and to end her life truly poor. For she desired so deeply to possess perfect poverty that for this purpose alone, that St. Peter the Apostle might acquire for her from Christ complete poverty, she went to Rome to ask St. Peter to seek this grace of complete poverty. When I listening read this part to her and she agreed that what it said was true although written with many defects, she added, "And when I neared Rome, I felt that divine grace granted it to me because I was seeking poverty." And when she then was going to the church of St. Francis she asked him, Blessed Francis, that is, that he might obtain that grace for her from the Lord Jesus Christ. And she told me many other things she asked for in that prayer she was saying as she went along. And when she got to the place between Spello and the steep path that comes after Spello and climbs up towards Assisi, there at the crossroads it was said to her, "You asked my servant Francis, but I did not want to send another messenger. I am the Holy Spirit, who come to you so that I may give you a consolation which you have never tasted. And I will go with you until you reach St. Francis"—and she added as if she were meditating on something—"and I want to come along speaking with you on the way and I will not put an end to speaking. And you will not be able to do anything, for I have raised you up. And I will not leave you until you come a second time to the church of St. Francis. And then I will leave you as far as this consolation is concerned, but I will not leave you ever from now on if you love me." And he began to say, "My daughter sweet to me, my daughter, my beloved, my temple; my beloved daughter, love me, for you are very loved by me, much more than you love me." And very often he said, "Daughter and bride, sweet to me." And he said, "I cherish you very much. I have rested within you, and now you may rest yourself in me. You prayed to my servant Francis. And since my servant Francis loved me very much, I did much for him. And if now there were any person who would love me more, I would do more for him."

At these words I began to doubt, and my soul said to him: "If you were the Holy Spirit you would not say this to me, for it is not appropriate. I am weak, and I could feel vainglory at this." And he replied, "Now think if from all these things you can feel any vainglory which makes you proud. And leave these words if you can." I began and tried to want to feel vainglory, so that I could prove whether what he said was true, and if he was the Holy Spirit. And I began to look around at the vineyards so that I might leave that, that is, that locution. And wherever I looked, he said to me, "This is my creature." And I felt ineffable divine sweetness. All my sins and vices were brought to mind, and on the other hand, I saw nothing in myself but sins and defects. I felt in myself so much humility, more than I had ever felt. And nevertheless I was told that the Son of the Virgin Mary had lowered himself to me. And he said, "If the whole world were to come with you now, you could not speak to them; for with you came the whole world." And in order to give me security in my doubt, he said, "I am he who was crucified for you, and I had hunger and thirst for you, and I shed my blood for you, so much have I loved you." And he spoke about his whole Passion. And he said, "Seek whatever grace you wish for yourself, and for your companions, and for whomever you wish. And make yourself ready to receive it, for I am much more prepared to give than you are to receive." And I said, and my soul cried out, "I don't want to ask, for I am not worthy." And my sins all returned to my mind. And my soul said, "If you are the Holy Spirit, you would not say such great things to me. And if you say them to me, it ought to be so great a joy that my soul ought not to be able to endure it." And he replied, "Nothing is, nor can be, unless I will it; now I do not give you more joy than this. I said less than this to someone, and he fell down, neither feeling nor seeing anything. And you come with companions, and no one knows; and now I have not given you greater feelings. And I give you this sign: try to speak with your companions, and think something else, good or evil, and you will not be able to think of anything except God. And I do all this not for your merits." And then all my evil faults came back into my memory, and I saw that I was more worthy of hell than ever. And he said, "I do this because of my goodwill; and if you had come with other people, unlike these, I would not have done this for you." For in some way they knew about my languor, because at every word I received the greatest

sweetness, and I did not want ever to arrive at Assisi or that the road should ever end, in all the time of the world. And I could not estimate how much was the joy and sweetness of God that I felt, especially when he said, "I am the Holy Spirit, who enter into you." And likewise when he said all the other things I felt great sweetness. And in my zeal I said, "Here it will be seen if you are the Holy Spirit, if you come with me as you said." And he said to me, "I will leave you as far as this consolation is concerned, when you come to the church of St. Francis for the second time, but I will not leave you from now on if you love me." And he came with me until St. Francis, as he had said, and he did not leave me when I entered the church and stood in the church, but he stayed with me until after the meal, when for the second time I came into the church of St. Francis. And then . . . at once when I genuflected at the entrance of the church and saw St. Francis depicted in the bosom of Christ, he said to me, "Thus embraced shall I hold you, and much closer than you can imagine with the eyes of the body. And now is the hour, sweet daughter, my temple, that I fulfill what I said to you, for I leave you after this consolation. But I will not ever leave you if you love me." And then, however bitter this word might be, nevertheless at the time I felt so much sweetness in that word that it was very soothing. And then I looked, that I might see even with the eyes of the body and the mind. And when I, the friar-scribe, asked her and said, "What did you see?" she responded by saying, "I saw something full, immense majesty, which I do not know how to describe. But it seemed to me that it was the sovereign good. And many words of sweetness he said to me when he departed, and with immense gentleness and with gentle delays he departed. And then after his departure I began to scream or shriek loudly, without any shame I screamed, crying, and I said these words, "Unknown love! Why have you left me? Why?

Why?" But I could not, or I was not, saying anything more except that without any shame I was shouting those words—"Unknown love! Why? Why?" These words so suffocated in my throat that the words could not be understood, and then I was left with certitude and without any doubt that this was surely God. And I wanted to die while I was crying out. And for me the great pain was that I was not dying and was staying behind. And then all my joints were loosened.

And after this, I returned from Assisi with that greatest sweetness, as I came along the road home. And on the way I went speaking of God, and it was very painful for me to keep silent, but I tried to abstain from talking as much as I could because of the company. On the return road from St. Francis, he said this to me among other things: "I give you this sign that it is me who speaks and has spoken to you; that is, I give you the cross and the love of God within you, and this sign will be with you for all eternity." And I immediately felt that cross and that love in the depths of my soul; and I felt that cross bodily, and feeling it my soul melted in the love of God. And he had said to me on the road going to Assisi—"All your life, your eating and drinking, sleeping and all your living is pleasing to me."

ST. CATHERINE OF SIENA   (1347–1380; Italy)

Letters

Translated by Elizabeth Petroff

To Blessed Daniella of Orvieto, Dressed in the Habit of Saint Dominic

. . . You see, then, that these people enjoy in this life the pledge of life eternal. They receive an advance, a pledge, but not the full payment, not waiting to receive it in the life everlasting, where there is life without death, fullness without discomfort and hunger without pain. The pain of hunger is far away, for they completely possess what they desire, and the discomfort of being full is far away, for He is the food of life without any lack. Indeed in this life one begins to taste the pledge in this way, that the soul begins to be hungry for the food of the honor of God and the salvation of souls. What it is hungry for, that is what it feeds on; that is, the soul nourishes itself on the love of its neighbor, for whom it feels hunger and desire. This is a food that never satisfied those nourished on it.—It is insatiable—and so continual hunger remains. Just as an advance is an anticipation of the security that one gives someone, in token of which he expects to receive the full payment (not that the advance is complete in itself, but good faith gives the assurance of reaching the fulfilment) so the soul enamoured of Christ, that has already received in this life the pledge of love for God and for one's neighbor, is not perfect in itself, but awaits the perfection of the immortal life. I say that this pledge is not perfect; that is, the soul that tastes it has not yet reached the perfection of not feeling suffering in itself and in others—suffering in itself for the offense that it gives to God, by the perverse law that is bound into our bodies, and suffering in others, from the offense of one's neighbor. It is, to be sure, perfect in grace, but not at the level of perfection of the saints who are in eternal life, as I said, for their desires are without suffering, and ours come with suffering. Do you know how it stands with the true servant of God, who is fed at the table of holy desire? He is blessed and grieving, as was the Son of God on the wood of the most holy cross: because the flesh of Christ was grieving and tortured, and the soul was blessed, through its union of our desire in God, and being clothed with his sweet will; and grieved, out of compassion for his neighbor, and for depriving us of delights and sensual comforts, mortifying his own sensuality.

But pay attention, daughter and beloved sister. I have spoken about you and me in general, but now I will speak to you and me in particular. I want us to do two special things so that ignorance doesn't impede the perfection to which God calls us and so that the devil, under the cloak of virtue and charity for one's neighbor, doesn't feed the root of presumption within the soul. Because of this we will fall into false judgments, seeming to ourselves to judge correctly and we will be judging wrongly; and often by following our own impressions, the devil would make us see many truths to lead us into falsehood. This happens because we make judgments about the minds of our fellow creatures, which God alone ought to judge.

This is one of those two things from which I wish us to free ourselves totally. But I want it to be done properly, not improperly. The proper way is this: if God specifically, not one time or two but many times, reveals in our mind the fault of a neighbor, we must never speak about it specifically to the person whom it concerns, but we should correct in general the vices of those who may have come to us for judgment, and plant virtues lovingly and with

goodwill. Severity in good will, when it's needed. And if it should seem that God frequently revealed to us the faults of another, if there was no express revelation, as I said, stay on the safe side, so that we may flee the deception and malice of the devil—because with this hook of desire he would catch us. On your lips let there be silence, and holy discourse about the virtues and disdain of vice. And the vice that you might have seemed to recognize in others, ascribe to them and to you together, always using true humility. If truly that vice does exist in such a person, he will correct himself better seeing himself understood so sweetly, and he will say to you what you wanted to say to him. And you will be safe in doing this, and you will cut off the pathway for the devil, so that he can't deceive us nor hinder the perfection of your soul. And know that we ought not to trust in every appearance, but we ought rather to put it behind us, and dwell only on seeing and recognizing ourselves.

If the situation should ever arise that we were praying particularly for some fellow-creatures, and while praying we saw in some of those for whom we were praying some light of Grace, but not in another, although he too was a servant of God, yet you seemed to see him with a mind deceived and sterile, we should not take that as a judgment of a defect due to a grave sin in him. It could be that your judgment was false. It sometimes happens that, praying for the same person, one time will find him with an illumination and with a holy desire in the presence of God, so much that it seems that the soul is fattening on its good, and another time you will see him when it will seem that his mind is far away from God, all full of shadows and troubles, so that it will seem hard work for the one who's praying to hold him in the presence of God.

This sometimes happens because of a failing that may be in him who is being prayed for; but more often it won't be because of a fault but will be because of God's having withdrawn himself from that soul. That is, God will have withdrawn as far as the feeling of sweetness and consolation is concerned, but not in respect to grace. So the mind remains sterile, dry, pain-filled—which God causes the soul praying about this person to perceive. God does this out of mercy for that soul receiving the prayer, so that together with him you can help to dissolve the cloud. Thus you see, my sweet sister, how ignorant and worthy of rebuke our judgment would be, if we, simply on the basis of appearances, judged that there were sin in that soul. Therefore, if God should show us this person for whom we were praying as so gloomy and dark, we have already observed that he is deprived not of grace but of the perception of the sweetness of feeling God. . . . I pray you then, you and me and every other servant of God, that we devote ourselves to understanding ourselves perfectly, in order that we may more perfectly recognize the good will of God, so that, enlightened, we may abandon judging our neighbor, and acquire true compassion, with a hunger for proclaiming virtues and reproving vice in ourselves and in them, according to the way described above.

We have spoken of the one matter I mentioned, but now I speak to you about the other (which I beg you we rebuke in ourselves), which occurs if some time the devil, or our own very evil construction of matters, has tormented us by making us want to send or to see all the servants of God walking on that path we are taking. For it often happens that seeing oneself advancing by the path of much penance, one would like to send everyone by that same path; and if one sees that someone doesn't go that way, one is displeased and shocked, feeling that he is not doing right. Sometimes it will happen that he will do better and will become more virtuous, even, let's say, the one who doesn't do as much penance as the one that's criticizing. For per-

fection does not consist in mortifying and killing the body, but in killing perverse self-will. And this path of the submerged will, subjected to the sweet will of God, we ought to desire for everyone, for all bodies are not equal. Also because it often happens that a penance that is begun has to be given up from many accidents that can happen. If we made or caused others to make penance their foundation, the penance might dwindle to nothing and would be so imperfect that consolation and virtue would be lacking in the soul, because these could be derived from what it loved, and had made of prime importance. The soul would seem to be deprived of God; and seeming deprived of God, would fall into irritation and the greatest sadness and bitterness, and then in the bitterness of the soul would lose the spiritual exercises and the fervent prayer to which it was accustomed. So you see how much evil would follow from making penance one's chief goal. We should be ignorant and should fall into a complaining attitude, and from this we will come to be irritated and bitter. We should study to give only finished works to God, who is infinite Good, and who asks of us infinite desire. It is necessary for us to build the foundation out of killing and drowning perverse self-will; and with this will submitted to the will of God, we will devote sweet, hungry, infinite desire to the honor of God and the salvation of souls. And thus we will feed ourselves at the table of this holy desire, desire which is never shocked, neither by itself nor by its neighbor, but enjoys and finds fruit in everything. Miserable me, I grieve that I never followed this true doctrine. Rather I've done the opposite, and consequently I feel that I have many times fallen into dislike and judgment of my neighbor. For this reason I pray you, by the love of Christ crucified, that healing may be found for this and for every other weakness of mine. So today let us, you and I, begin to walk in the way of truth, enlightened in making a true foundation in holy desire, and not trusting to impressions and appearances, so that we don't facilely neglect ourselves and judge the faults of our neighbor, except with compassion and by general rebuke.

We will accomplish this, nourishing ourselves at the table of holy desire—we can do it no other way. From desire we have light, and light gives us desire, and the one nourishes the other. And thus I said that I desired to see you in the true light. I say no more. Remain in the holy and sweet affection of God. Sweet Jesus, Jesus love.

To Sister Daniella of Orvieto, clothed with the habit of St. Dominic, who being unable to carry out her great penances, had fallen into grave affliction

In the name of Jesus Christ Crucified and of sweet Mary.

Dearest sister and daughter in Christ sweet Jesus, I, Catherine, servant and slave of the servants of Jesus Christ, write to you in his precious blood, with the desire of seeing in you the holy virtue of discretion which it is necessary to possess if we wish our own salvation. Why is discretion so necessary? Because it issues from the knowledge of ourselves and of God. In this house are planted its roots. Discretion, properly speaking, is a child born to Charity and an illumination and recognition that the soul has of God and of itself, as I said. The main thing it does is this: having seen with the light of reason to what it is a debtor and what it owes, it renders this at once with perfect discretion. Thus to God the soul renders glory, and praise to his name; and all the works that the affection of the soul performs it does by this illumination—that is, all are done to this end. Thus to God it gives the due of honor. It does not act like the indiscreet robber who wants to give honor to himself, and in seeking his own honor and pleasure

doesn't mind insulting God and harming his neighbor. Because the root of affection in the soul is corrupted by indiscretion, all its works are corrupt, whether in itself or in others. In others, I say, because it imposes burdens indiscreetly, and commands others—either secular or spiritual people—or of whatever rank they may be. If it admonishes or gives counsel, it does so indiscreetly, and wants to burden everyone with the same load with which it is weighed down. The discreet soul, that sees its own need and that of others, does the opposite. After it has rendered to God its due of honor, it renders its own due to itself, that is, hatred of sin and of its own sensuality. What is the reason for this? It is the love of virtue, loving it in itself. With this same illumination, by which it renders what is due, it renders its due to its neighbor. And therefore I said, "in relation to itself and to others." So it renders benevolence to its neighbor, as it is obliged to do, loving the virtue in him and hating the vice. It loves him as a being created by the highest and eternal Father. And according to what it has in itself, the soul renders more or less perfectly the affection of charity. So this is the principal result which the virtue of discretion achieves in the soul, for with illumination it has seen what it ought to render, and to whom.

These are the three principal branches of this glorious child discretion which issues from the tree of charity. From these branches come forth infinite and varied fruits, all delightful and of the greatest sweetness, which nourish the soul in the life of grace, when with the hand of free will and kindled desire it picks them. Whatever condition a person may be in, he tastes these fruits, if he has the light of discretion—in various ways, according to varying conditions. He whose condition is to be placed in the world, and who has this light, gathers from the tree of discretion the fruit of obedience to the commandments of God, and dislike for the world, mentally divesting himself of it, even if, let's suppose, he is actually clothed with it. If he has children, he gathers the fruit of the fear of God, and with his holy fear he feeds them. If he is a nobleman, he collects the fruit of justice, because he wishes discreetly to render his due to each person, so with the rigor of justice he punishes the unjust man, and rewards the just, tasting the fruit of reason, and neither for flatteries nor for servile fear does he depart from this path. If he is a subject, he gathers the fruit of obedience and reverence towards his lord, rejecting the cause and the way by which he might offend him. If he had not seen with this illumination he would not have rejected these things. If men are in religious orders or are prelates, from discretion they derive the sweet and pleasant fruit of being observers of the Rule of their order, enduring and putting up with one another's faults, embracing shames and annoyances, putting on their shoulders the yoke of obedience. The prelate receives from this tree the fruit of hunger for the honor of God and for the salvation of souls, throwing out to them the baited hook of doctrine and an exemplary life. In how many diverse ways and by what diverse creatures are these fruits gathered! It would be too lengthy to describe them; one could not explain them with the tongue.

But let us see, dearest daughter (let's speak in particular now—and speaking in particular will be speaking in general) what rule that virtue of discretion gives to the soul. It seems to me that it gives this rule both to the soul and to the body, in people who want to live spiritually, in action and in thought. Surely it regulates every person and orders him in his rank and his place. But now let's speak to ourselves. The first rule discretion gives to the soul is that one we have mentioned, to render honor to God and benevolence to one's neighbor, and to itself hatred of vice and of its own sensuality. Discretion orders this charity toward one's neighbor, for it does not wish to sacrifice its soul; that is, it isn't willing to offend God for the sake of providing his neighbor with utility or pleasure. But it discreetly flees guilt, and disposes its body to endure every pain and torment, even to death, to rescue a soul—and as many as it can rescue—from the hands of the devil. It is prepared to give up its earthly substance to help and rescue the body of its neighbor. Charity does this with the illumination of discretion, which has ordered it discreetly in charity for one's neighbor. The indiscreet person does just the opposite, for he doesn't mind offending God, nor losing his soul in order to indiscreetly provide pleasures and services for his neighbor, sometimes by keeping him company in wicked places, sometimes by bearing false witness, and in various other ways, as situations arise every day. This is the rule of indiscretion, which issues from pride and from the perversity of self love, and from the blindness of having recognized neither oneself nor God.

And when measure and rule have been found in regard to charity for one's neighbor, discretion rules in that which maintains and increases charity in the soul, that is, in humble, faithful, and continual prayer, putting over it the mantle of the love of virtue, so that the soul is not harmed by lukewarmness, negligence and self love, spiritual or corporeal. Therefore discretion gives the soul this love of virtue, so that love is not placed in anything by which it might be received.

Also discretion orders and rules the creature bodily in this way: the soul which is disposed to want God makes its beginning in the way we have described, but because it has the vessel of the body, it is necessary that this light of discretion impose a rule on the body (as it has placed one upon the soul) as the instrument it is meant to be to increase virtue. The rule is this, that discretion withdraws the body from the charms and delicacies of the world, and from the conversation of worldly people, and offers it instead the conversation of the servants of God; it pulls the soul out of dissolute places, and keeps it in locations that inspire it to devotion. It gives order to all the members of the body, so that they become modest and temperate. Let the eye not look where it should not, but envision earth and heaven before it; let the tongue flee idle and vain speaking, and be disciplined to announce the word of God for the salvation of its neighbor, and to confess its sins. Let the ear flee pleasing, flattering, dissolute words, and words of slander that might be said to it, and be alert to hear the word of God, and the need of its neighbor, that is, willingly listening to his necessity. So also the hand in touching or working, the feet in going—to all discretion gives a rule. And so that these instruments are not raised up for the purpose of the disorder that the body wages against the spirit, it imposes a rule of the body, mortifying it with vigils, fasts, and other exercises, all intended to curb our body.

But note that it does all this not indiscreetly, but with the gentle light of discretion. And in what does it show this? In this: that the soul does not impose any act of penance as its chief desire. So that it may not fall into such a mistake—of making penance the principal desire—the light of discretion looks ahead to clothing the soul with love of virtue. To be sure, penance ought to be used as a means, in regulated times and places, according to need. If out of too much strength the body should be recalcitrant toward the spirit, discretion takes the rod of the discipline, and fasting, and the hair shirt with many knots, and great vigils, and it puts enough burdens on the body that it becomes less resistant. But if the body is weak, fallen into sickness, the rule of discretion does not want it to behave like this. Rather, not only ought fasting to be put aside, but meat should be eaten, and if once a day isn't enough, let it be eaten four times a day. If one cannot stand up, let him stay in bed; if he can't

kneel, let him sit or lie down if he needs to. This is what discretion wants. And for this reason discretion proposes that penance be done as a means and not as a principal desire.

Do you know why discretion doesn't want this? So that the soul may serve God with something that cannot be taken away from it and that is not finite—but with something infinite, that is, with holy desire, for it is infinite by the union it has made with the infinite desire of God, and with the virtues, which neither the devil nor any creature nor any infirmity can take away from us, if we don't want to to. Rather, in infirmity you make trial of the virtue of patience; in the battles and troubles of the demons you make trial of strength and long perseverance; and in the adversity that you receive from creatures, your humility, patience, and charity are tested. And likewise God permits all the other virtues to be tested by their many opposites— but never to be taken away from us if we don't wish it. In these infinites, holy desire and the love of virtues, we must make our foundation, and not in penance. The soul cannot have two foundations; one or the other must by necessity fall to the ground. That which is not principal use as a means. If I make my principal desire bodily penance, I build the city of my soul on sand, so that every little wind can blow it down, and no building can be erected on it. But if I build on the virtues, my soul is founded on the living rock, sweet Jesus, and there is no building so tall that it cannot stand firmly, nor wind so contrary that it will ever pull it to earth.

Because of these things and many other difficulties that arise from them, it is not desirable that penance be used otherwise than as a means. I have already seen many penitents who were not patient nor obedient, because they studied to kill the body, but not the will. The rule of indiscretion has done this. Do you know what comes of it? All their consolation and their desire is placed in doing penance in their way, and not in that of anyone else. Their own will is being fed in them—while they may be fulfilling their penance, they have consolation and cheerfulness, and they seem to themselves to be full of God, as if they are falling prey to their own opinion, and into a judgmental attitude. For if everyone does not go by their same path, it seems to them they are in a state of damnation, an imperfect state. Indiscreetly, they want to measure all bodies by the same yardstick, that is, with that with which they measure themselves. And if one wishes to pull them away from this, either to break their will or through some need that they may have, they maintain their will harder than a diamond. They are living in such a way that at the moment of testing either by a temptation or by an injury, because of this perverse will, they find themselves weaker than straw.

Indiscretion convinced them that penance curbed wrath, impatience, and the other movements of vice that arise in the heart; and it is not like that. This glorious light of discretion teaches you that you will kill sin in your soul and pull it up by the roots with hatred and dislike of yourself, with aggravating your sin with reproof, with the consideration of who God is whom you are offending, with the reminder of death, and with the love of virtue. Penance cuts off the top of sin, but you will always find the root in you, ready to sprout; virtue, however pulls it up. This ground in which sins have once been planted is always ready to receive them again if self will with free choice puts them there; but otherwise no, because the root has been pulled up.

In some cases, it may happen that perforce a body that is sick is obliged to give up its habitual practices, and then it swiftly reaches irritation and mental confusion, deprived of every gladness, and it seems to itself to be damned and confounded, and it does not find sweetness in prayer, as it seemed to have in its time of penance. And where has it gone? With the personal will, on which it was based. This will cannot be gratified, and being unable to be gratified, it feels pain and despair from this. And why have you come to so much confusion and near-desperation? And where is the hope that you used to have in the kingdom of God? It is gone with the attachment to penance, by which means it hoped to have life eternal; no longer having the former, it seems to be deprived of the latter.

These are the fruits of indiscretion. If the soul had the illumination of discretion, it would see that only being deprived of the virtues took God away from it and that by means of virtue, through the blood of Christ, it has life eternal. Let us rise above every imperfection, and put our desire toward true virtue, as I said, which is of such great delight and enjoyment that the tongue cannot express it. There is no one who can cause pain to the soul founded in virtue, or who can take away the hope of heaven, because the soul has killed in itself its own will concerning spiritual things as well as earthly; because its love is not grounded in penance nor in its own consolations or revelations, but on endurance through Christ crucified and through the love of virtue. Thus it is patient, faithful; it puts its hope in God and not in its own workings. It is humble and obedient, believing in others rather than itself, because it has no presumptions about itself. It opens wide the arms of mercy, and with them chases away mental confusion.

In darkness and battles it holds up the light of faith, laboring manfully with true deep humility, and in gladness it enters into itself, so that the heart does not come to vain mirth. It is strong and persevering, because it has deadened in itself its own will, which made it weak and inconstant. And any time is the right time for it, any place the right place. If it is in a season of penance, this is a time of gladness and consolation, using penance as a means;

and if out of necessity or obedience it is necessary to let it go, the soul rejoices, because the principal foundation of the love of virtue cannot be and is not taken away; and because self-will is seen to be drowned, for the soul has seen with illumination that self-will must always be resisted with great diligence and solicitude.

This soul finds prayer in every location, because it always carries with it the place where God dwells by grace, and where we ought to pray, that is, the house of our soul, where holy desire prays ceaselessly. This desire is raised up with the light of the intellect to be mirrored in itself, and in the inestimable fire of divine charity, which it finds in Christ's shed blood. By the largess of love this blood is found in the vessel of the soul. To this it applies itself and should apply itself to know, so that it becomes drunk with the blood, and burns and consumes its own will in the blood—rather than applying itself simply to complete the total of so many paternosters. Thus we will make our prayer continuous and faithful; because in the fire of his charity we know that he has the potency to give us what we are asking. He is highest wisdom, who knows how to give and discern what is needful for us. And he is a most clement and pitying father, who wants to give us more than we desire, and more than we know how to ask for, for our own needs. The soul is humble, for it has recognized the faults in itself, and that in itself it is not. This is the prayer by means of which we come to virtue and maintain in ourselves the love of this virtue.

What is the beginning of so great a good? Discretion, the daughter of charity, as I said. And the good which it has itself it extends to its neighbor. So the foundation which it has made, and the love and the doctrine that it has received in itself, it wishes to extend, and does extend, to fellow creatures, and to show them by living example or through teaching; that is, giving counsel when it sees the necessity or

when advice was requested. It comforts the neighbor's soul and does not confound him by leading him to desperation when he had fallen through some fault, but tenderly it participates in its infirmity, giving him whatever remedy it can, and expanding in him hope in the blood of Christ crucified.

The virtue of discretion gives these and many other fruits to its neighbor. Therefore, since it is so useful and necessary, dearest and most beloved daughter and my sister in Jesus sweet Christ, I invite you and me to do that which in time past I confess I haven't done with that perfection that I should. To you it has not come to pass as it has for me, that is to have been and to be so full of defects, nor to have gone along being too lax rather than strict, through my fault; but you, like a person who has wanted to subdue the youthfulness of your body so that it not be rebel to the soul, have chosen a life so extreme in this mode that it seems to have gone beyond the limits of discretion—so much so that it seems to me that indiscretion wants to make you sense its fruits and to make you live out in this your own will. And with you leaving the penances you used to do, it seems that the devil is trying to make you believe that you are damned. This makes me very displeased, and I think it is a great offense against God. Therefore I wish, and beg you, that our beginning and foundation be made in the love of virtue, with true discretion, as I said. Kill your will, and do that which you are made to do. Be more attentive to how things look to others rather than to you. You feel your body to be weak and sick—every day take the food that is necessary to restore nature. And if your illness and weakness are alievated, take up a life ordered with moderation, not immoderation. Don't wish for the lesser good of penance to hinder the greater good; don't dress yourself in it as your chief desire, for you would find yourself deceived. I wish that we may sincerely run along the beaten path of virtue, and that we guide others along the same, breaking and shattering our own wills. If we have in ourselves the virtue of discretion, we will accomplish this—otherwise, no.

And therefore I said that I was wanting to see in you the holy virtue of discretion. I say no more. Remain in the holy and sweet affection of God. Forgive me if I have talked too presumptuously: the love of your salvation, for the honor of God, is my reason. Sweet Jesus, Jesus love.

To Sister Daniella of Orvieto   Tommaso
LXXX VII
Nov 1378   p. 449

In the name of Jesus Christ crucified and of sweet Mary.

Dearest daughter in Christ sweet Jesus: I, Catherine, servant and slave of the servants of Jesus Christ, write to you in his precious blood, with the desire of seeing you with the true and most perfect light, so that in perfection you may know the truth. O dearest daughter, how necessary is this light for us! For without it we cannot go on the path of Christ crucified, a shining path which gives us life; without it we will walk in the shadows, and will remain in the greatest tempest and bitter sorrow. If I weigh it carefully, I see that one needs to have this light in two ways. There is a general light that every rational creature ought to have in order to see and know what he ought to love, and whom he should obey, perceiving in the light of his intellect, with the pupil of holy faith, that he is bound to love and serve his creator, loving him with all his heart and all his affection without intermediaries, and obeying the commandments of the law, to love God above everything else, and our neighbors as ourselves. These are the principal laws to which all others are bound. This is a general light, to which we are all obligated; without it we would die, and deprived of the light of grace, would follow the darkened path of the devil.

But there is another light, which is not separated from this but united to it; indeed, from the first one attains the second. There are those who, observing the commandments of God, grow into another most perfect light; they rise from imperfection with great and holy desire, and they come to perfection, observing both the commandments and the counsels mentally and physically. This light must be exercised with hunger and desire for the honor of God and the salvation of the soul, mirroring oneself with this light in the light of the sweet and amorous Word; where the soul tastes the ineffable love that God has for his creature, shown to us through that Word who ran, like someone in love, to the shameful death of the cross, for the honor of the father and our salvation.

When the soul has known this truth with perfect light, it rises above itself, above the bodily instincts. With sweet love-agonies and amorous desires it runs, following the footprints of Christ crucified, bearing pains, disgraces, ridicule, insults, with much persecution from the world, and oftentimes from the servants of God under color of virtue. Hungrily the soul seeks the honor of God and the salvation of souls, and it so delights in this glorious food that it disdains itself and everything else: this alone does it seek and abandons itself. In this perfect light lived those glorious virgins and the other saints, who delighted only in receiving this food with their Bridegroom at the table of the cross. Now to us, dearest daughter and my sweet sister in Christ sweet Jesus, he has shown such grace and mercy that he has placed us in the number of those who have advanced from the general light to the particular. That is, he has caused us to elect the perfect state of the counsels. Therefore we ought to follow that sweet and straight way perfectly, in true light, not looking back for any reason whatsoever, and not going in our own fashion but only in God's fashion, enduring suffering without fault even until death—to rescue the soul from the hands of the devil. Because this is the way and the rule that eternal truth has given you. And he wrote it on his own body, not with ink but with his blood, with letters so large that no one is of such low intelligence that he is excused from reading them. You can clearly see the initial letters of this book, they are so large, and they all demonstrate the truth of God the Father, the ineffable love with which we were created—this is the truth—only so that we might participate in the highest and eternal good. This master is raised high on the pulpit of the cross, so that we may better study him, and that we may not deceive ourselves by saying, "He taught me on earth, and not on high." It is not so. He climbed up on the cross, and uplifted there with pain seeks to exalt the honor of the Father, and to restore the beauty of souls. Then let us read heartfelt love, founded on truth, in this book of life. Lose yourself entirely; the more you lose, the more you will find. God will not disdain your desire. Rather, he will guide you and instruct you in what you ought to do, and he will enlighten him to whom you were subject, if you act by his counsel. Because the soul that prays should have a holy jealousy, and let it always delight in doing whatever it does with the aid of prayer and counsel.

You write to me, and according to what I understood in your letter, it seems you are very troubled. And it is not a small thing—rather, it is a powerful feeling, greater than any other, when from one side in your mind you hear yourself called by God to new ways, and his servants put themselves on the opposing side, saying that this is not good. I feel great compassion for you, for I know there is no exhaustion like that, from the jealousy that the soul has for itself. For it cannot resist God, and it would like to fulfill the will of his servants, having more confidence in their light and understanding than in its own. Nevertheless it seems it cannot do so. Now I respond to you simply according to my lowly and limited sight. Don't make up your mind obstinately, but as you feel yourself called without self-interest, respond. Therefore if you see souls in danger, and you can help them, don't close your eyes, but with perfect solicitude exert yourself in helping them to the point of death. And don't pay attention to your past resolutions, neither of silence nor of anything else, so that it cannot be said of you afterwards, "You are cursed, for you kept silent." Our every beginning and foundation is made only in the charity for God and one's neighbor: all other activities are instruments and buildings placed on this foundation. Therefore you must not, in delight at the instrument or the building, neglect the principal foundation of the honor of God and love of your neighbor. Work then, my daughter, in that field where you see God calls you to work, and do not become pained or irritated in your mind over what I've told you, but keep going manfully. Fear and serve God, without concern for what people say, except to have compassion on them.

Concerning the desire you have of leaving your house and being in Rome, leave it up to the will of your Bridegroom. If it is to his honor and your salvation, he will show you the means and the way that you cannot think of now, in a way that you would not have imagined. Leave it all to him, and lose yourself, but take care that you do not lose yourself anywhere but on the cross, and there you will find yourself most perfectly. But you cannot do this without perfect illumination. For this reason I told you that I wanted to see you with the true and perfect light, in addition to the general light, as I said before.

Let us sleep no more, let us wake up from the sleep of negligence, groaning with humble and continuous prayer for the mystical body of holy church, and for the vicar of Christ. Do not cease praying for him, so that he will be given the light and strength to resist the blows of the incarnate devils, lovers of themselves, who want to contaminate our faith. It is a time of weeping.

Concerning my coming in your direction, pray the highest eternal sovereign good of God to do what may be to his honor and the salvation of souls, and pray particularly for me, when I am about to go to Rome to fulfill the will of Christ crucified and of his vicar. I don't know what path I will take. Pray Christ sweet Jesus to send us by the way which is most to his honor, with peace and rest for our souls. I say nothing else to you. Remain in the holy and sweet loving of God. Sweet Jesus, Jesus love.

To Brother Raymond of Capua of the Order of Friars Preachers June 1375 VII (Tommas) p. 59

In the name of Christ Jesus Crucified and of sweet Mary.

Most beloved and dearest father and my dear son in Jesus Christ, I Catherine, the servant and slave of the servants of Jesus Christ, write to you commending myself to you in the precious blood of the Son of God, with the desire of seeing you aflame and drowned in this his sweetest blood, drenched with fire of his most burning charity. This my soul desires—to see you in this blood, you and Nanni and Jacomo my son. I see no other remedy by which we may come to those chief virtues which are necessary for us. Sweetest father, your soul, which had made itself food for me (and no moment of the time passes that I do not receive this food at the table of the sweet lamb who bled to death with so much very ardent love) I say, your soul would not attain the little virtue of true humility if it were not drowned in blood. This virtue shall be born from hatred, and hatred from love. Thus the soul is born with the most perfect purity, as iron comes forth purified from the furnace.

I wish therefore that you lock yourself up in the open side of the Son of God, which is an open storehouse, so full of fragrance that there sin becomes perfumed. There the sweet Bride rests on the bed of fire and of blood. There is seen and manifested the secret of the heart of the Son of God. He is a winecask which, when it is broached, gives drink and inebriates every enamored desire, and gives mirth and illumines every intelligence and refills every memory, that struggles so hard to comprehend, so much so that it cannot retain, nor mean, nor love anything else, except this good and sweet Jesus. Blood and fire, priceless love! Since my soul will be blessed in seeing you so drowned, I wish you to do like him who gets water with a pail and pours it over something else; thus do you pour out the water of holy desire on the heads of your brothers, that are our members, bound to us in the body of the sweet Bride. And beware lest—either through illusion of the devils (which I know have given you trouble and will continue to do so) or through the words of some fellow creature— you should ever draw back, but always persevere every hour, even when things look most bleak, to the end that we may see blood shed with sweet and amorous desires.

Up, up, my sweetest father! Let us sleep no more. For I hear such news that I no longer wish either repose or rank. I have already received a head in my hands, which was of such sweetness to me that the heart cannot think it, nor the tongue speak, the eye see, nor the ear hear it. The desire of God preceded the other mysteries that were performed, which I do not describe, for it would take too long.

I went to visit him whom you know, from which he received such strengthening and consolation that he made his confession and prepared himself very well. He made me promise by the love of God that when the moment of justice came, I would be there with him. And thus I promised and did. Then in the morning, before the church bells, I went to him and he received great consolation. I led him to hear Mass, and he received Holy Communion, which he had never before received. His will was accorded and submitted to the will of God, and there only remained a fear of not being strong enough when the time came. But the immeasurable and enkindled goodness of God played a trick on him, creating in him such affection and love in the desire for God that he knew not how to be without him, saying, "Stay with me, and don't leave me, and so it will be no other than good for me, and I die happy." And he leaned his head on my breast. Then I heard a jubilation and smelled his blood. It was not without the odor of mine which I wish to shed for the sweet bridegroom Jesus. And the desire in my soul increasing, and feeling his fear, I said, "Take comfort, my sweet brother, for very soon we will arrive at the wedding. You shall go there bathed in the sweet blood of the Son of God, with the sweet name of Christ which I want never to leave your memory. And I will be waiting for you at the place of justice."

Now reflect, father and son, that his heart then lost every fear, and his face was transformed from sorrow to joy, and he rejoiced, he exulted, and he said, "From where does such grace come to me, that the sweetness of my soul will wait for me at the holy place of justice?" See how he had reached such illumination, that he was calling the place of justice holy! And he said, "I shall go wholly glorious and strong, and it will seem to me a thousand years until I come there, thinking that you are there waiting for me." And he was speaking words about the goodness of God so sweet that it would break your heart.

So I waited for him at the place of justice, and I waited there with continual prayer and in the presence of Mary and of St. Catherine, virgin and martyr. But before I attained that, I prostrated myself and stretched out my neck on the block, but it did not happen, but I had my desire full of myself. I prayed, and constrained her, and cried "Mary," for I wished this grace, that at the crucial point she would grant him a light and a peace in his heart, and then I would see him return to his goal. My soul was so full then that although a great crowd of people was there, I couldn't see a single creature, for the sweet promise made to me.

Then he arrived, like a gentle lamb, and seeing me he began to smile, and wanted me to make the sign of the cross. And when he had received the sign, I said, "Down! To the wedding, my sweet brother! Soon you shall be in the enduring life." He prostrated himself with great meekness, and I stretched out his neck, and bent myself down, and reminded him of the blood of the Lamb. His mouth said nothing except "Jesus" and "Catherine." And while he was speaking, I received his head in my hands, closing my eyes in the divine goodness, and saying, "I will."

Then was seen God-and-Man, as if the brightness of the sun were seen, and his side remained open and received the blood; in his blood a fire of holy desire, given and hidden in his soul through grace. Christ received it in the fire of his divine charity. When he had received his blood and his desire, he received his soul, which he put into the open storehouse of his side, full of mercy; the Primal Truth showing that by grace and mercy alone he received it, and not for any other deed. O how sweet and priceless it was to see the goodness of God! With how much sweetness and love he waited for that soul departed from the body. He turned the eye of mercy toward the soul, when it came to enter within his side bathed in his blood, which availed through the blood of the son of God. Thus he was received by God the Father through power (powerful is he to accomplish his ends!); and the Son, Wisdom the Incarnate Word, gave him and made him to participate in the crucified love through which he received painful and shameful death, through the obedience toward the

Father that he observed for the benefit of human nature and generation; and the hands of the Holy Spirit locked him within.

But he made a gesture sweet enough to draw a thousand hearts. I do not wonder, for he was already tasting the divine sweetness. He turned back, as does the bride when she has reached the door of her bridegroom, who turns back her glance and her head, bowing to one who has accompanied her, and with that gesture makes a sign of her thanks.

When he was at rest, my soul so rested in peace and quiet, in such a fragrance of blood, that I couldn't bear to remove from me the blood that had fallen on me from him.

Woe is me, miserable! I don't want to say any more. I remain on earth with the greatest envy. And it seems to me that the first new stone has already been put in place. And therefore do not wonder if I impose on you nothing except to see you drowned in the blood and fire that the side of the Son of God pours out. Now then, no more negligence, my sweetest sons, because the blood is beginning to pour, and to receive the life. Sweet Jesus, Jesus love.

VII

Women, Heresy, and Holiness
in Early Fourteenth-Century France

*Na Prous Boneta, Marguerite d'Oingt,
and Marguerite Porete*

*T*HREE VERY DIFFERENT female voices speak to us from early fourteenth-century France—different from one another and also from the women who preceded them. I will begin with Na Prous Boneta, whose experience seems most closely related to that of women in Italy and will then turn to Marguerite d'Oingt and Marguerite Porete. Na (for Domina) Prous Boneta,[1] a Spiritual Franciscan, follower of Peter John Olivi and in her own right leader of a heretical group of laypeople seems to have much in common with other women mystics of the thirteenth and fourteenth centuries except for two crucial facts. She was burned at the stake for her beliefs, and the only account we have of her life is her statement to the Inquisition in Montpellier shortly before her death in 1325.[2] Na Prous was probably born about 1290, and when she was young a number of events took place that became a part of the visionary myth she preached. The Spiritual Franciscans in southern France had been led by the noted Franciscan Peter John Olivi, and by the time he died in 1297 his apocalyptic theology and radical social message about the necessity for poverty caused him to be seen by some as a second Christ. Although he died quietly, at peace with the church, and was immediately acclaimed as a saint, there were those who said his bones were dug up and burned a few months after interment.[3] When elected in 1317, Pope John XXII declared the Spirituals' teaching on apostolic poverty to be a formal heresy, and intensive prosecutions of recalcitrant Spirituals and affiliated Beguines quickly followed. But persecution of the Spirituals had been going on since the 1280s, and as early as 1315 Na Prous had been connected with them, for in that year she was caught and imprisoned by the Inquisition at Montpellier, then released. In 1317 she may have seen Beguines burned at Narbonne, and in 1318 four friars were burned at Marseilles. After their deaths they were publicly venerated as martyrs by those sympathetic to the cause of the Spirituals. Na Prous and her sister Alisette made their home in Montpellier a center for radical religious ideas and activities, giving refuge to many fugitives.

As persecution got hotter, her exaltation increased. In 1320 she commenced to have visions and ecstasies in which she was carried to heaven and had interviews with Christ. Finally, on Holy Thursday, 1321, Christ communicated to her the Divine Spirit as completely as it had been given to the Virgin.... Thus the promises of the Everlasting Gospel were on the point of fulfillment, and the Third Age was about to dawn. Elijah, she said, was St. Francis and Enoch was Olivi; the power granted to Christ lasted until God gave the Holy Spirit to Olivi, and invested him with as much glory as had been granted to the humanity of Christ. The papacy has ceased to exist, the sacraments of the altar and of confession are superseded, but that of matrimony remains. That of penitence, indeed, still exists, but it is purely internal, for heartfelt contrition works forgiveness of sins without sacerdotal intercession or the imposition of penance.[4]

Like the more orthodox women whose works are included here, Na Prous was first a visionary, then a leader. But she goes further than the others—she has come to believe in herself as a herald of a new age, that she *is* in some way the Holy Spirit, and that people can be saved only if they believe in her. All else that she believed in has been taken away from her. Convinced that Christ's poverty in the Gospels is the only true model for humankind, she cannot believe in a Papacy that declares such a belief heretical. Peter John Olivi had died after years of struggle over his ideas, and the other leaders had either died, recanted, or disappeared into hiding. Even the laws of decency seem to have been suspended by the church, which approved of the mass burning of lepers in France in 1321 and 1322; this manifestation of hysteria, which only the Spirituals seem to have opposed, she sees as the equal of Herod's slaughter of the innocents. Since the persecution of the Spirituals and the burning of the books written by Olivi, the sacraments have no more validity for her, and the pope who has done this is the Antichrist.[5] Some of her beliefs are borrowed from the apocalyptic ideas of Joachim da Fiore as well as from Olivi, but some are clearly her own, and she believes in them enough to die for them. The notary who takes down her words for the Inquisition is damned, as are all her accusers, but she is confident she will soon be in heaven, "a glorious martyr in Paradise."

We know that Na Prous was unable to read Latin because she tells us that she says thirty Pater Nosters for each of the canonical hours; although there were many banned Spiritual Franciscan books and prophecies written in the vernacular and circulating in southern France, she gives us no indication that she has read them.

Na Prous dictated to the court notary in Provençal; her statements were taken down in Latin, with occasional phrases left in Provençal untranslated. The text was read back to her as the interrogation proceeded, and she would be asked to confirm what it said. The questions she was asked would have followed a standard protocol designed to elicit a confession along particular lines; in this case, her questioners wanted a confession that she shared the beliefs of the "begghini combusti" (the burned Beguines) of earlier years. Nevertheless, Na Prous manages to make her vision of the world dominate the proceedings, and her courage in knowingly condemning herself after ten years of resistance to the Inquisition is very moving.

Marguerite d'Oingt, the second of the women writing in France to be considered here, belongs to a more privileged world than Na Prous. Although Marguerite d'Oingt has been neglected by modern scholarship,[6] she may have been fairly well known in Na Prous's time, for her works were translated into Provençal and circulated in the region around Albi. We know almost nothing about her except what can be inferred from her writings. Her family was one of the most ancient and powerful families in the Lyonnais, with family records going back to about the year 1000. In her immediate family there were two sons and four daughters, three of whom entered convents. The family died out in the second half of the fourteenth century. Marguerite was venerated locally as a saint until the French Revolution, and her canonization is still pending. She was prioress of the Carthusian convent of Pelotens, modern Poleteins, by 1288, and had begun to write her Latin *Meditations* two years earlier.[7] She is mentioned in her parents' wills in 1297 and 1300, and the anonymous copyist of her works gives her death as occurring in 1310. She was the fourth prioress of a house that had been founded in 1225–26, the time of greatest popularity for the feminine branch of the Carthusian order.[8]

Marguerite's editors stress that she began to write only because she was so overwhelmed by her visionary experiences that she became ill. She was cured only by the act of writing down her experiences, and she continued to write only under pressure from her superiors. It is true that in one of her letters, perhaps to her spiritual director, Marguerite speaks of the origin of her writing in these terms. But there is more to her motivation than this; she is not simply saying that she had to write. Two unique characteristics of her writing point to the presence of a strong authorial consciousness: the fact that she writes in three languages suggests that she composed her texts with a specific audience in mind, and her dominant use of metaphors associated with writing and book production indicates that for her all communication was a form of writing, of inscription. Hildegard of Bingen heard God tell her to speak and write her visions; Gertrude the Great wrote down what she had memorized in her heart, but Marguerite writes what is written in her heart. When she defends her writing by saying

> [Her visions] . . . were all written in her heart in such a way that she could not think about anything else. . . . She thought that if she were to put these things in writing, as Our Lord had sent them to her in her heart, her heart would be more relieved for it. She began to write everything that is in this book . . . and as soon as she put a word in the book, it left her heart . . . I firmly believe that if she had not put it in writing she would have died or become crazy. . . .[9]

She is bringing two new perspectives to mystical writing by women. The first is the idea that the visionary is not a vessel but a text, a body in whom or on whom a text is inscribed. The second point is her emphasis on the act of writing; the text written within her is physically transferred by her to the pages of a book—"as soon as she put a word in that book, it left her heart." As we will see in her *Speculum* or *Mirror*, Christ is also a text; his wounds are inscribed on his body, and she reads the message of his Passion. This view of writing implies that the body and its experiences will also be central to her expression, which comes through very clearly in her first written work, the *Meditations*.[10]

She titled this work *Pagina Meditationum*, "Page of Meditation," and began with her conversion experience in 1286. As she was listening to the Mass, certain lines stood out to her, and she began to meditate on them. She decided to write down her thoughts (*cogitationes*) in order to remember them better and to be able to return to them during prayer. She then addresses herself directly to God; in the course of a recreation of Christ's Passion, she reflects on the love God manifests to human beings. It is near the close of this section that she speaks of God as her mother:

> For are you not my mother and more than my mother? The mother who bore me labored in delivering me for one day or one night but you, my sweet and lovely Lord, labored for me for more than thirty years. Ah, ... with what love you labored for me and bore me through your whole life. But when the time approached for you to be delivered, your labor pains were so great that your holy sweat was like great drops of blood that came out from your body and fell on the earth ... when the hour of your delivery came you were placed on the hard bed of the cross ... and your nerves and all your veins were broken. And truly it is no surprise that your veins burst when in one day you gave birth to the whole world.[11]

The conclusion to this meditation is a statement of her love for God and her desire to be saved by him when she dies. The meditation is almost entirely in Latin but occasionally, as here, she breaks into dialect to express her desire to leave the body and be with Christ.

The second meditation works through her thoughts on sin and the fear of hell. This leads her to a fierce attack on the vices of religious people in her day, in which she quotes some of St. Francis' criticisms. From this she moves to a contemplation of what will happen to such people in hell. She visualizes such sinners before the throne of God on the Day of Judgement, their sins parading before them and their consciences suddenly reawakening to realize with horror the judgment of God. Her description of the sufferings in hell is filled with storms, screams, flames; the sinners are clothed in burning pitch that sticks to their flesh and eats through to their bones; they then go on to other punishments—hunger so severe that they eat their own hands; they will bellow like beasts and their only bonds with each other will be hatred and envy. After this, Marguerite's attention turns to God's judgment for the elect, and she has a glimpse of heaven. The meditation closes with thanks to God for the spiritual gifts he has sent her and a request: "Sweet Master, write in my heart that which you wish me to do; write your laws there; write your commandments so that they can never be erased."

In the *Speculum,* her major work, we find a remarkably concise use of visionary experience as the ground for instruction in meditation. Marguerite, writing in the last decade of the thirteenth century (we know the book was presented to the Carthusian General Chapter in 1294 by Hugues, prior of Valbonne), organizes her *Mirror* into three chapters, each based on a different vision. In each chapter she first tells the content of her vision, its central images and metaphors, and then shows how she meditated on the details, with the results of those meditations presented as models to be followed by her readers. She speaks of the self having the visions in the third person and uses the first person for her reflective narration. She addresses her readers directly as *vous,* often using imperatives—think about this; meditate on this. The vision of Chapter 1 is of Christ, holding a closed book in his hand as if to teach from it, an image also found in statues of Christ in this period. On the book she notes letters in three colors: white, black, and silver-gilt. The book *in toto* suggests a number of themes for meditation: Christ's generosity in joining his divinity to our human misery; his humility; his desire to be persecuted;

his poverty, patience, and obedience. These meditations cause her to turn to another book, the book of her conscience, in which she finds her own inadequacies. Through the contrast between the two books, she is moved to amend her life to conform more closely to the pattern suggested by Christ's book. The colored letters, which seem to suggest historiated initials, have further contents to be meditated on. The white letters inscribe Christ's life on earth, the teaching he lived out for us. The black letters inscribe the evil done to Christ, and from them she learns to suffer adversity in patience. The silver-gilt letters, in which were inscribed the wounds of Christ and the shedding of his blood, become red in her meditations, and in them she discovers joy in tribulation and adversity, so that "it seemed to her that there was nothing in the world as sweet and as worthy as suffering the pains and torments of this age for the love of her Creator."

On the clasps, where the titles of medieval books were written, she sees letters of gold in her vision; two phrases from the Bible are found there. The first comes from First Corinthians 15, "God shall be all in all"; the second comes from Psalm 67.36, "God is marvelous in his saints." Both phrases lead her thoughts to the things of heaven, but she finds her mind is still too darkened to sustain such meditation, and she is forced to return to meditating on the life of Christ as she seeks to amend her own life.

In her second vision, she sees that the book is opened; it is like a beautiful mirror, and it has only two pages. In this book-mirror she sees a lovely place, larger than the world, with a glorious tripartite light. This place is the source of all good: wisdom, power, charm, strength, kindling of love, unthinkable joy. The angels and saints look on God and sing forever a new song; they are within God like the fish within the sea, and just as waves go to the sea and flow back again to the shore, so all beauty and sweetness pour forth from the Lord and flow back to him. The meditations on this vision allow Marguerite to understand better what is meant by the two phrases on the two clasps, for she has seen in her vision just how God is all in all, and how he is marvelous among his saints.

In the third vision, as Marguerite attempts again to meditate on Christ seated next to God the Father, she is ravished into heaven itself, again the place larger than the world, filled with a brilliant light, full of handsome and glorious beings. She sees that Christ is there, and that his wounds transmit the light, and she sees how he has made his friends like himself.

Marguerite d'Oingt's prose is simple, concise, and lyrical. Whether she is writing in Latin or Franco-Provençal, the rhythms of her phrases are incantatory. In the *Meditations* she demonstrates a remarkable ear for colloquial speech, and in the *Speculum* it is her visual imagination that dominates.

Marguerite Porete is also a poet, but of a very different sort. In comparison with the serenity and poise of Marguerite d'Oingt's style, which may reflect in some ways her social standing and the privileged Carthusian priory that she directed, Marguerite Porete's style seems much more impassioned and no less lyrical. Marguerite Porete is a compelling historical figure and a remarkable writer. A Beguine from Hainaut, she was one of the first writers to be associated with the Free Spirit movement.[12] Sometime between 1296 and 1306 she wrote a book, *The Mirror of Simple Souls*, which was soon condemned and burned by the Inquisition. By 1310 she had been declared heretical and was burned; during a year and a half in prison she refused to give any testimony so the Dominican Inquisitor extracted a list of articles from her book and submitted them, out of context, to the theological regents of the University of Paris. The regents declared the articles heretical, and she was swiftly judged a "relapsed" heretic (for she had been arrested several times before) and solemnly executed in the Place de Grève in Paris. While she was being pursued by the Inquisition, she sent her book to three noted scholars, who all approved of it. The text, in spite of being condemned, circulated widely, and by the latter half of the fourteenth century was translated into Latin, Italian, and Middle English. It seems likely that such circulation was possible because the *Mirror* was either falsely attributed to more respectable mystics or thought to be anonymous; correct attribution was not made until fairly recently, when Romana Guarnieri announced her discovery of an Old French manuscript of the *Mirror* explicitly identifying its author as Marguerite Porete.[13]

In her introduction to her edition of the *Mirror*, Guarnieri, seeking the origins of the heresy of the Free Spirit, the freedom from sin of the soul joined to God while still on earth, places Marguerite Porete's thought in a tradition first announced by St. Bernard (d. 1150) in his concept *gratia et libero arbitrio* and found in William of St. Thierry's (d. 1148) notion of the contemplative's *libertas spiritus*. The same ideas and phrases occur in Beatrijs of Nazareth, Marie d'Oignies, Christina Mirabilis, Ivetta of Huy, Juliana of Mont Cornillon, Mechthild of Magdeburg, and Hadewijch of Antwerp, according to Guarnieri;[14] all of these women were associated in some way with Beguine groups and with Cistercian spirituality. If Marguerite Porete's ideas can be seen to be, in general outline, consonant with the works of these writers, writers who were accepted by the church (although not without misgivings in a few instances), why was Marguerite's book condemned? Lerner suggests the following:

> Provisionally it may be said that *The Mirror* describes a completer union between the soul and God this side of paradise than would have been accepted by most mystics and it talks of a state of complete passivity that goes beyond and then ignores the spiritual ministrations of the Church. But it postulates Grace rather than nature as the motive force propelling the soul toward God and it avoids the antinomian or libertine conclusions traditionally associated with the heresy of the Free Spirit. Marguerite was probably a heretic, but had she been submissive and content to enter a cloister, like Mechthild of Magdeburg, with whom she is compared, she probably would have attracted little notice. Her active life, her pertinacity, and the political situation surrounding her arrest certainly contributed to her death.[15]

Peter Dronke, who provides an extended and stimulating analysis of Marguerite Porete's importance as a writer, compares her to Hildegard and Angela of Foligno.

> Like Angela, Marguerite tells of divine love and how she experiences it; like hers, Marguerite's language to evoke that love can be provocative and deliberately shocking. The reason she was persecuted and condemned, however, had little to do with this. It was rather that, unlike Angela, she laid claim to new perceptions of the divine realm, and of the Church. So too, in a sense, had Hildegard of Bingen—yet Hildegard advanced such thoughts only in her recognized function as messenger of the divine light. Here Marguerite showed a fateful audacity: like Hildegard, she castigated those in all ranks of the clergy

who failed to welcome her unique insights; but where Hildegard did this with a prophet's safe-conduct, Marguerite did so of her own accord, speaking only in the name of the "simple souls," the "free souls"—an invisible ideal community to which she aspired to belong and which she was certain should guide and judge the "Little Church" that is established on earth, Sainte Eglise la Petite.[16]

Her crime, then, was that she insisted on speaking publicly, teaching her ideas publicly, and that she did so in her own voice and that of others like her. She may have been heretical in her views—although the very evolved spirituality she is presenting seems no more or less dangerous than the spiritual teachings of Beatrijs or Hadewijch—but she was much more visible than they were, for she refused to hide behind God's voice or to submit to the church.

Formally, this long book (60,000 words) is a dialogue between Love (Amour) and Reason (Raison) concerning the conduct of a Soul (Âme). The dialogue is often interrupted by various allegorical figures and is commented on by verses and exempla. The section included here comes near the end and contains the crux of Marguerite's argument—the seven states of grace that lead up to the union of the soul with God. In the first state (or estate or being), the soul observes the Commandments; in the second it moves on to follow the evangelical perfection epitomized by Christ's life; and in the third it gives up good works and destroys its own will; by this it is enabled to reach the fourth state, a level of contemplation in which the soul is wholly absorbed in love. The fifth state lowers the soul to the depths of humility and nothingness, and in this abyss it sees and wants nothing. In the sixth state a further transformation takes place, and the soul is clarified, liberated, and purified. The seventh step, perfection, can take place only in heaven after the soul has left the body. It is the fifth and sixth stages that are controversial, for there the annihilated or liberated soul is said to be like the angels, with no intermediaries between its love and divine love. Wherever it looks, God is to be found, and it finds God within itself without even looking. This prose narrative, spoken by L'Âme, is followed by several lyrical exchanges between Vérité (Truth), L'Âme, and Holy Church.

Until recently, the only English translation available has been that of Clare Kirchberger. This remains the only complete translation, but it is based on the Middle English translation of the original Old French, not on the Old French text itself, which had not been discovered in 1927. The French text is not easily available although Dronke reproduces some sections. In addition to the translation included here, there is a partial translation in the recent Wilson volume.[17]

Marguerite Porete quite consistently (though not exclusively) addresses her book to women;[18] her public execution must also have been a direct message to women in particular as well as to heretical or fringe groups in general, a warning of the consequences of speaking *in propria persona*. Yet the spiritual corruption of the church and the lack of enlightened guidance by the clergy made it inevitable that other women would emerge as leaders and would be called to new and more public kinds of vocations. Some of those careers will be examined in the sections that follow.

NOTES

1. There is very little scholarship on Na Prous Boneta; the text of her confession (here abridged in translation) was edited by William Harold May, "The Confession of Prous Boneta, Heretic and Heresiarch," in *Essays in Medieval Life and Thought*, ed. John H. Mundy et al. (New York: Columbia University Press, 1955) pp. 3–30. Henry Charles Lea devotes a few pages to her in *A History of the Inquisition of the Middle Ages*, vol. III (New York: Harper and Brothers, 1887), pp. 80–83. She is mentioned by Marjorie Reeves in *The Influence of Prophecy in the Later Middle Ages: A Study in Joachimism* (Oxford: Clarendon Press, 1969), who groups her with a prophetess named Manfreda. Their preaching, says Reeves, was based on the "daring logic that, if the revolution was to be absolute there must be a new incarnation of the Godhead, and this must be in the opposite sex" (pp. 248–49).

2. This is the text edited by May cited in note 1.

3. Lea, *History of the Inquisition*, p. 45.

4. Lea, *History of the Inquisition*, p. 82.

5. May, "Confession of Prous Boneta," p. 4.

6. The only modern edition of her works was published in 1965, based in part on earlier transcriptions collated with other manuscripts: Antonin Duraffour, Pierre Durdilly, and Paulette Gardette, *Marguerite d'Oingt: édition critique de ses oeuvres* (Paris: Les Belles Lettres, 1965). Marguerite is identified by Bynum as one of the mystics whose works suggest a theology of Jesus as Mother.

7. *Marguerite d'Oingt*, pp. 9, 13.

8. *Marguerite d'Oingt*, pp. 11, 15.

9. *Marguerite d'Oingt, Letters*, pars. 137–38, p. 143.

10. *Marguerite d'Oingt*, pp. 71–88.

11. Caroline Bynum, *Jesus as Mother* (Berkeley and Los Angeles: Univ. of California Press, 1982), p. 153.

12. Robert E. Lerner, *The Heresy of the Free Spirit in the Later Middle Ages* (Berkeley: University of California Press, 1972), pp. 67–78, 200–8.

13. Romana Guarnieri, "Il Movimento del Libero Spirito," in *Archivio Italiano per la storia della pietà* 4 (1965), pp. 351–708. This contains a long introduction and the complete Old French text. See her discussion of the manuscript tradition, pp. 504 ff. There are three Old French mss., twelve mss. in translation. Five of these are in Latin translated directly from the Old French; three are in Middle English directly from Old French; there are also a Latin translation based on the Middle English version, two different Italian versions based on a Latin text, one of which has three copies. This is an unusual number of surviving manuscripts.

14. Guarnieri, "Il Movimento," pp. 358–59.

15. Lerner, *Heresy of the Free Spirit*, p. 208.

16. Peter Dronke, *Women Writers of the Middle Ages* (Cambridge: Cambridge Univ. Press, 1984), p. 217. His discussion is found on pp. 217–28. Lyrics from *Le mirouer* are found in the original Old French on pp. 275–78.

17. Clare Kirchberger, trans., *The Mirror of Simple Souls* (London and New York; Burns, Oates & Washbourne, 1927). This translation, based on an anonymous translation of a then anonymous work, was given the imprimatur. It was only in 1965 that the *Mirror* was definitely attributed to Marguerite Porete. For another translation of selections, see Gwendolyn Bryant, "The French Heretic Beguine: Marguerite Porete," in Katharina Wilson, ed., *Medieval Women Writers* (Athens, Ga.: Univ. of Georgia Press, 1984), pp. 204–26. Bryant provides an excellent bibliography.

18. Lerner, *Heresy of the Free Spirit*, pp. 200–2.

NA PROUS BONETA   (1290–1325; Carcassone, France)

The Confession of Na Prous Boneta, Heretic and Heresiarch, Carcassone, France, 6 August 1325

Translated by Elizabeth Petroff

Na Prous (Lady Prous) Boneta, the daughter of Duradus Bonetus, of the parish of St. Michael de Cadyera, in the diocese of Nîmes, who was an inhabitant of Montpellier from about the age of seven years, as she says, and who was arrested there, accused and suspected of the heresy of the burned Beguines, was brought to the city wall of Carcassone, so that her confession made in court might be established legitimately, and set down freely, willingly, and without interrogation. In the year of our Lord 1325, on the sixth of August, she said and claimed that on Good Friday four years ago from her confession made in court as written below, while she was in the church of the Franciscans in Montpellier where she was listening to the service with some other people, she adored the crucifix, as it is customary to do. When she had made her adoration in this way, and had returned to her seat, the office being completed and the church emptied of most of the people, the Lord Jesus Christ transported her in spirit, indeed in her soul, up to the first heaven. When she was there she saw Jesus Christ in the form of a man as well as in his divinity; he appeared to her who is speaking, and showed her his heart, perforated almost like the little openings in a small lantern. From this heart there went out solar rays, indeed, rays brighter than the sun, which shone all around her. All at once she saw, clearly and openly, the divinity of God, who in spirit gave her his heart.

She drew near to him, and put her head on the body of Christ, and she saw nothing but such great clarity as Christ gave to her in those rays. Then she was returned to the place where she first saw that clarity and looked on Christ himself, and thus gazing at the rays, little by little, that is *petit a petit*, they covered the whole of Christ's body. When this had been seen and done, Christ replaced her in her seat as she had been before. When she came to herself in the greatest tears and weeping, in great warmth and love toward God, she wanted her other women companions and people to know what had happened. She didn't move from there until her companions called her. Then she got up and went out of the church, and in the cemetery she saw for the second time the Man with whom she wanted to sojourn, and rays again surrounded her, like the first time.

When she was at home and at table with her companions, and they were talking about the sermon they'd heard, the rays again shone all about her, and because of them she was so kindled with fervor and love that she couldn't eat. Leaving the table, she went up to the solar and began to pray. Afterwards, they went to the Tenebrae service, and there, in the same church as before, she saw a certain lady who spoke to her and immediately vanished.

She also said and claimed that on the following Holy Saturday, when she was again there in the church for the service, at the time of the elevation of the Host or a little before, God the Father appeared to her. High contemplation was given to her by God, and the grace of contemplating heaven and of seeing our Lord Jesus Christ, as well as continuous prayer and a continual sensing of Our Lord. From then on, so she claims, very often our Lord God said to her, "I myself have given Him to you, as to the Virgin, and I have kept Him with me." She claims that she frequently saw the Lord God to face, and he came there in the form and species of a man. Afterwards there was preached an indulgence at Magalone, to which she wanted to go, but the Lord prevented her from going, and said to her who is telling this, "Do you remember I shall be the Lord of one soul?" God then added, "Saint John the Baptist was the herald of the advent of Jesus Christ's holy baptism, and you are the herald of the advent of the Holy Spirit."

After she heard this, she realized that the Lord was comparing her first to the Virgin and then to Blessed John the Baptist, and in her heart she thought that she was unworthy of being compared with the Virgin and of being called the handmaiden of Christ, and unworthy of being compared with St. John, a voice crying in the wilderness. So she replied to the Lord, "Lord, I am truly nothing, for I feel myself to be a sinner and sin is nothing." She gave herself to contemplation, and prayed God to give that grace to another.

At length the Lord responded, "Whether you are willing or unwilling, this shall be yours." And the Lord added, "I myself give Him to you, and I myself retain Him." But this time He didn't say "as to the virgin" as he had said above, but he said it as she said.

She also claimed that she was accustomed to say prayers: in a loud voice she cried out to God three times, "Friend, friend, friend," but God the Lord didn't reply until the third cry and then he showed himself in a cloud and said this:

"And you, what do you want?"

She answered, "Lord, may you have mercy on all the sins of the Jews, the Saracens, and all the peoples of the world. Lord, grant this to us by your great mercy, and by the merit of your good works, that we may always live faithfully in your trust. Also, Lord, may you have mercy on yours and your poor family. May honor and glory be granted unto you, Lord."

When this prayer was over, the Lord God replied, "I know whom I have chosen." And however many times she completed this prayer, she fell into ecstasy, so she said, for she desired so much that God be loved and honored, and she was so indebted that frequently she slipped away while still speaking.

For a year she kept all this hidden and revealed it to no one, until she had a guilty conscience, for she could no longer say her hours as completely and perfectly as she had been able to before, that is, the thirty paternosters that she used to say for Matins, and so on. Finally, when she wished to reveal all this to a certain religious man whom she named, the Lord prevented her from revealing it. At length, she revealed it to a certain person whom she named, with the permission of the Lord Jesus Christ. Afterward, God rebuked her for having spoken to this person, who was a man.

Then she spoke as follows to the Lord God: "Lord, you are a man as he is, yet in other respects do you not come from within?"

The Lord replied, "I am not as other men, for divinity took on human nature, and the root of the person of Christ is divinity, and you are other, and were of the root of sin." After He said this, the Lord fashioned a fire for her, saying, "See this fire, how it converts the whole matter and substance of the wood into its nature. In the same way the nature of divinity converts into itself souls it wishes for itself." Thus God proved that he could better come to the home of her telling this than the said man.

Shortly afterwards she saw two other persons like God himself, who were joined in order one after the other; one of them began to run, and on his way put himself on the neck of her who is telling this, and another placed himself on her right arm. From then on the three persons of the Trinity came to her, and she saw them; this seeing was spiritual and not corporeal, just as sometimes something is seen by one person mentally which is seen physically by another—but she saw only spiritually. She also claimed that God frequently said to her, "I go away totally and I return, for I have chosen and made my chamber in you."

Also one time the Lord leapt on her neck and fashioned a white horse with a man on it for her, saying, "See how this man controls this horse however he wishes. Thus am I above all nature, and I rule you as I will, and I am with you wherever you are."

She further claims that the divinity which God gave to her telling this formed for itself a body of more precious and more pure understanding than the one she had, and there was no angel nor archangel nor saint in paradise who might have administered or impeded this. She likewise claims that the spirit which God gave her at another time despoiled hell and repaired all human nature. Also that God said to her, "The Blessed Virgin Mary was the donatrix of the Son of God and you shall be the donatrix of the Holy Spirit."

When she who is telling this heard this, she grew afraid and prayed God, saying, "Lord God, guard me from that sin of pride through which the angel Lucifer fell from heaven."

And the Lord God replied, "I shall hear your prayer."

She also claimed that God told her that Christ had two natures, one human and the other divine, and that the Gospel being destroyed is against his human nature, and that the destruction of the writing of the Holy Spirit given to Friar Peter John is against His divine nature.

Also Christ told her that the pope preceding the present one was like that good man who placed the body of Christ crucified in the tomb, and that this present pope, John XXII, is like Caiaphas, who crucified Christ. The poor Beguines who were burned, and also the burned lepers, were like the innocents beheaded by the command of Herod; likewise, just as Herod procured the death of innocent boy children, thus this Herod, the devil, procured the death of these burned Beguines and lepers. Similarly she claimed that Christ told her that the sin of this pope is as great as the sin of Cain, and a fourth part of it is as great as the sin of Caiaphas, and a fifth part as great as was the sin of Simon Magus, and another part as great as was the sin of Herod.

Christ also told her, as she claims, that the sin of this pope, when he betrayed the Franciscan friars to death, was as great as the sin of Adam when he ate the apple. And that when he condemned the Gospel, the sin of this pope was as great as the sin of Adam when he tasted the apple and took it out of greed, perceiving that he sinned; for it was then that he ought to have sought mercy from the Lord God our God.

Also that the sin of this pope, when he condemned the writing of Friar Peter John, the holy father, was as great as the sin of Adam when he ate the apple and on account of that accused the woman Eve, imputing to Eve the blame for this—that he had eaten the apple offered to him by her, for he ought to have ruled her, when he is the head of the woman, and instead he accused her. This pope is similar, for as head of the holy church of God, he should have ruled the church according to the will of God, that is, the will of our Lord Jesus Christ. And in just the same way as Adam, on account of this sin, lost the grace earlier given to him by God, so this pope, on the account of his sin, lost the grace given to him by the Lord Jesus Christ, for the punishment is equal to the sin, and consequently the sacraments have lost their virtue. Also, just as Adam could never regain the grace which he had lost, so this pope shall never regain the grace he lost, that he had at first; for just as the whole human nature was dead spiritually on account of the said Adam, the first man, so Christianity as a whole is dead spiritually because of this pope's sin.

Since the pope destroyed the writing of Friar Peter John, written by the hand of divinity, the sacrament of the altar lost its virtue and power, which it shall never recover. For this reason God took away from the pope and all others the grace of the sacraments. Likewise Jesus Christ told her, as she claimed, that St. Peter had confessed that Jesus Christ was the true Son of the living God, and that this pope confessed Christ to be a sinner, in that he said that Christ owned things in common with others and personally for his own use.

Jesus Christ told her that St. Francis began his order in that same perfection and altitude as had Christ, when he began with his apostles to hold to poverty, in that same perfection and altitude St. Francis began to hold to poverty with his brothers.

Whatever men and women who had vowed virginity and chastity and afterwards were given husbands or wives were discarded and led to evil by the pope; this pope similarly carried away from Christ all those men and women who, on account of the fear of those works that are going on presently [that is, the Inquisition and persecution of the Spiritual Franciscans], are given over to doing evil and saying and swearing ignobly concerning God.

Jesus Christ told her, as she claimed, that since this pope had produced so much wind and stupidity, so much malice and evil, therefore, as Christ had at first given him a name more beautiful than all the men of this world, so Christ himself afterwards gave the same pope the name more horrifying than all the men of this world; for first he was called apostle or pope, and afterwards Christ gave him this more terrifying name, that is, Antichrist, which name Christ imposed on him, as she asserted, on the next to the last Friday before the feast of the Lord's Nativity just passed.

Christ said to her, as she claimed, that there is no layperson who should despise clerics, but clerics and laypeople should love each other with that spiritual friendship with which Adam and Eve loved each other before they sinned, for when God ejected Adam and Eve from the earthly paradise, they were both still virgins. Likewise Christ told her that clerics and lay people should love each other spiritually in that very same spiritual friendship with which Christ and the apostles loved each other. Likewise in that same spiritual friendship in which the faithful loved each other clerics and lay persons ought to love each other.

Likewise Christ told her that by the counsel of the whole Trinity, he sent his son to the Virgin Mother and that God sent his son into the Virgin in such a way and manner that God himself did not diminish himself. Likewise, that divinity which was given to the Virgin formed for itself a body of the more precious and pure blood that might be in the Virgin; and there was no angel nor archangel nor saint in paradise who could have intromitted this, but only Jesus Christ himself formed his body; likewise that Christ did not return to God the Father until he had fulfilled everything that the whole Trinity had or has established, and that the whole Holy Trinity has established that Christ had to to receive human flesh in the Virgin, and that he was God and man, and that he should return to man that which man had lost, that is, the terrestrial paradise.

Likewise she testified that Christ said that by virtue of his passion, Christ himself ordained the terrestrial paradise, and with the ten commandments enclosed the terrestrial paradise; that is, that in this paradise be placed the seven sacraments and the seven gifts of the

Holy Spirit and the four cardinal virtues; likewise that in the terrestrial paradise, that is, in the church, a man may confess his sins with such bitterness of heart that all things are forgiven by God; likewise that man in that earthly paradise could see the body of Christ in such reverence that all his sins were forgiven; likewise that in so much reverence a man might hear mass that all his sins were remitted for him. Likewise that in that earthly paradise a man could receive the body of Christ with such reverence that all his sins would have been remitted, even forgotten [thus unconfessed] mortal sins.

Likewise the Lord Jesus Christ said to her, as she claims, that a certain notary whom she names—with whom Na Prous set forth and related the aforesaid things, who was unwilling to believe her, along with those who held to the opinion of this notary—publicly crucified the Lord Jesus Christ in spirit, and that a certain apostate friar whom she named, to whom she revealed the aforesaid things, and those who maintained themselves in the opinion of the said apostate (whom she did not call an apostate), crucified the Lord Jesus Christ secretly. Declaring this similitude, she said that in the same way as God first sent his Son to the legal experts among the Jews, so God first sent the Holy Spirit to the legal experts of the Christians, that is, to the aforesaid notary, and thus it is obvious that just as the legal experts among the Jews knew the Son of God, equally the legal experts of the Christians knew the Holy Spirit of God, for in the same way as the Jews crucified the Son of God in person, so did these, that is, the legal experts of the Christians, crucify the Holy Spirit in person, that is, in the person of Na Prous, who is speaking. Accordingly all these things, as she claims, the Lord God said to her, the same God who, as she said above, gave her the Holy Spirit.

Likewise that God, when he ordained the orders of St. Francis and St. Dominic, did a great work, as great as when he created the world.

Likewise that as many souls as he has saved from the creation of the world up to that time in which he established the two orders, so many souls will he save until the end of the world. Likewise that as many saints as there were up to the aforesaid time, so many and such great saints shall there be until the end of the world.

Likewise, that St. Francis is as great a saint in paradise as is Blessed John the Baptist, for just as Blessed John prepared the way before the Lord, so St. Francis prepared the way before the Holy Spirit. Likewise the Lord told her, as she claims, that as many graces and as much glory as the Lord gave to Brother Peter John, so much and so many he gave to the Son of God in person, that is, to the extent that he was man and not to the extent that he was God; and for this reason it will now be necessary to believe that the Lord God gave to the said Friar Peter John the spirit completely, for otherwise men and women would not be saved. For she claims accordingly that God told her that in the body of Jesus Christ and in the body of his Mother, that is, the Virgin Mary, there was not any mingling of natures, when the whole might be everywhere the same. Likewise between the spirit in the body of the said friar Peter John and the spirit in the body of the one speaking, Na Prous, there is no mingling, for the spirit of friar Peter John and the spirit of Na Prous are one and the same, since the whole descends from God, as she said.

Likewise the Lord told her that in the same way as he, God, ruled the Church through the two bodies of flesh, that is, the bodies of Christ and of his mother the Virgin Mary, so in the same way he rules from henceforth the church through the two bodies of the spirit given to the aforesaid friar Peter John and to her speaking, Na Prous, both of which spirits are one, as she said.

Likewise she claimed that the Lord told her that it is necessary that whoever wishes to save himself must believe the words of the writing of the said friar Peter John, when they are written by the virtue of the Holy Spirit, and likewise that one must believe the words of this Na Prous, when they are spoke by virtue of the Holy Spirit, as she said. Afterwards, when they shall have known these things, another man cannot be saved, and moreover, he who does not believe in the words of Na Prous shall die an eternal death.

Likewise, the Lord God shall give two things to every person who believes in the words of Na Prous; that is, he will forgive the sins of the believing person, and he will give him the Holy Spirit.

Likewise, he who created the world redeemed me, and shall renew it. Likewise God sent his Son to a virgin to redeem human nature, and the Son of God sent the Holy Spirit to another virgin for redeeming human nature; saying that God gave her to understand clearly that she is the virgin to whom God sent the Holy Spirit to redeem human nature.

Likewise she said and claimed that the Lord God told her that that book which Blessed John said he had seen sealed with seven seals, she herself, Na Prous, opened. And that the first seal was opened by the notary of whom she spoke above, and the second was opened by a certain apostate Minorite friar, of whom she spoke above, and the third seal was opened by a certain other person whom she names, and moreover that the whole book was opened for me, Mennetus the notary, who writes this.

Likewise she said that if this pope who now is, that is Pope John XXII, and the cardinals, prelates, and doctors of the sacred page should say to her and demonstrate by reasonings and by the authority of holy scripture that the aforesaid things, which she holds and claims herself to believe and hold, are erroneous and heretical, and if they were to warn her to revoke the aforesaid errors, she would neither believe nor obey them, for, as she said, the Lord Jesus Christ, who told her the aforesaid things, is more experienced and more prudent than all the men of the whole world.

Likewise she said that if the pope should excommunicate her on account of that disobedience, she would not think herself to be excommunicated nor would she even believe herself to be damned, if she were to die under the aforesaid excommunication, for God has made her certain in another way, as she said, claiming that whoever should condemn her and burn her on account of the foregoing, she would believe herself to be saved and a glorious martyr in paradise.

Likewise she said that it shall be necessary henceforth for whoever shall wish to save himself to believe in the works of the Holy Spirit given to Friar Peter John and to her speaking, indeed that he believe in the words that are in the writing of the said Friar Peter John and in the words that she herself said; which words are all the work of the Holy Spirit. She says that now she had great discomfort, for it was necessary to say such things about herself that would seem to be able to be said out of vainglory, for she would prefer, as she claims, to be torn in pieces with swords, or that lightning from heaven should fall upon her and lay her stretched out upon the ground, rather than to say such things about herself, and that she would rather speak about any other creature, but for this God wishes and commands her, as she claims, that whoever shall have believed the writings of the said Friar Peter John and the words of the same Na Prous, and shall have preserved his commands, shall be baptized in the Holy Spirit, and the Lord will forgive his sins.

Likewise, when interrogated, she said that God commanded the sacrament of matrimony to be maintained and observed in that way by which it was done between Adam and Eve and in St. John, and in the same way in which was made the marriage when Christ was present in the nuptials with the Blessed John, although, when questioned, she said she didn't know in what way that matrimony was done.

Likewise she said that every day and night and every hour she sees God in the spirit, and he never leaves her; she says that Christ himself wishes to be head of the church and to guide souls, and that now he shall not permit souls to be ruled by any pope, even if another be elected by the cardinals, since the papacy is annulled for perpetuity. When questioned as to what way God rules souls, she said that by the Holy Spirit and by the work of the Holy Spirit he does this. Likewise she said and claimed that the Lord told her that Christ himself took his body of flesh from a poor virgin, so that poor people and rich would not fear to find fault with him and finally to crucify him, and so that no one should feel to crucify him; and that likewise Christ himself took a body of spirit in a poor virgin to the end that poor and rich should not fear to find fault

with him and persecute him and finally to crucify him in the spirit, for, as God told her, as she claims, he took his body from a virgin, for her, Naprous, he took the word, for just as much as Christ was vituperated in the body which he took in the Virgin, so it is necessary that he be so much vituperated in that body of the words of her speaking, that is, in spirit.

When asked if God told her those words which she had recited above, she said yes, but that she would not say them to anyone living except when she was compelled by God himself.

The aforesaid woman made her deposition and confessed freely and willingly, and as many times as her testimony was read to her in the vernacular, she confirmed and approved it. And having been warned, called, and urged many times in court and elsewhere, to revoke and objure all the aforesaid things as erroneous and heretical, she persevered in them, claiming that in the aforesaid, as in the truth, she wishes to live and die.

MARGUERITE D'OINGT   (died 1310; Poleteins near Lyon)

The Mirror of St. Marguerite d'Oingt

Translated by Richard J. Pioli

CHAPTER I

1. I think you have heard it said that, when you have listened to the story of some grace given by our Lord to certain friends of his, you become better for it for a long time. Since I desire your salvation as much as I desire my own, I will tell you, as briefly as possible, a great favor which our Lord gave—not long ago—to a person I know. And so that you may

gain the most profit from it, I will tell you the reason why, according to me, God granted it to her.

2. By the grace of Our Lord, this creature had inscribed in her heart the holy life that God, Jesus Christ, led on earth, his good example and good teaching. So firmly had she placed sweet Jesus Christ in her heart that it

sometimes seemed to her that he was present and that in his hand he held a closed book for teaching.

3. This book was written on the outside entirely in black, white and silver-gilt letters; the clasps of the book were written in gold letters.

4. In the white letters was written the holy life of the blessed Son of God, who was completely white by virtue of his very great innocence and holy works. In the black letters were written the blows and slaps and filthy things that the Jews threw in his face and on his noble body, to such an extent that his body looked like a leper's. In the silver-gilt letters were written the wounds and the precious blood that was poured out for us.

5. There were also two clasps which closed the book; they were written in letters of gold. On one was written: "God shall be All in All." On the other was written "God is marvelous in his saints."

6. Now I'd like to tell you briefly how this creature applied herself to the study of this book. When morning came, she began to think about the way in which the blessed Son of God wished to descend to the misery of this world and to take our humanity and join it to his divinity, to the extent that one might say that God, who was immortal, died for us. Next she thought about the great humility that was in him. Then she meditated on how he always wished to be persecuted. Finally she thought about his great poverty and his great patience, and how he was obedient unto death.

7. When she had looked at this book thoroughly, she began to read in the book of her conscience, which she found quite full of falsity and lies. When she considered the humility of Jesus Christ, she found herself full of pride. When she thought how he had wished to be despised and persecuted, she found the complete opposite in herself. When she reflected on his poverty, she did not find that she wanted to be so poor that she was despised for it. When she reflected on his patience, she did not find it in herself at all. When she thought about how he was obedient to the point of death, she did not find herself as obedient as she should have been.

8. There were white letters in which was written the behavior of the blessed Son of God. Afterwards, when she had thoroughly examined all her faults, she endeavored to correct them, as much as she could, according to the example of the life of Jesus Christ.

9. Next she devoted herself to the study of the black letters, in which were written the villanies which had been done to Jesus Christ. In these letters, she learned how to suffer tribulations with patience.

10. Then she devoted herself to the study of the red (silver-gilt in the initial vision) letters, in which were written the wounds of Jesus Christ and the shedding of his precious blood. In these letters she learned not only to suffer tribulation with patience, but even to rejoice in it, to the point that all the pleasures of this world became hateful to her, so that it seemed to her that there was nothing in the world as worthy and as sweet as suffering the pains and torments of this age for the love of her creator.

11. Next she devoted herself to the study of the letters of gold. There she learned to desire the things of heaven.

12. In this book she found written the life which Jesus Christ led on earth, from his birth until he ascended to heaven.

13. Then she began to meditate on how the blessed Son of God is seated at the right of his glorious Father. But she still had the eyes of the flesh, too darkened for her to be able to contemplate our Lord in heaven. Thus she was always obliged to return to the beginning of the life that Our Lord Jesus Christ led on earth, until she had thoroughly amended her life according to the pattern of this book. For a long time she meditated in this fashion.

CHAPTER II

14. Not long ago she was in prayer after Matins and she began to look at her book as was her custom. Just as she was looking attentively, it seemed to her that the book opened. She had only seen the outside of it earlier.

15. On the inside, the book was like a lovely mirror, and there were only two pages. Of what she saw in the book, I can only tell you about a few things, for I have neither the intelligence that can conceive them nor the lips that know how to recount them. Still I will tell you something, if God will grant me the grace.

16. Inside this book there appeared a delightful place, so large that the whole world is only a little thing in comparison. In this place there appeared a very glorious light that was divided into three parts, as into three persons, but the mouth of a man is not capable of speaking of it.

17. From there came all possible good things. From there came the true wisdom by which all things are made and created. There was the power, to whose will all things submit. From there came such great charm and such strengthening that the angels and the souls were so satiated that they could desire nothing more. Such a delightful odor came forth from there that it drew to itself all the virtues of the heavens. Such a great kindling of love came from there that all the loves of this world are but sorrow and bitterness in comparison with this love. From there comes a joy so great that there is no human heart capable of imagining it.

18. When the angels and the saints look on the great beauty of Our Lord and feel his kindness and his very great charm, they feel so much joy that they cannot keep themselves from singing, but they make a completely new song, so sweet that it is a great melody. This sweet song passes through all the orders of angels and saints, from the first to the last.

And this song has not quite ended when they sing another, completely new. This song will last without end.

19. The saints will be within their creator just as the fish in the sea; they will drink all they want, without becoming tired and without lessening the amount of water. The saints will be just like this, for they will drink and eat the great sweetness of God. And the more they receive of this sweetness, the more will be their hunger for it. This sweetness cannot be decreased any more or less than can the water of the sea. For just as the waves all go toward the sea and all come back, just so the beauty and the sweetness of Our Lord, even though they are poured forth everywhere, always return to him. And for that reason they can never diminish.

20. Even though the saints shall never do other than think about his great goodness, they will not be able to visualize perfectly the very great charity in virtue of which the good Lord sent his blessed Son to earth.

21. Now think that all other goods are contained in him. He is all that one may think and desire in all the saints. And this is the inscription that was on the first clasp of the book where there was written, "God shall be All in all."

22. On the second clasp of the book was written "Mirabilis Deus in sanctis suis," "God is marvelous in his saints." There is no human intelligence that can conceive how marvelous God is among his saints.

CHAPTER III

23. Not long ago, someone I know was in prayer before or after Matins. She set to thinking about Jesus Christ, how he is seated on the right of God the Father. And at once her heart was ravished to such a degree that it seemed to her to be in a place larger than the

entire world, and more brilliant than the sun in all its parts; and this place was full of people so handsome and so glorious that human speech cannot utter it.

24. Among others she seemed to see Jesus Christ, so glorious that there is no human heart capable of conceiving it. He was clothed in that glorious vestment that he acquired in the very noble body of Our Lady. On his most noble hands and feet appeared the glorious wounds that he suffered for love of us. From these glorious injuries there gushed forth a light so brilliant that one was stunned by it: it was as if all the beauty of divinity were transmitted by means of the wounds. This glorious body was so noble and so transparent that one could see very clearly the soul inside. This body was so noble that one could see oneself there more clearly than in a mirror. This body was so lovely that one saw in it the angels and the saints as if they were painted there. His expression was so graceful that the angels who had contemplated it since their creation could not be satiated with the sight, but had always the desire to look on it.

25. Surely if one conceived and considered his beauty and the goodness that is in him, one would love him so much that all other things would seem bitter in comparison. For he is so good and so sweet and so courteous that he has shared with his friends everything that he has of value.

26. Now imagine his very great beauty, so great that he has given to all the angels and to all the saints who are his members, the property of being more brilliant than the sun. You can imagine how lovely the place is where there is so much light.

27. For God is so great that he is everywhere, and that property belongs to him alone. He has given to his friends in heaven an agility so swift that they go in an instant there where they may wish; in effect, whereever they may be, they are everywhere present with him.

28. God is very strong and very powerful and because of this he has given his friends so much power and so much strength that they can do everything they wish: if they wished to raise up the whole entire world on a little finger, they could do it easily.

29. God is totally free, and because of that he has made his friends so free, subtle, and immaterial that they may enter and leave, even through closed doors, without any impediment, as did Jesus Christ after the resurrection.

30. God is invulnerable, and cannot have in himself any infirmity, and because of that he has given to his friends health so great that they can never be sick nor dejected nor suffering, neither in soul nor in body.

31. God is the highest joy, and there is no delight nor honest joy that does not come from him. He is the sweet electuary in which are all delicious flavors. He is so good that for those who taste him, the more they receive the greater will be their hunger, and they will not dare to desire anything other than the sweetness which they re-experience in him.

32. God is full of wisdom, and he has given so much of it to his friends that they will never need to ask anything more, for they will have all that they may wish.

33. God is love, and he has given so much to the saints that they love themselves as one member can love the other, and whatever one wishes, all the others wish.

34. God is eternal and because of that he has made his friends of such noble matter that they cannot corrupt nor age, but they will live eternally with him.

35. Now you can represent to yourself the very great goodness that is in him, who has given all that he has to his friends. He has done more for them, for he has given himself. He has made them so lovely and so glorious that each one sees the Trinity in him, as one sees in a fine mirror that which is before it. And this is the inscription that was on the

second clasp, where it was written "Mirabilis Deus in sanctis suis."

36. And just as the saints take pleasure in seeing the beauty of Our Lord, our good Creator takes pleasure in the beauty and love of his lovely creatures whom he has made in his image and in his likeness, as a good master painter willingly looks at a fine picture, when he has done it well.

37. In my opinion, he who will undertake to reflect on the very great beauty of Our Lord and on the glory which he manifests in his saints, will be able to say with reason that these are true marvels, and I think he will fall into a swoon. He may say that God has granted to his saints the promise he made to them by the prophet David, "I said, you shall be Gods." For it will seem to each to be a little god, for they will be his sons and his heirs.

38. Certainly I don't believe that there is anywhere in the world a heart so cold that it would not be totally inflamed with love if it could imagine and know the very great beauty of Our Lord. But there are some hearts so debased that they are like piglets that prefer the smell of the mire to that of a lovely rose. Those who love better to apply their spirit to things of this world and find there more comfort than in God behave like this. And they are so full of darkness that they see nothing.

39. And the people who have so little purity do not have the capability to love God nor to know him. In effect, God says in the gospel that no one knows the Son except the Father, nor the Father except the Son, and those to whom he wishes to reveal him. I believe that the Son of God does not reveal his secrets to those people who are not pure, and that is why the pure of heart are blessed, for they shall see God in all clarity. God himself promises in the Gospel and says that the pure in heart are blessed, for they shall see God face to face in his great beauty. May Jesus Christ grant us to live in such great purity of heart and of body that when our souls shall leave our bodies, he will deign to show us his glorious face. Amen.

MARGUERITE PORETE   (died Paris, 1310)

The Mirror of Simple Souls Who Are Annihilated and Who Only Remain in the Will and Desire for Love

Translated by Don Eric Levine*

CHAPTER CXVIII. Of the seven states of the devout Soul, which are otherwise called beings

I have promised, says this Soul, with regard to being taken by Love, to say something about the seven states that we call beings—because that is what they are. And these are the degrees by which one climbs from the valley to the mountain top which is so abandoned that there one sees only God—and each degree has its proper order of existence.

The first state, or degree, is when the Soul, which God has touched with grace and deprived of its power to sin, intends to keep the commandments that God has ordained in the Law for life, that is to say for death, and in this regard such a Soul considers with great fear that God has commanded it to love Him with all its heart and its neighbor as well as its self. This seems to this Soul enough labor for all it knows how to do; and it seems to it that even if it must live a thousand years its power has enough to do to keep and hold the commandments.

At this point, says the Open Soul, and in this state I have found myself for some time. Now I in no way fear to gain the height, nor should anyone if you have a gentle heart and are full of noble courage; but a small heart doesn't dare to undertake great things and through default of love cannot climb high. Such people are great cowards; but this is not astonishing because they live in a laziness that never allows them to search for or desire God who will never be found if he is not diligently searched for.

The second state or degree is when the Soul sees that God counsels his special friends beyond what he commands; and this Soul is not at all a friend if it refrains from accomplishing all that it knows will please its Beloved, and thus abandons its creatural self and forces itself above all to do all that men counsel in the way of mortifying nature, despising riches, delights, and honors, in order to accomplish to perfection the counsel of the Gospel, of which Jesus Christ is the example. Thus this Soul doesn't fear the loss of things, nor the words of men, nor the weakness of the body, because its Beloved never fears them; that Soul which is taken by him cannot act otherwise.

In the third state the Soul sees the feeling of love in itself as a work of perfection, and its spirit causes to arise in itself a burning desire for the love of multiplying such works, this being the knowable subtlety of the meaning of its love, a love which doesn't know what to offer its Beloved to comfort him except that which he loves. For no other gift is prized in love except to give the Beloved that which is most loved.

Thus it is that the will of this creature only

---

*Porete's prose style is marked by long sentences made up of series of usually short clauses. I have kept most of these sentences intact in order to give a feeling of her style. Since she is describing a series of highly abstract steps in the mystical ascent, she tries to give the whole process a syntactical feel of logical progression and inevitability; thus she uses words such as "therefore," "thus," and "because" a great deal and often repeats for the sake of emphasis and clarity. She indicates toward the end of this chapter that this is at least as much a heard as a written text. This may in part account for the great and serious verbal wit, in the seventeenth-century sense of the word. Indeed, if the quality of Porete's prose rings any echoes, it is likely to be the later ones of John Donne's sermons.

The vocabulary is borrowed from the *Roman de la Rose* (one of the most popular books of the Middle Ages), from what is often referred to as "the Courtly Love tradition" and from the language of chivalry: examples—Open Soul, "Ame Franche;" gentle heart, "coeur gentil;" noble courage, "noble courage;" coward, "couars;" Beloved, "Ami;" delight, "delit;" the danger, nobility, and other qualities of the Soul; touch; pride; lordship, "seigneurie;" and, most interestingly, pure love, "fine amour," which is the troubadour's term for the kind of love they were describing.

Porete is very fond of indirect pronouns, and I have felt free to keep or not keep these as the sense warranted. Thus, while the original French text is littered with the word "elle" ("she" or "it" feminine) referring to the Soul or to Love (both of which are feminine in the text), I have always translated this as "it," in accordance with current English usage. I have always kept Porete's capitalized nouns since they are part and parcel of the meaning. All words and phrases in parentheses are Porete's, and not interpolations on the part of the translator.

Finally, the English reader should be aware that one of the most often used and most important phrases in this chapter would be far more available to a contemporary French reader. The seven states of the Soul, the "états d'âme," have lost their number and been totally laicized in current French usage, but they are there as an inner state of being or feeling.

loves to do works of goodness, through the harshest of projects involving great work, by means of which it can nourish its spirit. Thus it truly seems that the will only loves to do works of goodness, for it doesn't know what to give to Love if it doesn't make him this sacrifice; because no death would be a martyrdom for it compared to abstaining from the work it loves, which is the delight of its pleasure and the life of the will, and is that which nourishes. After this the Soul forgoes the works which had been such a delight, and kills off the will to live, and forces itself as an act of martyrdom to be obedient to the will of others, to abstain from work and from will, and by fulfilling the will of others to destroy its own will. And this is more difficult, vastly more difficult than the two prior states, because it is harder to conquer the works of the will of the spirit than it is to conquer the will of the body in order to accomplish the will of the spirit. Thus it is fitting and necessary that the soul pulverize by breaking and shattering itself, in order to enlarge the place where Love wishes to be, and to burden itself with several beings in order to unburden itself, in order to attain its being.

In the fourth state the Soul is drawn by high love into the delight of meditative thought, and gives up all outward work and obedience to others through its high level of contemplation. Thus the Soul is so severe, noble, and full of delight that it cannot allow anything to touch it but the touch of Love's pure delight which makes the Soul charming and happy, full of pride at the abundance of love. Thus the Soul is mistress of this shining (that is to say, of the brightness of its soul which has marvellously filled it with love of great faith), through harmonious union which has put it in possession of these delights.

Then the Soul holds that there is no higher life than to have this over which it has lordship; for Love has so greatly fed it with his delights that it doesn't believe that God has any greater gift to give to a soul in this life than such a love as Love has spread through love within the Soul.

Ah, it is not astonishing if this Soul is caught unawares because Gracious Love has made it completely drunk, so drunk that Love doesn't let it attend to anything other than Love, so great is the power by which Love delights it. And because of this the Soul cannot occupy itself with any other being; the great brightness of Love has so dazzled its gaze that it cannot see anything other than its love. And there the Soul is deceived, because there are two other states in this life, given by God, which are greater and more noble than this one; but Love has deceived many a soul by the sweetness of the pleasure of its love which catches the Soul unawares as soon as it comes near. No one can resist such power: this that Soul knows which has been raised on high beyond itself by means of pure love.

In the fifth state the Soul sees that God is who is and thus every thing is, and that the Soul is not, except as every thing is. And these two considerations marvellously astonish the Soul, and it sees that he who has put free will in the Soul, which by itself is nothing but complete wickedness, is himself all goodness.

Now by means of pure divine goodness the divine Goodness has placed free will in the Soul. Now, in that which is nothing, though strong in wickedness, and which is thus all wickedness, free will is enclosed, that comes from the being of God who is being, and who wishes that that which has no being receive it from his gift. And therefore the divine Goodness pours forth in a ravishing rapid dilation of the movement of divine Light. This movement of divine Light, which is diffused throughout the Soul by light, is disclosed to the Will. [The Will wishes that the state of being of the Soul]* be moved from that place where it is, and where it shouldn't be, to there

*Gap in the original French manuscript supplied from the Latin translation.

where it isn't, and from where it came, there where it should be.

Now the Will sees by the light of the diffused divine Light, and this Light gives itself to the Will in order to replace this Will in God (this Will which cannot return without such Light), because the Will cannot profit from itself or dispose of itself through its own will; because its nature is wretched by inclination and the will has reduced that nature to less than nothing. Now the Soul sees this inclination and this perdition of the nothingness of its nature and of its own will, and in this way sees by means of light that Will ought to will the one divine will, without any other will, and this is the purpose for which this will was given. And therefore the Soul parts from this will and the Will parts from this Soul, and then it replaces and gives and yields itself to God, there from where it was first removed, without retaining anything belonging to him, in order to fulfill the perfect divine will, which cannot be fulfilled in the Soul without such a gift, so that the Soul may have neither war nor faintness. This gift makes perfection in the Soul and thus transforms it into the nature of Love which delights it with replenished peace, and satiates it with divine nourishment. And therefore it no longer need protect itself against Nature's war, because its will is nakedly laid in the place from which it was once taken, there where by right it ought to be. And this Soul was always at war as long as it held Will back from its true place.

Now this Soul is a blank, because it sees its nothingness by fullness of divine knowledge, which makes it blank, makes it a void. And thus it is all, because it sees by means of the depth of the knowledge of its own wickedness, which is so deep and so great that the Soul can't see either its beginning or size or end but only an unmeasurable, bottomless abyss; there the Soul finds itself, without finding and bottomless. A person finds nothing who cannot attain this state; and he who sees more of himself in such knowledge of wickedness has

more truthful knowledge than he who doesn't recognize his wickedness, not even the least part of it—thus this Soul is an abyss of wickedness, and a gulf of such lodging and such provision that it is like a deluge of sin, and it contains in itself all perdition. This is the way this Soul sees itself, without sight. And what makes it see itself? It is the depth of the humility that sits in the flesh and rules without pride. There pride cannot dig in at all since the Soul sees itself and doesn't see; and this non-seeing makes it see itself perfectly.

Now this Soul is seated on the bottom of the depths, there where there is no bottom and thus it is deep; and this depth makes the Soul see very clearly the true Sun of the lofty goodness because nothing obstructs its view. This divine Goodness shows itself to the Soul through goodness which draws, transforms, and unites the Soul by a joining of goodness in pure divine Goodness of which goodness is the mistress. And the knowledge of these two natures of which we have spoken (of divine Goodness and of the Soul's wickedness) is the means with which such goodness has endowed the Soul. And because the Bridegroom who is whole only wishes his young bride whole and entire, Mercy has made peace with enclosed Justice, and the Bridegroom has transformed this Soul in his goodness. Now the Soul is all and it is a blank, because its Beloved has made it one.

Now the Soul is fallen from love into nothingness, and without this nothingness it cannot be all. This fall is such a deep fall, if it be rightly fallen, that the Soul cannot arise from this abyss; and also it should not arise; on the contrary it ought to remain there. And there the Soul loses pride and youth, because the spirit has become old and no longer lets the Soul be either charming or pretty, because the will has left it, the will which had so often made it proud and arrogant through a feeling of love when at the height of contemplation or fourth state. But the fifth state has regulated the account, and shown this Soul its self. Now it sees itself from its self, and knows divine Goodness, and this knowledge of divine Goodness makes it re-see itself; and these two sights root out of it will and desire and good works, and thus the Soul is completely at rest, and come into possession of free being which forces the Soul away from all things by means of excellent nobility.

In the sixth state the Soul doesn't see at all because of whatever abyss of humility the Soul has in itself; nor does it see God for whatever high goodness he has. But God by his divine majesty sees himself in the Soul, and this purifies the Soul so that it sees that nothing exists except God himself, who is and therefore everything else exists, and that what truly is is God himself; and therefore the Soul only sees itself, because one who sees what is sees only God, God who sees himself in this very Soul by means of his divine majesty. And thus the Soul in the sixth state is freed of all things, clean and purified—and not glorified; because glorification belongs to the seventh state that we will have in glory, thus no one can speak of it. But this Soul, thus clean and purified, sees neither God nor itself, but God sees himself in it, for it, without it; which (that is, God) shows it that there is nothing but him.

And therefore this Soul knows only him, and loves only him, praises only him, for there is only he. Because what is exists by his goodness, and God loves his goodness whenever he has bestowed it, and his goodness bestowed is God himself, and God cannot depart from his goodness so that it doesn't dwell in him, thus he is what goodness is and goodness is what God is. And therefore Goodness sees itself by means of his goodness through divine light in the sixth state, by which the Soul is purified. And nothing is except he that is, who sees the divine majesty of himself in such a being (the Soul), and this happens by alteration of the love of goodness, spread out and dissolved in the Soul. And therefore he sees himself in such a creature without appropriating anything of the creaturely; everything is of his own substance, his very self. This is the sixth state of which we have promised to speak to our auditors, the sixth state of being taken by Love, and Love has by himself and by means of his high nobility paid this debt.

And the seventh state Love keeps within itself, to give us in everlasting glory, and of which we will have no knowledge until our soul has left our body.

VIII

Women Writers of the Late Fourteenth Century—Seeking Models

Julian of Norwich, Margery Kempe,
Doña Leonor López de Córdoba, and Christine de Pizan

*T*HE FOUR WOMEN WRITERS of the late fourteenth century covered in this chapter have in common a driving need to write down their own life experiences and a profound awareness of their difference from other women and from the role models offered by their society. All were born into a world devastated by repeated outbreaks of the plague, where food and labor were scarce, and death always nearby. Each felt a new kind of vocation; Julian of Norwich articulates a new vision of Christ, emphasizing his motherhood and his loving kindness; Margery invents a unique active vocation, pilgrim-mystic; Doña Leonor, stunned by the suffering she has witnessed since childhood, creates a devotional memoir to try to come to terms with her experience; Christine de Pizan becomes the first professional woman writer in France, taking up her pen in defense of women. She, like Margery, turned to the past for earlier models, identifying a community of women with similar courage and independence.

Late medieval England produced two unusual women mystics in Julian of Norwich (1343–1413) and Margery Kempe (1373–1439). Julian is far better known, more orthodox, and better educated.[1] She was a recluse[2] attached to the Church of St. Julian in Norwich although she may not yet have been enclosed when she had her first visions, or showings, in 1373 at the age of thirty; for she tells of her mother standing near her to close her eyes when she seemed to be dying. Although Julian makes the usual apologies for her lack of formal education, her work indicates that she was quite well read. Her book of revelations, *The Showings*, exists in two different redactions. The short text must have been written soon after her experience. Each vision included is described in careful sensual detail, and then brief comments are provided concerning the spiritual meaning. We learn from reading the long text that certain visions or narrative scenes were not included at first because they were not yet understood by Julian; it was only in 1388 that she finally reached an understanding of some of her early experiences and then developed them further as she wrote them down in 1393. In her commentaries on the meaning of each vision, she reveals much about her own questions about Christianity and shows us the process by which she worked through to an understanding of theological questions. She "reads" each vision as a kind of allegorical drama in which every detail of the imagery and the dialogue is significant—the color of clothing, the movements and gestures of the characters, the similes that occur to her as she observes her recollections, which sometimes take the form of static, hieratic images but more often are visualized as scenes dramatizing parables original with her. Her powers of observation are acute, and she draws on a wide variety of experience to illustrate her perceptions. For example, we may look at her summary of the details of a vision of Christ's head crowned with thorns:

> And during all the time that our Lord showed me this spiritual vision which I have now described, I saw the bodily vision of the copious bleeding of the head persist. The great drops of blood fell from beneath the crown like pellets, looking as if they came from the veins, and as they issued they were a brownish red, for the blood was very thick, and as they spread they turned bright red. And as they reached the brows they vanished; and even so the bleeding continued until I had seen and understood many things. Nevertheless, the beauty and the vivacity persisted, beautiful and vivid without any diminuition. . . . The drops were round like pellets as the blood issued, they were round like a herring's scales as they spread, they were like raindrops off a house's eaves, so many that they could not be counted.[3]

In her method of narrating a vision Julian is probably most similar to Hildegard of Bingen although she surpasses Hildegard in providing much more information concerning the process and development of her thought. She is probably best known to us for her teaching on the Motherhood of Christ. The idea was not completely new; it is found in the Greek fathers, and was explored in twelfth century writings on monastic spirituality. As Bynum summarizes

> In spiritual writers from Anselm to Julian, we find three basic stereotypes of the female or the mother: the female is generative (the foetus is made of her very matter) and sacrificial in her generation (birth pangs); the female is loving and tender (a mother cannot help loving her own child); the female is nurturing (she feeds the child with her own bodily fluid).[4]

Yet, Bynum adds, "the theme of God's motherhood is a minor one in all writers of the high Middle Ages except Julian of Norwich."[5] Motherhood is only one of the affective relationships epitomized in God, however. A passage from the middle of the long text will illustrate the complexity of Julian's thinking.

> For in the same time that God joined himself to our body in the maiden's womb, he took our soul, which is sensual, and in taking it, having enclosed us all in himself, he united it to our substance. In this union he was perfect man, for Christ, having joined in himself every man who will be saved, is perfect man.
>
> So our Lady is our mother, in whom we are all enclosed and born of her in Christ, for she who is mother of our saviour is mother of all who are saved in our saviour; and our saviour is our true Mother, in whom we are endlessly born and out of whom we shall never come.[6]

Julian was widely sought out as a spiritual counselor and teacher. Margery Kempe of Lynne,[7] thirty years younger, visited her when she sought validation for her own vocation; and her account of their meeting, brief as it is, gives us a good idea of the kind of guidance Julian provided. Margery was bidden by God to go to Julian and to reveal to her all her experiences of God: "compunction, contrition, sweetness and devotion, compassion with holy meditation and high contemplation, and full many holy speeches and dalliance that Our Lord spoke to her soul."[8] This she does, "to find out if there were any deceit in them, for the anchoress was expert in such things and could give good counsel."[9] Julian gives more than is asked.

> Said she: "The Holy Ghost never moves contrary to charity, for if he did, he would be contrary to his own self for he is all charity. Also he moves a soul to all chasteness, for chaste livers are called the temple of the Holy Ghost, and the Holy Ghost makes a soul stable and steadfast in the right faith, and the right belief. . . . Any creature that has these tokens may steadfastly believe that the Holy Ghost dwells in his soul. And much more when God visits a creature with tears of contrition, devotion, and compassion, he may and ought to believe that the Holy Ghost is in his soul . . . I pray God grant you perseverance. Set all your trust in God and fear not the language of the world, for the more despite, shame, and reproof that you have in the world, the more is your merit in the sight of God. Patience is necessary to you, for in that you shall keep your soul."[10]

This confirmation that Margery's emotional outbursts were not against the Spirit, as her enemies would have it, but a sign of the indwelling of the Holy Spirit was the comfort that Margery needed, voiced by an authority that Margery's world was compelled to acknowledge.

Margery Kempe was the daughter of the four-times mayor of Lynne and married at twenty to John Kempe. In order to tell her story, she invented the first autobiography in English just as in her life she invented a new religious role, a blend of personal asceticism, public apostolate, and pilgrimage. Shortly after her book was discovered, an enthusiastic reviewer commented, in a 1937 journal article:

> She trod the roads of England, south, east, and west, travelled in heavy wains and occasionally rode on donkey back. From her native Lynn in Norfolk she goes north to York; Norwich and Lincoln and Leicester flit by in the course of her narrative; she sits with the Primate in his garden at Lambeth discoursing on heavenly things till the stars come out over their heads; she goes down to Sheen Charterhouse to gain the Portiuncula Pardon, lodges in a German hostelry at Canterbury, takes shipping at Yarmouth and Ipswich for the Continent and lands at Dover on her way home. From Zierickzee she wanders across North Germany as far as Dantzig and Stralsund; Venice, Bologna, Assisi and Rome knew her presence, and she gained the Holy Land as well as Compostella, reached from Bristol after a week's sail.[11]

This passage captures one of the two essential qualities of Margery's presentation of self: movement. Her vocation is an active one, and she is constantly in motion. She and her husband are walking through a field when they finally come to an agreement about celibacy; when she meditates on the infancy of Christ and the flight into Egypt, she bustles about fetching things for Mary and Joseph, begging for food for them. During her difficult times, however, motion is denied her; her milling business fails because the horses won't move, and after her first child is born, she seems so mad that she is tied up.

The other motif in self-presentation is her crying, and this, too, is a very active process for her. She first acquires her tears during her pilgrimage to the Holy Land; they come to her in violent seizures that she has no power to resist, and they are mightily disruptive to those around her. The world and her fellow pilgrims won't let her preach (in fact, they forbid her to speak and then abandon her), but through her identification with Christ, the suffering Christ, she cries. Her tears are an expression of an ancient female role, that of mourner for the dead; they are her own personal "imitatio Christi," and they remind others of Christ's Passion. Through her tears she identifies with other women mystics of the past, particularly Marie d'Oignies. The extent of Margery's martyrdom can be measured by the number of times she reports being told to shut up—yet she was a gifted storyteller and well able to use words to protect herself as her demeanor, when she is accused of heresy, proves.

Mary G. Mason, in summarizing differences and similarities between Julian of Norwich and Margery Kempe, suggests that their deepest level of commonality is that their identities are determined by their relation to the divine.

> Both Julian and Margery Kempe, writing in the mystical tradition of personal dialogue with a divine being who is Creator, Father, and Lover, discover and reveal themselves in discovering and revealing the Other. Speaking in the first person with a singleness of vision that allows for no distractions or ambivalence, Julian establishes an identification with the suffering Christ on the cross that is absolute, yet . . . Julian is in no way obliterated as a person.
>
> Margery . . . speaks in the third person . . . to a Christ who, when he is not her infant, is her manly bridegroom. Unlike Julian's single-visioned *Revelations*, *The Book of Margery Kempe* displays a dual sense of vocation: the wife-mother, pilgrim-mystic roles . . . both of which, however, are ultimately determined by their relation to the divine.[12]

Doña Leonor López de Córdoba[13] was about a decade older than Margery Kempe, born about 1362; she died around 1412, but her autobiography, *Las Memorias* (Memories or Reminiscences) only takes her life up to about 1390.[14] Doña Leonor was a noblewoman of the Spanish kingdom of Castille. Her mother, niece of King Alfonso XI, died before Leonor was old enough to remember her; perhaps because of this, Leonor was married very early, at age seven, to Ruy Gutierrez de Henestrosa. He was also of very noble lineage, so rich that he possessed, among other things, "forty strings of pearls as fat as chickpeas."

Perhaps within a year of this child-marriage, Leonor's father, as a loyal supporter of King Pedro, was publicly beheaded in Seville after a successful coup by Pedro's illegitimate half brother Enrique. Leonor, her husband, her brother, sisters, and brothers-in-law were all imprisoned. The imprisonment finally ended in 1379, when King Enrique died, but meanwhile plague had swept through the prison, killing all but Leonor and her husband. After their release, Leonor and her husband separated; she went to live with her maternal aunt in Córdoba, and her husband Ruy began the attempt to recover his estate. When he realized his wealth was irretrievably lost, he "disappeared, and walked for seven years through the world, a wretch." Just as Leonor, believing herself abandoned, tried to enter a convent, Ruy returned, and they moved into a house next door to her aunt, miserably poor and ashamed around other members of the nobility.

Leonor does not give many details of her life until the next tragedy struck. There was another epidemic of the plague, and to escape it she moved from Córdoba to Aguilar. There she adopted a young boy, either a Moor or a Jew. In her mind this adoption is connected to a dream she had of an arch through which she entered a garden, where she gathered flowers. She had dreamed that she saw this arch on a particular plot of land, which she was determined to buy; there she planned to build a home for herself and a chapel dedicated to King Alfonso. "It was because of the charity I performed in raising the orphan in the faith of Jesus Christ that God helped me by giving me that beginning of a house."

But flight from this place of refuge was necessary because of the plague, and her adopted son, whom she had sent to Ezija, caught up with her in Aguilar, very obviously a victim of the plague: "with two small tumors in his throat and three carbuncles on his face, and with a high fever." Leonor kept trying to find people who could take care of the dying child, and "through my sins, thirteen persons who watched over him by night all died." The worst of it was that her biological son also died.

> My son, who was called Juan Fernandez de Henestrosa like his grandfather, and who was twelve years and four months old, came to me and he said to me, "Lady, is there no one to watch over Alonso tonight?" And I told him, "You watch over him, for the love of God." He replied to me, "Lady, now that the others have all died, do you want to kill me?" And I said to him, "For my charity, God will take pity on me." And my son, so as not to disobey me, went to keep vigil. Through my sins, that night he was given the pestilence, and another day I buried him. The sick one lived after all the others had died.[15]

Doña Leonor ends her narrative with her feelings of shame and guilt at these deaths. Personally she seems to have experienced a crisis of faith, which the autobiography may have been an attempt to resolve. Publicly, she was cast out by her aunt, evidently because she seemed fated to bring so much suffering with her; the people in the streets commiserate with her, but it is a humiliating kind of pity, for they cry, "See the most unfortunate, forsaken, and accursed woman in the world." Doña Leonor's *Memorias* express the guilt of a survivor and illustrate the spiritual disorientation of someone who has lived through a kind of holocaust.

Christine de Pizan was born in 1364, nine years before Margery Kempe and two years after Doña Leonor.[16] At first glance it would seem that Christine de Pizan could have little in common with Margery or with Julian of Norwich except for the coincidence of chronology. In fact, Christine seems unlike most other women of her time. Born in Italy of a Venetian mother and a Bolognese father, she came to France with her mother when she was about four to rejoin her father, who was court astrologer for Charles V. This position of privilege and security did not last; she was married at fifteen to Etienne de Castel, whom she greatly loved and with whom she had two children, but then tragedy struck. Her father died when she was twenty, and then her husband died of the plague when she was twenty-five. She was the head of a family that included her mother and three small children; her father's and husband's financial affairs were in disarray, and the family was being cheated by creditors, and Christine had to pull it all together if the little group were to survive. She did pull it together, supporting herself by writing. She became France's first professional woman author, and used her writing to defend the status of women. Her breadth of lived experience and her education (she was self-taught after her widowhood, but she had access to a remarkably wide range of books) were unusual for a woman of the late fourteenth century. Her only real peers may have been in the past: Hrotsvit or Hildegard of Bingen or Heloise, not in her own time.

> Her female contemporaries, for example, Margery Kempe and Julian of Norwich, were primarily religious mystics and visionaries: they experienced nowhere near the breadth of events influencing Christine. Other impressive women of that period were mostly business women and enlightened noble-women—not self-supporting writers. . . . What is special about her is that she, in a single lifetime, not only encompasses the different trends of her time but also manages to articulate them as no male author has. It would seem that she uses the circumstances of her oppression, converting them into sources of a privileged viewpoint. This aspect also forms part of her feminine voice.[17]

It seems to have taken Christine about ten years to come into her own as a writer, and over the next six years she produced a remarkable series of writings defending, protecting, inspiring, and educating women. In 1399 she wrote *L'Epistre au Dieu d'Amours*, which initiated the debate over the *Roman de la Rose*. This poem, begun a century and a half earlier by Guillaume de Lorris and completed around 1305 by Jean de Meun, is an elaborate courtly allegory that depicts a young man falling hopelessly in love with a rose (the part written by Guillaume) and then planning and carrying out his successful capture of her favors. "The purpose of both Ovid and Jean de Meun, she argues, is to effect on aristocratic maidens what the knights did by rape or fast talk with peasant girls."[18] This is bad enough, but what is worse in Christine's eyes are the long antifeminist digressions, particularly those spoken by the Jealous Husband.

> Whether Jean de Meun really intended his poem to be read as an art of seduction is not so important as the fact that Christine felt he was doing so, and that she as a Christian and as a woman ought to do something about it. . . . To blame all the faults of the world, especially those connected with love, on women, as the Jealous Husband does . . . is a comfortable masculine prerogative, made credible by masculine control of literature.[19]

The debate continued in the *Epistres du débat sur le Roman de la Rose* (1401–03), the first of Christine's prose works. The translation included here, a letter to Jean de Montreuil condemning the *Roman* and its readers, is from that collection. In April 1400, Christine wrote *Le Livre du dit de Poissy* after her visit to her daughter in the Dominican convent of Saint-Louis in Poissy. This was followed by three major works around 1405, *Le Livre de la Cité des Dames* (*The City of Ladies*), *Lavision Christine*, and *Le Livre des Trois Vertus* (*The Book of the Three Virtues*). Thanks to the recent translation by Richards,[20] *City of Ladies* is now easily available to modern readers, and it is unnecessary to go into detail here except to underscore two aspects of the book that link it closely to the other works by women writers in this anthology. Those two aspects are Christine's didactic purpose and her understanding of women's conflicts over writing. Her didactic purpose is well expressed by Marina Warner as follows:

> she is casting herself as a moral tutor, rather than a poet; she is writing to instruct us, to shape our thinking and so incline us to right-thinking and right-doing. When she pleads for education for women, she gives as her reason education's close correlation with good conduct.[21]

This is a humanist aim but one that allows for continuity and expansion of women's education; Christine is advocating not a break with the past for women but a truer continuity, based on what women have done and can do, "demonstrating women's intellect, courage and moral virtue."[22]

Her understanding of women's conflicts over writing is best illustrated in the opening to *City of Ladies*. The persona of Christine has been reading an antifeminist tract by one Matheolus, which makes her question if such a consistent body of male opinion about women could possibly be incorrect. Her own intuition and experience tell her these slanders are not true, but doubt remains:

> Although my intellect did not perceive my own great faults and, likewise, those of other women because of its simpleness and ignorance, it was however truly fitting that such was the case. And so I relied more on the judgment of others than on what I myself felt and knew. I was so transfixed in this line of thinking such a long time that it seemed as if I were in a stupor. Like a gushing fountain, a series of authorities, whom I recalled one after another, came to mind, along with their opinions on this topic. And I finally decided that God formed a vile creature when he made woman. . . . As I was thinking this, a great unhappiness and sadness welled up in my heart, for I detested myself and the entire feminine sex, as though we were monstrosities in nature.[23]

In response to this despair, Lady Reason appears, called into existence by Christine's determination to think through this dilemma. Together Christine and Lady Reason build the foundations for the city:

> First they dig out all the ugly distorted rocks, which represent antifeminist writers. Then they build a strong outer wall, using the biographical "material" of women who excelled in government, war, learning and the arts.[24]

It is exactly this kind of digging up that engages Christine in the *Roman de la Rose* debate, and it is on this foundation that she can build her next works. This is not to say that she issued from these public debates unscathed. In fact, the notoriety she attained taught her all too well the need for self-defence: although the insults directed toward her "appear to have scarred her self-image, they nevertheless hardened her resolve to write in defense of her sex and of the poor."[25]

Commentators on Christine de Pizan have often noted that her feminism did not extend to recommending scholarly pursuits for other women. Bell has suggested two possible reasons for this reluctance to use her own life as an explicit model for learning. First, Christine values what women are already contributing to society; because of the military and political situation of her day, "more and more women were entirely in charge of their household, defenses, and production in the absence of their male relatives."[26] The other reason is that her personal position in society is isolated and lonely. She is set apart by the loss of her husband and father, by her nationality, by her nonaristocratic status, by the fact that she is paid for her work. She is a woman doing a man's work, estranged from "the essential female network of her society."[27] In her writings she can create the ideal female community in which women such as herself would not feel alienated, and this ideal community has much in common with the monastic life as she observed it at Poissy and with the convents and beguinages of the Middle Ages. The City of Ladies, when it is completed, has farseeing high towers and defensive battlements; the Virgin Mary is its queen, and piety and chastity ("the most sovereign virtue" of women) reach fruition there.[28]

NOTES

1. The modern English translation is *Julian of Norwich Showings*, translated and edited by Edmund Colledge and James Walsh (New York: Paulist Press, 1978). The short text is on pp. 123–72; the long text is on pp. 173–348. The original Middle English text is *A Book of Showings to the Anchoress Julian of Norwich*, ed. Edmund Colledge and James Walsh (Toronto: Pontifical Institute of Medieval Studies, 1978). See also Paul Molinari, *Julian of Norwich* (London: Longmans, Green, 1958).

2. The recluse tradition seems to have been particularly vital in England during the Middle Ages; see Rotha Mary Clay, *The Hermits and Anchorites of England* (Detroit: Singing Tree Press, 1968; first published 1914). The medieval guide to the anchoress' life is *The Ancrene Riwle*, trans. and ed. M. B. Salu (London: 1955).

3. Julian, *Showings*, long text, pp. 187–88.

4. Caroline Bynum, *Jesus as Mother* (Berkeley and Los Angeles: Univ. of California Press, 1982), p. 131.

5. Bynum, *Jesus as Mother*, p. 168.

6. Julian, *Showings*, long text, p. 292.

7. The original text of Margery Kempe's book is *The Book of Margery Kempe*, ed. Sanford Brown Meech and Hope Emily Allen (Oxford: Oxford University Press, 1940, 1961), for the Early English Text Society, Orig. Ser. vol. 212. The owner of the manuscript published a modernized version shortly after the manuscript was identified: *The Book of Margery Kempe*, trans. W. Butler-Bowden (New York: Devin-Adair, 1944). Studies of Margery Kempe include Clarissa W. Atkinson, *Mystic and Pilgrim: The Book and the World of Margery Kempe* (Ithaca: Cornell University Press, 1983); Claire Cross, "Great Reasoners in Scripture: The Activities of Women Lollards 1380–1520," in *Medieval Women*, ed. Derek Baker (Oxford: Basil Blackwell, 1978), pp. 359–80; Susan Dickman, "Margery Kempe and the English Devotional

Tradition," in *The Medieval Mystical Tradition in England*, ed. Marion Glasscoe, pp. 156–72 (Exeter: University of Exeter, 1980); Anthony Goodman, "The Piety of John Brunham's Daughter, of Lynn" in *Medieval Women*, ed. Baker, pp. 347–358, Mary G. Mason, "The Other Voice: Autobiographies of Women Writers," in James Olney, ed. *Autobiography: Essays Theoretical and Critical* (Princeton: Princeton University Press, 1980), pp. 207–35; Louise Collis, *Memoirs of a Medieval Woman: The Life and Times of Margery Kempe* (New York: Harper & Row, 1983; first published 1964).

8. "Dame Julian of Norwich and Margery Kempe," in *Women and Religion, A Feminist Sourcebook of Christian Thought*, ed. Elizabeth Clark and Herbert Richardson (New York: Harper & Row, 1977), p. 112.

9. "Dame Julian . . .," p. 112.

10. "Dame Julian . . ." pp. 112–13.

11. Henry Chester Mann, "Margery Kempe," in *Pax* (February 1937), pp. 257–60 and 276–79. This is from pp. 257–8.

12. Mary G. Mason, "The Other Voice," in James Olney, ed., *Autobiography: Essays Theoretical and Critical* (Princeton, N.J.: Princeton University Press, 1980), pp. 207–35. This passage is from pp. 210–11.

13. Reinaldo Ayerbe-Chaux, "Las Memorias de Doña Leonor López de Córdoba," in *Journal of Hispanic Philology* 2 (February 1977–78), pp. 11–33.

14. See Joseph F. O'Callaghan, *A History of Medieval Spain* (Ithaca, N.Y.: Cornell University Press, 1975), pp. 410, 414, 419–27, 523–26; Manuel Serrano y Sanz, *Apuntes para una biblioteca de escritores españolas*, II (Madrid: Atlas, 1975; reprint of 1903 ed; volumes 268–71 of Biblioteca de autores españoles), pp. 16–18; and Ramon Menendez Pidal, *Crestomatia del español medieval* (Madrid: Gredos, 1966), p. 522.

15. "Las Memorias de Doña Leonor López de Córdoba," p. 24, trans. Kathleen Lacey.

16. There is much recent scholarship on Christine de Pizan. For biographical details, see Suzanne Solente, "Christine de Pizan," *Histoire littéraire de la France* 40 (1974), pp. 335–422. Among articles by Charity Cannon Willard are "The Manuscript Tradition of the *Livre des Trois Vertus* and Christine de Pizan's Audience," *Journal of the History of Ideas* 27 (1966), pp. 433–44, and "A Fifteenth Century View of Women's Role in Medieval Society: Christine de Pizan's *Livre des Trois Vertus*," in *The Role of Women in the Middle Ages*, ed. Rosmarie Thee Morewedge; see also Astrik L. Gabriel, "The Educational Ideas of Christine de Pizan" in *Journal of the History of Ideas* 16:1 (January 1955), pp. 3–21. Charity Cannon Willard, *Christine de Pizan: Her Life and Works* (New York: Persea Press, 1985) provides the best introduction and overview of Christine's importance.

17. Nadia Margolis, Introduction to an unpublished study on Christine de Pizan as a French Humanist.

18. F. Douglas Kelly, "Reflections on the Role of Christine de Pizan as a Feminist Writer," *Sub-stance* 2 (1972), pp. 63–71. This is on p. 67.

19. Kelly, "Reflections," pp. 68, 70.

20. *The Book of the City of Ladies, Christine de Pizan*, trans. Earl Jeffrey Richards, foreword by Marina Warner (New York: Persea Books, 1982).

21. Marina Warner, foreword to *City of Ladies*, p. xv.

22. Susan Groag Bell, "Christine de Pizan (1364–1430): Humanism and the Problem of the Studious Woman," in *Feminist Studies* 3: 3–4 (Spring–Summer 1976), pp. 173–84. This is on p. 176.

23. *City of Ladies*, trans. Richards, pp. 4–5.

24. Diane Bornstein, ed., *Distaves and Dames: Renaissance Treatises For and About Women* (Delmar, N.Y.: Scholar's Facsimilies and Reprints, 1978). This is from the Introduction, p. xv.

25. Margolis, conclusion to the unpublished manuscript cited in note 16.

26. Susan Groag Bell, "Christine de Pizan," p. 180.

27. Bell, "Christine de Pizan," p. 181.

28. Jill Freeland first pointed out to me the connections between Christine's description of Poissy, the City of Ladies, and medieval women's communities.

JULIAN OF NORWICH   (1343–1413; England)

Showings (Long Text)

Translated by Edmund Colledge and James Walsh

The Fifty-first Chapter

And then our courteous Lord answered very mysteriously, by revealing a wonderful example[1] of a lord who has a servant, and gave me sight for the understanding of them both. The vision was shown doubly with respect to the lord, and the vision was shown doubly with respect to the servant. One part was shown spiritually, in a bodily likeness. The other part was shown more spiritually, without bodily likeness. So, for the first, I saw two persons in bodily likeness, that is to say a lord and a servant; and with that God gave me spiritual understanding. The lord sits in state, in rest and in peace. The servant stands before his lord, respectfully, ready to do his lord's will. The lord looks on his servant very lovingly and sweetly and mildly. He sends him to a certain place to do his will. Not only does the servant go, but he dashes off and runs at great speed, loving to do his lord's will. And soon he falls into a dell and is greatly injured; and then he groans and moans and tosses about and writhes, but he cannot rise or help himself in any way. And of all this, the greatest hurt which I saw him in was lack of consolation, for he could not turn his face to look on his loving lord, who was very close to him, in whom is all consolation; but like a man who was for the time extremely feeble and foolish, he paid heed to his feelings and his continuing distress, in which distress he suffered seven great pains. The first was the severe bruising which he took in his fall, which gave him great pain.

The second was the clumsiness of his body. The third was the weakness which followed these two. The fourth was that he was blinded in his reason and perplexed in his mind, so much so that he had almost forgotten his own love. The fifth was that he could not rise. The sixth was the pain most astonishing to me, and that was that he lay alone. I looked all around and searched, and far and near, high and low, I saw no help for him. The seventh was that the place in which he lay was narrow and comfortless and distressful.

I was amazed that this servant could so meekly suffer all this woe; and I looked carefully to know if I could detect any fault in him, or if the lord would impute to him any kind of blame; and truly none was seen, for the only cause of his falling was his good will and his great desire. And in spirit he was as prompt and as good as he was when he stood before his lord, ready to do his will.

And all this time his loving lord looks on him most tenderly, and now with a double aspect, one outward, very meekly and mildly, with great compassion and pity, and this belonged to the first part; the other was inward, more spiritual, and this was shown with a direction of my understanding towards the lord, and I was brought again[2] to see how greatly he rejoiced over the honourable rest and nobility which by his plentiful grace he wishes for his servant and will bring him to. And this belonged to the second vision.[3] And now my understanding was led back to the first, keeping both in mind.

Then this courteous lord said this: See my beloved servant, what harm and injuries he has had and accepted in my service for my love, yes, and for his good will. Is it not reasonable that I should reward him for his fright and his fear, his hurt and his injuries and all his woe? And furthermore, is it not proper for me to give him a gift, better for him and more honourable than his own health could have been? Otherwise, it seems to me that I should be ungracious.

And in this an inward spiritual revelation of the lord's meaning descended into my soul, in which I saw that this must necessarily be the case, that his great goodness and his own honour require that his beloved servant, whom he loved so much, should be highly and blessedly rewarded forever, above what he would have been if he had not fallen, yes, and so much that his falling and all the woe that he received from it will be turned into high, surpassing honour and endless bliss.

And at this point the example which had been shown vanished, and our good Lord led my understanding on to the end of what was to be seen and shown in the revelation. But despite this leading on, the wonder of the example never left me, for it seemed to me that it had been given as an answer to my petition. And yet at that time I could not understand it fully or be comforted. For in the servant, who was shown for Adam, as I shall say, I saw many different characteristics which could in no way be attributed to Adam, that one man; and so at that time I relied greatly on three insights, for the complete understanding of that wonderful example was not at that time given to me. The secrets of the revelation were deeply hidden in this mysterious example; and despite this I saw and understood that every showing is full of secrets. And therefore I must now tell of three attributes through which I have been somewhat consoled.

The first is the beginning of the teaching which I understood from it at the time. The second is the inward instruction which I have understood from it since. The third is all the whole revelation from the beginning to the end, which our Lord God of his goodness freely and often brings before the eyes of my understanding. And these three are so unified, as I understand it, that I cannot and may not separate them. And by these three as one I have instruction by which I ought to believe and trust that our Lord God, that out of the same goodness and for the same purpose as he revealed it, by the same goodness and for the same purpose will make it clear to us when it is his will.

For twenty years after the time of the revelation except for three months, I received an inward instruction, and it was this: You ought to take heed to all the attributes, divine and human,[4] which were revealed in the example, though this may seem to you mysterious and ambiguous. I willingly agreed with a great desire, seeing inwardly with great care all the details and the characteristics which were at that time revealed, so far as my intelligence and understanding will serve, beginning with when I looked at the lord and the servant, at how the lord was sitting and the place where he sat, and the colour of his clothing and how it was made, and his outward appearance and his inward nobility and goodness; and the demeanour of the servant as he stood, and the place where and how, and his fashion of clothing, the colour and the shape, his outward behaviour and his inward goodness and willingness. I understood that the lord who sat in state in rest and peace is God. I understood that the servant who stood before him was shown for Adam, that is to say, one man was shown at that time and his fall, so as to make it understood how God regards all men and their falling. For in the sight of God all men are one man, and one man is all men. This man was injured in his powers and made most feeble, and in his understanding he was amazed, because he was diverted from looking on his lord, but his will was preserved in God's sight. I saw the lord[5] commend and approve him for his will, but he himself was blinded and hindered from knowing this will. And this is a great sorrow and a cruel suffering to him, for he neither sees clearly his loving lord, who is so meek and mild to him, nor does he truly see what he himself is in the sight of his loving lord. And I know well that when these two things are wisely and truly seen, we shall gain rest and peace, here in part and the fulness in the bliss of heaven, by God's plentiful grace.

And this was a beginning of the teaching which I saw at the same time, whereby I might come to know in what manner he looks on us in our sin. And then I saw that only pain blames and punishes, and our courteous Lord comforts and succours, and always he is kindly disposed to the soul, loving and longing to bring us to his bliss.

The place which the lord sat on was unadorned, on the ground, barren and waste, alone in the wilderness. His clothing was wide and ample and very handsome, as befits a lord. The colour of the clothing was azure blue, most dignified and beautiful. His demeanour was merciful, his face was a lovely pale brown with a very seemly countenance, his eyes were black, most beautiful and seemly, revealing all his loving pity, and within him there was a secure[6] place of refuge, long and broad, all full of endless heavenliness. And the loving regard which he kept constantly on his servant, and especially when he fell, it seemed to me that it could melt our hearts for love and break them in two for joy. This lovely regard had in it a beautiful mingling which was wonderful to see. Part was compassion and pity, part was joy and bliss. The joy and bliss surpass the compassion and pity, as far as heaven is above earth. The pity was earthly and the bliss was heavenly.

The compassion and the pity of the Father were for Adam, who is his most beloved creature. The joy and the bliss were for the falling of his dearly beloved Son, who is equal with the Father. The merciful regard of his lovely countenance filled all the earth, and went down with Adam into hell, and by this continuing pity Adam was kept from endless death. And this mercy and pity abides with mankind until the time that we come up to heaven. But man is blinded in this life, and therefore we cannot see our Father, God, as he is. And when he of his goodness wishes to show himself to man, he shows himself familiar, like a man, even though I saw truly that we ought to know and believe that the Father is not man. But his sitting on the ground, barren and waste, signifies this: He made man's soul to be his own city and his dwelling place, which is the most pleasing to him of all his works. And when man had fallen into sorrow and pain, he was not wholly proper to serve in that noble office, and therefore our kind Father did not wish to prepare any other place, but sat upon the ground, awaiting human nature, which is mixed with earth, until the time when by his grace his beloved Son had brought back his city into its noble place of beauty by his hard labour.

The blueness of the clothing signifies his steadfastness; the brownness of his fair face with the lovely blackness of the eyes was most suitable to indicate his holy solemnity; the amplitude, billowing[7] splendidly all about him, signifies that he has enclosed within himself all heavens and all endless joy and bliss; and this was shown in a brief moment, when I perceived that my understanding was directed to the lord. In this I saw him greatly rejoice over the honourable restoration to which he wants to bring and will bring his servant by his great and plentiful grace. And still I was amazed, contemplating the lord and the servant as I have said.

I saw the lord sitting in state, and the

servant standing respectfully before his lord, and in this servant there is a double significance, one outward, the other inward. Outwardly he was simply dressed like a labourer prepared to work, and he stood very close to the lord, not immediately in front of him but a little to one side, and that on the left; his clothing was a white tunic, scanty, old and all worn, dyed with the sweat of his body, tight fitting and short, as it were a hand's breadth below his knee, looking threadbare as if it would soon be worn out, ready to go to rags and to tear. And in this I was much amazed, thinking: This is not fitting clothing for a servant so greatly loved to stand in before so honourable a lord. And, inwardly, there was shown in him a foundation of love, the love which he had for the lord, which was equal to the love which the lord had for him. The wisdom of the servant saw inwardly that there was one thing to do which would pay honour to the lord; and the servant, for love, having no regard for himself or for anything which might happen to him, went off in great haste and ran when his lord sent him, to do the thing which was his will and to his honour; for it seemed by his outer garment as if he had been a constant labourer and a hard traveller[8] for a long time. And by the inward perception which I had of both the lord and the servant, it seemed that he was newly appointed, that is to say just beginning to labour, and that this servant had never been sent out before.

There was a treasure in the earth which the lord loved. I was astonished, and considered what it could be; and I was answered in my understanding: It is a food which is delicious and pleasing to the lord. For I saw the lord sitting like a man, and I saw neither food nor drink with which to serve him. This was one astonishment; another astonishment was that this stately lord had only one servant, and him he sent out. I watched, wondering what kind of labour it could be that the servant was to do. And then I understood that he was to do the greatest labour and the hardest work there is. He was to be a gardener, digging and ditching and sweating and turning the soil over and over, and to dig deep down, and to water the plants at the proper time. And he was to persevere in his work, and make sweet streams to run, and fine and plenteous[9] fruit to grow, which he was to bring before the lord and serve him with to his liking. And he was never to come back again until he had made all this food ready as he knew was pleasing to the lord; and then he was to take this food, and drink, and carry it most reverently before the lord. And all this time the lord was to sit in exactly the same place, waiting for the servant whom he had sent out.

And still I wondered where the servant came from, for I saw in the lord that he has in himself endless life and every kind of goodness, except for the treasure which was in the earth, and that was founded in the lord in a marvellous depth of endless love. But it was not wholly to his honour until his servant had prepared it so finely and carried it before him into the lord's own presence. And except for the lord, there was nothing at all but wilderness; and I did not understand everything which this example meant. And therefore I wondered where the servant came from.

In the servant is comprehended[10] the second person of the Trinity, and in the servant is comprehended Adam, that is to say all men. And therefore when I say "the Son," that means the divinity which is equal to the Father, and when I say "the servant," that means Christ's humanity, which is the true Adam. By the closeness of the servant is understood the Son, and by his standing to the left is understood Adam. The lord is God the Father, the servant is the Son, Jesus Christ, the Holy Spirit is the equal love which is in them both. When Adam fell, God's Son fell; because of the true union which was made in heaven, God's Son could not be separated from Adam, for by Adam I understand all mankind. Adam fell from life to death, into the valley of this wretched world, and after that into hell. God's Son fell with Adam, into the valley of the womb of the maiden who was the fairest daughter of Adam, and that was to excuse Adam from blame in heaven and on earth; and powerfully he brought him out of hell. By the wisdom and the goodness which were in the servant is understood God's Son, by the poor labourer's clothing and the standing close by on the left is understood Adam's humanity with all the harm and weakness which follow. For in all this our good Lord showed his own Son and Adam as only one man. The strength and the goodness that we have is from Jesus Christ, the weakness and blindness that we have is from Adam, which two were shown in the servant.

And so has our good Lord Jesus taken upon him all our blame; and therefore our Father may not, does not wish to assign more blame to us than to his own beloved Son Jesus Christ. So he was the servant before he came on earth, standing ready in purpose before the Father until the time when he would send him to do the glorious deed by which mankind was brought back to heaven. That is to say, even though he is God, equal with the Father as regards his divinity, but with his prescient purpose that he would become man to save mankind in fulfillment of the will of his Father, so he stood before his Father as a servant, willingly taking upon him all our charge.[11] And then he rushed off very readily at the Father's bidding, and soon he fell very low into the maiden's womb, having no regard for himself or for his cruel pains.

This white tunic is his flesh, the scantiness signifies that there was nothing at all separating the divinity from the humanity. The tight fit is poverty, the age is Adam's wearing, the wornness is the sweat of Adam's labour, the shortness shows the servant-labourer.

And so I saw the Son stand, saying in intention: See, my dear Father, I stand before you in Adam's tunic, all ready to hasten and run. I wish to be on earth to your glory, when it is your will to send me. How long shall I desire it? Very truly the Son knew when was the Father's will, and how long he would desire it, that is to say as regard his divinity, for he is the wisdom of the Father. Therefore this meaning was shown for understanding of Christ's humanity. For all mankind which will be saved by the sweet Incarnation and the Passion of Christ, all is Christ's humanity, for he is the head, and we are his members, to which members the day and the time are unknown when every passing woe and sorrow will have an end, and everlasting joy and bliss will be fulfilled, which day and time all the company of heaven longs and[12] desires to see. And all who are under heaven and will come there, their way is by longing and desiring, which desiring and longing was shown in the servant standing before the lord, or, otherwise, in the Son standing before the Father in Adam's tunic. For the longing and desire of all mankind which will be saved appeared in Jesus, for Jesus is in all who will be saved, and all who will be saved[13] are in Jesus, and all is of the love of God, with obedience, meekness and patience, and the virtues which befit us.

Also in this marvellous example I have teaching within me, as it were the beginning of an ABC, whereby I may have some understanding of our Lord's meaning, for the mysteries of the revelation are hidden in it, even though all the showings are full of mysteries.

The sitting of the Father symbolizes the divinity, that is to say to reveal rest and peace, for in the divinity there can be no labour; and that he shows himself as a lord symbolizes our humanity. The standing of the servant symbolizes labour, and that he stands to the left symbolizes that he was not fully worthy to stand immediately in front of the lord. His rushing away was the divinity, and his running was the humanity; for the divinity rushed from the Father into the maiden's womb, falling to accept our nature, and in this falling he took great hurt. The hurt that he took was our flesh, in which at once he experienced mortal pains. That he stood fearfully before the lord and not immediately in front symbolizes that his clothing was not seemly for him to stand in immediately in front of the lord, nor could nor should that be his office whilst he was a labourer; nor, further, might he sit with the lord in rest and peace until he had duly won his peace with his hard labour; and that he stood to the left symbolizes that the Father by his will permitted his own Son in human nature to suffer all man's pain without sparing him. By his tunic being ready to go to rags and to tear is understood the rods and the scourges, the thorns and the nails, the pulling and the dragging and the tearing of his tender flesh, of which I had seen a part. The flesh was torn from the skull, falling in pieces until when the bleeding stopped; and then it began to dry again, adhering to the bone. And by the tossing and writhing, the groaning and moaning, is understood that he could never with almighty power rise from the time that he fell into the maiden's womb until his body was slain and dead, and he had yielded his soul into the Father's hand, with all mankind for whom he had been sent.

And at this moment he first began to show his power, for then he went down into hell; and when he was there, he raised up the great root out of the deep depth,[14] which rightly was joined to him in heaven. The body lay in the grave until Easter[15] morning; and from that time it never lay again. For then the tossing about and writhing, the groaning and the moaning[16] ended, rightly; and our foul mortal flesh, which God's Son took upon him, which was Adam's old tunic, tight-fitting, threadbare and short, was then made lovely by our saviour, new, white and bright and forever clean, wide and ample, fairer[17] and richer than the clothing which I saw on the Father. For that clothing was blue, and Christ's clothing is now of a fair and seemly mixture, which is so marvellous that I cannot describe it, for it is all of true glory.

Now the lord does not sit on the ground in the wilderness, but in his rich and noblest[18] seat, which he made in heaven most to his liking. Now the Son does not stand before the Father as a servant before the lord, pitifully clothed, partly naked, but he stands immediately before the Father, richly clothed in joyful amplitude, with a rich and precious crown upon his head. For it was revealed that we are his crown,[19] which crown is the Father's joy, the Son's honour, the Holy Spirit's delight, and endless marvellous bliss to all who are in heaven.

Now the Son does not stand before the Father on the left like a labourer, but he sits at the Father's right hand in endless rest and peace. But this does not mean that the Son sits on the right hand side as one man sits beside another in this life, for there is no such sitting, as I see it, in the Trinity; but he sits at his Father's right hand, that is to say right in the highest nobility of the Father's joy. Now the spouse, God's son, is at peace with his beloved wife, who is the fair maiden of endless joy. Now the Son, true God and true man, sits in his city in rest and in peace, which his Father has prepared for him by his endless purpose, and the Father in the Son, and the Holy Spirit in the Father and in the Son.

NOTES

1. That is, an illustrative story or parable such as a preacher might use.
2. This perhaps refers to Revelation IX, Chapter 22 where Julian describes how her understanding was lifted up into heaven. On this difficult passage (which defeated the 55 scribes) see *Showings*, II, 517 note 42.
3. That is, the second "part" of it.
4. Literally, "to all the properties and the conditions;" see *Showings*, II, 520 and note 88.
5. "Our Lord," that is, God the Father.

6. Literally, "high."

7. "Flammyng" (P), "flaming" (C), "flamand" (SS); the word might also mean "shining," or all the readings may be corrupt.

8. On the double entendre here, see *Showings*, II, 529 note 182.

9. So SS; P, C: "fine plentiousness."

10. Julian appears to use "comprehend" in the same ambiguous sense which is found in John 1.5, to suggest both "include, surround" and "understand."

11. Again, the word is calculatedly ambiguous and seems to suggest "burden," "cost," "responsibility."

12. So C; P: "or"; Om. SS: "and desires."

13. So SS, which seem superior to P, C: "are saved."

14. For the scriptural allusions and the rhetorical devices here, see *Showings*, II, 542 notes 301 and 302.

15. So C, SS; P: "after."

16. So SS; P, C: "morning" (or "mourning").

17. So C, SS; P: "fair."

18. So SS; P, C: "noble."

19. What follows differs from the short text SS: "surely."

MARGERY KEMPE   (1373–1439; England)

From The Book of Margery Kempe

Translated by Susan Dickman

Margery's First Vision: A Woman's Desire for Spiritual Autonomy

When this creature was twenty years old or somewhat more, she was married to an honorable townsman[1] and she conceived a child after a short time, as these things happen. And, after she conceived, she was troubled by severe illness until the child was born, and then, on account of the trouble she had in childbirth and the illness before, she despaired of her life, thinking she might not live. And then she sent for her confessor[2] for she had something on her conscience which she had never revealed before in her life. She was always prevented by her enemy, the Devil, who kept telling her while she was in good health that she did not need confession but could do penance by herself alone, for God is merciful enough. And therefore this creature did penance many times, fasting on bread and

water and doing other good deeds with devout prayers, but she never revealed in confession the thing she had done. And whenever she was sick or diseased, the Devil said in her mind that she would be damned, for she had not been forgiven for her sin. So, after her child was born, she, fearing for her life, sent for her confessor as told above, determined to be forgiven for all the sins of her life. And, just when she came to the point of saying the thing that she had concealed for so long, her confessor was a little too hasty and began to reprove her sharply before she had finished saying what she intended, and then she would say no more, no matter what he did. And, between the dread she had, of damnation on the one side and of her confessor's reproof on the other, this creature went out of her mind and was incredibly vexed and troubled by spirits for half a year, eight weeks and some odd days.

And day and night during this time she thought she saw devils with open mouths all a-flame with burning waves of fire as though they would swallow her, sometimes raging at her, sometimes threatening her, sometimes pulling her and grabbing her. And the devils also cried out dire threats and demanded that she forsake her Christianity and her faith, and deny her God, his Mother, all the saints in Heaven, her good works and all the virtues, her father, her mother and all her friends. And so she did. She slandered her husband, her friends and her own self; she spoke many a hard and scolding word; she knew no virtue or goodness; she desired all wickedness. Exactly what the spirits tempted her to say and do, she said and did. She would have destroyed herself many times and been damned with them in Hell, and to show that, she bit her own hand so hard that the mark could be seen for the rest of her life. And she tore the skin over her heart spitefully with her nails because she had nothing else. And she would have done worse but she was bound and restrained both night and day so she could not have her way.

And after she had been troubled by these temptations and others so long that men thought she would never recover or live, when she was lying all alone and her keepers were away, our merciful Lord Jesus Christ, who is ever to be trusted, worshipped be his name, never forsaking his servant in time of need, appeared to this creature who had forsaken him. In the likeness of a man, the most handsome and beautiful and amiable that might ever be seen, wearing a purple cloak, sitting on her bedside, looking upon her with such a blessed expression that she felt strengthened in her spirits, he said these words to her: "Daughter, why have you forsaken me and I never forsook you?" And as soon as he said these words, she actually saw the sky open like a flash of lightning; and he climbed up into the air, not too quickly or hastily, but gracefully and easily, so that she could see him in the sky until it closed again.

And immediately this creature was as sound in her wits and her reason as she had ever been before. As soon as he came to her, she asked her husband for the keys to the pantry so she could take her meat and drink as she had before. Her serving women and her keepers told him not to give her the keys. They expected that she would give away the things that were there, for they thought she did not understand what she was saying. Nevertheless her husband, who was always filled with tenderness and compassion for her, commanded them to give her the keys. And she took her meat and drink as her strength returned. And she recognized her friends and the members of her household and all the other people who came to visit her to see how our Lord Jesus Christ had wrought his grace in her, blessed may he be who is always near in tribulation. When men think he is far from them, he is very near with his grace. Afterwards this creature did everything she was expected to do wisely and earnestly enough, but she was not truly drawn to our Lord.[3]

Margery Negotiates a Victory: The Kempes' Vow of Chastity

It happened on a Friday, Midsummer's Eve, in very hot weather, as this creature was coming from York carrying a bottle of beer in her hand while her husband carried a cake in his arms, that he asked his wife this question: "Margery, if there was a man with a sword who would cut off my head unless I had sex with you as I used to, tell me the truth—for you say you do not lie—whether you would let my head be cut off or let me meddle with you as I did before." "Alas, sir," she said, "why does this worry you when we have been chaste for eight weeks?" "Because I want to know the truth of your heart." And then she said with great sorrow: "Truthfully, I would rather see you slain than that we should turn again to uncleanness." And he replied, "You are not a good wife." And then she asked her husband why he had not had sex with her during that last eight weeks, since she lay with him in his bed every night. And he said he felt so fearful when he wanted to touch her that he did not dare. "Now, good sir, change your ways and ask God's mercy, for I told you almost three years ago that you would suddenly be killed, and now this is the third year; and yet I hope I shall have my desire. Good sir, give me what I ask, and I shall pray that you be saved through the mercy of our Lord Jesus Christ, and you shall have more reward in Heaven than if you wore a hair shirt or a habergeon.[4] I beg you let me make a vow of chastity before whichever bishop God chooses."[5] "No," he said, "I will not grant you that, for now I may use you without mortal sin but then I might not." Then she replied: "If it is the will of the Holy Ghost to do what I've said, I pray you may consent; and, if it is not the will of the Holy Ghost, I pray you never consent."

Then they went on toward Bridlington, in hot weather, the aforesaid creature having great sorrow and great fear for her chastity. And, as they came to a cross, her husband sat himself beneath it, calling his wife to him and saying these words to her: "Margery, grant me my desire, and I shall grant you your desire. My first desire is that we shall still lie together in one bed as we have before; the second is that you pay my debts before you go to Jerusalem; the third is that you eat and drink with me on Fridays as you used to do." "No sir," she said, "I will never break my Friday fast for you as long as I live." "Well," he said, "then I shall have sex with you again." She asked him to let her say her prayers and he willingly agreed. Then she knelt down beside a cross in the field and prayed in this manner with a great abundance of tears: "Lord God, you know all things. You know what trouble I've had trying to be chaste for you these three years, and now I might have my desire and I dare not for love of you. For, if I could break the fast from meat and drink which you commanded me to keep on Fridays, I should have my desire. But, blessed Lord, you know I will not oppose your will and my sorrow will be great unless I find comfort in you. Now, blessed Jesus, make your will known to me, unworthy though I am, so I may follow it and fulfill it with all my might." And then our Lord Jesus Christ spoke to this creature with great sweetness, commanding her to return to her husband and to ask him to grant her what she desired. "And he shall have what he desires. For, my beloved daughter, this was the reason that I asked you to fast, so that you would get and obtain your desire sooner; and now it is granted you. I want you to fast no longer and I bid you in the name of Jesus to eat and drink as your husband does." Then this creature thanked our Lord Jesus Christ for his grace and his goodness, and afterwards got up and went to her husband, saying to him: "Sir, if you like, you shall grant my desire, and you shall have your desire. Promise me you will not come into my bed, and I promise to repay your debts before I go to Jerusalem. Make my body free for God and never again force me to refuse by asking the debt of matrimony as long as you live; and I shall eat and drink on Fridays as you want." Then her husband replied: "May your body be as free to God as it has been to me."

This creature thanked God, rejoicing that she had what she desired, and asked her husband to say three Our Fathers in honor of the Trinity for the great grace he had granted them. And so they did, kneeling under a cross, and afterwards they ate and drank together in great gladness of heart. This was on a Friday, Midsummer's Eve. Then they went on to Bridlington and later to many other places, and spoke with God's servants, both anchorites and recluses, and many other people who love our Lord, with many worthy clerics, bachelor and doctors of divinity. And this creature showed her feelings and her contemplations to several of them, as she was commanded to do, to find out if there was anything wrong with what she felt.[6]

Margery's Pilgrimage to Jerusalem Where She Cries Her First Tears of Devotion

The same company of pilgrims who had excluded the aforesaid creature from their meals, so she no longer ate with them, also chartered a ship to sail in.[7] They bought containers for their wine and found bedding for themselves, but not for her. Seeing their unkindness, she went to the same supplier as they had and arranged for bedding and came back to where they were and revealed what she had done, intending to sail with them in the ship they had chartered. Afterwards, while this creature was praying, our Lord warned her inwardly that she should not sail in that ship and he assigned her another ship, a galley, to sail in. Then she told this to some of the company and they told it in turn to their companions, and then they did not dare to sail in the ship they had chartered. They sold the containers they had bought for their wines and decided to sail on the galley she was on. So, although it was against their will, she was included in their company, for they did not dare do otherwise.

When it was time to make up their beds, they locked up her bedclothes, and a priest who was in the company took a sheet from the aforesaid creature and said it was his. She swore to God that it was her sheet. Then the priest swore a great oath, by the book in his hand, that she was utterly false. And he despised her and rebuked her. So she suffered much tribulation until she arrived in Jerusalem. And before she arrived there, she said to those whom she thought were displeased with her, "I pray you, sirs, be in charity with me, for I am in charity with you, and forgive me if I have displeased you on the way. And, if any of you have trespassed against me, may God forgive you as I do."

And so they proceeded into the Holy Land until they could see Jerusalem. And when this creature, who was then riding on an ass, saw Jerusalem, she thanked God with all her heart, praying him for his mercy that just as she had been allowed to see the earthly city of Jerusalem, he would grant her the grace to see the blissful city of Jerusalem above, the city of Heaven. Our Lord Jesus Christ responded to her thoughts and granted her desire. Then, because of the joy she had and the sweetness she felt in the dalliance[8] of our Lord, she almost fell off her ass, for she could not bear the sweetness and grace God worked in her soul. Then two Dutch pilgrims, one of whom was a priest, went to her and kept her from falling. He put spices in her mouth to comfort her, thinking she was sick. And so they helped her to Jerusalem. And when she came there she said, "Sir, do not be displeased if I weep bitterly in this holy place where our Lord Jesus Christ was both alive and dead."

Then they went to the Temple in Jerusalem and they were allowed in one day at the time of evensong and remained there until the next day at the same time.[9] Then the friars lifted up a cross and led the pilgrims around from one place to the next where our Lord suffered his pains and his passions. Every man and woman carried a wax candle in their hand. And, as they went from place to place, the friars told them what our Lord had suffered there. And the aforesaid creature wept and sobbed as much as if she had physically seen our Lord suffering his Passion at that very time. She saw him before her in contemplation in her soul, and that sight caused her to feel compassion. And, when they came to Mount Calvary, she could not stand or kneel but fell down and turned and twisted her body, spreading her arms out, and cried with a loud voice as though her heart would break; for, in the city of her soul, she saw truly and vividly how our Lord was crucified. In her spiritual sight she saw and heard the mourning of our Lady, of St. John and Mary Magdalene before her eyes.[10] And she felt such deep compassion and such pain to see our Lord's pain that she could not keep herself from crying and roaring, although she might have died from it. And this was the first cry she ever cried in contemplation.

This kind of crying lasted for many years afterwards, no matter what anyone did, and she suffered much embarrassment and shame on account of it. The crying was so loud and so strange that it astonished people unless they had heard it before or knew what caused it. And she had these cries so often that they made her physically weak, especially if she heard our Lord's Passion mentioned. And sometimes, when she saw the crucifix, or if she saw a man or a beast with a wound, or if a man beat a child in front of her or hit a horse or another animal with a whip, whether she saw it or heard it, in the fields as well as in the town, by herself as well as among other people, she thought she saw our Lord beaten or wounded just like the man or beast.

When she first had her crying spells in Jerusalem, she had them often; and often in Rome as well. And, when she first came home to England, they did not happen so often, perhaps once a month, then once a week, and afterwards, every day. Once she had fourteen in a day, and another day she had seven. And so, as God wanted, he would send her crying spells, sometimes in church, sometimes in the street, sometimes in her room, sometimes in the fields. She never knew the time or the hours they would come. And they never came without great sweetness of devotion and high contemplation. And as soon as she knew she

was going to cry, she would hold it in as much as she could, so that people would not hear her and be annoyed. For some said she was troubled by a wicked spirit; some said it was a sickness; some said she had drunk too much wine; some would have nothing to do with her; some wished she were drowned in the harbor; some wished she were put to sea in a bottomless boat; and so on, each according to his prejudice. Other spiritual men loved her and honored her more. Some important clerics said our Lady never cried that way, nor any saint in Heaven. But these clerics knew little of what she felt, and they would not believe that she could not keep from crying if she wanted and, therefore, when she knew she was going to cry, she held it in as long as she could and did everything she could to withstand it or put it away, until she grew blue as lead. And it labored in her mind until it finally burst out. And, then, when the body could no longer stand the spiritual labor but was overcome with unspeakable love working fervently in the soul, then she fell down and cried incredibly loudly. And the more she tried to hold it in or to put it away, the more and the louder she would cry.

And thus she cried on Mount Calvary as written above. In contemplation she saw an image in the sight of her soul, as if Christ had hung before her physical eye in his manhood. And, when through the dispensation of the high mercy of our Sovereign savior Christ Jesus it was granted this creature to see his precious, tender body, all torn and rent with scourges, more full of wounds than a dovecote is full of holes, hanging upon the cross with the crown of thorns on his head, his blissful hands, his tender feet nailed to the hard tree, the rivers of blood flowing out of every limb, the grisly and grievous wound in his side shedding blood and water for her love and her salvation, then she fell down and cried in a loud voice, turning and twisting her body every which way, spreading her arms as if she would have died. These bodily movements were on account of the fire of love which burned so fervently in her soul with pure pity and compassion.

Margery's Good Friday Meditation, elaborated in the Popular Fashion of the Meditations Vitae Christi

When our Lord was buried, our Lady fell down in a dead faint, as though she had just come from the grave, and St. John took her up into his arms, and Mary Magdalene went on the other side to support and comfort her as much as could be. Then the said creature, who desired to remain by the grave of our Lord, mourned, wept and sorrowed with loud cries because of the tender love and pity she felt for our Lord's death and many other sad feelings which God put into her mind at that time. People were curious about her on that account, wondering what was wrong with her; for they had little idea of the cause. She thought she never wanted to leave the grave and desired to die right there and to be buried with our Lord.[11]

Next the creature thought she saw our Lady returning home. And, as she went, many good women came to her and said, "Lady, we are distressed that your son is dead and that our people have shamed him so." And then our Lady, bowing her head, thanked them meekly with her eyes, for she could not speak, her heart was so heavy. Then this creature thought that our Lady came home and lay down on a bed and that she made our Lady a fortifying drink[12] and brought it to her to comfort her. And then our Lady said to her, "Take it away, daughter. Give me no food but my own child." Then the creature replied, "Ah, blissful Lady, you must take comfort and quit sorrowing." "Ah, daughter, where can I go, where can I live without sorrow? I tell you truly there never was a woman on earth with such reason for sorrow as I have, for there never was a woman in this world who bore a better child or one meeker to his mother than my son was to me." And just afterwards, she thought she heard our Lady crying with a sad voice, "John, where is my son Jesus Christ?" And St. John replied, "Dear Lady, you know he is dead." "Ah, John, she said, "that is painful news for me." The creature heard this answer in her spiritual understanding as clearly as she would have understood one man speaking to another.

And then the creature heard St. Peter knocking at the door, and St. John asked who was there. Peter answered, "I, sinful Peter, who forsook my Lord Jesus Christ." St. John wanted him to come in, and Peter would not until our Lady asked him in. And then Peter said, "Lady, I am not worthy to come in," and he stood on the doorstep. Then St. John went to our Lady and told her that Peter was so ashamed that he would not come in. Our Lady asked St. John to go quickly to St. Peter and ask him to come to her.

And then the creature saw in her spiritual sight how St. Peter came to our Lady and fell down on his knees with great weeping and sobbing, and said, "Lady, I beg for mercy, for I have forsaken your beloved Son and my sweet master who loved me well, and therefore, Lady, I am not worthy to look at him or at you, unless you are merciful." "Ah, Peter," said our Lady, "do not fear, for, although you have forsaken my sweet son, he never forsook you, Peter, and he shall come again and comfort us all. He promised me, Peter, that he would come again on the third day and comfort me. Ah, Peter", said our Lady, "I shall find the time very long until that day comes and I see his blessed face."

Then our Lady lay quietly on her bed and heard the friends of Jesus talking about their sorrows. And our Lady lay quietly, mourning and weeping with great sadness, and at last Mary Magdalen and our Lady's sisters left her to go and buy ointment to anoint our Lord's body. Then the creature lay quietly with our Lady, and it felt like a thousand years to her before the third day came. And that day she was present with our Lady in a chapel where our Lord appeared to her and said, "Salve, sancta parens." And then the creature thought inwardly that our Lady said, "Are you my sweet son, Jesus?" And he said, "Yes, my blessed mother, I am your son Jesus." Then he held his mother and kissed her very sweetly. And then the creature thought she saw our Lady feeling and touching our Lord's body everywhere, including his hands and feet, to see if there was hurt or pain. And she heard our Lord say to His Mother, "Dear Mother, my pain is all gone, and now I shall live forever. And, Mother, so shall your pain and sorrow be turned into great joy. Mother, ask whatever you want to know and I will answer you." And when he had allowed his mother to ask what she wanted and he had answered her questions, then he said, "Mother, with your permission I must go speak with Mary Magdalene." Our Lady said, "That is well done, Son, for she has sorrowed for your absence. And, I beg you, do not be long from me."

On Easter day and on other days when our Lord visited her with his grace, these spiritual sights and understanding caused the creature to weep, to sob, and to cry so loudly that she could not control it or restrain herself. And afterwards in her contemplation, this creature was present with Mary Magdalene, mourning and seeking our Lord at the grave, and she heard and saw how our Lord appeared to Mary in the likeness of a gardener, saying, "Woman, why do you weep?" Mary, not knowing who he was, and all enflamed with the fire of love, replied, "Sir, if you have taken my Lord away, tell me and I will take him back." Then our merciful Lord, filled with pity and compassion for her said, "Mary." And with that word she recognized our Lord

and fell down at his feet and tried to kiss them, saying, "Master." Our Lord said to her, "Touch me not." Then this creature thought that Mary Magdalene said to our Lord, "Ah, Lord, I see you do not want me to be as much at home with you as I was before," and became sad. "Yes, Mary," said our Lord, "I shall never forsake you but I shall be with you without end." Then our Lord said to Mary Magdalene, "Go tell my brothers and Peter that I have risen." And then the creature thought that Mary went forth with great joy, and it was amazing to her that Mary rejoiced, for if our Lord had spoken to her as he did to Mary, she thought she could never have been merry. That was when she wanted to kiss his feet, and he said, "Do not touch me." The creature felt such sorrow and sadness in that phrase that whenever she heard it in a sermon, as she often did, she wept, she sorrowed, and she cried, as though she would have died of the love and desire she felt to be with our Lord.

The Trial at York, 1417: Margery Acquits Herself of Heresy and Proves Herself the Equal of Many Clerics

There was a monk who was going to preach in York who had heard much slander and evil spoken about the said creature. And, when he was due to preach, there was a great crowd of people came to hear him, and she was there as well. And so, when he gave his sermon, he said some things so pointedly that people understood he meant her. Her friends who loved her were sorry and sad, but she was much the merrier, for she had something to test her patience and her charity, by which she hoped to please our Lord Christ Jesus. When the sermon was over, a doctor of divinity who loved her came to her with many other people and said, "Margery, how are you today?" "Sir," she said, "very well, praise God. I have reason to be merry and glad in my soul if I suffer anything for his love, for he suffered much more for me.'' Immediately afterwards a man of good will who loved her well came with his wife and several others, and led her seven miles to the Archbishop of York. They took her into a handsome room, and a clerk came, saying to the good man who had brought here there: "Sir, why have you and your wife brought this woman here? She will slip away from you and you will be embarrassed by her." The good man said: "I dare say she will stay and answer with good will."

On the next day she was taken into the Archbishop's Chapel, and many of the Archbishop's household came, despising her and calling her Lollard and heretic.[13] And they swore many horrible oaths that she should be burned. And she replied to them through the strength of Jesus: "Sirs, I fear you shall be burnt in Hell without end unless you quit your swearing, for you do not keep the commandments of God. I would not swear as you do for all the things of this world." Then they went away as though they were ashamed. She prayed inwardly, asking to be judged that day as was most pleasing to God and good for her own soul and the best example to her fellow-Christians. Our Lord, answering her, said all would be well. At last the Archbishop came into the Chapel with his clerks and he said sharply to her: "Why do you dress in white? Are you a virgin?" Kneeling before him on her knees, she said, "No, sir, I am no virgin; I am a wife." He commanded his men to fetch a pair of fetters and said she should be fettered because she was a false heretic. And then she said, "I am no heretic, nor shall you prove me one." Then the Archbishop went away and left her standing all alone. Then she prayed for a long time to our Lord God Almighty to help her and succour her against all her enemies, spiritual and physical. And she trembled and shook so much that she wanted to hide her hands in her sleeves so no one could

see. Afterwards the Archbishop came back to the Chapel with many worthy clerics, among whom were the same doctor who had examined her before and the monk who had preached against her just a little while before in York. Some people asked if she were a Christian woman or a Jew; some said she was a good woman and some said she was not.

Then the Archbishop took his seat and his clerks did so too, each according to his degree, since many people were there. And the whole time, while people were gathering together and the Archbishop was taking his seat, the said creature was standing at the back praying for help and succour against her enemies. She prayed so devoutly for so long that she melted into tears. And, finally, she began to cry so loudly that the Archbishop and his clerics and many people were astonished, for they had never heard such crying before. When her crying had passed, she came before the Archbishop and fell down on her knees, and the Archbishop said sharply to her: "Why do you weep this way, woman?" She replied, "Sir, someday you will wish you had wept as bitterly as I." And then, after the Archbishop questioned her on the Articles of our Faith, which God gave her the grace to answer well and truly and readily without any hesitation, so that the Archbishop could not find fault with her, he said to the clerics: "She knows her Faith well enough. What shall I do with her?" The clerics said: "We know she knows the Articles of Faith, but we will not let her live among us, for the people have faith in what she says and perhaps she will mislead some of them." Then the Archbishop said to her, "I have heard evil things about you; I hear tell you are a very wicked woman." And she replied: "Sir, so I hear tell that you are a wicked man. And if you are as wicked as men say, you will never get to Heaven unless you change your ways while you are here." Then he said angrily: "Why, you wretch, what do men say about me?" She answered: "Other men, sir, can tell you well enough." Then an important cleric with a furred hood said, "Peace, speak for yourself and let him be."

Afterwards, the Archbishop said to her: "Lay your hand on the book before me and swear you will go out of my diocese as soon as you can." "No sir," she said, "give me leave to go back to York to say goodbye to my friends." Then he gave her permission to stay for a day or two. She thought it too short a time, so she replied: "Sir, I cannot leave this diocese that fast. I must stay and speak with certain good men before I go. I must sir, with your leave, go to Bridlington and speak with my confessor, a good man, who was the confessor of the good Prior who is now canonized."[14] Then the Archbishop said to her, "You must swear that you will not teach or challenge the people in my diocese." "No, sir, I will not swear," she said, "I shall speak of God where I want and reprove those who swear great oaths until the Pope and Holy Church ordain that no one shall be so bold as to speak about God; for God Almighty does not forbid us, sir, to speak of him. And also the Gospel mentions that when the woman heard our Lord preach, she came to him and said in a loud voice, 'Blessed be the womb that bore you and the breast that gave you suck.' Then our Lord replied, 'Truly, they are blessed who hear the word of God and keep it.'[15] And therefore, sir, I think the Gospel gives me leave to speak of God." "Sir," said the clerics, "we know she has a devil inside her, for she speaks of the Gospel." Quickly, an important cleric brought out a book and quoted St. Paul saying that women should not preach.[16] Answering that, she said: "I do not preach, sir, I do not use a pulpit. I rely on good words and good deeds only, and that I will continue to do as long as I live." Then the doctor who had examined her previously said, "Sir, she told the worst tales about priests that I ever heard." The Bishop commanded her to tell the tale.

"Sir, I spoke only about one priest by way of example. As I heard it, one day he wandered, lost in the woods, as God would have it for the good of his soul, until night fell. Without anywhere to stay, he found a pretty arbor, where he could rest, which had a pear tree in the middle, flourishing and covered with flowers and blossoms, which were lovely to look at. Then a bear arrived, huge and violent and ugly, and shook the pear tree so the flowers fell. Greedily, the horrible beast ate and devoured the beautiful flowers. And when he had eaten them, turning his tail to the priest, he voided them out of his hind quarters."

The priest, disgusted by this abominable sight, and confused about what it meant, wandered on his way the next day in a sad and thoughtful mood. He chanced to meet an old man, rather like a palmer or pilgrim, who asked him why he was so serious.[17] The priest, explaining the above, said he began to dread and doubt when he saw the horrible beast defoul and devour such beautiful flowers and blossoms and then void them so horribly from his tail-end. He did not understand what it meant. Then the palmer, showing himself to be God's messenger, enlightened him.

"Priest, you yourself are the pear tree, flourishing and flowering in many ways because you say the service and minister the Sacraments. But you do it without devotion; you take little care how you say your Matins and the service, as long as you blabber it somehow to the end. You go to Mass without devotion and you have little contrition for your sins. You receive the fruit of everlasting life, the Sacrament of the Altar, in the wrong spirit. The whole day after, you waste your time; you devote yourself to buying and selling, bargaining and bartering as though you were a worldly man. You sit and drink ale, giving in to gluttony and excess, as well as to lust, through lechery and uncleanness. You break God's commandments, swearing, lying, detracting, backbiting, and sinning in other ways. Thus, your misbehavior is like the horrible bear, you devour and destroy the flowers and blossoms of virtuous living. It will be your endless damnation and a hindrance to many other men unless you receive the grace to repent and change your ways."

The Archbishop liked the story and praised it, saying it was a good story. And the cleric who had examined her earlier without the Archbishop said, "Sir, this story pierces me to the heart." The aforesaid creature said to the cleric, "There is a honorable doctor, sir, in the place where I generally live, who is a worthy cleric, and a good preacher, and who speaks out boldly against people's misbehavior and will flatter no one. He has said many times in the pulpit, "if any man is not pleased by my preaching, notice who he is, for he feels guilty." And just so, sir," she said to the cleric, "you have responded to me, may God forgive you." The cleric did not know what he could say to her then. Afterwards, he came to her and begged forgiveness for having been against her. Also he asked her specially to pray for him.

And then immediately afterwards the Archbishop said, "Where can I find a man who will lead this woman away from here?" Quickly, many young men jumped up and every one of them said, "My Lord, I will go with her." The Archbishop answered, "You are too young; I cannot use you." Then a good, earnest man from the Archbishop's household asked what he would be given for it and where he should lead her. The Archbishop offered him five shillings and the man asked for a noble.[18] The Archbishop answered, "I will not stake that much on her body." "Yes, good sir," said the creature, "our Lord will reward you well in return." Then the Archbishop said to the man, "See, here is five shillings. Lead her out of here immediately." Asking her to pray for him, he blessed her and let her go. Then she returned to York and was well received by many people and many worthy clerics, who rejoiced in Our Lord, who had given an unlettered woman the wit and wisdom to answer so many learned men without mistake or fault.

Margery's Conflict with the Preaching Friar: The Case For and Against a Woman's Holy Tears

Then a friar came to Lynn who was commonly held to be a holy man and a good preacher.[19] His name and his perfection in preaching were very widely spread and known. Good men came to the said creature with all charity and said, "Margery, now you will have preaching enough, for one of the most famous friars in England has come to town, to be in the convent here." Then she was merry and glad and thanked God with all her heart that such a good man had come live amongst them. Shortly after that, the friar gave a sermon in the chapel of Saint James in Lynn, where many people had gathered to hear him. And, before the friar walked to the pulpit, the parish priest of St. James where he was about to preach, went up to him and said, "Sir, I beg you not to be displeased. A woman will come to your sermon who often weeps and sobs and cries when she hears the Passion or any high devotion, but it does not last long. And, therefore, good sir, if she makes some noise during your sermon, suffer it patiently and do not be abashed."

The good friar went on to give his sermon and preached very piously and devoutly and spoke so much about our Lord's Passion that the said creature might bear it no longer. She kept herself from crying as long as she could and then at last she burst out with a great cry and cried very bitterly. The good friar suffered it patiently at the time and said not a word. Shortly after that he preached again in the same place. The said creature being present and seeing how fast people came running to hear the sermon, rejoiced in her soul, thinking to herself, "Ah, Lord Jesus, I think if you were here to preach in person, people would rejoice to hear. I beg you, Lord, make your holy word settle in their souls as I would have it settle in mine, and may as many be moved by his voice as would be by your voice if you preached yourself." And with such holy thought and holy mind, she asked God's grace for the people at that time. And afterwards, what with the holy sermon and her own meditation, the grace of devotion worked deeply in her soul that she fell into a fit of violent weeping. Then the good friar said, "I wish this woman were out of this church; she annoys other people." Some of her friends answered, "Sir, excuse her. She cannot control it."

Then many people turned against her and were very glad that good friar opposed her. Then some men said that she had a devil inside her. They had said so many times before, but now they were bolder because they thought their opinion was considerably strengthened and fortified by this good friar. He would not allow her at his sermons unless she stopped her sobbing and crying.

At that time there was a good priest who had read much good scripture to her and knew the cause of her crying. He spoke to another good priest who had known her many years and told him that he intended to go to the good friar and see if he could soften his heart. The other good priest said he would happily go with him to help get the friar's grace if he could. So both priests went together and begged the friar as heartily as they could to let said creature come quietly to his sermons and bear it patiently, as other good men had before, if she happened to sob or cry. He replied shortly, if she came to any church where he was preaching and she made any noise in the way she usually did, he would speak sharply to her; there was no way he would let her cry.

Afterwards an honorable doctor of divinity—a White Friar, a solemn cleric and an old doctor, who was well thought of and who had known said creature for many years and believed that God worked his grace in her—took a worthy man, a bachelor of law, a man well-grounded and long versed in scripture, who was said creature's confessor, and went to the good friar as the good priests had before. They sent for wine to placate the friar, and asked him to look kindly on the works of our Lord in said creature out of charity and to treat her benevolently by supporting her if she happened to cry or sob while he was giving a sermon. And these worthy clerks told him that her crying was a gift from God which she had only when God sent it, and which she had not power to control when it was sent, and which God would withdraw when he wished (for she had that information by revelation and it was unknown to the friar). Believing neither the doctor's words nor the bachelor's, and trusting his own popularity, the friar said he would not look kindly on her crying no matter what anyone did or said, for he could not believe that it was a gift from God. But he said, if she could not control it, he believed it was a cardiac illness or some other disease;[20] and if she wanted it to be identified that way, he said he would take pity on her and get the people to pray for her, and under this condition he would have patience and let her cry all she wanted but only if she would agree that it was an ordinary, natural disease. And she herself knew through revelation and by the way it felt that her crying was no sickness, and she would not say something other than what she felt, for all the world. And therefore they did not agree. Then the honorable doctor and her confessor advised her not to go to the friar's sermons, and that hurt her.

Then another man, an honorable townsman

who was mayor of Lynn a few years later, went to the friar and begged as the clerics had done before, and he received the same answer they had. Then she was ordered by her confessor not to go where the friar was preaching, but when he preached in one church, she should go to the other. She was so filled with sorrow that she did not know what to do, for she was excluded from sermons, which were her highest comfort on earth whenever she heard them and, conversely, her greatest pain on earth when she missed them. When she was alone by herself in one church and he was preaching to the people in the other, she cried as loud and as violently as when she was surrounded by people.

For years she was not allowed to go to this friar's sermons, because she cried whenever it pleased our Lord to give her thought and actual visions of his bitter Passion. But she was not excluded from other clerics' preaching, but only from the good friar's, as has been said, although many honorable doctors and other worthy clerics, both religious and secular, preached during that time, and at their sermons she often cried very loudly and sobbed violently. And yet they bore it patiently, and some who had spoken with her before and had knowledge of her manner of living defended her when they heard rumors or complaints about her.

Afterwards the good Friar (at the time he was neither a bachelor nor doctor of divinity) preached on St. James Day in the St. James Chapel yard in Lynn, where there were many people and a large audience, for he had a holy name and was a great favorite of the people. When they knew that he was going to preach in the area, some men would go with him or follow him from town to town, they were so delighted to hear him. And so, praise God, he preached very devoutly and piously. Nevertheless this day he preached against said creature, not mentioning her by name but

explaining things so people clearly understood that he meant her. Then there was much grumbling among the people, for many men and many women trusted and loved her and were both sad and sorry that he spoke against her as he did, and they wished they had not heard him that day. When he heard people grumbling and murmuring, anticipating that her friends would reply to him another day, he said, pounding his hand on the pulpit, "If I hear these matters discussed again, I shall hit the nail on the head so it will shame all her supporters."

And then many of those who pretended to be her friends turned against her on account of a little vain fear of the friar's words and did not speak to her. The priest who afterwards wrote this book was one of these and he intended never to believe in her feelings again. And yet our Lord, praise him, brought him back in a short time, so that he loved her and had more faith in her weeping and crying than he ever did before. For afterwards he read of a woman named Mary of Oignies,[21] of her manner of living, of the wonderful sweetness she felt when she heard the words of God, of the wonderful compassion she had when she thought of the Passion, and of the copious tears she wept, which made her feel so feeble and so weak that she couldn't bear to see the Cross or to hear the story of the Passion repeated without dissolving into tears of pity and compassion.

He deals with the subject of the grace of her tears in the nineteenth chapter of the book mentioned above,[22] which begins, "Bonus es, domine, sperantibus in te," and in the nineteenth chapter, where he tells how a priest requested not to be troubled or distracted by her weeping and sobbing while he was serving Mass, and how she went out the church door, crying in a loud voice that she could not help herself. And our Lord visited the priest who was serving Mass with such grace and such devotion that when he was supposed to read the Holy Gospel he wept so much that he wet his vestments and the ornaments on the altar. He could not control his weeping or sobbing, it was too abundant, or restrain it, or even stand at the altar. Then he truly believed that the good woman, for whom he had so little affection before, could not control her weeping, her sobbing or her crying, since she felt more grace beyond all comparison than he ever did. Then he understood that God sends his grace to whomever he wants. It was through suggestion of a worthy cleric and a bachelor of divinity that the priest who wrote this treatise saw and read the above, but it was written much more seriously and effectively than it is in this treatise (here there is only a little of the effect, because he could not remember the said matter clearly when he wrote this treatise, and so he wrote less of it).

Then he drew and inclined towards said creature more earnestly, though he had fled and avoided her on account of the friar's preaching as written above. Also the same priest afterwards read the following words in the second chapter of a treatise which is called the *Prick of Love*, written by Bonaventure himself,[23] "Ah, Lord, what more shall I call or cry. You delay and you do not come and I, weary and overcome with desire, begin to go mad, for love governs me and not reason. I run with a hasty course wherever you want. I bow, Lord, and those who see me are troubled and rueful, not knowing that I am drunk with your love. Lord, they say, 'Lo, that madman cries in the streets,' but they cannot see the great desire of my heart."

He also read similar things about Richard Hampole, the hermit, in *Incendium Amoris*,[24] which moved him to believe said creature. Also, Elizabeth of Hungary[25] cried in a loud voice, as is written in her treatise. And many others who had forsaken her on account of the friar's preaching repented and turned toward her again in time, although the friar main-

tained his opinion. And he always had a part of his sermons condemning her, whether she was present or not, and he caused many people to think badly of her for a long time. For some said she had a devil inside her, and some said to her face that the friar should have driven the devils out of her. Thus she was slandered and eaten and gnawed by the people on account of the grace of compassion and devotion and compunction which God worked in her. Through the gift of these graces she wept, sobbed and cried completely against her will, she could not choose, for she would have wept softly and privately instead of openly if it had been in her power.

John Kempe's Fall: Margery Combines Her Vocations As Pious Woman and Provincial Housewife

Once, when the husband of the said creature, an old man past sixty, was coming down from his bedroom with bare feet and bare legs, he slipped or lost his footing and fell headfirst to the ground from the steps. His head was so badly broken and bruised that he had five dressings on his head for many days while it healed. And, as God would have it, some of his neighbors knew that had fallen from the steps, perhaps on account of the noise and the violence of the fall. And so they came to him and found him lying with his head under him, half alive, all covered with blood and not likely to live long enough to speak with a priest or cleric without special grace or a miracle. Then the said creature, his wife, was sent for, and so she came to him. Then he was lifted up and his head sewn up, and he was sick so long afterwards that men expected he would die.

And the people said, if he died, his wife deserved to be hanged for his death, because she might have looked after him but she did not. They did not live together, nor did they sleep together, because, as written above, they had both vowed to each with free will, to live chaste. And, in order to avoid problems, they lived and stayed in separate places where there could be no suspicion of the incontinence. For, after they first made their vow, they lived together, and then people slandered them and said they satisfied their lust and desire just as they had before they made their vow. And when they went on pilgrimage or to visit other spiritual people, many evil folk (whose tongues were their own undoing, since they lacked the dread and love of our Lord Jesus Christ) said that they went instead to the woods, groves or valleys to satisfy their lust where other people would not see them or know about it. Knowing how prone the people were to think evil of them, and desiring themselves to avoid every opportunity for evil they could, they agreed to part company for room and board and went to live in different places. And this was one reason that she was not with him. And, also, she would not be kept from contemplation.[26]

And so when he had fallen and was so badly injured, as was said before, people said, if he died, it was right that she should answer for his death. Then she prayed to our Lord that her husband might live a year and that she might be rescued from slander, if it were his will. Our Lord said to her: "Daughter, you shall have your wish, for he shall live, and I have done a great miracle for you that he has not died. And I ask you to take him home and take care of him for my love." She said: "No, good Lord, for I shall not attend to you then as I do now." "Yes, Daughter," said our Lord, "you shall have as much reward for looking after him and helping him in his need at home as if you were in church saying your prayers. And you have said many times that you would like to serve me. I pray you to serve him now for my love for in the past he has done both your will and mine; and he has freed your body for me so that you could serve me and live chaste and clean; and therefore my will is

that you be free to help him in his need in my name." "Ah, Lord," said she, "for your mercy, grant me the grace to obey your will and fulfill your will and never let my spiritual enemies have any power to keep me from fulfilling your will."

Then she took her husband home with her and looked after him for as long as he lived. And she worked very hard for in his last days he turned childish again and lost touch. So he could not control his bowels and use a seat, or else he would not, but like a child he voided in his linen at the fire or at the table, wherever he was sitting; he spared no place. And therefore she had much more work washing and wringing and much more expense in drying, and she was kept to a great extent from contemplation. Many times she would have resented her work, except she remembered the many delectable thoughts, fleshly lust and inordinate love she had for him in her youth. And therefore she was glad to be punished with the same person and she took it more easily and served him and helped him, she thought, as she might have done Christ himself.

NOTES

1. The Middle English is "burgeys," the citizen of a town.

2. Margery calls her confessor her "gostly fadyr," the common term and one much more suggestive of the nature of the relationship than the modern English equivalent.

3. Margery says, "sche knew not veryli þe drawt of owyr lord." "Drawt" is a common word in mystical treatises meaning "spiritual call" or "attraction" and Margery Kempe uses it repeatedly to describe God's action in her life.

4. A habergeon was a shirt of chain mail which might be worn as a garment of penance like a hair shirt.

5. The vow Margery so desired was not a private agreement but a sacramental vow made before a bishop.

6. Like most medieval mystics, Margery worried about the "truth" of her feelings and revelations.

Throughout her life, she explained them to various experts to assure herself they were divine rather than diabolical in origin. This problem, commonly known as "the discernment of spirits," was much discussed in the fourteenth century when the number of mystics grew phenomenally. Jean Gerson (1363–1424), Chancellor of Paris, produced one of the standard works on the subject, *De distinctione verarum visionum a falsis*, for the rehabilitation of Joan of Arc, in which he details the criteria by which true and false spirits can be distinguished. See *Opera*, ed. Petri de Alliaco, Iacobi Almaini, and Iannis Majoris. Paris 1606, column 595 ff.

7. Margery and her fellow pilgrims chartered their ship in Venice. They would have landed in Jaffe, and for their entire sojorn in the Holy Land had been watched by Moslem guards.

8. "Dalliance" is the word Margery most often uses to describe our Lord's conversations with her. In Middle English, as in modern English, it suggests an intimate kind of love talk.

9. The Church of the Holy Sepulcher was guarded by Moslem officials, who allowed Christian pilgrims to enter once a day. They locked the pilgrims in for a twenty-four hour vigil. Inside were two chambers, one containing the supposed tomb of Jesus. Also in the floor of the northern part, there was a hole where the cross was supposed to have been erected. The south was believed to be the site of the nailing of Christ to the cross. See W. Harvey, *The Church of the Holy Sepulchre, Jerusalem* (Oxford, 1935).

10. Mary's sorrow at the crucifixion, though it has no warrant in the synoptic Gospels, was taken as a model of Christian feeling from the time of St. Anselm (d. 1109) onward.

11. Margery's meditation follows Nicholas Love's meditation for Good Friday in his English translation of the *Meditationes, Myrrour of the Blessed Lyf of Jesus Christ*, very closely. But it is not a paraphrase and Margery elaborates the scene in her own distinctive way, imagining herself giving the virgin a hot drink. For Love's version of this scene, see *The Myrrour of the Blessed Lyf of Jesu Christ*, (London: Roxborough Club, 1908), pp. 254 ff.

12. Margery specifically mentions a "caudle," a warm drink of gruel, sugar, spices and wine given to invalids and to women in childbirth.

13. Margery's trial took place in 1417, when she was returning to Lynn from her two-year pilgrimage to Jerusalem and Rome. Her white clothing may have suggested to some that she was a member of the Flagellants, proscribed in England since 1399. But it was probably her habit of moralizing

and talking constantly about the love of God which led people to suspect she was a "heretic and a Lollard." Popular Lollardry emphasized lay preaching and reading of the Bible and was a strong, underground movement in the counties near Lynn in the early fifteenth century. See J. A. F. Thomson, *The Later Lollards* (Oxford: 1965). While Margery's piety with its emphasis on the Eucharist is ultimately very different from the Lollard's, the ease with which she was mistaken for a Lollard makes her insouciance in York all the more remarkable.

14. The confessor in question is Sleytham; and the canonized prior, St. John of Bridlington, whom Julian of Norwich also mentions. He died in 1379. See "De S. Iohanne Bridlingtoniensi Collectanea" in *Analecta Bollandiana*, IV (1935), pp. 101–29.

15. Luke XI, 27–28.

16. The issue here is Margery's supposed Lollardry, though the verse from St. Paul (I *Cor.* XIV, 34–35) the cleric quotes was used against proponents of feminists generally, not just Lollards.

17. Palmer, a pilgrim returning from the Holy Land with a palm leaf.

18. A noble was six shillings, eight pence.

19. This preacher, probably William Melton, came to Lynn in 1420.

20. A precise medical term "cardiacyl" is attributed to the friar.

21. Mary of Oignies (d. 1213) was one of the original *mulieres sanctae*. She lived in the diocese of Liége. Like Margery, she was married, but she left her husband, with his consent, to live in a cell near the church in Oignies. She gathered about her a group of like-minded women, who wished to live chastely, performing works of mercy in the world. Her life was written by her confessor, Jacques de Vitry, who wished to promote this new model of female sanctity. See Brenda M. Bolton, "Mulieres Sanctae," in *Medieval Women, Studies in Church History*, vol. 10, edited by Derek Baker, pp. 77–88. (Oxford: Basil Blackwell, 1978).

22. Here the priest loses track of his thoughts. He has not told us which book he is referring to, but it is surely the *Life of Mary of Oignies* by Jacques de Vitry. It was known in England in the fourteenth century; see the text in *Anglia VIII*, 138. The passage which follows is difficult to follow and exhibits the priest's habit of vague pronoun references as well as his digressive style.

23. A reference to *Stimulus Amoris*, now attributed to Friar James of Milan. Translated by Walter Hilton into English, it sets out a combination of affective prayer and speculative instruction designed to bring the soul to God.

24. The reference is to the *Incendium Amoris* of

Richard Rolle, the English mystic whose paramystical experiences most resemble Margery's. In this treatise, Rolle describes the physical fire, as well as the cries which were part of his experience of divine love.

25. Elizabeth of Hungary (1207–1231), wife of the Landgrave Ludwig IV of Thuringia and a Franciscan Tertiary. A married mystic whose life and meditations were known in England, she was known for care for lepers, as well as her tears. Her life was known at Margery's time. See Osbern Bokenham, *Legends of Holy Women*, EETS No. 206, ed. Mary S. Serjeantson.

26. After her return from pilgrimage, Margery apparently devoted her days to prayer and meditation. Though Margery does not say, she apparently nursed John Kempe for six years until he died. His name is not recorded in municipal records after 1431.

DOÑA LEONOR LÓPEZ DE CÓRDOBA

(c. 1362–c. 1412; Spain)

The Memories of Doña Leonor López de Córdoba

Translated by Kathleen Lacey

In the name of God the Father, and of the Son, and of the Holy Spirit, three persons and one true God in Trinity, to whom all glory is given, to the Father and to the Son and to the Holy Spirit, as it was in the beginning, is now and forever. Amen. In the name of the Lord and of the Virgin, St. Mary his mother, lady and advocate of sinners, and in honor and praise of all the angels and saints of the court of heaven. Amen.

Therefore, may whoever reads this document know that I am Doña Leonor López de Córdoba, the daughter of my lord, Master Don Martín López de Córdoba, and Doña Sancha Carrillo, to whom God gave glory and paradise. I swear, by the meaning of the cross that I adore, that all that is written here is true, that I saw it, and it happened to me. I write it for the honor and glory of my Lord Jesus Christ, and of the Virgin, St. Mary his mother, who gave birth to him, so that all creatures that were in tribulation may be secure—as I put my faith in her mercy—that if they commend their hearts to the Virgin St.

Mary, she will console and succor them, as she consoled me. And so that whoever hears this knows the story of the deeds and miracles the Virgin St. Mary showed me, and as it is my intention that these deeds and miracles be remembered, I ordered this to be written, as you see.

I am the daughter of the said master who was Lord of Calatrava in the time of King Pedro. The king did my father the honor of giving him the commission of Alcantara, which is in the city of Seville. The king then made him master of Alcantara and, in the end, of Calatrava. This master, my father, was a descendent of the house of Águilar, and the nephew of Don Juan Manuel, son of his niece who was the daughter of two brothers. He rose to a very high estate, as can be discovered in the chronicles of Spain. And as I have said, I am the daughter of Doña Sancha Carrillo, niece and ward of King Alfonso of most illustrious memory, to whom God granted paradise, who was the father of King Pedro.

My mother died very early, and so my

father married me at seven years old to Ruy Gutierrez de Henestrosa. He was the son of Juan Fernandez de Henestrosa, King Pedro's head valet, his chancellor of the royal seal, and head majordomo of Queen Blanca his wife; Juan Fernandez married Doña María de Haro, mistress of Haro and the Cameros. To my husband were left many of his father's goods and several estates. He received three hundred mounted soldiers of his own, and forty strands of pearls as fat as chick-peas, and five hundred Moorish servants, and silver tableware worth two thousand marks. The jewels and gems of his house could not be written on two sheets of paper. All this came to him from his father and mother because they had no other son and heir. My father gave me twenty thousand *doblas* as a dowry; we lived in Carmona with King Pedro's daughters, my husband and I, along with my brothers-in-law, my sisters' husbands, and with one brother of mine, who was named Don Lope López de Córdoba Carrillo. My brothers-in-law were named Fernán Rodriguez de Aza, Lord of Aza and Villalobos, and Ruy García de Aza, and Lope Rodriguez de Aza. They were the sons of Alvaro Rodriguez de Aza and Doña Costanza de Villalobos.

That was how things stood when King Pedro was besieged at the castle of Montiel by his brother, King Enrique. My father went down to Andalusia to bring people to aid King Pedro, and on the way he discovered that the king was dead at the hands of his brother. Seeing this disgrace, he took the road to Carmona where the princesses were, King Pedro's daughters, who were very close relatives of my husband, and of myself through my mother. King Enrique, becoming King of Castile, came to Seville and surounded Carmona. As it is such a strong town, it was surrounded for many months.

But by chance my father had left Carmona, and those of King Enrique's camp knew how he was gone, and that it would not remain so well protected. Twelve knights volunteered to scale the town, and they climbed the wall. They were captured, and then my father was informed of what had happened. He came to Carmona then, and ordered them to be beheaded for their audacity. King Enrique observed this, and because he could not enter Carmona by force of arms to satisfy himself about this deed, he ordered the constable of Castile to discuss terms with my father.

The terms that my father put forward were two. First, King Enrique's party was to free the princesses and their treasure to leave for England, before he would surrender the town to the King. (And so it was done. He ordered certain noblemen, his kinsmen and natives of Córdoba bearing his family name, to accompany the princesses and the rest of the people who intended to leave with them.) The second condition was that my father, his children, his guard, and those in the town who had obeyed his orders would be pardoned by the king, and that they and their estates would be considered loyal. And so it was granted him, signed by the constable in the king's name. Having achieved this, my father surrendered the town to the constable in King Enrique's name, and he left there—with his children and the rest of the people—to kiss the king's hand. King Enrique ordered them to be arrested and put in the dungeon of Seville. The constable, who saw that King Enrique had not fulfilled the promise he had made in his name to this master (my father), left the court and never returned to it.

The king ordered my father to be beheaded in the Plaza de San Francisco in Seville, and his goods confiscated, as well as those of his son-in-law, guardsmen, and servants. While he was on his way to be decapitated, my father encountered Mosen Beltran de Clequin, a French knight, the knight, in fact, whom King Pedro had trusted and who had freed him when he was trapped in the castle of Montiel, but who had not fulfilled his promise, and instead surrendered him to King Enrique to be killed. As Mosen Beltran met with my father, he said to him, "Master, didn't I tell you that your travels would end in this?" And my father replied, "Better to die loyal, as I have done, than to live as you live, having been a traitor."

The rest of us remained in prison for nine years, until King Enrique died. Our husbands each had seventy pounds of iron on their feet, and my brother, Don Lope López, had a chain between the irons in which there were seventy links. He was a boy of thirteen years, the most beautiful creature in the world. My husband especially was made to go hungry. For six or seven days he neither ate nor drank because he was the cousin of the princesses, the daughters of King Pedro.

A plague came into the prison, and so my brothers and all of my brothers-in-law and thirteen knights from my father's house all died. Sancho Miñez de Villendra, my father's head valet, said to my brothers and sisters and me, "Children of my lord, pray to God that I live for your sakes, for if I do, you will never die poor." It was God's will that he died the third day without speaking. After they were dead they took them all out to the smith to have their chains taken off, like Moors.

My poor brother, Don Lope López, asked the mayor who had us in his charge to tell Gonzalo Ruíz Bolante that much charity was shown to us, and much honor, for the love of God. "Lord Mayor, it would be merciful of you to take off my irons before my soul departs, and not to take me to the smith." The mayor replied to him as if to a Moor, "If it were up to me, I would do it." At this, my brother's soul departed while he was in my arms. He was a year older than I. They took him away on a slab to the smith, like a Moor, and they buried him with my brothers and my sisters and my brothers-in-law in the church of San Francisco of Seville.

Each of my brothers-in-law used to wear a gold necklace around his throat, for they were five brothers. They put on those necklaces in Santa María de Guadalupe, and they vowed not to take them off until all five lay themselves down in Santa María. Because of their sins, one died in Seville, and another in Lisbon, and another in England, and so they died scattered. They ordered that they be buried with the gold necklaces, but the monks, after burying them, greedily removed the necklaces.

No one from the house of my father, Master Don Martín López, remained in the dungeon except my husband and myself. At this time, the most high and illustrious King Enrique, of very sainted and illustrious memory, died; he ordered in his will that we were to be taken out of prison, and that all that was ours be returned. I stayed in the house of my lady aunt, Doña María García Carrillo, and my husband went to demand his goods. Those who held them paid him little attention, because he had no rank or means to demand their return. You already know how rights depend on one's petition being granted. So my husband disappeared, and wandered through the world for seven years, a wretch, and never discovered relative nor friend who would do him a good turn or take pity on him. After I had spent seven years in the household of my aunt, Doña María García Carrillo, they told my husband, who was in Badajoz with his uncle Lope Fernandez de Padilla in the Portuguese War, that I was in good health and that my relatives had treated me very well. He mounted his mule, which was worth very little money, and the clothes he wore didn't amount to thirty *maravedis*, and he appeared at my aunt's door.

Not having known that my husband was wandering lost through the world, I requested my lady aunt, my lady mother's sister, to speak with Doña Teresa Fernandez Carrillo, who was a member of the Order of Guadalajara, which my great grandparents founded;

they have given an endowment to support forty wealthy women of their lineage who should join the order. I sent my aunt to petition that Doña Teresa would wish to receive me into that order, for through my sins my husband and I were lost. She, and all the order, agreed to this, for my Lady mother had been brought up in their monasteries. King Pedro had taken her from there and had given her to my father in marriage because she was the sister of Gonzalo Díaz Carrillo and of Diego Carrillo, sons of Don Juan Fernandez Carrillo and Doña Sancha de Rojas. Because these uncles of mine were afraid of King Pedro, who had killed and exiled many of his lineage and had demolished my grandfather's houses and given his property to others, these uncles of mine left there, in order to serve King Enrique when he was count, because of this outrage. I was born in Calatayud, in the king's house. The lady princesses, his daughters, were my godmothers, and they brought me with them to the fortress of Segovia, along with my lady mother, who died there. I was of such an age that I never knew her.

And after my husband arrived, as I said, I left the house of my lady aunt, which was in Córdoba next to San Ipólito, and my husband and I were received into some houses there, next to hers, and we came there with little rest.

For thirty days I prayed to the Virgin Saint Mary of Bethlehem. Each night on my knees I said three hundred Ave Marias, in order to reach the heart of my Lady aunt so she would consent to open a postern to her houses. Two days before my praying ended, I demanded of my lady aunt that she allow me to open that private entrance, so that we wouldn't walk through the street, past so many nobles that there were in Córdoba, to come eat at her table. In her mercy she responded to me and granted it, and I was greatly consoled. Another day, when I wanted to open the postern, her servants had changed her heart

and she would not do it. I was so disconsolate that I lost patience, and she that had caused me the most trouble with my lady aunt died at my hands, eating her tongue.

Another day, when only one day remained to complete my prayer, a Saturday, I dreamed I was passing through San Ipólito touching the alb. I saw in the wall of the courtyard an arch, very large and very tall. I entered through it and gathered flowers from the earth, and saw a very great heaven. At this I awoke, and I was hopeful that my Virgin St. Mary would give me a home.

At this time there was a robbery in the Jewish quarter, and I took in an orphan boy who was there, so that he would be instructed in the faith. I had him baptized so that he would be instructed in the faith.

One day, coming with my lady aunt from mass at San Ipólito, I saw being distributed among the clerics of San Ipólito those grounds where I had dreamed there was the great arch. I implored my lady aunt, Doña Mencia Carrillo, to purchase that site for me, since I had been her companion for seventeen years, and she bought it for me. She gave these grounds to me with the condition—which she indicated—that I build a chapel (erected over the houses) for the soul of King Alfonso, who built that church in the name of St. Ipólito because he was born on that saint's day. These chaplains have another six or seven chapels built by Don Gonzalo Fernandez, my lady aunt's husband, and Don Alfonso Fernandez, lord of Aguilar, and by the children of the marshal. Then, when I had done this favor, I raised my eyes to God and to the Virgin Mary, giving them thanks.

There came to me a servant of Master Don Martín López, my lord and father, who lives with Martín Fernandez, mayor of the doncels, who was there hearing mass. I sent a request with this servant to Don Martín Fernandez that, as a kinsman, he thank my lady aunt for the kindness she had shown me. He was greatly pleased, and so he did it well, saying that he received her kindness to me as if it were shown to him.

Now that possession of these grounds had been given to me, I opened a door on the very place where I had seen the arch which the Virgin Mary showed me. It grieved the abbots to hand over that site to me, for I was of a great lineage, and my children would be great. They were abbots, and had no need of great knights so near them. This I heard from a reliable voice, and I told them to hope in God that it would be so. I made myself so agreeable to them that I opened the door in the place that I wanted. God helped me by giving me that beginning of a house because of the charity I performed in raising the orphan in the faith of Jesus Christ. For thirty days before this, I had gone at Matins to the image of St. Mary the Fainting, which is in the Order of San Pablo of Córdoba, barefoot and with tears and sighs, and I prayed to her the prayer that follows sixty-three times, with sixty-six Ave Marias, in reverence for the sixty-six years that she lived with bitterness in this world, so that she would give me a home, and she gave me a home, and houses better than I deserved, out of her mercy. Here begins the prayer: "Mother St. Mary, your well-taught son took on great pain for you. You saw him tormented with great tribulation; your heart fainted after his tribulation. He gave you consolation; Lady, you who know my pain, give the same to me." It was the Virgin St. Mary's will that with the help of my lady aunt, and by the labor of my hands, I built in that yard two mansions, and an orchard, and another two or three houses for servants.

In this period of time a very cruel plague came. My lady aunt did not want to leave the city; I requested of her the kindness to permit me to flee with my children so that they would not die. She was not pleased but she gave me leave. I left Córdoba and went to Santa Ella with my children. The orphan that I raised lived in Santa Ella, and he lodged me in his house. All of the neighbors of the town were delighted by my coming. They received me with warm welcome, for they had been servants of the lord my father, and so they gave me the best house there was in that place, which was that belonging to Fernando Alonso Mediabarba. Being without suspicion, my lady aunt came there with her daughters, and I withdrew to a small room. Her daughters, my cousins, never got on well with me because of all the good their mother had done me. I suffered so much bitterness from them that it cannot be written.

The plague came there, so my lady left with her people for Águilar, and she took me with her as one of her own daughters, for she loved me greatly and said great things of me. I had sent the orphan that I raised to Ezija. The night that we arrived in Águilar, the boy came from Ezija with two small tumors in his throat and three carbuncles on his face, and with a high fever. In that house there were Don Alonso Fernandez, my cousin, and his wife and all of his household. Though all of the girls were my nieces and my friends, knowing that my servant came in such a condition, they came to me and said, "Your servant, Alonso, comes with the plague, and if Don Alonso Fernandez sees it he will be furious at his being here with such an illness."

And the pain that reached my heart anyone who hears this history can well understand. I became worldly wise and bitter. Thinking that through me such great sorrow had entered that house, I had Miguel de Santa Ella called to me. He had been a servant of the master, my lord and father, and I begged him to take that boy to his house. The wretched man was afraid, and he said, "Lady, how can I take him with the plague, which will kill me?" And I said to him, "Son, God would not want that." Shamed by me, he took the boy; and through my sins, thirteen persons who watched over him by night all died.

I made a prayer which I had heard, which a nun said before a crucifix. It seems that she was a great devotee of Jesus Christ, and she says that after she had heard Matins she came before a crucifix. On her knees she prayed seven thousand times "Pious Son of the Virgin, may piety conquer you." One night, when the nun was near that place, she heard that the crucifix answered her, and it said, "Pious you called me, and pious I will be for you." I found great devotion in these words. I prayed this prayer each night, begging God to free me and my children, and if he had to take someone, let it be the eldest, for he was very sick.

One night it was God's will that there was no one to watch over that sorrowful boy, for all who had until then watched over him had died. My son, who was called Juan Fernandez de Henestrosa like his grandfather, and who was twelve years and four months old, came to me and said, "Lady, is there no one to watch over Alonso tonight?" And I told him, "You watch over him, for the love of God." He replied to me, "Lady, now that the others have all died, do you want to kill me?" I said to him, "For my charity, God will take pity on me." And my son, so as not to disobey me, went to keep vigil. Through my sins, that night he was given the pestilence, and another day I buried him. The sick one lived after all the others had died.

Doña Teresa, the wife of my cousin Don Alonso Fernandez, became very angry because my son was dying in her house at that time. She ordered that he be removed from the house on account of his illness. I was so transfixed by grief that I could not speak for the shame that those words caused me. My poor son said, "Tell my lady Doña Teresa not to cast me away, for my soul will leave now for heaven." He died that night. He was buried in Santa María la Coronada, which is in the same town. Because Doña Teresa felt very hostile to me, and I did not know why, she ordered that he not be buried within the town. When they took him to be buried, I went with him. As I went through the streets with my son, people came out, making a great hue and cry, ashamed for me. They said, "Come out, lords, and see the most unfortunate, forsaken, and accursed woman in the world!" with shouts that trespassed the heavens. Like those of that place, all who were there in that crowd were servants of the lord my father, and had been brought up by him. Although they knew that it grieved their present lords, they made a great lament with me as if I were their lady.

This same night, after I came from burying my son, they told me to return to Córdoba. I went to my lady aunt to see if she had ordered this. She said to me, "Lady niece, I cannot fail to do it, for I have promised my daughter-in-law and my daughters, for they are acting as one. In the meantime, it distresses me to have you leave, although I have granted permission. I do not know what annoyance you have caused my daughter-in-law Doña Teresa, that makes her so hostile to you."

I said to her with many tears, "Lady, if I have deserved this, may God not save me." And so I returned to my house in Córdoba.

CHRISTINE DE PIZAN   (1363–1429? France)

Selections from the Works of Christine de Pizan
The Lavision-Christine, 1405

Translated by Nadia Margolis

Christine's Complaint to Lady Philosophy

Most revered Lady, whom I hope not to annoy by my prolixity but rather to betoken my obeisance to your most serene highness by the narration of my adventures, may it please you to extend the grace of your wise counsel to succor the wretchedness of my state of mind. Oh, my dear Lady, may you wish to note how Fortune the variable has always been, as it is said, a most bitter and cruel mother to me, especially considering the circumstances into which I was born. For I was born of noble parents in the land of Italy in the city of Venice, where my father, born in Bologna, where I was since then nourished, went to marry my mother, who was also born there, this marriage having been arranged through the longtime acquaintance of my father with my mother's father, a scholar with both master's and doctorate born in the town of Forlì and a graduate of the institute of Bologna, who then was a salaried counsel to the above-mentioned city where I was born. Because of this relative my above-mentioned father had come to know the Venetians and was, because of the extent and reputation of his knowledge, apparently retained as a salaried counsel of the said city of Venice during which time he resided in that city amidst wealth and many honors.

Now, I say to myself, was it not Fortune who made my father gifted for certain tasks and who caused him to move his possessions to live in the said city of Bologna? In which city there came to him soon thereafter news and messages all at once from two most excellent kings, these sending for him and promising sizeable salaries and perquisites for his great renown and the authority of his learning, each king wishing him to come to his court, one of whom was the sovereign Christian King of France, Charles the Wise, the fifth by this name. The other was the King of Hungary, the one whose worth and merit lived on after him such that he was called the Good King of Hungary.

Now since the importance of these emissaries to the esteem and dignity could not be set aside and forgotten, my father deliberated over the one party to which he would pledge his obedience. That is to say, which would be the most worthy, as well as his desire to see the colleges of Paris and the high status of the French court: he thus decided to come to the French king, expecting to serve the King on a temporary basis and visit the said institutes over the space of one year and then return to his wife and family, whom he bade stay in Bologna with all of their possessions and belongings. And all of these things having been arranged with permission from the said lords of Venice, he left and came to France, where he was most grandly received and honored by wise King Charles. And soon afterward, verification of his learning and knowledge established him as the King's special adviser and private counsel, whom he held in such high regard that after the beginning of the following year my father was not granted his leave (as originally planned), for the King desired to keep him at all costs and thus generously, at his own expense, sent him to bring back his wife, children and other family to live all of their lives in France and to be near him, promising them adequate revenues and pensions to ensure the honorable status of their estate. Nevertheless, my father, still expecting to return, delayed the move for almost three years, after having finally agreed to the situation. And so, as said before, we were transported from Italy to France: how grandly were received the wife and children of your kindred philosophical spirit, Master Thomas, my father, upon their arrival in Paris. Dressed in the rich Lombard garments as befitted women and children of their estate, these the most benign and wise King wished to see and receive joyously, which was done right after their arrival to the Louvre palace in Paris in the month of December. There was the King at the presentation of the said household to the beautiful and honorable company of relatives manifest before his eyes as he welcomed the wife and family most warmly.

Here Christine Tells of Her Good Fortune

Fortune was most favorable to us during the life of the above-mentioned good, wise King Charles. And with the other rewards of prosperity came a joyous, productive and peaceful life in marriage, as is natural for any good and loyal servant given the prosperity of his good master by the grace of God. From the time of his arrival in the service of the king, my father exerted some influence even over military warfare by administering his wise counsel according to the science of astrology. The King's success grew in value as he took many victories and triumphs over his enemies, and to prove these things to be true I refer to those princes still alive and others from that time who knew of these deeds. The aforementioned wealth of the prince was the culminating mark of his satisfaction with his above-mentioned loyal servant although philosophers did not customarily benefit from the remuneration and wealth bestowed upon my father; this matter, with all due respect, I would never condone as praiseworthy in the estate of married people, whose concern it should be that their estate and household should not fall victim to privation resulting from any prodigality after them. In any case, despite his customary generosity, the providence of the good King never allowed the edifice of his soul to fail in any of the necessary virtues.

To return to the point in my own fortunes, the time came whereupon I was approaching the age when it is customary for young ladies to take a husband. Although I was still quite a young thing, I was much sought after by knights and other nobles and wealthy clerics, may this not be taken as boasting on my part. For the honorable reputation and the great love that the King demonstrated toward my father was never but for the reason that my father considered a man worthy not by material wealth but by his knowledge and good character. He thus had in mind a young scholar, recently graduated, of good birth from noble parents of Picardy, whose qualities met with my father's approval as his son, to whom I was given in marriage. In this matter, I do not complain to Fortune, for to choose the right person in all ways I myself could have done no better than that person. Soon after our marriage, the good King, who thought highly of him, gave him the position, as it was vacant at that time, of notary and secretary in financial affairs and retained him at his court as a most beloved servant.

Christine Begins to Speak of Her Bad Fortune

Thus endured this prosperity for several years, but as Fortune showed herself to be envious of our success, she sought to restrain the source from which it came, and were it not for this dear lady the kingdom truly would not have suffered the grave misfortunes that made themselves felt in the household of Master Thomas. It was then that the most wise good prince, ravaged not by the natural course of things, but who, at the rather young age of forty-four years, fell to a rather brief illness from which he passed away. Alas, it indeed happens that good things last but a short while. For still today, if only it had pleased God to have let his life continue, a life so necessary to this kingdom whose government and state have since then been so badly ravaged. Now the door was open to our misfortunes, and I, being still quite a young woman, found myself entering through it. And as it is the custom with powerful men to keep secrets to themselves, great are the transformations and upheavals within their courts and domains, which cause conflicts of will on several fronts. This could hardly be otherwise unless great discretion is used as a remedy. Just as in the case of Alexander the Great, about whom various writings attest that, despite all of the lands he divided amongst them, his barons quarrelled nonetheless.

So thus did my father's large earnings diminish: the 100 francs per month, plus books and other gifts, did not amount to what he had originally expected from the good King for himself and his heirs: the 500 pounds in books and many other material goods which the King had forgotten to promise him on paper before his untimely death so that he was retained by the governing princes on a sadly diminished salary. In addition to which, he had already reached old age, so that he soon took ill and became incapacitated through which many privations threatened, rendering us less financially independent. For this reason, I believe that it is careful financial management in youth that provides us with security in old age. All the while when he was of sound mind, my father, as a true catholic,

recognizing his creator to the end, passed away at the hour he had previously predicted, for which, among scholars, he would be renowned such that over the past century no man had ever lived who was possesed of such lofty intelligence in mathematics, science, or judicial astrology. With this, among the princes and others who knew him well, his honest reputation as a worthy, distinguished man, his good works, his loyalty, honesty and other virtues without reproach caused him to be mourned and sadly missed. If he were at times too liberal, he was also generous with the poor; never refusing a poor man with wife and child. I only say in the interests of truth that, even to this day, he was lamented and mourned by princes and others as one worthy of being among them.

More of the Same

Now there remained as head of the household my husband, young and courtly, wise and moderate and much loved by princes and all people who came into contact with his office, which, because of his good sense, sustained the estate of the said family. But since Fortune had already set about moving her wheel downward, disposed toward pain, in order that she might strike me down to the lowest point, she could not bear that this very good person should endure for me. Because of Fortune, he died when in the flower of his abilities, wisdom, and promise in his position so that he could have risen to high office. She took him from me in the flower of his youth at the age of thirty-four and when I was twenty-five, having to care for three small children and an extensive household. I was thus with good reason full of bitterness, lamenting the loss of his sweet companionship and our past happiness that had only lasted ten years for me. Seeing arrive the great flood of tribulation rushing toward me, I desired more to die than to live, without forgetting my faith or my promise given to him in love never to take another husband.

And so I had fallen into the valley of tribulation. For just as Fortune, when she wishes to bring something into decline, whether it be a city, an empire, or an individual person, searches far and wide for all possible obstacles in order to guide that person upon whom she has chosen to vent her anger to the point of utter unhappiness, so this happened to me. I was therefore not present at the death of my husband, who was suddenly stricken by a rapid epidemic. Nevertheless he met his end a good catholic in the city of Beauvais where he had gone with the King, and was accompanied only by his servants and an entourage of strangers so that the precise state of his possessions could not be known. For it was the custom for married men not to talk about or declare the complete state of their affairs to their wives, from which often comes harm as it was to happen to me in my experience, and it makes no sense unless women, instead of being ignorant, learn wise management of such matters. I know well that it was not clear to me all that he had. Now it was necessary for me to go to work, something which I, nurtured on the finer things of life, had not learned, and to be the navigator of our ship cast out to sea in a storm without a captain, that is, our bereaved household without hearth nor country. I was thereupon beset by troubles from everywhere. And as is the case with all widows, legal complaints and trials surrounded me from all sides. Even those who owed me assailed me so that I would not try to ask them for anything. And Heaven only knows that it was true that many took advantage of the disarray of my husband's papers so as to collect fraudulent debts and other benefits to be obtained by liars. I was thus early on deprived of my rightful inheritance from my husband. . . . Other troubles plagued me concerning inheritance, on which they asked for back rent and large arrearages never mentioned in the origi-

nal decrees . . . I came upon the culmination of my adversities when I was stricken like Job by a lengthy illness . . . it is a wonder to what extent Fortune was unleashing herself against me. . . . So you might be able to know if for me, a fragile and naturally timid woman, making virtue out of necessity was a costly and dangerous task. . . .

Christine Tells of How She Changed Her Way of Life

After these things had happened during my youth as well as my greatest occupations outside, I returned to the life that pleased me the most. That is to say, solitary and calm, and so in solitude first came to me ruminations on Latin and the orators of beautiful learning and various sententiae and polished rhetoric that I had heard in the past when my friends, my father and husband were alive, although I retained but little of these because of my youthful frivolity. For even though I had been naturally since birth inclined to study, family affairs common to married folk took me away from such pursuits, and also the frequent bearing and care of children; and with this, too flagrant youth—the all too charming enemy of good sense—that often leaves children with only the mind for play, while they frequent their studies only for fear of beatings. But because I did not have this fear, the will to play mastered that of intelligence and understanding, so that I could never consistently apply myself to the labor of learning.

The Pleasure Christine Derives from Study

Now was the state of my life transmuted in another disposition. But not so much as to change my bad fortune. Thus, while suffering, I was able, through the solace and productivity of my solitary and speculative life, to persevere through the malevolence not only to my person but also to that of those closest to me, which I attributed to the pattern of my adversities. And I will tell you how, by taking my good friends away from me as always, she repulsed my progress and prosperity. Fortune did not suffer them to live long. It is true that, as rumors ran here and there among the princes of the order and manner of my way of life, that is, at study, and although I wished to keep it secret, I made them a present of my new volumes, however feeble and meager they were, on various subjects which, through their grace as benign and humble princes, they saw willingly and accepted with great pleasure. And the more I held to my unaccustomed image of a woman of letters, the more esteem came and with it, dignity, so that, within a short time, my said books were discussed and circulated in various parts and countries.

CHRISTINE DE PIZAN
The One Hundred Ballads (1393–1399?)

Translated by Nadia Margolis

Here Begin the One Hundred Ballads

I

Several people request that I compose
Some lovely verses that to them I'll send,
For when it comes to verses, they suppose
I possess a gift, but I don't pretend
To make fine or good poems, now and then,
Since they have asked me to do my best,
The small sum of my talents I'll extend,
To try to comply with their kind request.

Yet I've neither the feeling nor repose
To write words of joy and solace for them;
For my grief, which never fails to expose
Its dreary self, seeks my joy to upend;
So that sorrow retains me to the end,
All of my eloquence I could invest,
Were this the subject on which I should pen
To try to comply with their kind request.

And to those who wish that I might disclose
My life's secret sadness, I'll just pretend
That this is what death dealt by unseen blows;
Struck down the one upon whom I depend
Whose death the whole course of my life
    would amend
To despair; nor has my health been its best;
From this I shall write, since they so intend,
To try to comply with their kind request.

Princes, these verses to you I commend,
The work of a novice, at the behest
Of many who wished them, these I extend,
To try to comply with their kind request.

Rondeau LXII

A fountain of tears, a sorrowful stream,
Sea full of bitterness, river of pain,
Surround me, subjecting to merciless strain
My poor heart in which such miseries teem.

Thus I am plunged into violent dreams;
For through me there run with more force
    than the Seine,
A fountain of tears, a sorrowful stream.

So their waves fall in cadence supreme,
As though ushered in from Fortune's domain,
All breaking upon me; so, to regain
Dignity, must I suffer to extreme
A fountain of tears, a sorrowful stream.

Virelay I

I sing from behind a veil,
For 'tis better my eyes shed tears
Than to reveal the fears
That make my poor heart pale.

For this I hide my pain;
I shall not seek to flaunt,
Their pity I shan't want;
Such friendships as I retain.

For this I do not wail,
Nor grieve among my peers;
I laugh—so it appears—
In case all rhyme should fail,
I sing from behind a veil.

There is but little gain
In showing wretched want,
Since 'tis a foolish game
Of those who wish to taunt.

I thus care not to fail,
Whatever question nears,
To hide my obscure fears,
And my will to curtail,
I sing from behind a veil.

CHRISTINE DE PIZAN   Romance of the Rose

Christine's Response to the Treatise on the Romance of the Rose by John of Montrevil, June–July 1401: The First Extant Combative Document in the Debate

Translated by Nadia Margolis

To that most adept and knowledgeable person, Master John Johannes, secretary to our lord, the King.

Most reverend, honorable sir, to you my lord Provost of Lille, dearest sire and master, wise in all customs and morals, lover of science, learned in holy matters and expert in rhetoric, from me, Christine de Pizan, a woman ignorant of subtle understanding and agile sentiment—for which things your wisdom has never held the paltriness of my reasoning in contempt, I thus wish to beg your indulgence despite my feminine debility. And since it has pleased you to send me, for which I thank you, a small treatise composed in fine rhetoric and convincing arguments (this done in your own words in reproving, or so it seems to me, several of those finding fault with the compilation of *The Romance of the Rose* in several places and vigorously defending and approving this work and its authors, especially Meun), I, having read and considered your aforementioned prose and understood its meaning inasmuch as the feebleness of my paltry intellect would enable me—to the extent that, without a response having been requested of me, I, moved rather by my contrary opinion of your words and in accord with the especially astute and discerning cleric to whom your epistle is addressed—mean to say, divulge and manifestly uphold that, your good grace notwithstanding, you have committed a great error without reason in giving such perfect praise to the aforesaid work, which could better be called utter idleness than a useful work, in my judgment. And how often you reprove those who would contradict your opinion, saying that "it is a great thing thus to understand that which another says to be true; he has better constructed and held up his assumptions by dint of long and diligent study," etc., may I not be judged presumptuous in daring to repudiate and reprove so serious and subtle an author; but let it be noted that the firm and forceful conviction that moves me against several particularities which are or are said to be understood—and, moreover, a thing that is said out of inner conviction and not by order of the law can be argued without prejudice. And however much I do not possess great knowledge nor am I schooled in the use of subtle styles of language

(from which I might know how to arrange words pleasingly and in polished style and order to make my ideas shine forth), I will not allow to be said in any way whatsoever a vulgar opinion of my understanding, merely because I do not know how to express it in ornate, well-ordered words.

So why have I said above that this work "could better be called idleness . . ."? Without fail it seems to me that anything without worth, although it has been treated, done and accomplished by great labor and trouble, can be called idle or worse than idle inasmuch as worse evil comes of it. And since already for a long time for the great common renown of the said romance I have desired to see it, after knowledge and recognition had caused me to understand somewhat these subtle matters, I read and considered it at length and in great detail to the best of my understanding. It is true that for the material that was not to my liking in several areas I hopped over it like a bird over a snare: I thus did not dwell on it much. Nevertheless there remained in my memory several matters treated in it that my judgment greatly condemned and still cannot approve in spite of the contrary praise of other people. It is very true that my paltry understanding considers that which is expressed with levity and delight, in several sections, to be rather solemn discourse in what it really means—and in very attractive terms and graceful leonine verses: nor could it be said more subtly nor in more measured terms than that means by which he intends to treat his subject. But in dealing with the disputed position, without fail, in my opinion, he treats this dishonestly in several parts—and equally in the character which he calls Reason, who names the secret parts of the body explicitly. And to the extent to which you defend and convey his position, and allege that in all things God has created there is no ugliness and consequently their names must not be evaded, I say and confess that God did indeed create all things pure and clean in themselves, and at that time it was not unseemly to name them: but by the pollution of sin did man become impure, from which the original sin still inhabits us (so testify the Holy Scriptures). Thus by way of comparison I can allege: God made Lucifer the most beautiful of all the angels and gave him a solemn and beautiful name, he who was then by his sin dragged down to hideousness; in his case the name as beautiful as it was originally now strikes terror in the ears of all who hear it because of the reputation of its bearer.

Moreover you propose that Jesus Christ, "In speaking of female sinners, called them *meretrix*," etc. And that in his calling them by this name I can deduce via your argument that this term *meretrix* is not at all unsuitable for naming the vileness of the thing itself—for in Latin it can be said in still more vile terms. And that shame must be pushed aside in speaking publicly of those things of which nature herself is ashamed, I reply that, given the esteem in which both you and the author are held, you are commiting a great error against the noble virtue of shame, which by its very nature refrains from libertinage and dishonesty in sayings and deeds; and that it is a great vice beyond the realm of honest practice and good morals as found in many places throughout the Holy Scriptures. And that the name should not be repudiated "any more than if it were the holy relics themselves being named," I confess to you that it is not the name which makes a thing dishonest, but the thing that makes a name dishonest. For this reason, to my fragile mind, it should be spoken of with sobriety—and not without necessity—for a particular reason, as in the treatment of illness or other such necessity. And just as our ancestors hid them, so should we in deed and in word.

And I still cannot remain silent about that which disturbs me: that the lofty personage of Reason, whom he himself calls the daughter of God, must be the one to enunciate in such words and in the form of a proverb that which I have noted in this chapter, wherein she says to the Lover that "in the battle of love . . . it is better to deceive than be deceived." I daresay here that John of Meun's Reason abjures her Father in so saying, for she has given herself too much to another doctrine. For if one were better than the other, it would follow that both were worthy: which cannot be. I thus hold to the contrary that, to tell the truth, it is less bad to be deceived than to deceive.

Now let us go further in considering the material or the manner of speaking, which has caused many to reproach on good advice. Great Good Lord! What horribleness! What dishonesty! And such contradictory teachings does he record in the chapter on the Duenna! But for Heaven's sake! What else can one find here but sophistic exhortations full of ugliness and utterly vile reminiscence? Look here! Among you who have beautiful daughters and wish to initiate them to a life of virtue, take them under your wing, and procure for them and advise them to read *The Romance of the Rose* in order to teach them to discern good from evil—what am I saying? But evil from good! And what use or advantage can it be for the listener to hear such vileness? Then in the chapter on Jealousy, good Lord! What great benefit can be noted, what need to record the dishonest and ugly words which are are all too frequently on the lips of those unfortunates smitten with this malady? What good example or initiation can this possibly provide? And the ugliness noted down there about women, some say that in justifying this by saying that it is spoken by the Jealous Husband, and truly it is as if God were speaking through Jeremiah. But unfailingly, whatever deceitful additions he may have added, they cannot—thank God!—in any way make conditions for women more bitter or unfavorable. So much for that! And when I think of the ruses, false appearances, and hidden deceptions in marriage or in other situations that one may gather from this treatise, I adjudge these most certainly to be good and worthwhile narratives to hear!

But the character whom he names Genius the priest says marvelous things: no doubt the works of Nature would all have failed long ago if he had not commended them! But for Heaven's sake! Who is this man who has the nerve to assure me that this great progression full of vituperation that he calls a sermon could possibly be worthwhile, as though in derision of holy predication, which he says Genius is doing, wherein you find so much dishonesty, sophistic names and words provoking Nature's secrets—those which should be kept in silence and not named, since one does not see at all discontinued the activities that maintain the common order which cannot fail: for, if it were otherwise, it would be well and good for the perpetuation of the human race, to find and speak those provocative and exciting words to urge mankind to continue such activity.

The author goes on to say, as far as I can remember, to what end I cannot cease to marvel: for to the aforementioned sermon he joins, as a kind of figure, Paradise and the pleasures found within it. He says rightly that here is where the virtuous shall go, and then concludes so that all may understand—without sparing man or woman—how to accomplish and put to practice the works of Nature; not in that it goes against the law, as one would expect him to say—but very plainly!—that in so doing they will be saved. And in this he seems to wish to maintain that there is no sin in *Luxuria*, that it is thus a virtue—which is an error and contrary to the laws of God. Oh! What sowing and what doctrine! What can one expect to reap from all this! I believe that many people have retreated from the world and entered religion or have become hermits for this holy reading, or have withdrawn from a life of wrongdoing to be saved from such advice, which never comes, I daresay at the risk of offending someone, except through abandonment of one's character to corruption and vice—which may cause great suffering and sin.

And still, for the sake of God! Let us look a little beyond: in what manner valuable or constructive can he be justified in so excessively, impetuously, and most dishonestly accusing, blaming and slandering women as committing many serious vices and whose habits are full of every kind of perversion; and by so many attacks as conveyed by as many characters as one could ever hope to absorb. For if you wished to tell me that the Jealous Husband acts out of passion, I would not understand him to be in the service of Genius, who so often recommends and counsels one to sleep with women without forgetting that activity which he so frequently praises; and this same character says to all others many vituperations against women, and says in fact: "Flee! Oh flee the venomous serpent!" and then says to continue as before with that activity. There is here a great and evil contradiction in commanding us to flee that which he wishes us to follow and to follow that which he wishes us to flee. Rather, if women are that perverse, one should not order us to approach them at all; for whoever fears trouble should take pains to evade it.

And because of this he strongly forbids telling secrets to women—about whom he is so desirous to know, as he records, such that I do not believe that devils can find as much hodgepodge, rubbish, and wasted words to equal that so carefully arranged therein—yet I beg of those who make such opinions a reality and who uphold them to tell me when they have once seen men accused, dead, hanged, or attacked in the street because of accusations made by their wives: I think they will find them to have suffered for other reasons. Notwithstanding that it is good and praiseworthy advice that everyone should keep his secrets close for safety's sake, for there are vicious people everywhere; and that in many cases, as I have heard tell, someone has been accused and then hanged because of having been betrayed by a friend in whom he had placed his confidence, but I think that before justice there have been few such rumors, or complaints of horrible evils, or great betrayals and diabolical behavior as he maliciously and secretly knows women to have committed—what kind of secret is it that is true of no one! And as I have said earlier on this subject in a poem of mine called *The Epistle to the God of Love*: where are the countries or kingdoms which exile people for their evil deeds? But without speaking in common agreement, let us say of those great crimes one can accuse even the worst those who deceive the most: what can these women do if you don't give them a chance to deceive you? If they ask you for the silver from your purse, which they do not take nor steal from you, don't give it to them if you do not wish to! And if you say that you were besotted at the time, don't let yourself get drunk! What are these women going to do, track you down in your home and take it from you by force? It would be good to know just how women deceive you.

And moreover, he spoke so superfluously and offensively about married women who deceived their husbands—a situation he could not know firsthand and so spoke of it in so many generalizations: to what good end can this lead, what good can come of it? I know not what to think other than that it prevents happiness and harmony, and renders husbands who hear so much rubbish and twaddle, if they decide to believe it, suspicious and unloving with their wives. Heavens! What an exhortation! How worthwhile it is! Actually, since he blamed all women in general, I am forced to believe that he has never made the acquaintance nor known the company of an honorable and virtuous woman, but rather has frequented only dissolute and disreputable

ones—as self-indulgent men are wont to do—and thus claims that all women are of the lowly kind, since he has never known the other. If only he had criticised the dishonest ones and had advised the avoidance of this sort alone, his teachings would be good and just. But no! He accuses all women of this without exception. But if the author takes it upon himself so much beyond the limits of reason to accuse them or judge them untruthfully, no blame should be imputed to them but rather to him who tells a lie so far beyond the boundaries of truth that it is totally unbelievable, as the contrary manifestly appears. For if he and all his accomplices in this matter had sworn to it, none would suffer, for there have already been, there are and will be many of the most valiant women, more honest, better raised and even more learned, whose greatest worth is revered throughout the world where that author has never been—even in worldly affairs and most refined customs—and several who were the cause of reconciliation of their husbands, and conducted their affairs for them and kept their inner passions and secrets within, even though their husbands were crude and unloving. Of this one finds proof enough in the Bible and in other ancient histories, such as Sarah, Rebecca, Esther, Judith, and many others; even in our time have we seen in France many valiant women, great ladies and others of our ladies of France: the holy devoted Queen Joan, Queen Blanche, the Duchess of Orléans, daughter of the King of France, the Duchess of Anjou who is now named the Queen of Sicily—all of whom had such beauty, chastity, honesty, and wisdom—and still others; and the least known valiant noblewomen, such as my lady of Ferte, the wife of my lord Peter of Craon—who performed many laudable deeds, and several others, all of whom would make too long an account to relate here.

And do not believe, dear sir, that no one else could have an opinion on this matter, or that I say or put in order these said defenses for the purpose of gaining favorable treatment as a woman: for in truth my motive is nothing more than to uphold pure truth, since I know a certain body of accepted knowledge to be contrary to the aforementioned points denied by me; and in that I am indeed a woman, I can better bear witness on this aspect than he who has no experience of it, and who thus speaks only out of supposition and haphazard guessing.

By all means, for the love of Heaven!—let this be considered the end of this said treatise. For as the proverb says, "At the end all things are finished." So let it be seen and noted to whom it may be useful the most horrible and shameful conclusion—and I do mean shameful!—but so dishonest that I dare say that no one loving virtue and honesty would hear it without being confounded by shame and outraged at thus hearing discerned and disjointed and put into dishonest fictions that which reason and shame should restrain good people from even thinking; moreover, I daresay that even the Goliards would be shocked to read or hear it in public, in proper places, or before people of virtuous reputation. What is the point of a work one dares not read or speak of in proper form at the table of queens, princesses and worthy noblewomen—without their having to cover their faces as they blush with shame! And if you wish to excuse this by saying that it was in the style of a lovely novella that it pleased him to represent the goal of love by these figures, I'll reply to you that there's nothing new in what he's telling us! Don't we already know how men inhabit women by nature? If he were to relate to us how bears or lions or birds or other strange beasts came to be, that would serve to make us laugh in a fable, but he still tells us nothing new. No doubt such occurrences have been related more pleasantly, much more sweetly, and in more courtly terms, more likely to please charming honest lovers and all other virtuous people.

Thus, according to my limited abilities and feeble judgment, without being more prolix in language, although more can be said and better, I cannot attribute any good use to the said treatise; for so much do I seem to notice in it that many pains were taken to no advantage. Although my judgment confesses Master John to be a very great cleric, subtle and eloquent, capable of producing a work of great merit and lofty sentiment if he were to apply himself to it—in this case it's a pity—I suppose that the great carnality with which his work is filled caused him to abandon at will that which would have led him to a profitable end, as all operations come to be known by their inclinations. This notwithstanding, I would never reprove the *Romance of the Rose* as a whole, for there are certainly some good things well stated in it. And this moreover is the work's greatest danger: for evil is rendered more believable by putting it together with good to make it more respectable; in this way many subtle authors have on several occasions planted the seeds by error by mixing and coating it with bits of truth and virtue. Just as his priest Genius says: "Flee! flee woman, the evil serpent lurking under the grass!" I can say: "Flee! flee the covert malice beneath the shadow of goodness and virtue!"

For this reason I say to you, in conclusion, most dear sir, and to all of your allies and accomplices who praise it so much and who wish to magnify its worth to such an extent that you would devalue all other volumes and would dare lower your esteem of them before it, that it is not worthy of a judgment being imputed to it, with all due respect to your good grace; and that you do a great injustice to all valuable books: for a work without usefulness to the common or private good—no matter how delightful or at what labor and cost—is not worthy of praise. And just as in olden times when the triumphant Romans would give neither praise nor honors to anything that was not useful to the public, let us look at their example before attempting to crown this romance. For I find, it seems to me, these aforementioned things and others considered, better that it be shrouded in fire than crowned with laurel, even though you call it a "mirror of good living, a model for political self-government and for living religiously and wisely;" on the contrary, with all respect, I say that it is an exhortation to vice seeking to comfort a dissolute life, a doctrine full of deception, a path to damnation, public defamation, a cause of suspicion and heresy, shame in several people, and perhaps a source of error.

And I well know that on this point in excusing it you will answer me that in it good deeds are extolled and that evil is presented only so as to be avoided. Likewise I can explain to you by means of a better reason that human nature, which in itself is inclined toward evil, has no need for us to call attention to the lame foot in order to learn to walk more correctly; and as for speaking of all the good that can be noted in said book, certainly too many virtuous things, better said, more respectable and more useful—even in political and moral life—are found in many other volumes done by philosophers and doctors of our faith, such as Aristotle, Seneca, Saint Paul, Saint Augustine, and others—this you know—which more validly and completely attest and teach virtue and how to flee vices than Master John of Meun would know to do: but not so willingly are these authors seen or retained by mortals of the flesh, as when it greatly pleases the drunkard taken ill for whom the physician prescribes that he drink plenty of fluids, and so willingly for the pleasure of drinking does he allow himself to believe it will no longer do him any harm. And so I become certain that you—to whom God has prescribed it!—and all others returned to the light and purity of a clear conscience by the grace of God, without the blemish or pollution of sin nor even its intention, if you clean by the sting of contrition (an act causing to be seen clearly the secret of conscience and condemning free will as the arbiter of truth), you will make another judgment of the *Romance of the Rose* and might even wish, perhaps, that you had never seen it.

So it should thus suffice. And may folly, arrogance, or presumption not be imputed to me for daring, I a woman, to take up and refute such a subtle author and whittle down the praise of him, when he, only one man, dared to undertake the defamation and blasphemy, without exception, of an entire sex.

IX

Individual and Collective Reformation at the End of the Middle Ages

Magdelena Beutler of Freiburg and Mary of Nijmeghen

IN THE FINAL TWO WORKS in this collection, we find some of the same interpenetration of secular and spiritual worlds found in Christine de Pizan's work. The mystic and reformer Magdalena Beutler of Freiburg[1] was herself the daughter of a mystic, and she had her first experiences of visions and mystical death when her mother left her alone as a very small child so she could pursue her own spiritual practices. Her mother moved in Dominican circles, and Magdalena's allegiances were to the Franciscans and specifically devoted to a reform of the house of Clarisses in Freiburg. Her life has been studied, and one of her major writings edited by Karen Greenspan, who also discovered the manuscript. The text included here is taken from a manuscript in Freiburg. Magdalena's major writings are *Die Goldene Litanie* and the *Erklaerung des Vaterunsers* (*The Golden Litany* and *Meditations on the Paternoster*). The section from her biography included here stresses the public character of her mission; at the time that she prophesied her own mystical death, Magdalena was only twenty-three. Yet she was already important enough, not just to her convent but also to the town, that all the municipal officials came to the church to witness her death. Hundreds of ordinary people were also there; the town council put the cloister under a guard of honor, and several city councilmen, along with leaders of the various religious groups in the town, requested permission to enter the cloister where Magdalena lay dying. All told, seventeen authority figures from the town were present early Friday morning, Twelfth Night 1430. Neither the religious nor the secular authorities seemed to have been particularly well equipped to understand the situation. Though Magdalena did not die, the event was not a failure. In fact, her influence seemed to grow in the community after this scene and a similarly public disappearance a few days later. It would seem that Magdalena's "death" is actually the occasion on which she receives the stigmata in her hands and feet. This would account for the success of the event, particularly following her successful restoration of her convent of Poor Clares to a rule closer to that of St. Francis' time.[2]

These events seem almost to come from an earlier time, an older mentality—the early thirteenth century of Marie d'Oignies and Christina Mirabilis, perhaps—except for Magda-

347

lena's emphasis on writing. She wishes to disappear behind her written words—written communication is much more to be trusted than the memory of spoken words. She had prepared letters (to be read aloud after her death) and they were read publicly while she was lying in her coffin in the cloister. The previous year (1429) she had mysteriously disappeared but had remained in touch with her sisters in the convent by secretly dropping into the choir letters written in blood stating what must be done to bring about the reform of the convent. Others had tried to reform the convent, but only Magdalena's efforts met with success. Although her biography seems to us violent and overdramatic, Magdalena's style may have been exactly what was needed for her time, for we are told that "there was no one so wild who saw or heard her, but received special grace from her."

The final work of this collection is a play, Marika or *Mary of Nijmeghen*,[3] which has been attributed to the Antwerp poet Anna Bijns. The translator, Eric Colledge, believes that, if not by her, it is certainly by someone associated with her group. It is a remarkable piece, with parallels to Hrotsvit's play of Mary, the niece of Abraham. Here, too, Mary is being brought up by an uncle, Sir Gilbert—a priest rather than a hermit. Mary is sent to the nearby town to do some shopping, and since it is late, her uncle advises her to stay overnight with her aunt who lives in town. By the time Mary finishes her tasks, it is indeed dark, and she is afraid of being attacked as she walks home. Her aunt refuses to let her stay and accuses her of promiscuity. In rage and despair, not caring what happens to her, Mary begins to walk home, and of course the devil accosts her. She accepts his invitation to live with him and be his love, on the terms that he will teach her necromancy or the next best thing, the seven liberal arts. They live a low life in the taverns of Antwerp for some time, where she astounds the guests with her mathematical wizardry and her rhetorical skills, including a fine poem in defense of the artist. The only negative aspect for her is the number of dead bodies the two of them leave in their wake, the victims of quarrels and rivalries catalyzed by the demonic presence.

The second movement of the play begins with Mary's regretting the choice she has made although she feels she has gone too far to turn back. Nevertheless, she wants to return to her home town and see Sir Gilbert, her uncle. When she and the devil Moenen arrive, the traditional Rogation Day play is being performed, a play that opens with a devil Mascaron presenting the overwhelming forgivingness of God. From the devil Mascaron's point of view, such compassion is maddening, and he longs for a return to the old days when a sin was a sin, and you always knew how it would be punished. Watching the play, Mary feels true contrition and desires to be a Christian again. The devil, aware he has lost her, flies up to the steeple with her and throws her down bodily, hoping to break her neck. Only as her body comes hurtling through the crowd from on high does her uncle become aware of her, and he hastens to her side. She lives through the fall, and he supervises her penitence. But, having lived as man and wife with the devil, her sin is so great that no priest feels competent to absolve her.

> After this, Sir Gilbert went with his niece to all the most learned priests in the town of Nijmeghen; but no priest, however learned, however experienced, however holy or devout, once he had understood the case, dared in any way be so bold as to absolve her or impose on her any penance for her sins, which were so dreadful and so unnatural, and so they were all greatly oppressed.[4]

Even the pope, when they reach him, is hesitant when he thinks about the fact that she really had sex with the devil, but he fastens iron rings about her body as her penance. Mary is very straightforward about the seriousness of her sin: "I am the devil's mistress, and I have been for more than seven years . . . I have done with him that which man and wife do. Have I not reason to feel horror at myself?" She is equally honest when the shocked pope asks her how she could possibly have had sex with the devil knowing who he was. "Father, it was the good times, all the money and the presents . . . and now it makes me shudder."[5] She completely accepts her penance, iron rings about her neck and arms, believing that when these rings fall off, she will be freed from the burden of her sins. In time the rings do fall off, and she is forgiven. Next to the convent for converted prostitutes in Maestricht, Mary's grave still bears three rings over it and a written sign that tells her story.

The first time one reads this play, two things stand out: that it is a variant of the Faust story, with a female protagonist, and that the conversion scene, a play within a play, seems remarkably effective. Whether it dates from the fourteenth or the fifteenth century, the degree of dramatic complexity is surprising. So are the tolerance and the humor expressed in the entire play. Only upon rereading does one notice that Mary is, in fact, a witch although never identified as such; her confession of having had sex with the devil, acquiring knowledge from him and then causing the deaths of innocent people is exactly what witchcraft inquisitors of that time were trying to extract from their victims in less tolerant areas of Europe. Even the quarrel with her aunt is the kind of detail that often turns up in witchcraft documents as the motivation for someone's turning to witchcraft. Still, one cannot say there is a witchcraft theme in this play. Mary is a Faust figure—she is not sex-typed as female in her response to the devil's offers. There is a surprisingly noninflammatory tone to the presentation of Mary's sin. It's also very funny. The fall from the steeple into her uncle's sight is his wonderfully belated recognition of her fall from grace. Like Maria's uncle Abraham, Sir Gilbert has not done a very good job protecting his ward from such a fall, and so he shares in her penitential journey. The urbanity, compassion, and humor of this play about sin make it the ideal conclusion to this collection of writings by medieval women.

NOTES

1. Karen Greenspan, *Erklaerung des Vaterunsers: A Critical Edition of a Fifteenth Century Mystical Treatise by Magdalena Beutler of Freiburg*. Ph.D. thesis, University of Massachusetts at Amherst, 1984.

2. In the opening paragraph of the selection included here, we are told Magdalena "will undergo the same suffering as her redeemer" and that God will "give her the signs of love on her body." She understands the "temporal death" to mean her soul will be separated from her body. She seems to really believe in the reality of her coming death and has prayed that no one who witnesses it will be lost. After several attempts are made to get her to speak while she is dying, she seems to return to health, and the Passion is read to her that night. Suddenly she cries out in pain as a wound breaks out on her foot, and then the same thing happens to her hands. The crowd waiting outside is told what has happened, and "when these folk heard of the great miracle, they were greatly moved. . . ." For Greenspan's discussion of the significance of the stigmata here, see *Erklaerung*, p. 29.

3. *Mary of Nijmeghen* was translated by Eric Colledge in *Mediaeval Netherlands Religious Literature* (New York: London House and Maxwell, 1965), pp. 191–224.

4. *Mary of Nijmeghen*, p. 219.

5. *Mary of Nijmeghen*, p. 221.

MAGDALENA BEUTLER OF FREIBURG

(1407–1458; Germany)

From The Life of Magdalena Beutler

Transcribed and translated by Karen Greenspan

At a certain time, three great things were revealed to Magdalena. The first was that she should undergo the same suffering as her Redeemer; the second, that God wished to give her the signs of love on her body; the third, that God had chosen her to possess a martyr's reward. One should not understand this to mean that she was to be martyred by the sword, but rather that God wished to send her much affliction and distress, through which he would make her more pleasing to himself.

In that year (which is counted 1430) she was one day in deep inward prayer, when God Almighty spoke to her: "Prepare yourself, for on Twelfth Night you will undergo a temporal death." She understood by this that her soul would be separated from her body. So she prayed with all the earnestness of her heart, and said, "Holy, worthy Creator, I beg you that unto those who honor your holy name through me, your poor creature, or do a good deed on account of my life or after my death, you impart your special grace, and release them from all their sins, and heal them, soul and body; and also that of all who are present at my end, none may ever be lost; and also, at the hour of my death, that all believing souls be rescued from the torments of Purgatory."

God heard her and answered forthwith, "My dearest spouse, what you have begged of me shall be granted unto you."

When she saw her sisters afterward, she told them, "In three days I shall become very ill and in thirty-four days I shall die." And so it

came to pass. And when the sisters heard that she would be parted from them, who can describe their hearts' great pain? Day and night they wept and mourned, as if she had been their true mother.

Now, she lay seventeen days in the infirmary, in grave illness. And in her illness, she thanked God for His grace and desired from all her sisters that they help her in praising God, which they did. And she often desired that God be praised in her presence with singing and reading. She helped them with this as much as her illness permitted her.

God granted her many great favors during this time. Among them was a vision, in which she saw Our Lady sitting upon an altar, wearing two crowns on her head. Then God's mother took one of the crowns from her head and, leaning toward the dear Magdalena, set it upon her head, saying, "This crown is yours, my dear child, which has been prepared for you since the beginning of the world." After this, for a time, Magdalena required no bodily food at all.

When seventeen days had passed, however, she received the holy, worthy sacrament and the holy anointment* with great earnestness and devotion. She then lay in a trance until nightfall, at which time she came to herself and asked after all her sisters, and looked upon them and said, "My lord Jesus Christ has done me a great favor and has instructed me in what manner I am to pass the next fifteen days. And I commend unto you most especially the praise of God, and that you love

*Extreme unction.

one another, as Christ commanded his disciples. And what you desire that others do unto you, that should you yourself do unto others. And practice holy poverty; for wherever holy poverty is, there you have riches. And I also commend unto you that inward piety and turning of the heart toward God, which are very pleasing to Him. And pray to God for me, which I will also do for you eternally." The sisters desired the same of her, and amid great sorrow and weeping they conversed a long time with her; and after much speech, several sisters begged her, "Tell us something that the Lord has revealed to you today."

She answered them, saying, "I will tell you one thing. It seemed to me that I stood before the Heavenly Father and lamented my impending death and the torment of my illness. He answered me, saying, 'I wished to harbor salvation in my only-begotten Son and in the pain of the Cross until the Last Judgment, and I wanted my Son to give himself up to it willingly. I want the same thing of you.'" And she said, "My dearest sisters, let whatever pleases God please you also. For know ye, that I must remain on my prayer-stool these next fifteen days, by myself all alone." And so it came to pass that the sisters led her into the choir, where she remained fifteen days without any bodily food. But every day she received the body of Our Lord—that was her manner of her abiding during that time.

And on holy Christmas Eve a wondrous thing happened, which was that God granted something to her in her illness which gave her strength enough to sing with the other women. And she sang nine lessons by herself, in a high, festive voice, and after the *Te deum laudamus*, the sisters took her back to her prayer-stool and she became as ill again as she had been before.

By this time, the news that she was to die had gotten out and many hundreds of people from the towns and villages came, desiring with great devotion to be present at her end;

and so it came to pass. And they brought a great many wax tapers and an untold number of tallow candles to be burned at her end. The news came to her that now all the people desired that she pray to God for them. She praised God in Heaven then and gave all honor to Him, her Creator, and accepted no worldly praise for herself, but only desired intensely all that led to the healing of mankind. And she bethought herself of the great favor that she had obtained of God, that of all the people who came to her death, none should ever be lost. And even those people that scorned God's grace and gifts and mocked her with hard words, who were present at her end, would certainly receive grace at their death.

Shortly after this, the women sent for their Father Provincial. He came, bringing several friars of his order with him. The town council put the cloister under a guard of honor, and several of the city councilmen and other folk, both secular and religious, came to the Provincial and entreated him most earnestly to take them into the cloister with him. He conceded to this and he took them into the cloister, along with sixteen brothers of his order, which was indeed unheard of.

In 1431, Twelfth Night fell on a Friday. On Thursday evening, since the next day was that very Friday, Magdalena arose from her prayer-stool and went to the sisters in the choir, desiring to eat with them one last time in the spirit of love, as Christ ate with his disciples. This the sisters did and held the ceremony with her in the choir. She read the holy prayers herself at table, and after the meal she blessed all the sisters and desired them to take the holy sacrament with her the next day. They agreed to this, and at Compline the sisters led her before the altar. She lay there the whole night long in great illness and great agony; and the sisters stayed by her in the choir and prayed all night.

Early in the morning the Provincial came

into the cloister with the following people, both worldly and religious, who had been appointed to observe this matter clearly, to see and to hear; and these are the people by name: Graf Bernhart von Tierstein, Junker Hanns Erhart von Schefenberg, the deacon of Freiburg, the deacon of Rheinfelden, the reading-master of the Augustinians, the holy lords the Prior of the Carthusians of Freiburg and the Prior of the Carthusians of Basel, and the Burgermeister of the city, called Junker Heitze Kichle, and Junker Jerg von Kippenheim, the old Burgermeister, and the foremost among the city councillors, Ulrich Ruber, Haman von Todnau, Rudolf von Kilchen, Master Paulus Gloterer, the doctor, Hamann Schnidke, the city secretary, Anderes Henenberg, and Ehrhart Hesle. All these people went into the cloister early on that Friday.

When they came into the choir, they found the lady Magdalena lying before the altar on the bare ground, in grave illness, though fully conscious. They dutifully observed her and saw how she often turned herself about, sometimes one way, sometimes another. She lay in this fashion until the clock struck twelve. As soon as the clock began to strike, she altered in such a way that the people knew it could mean nothing else but that she had departed this life; but, so that they might render a reliable report of the matter, they continued to observe her with great diligence. After a little while a tiny movement was discovered in her heart, but the people discerned no possibility of a recovery in it, nor any expectation of life. Having ascertained this, they left her to lie and went from her to read several letters, written by her for the benefit of all, which she had directed them to read after her death. When the last letter had been read, she let out a cry, which sounded to them as if she said, "Coffin, coffin!" And after a little time, they laid her in a coffin, as she desired, and there she held herself all motionless. And, as she remained motionless, they went away from her; and

after a little while, the Provincial of the order and several other noble people came over to the coffin to look at her. They found her as unmoving as they had left her, and the Provincial decided with the others that he would admonish her by her vow of obedience. Kneeling humbly by the coffin, he said, "My dear daughter Magdalena, I admonish you by the honor of the Holy Trinity and by the worthy death of Jesus Christ and by the vow of holy obedience, which you have vowed to honor in your holy, worthy order, that you tell us, if it is possible, how it goes with you." He made this admonition three times. At the first admonition she remained motionless as before; at the second, she moved her head a little bit; at the third, she let out a cry which no one understood. Upon this, her superior was advised by several people to try the threefold admonition again.

At the next admonition, she uttered something which they understood as, "My body is dead but my heart still lives." Those who were there as witnesses then sent for others who had not been present, that they might be perfectly sure of what was taking place. When these people came, the command was repeated for a third time; at the admonition, it was perceived that she spoke with her mouth, in full voice, "God has worked such a thing in my heart, that I may not die." And that was heard by everyone who was there. And afterward she was left alone by all those people, who forsook the cloister to bring the matter before the city council. It was arranged that several of the same councilmen, both worldly and religious, were to go into the cloister again, for the perfect observation of the following miracle of God.

They returned to the cloister at the eighth hour of the night and found her in the coffin exactly as they had left her. After a little time one of them went over to the coffin and, noticing that she stirred slightly, spoke to her and bade her most earnestly to tell him what she required. She was greatly distressed by this, and with an outpouring of hot tears and a loud cry she said that nothing had brought greater affliction upon her at this time than the annoyances of stupid people. And after these aforementioned things had passed, she was taken out of her coffin in obedience to the command of her superior, and laid before the altar in severe illness and distress. She wept intensely while the observers and her sisters stayed by her in the choir the whole night long.

The next morning at the twelfth hour of day, the people again left the cloister; and when they came before the council, it was decided that they, along with other, more noble people, should return to the cloister. And so, at the fourth hour after midday, they returned and found her in quite good health. She remained well until the eleventh hour of the night. Then the Passion of Our Lord was read and at the end of it, when they read, "All things are complete; Father, into Thy hands I commend my spirit," she cried out, "O woe, woe, how my foot pains me!" and her foot was shown to those who stood by. Then a wound broke out on her foot, from which fresh blood ran out on to the ground, and the same thing happened to her hands. This was seen by the people who had been sent by the city council as witnesses.

Thus she remained afterward in a state of decided illness, in which she demanded and received the holy sacrament. And after communion, she turned to rest. And, while resting, she was given to understand the mercy of God, and she said, "Help me to the place where I was before last Friday, to my prayer-stool, for there the Lord will work his works." And so it came to pass; they carried her to her prayer-stool in the choir, and she lay there without moving.

On Monday morning, the people all went out of the cloister and left her lying motionless, and informed the council of all that had passed. They conferred among themselves and decided that the matter should be proclaimed publically from the pulpit. A worthy spiritual lord, the reading-master of the Augustinians, who had heard and seen these things himself, was chosen; and all the people who had been present, and who now stood together with him, he named as witnesses of the event. And three signs were posted at the entrance to the church, as for a sermon; such a throng gathered that they feared the people would crush each other to death. When these folk heard of the great miracle, they were greatly moved within themselves and praised God for His mercy.

And just as the witnesses had left the blessed Magdalena lying on Monday, so she remained until Tuesday morning without moving. And on Tuesday morning she came to herself again, and she spoke with her sisters and desired that she be given the holy sacrament. The Provincial himself gave it to her. She received new strength from it, at which they all marvelled.

And shortly afterward* her Provincial ordered her to speak with him about the matter, which greatly disturbed her. And that night she made a very earnest prayer to God, her beloved, three times, and when she had made this prayer for the last time, she was instructed by God to go before the altar alone on the morrow and to give herself entirely to the will of God. This came to pass, and in the morning at the eighth hour, the Provincial was in the cloister and saw Magdalena, and commanded two respectable nuns, Clara von Cipenheim and Lady Sufei von Blumeneck to watch over her while he held chapter meeting with the other women. This they did, and the two women remained with her in the choir. And while he was holding chapter meeting,

*Several days pass between her revival and the following events.

Magdalena asked these two women, among other things, to go before the choir door for a little while, which they did. Then she went before the altar and gave herself completely to the will of God. And a great light came and engulfed the altar and her, which frightened her greatly, and she knew no more. She was rapt up in body and soul and came out of the choir without any human aid. And when the women came into the choir again and could not find her, they were sorely afraid and told the story to the Provincial. And he was also afraid, and humbly begged God for His mercy, and put ashes on his head. And he gave them all ashes for their heads and bade them to go humbly on with the service. This they did and prayed to God to give them back their dear sister.

That same Friday and Saturday having passed, several sisters sat in the choir on Sunday night after Matins and saw with their eyes how she was given back to them in the choir bodily, without human aid. Who can describe or pronounce the great joy of the sisters or the great praise of God with which they passed the rest of the night in singing and reading?

In the morning, the Provincial came joyfully into the cloister and spoke to her. "Magdalena, my dear daughter, how goes it with you? Tell me, for what reason did God take you away from us?" She answered and said, "That I was taken away from you was done for many reasons, by God's authority alone, so that He might demonstrate His external authority. That I still live, however, is a miraculous hidden thing and a judgment of God, which I can make no human understand."

And she was questioned further about what things her death had revealed to her. She answered and said, "The prophecy of death was made for many reasons; and also that my name might be forgotten for a little while and held to be sinful and thought to be dead; and also, that I might thereby suffer great slander

and insult and scorn. I shall spend the remainder of the time that I live in illness and in toil. I have much more to tell you of the wonders of God; if it pleases God, He will give it to me to do so. God be praised today and forevermore, for He has worked great wonders, and that he has chosen to see such a sinful, useless creature saved is not to be spoken of. Hold God dear and serve Him gladly, for you will be well rewarded."

And everything happened as she had predicted, as it is written above, when she said, "I shall pass my time in illness and in toil." It was certainly true, for she suffered great agony and illness for a long time; and in spite of the severe pain that she suffered, she spared her tender, virginal body not at all. For her bed was the hard earth or a straw mat, and she lay upon twigs, and a scanty cloak was her blanket; and her food was not so much that she might have lived upon it, had God not maintained her supernaturally; and she subjected her tender body to much great abstinence. She also lashed herself with many hard disciplines, until her blood ran out. Her holy, blessed life was scoffed at and denied by many sinful people, and it was often taken as a sign that she was a sorceress. She bore this slander with great contentment and eagerness; when someone reproached her she was happy, and whoever offered her insult, for him she begged a special grace from God; but when she was praised she was seen to be grieved and unhappy.

There was a pious maiden living in a cloister of St. Bernard's order, to whom God revealed in a vision that Magdalena should die. The sister was persuaded, deeply exhorted in the name of God's love, to speak the pure truth as it had been revealed to her by God. She answered and said, "By the living God, this story is no lie. An angel of God came to me in a vision and proclaimed to me of the dear lady Magdalena: 'Know ye, that she shall pass away, and it pleases God that you pray to him to have her returned to life through the healing of holy Christianity.' And so I prayed, as God wished me to do, that she would be returned to life; and so I was given to understand that a tiny movement would be left in her heart, in order that she might suffer the more for sinners and bear penance." She spoke further and said: "She has died a natural death and is sanctified before God and is, furthermore, far greater than other people, for she is a living saint." And that for which Magdalena prayed to God, while she endured death, has certainly happened, as was written before.

Her great holiness shone forth and radiated from her, for her conduct was so kindly and gracious that she lightened the hearts of her sisters, and from living with her they often obtained great grace and devotion. There was no one so wild who saw or heard her, but received special grace from her. God also performed many wonders and signs through her during her lifetime, and every day she grew in holiness and the grace of God increased greatly in her; and she was rapt up daily, and in her rapture beheld things so high that they may be neither written nor spoken.

ANNA BIJNS ATTRIBUTED

(fourteenth or fifteenth century; Dutch)

Mary of Nijmeghen

Translated by Eric Colledge

Prologue

In the time when Duke Arnold of Gelderland was imprisoned at Grave by his son, Duke Adolf and his fellow-conspirators, there was living three miles away from Nijmeghen a holy priest called Sir Gilbert, and with him there lived a pretty young girl called Mary, the daughter of his sister who had died. This girl kept house for her uncle, pleasing him greatly by her honesty and hard work.

How Sir Gilbert sent his niece Mary to Nijmeghen

It happened that this Sir Gilbert wanted to send his niece Mary into the town of Nijmeghen, to buy there the things which they needed, and he spoke to her thus:

> *The Uncle*: Mary!
> *Mary*: What is your pleasure, sir?
> *The Uncle*: Listen, child, and pay attention to what I say. You must go to Nijmeghen, to buy in the provisions which we need: candles, and oil for the lamp, vinegar, salt and onions, and sulphur sticks, as you have told me yourself. Here is the money so go to Nijmehen and buy what we need. Today is market day, all the better for you to find what you want.
> *Mary*: Sir, you know that I am ready to do your bidding in all obedience.

© 1964, A. W. Sijthoff's Uitgerversmaatschappij, N.V., *Medieval Netherlands Religious Literature*, translated and introduced by Eric Colledge (New York: London House and Maxwell, 1965).

The Uncle: It will be too late to come back home again tonight, because the days are now very short, and it is two good miles from here to Nijmeghen, and it is now ten o'clock or later. Listen, child: if it takes you so long that you think you cannot comfortably get home in daylight, stay the night there and I shall be easier in my mind.

Go and sleep at your aunt's my sister's; she will not turn you away for just one night, and I would rather that you did that than came home alone in the dark across the fields. There are far too many thieves about the road, and you are a pretty young creature, the sort they would use filthy language to.

Mary: Sir, I shall do everything as you say, and nothing contrary.

The Uncle: My greetings to your aunt, my sister, and now good-bye. See that you get good measure and weight in what we need.

Mary: I shall, sir, good-bye.

The Uncle: Good-bye Mary, my dear niece. May God's grace be always with you! Lord God, why is my heart so heavy? Is it because there is so much trouble here in the land, or is it because my niece has left me? How is it that I am so heavyhearted? It is a strange thing, but just as the child went off, something which I do not understand came into my mind; and I thought that some mishap would come to her or to me. I wish that I had kept her at home! It is madness to allow young women or girls to walk about the countryside alone, for the world is full of crime.

How Mary was very unkindly received by her aunt

When Mary had taken leave of her uncle, she went to Nijmeghen, where she bought what she and her uncle needed. And on the very day on which she came to Nijmeghen, her aunt had quarrelled with four or five other women about Duke Adolf, who had put his father in prison, and she seemed more like a mad-woman or a raging she-devil than a Christian, because she was on the side of the young Duke, and afterwards she destroyed herself when she learned that the old Duke had been freed from imprisonment by the help of the keeper of the castle at Grave, as you will presently hear. Mary, seeing that it was almost evening when she had done her errands, said to herself in this way:

Now I have had everything which we needed weighed and measured to my satisfaction, and I have bought and paid the proper price; but it seems to me that I have stayed so long that over there night is approaching fast. There is a sundial: what time can it be? Already it is half past four. I must stay here in the town tonight; there is only another hour of daylight left, and it will take me all of three hours to walk from here to my uncle's. No, I had far better stay. My aunt lives close by. I will go to her and ask her for a bed, and in the morning, as soon as I wake, I shall hurry back home and get to work. I can see my aunt standing outside her door. I shall go and greet her politely. Aunt, may Christ sweeten all your sorrows, and guard all those you love from harm.

The Aunt: Well, welcome to the devil: how are things in hell? Well, my fine lady, what do you want here?

Mary: My uncle sent me when it was nearly noon to buy candles and mustard and vinegar and bitter essence and all the other things we needed at home, and by the time that I had been from one shop to the other and had found everything and bought it, it was so late; and you will not mind giving me a bed for the night, if you please. I would still go back home, but sometimes when it is dark a young girl can be watched and spied upon, and shamefully molested, and I am afraid of this.

The Aunt: Bless us and save us, you silly chit! For God's sake, are you so anxious about your virginity? My dear niece, it wasn't just yesterday that you found out how you were conceived, even if you are so coy about it now; and I do not think that it is only shopping that has kept you busy since noon.

Mary: Truly, it was, Aunt.

The Aunt: You have been busy sitting somewhere in a corner drinking your fill. Niece, there are Tom and Dick and Harry who all know how to walk you country girls down into the cornfields, and when you play games in the evenings, Betty will always find a Jack to treat her. Yes, niece, you know all about it, for where you live there are plenty of lively lads.

Mary: Why do you talk like this, Aunt?

The Aunt: Ah, you two-faced thing! Even if we must not say the truth, you have danced many a measure for which the piper was not paid in money. You may play this game for a long time yet: we are all virgins till our bellies swell.

Mary: It wounds me to the heart that you should say such shameful things which I do not deserve.

The Aunt: I have talked to people who will swear that they have seen you doing things with your own uncle so shameless that it would be disgraceful for me to repeat them. You are bringing our whole family into disgrace. You will become a byword, you wretched creature, and I cannot bear to look at you.

Mary: Oh, God, what sorrow is in my heart! The blood suddenly runs cold in all my body. To have to listen and to suffer guiltlessly such shameful words! Aunt, please tell me if you will let me have a bed, only for tonight and no longer.

The Aunt: I would rather seeing you lying as deep in the river Maas as the height of this house, to feed all the fish swimming in it. Be off from here before you are sorry! I am shaking like a leaf with rage.

Mary: Aunt, what you say is most unjust.

The Aunt: Wait, this accursed bitch will not leave me in peace. Would you like me to pull down your plaits? She stirs up the maggots in my brain. I could lead the devil astray, I am in such an evil mood; I could tie him to a pillow as if he were a babe. I am in such a furious rage, I don't know whether I am on my head or my heels. I am in so foul a mood that everyone who meets me today will get the same answer that the devil gives his mother.

Mary: Poor me, I am in for sad times. I stand here so amazed that I can give no account of myself. I am in such confusion I had best clear out of the town, even if there are thieves and footpads, and make a bed for myself under the leaves. I will ask no one else on earth for help, and if the devil himself came to me I would not trouble to speak to him. I shall sit down underneath this hedge; and I commend myself into God's hands, or else to the devil of hell.

How Mary left her aunt and went out of Nijmeghen

So this young girl Mary left her aunt, and went out of the town of Nijmeghen as night came on, weeping and very distressed, and walked on until she came to a great thick hedge. Then she sat down in great sorrow and wept and cried aloud, and often commended herself to the devil, saying to herself with sorrowful heart:

Mary: Alas! weeping and crying and wringing my hands and calling myself accursed is now my only consolation. I have been shamefully used by my aunt, and can it be wrong for me to resent having such words to suffer when I have done no harm? Truly, no. Such resentment is growing in my heart that I sit here in evil mood, ready to curse myself everlastingly. Help! what temptations leap out upon me? Do I want to hang myself or cut my throat? Oh, youth, cannot you exercise control, cannot you act reasonably? How should I bear such words when I have not deserved them? I do not think that there is anyone living who could endure this without having earned it. I say all this in the despair which comes to afflict me. Come now to me and help me to lament, God or the devil, it is all the same to me.

The devil, who always spreads his traps and nets as he plots the damnation of souls, hearing these words said to himself as follows:

The Devil: These words commend this soul to me. I have already disguised myself as if I were a man, and all this is by the sufferance of God; and everything is as it should be, except for my one eye, and that is because of some spell. We evil spirits have not the power, nor can we obtain it, to make ourselves perfect human beings, under any condition. Always there has to be something missing, in head or in hand or in foot. Now let me make my voice as sweet as I can, and speak so charmingly and gently that I do not scare this little darling. Gently does it with the women. Pretty child, why are you sitting here so forlorn? Has anyone harmed you, whether justly or not? I shall avenge you, as any decent fellow would. I cannot think that you have done any wrong, and therefore I offer myself as your comforter.

Mary: God, help! Why am I so terrified? What is happening to me? I hardly can account for myself, but since I set eyes on this man, how faintly my heart is beating.

The Devil: Pretty child, do not fear any harm or sorrow. I shall do you no injury nor trouble you. But I promise you that if you will act by my advice and come with me, you may be sure that that before long I shall make you a lady of ladies.

Mary: Friend, I am sitting here almost out of my mind, so upset and so discomposed by the scolding words that I have had to endure without any fault of mine—"whore, slut,

bitch"—that I would as gladly entrust myself to the devil as to God, for I sit here half mad.

The Devil: By Lucifer, I cannot lose! She has swallowed down her draught of wrath, and now sits as if turned to stone by despair. I need not complain, for I may well hope to win. Pretty child, let me ask you if you will be my friend?

Mary: Who are you, friend?

The Devil: A Master of Arts, and I never fail in what I undertake.

Mary: It is all the same to me whom I go with: I'd as soon go with the worst as with the best.

The Devil: If you would give your love to me, I would teach you the arts as no one else could: the seven liberal arts, rhetoric, music, logic, grammar, geometry, arithmetic and alchemy, all of which are most important arts. There is no woman upon earth so proficient in them as I shall make you.

Mary: You seem indeed to be a man full of art. Who are you then?

The Devil: What does that matter to you? It would be better for you not to ask me who I am. I am not the best of my family, but no one could love you better than I.

Mary: What is your name, friend?

The Devil: One-eyed Moenen; and I have lots of good friends who know me well.

Mary: You are the devil out of hell.

The Devil: Whoever I am, I shall always be good to you.

Mary: I feel no fear of you, no terror or horror. Though Lucifer himself were to come up out of hell, I should not run away from him. I am not touched by any fear.

The Devil: Well, my pretty, let us not waste time. If you will come with me and truly do my will, I shall teach you everything which you can possibly think of, as I told you before; and you will never again be without riches and jewels and money.

Mary: That is well said, but whilst we are now talking, before you and I are joined in friendship, teach me the seven liberal arts, for I take great delight in all such things. You will teach them to me, won't you?

The Devil: You can trust me for that! I shall teach you everything you need to know.

Mary: Necromancy, that is a fine art. My uncle knows a lot about it, and sometimes he does marvels which he gets out of a book. I do not think that he has ever failed. They say he can make the devil crawl through a needle's eye, whether he likes it or not. That is an art that I would like to learn.

The Devil: Pretty innocent, everything which I know is at your disposal, to make you happy; but I never learned necromancy, which is a very complicated and difficult art, in which are many dangers. If you were beginning to recite a spell with your pretty red lips, and you were to forget a word or a letter, so that you could not at once say the right thing to the spirit whom you had conjured, he would break your neck straight away. You can see how dangerous it is, my pretty flower.

Mary: If that is the case, I shall not begin it: I do not want to learn anything which could kill me.

The Devil: Ah ha! that has put her off the scent! The idea of her wanting to learn necromancy! If she had learned necromancy, the danger would be in case she were to call up all hell and put them in danger, and even to exercise her powers over me if she chose, or get me into some tight place. I teach her necromancy? Not likely! I shall do what I can to make her forget the idea. Now listen to what I shall teach you, my pretty love, if you will just give necromancy up.

Mary: What else shall I learn?

The Devil: I'll tell you now. I shall teach you all the languages in the world, so that the whole world will honour and pay tribute to you, for you have no idea what an achievement this is, then, because you also know the seven liberal arts, you will be high in every man's esteem.

Mary: The sorrows which oppress me lessen as I listen. I shall be most obedient to your will, if you will do this.

The Devil: Yet there is one other request I have to make of you, my pretty sweet. Do this for me and it will greatly benefit you.

Mary: What request is that?

The Devil: That you will give up your name and take another from now on. "Mary" is not a name I like to hear: there was once a Mary who did great harm to me and my friends, so that we have always disliked the name since then. Call yourself "Lina" or "Peggie" or "Lizzie:" do that, and before the year is out it will get you more than you ever had from your friends or relatives.

Mary: Alas, why should this name displease you? It is the noblest and sweetest name in the world, and pleasing to everyone. "Mary" or "Maria," how could you hate this name? I will not take another name for all the world. I do not think that anyone could find a sweeter name.

The Devil: Indeed, I have just been wasting my time if I cannot make her change her name! Listen, my dear, if we are to go travelling together, you must change your name, however little you may like it, or else we must part; and there is something else which you must promise me. Do not argue; a promise is a debt.

Mary: What must I promise?

The Devil: That you will never again make the sign of the cross. Whatever happens, however much it may hurt you, you must not bless yourself.

Mary: I will gladly promise. I do not attach great importance to the sign of the cross; but I cannot bear to deny my own name, for Mary, after whom I am called, is all my consolation and hope, and whatever sorrow or danger I am in, I call upon her at once for succour, and daily I honour her with the prayer that I learned as a child: "Mary, Mary, be blessed by me." As long as I have life, I shall never fail to do this; though I may go astray and live a bad life, I shall never forget to sing her praises.

The Devil: Well, if you are so attached to the name. I shall modify my wishes. I shall be satisfied for you to keep the first letter, the "M" of your name; and so, dear lady, you shall be called "Emma." In your part of the world there are many girls and women called that.

Mary: Very well, Moenen, since I cannot keep my own name, better let me be satisfied with the first letter than that we should part. Everywhere we go I shall be called "Emma," although I do not like it.

The Devil: Yet be content: if you are not the mistress of all you long for within a year, I shall answer to you for it. Let us go to Bois-le-duc at once, and after that we shall have much to do. As soon as we please we may go to Antwerp, and there we shall give them all a surprise. Before we arrive there you will know all the languages you want to learn, as I promised you, and the seven liberal arts, as you required. Bastard and Malmsey will be your only drink; and if you keep my love and my gratitude, you will achieve still more wonderful things. But finally I hope that your soul will perish.

After these words Emma and Moenen set off for Bois-le-duc, where they stayed for several days faring very well and paying for each one of the people who came to eat or drink with them. Now let us turn from Emma and Moenen, and speak about Sir Gilbert, Emma's uncle. After Mary, whom we now call Emma, had been absent for a few days, her uncle Sir Gilbert was very surprised at her long absence, saying to himself as follows:

The Uncle: Oh anxiety, crying so loudly inside me, how you trouble my heart and mind and understanding, because Mary, my niece, whom I sent to Nijmeghen marketing, has been absent so long. It is true that I told her, if the night should overtake her or if anything should alarm her, that she should go to sleep at my sister's, because when I come to Nijmeghen I always stay there. I shall have no happiness or peace of mind until I know how she is. If some frightful thing were to have happened to her, I should die hopeless and disconsolate, for that child is all my consolation, and I reared her from her infancy. I could not bear any harm to come to her; but young girls are very easily led astray. I must go to Nijmeghen without delay to get proper news of her. Bad news would be better than no news.

With these words Sir Gilbert went to his sister's house to ask about Mary, niece to him and to her aunt, who became very angry and swore she knew nothing of her. At which he became very sad and said to her thus:

The Uncle: Alas, sister, you are deceiving me, telling me that you know nothing about Mary.

The Aunt: My good man, I do not, believe me.

The Uncle: Alas, sister, you are deceiving me.

The Aunt: I expect she'll be tucked away safe and sound, somewhere where roast chickens like her are had cheap.

The Uncle: Alas, sister, you are deceiving me, telling me that you know nothing about her. You behave as if you are troubled and ill at ease, merely because I ask you quietly if you have seen her.

The Aunt: Of course I am troubled when you behave as if I had been responsible for her. It is eight or ten days ago since she came here, saying, "Auntie, let me have a bed for tonight. I dare not go home for fear of being followed by thieves, the sort who like to ill-use young girls;" and I told her that she should go and lodge where she had been sitting drinking all day long.

The Uncle: What? Had she been sitting drinking all day?

The Aunt: You can believe me, she had not been wasting her time, and she came here with a face as red as a well-thrashed backside, and when I told her what I thought of her, she nearly bit my head off, and she cleared off cursing and shouting, and that was the last I saw of my fine lady.

The Uncle: Alas, what will become of me? O God in Trinity, where has the child gone?

The Aunt: My good man, she will have gone where there is plenty of drink, and plenty of boon companions.

The Uncle: Alas, sister, it makes me weep to hear such words from you.

The Aunt: If you had locked her up in a box you could have saved yourself this trouble. Good heavens, my poor man, what harm is it going to do her if she does go her own way for a while? It will cost her nothing and do her no harm; she won't go round maimed for the rest of her life.

The Uncle: Oh, it grieves me so to listen to you that I feel that my heart is breaking. I must turn around and wipe my eyes, for the tears are running down my cheeks. Oh, Mother of our Lord, whom I have visited at Aachen every year with great devotion, help me now in my need. And you, St. Servatus, whose body lies at Maestricht, where each year I have caused many a fine light to be lit in devotion to you, I hope that now you will not fail me. When we are in need we must seek comfort from our friends. Now I shall have her searched for in every place, whether anyone has heard of her. Horrified as I am, it is no wonder though I grieve. No one is glad to be parted from what he loves.

After this Sir Gilbert left his sister with a sorrowful mind, because he had gained no news of his niece Mary.

How Mary's aunt cut her throat

In the meantime the keeper of the castle at Grave had released the old Duke Arnold from imprisonment and had conducted him to the town of Bois-le-duc, where he was hospitably received by the lord of the town. And when Mary's aunt heard of this, she became so angry in her venemous heart that she almost burst with spleen, saying:

The Aunt: Help, liver, lungs and spleen, teeth, heads, all is going badly for me. Anger will make me burst or melt, for I am swelling with spleen like a spider. I am going raging mad, I am losing my mind at the news which I have heard. That old thief who was safely locked up at Grave has been released and turned loose. This is the end of all my joys, for our young Duke, on whose side I am, will soon have the worst of it, I fear. This has so shaken me that I could easily give myself up, body and soul, and call all the devils that exist to come to my help.

The Devil: Ha ha, I ought to gain some profit out of this undertaking! This soul will be mine if I can spend just half an hour with her.

The Aunt: Is this not shameful?

The Devil: It is, and a great harm for those who are on the side of the young Duke.

The Aunt: Truly, who could it be who was not satisfied with so fine a fellow? Even if I have to burn in hell forever, I shall cut my throat out of spite, and so I shall be rid of these miseries. Oh, farewell, adieu, fine young prince! If you can rule again as duke, then it is nothing to me that I cut my life short. And so I stick this knife into my throat, and with this blow let me kill myself. Partizanship has destroyed many a soul.

The Devil: In the rabble of Hell, in endless torment shall I under Lucifer roast this soul. What fools they are, who for the sake of princes or lords destroy themselves out of partizanship. All who show themselves so obstinate end by being ours. Faction and strife provide Hell with many millions in the year, let him sorrow for it who will.

How Emma and Moenen travelled to Antwerp, where much harm came to the people through them

After Emma and Moenen had been at Bois-le-duc for some days, they set off for Antwerp and soon arrived there. And Moenen said to Emma thus:

Moenen: Now we are in Antwerp, where you wanted to be, and we shall have a great success here and live like princes. Let us go into The Tree for a pint of Rumney.

Emma: To The Tree, you say?

Moenen: Yes, love, and there you will see all the spendthrifts who waste their lives, all the daughters of joy and the whores who gamble with their lives. The freemen sit up above, the craftsmen below, and they all prefer to receive rather than give.

Emma: That is the life I love to see; nothing pleases me more.

Moenen: Let us have a drink in the Gold Room before we go, if you like. Sit down, love. Landlord, broach a new barrel: it would be a shame for it to go sour.

(*The Potboy*: What wine would you like, sir?)

Moenen: A pint of Grenade, and a pint of Ypocras for my wife, and a pint of Rumney. There's nothing like it for warming you up; it raises your spirits, however low they are.

The Potboy: You're right, and here it is, a broach, a broach; the very best, the very best, and good measure.

First Drinker: Look, Jack, there's a fine wench over there.

Second Drinker: True, and an ugly-looking devil with her.

First Drinker: Let us take our drink over to them and if we find out that she is only his strumpet, we'll have her for ourselves.

Second Drinker: Tonight he can sample my knife, because he's an ill-favoured lout, but the girl is as pretty as can be. If she's only his whore, she is mine tonight. Will you help me?

First Drinker: I swear I will; and I will stick close to your side. God bless you, friend!

Moenen: Come and drink with us, good fellows!

First Drinker: No, friend, we have plenty here, but may we come and sit with you?

Moenen: Yes, and sit as long as you like. Good company does me no harm.

First Drinker: Excuse me, where do you two come from?

Moenen: From Bois-le-duc or thereabouts.

Emma: Moenen dear, would it be through geometry if I were to be able to count exactly how many drops of wine there are in a pot?

Moenen: Yes, dear, but have you remembered how to do it? That was something I taught you yesterday.

Emma: That is true, indeed, and you also taught me logic, and I have remembered all that as well.

A Drinker: Friend, what is that your wife says? Can she really calculate exactly how many drops of wine went into this pot? I have never heard anything to equal it.

Moenen: That is nothing to some of the things she can do. You never saw the like of her in all your life. She understands all the seven liberal arts, astronomy and geometry, arithmetic, logic and grammar, music and rhetoric, the most ancient of them all. She could hold her own against the cleverest scholar who studied in Paris or Louvain.

The Second Drinker: My good friend, I beg you to allow us to see or hear something of her skill.

The First Drinker: Yes, please, and I will buy you each a pint of wine, and I swear that if anyone tries to interrupt you, we shall fight them for you, if they give you trouble.

Moenen: The poem you made up yesterday when we were walking in the High Street at noon, say that for them.

Emma: Please excuse me. I am a very dull scholar at rhetoric, much as I should like to practise it, so as to master all the seven liberal arts; it requires more than industry for rhetoric, which is an art which must come of its own accord. All the other arts can be learned by application and instruction, if one will work hard at them, but rhetoric is to be esteemed above them all. It is a gift of the Holy Spirit, and though one finds many ignorant creatures who despise it, that gives great sorrow to lovers of rhetoric.

The Second Drinker: Well, my dear, how many times do you want us to ask you?

The First Drinker: Recite something for us that you know: it is only for fun, and we shall be satisfied, and then I shall recite something too.

Emma: Then be quiet, and I shall sing you a song as well as I can; rhetoric has to be listened to and taken in, so do not let us have any chattering.

O rhetoric, o true and lovely art, I who have always esteemed thee above all, I lament with grief that there are those who hate you and despise you. This is a grief to those who love you. Fie upon those who count you merely folly. Fie upon them who do so, for I wholly despise them. But for those who support you, life is full of hurt and sorrow. Ignorant men are the destruction of art.

They say in the proverb that through art grows the heart, but I say that it is a lying fable, for should some great artist appear, those who are unskilled and know not the first thing about art will make their opinion prevail everywhere, and artists will be reduced to beggary. Always it is the flatterer who is preferred, and always artists suffer such harm, and ignorant men are the destruction of art.

Fie upon all crude, coarse, common minds, trying to measure art by your standards: everyone should pay honour to pure art, art which is the ruler of many a pleasant land. Honour be to all who are the promoters of art, fie upon the ignorant who reject art, for this is why I proclaim the rule that ignorant men are the destruction of art.

Prince, I will devote myself to art, and do everything in my power to acquire it. But it is to all lovers of art a sorrow that ignorant men pay so little honour to art.

Many people assembled to listen to this poem, and seeing this, Moenen showed his cunning, and organized such an uproar that one of the company was stabbed to death, and he who did it had his throat cut. So Emma and Moenen lived at The Golden Tree in the market place, where every day, through their instrumentation, murders and killings and other evil deeds were done. And Moenen had great joy of this, saying to himself thus:

The Devil: What marvels I can perform! I hope that Hell will gain some profit from it. If I am in charge here for a while, I shall thrust still more down into the mouth of Hell. It would be a pity for us to leave this inn, for all who come here to spend their time, tricksters, duellers, profligate strumpets, pimps, whoremongers, are all found in great plenty; and they are the sort of people who bring me profit. So I must stay where I am in this house. I shall go at once and ask the landlord what he will charge for the two of us. If I lodge here, I shall have everything here which I require just as I want it, and if there is any secret into which I can pry, I shall always seek to stir up strife. In this next year I shall have a hundred stabbed to death, for Lucifer to welcome into the pleasure-gardens of Hell. I shall disguise myself as a quack, so that everyone will esteem me, and I shall say that I know how to lead people to hidden treasure, for which great honour will be paid to me. I shall know just how to describe all the events which have happened to men. Before a month is out people will be following me by the thousand because of my arts, and I shall gain riches as no man ever did. My dear Emma will love me more and more, and if the Almighty does not hinder me, I shall before a year is past trap more than a thousand souls. But should it be His will, all my work will have been in vain.

How Emma began to lament her sinful life

So Emma, living in Antwerp and seeing that she was leading a very evil and sinful life, because for her sake Moenen was every day the cause of very much harm, said to herself thus:

Emma: O memory and understanding, if you were to think upon the life which I am living now, it would seem sinful and foul to you. I have forsaken the light of Heaven, and I walk the road to Hell, which is very hideous. I see and observe how nearly every day someone here is injured or killed because of me, and I know well that it is this man Moenen who is the cause of this harm. And he is a bad lot, and this is the root of it. I feel it strongly, though he does not himself say it straight out, that he must be a devil or little better. Oh, Aunt, those great and cruel reproaches of yours will make me into a damned whore, eternally expelled from the grace of Almighty God. Alas, the most lamentable part of my situation is that I have gone too far, however much I may wish to turn back. Once I used to serve Mary every day with my prayers or some other service pleasing to her, but now my devotion is all gone, and Moenen would not endure it, for he will not suffer me even to make the signs of the cross. By that one can feel that he is evil, when he shuns the cross's blessing. Consider how I could possibly repent—things have gone too far now for repentance! Aha! there are two fellows over there who stood me a drink

yesterday. I'll go over to them and wet my whistle.

And with this she went to sit and drink with her boon companions, and Moenen so contrived it that one of them got his death. And the one who did it was led by Moenen outside the town, where he murdered another man by counsel of Moenen, who had told him that the man he murdered had much money, for which he ought to kill him. At which Moenen was very glad, saying:

The Devil: With the aid of Lucifer's traps and the pit of Hell, how I am destroying these people every day! They think that I am a fine lord, and I know just what to say to take them in, and so they all come flocking after me. I know how to give them clear advice, and so I whisper to the women how to drive men mad for love of them, or I tell them how to feed them so they do not live another week. I have done this more than once, and Lucifer has not lost one of them, believe me. And now I am beginning to teach people how to find hidden treasure; and only yesterday it cost one of them his life. I told him where there was a treasure hidden and growing mouldy, in a stable, underneath a beam on which the whole weight of the stable was resting. I told him that he would have to dig deep into the ground, and he would find pound upon pound of the hidden treasure. At once he started to dig there, but as soon as he had dug so far that he undermined the beam and the posts supporting it, the beam fell to the ground and crushed this poor idiot under it! This is nothing to what I shall do soon, if I am not hindered from on high. They will believe that I am a god, and I shall lead them down into Hell in troops.

After Emma and Moenen had lived at The Golden Tree in Antwerp for about six years, and an astonishing amount of harm had been caused by them, Emma began to long to visit her uncle and her other dear ones in Gelderland, and to ask Moenen to allow her to do this and to travel with her. To which he replied:

The Devil: Emma, I do not refuse what you ask. Do you want to visit your friends, you say?

Emma: I do ask you for this, if it were your pleasure.

The Devil: Dear one, I do not forbid it.

Emma: I have not seen my aunt at Nijmeghen or my uncle at Venloo for six or seven years.

The Devil: That is why I do not refuse you. Certainly, let us go to visit your friends.

Emma: Those who were nearest to me do not know where I went, any more than if the ground had swallowed me up. And my uncle thought the world of me; I know that he has shed many a tear for me.

The Devil: That old hypocrite's prayers have often hindered me, when I should have liked to break every bone in her body. I should have broken her neck long ago, but his prayers to that woman all in white have always stopped me. I never once was able to get the opportunity I wanted.

Emma: What do you say, Moenen?

The Devil: Nothing, Emma my dear. I give you permission, just as you ask, to see your friends as you wish to. So go now and pay our account with the landlord at The Tree, where we have been lodging, and tomorrow we shall go to your uncle's, or to your other friends, wherever you take me. I am quite ready.

Emma: I shall go and ask how much is still outstanding on our bill, and pay it all.

The Devil: Do that, my darling, pay everything they ask, down to the last halfpenny. I can be sure that I am not going to lose by this, when we go to her uncle the parson's. Just let me catch him once off his guard, and I shall have it all my own way. Then I shall break the hypocrite's neck, for if he were once out of the way, the girl would be wholly in my power.

But whatever I plan or say, it is all in vain if the Almighty does not give me His full consent: I cannot touch a hair of his head against God's will.

How Emma and Moenen went to Nijmeghen

So Emma and Moenen went to Nijmeghen, where they arrived in time for the Rogation Day procession; and Emma was very glad, and Moenen said to her thus:

The Devil: Well, Emma, here we are, just as you asked me, in Nijmeghen, and today is Rogation Day, too. You said that your aunt used to live here. Do you not want to go to visit her?

Emma: To go to visit her is one thing, but I would not dream of asking her for shelter, or any food or drink. She would only give me shameful language and furious anger, as she did once before with no hesitation. It was what she said in her folly and ignorance which led me first to this life of shame that I am leading now, alas!

The Devil: I hardly think you need to go there, my dear, my joy. It is time that you know that your aunt has been dead for three years.

Emma: What do you say? Dead?

The Devil: Yes, dearest heart.

Emma: How do you know that, Moenen?

The Devil: I know it for certain.

Emma: This is a great sorrow to me.

The Devil: Truly, it is.

Emma: Wait, what do I see over there? Let us watch before we go away. Look, look, a great crowd of people is gathering. Is something happening? Go and ask someone quickly.

The Devil: No, love, they are just going to play a pageant on wheels.

Emma: That happens every year on this

day. Now that I remember, this is the play of Mascaron. I cannot tell you how good it is. My uncle always used to come to see it. Oh, Moenen, let us stay and listen to it.

The Devil: It is all a lot of nonsense. Do you really want to listen to such drivel? We had far better go look for a roast and some wine.

Emma: Oh, Moenen, it is always so good. There were times when I heard my uncle say that this play is better than all the sermons ever preached. Such plays often contain very good stories. My darling, if it would not bore you I should like to see it.

The Devil: I do not want to agree. By Lucifer's backside, I am very frightened! If she were to hear something in the play so forceful that she were seized with remorse or suspicion, by Lucifer, all my great plans would be useless.

Emma: Oh, Moenen, let me listen to it!

The Devil: Well, only till I tell you to come away, or I shall be angry.

Emma tormented Moenen so long, asking him to let her listen to the play, that in the end he agreed, but very grudgingly, as you have heard. And the play began as follows:

Mascaron: Hallo, here I am, Mascaron, Lucifer's advocate at law, come to plead my case before the Omnipotent Judge Himself, to ask Him why He shows more mercy and grace to the miserable human race than to us, poor spirits whom He has everlastingly rejected. Even if a human being had committed all the sins by himself which all the men in the world commit, if he has a good and heartfelt contrition and a good intention, he will attain mercy, but we poor spirits, who never sinned except by one brief thought, have because of it been cast into the abyss, without hope, into everlasting cruel torment. I, Mascaron, procurator of Lucifer, demand once more of You, God of mercy, why You have denied mercy to us more than to man, who daily commits unspeakable sins.

God: My mercy is withheld from no man who feels contrition before the end of his life, and who acknowledges, while there is yet time, that I am a merciful and just God. But those who persist in their shameful ill-doing, who never feel the qualms of conscience, they must sink down with Lucifer into the abyss, where there will be nothing but lamentation.

Mascaron: In many respects Your justice is imperfect, even though they call You a God just in all His ways. In the days of Abraham and Moses and David men could call You just, because then they saw You blaming and condemning and punishing men for a single unclean thought; but nowadays, even if a child were to rape its own mother, to strike its father down or tread him underfoot, or if one brother were to accuse another of every evil ever committed, if he has heartfelt contrition, at once he gains Your mercy.

God: Why did I die a death so disgraceful, so shameful, lifted up on the Cross, unless to obtain for every man, young and old, My Father's grace?

Mascaron: On this account You ought to be more angry and stern than you were before: naked, You died so shameful a death, so as to cleanse human nature; and yet men are more hardened than they were before in their horrible, disgraceful sins. One cannot describe them or conceal them. Reasonable men shudder when they reflect that things which men under the Old Law dared not think of, men today do without fear.

God: What you say is true, Mascaron. People are now so hardened in evil-doing that unless they will turn away from it, I shall punish them with the strokes of My mighty sword of justice, and send down My plagues which are cruel to suffer.

Our Blessed Lady: Oh my child, if You condemn man to punishment with plague, that will greatly afflict me. Let Yourself be entreated, leave mankind in peace for yet a little while. Send signs or warnings to the people first, as You have done before under such constraint: earthquakes or double suns or stars with tails, so that they can understand from such tokens that You are immeasurably angered. Then perhaps they will forsake their sins for fear lest they are more afflicted.

God: No, Mother, you waste your labours. Again and again I have sent such tokens, which ought to have struck terror into their hearts: pestilences, wars, famines, which should have made men to eschew the sins which offend My Divinity. But the more they have been afflicted, the more they have gone astray, never thinking of everlasting death, full of lamentation. All they ever say is: "Why should I trouble? One act of contrition at the end, and God, who is merciful, will have mercy on me."

Emma, listening to the play, began to reflect with sorrowful heart upon her sinful life, saying to herself:

Emma: Lord God, how am I moved, listening to this pageant? I hear such reasons and arguments that I am filled with pure contrition and remorse.

The Devil: Well, are we going to stay here all day? You, speak! What do you want to listen to this drivel for? Dear one, let us go.

Emma: No, it is no use shouting and tugging and pulling at me. As long as this play lasts, you will not move me from here—let those go who want to. This is better than a sermon.

The Devil: Lucifer's backside, help me! It is a torment to me to let her stand here. She will catch contrition, I think, if she stands here listening to all this prating. I shall wait a little longer, but if she will not come away I shall give her a good punching and get her away like that.

So Moenen would gladly have prevented Emma from listening to the play, but she stayed and heard it, whether he liked it or not. And the play continued so:

Mascaron: O guide of the heavens and of the elements, God throned on high in your justice, would You not permit and consent to Lucifer and his minions in Hell that we might chastize men for their misdeeds and their great wickedness? Otherwise You will never have an end to the evils in which they persist: Your hand of justice must chastize them, if You are to be acknowledged among mankind.

God: Mascaron, I shall give consent for mankind to be afflicted, because nothing instils fear into them, unless they feel a knife at their throats.

Our Blessed Lady: O son, mankind will improve in every way. Do not be too hasty in unleashing Your punishments. Think of the breasts that You sucked, think of the womb in which You lay, think of the Passion You suffered, think of Your bloody sweat in Your anguish. Was not all this for the sake of man? Was it not so that he might attain to Your Father's mercy? You have said this Yourself, so what will You do now? If one man had committed all the sins of the world, if he uttered one heartfelt cry for Your mercy, he would be received with open arms. This is what You said, and many a man knows it.

God: That is what I said, and I am not sorry for it, my Lady Mother, and I say again that though a man had committed every sin which one could imagine, if he calls upon Me with contrition, he shall be one of My chosen. And rather than that one soul should be lost, I would suffer all My torments again twice over which the Jews inflicted upon Me in days long past. O man, think well upon these things!

How Emma went on listening to the play, so that she repented even more of her sins, saying thus

Emma: Now at last the tears begin to run fast down over my face. Oh, what compunction have I felt, as I heard these words, oh Lord of lords! Could it be possible that if I were to repent I could attain to Your grace? I never suspected it until now. Could it be possible? I never thought so before. I have too gladly consented to what I have done, foolishly taking pleasure in my own wilful acts. Oh, earth, open and swallow me up, for I am not fit to tread upon you.

The Devil: Help, Modicat, my eyes grow fiery with rage! This girl is getting a bellyful of repentance. Let us go off to some pleasant part of the town and drink a pot of wine.

Emma: Leave me alone, and get away from me, you evil, cruel devil! Alas for me that it was you whom I summoned and called to, forgetting You who are divine and merciful. Oh, oh, I am filled with such heartfelt remorse that my heart will crack!

Oh, I am dying, my strength is failing me!

The Devil: Lucifer's liver and lungs and spleen, help me! Now may I well curse and shoot flames from my eyes and howl, for all my plans are going astray. What I have achieved will be little esteemed among the revellers in Hell. Get up, in the name of every devil, or I will carry you off as you are to fry in Hell!

Emma: Oh Lord, have mercy on me!

The Devil: Oh, indeed? Now I can hear remorse pulling at her placket! I will carry her off high above the roofs into the sky, and throw her down from there. If she ever draws breath again that will be her good fortune, the ugly wretch! Come on, come on, you are coming up into the sky with me.

After these words Moenen the devil lifted Emma up into the air, higher than any house or church, so that her uncle and all the people saw this, which greatly astonished them, not knowing what it could mean.

How Moenen threw Emma down from on high, and how her uncle recognized her

When Moenen the devil had carried Emma high up above all the houses, he threw her down into the street from above, intending to break her neck, which greatly terrified the people. And Sir Gilbert, her uncle, who was also listening to the play, was amazed to think what this could mean and how it was possible that anyone could fall from so high up, saying and asking one of those standing near him as follows:

The Uncle: If she has not broken her neck, that is her good fortune. There is unspeakable terror in my heart, as I see all the people looking at this person. Do I not know her? Who is the woman?

A Citizen: I want to see if I know her, but the people are crowding around her so that no one can get near her. Follow me, sir, and I shall make a way for us. If anyone thinks that I do not know how to push, he is wrong. Here you are, sir, the girl is lying here unconscious, all alone.

The Uncle: That is not surprising. Help, I could swear that there is no drop of blood left in all my body! The tears start from my eyes. My veins dry up, my face is white. I have never felt myself so weak. Oh, my friend, please look after me, I beg you.

The Citizen: Wait, what is the matter with you, sir? You are so changed you seem as if you were a dead man.

The Uncle: In this moment of horror I could wish to die. Oh, Atropos, come and put out my light!

The Citizen: Why are you lamenting like this?

The Uncle: Oh, this is my niece! I have already suffered enough on her account. This is she whom I have been seeking for over seven years, and now, alas, here she is lying with her neck broken. Oh, earth, open and swallow me up! No longer do I wish to stay here.

The Citizen: Are you sure that it is she?

The Uncle: Could I fail to recognize her? Or do you think that I am out of my mind?

The Devil: Help, all you ministrants of hellish joys: I could piss on my own tail out of sheer rage. I cannot think what to do in this business. This is her uncle: how shall I contrive it now? I could have easily broken her neck, but the prayers of this pious parson have stood in my way. If I only had the power I would carry him off to Hell this instant.

The Citizen: Look, sir, I see her moving.

The Uncle: If she would move, that would be the cure for much of my suffering. It is true, she is indeed moving.

Emma: Oh, what has happened to me? Where have I been, and where am I now? Oh, Lord, am I still in Your favour, so that I may attain to grace? Yes, truly, I am, for had You not taken me into Your omnipotent protection, I should have been thrust down for ever into eternal torment, banished body and soul from the Kingdom of the Lord.

The Uncle: If you can still speak, Mary, my niece, speak to me, who have sighed so many sighs for you and made so many laments, and asked for you high and low! And now I find you, in the middle of this crowd, and in this wretched state.

Emma: Oh, is it you, my uncle? Oh, if only God would grant that I could now be in the same state as I was when I last saw you, that I had never gone away! Oh, when I think of what I am, I am sure that I shall be everlastingly damned!

The Uncle: Niece, what you say is sinful, for no one is lost except him who gives himself up for lost. Why should you be damned? That would be a dreadful thing. But how do you come to be here? That is what I greatly want to know. A moment ago you were up there in the sky. Please tell me how this could be. I do not know that I have ever seen anyone so high up before.

Emma: Uncle, it would be impossible for me to give you a reasonable account of all my adventures. Once I surrendered myself wholly to the devil, and then I kept company with

him for some seven years. I cannot describe it all to you; I shall just tell you as briefly as I can how I have lived and what we have done during those seven years. They could indeed write books about it. There is no evil to compare with the evil I have done. But, at the end of all these strange events, I came back here to our own country to visit my friends, and as we passed through the town here and came into the market place, I saw the play about Mascaron being performed, and I approached to listen, and from the words I heard I was seized with such contrition that it angered him who was with me, and he carried me off up to where all the people saw me, high up in the sky.

The Uncle: Alas, alack, in this true, niece? Was the devil with you?

Emma: Yes, Uncle, and he has been with me now for about seven years, since I first put myself at his command and began to go around with him.

The Uncle: Help us, almighty God! To hear this fills my whole being with horror. We must drive this spirit away from you, if you are ever to attain to God's blessed kingdom.

The Devil: Ah, you hypocrite, that you cannot do; you cannot separate me from her. If I want to I shall carry her off, skin and bones and all, and take her to where they do not stint the sulphur and the pitch.

The Uncle: Will you, you evil spirit?

The Devil: Yes, I will, you whoreson hypocrite! She is mine, she has surrendered herself to me, she has forsaken Almighty God and she has bound herself to me, and so she must burn in the fires of hell; and if you were to try to snatch from me what is my possession, I would break every bone in your body.

The Uncle: Evil spirit, I shall stand in your way. Here in my breviary I have eight or ten lines written on a piece of paper, and they will soon make you laugh on the other side of your face.

The Devil: Oh, oh! My hackles rise, my hair

stands on end, as he reads it there. What shall I do now? By Modicat, if I lose this woman now, I shall be flogged with whips of fire. I grind my teeth for very rage, and I blow sparks from the fires of hell out of my ears and cheeks! All men can now see from me that we are less than powerless when what we plan is displeasing to the Almighty Lord. I think that this soul and I must now part.

The Uncle: Let us go, Mary my niece, and I shall take you to the deacon's, and have a fire lit for you. I think that you must be injured in every limb, since he took you up so high and let you fall down. You must be badly hurt.

Emma: I pay no heed to it at all. Uncle, I am willing to suffer ten thousand times this pain, for which there may be no cure at all, and more than any pen could write; if only God's mercy be not withdrawn from me, I do not care what becomes of me, if I may have His consolation and grace.

The Uncle: Do not let this resolution weaken, and I can assure you that you will gain what you wish for—the Kingdom of God. Daily we read in the Scriptures that to attain to God's perfect glory, nothing is needed more than a perfect final contrition.

After this, Sir Gilbert went with his niece to all the most learned priests in the town of Nijmeghen; but no priest, however learned, however experienced, however holy or devout, once he had understood the case, dared in any way be so bold as to absolve her or impose on her any penance for her sins, which were so dreadful and so unnatural; and so they were all greatly oppressed.

How Sir Gilbert travelled to Cologne with his niece

On the following day, very early in the morning, Sir Gilbert prepared himself as if he were about to celebrate Mass, and, taking the glorious, blessed and holy Sacrament in his hand, he set off with his niece Emma for Cologne. And Moenen the devil followed them from far off, but he did not dare to approach them or to come near to Emma, because of the might of the Holy Sacrament. Yet at times he would throw a split oak or some other tree after them, to break both their necks. But our Blessed Lord would not permit this, because Emma was accustomed every day to say a prayer in honour of our Blessed Lady. So in the end they had travelled so long and so far that they arrived at Cologne, where Emma made her confession to the Bishop. But she obtained no counsel for this, because her sin was so unnatural and so great that he had no power to absolve her from it.

How Emma and her uncle travelled to Rome, and how Emma made her confession to the Pope

After this, Emma and her uncle left the Bishop and travelled from Cologne to Rome, where they arrived after much travelling and great labour. And Emma said her confession before the Pope, saying with weeping eyes:

Emma: Oh viceregent of God, yes, God upon earth, as men teach us, the earth has not upon it a greater sinner than I, who am, I believe, eternally excluded from the heavenly Kingdom.

The Pope: Why is that, my child?

Emma: I am the devil's mistress, and I have been for more than seven years. I talked with him, walked with him, went with him where we pleased. Understand this matter well. I have done with him that which man and wife do. Have I not reason to feel horror at myself?

The Pope: What, my child, with the devil of Hell?

Emma: Yes, Holy Father!

The Pope: And did you know well when he came to you that it was the devil?

Emma: Yes, I did, and that is why I mourn!

The Pope: But how could you have commerce with the devil when you knew who he was?

Emma: Father, it was the good times, all the money and the presents which he gave me, you must know this, which made me do it, and now it makes me shudder. There was nothing which came into my mind which he did not give to me as I desired. And the worst of all, which afflicts me most and sends the greatest anguish to my heart, is that so many men lost their lives in the places which we frequented. More than two hundred, Holy Father, have been murdered and sent to their deaths for my sake, at one time or another.

The Pope: Help us, oh divine Lord! For such misdeeds you must indeed now live a life of sorrow.

Emma: Oh, Father, give me counsel, if that is possible, and lay penance on me before we part. I do not care how heavy it is.

The Pope: I hardly dare try so greatly the mercy of our Lord. For you to have lived with the devil! Never have such sins been confessed to me before, and then, more, that so many lives have been lost because of your vicious ways! I do not know what penance to give you which would be heavy enough for such sinful deeds. For you to have been with the devil—it is too beastly! Oh God, unfathomable well of grace, give me counsel in this matter, for my own mind is wholly oppressed. Oh righteous Judge, pour into me Your inspiration, out of Your great glory. Wait—it comes to my mind—it would be a great sorrow to me to reject you. Call the priest who came with you, and he shall hear what your penance is.

Emma: Where are you, uncle?

The Uncle: I have been standing here at the door, full of sorrow and fear until I know what is to happen.

The Pope: Then listen to my decision. It would be a sorrow to me, and it would be pitiful, for anyone to be lost if one could prevent it, nor would God gladly suffer it. Look there, at those three iron rings. The biggest of them you must lock round her neck, and the other two, without further delay, fasten tight and firm round her arms; and she must wear the rings until they wear through or fall off of their own accord. Then will all her sins have been forgiven her, and not until then will she be freed and quit.

The Uncle: I think that it will be a very long time before they fall off by themselves, for they are so thick and heavy and hard. In a hundred years not a quarter of their thickness would wear away.

The Pope: She may so free herself in complete and heartfelt penance of her sins that they may themselves fall from her arms and neck. But they must be firmly fastened on.

The Uncle: Good, Father, I shall have them fastened on so well and so firmly that they will never fall off, unless it be the work of God. Oh, you who are priest and cleric over all ranks, by your favour we will now leave you, and travel our own road back to our country, whence we came.

The Pope: May the Almighty, He who has reconciled us all, make your sufferings as sweet as they are prolonged.

Emma: Farewell, Holy Father!

The Pope: Go in God's keeping, daughter, and be resolute in your penance, for on high, in heaven's bliss, perfect penance is highly esteemed, and penance can cure many ills, more than all the other remedies of which we read.

So Emma received her penance from the Pope. And at once her uncle had the rings fastened so firmly around her neck and her arms that they would not have come off all her lifetime, had it not been by the consent and the miraculous intervention of our Blessed Lord.

How Emma left Rome, and how she became a nun in the house for converted sinners at Maestricht

When Emma had the rings on, as you have heard, she left the city of Rome with her uncle, and they travelled on until they came to Maestricht, where Emma became became a nun in the convent of converted sinners, and her uncle helped her in this. And after he had helped her in this matter, he took his leave of her and travelled to his own territory, where he lived for another twenty-four years, after he had helped his niece to enter the convent, and as long as he lived he visited her once a year.

How the angel of God took the rings off Emma's neck and hands

When Emma resided in the convent of which we have written, she lived so holy a life and performed such great penances that the merciful Christ forgave her all her sins, sending His angel to her, where she lay and slept, who took off her rings. At which Emma was very joyful, saying:

Emma: The long nights are seldom welcome to those whose hearts are oppressed with grief and heaviness. Their sleep is great disquiet or greater sorrow, with grievous dreams terrifying them with further terrors. Many such troubles come to me, and who shall tell me the true meaning of my dreams which have come to me as I lay? I thought that I was taken out of the fires of Hell, and borne up from there into Heaven, and many white doves came flying towards me, who with their wings struck off my bonds. Wait, what is this I see, O God full of blessings! Have I attained to this great grace? Yes, truly I have, my bonds are off, as I can see, and they lie here beside me! This is the work of God, of You who are our powerful shield and defence against our weakness! Never can I pay proper thanks to You for this. Oh man, full of misdeeds and sins, from this you can take example, and say eternal praises to Almighty God in honour of this unparalleled goodness. In your own poor and feeble way, pay fitting honour to Him in His temple.

The Epilogue

So, God's chosen friends, this happened once long ago, and it is true, though many think it a lie; and if you went to Maestricht, to the house of converted sinners, you would see Emma's grave, and over the grave the three rings hanging, and under the rings, written in letters still legible, the story of her life and of the penance which she suffered, and how and when it happened. These are the signs which convince me that it is true. She lived some two years more, after her rings fell off, it was told to me, always performing penances and exercises to gain the favour of the King of kings. Accept this thankfully and without complaint, this poor story, for it was written for love, that we may receive heavenly glory. Amen.

Bibliography

PRIMARY SOURCES

Abelard and Heloise

Abelard, Pierre. *Historia Calamitatum*. Edited by J. Monfrin. Paris: Librairie Philosophique J. Vrin, 1959. 2nd. 1962.

Jolivet, J., et al., eds. *Petrus Abaelardus (1079–1142): Person, Werk und Wirkung. Trierer Theologische Studien* 38 Trier: 1980.

McLaughlin, T. P. "Abelard's Rules for Religious Women." *Medieval Studies* 18 (1956): 241–92.

Muckle, J. T. "Abelard's Letter of Consolation to a Friend (Historia Calamitatum)." *Medieval Studies* 15 (1953): 240–81.

———. "Letter of Heloise on the Religious Life and Abelard's First Reply." *Medieval Studies* 17 (1955): 240–81.

———. "The Personal Letters of Abelard and Heloise." *Medieval Studies* 15 (1953): 68–94.

Radice, Betty, trans. *The Letters of Abelard and Heloise*. Baltimore and London: Penguin, 1974.

Angela da Foligno (1248–1309, Italy)

Angela da Foligno *L'autobiografia & gli scritti*. Edited by M. Faloci Pulignani. Translated by M. Castiglione Humani. Città di Castello: Il Solco, 1932.

Angela of Foligno. *Le Livre de la Bienheureuse Soeur Angèle de Foligno*. edited and translated by Paul Doncoeur. Paris: Librairie de l'art catholique, 1926.

———. *Le Livre de l'expérience des vrais fidèles*, M. J. Ferré and L. Baudry. Paris: E. Droz, 1927.

DeLuca, Don Giuseppe. "La Beata Angela da Foligno." In *Scrittori di Religione del Trecento volgarizzamenti*. Vol. 3. pp. 501–510. Torino: Einaudi, 1977.

Steegmann, Mary G., trans. *The Book of Divine Consolation of the Blessed Angela of Foligno*. New York: Cooper Square, 1966, reprint edition.

Baudonivia (sixth century, Frankish kingdom)

Baudonivia. *De vita S. Radegundis*. Edited by *MGH, Scriptores Rerum Merov*. II. pp. 364–95.

Beatrice of Nazareth (Beatrijs van Tienen) (1200–68, Antwerp)

Reypens, L. ed. *De autobiografie van de Z. Beatrijs van Tienen*. Antwerp: Ruusbroecgenootschap, 1964.

———, and J. van Mierlo, eds. *Seven manieren van Minne*. Leuven: 1926.

Vekeman, H. and J. Tersteeg. *Beatrijs van Nazareth. Van seuen manieren van heiliger minne*. (Zutphen: Thieme, 1970).

Vita Beatricis. Prologue. Ed. P. V. Bets, *Analects pour servir à l'histoire ecclésiastique de la Belgique*, vol. VI, 1870.

"Vita Beatricis," ed. Chr. Henriquez, in *Quinque Prudente Virgines*, Antwerp, 1630, pp. 1–167.

Bertha of Vilich (1056–57, Frankish Kingdom)

Vita Adelheidis Abbatissae Vilicensis. Edited by *MGH, Scriptores* XV2. pp. 755–63.

Birgitta, Saint (1303–73, Sweden)

Saint Birgitta. *The Revelations of Saint Birgitta*. Edited by William Patterson Cumming. London: Oxford University Press, 1929.

Bonaventure, Saint (pseud.)

Green, Rosalie B., and Isa Ragusa, ed. and trans. *Meditations on the Life of Christ: An illustrated manuscript of the 14th century*. Princeton: Princeton University Press, 1961.

Catherine of Gerberschweber (d. 1330, Germany)

Catherine of Gerberschweber. "Vitae Sororum" d'Unterlinden, in *Archives d'histoire doctrinale et littéraire du moyen age* 5 (1930) 317–509, ed. Jeanne Ancelet-Hustache.

Cathars

Borst, A. *Die Katharer. MGH*. Stuttgart, 1953.

Catherine of Genoa, Saint (1447–1510, Italy)

Catherine of Genoa. *Purgation and Purgatory: The Spiritual Dialogue* (Classics of Western Spirituality). Translated by Serge Hughes. New York: Paulist Press, 1979.

Catherine of Siena, Saint (1347–80, Italy)

Caterina da Siena. *Il Dialogo, ovvero Libro della divina dottrina*, ed. Giuliana Cavallini. Rome: Edizioni Caterinianae, 1968.

Caterina da Siena. *Le Lettere*. Edited by Piero Misciatelli. Siena: Bentivoglio, 1913–22. Reprinted by Marzocco, Florence, 1970.

Catherine of Siena. *The Dialogue* (Classics of Western Spirituality) Suzanne Noffke. New York: Paulist Press, 1981.

———. *The Orcherd of Syon* (15th cent. English trans. of *Dialogue*). Edited by Phyllis Hodgson and Gabriel M. Liegey. London: Oxford University Press, 1966. For E.E.T.S. o.s. 258.

Scudder, Vida D., ed. and trans. *Saint Catherine of Siena as Seen in Her Letters*. London: J. M. Dent, 1927.

Thorold, Algar, trans. *The Dialogue of the Seraphic Virgin Catherine of Siena*. Westminster, Md.: Christian Classics, 1973.

Christina Mirabilis (1150–1224, Brabant-Flanders)

De Cantimpre, Thomas. "Vita Beatae Christinae Mirabilis Trudonopoli in Hasbania," ed. J. Pinius. *AASS* Jul. t.5. Paris, 1868, pp. 637–60.

Christina of Markyate (ca. 1096–98 to 1160, England)

Talbot, Charles H., ed. and trans. *The Life of Christina of Markyate, A Twelfth Century Recluse*. Oxford: Clarendon Press, 1959.

Christine de Pizan (1363–1429? France)

Christine de Pizan. *Book of the Duke of True Lovers*. Introduction by Alice Kemp-Welch. London: Chatto and Windus, 1908.

———. *The Book of the City of Ladies*. Edited and translated by Earl Jeffrey Richards. New York: Persea Books, 1982.

———. *Le Débat sur le "Roman de la Rose,"* Edited by Eric Hicks. Paris, H. Champion, 1977.

———. *Le Livre de la Mutacion de Fortune*. 4 volumes. Edited by Suzanne Solente. Paris: A. J. Picard, 1959–66.

———. *Oeuvres poétiques de Christine de Pizan*. 2 volumes. Edited by Maurice Roy. Paris: Firmin Didot, 1886–91.

Clare of Assisi, Saint (1196–1253, Italy)

de Robeck, Nesta. *St. Clare of Assisi*. Milwaukee: Bruce, 1951.

Scripta. In *Concordantiae verbales opusculorum S. Francisci et S. Clarae*. pp. 167–218. Ed. I. M. Boccali. Assisi: 1976.

Saint Clare. *Legends and Writings of St. Clare of Assisi*. Edited by the Franciscan Institute. New York: St. Bonaventure, 1953.

Clemence of Barking (fl. 1163–69, Anglo-Norman England)

McBain, W., ed. *The Life of St. Catherine*. Oxford: Anglo-Norman Text Society, 1964.

Sodergard, O., ed. *La vie d'Edouard le Confesseur*. Uppsala: Almqvist & Wiksells, 1948.

Dhuoda (ca. 803–after 843, Frankish Kingdom)

Riche, P., ed. (*Liber Manualis*) *Manuel pour mon fils*. Translated by B. de Vergille and C. Mondesert. Paris: Sources Chrétiennes, 1975.

Douceline, Saint (d. 1282, Marseilles, Provence, France)

Albanes, Joseph Mathias Hyacinthe, ed. *La vie de Sainte Douceline, fondatrice des Beguines de Marseille*. Marseille: E. Camoin, 1879.

Egeria (fl. c. 381–84, Spain)

Prinz, O., ed. *Itinerarium (Peregrinatio Aetheriae)*. Heidelberg: Carl Winter, 1960.

Elisabeth of Schönau, Saint (1129–65, Germany)

Phillips, ed. *Sankt Elisabeth Fürstin, Dienerin, Heilige: Aufsätze, Dokumentation, Katalog*. Sigmaringen: Universität Marburg, 1981.

Roth, F. W. E., ed. *Die Visionen und Briefe der heiligen Elisabeth*. Brunn: Verlag der "Studien aus dem Benedictiner- und Cistercienser-Orden," 1884.

Gerontius

Gerontius. *Vie de Sainte Mélanie*. Edited and translated by Denys Gorce. Paris: Editions du Cerf, 1962.

Gertrude of Helfta, Saint (St. Gertrude the Great)
(1256 to 1301–12, Germany)

Hourlier, J., and A. Schmitt, eds. *Les exercices. Oeuvres Spirituelles* I. Paris: Sources Chrétiennes, 1967.

The Exercises of Saint Gertrude, by a Benedictine nun of Regina Laudis. Westminster, Md.: Newman Press, 1956.

Le héraut (Legatus) Oeuvres Spirituelles II-IV. Paris: Sources Chrétiennes, 1968. Autobiography is "Legatus," Book II, pp. 225–353.

The Life and Revelations of Saint Gertrude. Westminster, Md.: Newman Press, 1949.

Gospels

Schneemelcher, W., ed. *New Testament Apocrypha.* 2 vols. Introduction by E. Hennecke. Philadelphia: Westminster Press, 1965.

Gregory of Nyssa, Saint

Gregory of Nyssa, Saint. *Ascetical Works.* Translated by Virginia Woods Callahan. In *The Fathers of the Church, a New Translation.* Vol. 58. Washington, D.C.: Catholic University of America Press, 1947.

Hadewijch of Brabant (1st half of 13 century, Antwerp)

Hart, Mother Columba, trans. *Hadewijch: The Complete Works.* New York: Paulist Press, 1980.

Mierlo, Jozef van, ed. *Hadewijch, Brieven.* 2 vols. Antwerp: Standaard-Boekhandel, 1947.

———. *Hadewijch, Mengeldichten.* Antwerp: Staandard-Boekhandel, 1952.

———. *Hadewijch, Strophische Gedichten.* 2 vols. Antwerp: Standaard-Boekhandel, 1942.

———. *Hadewijch, Visioenen.* 2 vols. Louvain: Vlaamsch Boekenhalle, 1924–25.

Herrad of Hohenbourg (Herrad of Landsberg)
(1125/30–1195, Germany)

Green, Rosalie, et al., eds. *Hortus Deliciarum.* 2 vols. London: Warburg Institute, 1979.

Hildegard of Bingen (1098–1179, Germany)

Barth, Pudentiana, M. Immaculata Ritscher, and Joseph Schmidt-Gorg, eds. *Lieder: Nach den Handschriften herausgegeben.* Salzburg: O. Muller 1969.

Carlevaris, A., and A. Fuhrkotter. *Hildegardis Scivias.* Corpus Christianorum Continuatio Medievalis, 43–43A. Turnhot: Brepols, 1978.

Grant, Barbara L. "Five Liturgical Songs by Hildegarde von Bingen." *Signs* 5, 3 (Spring 1980): 566–67.

Hildegard. *Sanctae Hildegardis Revelationes* (*Lucca MS #1942*). Edited by A. R. Calderoni Masetti and G. Dalla Regoli. Lucca, 1973.

Hozeski, Bruce W. "*Ordo Virtutum*: Hildegarde of Bingen's Liturgical Morality Play." *Annuale Mediaevale* 13 (1978): 45–69.

Pitra, J. B., ed. "Liber vitae meritorum." In *Analecta Sacra VIII: Sanctae Hildegardis Opera*, pp. 1–244. Rome: Monte Cassino, 1882.

Steele, Francisca Maria, ed. and trans. *The Life and Visions of St. Hildegarde.* London: Heath, Cranton and Ousely, 1914.

Hrotsvit of Gandersheim (c. 932–c. 1000, Germany)

Bergman, Sister Mary Bernardine, ed. and trans. *Hrosvithae Liber tertius.* Covington, Ky.: Sisters of Saint Benedict, 1945.

Bonfante, Larissa. *The Plays of Roswitha.* New York: New York University Press, 1979.

———. trans. "*Callimachus*, A Play by Hroswitha." *Allegorica* 1,1 (Spring 1976): 7–51.

Haight, Anne L., ed. *Hroswitha of Gandersheim* (bibliography). New York: Hroswitha Club, 1965.

Homeyer, Hélene, ed. *Hrotsvithae Opera.* Munich: Schoningh, 1970.

Hrotsvit. *Hroswitha Opera.* Edited by Karl Strecker. Leipzig: Bibliotheca Teubneriana, 1930. Reprint of 1906 edition.

———. *Patrologiae Cursus Completus.* Tomus CXXXVII, Series Latina, Tomus I. Edited by J. P. Migne. Paris, 1853.

St. John, Christopher (pseudonym for Christabel Marshall). *The Plays of Roswitha.* New York: Cooper Square, 1966. Reprint of 1932 edition, the Medieval Library, London.

Wiegand, Sister Gonsalva M., OSF. "The Non-Dramatic Works of Hroswitha." Ph.D. dissertation, St. Louis University, 1936.

Wilson, Katharina M. *The Dramas of Hrotsvit of Gandersheim.* Saskatoon: Peregrina, 1985.

Hugeburc of Heidenheim (8th century Wessex, died Germany)

Vita Willibaldi Episcopi Eichstetensis. Edited by *MGH Scriptores XV, i*, pp. 86–106.

Vita Wynnebaldi Abbatis Heidenheimensis. Edited by *MGH Scriptores XV, i*, pp. 106–17.

Ida of Nivelles (c. 1190–1231, Belgium)

Vita Idae Nivellensis, 32, in Chrysostom Henriquez, *Quinque Prudentes Virgines.* Antwerp, 1630, pp. 199–297.

Vita Idae Nivellensis Acta Sanctorum, vol. 13 (October). Edited by D. Papebroeck. Paris, 1883.

Inquisition

Lea, Henry Charles. *The Inquisition of the Middle Ages.* Historical introduction by Walter Ullmann. New York: Harper and Row, 1969.

Jacobus de Voragine

Ripperger, Helmut, and Granger Ryan, trans. *The Golden Legend of Jacobus de Voragine*. New York: Arno Press, 1969.
Jacobus de Voragine. Legenda Aurea. Edited by Th. Graesse. Osnabruck: O. Zeller, 1965.

Julian of Norwich (1343–1413, England)

Colledge, Edmund, and James Walsh. *Julian of Norwich Showings*. New York: Paulist Press, 1978.
A Book of Showings to the Anchoress Julian of Norwich. Toronto: Pontifical Institute of Medieval Studies, 1978.

Leoba, Saint (c. 700–779, b. Wessex, d. Germany)

Talbot, Charles H., ed. and trans. *The Anglo-Saxon Missionaries in Germany*. New York: Sheed and Ward, 1954.

Doña Leonor López de Córdoba (c. 1362–c. 1412, Spain)

"Las memorias de Doña Leonor López de Cordoba." *Journal of Hispanic Philology* 2 (February 1978: 11–33). Ayerba-Chaux, Reinaldo.

Libellus

Constable, Giles, and Bernard Smith, eds. and trans. *Libellus de Diversis Ordinibus et Professionibus Qui Sunt in Aecclesia*. Oxford: Clarendon Press, 1972.

Magdalena Beutler of Freiburg (1407–58, Germany)

Greenspan, Karen. *Erklaerung des Vaterunsers: A Critical Edition of a Fifteenth Century Mystical Treatise by Magdalena Beutler of Freiburg*. Ph.D. thesis, University of Massachusetts at Amherst, 1984.

Margery Kempe (1373–1439, England)

Meech, Sanford Brown, ed. *The Book of Margery Kempe*. Vol. 1. Preface by Hope Emily Allen. London: Oxford University Press, 1940.

Marguerite d'Oingt (d. 1310, Poleteins near Lyon)

Duraffour, A., P. Durdilly, and P. Gardette. *Marguerite d'Oingt: édition critique de ses oeuvres*. Paris: Les Belles Lettres, 1965.

Marguerite Porete (d. 1310, Paris)

Colledge, E., and R. Guarnieri, eds. "The Glosses by 'M.N.' *Archivio italiano per la storia della pietà* V (1968): 357–82.
Doiron, M. "Margaret Porete: *The Mirror of Simple Souls*, A Middle English Translation." *Archivio italiano per la storia della pietà* V (1968): 241–355.
Fredericq, Paul. *Corpus documentorum inquisitionis haereticae pravitatis Neerlandicae*. 5 vols. Ghent: 1889–1903. Vol. 1, pp. 159–61; Vol. 2, pp., 64–66.
Kirchberger, Clare, ed. *The Mirror of Simple Souls*. London: Burns, Oates and Washbourne, 1927.
Porete, Marguerite. "Le Mirouer des simples âmes anienties et qui seulement demeurent en vouloir et désir d'amour." Edited by Romana Guarnieri. *Archivio Italiano per la storia della pietà* IV (1965).

Marie de France (12th century)

Ewert, Alfred, ed. *Lais*. Oxford: Basil Blackwell, 1963. Reprint of 1944 edition.
———, and R. C. Johnston, eds. *Fables*. Oxford: Basil Blackwell, 1966. Reprint of 1942 edition.
Ferrante, Joan, and Robert Hanning, trans. *The Lais of Marie de France*. Durham, N.C.: Labyrinth Press, 1982.
Menard, Philippe, ed. *Les Lais de Marie de France*. Paris: Presses universitaires de France, 1979.
Sienaert, Edgard. *Les Lais de Marie de France*. Paris: H. Champion, 1978.
Warnke, K., ed. *Espurgatoire S. Patrice*. Halle: M. Niemeyer, 1938.
———. *Die Lais der Marie de France*. Halle: M. Niemeyer, 1900, 1925.
———. *Les fables: Die Fabeln*. Paris, 1969.

Marie d'Oignies (1177–1213, Brabant-Flanders)

De Vitry, Jacques. "Vita Mariae Oigniacensis." Edited by D. Papebroeck. In AASS Jun. t.v. Paris, 1867, pp. 542–72.

Mechthild of Hackeborn (1241–c.1298, Germany)

Halligan, Theresa A., ed. *The Book of Gostlye Grace of Mechtild of Hackeborn*. Toronto: Pontifical Institute of Medieval Studies, 1979.
Solesmes Monks, eds. "Liber specialis gratiae." In *Revelationes Gertrudianae ac Mechtildianae II*. Paris: Oudin, 1877.

Mechthild of Magdeburg (c.1212–c.1294, Germany)

Menzies, Lucy, *The Revelations of Mechthild of Magdeburg (1210–1297) or The Flowing Light of the Godhead*. New York: Longman's, Green & Co., 1953.
Morel, Gall R., ed. *Offenbarungen, oder Das Fliessende Licht der Gottheit*. Regensburg: G. J. Manz, 1869.
Schmidt, M., intro. and trans. *Das Fliessende Licht der Gottheit*. Zurich and Cologne: Einsiedeln, 1955.
Solesmes Monks, eds. "Lux divinitatis." In *Revelationes Gertrudianae ac Mechtildianae II*, pp. 437–70. Paris: Oudin, 1877.

Mystics

Colledge, Eric. *The Medieval Mystics of England.* New York: Scribner and Sons, 1961.

———, ed. and trans. *Medieval Netherlands Religious Literature.* New York: London House and Maxwell, 1965.

Craveri, Marcello. *Sante e Streghe: Biografie e Documenti dal XIV al XVII secolo.* Milan: Feltrinelli, 1980.

Gardner, Edmund, ed. *The Cell of Knowledge: Seven Early English Mystical Treatises.* New York: Cooper Square, 1966. Reprint of 1910 edition, Chatto and Windus, (London), Duffield (New York).

Lewis, Agnes Smith, trans. *Select Narratives of Holy Women.* 2 vols. London: C. J. Clay, 1900.

Petroff, Elizabeth. *Consolation of the Blessed: Women Saints in Medieval Tuscany.* New York: Alta Gaia, 1980.

Pfeiffer, Frantz. *Deutsche Mystiker des 14 Jahrhunderts* II. Leipzig, 1857. Reprinted Göttingen: Vandenhoeck & Ruprecht, 1914.

Na Prous Boneta (1290–1325, Carcassone, France)

May, William Harold. "The Confession of Prous Boneta, Heretic and Heresiarch." In *Essays in Medieval Life and Thought,* pp. 3–30. Edited by John H. Mundy et al. New York: Columbia University Press, 1955.

Paula, Eustochium, Saints (4th century)

Ruiz Bueno, D., ed. "Letter to Marcella." In *Cartas de San Jerónimo.* 2 vols, pp. 318–34. Madrid, 1962. Epistle 46.

Perpetua and Felicity, Saints (d. Carthage, c.203)

Musurillo, Herbert, trans. *The Acts of the Christian Martyrs.* Oxford: Clarendon Press, 1972.

Owen, E. C. E., trans. *Some Authentic Acts of the Early Martyrs.* Oxford: Clarendon Press, 1927.

Shewring, Walter Hayward, trans. *The Passion of SS. Perpetua and Felicity.* London: Sheed and Ward, 1931.

Schwester Katrei (14th century)

Katrei, Schwester (attributed). *Deutsche Mystiker des 14 Jahrhunderts II,* pp. 448–75. Leipzig, 1857.

Sisters of Unterlinden (13th century, Colmar, Germany)

Ancelet-Hustache, Jeanne, ed. *Les "Vitae Sororum" d'Unterlinden.* Édition critique in *Archives d'histoire doctrinale et littéraire du moyen âge* 5 (1930), pp. 317–509. (Biographies of forty-four nuns in Dominican convent in Colmar.)

Trobairitz

Bec, Pierre, ed. *Anthologie des troubadours.* Paris, 1979.

Bogin, Meg. *The Women Troubadours.* New York and London: Paddington Press, 1976. New York: Norton, 1980.

Schultz-Gora, Oskar. *Die Provenzalischen Dichterinnen.* Leipzig: G. Fock, 1888.

Trotula of Salerno

Mason-Hohl, Elizabeth. *The Diseases of Women by Trotula of Salerno: A translation of "Passionibus Mulierum Curandorum".* New York: Ward Richie Press, 1940.

Rowland, Beryl. *Medieval Woman's Guide to Health: The First English Gynecological Handbook.* Kent, Ohio: Kent State University Press, 1981.

Umiliana (1303–30, Italy)

Da Cortona, Vito. "Leggenda della Beata Umiliana de' Cerchi." In *Scrittori di religione del Trecento Volgarizzamenti,* Vol. 3, pp. 365–410. Edited by Don Giuseppe de Luca. Turin: Einaudi, 1977.

Umiltà of Faenza, Saint (1226–1310, Italy)

Umiltà. *Sanctae Humilitatis de Faventia. Sermones.* Edited by T. Sala. Florence, 1884.

Zama, Pietro. *Santa Umiltà La Vita e i "sermones".* Faenza: Fratelli Lega Editori, 1974.

SECONDARY SOURCES

Abel, Elizabeth, ed. *Writing and Sexual Difference.* Chicago: University of Chicago Press, 1982.

Abels, Richard, and Ellen Harrison. "The Participation of Women in Languedocian Catharism." In *Mediaeval Studies* 41 (1979): 215–51.

Abrahamse, Dorothy. "Images of Childhood in Early Byzantine Hagiography." *History of Childhood Quarterly* 1 (1973): 497–517.

Aigrain, René. *L'Hagiographie: ses sources, ses méthodes, son histoire.* Paris: Bloud et Gay, 1953.

Ambrose, Sister Mary (Mullholland), B.V.M. "Statutes on Clothmaking: Toulouse, 1227." In *Essays in Medieval Life and Thought,* edited by John H. Mundy et al., pp. 167–80. New York: Columbia University Press, 1955.

Ancelet-Hustache, Jeanne. *Mechtilde de Magdeburg (1207–1282): Étude de psychologie religieuse.* Paris: H. Champion, 1926.

Angiolillo, Maria d'Elia. "L'epistolario femminile di S.

Bernardo." *Analecta Sacri Ordinis Cisterciensis* 15 (1959): 23–55.

Anson, John. "The Female Transvestite in Early Monasticism: The Origin and Development of a Motif." *Viator* 5 (1974): 1–32.

Aries, Philippe. *Centuries of Childhood*. Translated by Robert Baldick. London: Jonathan Cape, 1962.

Atkinson, Clarissa. *Mystic and Pilgrim: The Book and the World of Margery Kempe*. Ithaca: Cornell University Press, 1983.

Attwater, Donald. *The Penguin Dictionary of Saints*. Harmondsworth, England, and Baltimore: Penguin Books, 1965.

Auerbach, Erich. *Literary Language and Its Public in Late Latin Antiquity and in the Middle Ages*. Translated by Ralph Manheim. New York: Bollingen Foundation, and London: Routledge and Kegan Paul, 1965.

Bainton, Roland H. "Feminine Piety in Tudor England." In *Christian Spirituality: Essays in Honour of Gordon Rupp*, edited by Peter Brooks. pp. 63–77. London: S. C. M. Press, 1975.

Baker, Derek. *Medieval Women, Dedicated and Presented to Professor Rosalind M. T. Hill*. Published for the Ecclesiastical History Society. Oxford Basil Blackwell, 1978.

———, ed. *Schism, Heresy and Religious Protest. Studies in Church History*, Vol. 9. Cambridge: Cambridge University Press, 1972.

Baker, Derek, and J. J. Cummings, eds. *Popular Belief and Practice: Studies in Church History*. Vol. 8. Cambridge: Cambridge University Press, 1972.

Balsdon, John Percy Vyvian Dacre. *Roman Women: Their History and Habits*. New York: Barnes & Noble, 1983; first pub. New York: J. Day Co., 1963.

Banker, James R. "Mourning a Son: Childhood and Paternal Love in the Consolateria of Gianozzo Manetti." *History of Childhood Quarterly* 3:3 (Winter 1976): 351–62.

Banti, Ottavio. "Per la storia dell'eremitismo del Tre e del Quattrocentro." *Bollettino Storico Pisano* 33–35 (1964–66): 714–17.

Barber, Malcolm C. "Women and Catharism." In *Reading Medieval Studies*. Annual Proceedings University of Reading Graduate Centre for Medieval Studies. Vol. 3. Reading, England: Reading University Press, 1977, pp. 45–62.

Bartoli, Marco. "Analisi storica e interpretazione psicanalitica di una visione di S. Chiara d'Assisi." *Archivum Franciscanum Historicum* 73:4 (October–December 1980): 449–72.

Battistoni, Andrea. "Recenti studi sull'eremitismo dei secoli XII–XIII con particolare riguardo al territorio toscano." *Bollettino Storico Pisano* 33–35 (1964–66): 703–8.

Bauml, Franz H. "Medieval Texts and Two Theories of Oral-Formulaic Composition." *New Literary History* XVI (Autumn 1984) 31–50.

———. "Transformations of the Heroine: From Epic Heard to Epic Read." In *The Role of Woman in the Middle Ages*, ed. Rosmarie Thee Morewedge. Albany, N.Y.: SUNY Press, 1975, pp. 23–40.

———. "Varieties and Consequences of Medieval Literacy and Illiteracy." *Speculum* 55 (April 1980): 237–65.

Becker, Marvin. "Aspects of Lay Piety in Early Renaissance Florence." In *The Pursuit of Holiness in Late Medieval and Renaissance Religion*, ed. Heiko A. Oberman. Leiden: E. J. Brill, 1974, pp. 177–99.

Bell, Robert. "Metamorphoses of Spiritual Autobiography." *Journal of English Literary History* 44:1 (1977): 108–26.

Bell, Susan Groag. "Medieval Women Book Owners: Arbiters of Lay Piety and Ambassadors of Culture." *Signs* 7:4 (Summer 1982): 742–69.

———. *Women from the Greeks to the French Revolution*. Belmont, Calif.: Wadsworth, 1973.

A Benedictine of Stanhope. "Margery Kempe and the Holy Eucharist." *Downside Review* 56 (1938): 468–82.

Bennett, Henry Stanley. *Six Medieval Men and Women*. New York: Atheneum, 1962.

Benton, John F. "Clio and Venus: An Historical View of Medieval Love." In *The Meaning of Courtly Love*, edited Francis X. Newman, pp. 19–42. Albany: SUNY Press, 1972.

———. "The Court of Champagne as a Literary Center." *Speculum* 36:4 (October 1961): 551–91.

———. "Fraud, Fiction, and Borrowing in the Correspondence of Abelard and Heloise." In *Pierre Abélard-Pierre le Vénérable: Les courants philosophiques, littéraires et artistiques en Occident au milieu du XIIe siècle*. Actes et mémoires du colloque international, Abbaye de Cluny, 2 au 9 juillet 1972. Paris: Éditions du Centre national de la recherche scientifique, 1975.

Benton, John F., ed. *Self and Society in Medieval France: The Memoirs of Abbot Guibert of Nogent*. New York: Harper & Row, 1970.

Bergendoff, Conrad. "A Critic of the Fourteenth Century: St. Birgitta of Sweden." In *Medieval and Historigraphical Essays in Honor of James Westfall Thompson*, edited by E. N. Anderson and James L. Cate, Port Washington, N.Y.: Kennikat Press, 1966.

Bischoff, Bernhard. "Die Kölner Nonnenhandschriften und das Skriptorium von Chelles." In *Mittelalterliche Studien I*, pp. 16–34. Stuttgart: A. Hiersemann, 1966. Pp. 16–34.

———. "Wer ist die Nonne von Heidenheim?" In *Studien und Mitteilungen zur Geschichte des Benediktinerordens* 49 (1931): 387 ff.

Bloomfield, Morton W. "Joachim of Flora: A Critical Survey of His Canon, Teachings, Sources, Biography, and Influence." *Traditio* 13 (1957): 249–312.

Bolton, Brenda M. "Mulieres Sanctae." In *Women in Medieval Society*, edited by Brenda M. Bolton et al., pp. 141–58. Philadelphia: University of Pennsylvania Press, 1976.

———. "Tradition and Temerity: Papal Attitudes to Deviants, 1159–1216." In *Schism, Heresy and Religious Protest*, edited by Derek Baker, pp. 79–92. Cambridge: Cambridge University Press, 1972.

———. "Vitae Matrum." In *Medieval Women: Dedicated and Presented to Rosalind M. T. Hill*, edited by Derek Baker, pp. 253–73. Published for the Ecclesiastical History Society. Oxford: Basil Blackwell, 1970.

Bolton, Brenda et al. *Women in Medieval Society*. Philadelphia: University of Pennsylvania Press, 1976.

Bonfante, Larissa. *The Plays of Hrotswitha of Gandersheim*. New York: New York University Press, 1979.

Bosse, R. B. "Margery Kempe's Tarnished Reputation." *Fourteenth Century English Mystics Newsletter* 5:1 (1979): 9–19.

Boulding, Elise. *The Underside of History: A View of Women Through Time*. Boulder, Colo.: Westview Press, 1976.

Bouyer, Louis, Dom Jean Leclercq, and Dom François Vandenbroucke, *The Spirituality of the Middle Ages*. London: Burns and Oates, 1968. (Translation of *La Spiritualité du Moyen Age*. Paris: Aubier, 1961; trans. by the Benedictines of the Holme Eden Abbey, Carlisle, N.Y.)

Bowden, Betsy. "The Art of Courtly Copulation." *Medievalia et Humanistica* 9 (1979): 67–85.

Bowsky, William M. "The Impact of the Black Death upon Sienese Government and Society." *Speculum* 39:1 (January 1964): 1–34.

Boyd, Catherine E. *A Cistercian Nunnery in Mediaeval Italy: A Story of Refreddo in Saluzzo, 1220–1300*. Cambridge, Mass.: Harvard University Press, 1943.

Boyer, Regis. "An Attempt to Define the Typology of Medieval Hagiography." In *Hagiography and Medieval Literature*, pp. 27–36. Center for the Study of Vernacular Literature in the Medieval Ages). Odense, Denmark: Odense University Press, 1981.

Bradley, Ritamary. "Julian of Norwich: Writer & Mystic" in *An Introduction to the Medieval Mystics of Europe*, ed. Paul Szarmach. Albany, N.Y.: SUNY Press, 1984.

———. "The Motherhood Theme in Julian of Norwich." *Fourteenth Century English Mystics Newsletter* 2:4 (1974): 25–30.

Bridenthal, Renate, and Claudia Koonz. *Becoming Visible: Women in European History*. Boston: Houghton Mifflin, 1977.

Broner, Esther M., and Cathy N. Davidson. *The Lost Tradition: Mothers and Daughters in Literature*. New York: Frederick Ungar, 1980.

Brook, Christopher. "Heresy and Religious Sentiment: 1000–1250." *Bulletin of the Institute of Historical Research* (November 1968): 115–31.

Brooks, Peter, ed. *Christian Spirituality: Essays in Honour of Gordon Rupp*. London: S. C. M. Press, 1975.

Brown, Peter Robert Lamont. *The Cult of the Saints: Its Rise and Function in Latin Christianity*. Chicago: University of Chicago Press, 1980.

———. *The Making of Late Antiquity*. Cambridge, Mass.: Harvard University Press, 1978.

———. *Religion and Society in the Age of St. Augustine*. London: Faber, 1972.

———. "The Rise and Function of the Holy Man in Late Antiquity." *Journal of Roman Studies* 61 (1971): 80–101.

———. *Society and the Holy in Late Antiquity*. Berkeley: University of California Press, 1982.

———. "Society and the Supernatural: A Medieval Change." *Daedalus* 104:2 (Spring 1975): 133–51.

———. "Sorcery, Demons and the Rise of Christianity." In *Witchcraft Confessions and Accusations*, edited by Mary Douglas, pp. 17–46. London and New York: Tavistock Publications, 1970.

Browning, Robert. "The 'Low Level' Saint's Life in the Early Byzantine World." In *The Byzantine Saint*, edited by Sergei Hackel, pp. 117–27. University of Birmingham Fourteenth Spring Symposium of Byzantine Studies, 1980. London: Fellowship of St. Alban and St. Sergius, 1981.

Brownstein, Rachel M. *Becoming a Heroine: Reading About Women in Novels*. New York: Penguin, 1982.

Bryant, Gwendolyn. "The French Heretic Béguine Marguerite Porete." In *Medieval Women Writers*, edited by Katharina M. Wilson, pp. 204–26. Athens, Ga.: University of Georgia Press, 1984.

Budge, Ernest Alfred Wallis. *Paradise of the Fathers*. 2 vols. London: Chatto and Windus, 1970; reprint of 1910 edition, New York: Duffield and Co.

Bullough, Vern L. "Medieval Medical and Scientific Views of Women." *Viator* 4 (1973): 485–501.

———. "Transvestites in the Middle Ages." *American Journal of Sociology* 79 (May 1973): 1381–94.

Burgess, G. S. *Marie de France: An Analytical Bibliography*. London: Grant & Cutler, 1977.

Burr, David. "Olivi on Marriage: The Conservative as Prophet." *Journal of Medieval and Renaissance Studies* 2 (Fall 1972): 183–204.

Butkovitch, Anthony. *Revelations of St. Birgitta of Sweden*. Los Angeles: Ecumenical Foundation of America, 1972.

Bynum, Caroline. *Jesus as Mother: Studies in the Spirituality of the High Middle Ages.* Berkeley: University of California Press, 1982.

———. "The Spirituality of Regular Canons in the Twelfth Century: A New Approach." *Medievalia et Humanistica* 4 (1973): 3–24.

———. "Women and Eucharistic Devotion in the Thirteenth Century." Forthcoming *Women Studies.*

———. "Women's Stories, Women's Symbols: A Critique of Victor Turner's Theory of Liminality." In *Anthropology and the Study of Religions,* edited by Frank E. Reynolds and Robert Moore. Chicago: Center for the Scientific Study of Religion, 1984.

Bynum, David E. *The Daemon in the Wood: A Study of Oral Narrative Patterns.* Cambridge, Mass.; Center for the Study of Oral Literature, distributed by Harvard University Press, 1978.

The Byzantine Saint, edited by Sergei Hackel. University of Birmingham Fourteenth Spring Symposium of Byzantine Studies, 1980. London: Fellowship of St. Alban and St. Sergius, 1981.

Campbell, Jane. "Women Scholars of the Middle Ages." *American Catholic Quarterly Review* 43 (January–October 1918): 237–40.

Capitani, Ovidio, ed. *Medioevo Ereticale.* Bologna: Il Mulino, 1977.

Carlé, Birte. "Structural Patterns in the Legends of the Holy Women of Christianity." In *Aspects of Female Existence,* edited by Birte Carlé et al., pp. 79–81. Proceedings of St. Gertrud Symposium "Women in the Middle Ages," Copenhagen, September 1978. Copenhagen: Gyldendal, 1980.

Casagrande, Carla. *Prediche alle Donne del Secolo XIII.* Milan: Bompiani, 1978.

Casey, Kathleen. "The Cheshire Cat: Reconstructing the Experience of Medieval Woman." In *Liberating Women's History,* edited by Bernice Carroll, pp. 224–49. Urbana: University of Illinois Press, 1976.

Casolini, Fausta. "I Penitenti francescani in 'Leggende' e cronache del Trecento." In *I Frati Penitenti di S. Francesco nella società del 2 e 300,* edited by Mariano d'Alatri, pp. 69–85. Rome: Istituto Storico dei Cappuccini, 1977.

Cecchetti, Bartolomeo. "La Donna nel Medioevo a Venezia" *Archivio Veneto* (1886). Tomo 31:33–69; Tomo 32:307–349.

Chadwick, Henry. "Pachomius and the Idea of Sanctity." In *The Byzantine Saint,* edited by Sergei Hackel, pp. 11–24. University of Birmingham Fourteenth Spring Symposium of Byzantine Studies, 1980. London: Fellowship of St. Alban and St. Sergius, 1981.

Chitty, Derwas. *The Desert A City.* Oxford: Basil Blackwell, 1966.

Chojnacki, Stanley. "Patrician Women in Early Renaissance Venice." *Studies in the Renaissance* 21 (1974): 176–203.

Cholmeley, Katherine. *Margery Kempe, Genius and Mystic.* London: Longmans, Green and Co., 1947.

Chrisman, Miriam U. "Women and the Reformation in Strasbourg, 1490–1530." *Archive for Reformation History* 63:2 (1972): 143–68.

Clanchy, M. T. *From Memory to Written Record: England 1066–1307.* Cambridge, Mass.: Harvard University Press, 1979.

Clark, Elizabeth, and Herbert Richardson. *Women and Religion: A Feminist Sourcebook of Christian Thought.* New York: Harper & Row, 1977.

Clay, Rotha Mary. *The Hermits and Anchorites of England.* Detroit: Singing Tree Press, 1968; reprint of 1914 edition.

Cleugh, James. *Love Locked out: An Examination of the Irrepressible Sexuality of the Middle Ages.* New York: Crown, 1964.

Cohn, Norman. *Europe's Inner Demons.* New York: Basic Books, 1975.

———. *The Pursuit of the Millenium.* New York: Academy Library, 1969.

Colafemmina, Cesare. "Donne, ebrei e christiani." *Quaderni Medievale* 8 (1980): 117–25.

Coleman, Emily. "Infanticide in the Early Middle Ages." In *Women in Medieval Society,* edited by Brenda M. Bolton et al., pp. 47–70. Philadelphia: University of Pennsylvania Press, 1976.

———. "Medieval Marriage Characteristics." In *The Family in History,* edited by Theodore K. Rabb and Robert I. Rotberg, pp. 1–5. New York: Harper & Row, 1973.

———. "Medieval Marriage Characteristics: A Neglected Factor in the History of Medieval Serfdom." *Journal of Interdisciplinary History* 2 (Autumn 1971): 205–19.

Coleman, Janet. *Medieval Readers and Writers.* New York: Columbia University Press, 1981.

Coleman, Thomas William. *English Mystics of the Fourteenth Century.* Westport, Conn.: Greenwood Press, 1971; reprint of 1938 edition.

Collis, Louise. *Memoirs of a Medieval Woman: The Life and Times of Margery Kempe.* New York: Crowell, 1964.

Connel, Susan. "Books and Their Owners in Venice: 1345–1480." *Journal of the Warburg and Courtauld Institute* 35 (1972): 165–86.

Constable, Giles. "Twelfth Century Spirituality and the Late Middle Ages." *Medieval and Renaissance Studies* 5 (1971): 29–30.

Corcoran, Donald. "Contemporary Forms of Spirituality and Monastic Life." In *The Continuing Quest for God,* edited by William Skudlarek, O.S.B., pp. 242–56. Collegeville, Minn.: The Liturgical Press, 1982.

Corsi, Dinora. "Firenze 1300–1350: 'Non-conformismo' Religioso e Organizzazione Inquisitoriale." *Annali dell' Istituto di Storia, Università di Firenze, Facoltà di Magistero* 1 (1979): 29–66.

Crosby, Ruth. "Oral Delivery in the Middle Ages." *Speculum* 11 (January 1936): 88–110.

Cunningham, Lawrence. *The Meaning of Saints.* New York: Harper & Row, 1980.

Curschman, Michael. "Oral Poetry in Medieval English, French, and German Literature: Some Notes on Recent Research." *Speculum* 42 (January 1967): 36–52.

D'Alatri, Mariano. "'Eresie' perseguite dall'inquisizione in Italia nel corso del Duecento." In *The Concept of Heresy in the Middle Ages (11th–13th centuries)*, edited by Dr. W. Lourdaux and Dr. D. Verhelst, pp. 211–24. Mediaevalia Lovaniensia, Series 1, studia 4). The Hague: Leuven University Press, 1976.

———, ed. *I Frati Penitenti di S. Francesco nella società del 2 e 300.* Rome: Istituto storico dei cappuccini, 1977.

Daly, Mary *The Church and the Second Sex.* New York: Harper & Row, 1975.

Daniel, E. Randolph. "Spirituality and Poverty: Angelo da Clareno and Ubertino da Casale." *Medievalia et Humanistica* 4 (1973): 89–98.

Davis, Natalie Zemon. *Society and Culture in Early Modern France.* Stanford: Stanford University Press, 1975.

Deen, Edith. *Great Women of the Christian Faith.* New York and London: Harper & Row, 1976.

DeGanck, R. "The Cistercian Nuns of Belgium in the 13th Century." *Cistercian Studies* 5 (1970): 169–87.

Delany, Sheila. *Writing Woman: Women Writers and Women in Literature, Medieval to Modern.* New York: Schocken, 1983.

Delcourt, Marie. "Appendix: Female Saints in Masculine Clothing." In *Hermaphrodite: Myths and Rites of the Bisexual Figure in Classical Antiquity*, pp. 84–102. Translated by Jennifer Nicholson. London: Studio Books, 1961. French title *Hermaphrodite*.

Delehaye, Hippolyte. *The Legends of the Saints.* Translated by Donald Attwater. New York: Fordham University Press, 1962; original French edition, 1905; 4th French edition, 1955.

———. *Les passions des martyrs et les genres littéraires.* Brussels: Bureaux de la societé des Bollandistes, 1921.

———. "Problemi di metodo agiografico: le coordinate agiografiche e le narrazioni." In *Agiografia Altomedio-vale*, edited by Sofia Boesch Gajano, pp. 49–71. Bologna: Il Mulino, 1976.

Della Robbia, Enrica Viviani. *Nei Monasteri Fiorentini.* Florence: Sansoni, 1946.

Delooz, Pierre. "Per uno studio sociologico della santità." In *Agiografia Altomediovale*, edited by Sofia Boesch Gajano, pp. 227–58. Bologna: Il Mulino, 1976.

Demaitre, Luke. "The Idea of Childhood and Childcare in the Medical Writings of the Middle Ages." *Journal of Psychohistory* 4:4 (Spring 1977): 461–90.

Dembrowski, Peter. "St. Mary of Egypt and Problems of Development of Hagiography in Old French." Paper presented at the 1979 MLA Conference, San Francisco.

de Mause, Lloyd, ed. *The History of Childhood.* New York: Harper & Row, 1974.

De Robeck, Nesta. *Among the Franciscan Tertiaries.* London and Toronto: J. M. Dent, 1930.

———. *Saint Clare of Assisi* Milwaukee: Bruce, 1951.

De Troeyer, Benjamin. "Béguines et Tertiares en Belgique et aux Pays-Bas aux XIII–XIVᵉ siècles." In *I Frati Penitenti di S. Francesco nella società del 2 e 300*, edited by Mariano D'Alatri, pp. 133–39. Rome: Istituto Storico dei Cappuccini, 1977.

Dickman, Susan. "The Book of Margery Kempe." Unpublished translation.

———. "The Devout Imagination: Julian of Norwich and Margery Kempe." Unpublished manuscript.

———. "Margery Kempe and the English Devotional Tradition," in *The Medical Mystical Tradition in England* (Exeter: Exeter U.P. 1980) ed. Marion Glasscoe.

Dodwell, Charles Reginald, Otto Pächt, and Francis Wormald, eds. *The St. Albans Psalter.* London: Warburg and Courtauld Institute, 1960.

Downing, Christine. "Revisioning Autobiography: the Bequest of Freud and Jung." *Soundings* 60 (Summer 1977): 210–28.

Drijvers, Han J. W. "Hellenistic and Oriental Origins." In *The Byzantine Saint*, edited by Sergei Hackel, pp. 25–33. University of Birmingham Fourteenth Spring Symposium of Byzantine Studies, 1980. London: Fellowship of St. Alban and St. Sergius, 1981.

Drinker, Sophie Lewis. *Music and Women: The Story of Women in Their Relation to Music.* Washington, D.C.: Zenger Publishing, 1975.

Dronke, Peter. *Medieval Latin and the Rise of the European Love-Lyric.* Oxford: Clarendon Press, 1965.

———. *The Medieval Lyric.* New York: Harper & Row, 1969.

———. *Poetic Individuality in the Middle Ages: New Departures in Poetry 1000–1150.* Oxford: Clarendon Press, 1970.

———. "The Provençal *Trobairitz*: Castelloza" in *Medieval Women Writers*, ed. Katharina H. Wilson. Athens Ga.: University of Georgia Press, 1984, pp. 131–52.

————. *Women Writers of the Middle Ages: A Critical Study of Texts from Perpetua (+203) to Marguerite Porete (+1310).* Cambridge: Cambridge University Press, 1984.

Duggan, Joseph J., ed. *Oral Literature.* New York: Barnes & Noble, 1975.

Dunbar, Agnes B. C. *A Dictionary of Saintly Women.* 2 Vols. London: G. Bell and Sons, 1904–1905.

Dunn, Catherine E. "Popular Devotion in the Vernacular Drama of Medieval England." *Medievalia et Humanistica* 4 (1973): 55–87.

Eckenstein, Lina. *Women Under Monasticism.* Cambridge: Cambridge University Press, 1896.

Economou, George D. "The Two Venuses and Courtly Love." In *In Pursuit of Perfection,* by George D. Economou and Joan M. Ferrante, pp. 17–50. Port Washington, N.Y., and London: Kennikat Press, 1975.

Edna Mary, Sister. *The Religious Life.* Baltimore and London: Penguin, 1968.

Eifler, Margaret, ed. *Women in an Intellectual Context.* Rice University Studies 64:1. Houston: Rice University Press, 1978.

L'eremitismo in occidente nei secoli XI e XII. Miscellanea del Centro di Studi Medioevali. Vol. 5. Atti della seconda settimana internazionale di studio, Mendola, 30 Agosto–6 Settebre 1962. Milan: Vita e Pensiero, 1965.

Erickson, Carolly, *The Medieval Vision.* New York: Oxford University Press, 1976.

————, and Kathleen Casey. "Women in the Middle Ages: A Working Bibliography." *Medieval Studies* 37 (1975): 340–59.

Etienne, Robert. "Ancient Medical Conscience and the Life of Children." *Journal of Psychohistory* 4:2 (Fal 1976): 131–61.

Evans, Gillian R. "Two Aspects of Memoria in Eleventh and Twelfth Century Writings." *Classica et Mediaevalia* 32 (1980): 263–78.

Fell, Christine E. "Hild, Abbess of Streonaeshalch." In *Hagiography and Medieval Literature: A Symposium,* Edited by Hans Bekker-Nielsen, Peter Foote, Jorgen Hojgaard Jorgensen, and Tore Nyberg. Proceedings of the Fifth International Symposium organized by the Centre for the Study of Vernacular Literature in the Middle Ages, Odense University on 17–18 November 1980. Odense: Odense University Press, 1981.

Ferrante, Joan. "The Education of Women in the Middle Ages in Theory, Fact, and Fantasy." In *Beyond Their Sex: Learned Women of the European Past,* edited by Patricia H. LaBalme, pp. 9–42, New York: New York University Press, 1980.

————. "The French Courtly Poet: Marie de France", in Katharina Wilson, ed. *Medieval Women Writers.*

Athens, Ga.: University of Georgia Press, 1984, pp. 64–88.

————. *Woman as Image in Medieval Literature.* New York: Columbia University Press, 1975.

Fingarette, Herbert. "The Ego and Mystic Selflessness." *Psychoanalysis and the Psychoanalytic Review* 45 (Spring–Summer 1958): 5–40.

Finucane, Ronald C. *Miracles and Pilgrims: Popular Beliefs in Medieval England.* Totowa, N.J.: Rowman and Littlefield, 1977.

Fiorenza, Elisabeth Schussler. "Word, Spirit and Power: Women in Early Christian Communities." In *Women of Spirit: Female Leadership in the Jewish and Christian Traditions,* edited by Rosemary Reuther and Eleanor McLaughlin, pp. 29–70. New York: Simon & Schuster, 1979.

Fontaine, J. "Alle fonti dell'agiografia europea." *Rivista di storia e letteratura religiosa* 2 (1966): 187–206.

Forsyth, Ilene H. "Children in Early Medieval Art: Ninth Through Twelfth Centuries." *Journal of Psychohistory* 4:1 (Summer 1976): 31–70.

Franco, Sr. Maria Romana, M.S.C. *La Beata Umiliana dei Cerchi nella Firenze dugentesca.* Rome: Franciscan Congregation, Sisters of the Sacred Heart, 1977.

Frank, Roberta. "Marriage in Twelfth and Fifteenth Century Iceland." *Viator* 4 (1973): 473 ff.

Freed, John B. "Urban Development and the 'Cura Monialium' in Thirteenth Century Germany." *Viator* 3 (1972): 311–27.

Frugoni, Chiara. "L'Iconografia del matrimonio e della coppia nel medioevo." In *Il Matrimonio nella Società Altomedievale,* pp. 901–63. Spoleto: Centro Italiano di Studi sull'Alto Medioevo, 1977.

Furitano, Giuseppe. "Una Santa Donna del Duecento: Margherita Colonna." In *Fatti e Figure del Lazio Medievale,* pp. 387–95. Rome: Fratelli Palombi Editori, 1979.

Gaiffier, B. de. "Mentalité de l'hagiographie médiévale." *Analecta Bollandiana* 86 (1968): 391–400.

Gajano, Sofia Boesch, ed. *Agiografia Altomedioevale.* Bologna: Il Mulino, 1976.

————. "Il Culto di Maria Maddalena nell'Occidente Medioevale." *Rivista di Storia e Letteratura Religiosa* 15:3 (1979): 436–44.

————. "Introduzione." In *Agiografia Altomedioevale,* pp. 7–48. Bologna: Il Mulino, 1976.

Ganz, P. F. "'The Cancionerillo Mozárabe' and the Origin of the Middle High German Frauenlied." *Modern Language Review* 48 (1953): 301–9.

Garth, Helen Meredith. *Saint Mary Magdalene in Medieval Literature.* Johns Hopkins University Studies in History and Political Science, series 67, No. 3. Baltimore: Johns Hopkins University Press, 1950.

Geary, Patrick J. *Furta Sacra: Thefts of Relics in the*

Central Middle Ages. Princeton, N.J.: Princeton University Press, 1978.

Gies, Frances, and Joseph Gies. *Women in the Middle Ages.* New York: Crowell, 1978.

Gilbert, Sandra M., and Susan Gubar. *The Madwoman in the Attic: The Woman Writer and the 19th Century Literary Imagination.* New Haven and London: Yale University Press, 1979.

Ginzburg, Carlo. *I Benandanti. Ricerche sulla stregoneria e sui culti agrari tra cinquecento e seicento.* Turin: Giulio Einaudi, 1966.

Goldberg, Jonathan. "Cellini's *Vita* and the Conventions of Early Autobiography." *Modern Language Notes* 89 (1974): 71–83.

Goodich, Michael E. "Bartholomaeus Anglicus on Child-Rearing." *History of Childhood Quarterly* 3:1 (Summer 1975): 75–84.

———. "Childhood and Adolescence Among the Thirteenth Century Saints." *History of Childhood Quarterly* 1 (1973: 285–307.

———. "The Politics of Canonization in the Thirteenth Century: Lay and Mendicant Saints." *Church History* 44:3 (September 1975): 294–307.

Gougaud, Dom Louis. *Hermites et reclus: Études sur d'anciennes formes de vie religieuse.* Vienne: Abbaye Saint-Martin de Ligugé, 1928.

Grant, Barbara L. "Five Liturgical Songs by Hildegarde von Bingen," in *Signs* 5:3 (Spring 1980) pp. 560–67.

———. "An Interview with the Sybil of the Rhine: Hildegard von Bingen (1098–1179)." *Heresies* 3:2 (Summer 1980): 7.

Graus, Frantisek. "Le funzioni del culto dei santi e della leggenda." In *Agiografia Altomedioevale,* edited by Sofia Boesch Gajano, pp. 145–60. Bologna: Il Mulino, 1976.

Green, Carol Hurd, and Mary G. Mason, eds. *Journeys: Autobiographical Writings by Women.* Boston: G. K. Hall, 1979.

Gregoire, Reginald. "Il Matrimonio Mistico." In *Il Matrimonio nella Società Altomedievale,* pp. 701–817. Spoleto: Centro Italiano di Studi sull'Alto Medioevo, 1977.

Grundman, Herbert. "Die Frauen und die Literatur im Mittelalter: Ein Beitrag zur Frage nach der Entstehung des Schrifttums in der Volkssprache." *Archiv für Kulturgeschichte* 26 (1936): 129–61.

———. "Innocent III and the Heretics." In *Religious Dissent in the Middle Ages,* edited by Jeffrey Burton Russell, pp. 131–33. New York and London: Wiley, 1971.

———. *Religiöse Bewegungen im Mittelalter.* Vaduz: Kraus Reprint, 1965; reprint of 1935 edition, Berlin: E. Ebering.

Guarnieri, Romana. "Il Movimento del Libero Spirito."

Archivio Italiano per la Storia della Pietà 4 (1965): 351–08.

Gundersheimer, Werner L. "Bartolommeo Goggio: A Feminist in Renaissance Ferrara." *Renaissance Quarterly* 33:2 (Summer 1980): 175–200.

———. "Women, Learning, and Power: Eleonora of Aragon and the Court of Ferrara." In *Beyond Their Sex: Learned Women of the European Past,* edited by Patricia H. LaBalme, pp. 43–65. New York: New York University Press, 1980.

Gunther, Heinrich. "Psicologia della leggenda: aspetti e problemi." In *Agiografia Altomedioevale,* edited by Sofia Boesch Gajano, pp. 73–84. Bologna: Il Mulino, 1976.

Hackel, Sergei, ed. *The Byzantine Saint.* University of Birmingham Fourteenth Spring Symposium of Byzantine Studies, 1980. London; Fellowship of St. Alban and St. Sergius, 1981.

Hagiographie, Cultures et Sociétés, IVe–XIIe siècles. Actes du Colloque Organisé à Nanterre et à Paris (2–5 Mai 1979). Paris: Études Augustiniennes, Centre de Recherches sur l'Antiquité tardive et le haut Moyen-Âge, Université de Paris X, 1981.

Haight, Anne L., ed. *Hroswitha of Gandersheim.* New York: Hroswitha Club, 1965.

Hall, Donald John. *English Medieval Pilgrimage.* London: Routledge and Kegan Paul, 1966.

Halligan, Theresa A., ed. *The Book of Gostlye Grace of Mechtild of Hackeborn.* Studies and Texts 46. Toronto: Pontifical Institute of Medieval Studies, 1979.

Hanawalt, Barbara A. "The Female Felon in Fourteenth Century England." In *Women in Medieval Society,* edited by Susan Mosher Stuard. pp. 125–40. Pittsburgh: University of Pennsylvania Press, 1976.

Harvey, Rosemary. "The Political Saint of the Eleventh Century." In *The Byzantine Saint,* edited by Sergei Hackel, pp. 43–50. University of Birmingham Fourteenth Spring Symposium of Byzantine Studies, 1980. London: Fellowship of St. Alban and St. Sergius, 1981.

Healy, Elliott D. "Louise Labé and the Comtessa de Dia." In *Studies in Comparative Literature,* edited by Waldo F. McNeir, pp. 47–68. Baton Rouge, La.: Louisiana State University Press, 1962.

Helmholz, R. H. "Infanticide in the Province of Canterbury During the Fifteenth Century." *History of Childhood Quarterly* 2 (1975): 379–90.

Henrion, Albina. "Santa Chiara d'Assisi: La Cooperatrice di San Francesco." *Archivum Franciscanum Historicum* 19 (1926): 579–609.

Hentsch, Alice Adele. *De la Littérature didactique du Moyen Age s'adressant spécialement aux femmes.* Cahors: A. Coueslant, 1903.

Herlihy, David. "Family Solidarity in Medieval Italian

History." In *Economy, Society and Government: Essays in Memory of Robert L. Reynolds*, edited by David Herlihy, Robert S. Lopez, and Vsevolod Slessarev, pp. 173–84. Kent, Ohio: Kent State University Press, 1969.

————. "Life Expectancies for Women in Medieval Society." In *The Role of Women in the Middle Ages*, edited by Rosmarie Thee Morewedge, pp. 1–20. Albany: SUNY Press, 1975.

————. "The Natural History of Medieval Women." *Natural History* 87 (March 1978): 56–67.

————. "Women in Medieval Society." In pamphlet: *The Smith History Lecture*. Houston: University of St. Thomas, 1971.

Hilpisch, Stephanus. *History of Benedictine Nuns*. Translated by Sr. M. Joanne Muggli. Collegeville, Minn.: St. John's Abbey Press, 1958.

Hodgson, Phyllis. "'The Orcherd of Syon' and the English Mystical Tradition." In *Proceedings of the British Academy*. Vol. 50, pp. 229–49. London: Published for the British Academy by the Oxford University Press, 1965.

Holdsworth, Christopher J. "Christine of Markyate." In *Medieval Women, Dedicated and Presented to Professor Rosalind M. T. Hill*, edited by Derek Baker, pp. 185–204. Published for the Ecclesiastical History Society. Oxford: Basil Blackwell, 1978.

Howe, Elizabeth Teresa. "St. Teresa's *Meditaciones* and the Mystic Tradition of the Canticle of Canticles." *Renascence* 33:1 (Autumn 1980): 47–64.

Hozeski, Bruce W. "The Parallel Patterns in Hrotsvitha of Gandersheim, a Tenth Century German Playwright, and in Hildegard of Bingen, a Twelfth Century German Playwright." *Annuale Mediaevale* 18 (1977): 42–53.

Hughes, Diane Owen. "Urban Growth and Family Structure in Medieval Genoa." *Past and Present* 66 (February 1975): 3–28.

Hughes, Muriel Joy. *Women Healers in Medieval Life and Literature*. Freeport, N.Y.: Books for Libraries Press, 1968; reprint of 1943 edition.

James, Montague R. *The Apocryphal New Testament*. Oxford: Clarendon Press, 1924.

Jameson, Anna. *Legends of the Madonna as Represented in the Fine Arts*. Boston and New York: Houghton, Mifflin, 1895.

————. *Legends of the Monastic Orders as Represented in the Fine Arts*. London: Longmans, Green, and Co., 1880; reedition of corrected and enlarged edition of 1865.

————. *Sacred and Legendary Art*. 2 Vols. Boston and New York: Houghton, Mifflin, 1857.

Jeremy, Sister Mary. *Scholars and Mystics*. Chicago: Henry Regnery, 1962.

Jolliffe, P. S. *A Checklist of Middle English Prose Writings of Spiritual Guidance*. Toronto: Pontifical Institute of Mediaeval Studies, 1974.

Jonas, Hans. *The Gnostic Religion: The Message of the Alien God and the Beginnings of Christianity*. 2d rev. ed. Boston: Beacon Press, 1963. Originally published in 1923 as *Gnosis und spätanticus Geist*.

Jones, Rufus M. *The Flowering of Mysticism: The Friends of God in the Fourteenth Century*. New York: Hafner, 1971.

Jorgensen, Johannes. *Saint Bridget of Sweden*. 2 Vols. Translated from Danish by Ingeborg Lund. London and New York: Longmans, Green and Co., 1954.

Judd, Elizabeth. "Women Before the Conquest: A Study of Women in Anglo-Saxon England." *University of Michigan Papers in Women's Studies* 1:1 (February 1974): 127–49.

Kelly, Amy. *Eleanor of Aquitaine and the Four Kings*. Cambridge, Mass.: Harvard University Press, 1950.

Kelly-Gadol, Joan. "Did Women Have a Renaissance?" In *Becoming Visible: Women in European History*, edited by Renate Bridenthal and Claudia Koonz, pp. 137–64. Boston: Houghton Mifflin, 1977.

Kemp-Welch, Alice. *Of Six Medieval Women*. London: Macmillan, 1913.

Kieckhefer, Richard. *European Witch Trials: Their Foundations in Popular and Learned Culture, 1300–1500*. London: Routledge and Kegan Paul, 1976.

————. *Unquiet Souls: Fourteenth Century Saints and Their Religious Milieu*. Chicago: Univ. of Chicago Press, 1984.

————. "Radical Tendencies in the Flagellant Movement of the Mid-fourteenth Century." *Journal of Medieval and Renaissance Studies* 4 (1974): 157–76.

King, Margaret Leah. "Book-lined Cells: Women and Humanism In the Early Italian Renaissance." In *Beyond Their Sex: Learned Women of the European Past*, edited by Patricia H. LaBalme. pp. 66–90. New York: New York University Press, 1980.

————. "The Religious Retreat of Isotta Nogarola (1418–1466): Sexism and its Consequences." *Signs* 3:4 (Summer 1978): 807–22.

King, Margot H. *The Desert Mothers: A Bibliography*. Saskatoon, Sask., Canada: Peregrina Publishing Co., 1984.

————. *The Desert Mothers: A Survey of the Female Anchoretical Tradition*. Saskatoon, Sask., Canada: Peregrina Publishing Co., 1984.

Kirshner, Julius, and Anthony Molho. "Il Monte delle doti a Firenze dalla sua fondazione nel 1425 alla metá del sedicesimo secolo. Abbozzo di una Ricerca." *Ricerche Storiche* 10:2 (1980): 21–47.

Klawiter, Frederick C. "The Role of Martyrdom and Persecution in Developing the Priestly Authority of

Women in Early Christianity: A Case Study of Montanism." *Church History* 49 (1980): 251–61.

Knauf, Peggy. *Fictions of Feminine Desire: Disclosures of Heloise*. Lincoln, Nebr.: University of Nebraska Press, 1982.

Knowles, David. *From Pachomius to Ignatius: A Study in the Constitutional History of the Religious Orders (Sarum Lectures 1964–65)*. Oxford: Clarendon Press, 1966.

———. *The Religious Orders of England*. Cambridge: Cambridge University Press, 1848.

Kraemer, Ross S. "The Conversion of Women to Ascetic Forms of Christianity." *Signs* 6:2 (Winter 1980): 298–307.

Kraft, Kent. "The German Visionary Hildegard of Bingen." In *Medieval Women Writers*, edited by Katharina M. Wilson, pp. 109–30. Athens, Ga: University of Georgia Press, 1984.

Kristeller, Paul Oskar. "The Contribution of Religious Orders to Renaissance Thought and Learning." In *Medieval Aspects of Renaissance Learning*, edited and translated by Edward P. Mahoney, pp. 95–158. Durham: Duke University Press, 1974.

———. "Learned Women of Early Modern Italy: Humanists and University Scholars." In *Beyond Their Sex: Learned Women of the European Past*, edited by Patricia H. LaBalme. pp. 91–116. New York: New York University Press, 1980.

LaBalme, Patricia H., ed. *Beyond Their Sex: Learned Women of the European Past*. New York: New York University Press, 1980.

Larner, John. *Culture and Society in Italy, 1290–1420*. London: Batsford, 1971.

Lauter, W. *Hildegard—Bibliographie*. Alzey: n.p., 1970.

Lazzari, Francesco. *Mistica e ideologia tra XI e XIII secolo*. Milan and Naples: Riccardo Ricciardi Editore, 1972.

Lea, Henry Charles. *History of Sacerdotal Celibacy in the Christian Church*. 3d rev. ed. Hyde Park, N.Y.: University Books, 1966; reprint of *An Historical Sketch of Sacerdotal Celibacy in the Christ Church*, Philadelphia: 1867.

Leclerq, Dom Jean. "Feminine Monasticism in the Twelfth and Thirteenth Centuries." In *The Continuing Quest for God*, edited by William Skudlarek, O.S.B. pp. 114–26. Collegeville, Minn.: The Liturgical Press, 1983.

———. *The Love of Learning and the Desire for God*. Translated by Catherine Misrahi. New York: Fordham University Press, 1960.

———. "Modern Psychology and the Interpretation of Medieval Texts." *Speculum* 48:3 (1973): 476–90.

———. "Le monachisme féminin au Moyen Âge." *Cristianesimo nella Storia* 1:2 (April 1980): 445–58.

———. *Monks and Love in Twelfth Century France*. Oxford: Clarendon Press, 1979.

———. "The Spirituality of Medieval Feminine Monasticism." In *The Continuing Quest for God*, edited by William Skudlarek, O.S.B., pp. 127–38. Collegeville, Minn.: The Liturgical Press, 1982.

Leff, Gordon. *Heresy in the Later Middle Ages: The Relation of Heterodoxy to Dissent, c. 1250–1450*. 2 Vols. Manchester: Manchester University Press, and New York: Barnes & Noble, 1967.

Leff, P. "Autobiographies of the Middle Ages." *Transactions of the Royal Historical Society* 5:3 (1953): 41–52.

Le Goff, Jacques. "Cultura ecclesiastica e tradizioni folkoriche nella civiltà merovingia." In *Agiografia Altomedievale*, edited by Sofia Boesch Gajano, pp. 215–26. Bologna: Il Mulino, 1976.

Lemay, Helen Rodnite. "Some Thirteenth and Fourteenth Century Lectures on Female Sexuality." *International Journal of Women's Studies* 1 (July–August 1978): 391–400.

Lerner, Robert E. *The Heresy of the Free Spirit in the Later Middle Ages*. Berkeley and Los Angeles: University of California Press, 1972.

Lewis, C. S. *The Allegory of Love*. Oxford: Oxford University Press, 1955; reprint of 1938 edition.

Lewis, Ioan M. *Ecstatic Religion*. New York and London: Penguin, 1971.

Liebowitz, Ruth P. "Voices from Convents: Nuns and Repentant Prostitutes in Late Renaissance Italy." Paper presented at the Fourth Berkshire Conference on History of Women, 23 August 1978. Northampton, MA.

Little, Lester. "Intellectual Training and Reform." In *Pierre Abélard—Pierre le Vénérable: Les courants philosophiques, littéraires et artistiques en Occident au milieu du XIIᵉ siècle*, pp. 236–49. Actes et mémoires du colloque international, Abbaye de Cluny, 2 au 9 juillet 1972. Paris: Éditions du Centre national de la recherche scientifique, 1975.

Logan, Oliver. "Patronage and Collecting of Art." In *Culture and Society in Venice, 1470–1790: The Renaissance and Its Heritage*, edited by J. R. Hale, pp. 148–219. New York: Scribner's, 1972.

Lord, Albert B. "Perspectives on Recent Work on Oral Literature." In *Oral Literature: Seven Essays*, edited by Joseph J. Duggan, pp. 1–24. Edinburgh and London: Scottish Academic Press, 1975.

Lucas, Angela M. *Women in the Middle Ages: Religion, Marriage and Letters*. New York: St. Martin's Press, 1983.

Lungo, Isidoro Del. *La donna fiorentina del buon tempo antico*. Florence: R. Bemporad Figlio, 1906.

Lyman, Richard B., Jr. "Barbarism and Religion: Late Roman and early Medieval Childhood." In *The His-*

tory of Childhood, edited by Lloyd de Mause, pp. 75–100. New York: Harper & Row, 1974.

Maccarone, M. "Riforma e sviluppo della vita religiosa con Innocenza III." In *Rivista di storia della chiesa in Italia*, 16, (1962): 60–73.

McCall, Andrew. *The Medieval Underworld*. London: Hamish Hamilton, 1979.

McCurry, Charles. "Religious Careers and Religious Devotion in Thirteenth Century Metz." *Viator* 9 (1978): 325–33.

McDonnell, Ernest W. *The Beguines and Beghards in Medieval Culture*. New York: Octagon Books, 1969; reprint of 1954 edition, New Brunswick, Rutgers University Press.

McLaughlin, Eleanor. "Christ My Mother: Feminine Naming and Metaphor in Medieval Spirituality." *Nashotah Review* 15 (1975): 228–48.

———. "The Heresy of the Free Spirit and Late Medieval Mysticism." *Medievalia et Humanistica* 4 (1973): 37–54.

———. "Women and Medieval Heresy." *Concilium* 111 (1976): 73–90.

———, and Rosemary Reuther, eds. *Women of Spirit: Female Leadership in the Jewish and Christian Traditions*. New York: Simon & Schuster, 1979.

McLaughlin, Mary Martin. "Abélard as Autobiographer: The Motives and Meaning of His *Story of Calamities*." *Speculum* 42:3 (1967): 473–76.

———. "Peter Abélard and the Dignity of Women." In *Pierre Abélard—Pierre le Vénérable: Les courants philosophiques, littéraires et artistiques en occident au milieu du XIIᵉ siècle*, pp. 288–325. Actes et mémoires du colloque international, Éditions du Centre national de la recherche scientifique, 1975.

———. "Survivors and Surrogates." In *History of Childhood*, edited by Lloyd de Mause, pp. 101–81. New York: Psychohistory Press, 1974.

McNamara, Joann. "Sexual Equality and the Cult of Virginity in Early Christian Thought." *Feminist Studies* 3:4 (Spring–Summer 1976): 145–58.

McNamara, Joann, and Suzanne Wemple. "The Power of Women Through the Family in Medieval Europe." In *Clio's Consciousness Raised*, edited by Louise Banner and Mary Hartman, pp. 103–18. New York: Harper & Row, 1974.

———, and "Sanctity and Power: The Dual Pursuit of Medieval Women." In *Becoming Visible: Women in European History*, edited by Renate Bridenthal and Claudia Koonz. Boston: Houghton Mifflin, 1977.

Macrides, Ruth. "Saints and Sainthood in the Early Palaiologan Period." In *The Byzantine Saint*, edited by Sergei Hackel, pp. 67–87. University of Birmingham Fourteenth Spring Symposium of Byzantine Studies, 1980. London: Fellowship of St. Alban and St. Sergius, 1981.

Madaule, Jacques. *The Albigensian Crusade*, trans. Barbara Wall. Bronx, N.Y.: Fordham U.P. 1967; first published as *Le Drame Albigeois et le Destin français*, Paris: Bernard Grasset, 1961.

Magdalino, Paul. "The Byzantine Holy Man in the Twelfth Century." In *The Byzantine Saint*, edited by Sergei Hackel, pp. 51–66. University of Birmingham Fourteenth Spring Symposium of Byzantine Studies, 1980. London: Fellowship of St. Alban and St. Sergius, 1981.

Malvern, Marjorie M. *Venus in Sackcloth: The Magdalen's Origins and Metamorphoses*. Carbondale , Ill.: Southern Illinois University Press, 1975.

Mandel, Barrett J. "Truth and Reality in the *Life* of St. Teresa." *Renascence* 32:3 (Spring 1980): 131–45.

Mann, Henry C. "Margery Kempe." *Pax (Caldey Abbey, Tenby, England)* (1937): 257–60, 276–79.

Maranda, Pierre, and Elli Kongas Maranda, eds. *Structural Analysis of Oral Tradition*. Philadelphia: University of Pennsylvania Press, 1971.

Martines, Lauro. *The Social World of the Florentine Humanists 1390–1460*. Princeton: Princeton University Press, 1963.

———. "A Way of Looking at Women in Renaissance Florence." *Journal of Medieval and Renaissance Studies* 4 (Spring 1974): 15–28.

———, ed. *Violence and Civil Disorder in Italian Cities, 1200–1500*. Berkeley and Los Angeles: University of California Press, 1972.

Malvern, Marjorie M. *Venus in Sackcloth: The Magdalene's Origins and Metamorphoses*. Carbondale, Ill.: Southern Illinois University Press, 1975.

Mason, Mary G. "The Other Voice: Autobiographies of Women Writers." In *Autobiography: Essays Theoretical and Critical*, edited by James Olney, pp. 207–35. Princeton: Princeton University Press, 1980.

Mayr-Harting, H. "Functions of a Twelfth Century Recluse." *History* 60 (1975): 337–52.

Mazlish, Bruce. "Autobiography and Psycho-analysis." *Encounter* 35 (October 1970): 28–37.

Mazzamuto, Pietro. "Aspetti teologici e strutturali dell'epistolario Cateriniano." In *Studi in Onore di Alberto Chiari*, pp. 853–82. Brescia: Paideia Editore, 1972.

Mazzeo, Arturo. *Donne Famose di Romagna*. Bologna: Ponte Nuovo, 1973.

Mecklin, John Moffatt. *The Passing of the Saint: A Study of a Cultural Type*. Chicago: University of Chicago Press, 1941.

Meersseman, Gilles-Gerard. "La Riforma delle confraternite laicali in Italia prima del Concilio di Trento." In *Problemi di vita religiosa in Italia nel cinquecento*, pp. 17–30. Padua: Società Editrice Antenore, 1960.

Meiss, Millard. *Painting in Florence and Siena After the Black Death: The Arts, Religion and Society in the*

Mid-Fourteenth Century. Princeton: Princeton University Press, 1951.

Miller, Robert P. "The Wounded Heart: Courtly Love and the Medieval Anti-feminist Tradition." *Women's Studies* 2 (1974): 335–50.

Misch, George. *A History of Autobiography in Antiquity*. 2 Vols. Translated by E. W. Dickes in collaboration with the author. London: Routledge and Kegan Paul, 1950.

Mollat, Michel. *Les Pauvres dans la société médiévale: Études sur l'histoire de la pauvreté*. Paris: Publications de la Sorbonne, 1974.

———. *Popular Revolutions of the Late Middle Ages*. Translated by A. L. Lytton-Sells. London: Allen and Unwin, 1973.

Monfrin, Jacques. "Le Problème de l'authenticité de la correspondance d'Abélard et d'Héloise." In *Pierre Abélard—Pierre la Vénérable: Les courants philosophiques, littéraires et artistiques en occident au milieu du XII^esiècle*, pp. 409–24. Actes et mémoires du colloque international, Abbaye de Cluny, 2 au 9 juillet 1972. Paris: Éditions du Centre national de la recherche scientifique, 1975.

Monter, E. William. "The Historiography of Witchcraft: Progress and Prospects." *Journal of Interdisciplinary History* 2:4 (Spring 1972): 435–51.

———. "The Pedestal and the Stake: Courtly Love and Witchcraft." In *Becoming Visible: Women in European History*, edited by Renate Bridenthal and Claudia Koonz, pp. 119–36. Boston: Houghton Mifflin, 1977.

Moore, R. I. "Heresy As Disease." In *The Concept of Heresy in the Middle Ages (11th–13th Centuries)*, edited by Dr. W. Lourdaux and Dr. D. Verhelst, The Hague: Leuven University Press, 1976.

Moorman, John. *A History of the Franciscan Order from Its Origins to the Year 1517*. Oxford: Clarendon Press, 1968.

Morewedge, Rosmarie Thee, ed. *The Role of Woman in the Middle Ages*. Albany: SUNY Press, 1975.

Morris, Rosemary. "The Political Saint of the Eleventh Century." In *The Byzantine Saint*, edited by Sergei Hackel, pp. 43–50. University of Birmingham Fourteenth Spring Symposium of Byzantine Studies, 1980. London: Fellowship of St. Alban and St. Sergius, 1981.

Murray, Robert. "The Features of the Earliest Christian Asceticism." In *Christian Spirituality. Essays in Honour of Gordon Rupp.*, edited by Peter Brooks, pp. 63–77. London: S.C.M. Press, 1971.

Neuls-Bates, Carol, ed. *Women in Music, An Anthology of Source Readings from the Middle Ages to the Present*. New York: Harper & Row, 1982.

Newman, Francis X., ed. *The Meaning of Courtly Love*. Albany: SUNY Press, 1972.

Nichols, John A. "Male Supervisors and the English

Cistercian Nunneries." Unpublished paper, History Department, Slippery Rock State Teachers College, Slippery Rock, Pa. 16057.

Nicholson, Joan. "Feminae Gloriosae: Women in the Age of Bede." In *Medieval Women, Dedicated and Presented to Professor Rosalind M. T. Hill*, edited by Derek Baker, pp. 15–29. Published for the Ecclesiastical History Society. Oxford: Basil Blackwell, 1978.

Nolan, Barbara. *The Gothic Visionary Perspective*. Princeton: Princeton University Press, 1977.

Oberman, Heiko A. and Charles Trinkhaus, eds. *The Pursuit of Holiness in Late Medieval and Renaissance Religion. Studies in Medieval and Reformation Thought*. Vol. 10. Leiden: E. J. Brill, 1970.

O'Faolain, Julia, and Lauro Martines, eds. *Not in God's Image: Women in History from the Greeks to the Victorians*. New York: Harper & Row, 1973.

Oldenbourg, Zoé. *Massacre at Montsegur*. New York: Pantheon, 1962.

Olney, James, ed. *Autobiography: Essays Theoretical and Critical*. Princeton: Princeton University Press, 1980.

Ong, Walter. *Orality and Literacy: The Technologizing of the Word*. London and New York: Methuen, 1982.

———. "Orality, Literacy, and Medieval Textualization," *New Literary History*, XIV (Autumn 1984): 1–12.

Origo, Iris (Cutting). "The Domestic Enemy: The Eastern Slavs in Tuscany in the Fourteenth and Fifteenth Centuries." *Speculum* 30:3 (July 1955): 321–66.

———. *The Merchant of Prato*. London: J. Cape, 1957.

———. *Tribune of Rome; a Biography of Cola di Rienzo*. London: The Hogarth Press, 1938.

———. *The World of San Bernardino*. New York: Harcourt, Brace and World, 1962.

Ozment, Stephen. "Mysticism, Nominalism, and Dissent." In *The Pursuit of Holiness in late Medieval and Renaissance Religion*, edited by Heiko Oberman and Charles Trinkhaus, pp. 67–92. Leiden: E. J. Brill, 1970.

Pagels, Elaine. "What Became of God the Mother? Conflicting Images of God in Early Christianity." *Signs* 11 (Winter 1976): 293–303.

———. *The Gnostic Gospels*. New York: Random House, 1979.

Palladius. *Lausiac History*. Translated by Ernest A. Wallis Budge. London: Chatto and Windus, 1907.

Papi, Adriana Benvenuti. "Sante Patrone nel territorio Valdelsano e nel medio Valdarno: considerazioni attorno al caso di Santa Verdiana di Castel-Fiorentino." In *Atti del Convegno di San Vivaldo, 29 Septembre 1979*.

———. "Umiliana dei Cerchi—nascita di un culto nella Firenze del dugento." *Studi Francescani: Revista Nazionale Italiana* 77:1–2 (1980): 110–12.

Paschini, Pio. "I Monasteri femminili in Italia nel

cinquecento." In *Problemi di vita religiosa in Italia nel cinquecento*, pp. 31–60. Padua: Società Editrice Antenore, 1960.

―――. *Tre ricerche sulla storia della chiesa nel cinquecento*. Roma: Edizioni Liturgiche, 1945.

Patlagean, Evelyne. "Agiografia bizantina e storia sociale." In *Agiografia Altomediovale*, edited by Sofia Boesch Gajano, pp. 191–213. Bologna: Il Mulino, 1976.

Péano, Pierre. "Les Béguines du Languedoc ou la Crise du T.O.F. dans la France Méridionale (XIII–XIVᵉ siècles)." In *I Frati Penitenti di S. Francesco nella società del 2 e 300*, edited by Mariano D'Alatri, pp. 139–58. Rome: Istituto Storico dei Cappuccini, 1977.

Pereira, M. "Maternità e sessualità femminile in Ildegarda di Bingen." *Quaderni Storici* 44 (1980): 564–79.

Perera, Sylvia Brinton. *Descent to the Goddess: A Way of Initiation for Women*. Toronto, Canada: Inner City Books, 1981.

Petroff, Elizabeth. *The Consolation of the Blessed: Women Saints in Medieval Tuscany*. New York: Alta Gaia, 1980.

―――. "Discovering Biography in Hagiography: Lives of Women Saints," in *Lady-Unique-Inclination-of-the-Night*, Cycle 2 (Autumn 1977) pp. 34–45.

―――. "Landscape in Pearl: The Transformation of Nature." *Chaucer Review* 16: 2 (Fall 1981): 181–93.

―――. "The Paradox of Sanctity: Lives of Italian Women Saints 1200–1400." *Occasional Papers of the International Society for the Comparative Study of Civilization* I 1 (Fall. 1977): 4–24.

―――. "Transforming the World: The Serpent Dragon and the Virgin Saint." *Arché, Notes and Papers on Archaic Studies* 6 (1981): 53–70.

Phillips, Dayton. *The Beguines in Medieval Strasburg*. Ann Arbor, Mich.: University of Michigan Press, 1941.

Pierre Abélard―Pierre le Vénérable: Les courants philosophiques, littéraires et artistiques en occident au milieu du XIIᵉ siècle. Actes et mémoires du colloque international, Abbaye de Cluny, 2 au 9 juillet 1972. Paris: Éditions du centre national de la recherche scientifique, 1975.

Plaskow, Judith, and Joan Arnold Romero, eds. *Women and Religion*. Missoula, Mont.: American Academy of Religion and the Scholars' Press, 1974.

Plummer, J. F., ed. *Vox Feminae: Studies in Medieval Women's Songs*. Studies in Medieval Culture 15. Kalamazoo, Mich.: Medieval Institute Publications, 1981.

Policelli, Eugene F. "Medieval Women: A Preacher's Point of View." *International Journal of Women's Studies* 1:4 (1978): 281–96.

Power, Eileen. *Medieval English Nunneries 1275–1535*. Cambridge: Cambridge University Press, 1922.

―――. *Medieval Women*, edited by M. M. Postan. Cambridge: Cambridge University Press, 1975.

Pratt, Annis (with Barbara White, Andrea Loewenstein, and Mary Wyer). *Archetypal Patterns in Women's Fiction*. Bloomington: Indiana University Press, 1981.

Pruyser, Paul W. "Psychoanalytic Method in the Study of Religious Meanings." *Psychohistory Review* 6 (1978): 45–52.

Pullan, Brian. *A History of Early Renaissance Italy*. London: Allen Lane and Penguin, 1973.

―――. *Rich and Poor in Renaissance Venice: The Social Institutions of a Catholic State, to 1620*. Cambridge Mass.: Harvard University Press, 1971.

Putnam, Emily James. *The Lady: Studies of Certain Significant Phases of Her History*. Chicago: University of Chicago Press, 1969; reprint of 1910 edition.

Radcliff-Umstead, Douglas. ed. *Innovation in Medieval Literature*. Pittsburgh: Medieval Studies Committee of the University of Pittsburgh, 1971.

―――, gen. ed. *University of Pittsburgh Publications on the Middle Ages and the Renaissance*. Vol. 4 of *University of Pittsburgh Publications on the Middle Ages and the Renaissance*. Pittsburgh: Center for Medieval and Renaissance Studies, 1978.

―――, gen. ed. *The Roles and Images of Women in the Middle Ages and Renaissance*. Vol. 3 of *University of Pittsburgh Publications on the Middle Ages and the Renaissance*. Pittsburgh: Center for Medieval and Renaissance Studies, 1978.

Rader, Rosemary. "Christian Pre-Monastic Forms of Asceticism: Syneisaktism, or 'Spiritual Marriage.'" In *The Continuing Quest for God*, edited by William Skudlarek, pp. 80–87. Collegeville, Minn.: The Liturgical Press, 1982.

―――. "Early Christian Forms of Communal Spirituality: Women's Communities." *Signs* 7:4 (1982): 752+.

Reeves, Marjorie. *The Influence of Prophecy in the Later Middle Ages: A Study in Joachimism*. Oxford: Clarendon Press, 1969.

Reuther, Rosemary, ed. *Religion and Sexism: Images of Women in the Jewish and Christian Traditions*. New York: Simon & Schuster, 1974.

―――, and Eleanor McLaughlin. *Women of Spirit: Female Leadership in the Jewish and Christian Traditions*. New York: Simon & Schuster, 1979.

Riché, Pierre. *Instruction et vie religieuse dans le haut moyen âge*. Collected Studies 139. London: Variorum Reprints, 1981.

Rodini, Robert J. "The Festa and Theater." *Forum Italicum* 14:3 (1980): 476–84.

Rogers, Katharine M. *The Troublesome Helpmate: A History of Misogyny in Literature*. Seattle and London: University of Washington Press, 1966.

Roisin, Simone. "L'efflorescence cisterçienne et le courant féminin de piété au XIIIe siècle." *Revue d'histoire écclesiastique* 39:3-4 (1943): 342-78.

———. *L'hagiographie cistercienne dans le diocèse de Liège au XIIIe siècle*. Louvain: Bibliotheque de l'Université, 1947.

Rolt-Wheeler, Ethel. *Women of the Cell and Cloister*. London: Methuen and Company, 1913.

Romanello, Marina. *La Stregoneria in Europe*. Bologna: Il Mulino, 1978.

Rosenthal, Joel. *Purchase of Paradise*. Toronto: University of Toronto Press, 1972.

Roy, Bruno, ed. *L'Érotisme au moyen age: études présentées au troisième colloque de l'Institut d'études médiévales*. Montreal: Aurore, 1977.

Ruh, Kurt. "Beginenmystik: Hadwijch, Mechtild von Magdeburg, Marguerite Porete." *Zeitschrift für deutsches Altertum und deutsche Literatur* 106 (1977): 265-77.

Rusconi, R. "Espansione del franscescanesimo femminile nel secolo XIII." In *Movimento religioso femminile e francescanesimo nel secolo XIII*. Atti del VII Convengo Internazionale di Studi Francescani. Assisi: Studi Francescani, 1979.

Russell, Jeffrey Burton. *Witchcraft in the Middle Ages*, Secaucus, N.J.: Citadel, 1972.

———, ed. *Religious Dissent in the Middle Ages*. New York and London: Wiley, 1971.

Ryden, Lennart. "The Holy Fool." In *The Byzantine Saint*, edited by Sergei Hackel, pp. 106-13. University of Birmingham Fourteenth Spring Symposium of Byzantine Studies, 1980. London: Fellowship of St. Alban and St. Sergius, 1981.

Sawyer, Michael E., comp. *A Bibliographical Index of Five English Mystics*. Pittsburgh: Clifford E. Barbour Library, Pittsburgh Theological Seminary, 1976.

Saxer, Victor; *Le Culte de Marie Madeleine en occident, des origines à la fin du moyen âge*. 2 Vols. Paris: Clasvreuil 1959.

Schulberg, Jane Tibbets. "Sexism and the Celestial Gynaceum from 500-1200." *Journal of Medieval History* 4 (March 1978): 117-33.

Schutte, Anne Jacobsen. "Printing, Piety, and the People in Italy: the first 30 years." *Archiv für Reformationsgeschichte* 71 (1980): 5-20.

Secouet, J. P., O.C.D. "The Spanish Woman in the Sixteenth Century." *Contemplative Review* 10 (1975).

Serrano y Sanz, Manuel. *Apuntes para una biblioteca de escritoras españolas* II. Madrid: Establecimiento tipolitografico sucesores de Rivadeneyra, Madrid 1903. Reprinted Madrid: Atlas, 1975.

Shahar, Shulamith. *The Fourth Estate. A History of Women in the Middle Ages*. London & N.Y.: Methuen, 1983 (Trans of *Die Frau im Mittelalter*, Chaya Galai).

Shapiro, Marianne. "The Provençal *Trobairitz* and the Limits of Courtly Love." *Signs* 3 (1977-78): 560-71.

Showalter, Elaine. *A Literature of Their Own: British Women Novelists from Bronte to Lessing*. Princeton: Princeton University Press, 1977.

Sims-Williams, Patrick. "Cuthswith, Seventh Century Abbess in Inkberros." *Anglo-Saxon England* 5 (1976): 1-21.

Skudlarek, William, ed. *The Continuing Quest for God*. Collegeville, Minn.: The Liturgical Press, 1982.

Smith, Jacqueline. "Robert of Arbrissel: Procurator Mulierum." In *Medieval Women, Dedicated and Presented to Professor Rosalind M. T. Hill*, edited by Derek Baker, pp. 175-84. Published for the Ecclesiastical History Society. Oxford: Basil Blackwell, 1978.

Southern, Richard William. *The Making of the Middle Ages*. New Haven and London: Yale University Press, 1953.

———. *Western Society and the Church in the Middle Ages*. Baltimore, Md.: Penguin, 1970.

Spacks, Patricia Meyer. "Reflecting Women." *Yale Review* 63 (1973): 26-42.

———. "Stages of Self: Notes on Autobiography and the Life Cycle." *Boston University Journal* 25:2 (1977): 7-17.

———. "Women's Stories, Women's Selves." *Hudson Review* 30:1 (Spring 1977): 29-46.

Spengemann, William C. *The Forms of Autobiography: Episodes in the History of a Liberary Genre*. New Haven and London: Yale University Press, 1980.

Spitzer, Leo. "The Epic Style of the Pilgrim Aetheria." In *Romanische Literaturstudien 1936-56*, pp. 871-912. Tubingen: 1959.

———. "Mozarabic Lyric and Theodor Frings' Theories." *Comparative Literature* 4 (1952): 1-22.

Stevens, Martin. "The Performing Self in Twelfth Century Culture." *Viator* 9 (1978): 193-212.

Sticca, Sandro. "The Festa and Theater." *Forum Italicum* 14:3 (Winter 1980): 476-84.

———. "Sin and Salvation: The Dramatic Context of Hrotswitha's Women." In *The Roles and Images of Women in the Middle Ages and Renaissance*, edited by Douglas Radcliff-Umstead, pp. 3-22. Vol. 3 of *University of Pittsburgh Publications on the Middle Ages and the Renaissance*. Pittsburgh: Center for Medieval and Renaissance Studies, 1978.

Stiller, Nikki. "Eve's Orphans: Mothers and Daughters in Medieval English Literature." In *The Lost Tradition: Mothers and Daughters in Literature*, edited by Esther M. Broner and Cathy Davidson, pp. 22-32. New York: Frederick Ungar, 1980.

Stock, Brian. "Medieval Literacy, Linguistic Theory, and Social Organization," *New Literacy History* XVI (Autumn 1984) 13-30.

Stone, Robert Karl. *Middle English Prose Style: Margery Kempe and Julian of Norwich.* The Hague: Monton, 1970.

Stuard, Susan Mosher. "Dame Trot." *Signs* 1 (Winter 1975): 537–42.

Tavard, George T. *Woman in Christian Tradition.* Notre Dame and London: University of Notre Dame Press, 1973.

Taylor, Dennis. "Some Strategies of Religious Autobiography." *Renascence* 27:1 (Autumn 1974): 40–44.

Taylor, Henry Osborn. "Mystic Visions of Ascetic Women." In *The Medieval Mind.* 4th rev. ed. 2 Vols. Vol. 1, pp. 458–86. New York: Macmillan, 1925.

Thompson, James W. *The Literacy of the Laity in the Middle Ages.* Berkeley: University of California Press, 1939.

Thurston, Herbert. *Surprising Mystics.* Chicago: Henry Regnery, 1955.

Tillyard, Henry Julius Wetenhall, trans. *Plays of Roswitha.* London: The Faith Press, Ltd., 1923.

Tocco, Felice. "Guglielma Boema e i Guglielmiti." In *Reale accadem. Aei lincei, memorie della classe di scienze morali, storiche : filologiche atti, 5 Series 8.* pp. 25 ff. Rome 1902.

Trexler, Richard. "Le Célibat à la fin du Moyen Age: Les Religieuses de Florence." *Annales* 27 (November–December 1972): 1329–1350.

———. "Florentine Religious Experience: The Sacred Image." In *The Pursuit of Holiness*, edited by Heiko Oberman and Charles Trinkhaus, pp. 7–41. Leiden: E. J. Brill, 1970.

———. "Florentine Theater." *Forum Italicum* 14:3 (Winter 1980): 454–75.

———. "The Foundlings of Florence, 1395–1455." *History of Childhood Quarterly* 1 (Fall 1973): 259–84.

———. "Infanticide in Florence: New Sources and First Results." *History of Childhood Quarterly* 1:1 (Summer 1973) 98–116.

———. "In Search of Father: The Experience of Abandonment in the Recollections of Giovanni di Pagolo Morelli." *History of Childhood Quarterly* 3:2 (Fall 1975): 225–52.

———. "Ritual Behavior in Renaissance Florence." *Medievalia et Humanistica* 4 (1973): 125–44.

———. "Ritual in Florence: Adolescence and Salvation in the Renaissance." In *The Pursuit of Holiness*, edited by Heiko A. Oberman and Charles Trinkhaus, pp. 200–64. Leiden: E. J. Brill, 1974.

Underhill, Evelyn. *Mysticism.* New York: Dutton, 1961.

Vance, Eugene. "Augustine's *Confessions* and the Grammar of Selfhood." *Genre* (March 1973): 1–28.

Vauchez, André. "L'Ideale di santità nel movimento femminile francescano." In *Movimento religioso femminile e francescanesimo nel secolo XIII.* Assisi: Atti del VII Convegno Internazionale di Studi Francescani, 1979.

———. *Religion et societé dans l'occident médiéval.* Turin: Bottega d'Erasmo, 1980.

Veilleux, Armand, O.C.S.O. "The Origins of Egyptian Monasticism." In *The Continuing Quest for God*, edited by William Skudlarek, pp. 44–50. Collegeville, Minn.: The Liturgical Press, 1982.

———. "Pachomian Community." In *The Continuing Quest for God*, edited by William Skudlarek, pp. 51–60. Collegeville, Minn.: The Liturgical Press, 1982.

Vitz, Evelyn Birge. "The 'I' of the *Roman de La Rose*." *Genre* (March 1973): 49–75.

———. "Type et individu dans l'autobiographie médiévale," Translated by Phillippe Lejeune. *Póetique* 24 (1975): 426–45.

Volpe, Gioacchino. *Movimenti religiosi e sette ereticali* Florence: Sansoni, 1977.

von Franz, Marie-Louise. *The Passion of Perpetua.* Irving, Tex.: Spring Publications, 1980.

von Moos, Peter. "Le silence d'Héloise et les idéologies modernes." In *Pierre Abélard—Pierre le Vénérable: Les courants philosophiques, littéraires et artistiques en occident au milieu du XIIe siècle*, pp. 425–68. Actes et mémoires du colloque international, Abbaye de Cluny, 2 au 9 juillet 1972. Paris: Éditions du centre national de la recherche scientifique, 1975.

Vuarnet, Jean-Noel. *Extases féminines.* Paris: Les Éditions Arthaud, 1980.

Wakefield, Walter L. *Heresy, Crusade and Inquisition in Southern France.* London: G. Allen & Unwin, 1974.

Wakefield, Walter Legget, and Austin P. Evans, eds. and trans. *Heresies of the High Middle Ages.* New York: Columbia University Press, 1969.

Walsh, James, ed. *Pre-Reformation English Spirituality.* London: Burns and Oates, 1965.

Warner, Marina. *Alone of All Her Sex: The Myth and the Cult of the Virgin Mary.* New York: Knopf, 1976.

———. *Joan of Arc: The Image of Female Heroism.* New York: Knopf, 1981.

Watkins, E. I. "In Defense of Margery Kempe." *Downside Review* 69 (1941): 243–63.

Weinberger, Stephen. "Peasant Households in Provence, ca. 800–1100." *Speculum* 48:4 (1973): 247–57.

Weintraub, Karl J. "Autobiography and Historical Consciousness." *Critical Inquiry* 1:4 (1975): 821–48.

Wemple, Suzanne. *Women in the Frankish Kingdom.* Philadelphia: University of Pennsylvania Press, 1980.

Wessley, Stephen E. "The 13th Century Guglielmites: Salvation Through Women." In *Medieval Women, Dedicated and Presented to Professor Rosalind M. T. Hill*, edited by Derek Baker, pp. 289–305. Oxford: Basil Blackwell, 1978.

Willard, Charity Cannon, *Christine de Pizan: Her Life and Works*. New York: Persea Press, 1985.

Williams, Ann, ed. *Prophecy and Millenarianism. Essays in Honour of Marjorie Reeves*. London: Longman, 1980.

Williams-Krapp, Werner. "German and Dutch Legendaries of the Middle Ages: A Survey." In *Hagiography and Medieval Literature*, pp. 66–75. Odense: Odense University Press, 1981.

Wilson, Katharina, ed. *Medieval Women Writers*. Athens GA: University of Georgia Press, 1984.

Wilson, R. M. "The Contents of the Medieval Library." In *The English Library Before 1700*, edited by Francis Wormald and C. E. Wright, pp. 85–111. London: University of London Athlone Press, 1958.

———. "Three Middle English Mystics." In *Essays and Studies*, pp. 87–112. London: John Murray, 1956.

Wilson-Kastner, Patricia. "Macrina: Virgin and Teacher." *Andrews University Seminary Studies* 1 (Spring 1979): 105–17.

Winkler, Gabriele. "The Origins and Idiosyncrasies of the Earliest Form of Asceticism." In *The Continuing Quest for God*, edited by William Skudlarek, pp. 9–43. Collegeville, Minn.: The Liturgical Press, 1982.

Women and Literature: An Annotated Bibliography. Cambridge, Mass.: Women and Literature Collective, 1976.

Workman, Herbert B. *The Evolution of the Monastic Ideal*. Boston: Beacon Press, 1962. 1st pub. 1913.

Yarbrough, Anne. "Christianization in the Fourth Century: The Example of Roman Women." *Church History* 45 (June 1976): 149–65.

Zanni, L. "Gli Umiliati nei loro rapporto con l'eresia, l'industria della lana ed i communi nei secolo XII^c." In *Biblioteca historica Italia* Serie II, 2. Milan: 1911.

Zimmerman, T. Price. "Confession and Autobiography in the Early Renaissance." In *Renaissance: Studies in Honor of Hans Baron*, edited by Anthony Molho and John Tedeschi. De Kalb: North Illinois University Press, 1971.

Zumthor, Paul. "Autobiography in the Middle Ages?" *Genre* 6 (1973): 29–48.

———. "The Text and the Voice," *New Literary History* XVI (Autumn 1984) 67–92.

Index

Abbess, 50, 84, 235

Abelard, Peter (Pierre), 21, 177. *See also* autobiography

Abraham (play by Hrotsvit of Gandersheim), 348

absolution: not given by women, 21; in *Mary of Nijmeghen*, 348

Adam (in Julian of Norwich, *Showings*), 32

Agatha, disciple of St. Leoba, 85

Agatha, Saint, 60

aggression, 18; in women mystics, 18

Agnes, Saint, 60

Agnes of Assisi, Saint, 233, 235, 241 *n;* text, 245–46

Albi, 278

Albigensian(s), 172; Crusade, 55 *n,* 173

Aldobrandesca of Siena, Blessed, 17–18, 19

alienation, 35. *See also* isolation and alienation

Alisette Boneta, 277

allegorical exegesis, 141

allegory (in Julian of Norwich, *Showings*), 31, 300

amatory dialogue, 26

amour courtois, 174, 281

anchoress (female recluse or hermit), 301

Angela of Foligno, Blessed, 231ff; bibliography, 241 *n;* devotional meditations, 10, 11; dialogue, 26; ecstasy, 41; erotic visions, 13, 259–63; and Marguerite Porete, 281; path of penitence, 254ff; poverty, 255, 256, 257; text (*Liber de vere fidelium experientia*), 254–63; weeping, 259

Anna Bijns (attributed), 349; text (*Mary of Nijmeghen*), 355–71

Annunciation to Virgin Mary, Feast of, in Christina of Markyate, 137, 149

Anselm, Saint, 25

anti-feminism, 52

Antwerp, 348

apology, 42

apocalyptic theology, 276

apostolic fervor, 51

apostolic poverty, 231. *See also* poverty

Arabs, 90. *See also* Saracens

arena, death in, 61, 65. *See also* martyrdom

aristocracy, 5

Arnaldo, Fra (scribe and confessor of Angela of Foligno), 39–40, 237, 260

art, 8; as source of doctrine, 8

artist, woman visionary as, 6

Ascension of Christ, location of (in *Hodoeporicon*), 99

ascetic(s), 33, 60, 87, 240

ascetic self-sacrifice, 174

asceticism, 36, 44, 235, 239; advice on, 240. See also *Christina Mirabilis, Life of; Marie d'Oignies, Life of; St. Macrina, Life of*

Assisi, 232, 233

Assumption of Virgin Mary, Feast of, 19; in Elisabeth of Schönau, 19, 169–70; in *Hodoeporicon*, 99

audience: for devotional literature, 4; for Marguerite d'Oingt, 278. *See also* language; *specific women writers*

Auerbach, Erich, 46, 59 *n*

Augustine, Saint, 21, 24, 198

austerities, 37

authority (of writer), 4, 5; associated with celibacy, 32; of St. Macrina, 67; priest-like, 141; questioned (Hadewijch), 177; secular, 45; spiritual, 8; spiritual authority of women, 20

autobiography, 44ff; in fourteenth century, 299–301; medieval, 21; in writers: Angela of Foligno, 237; Christina of Markyate, 137; Christine de Pizan, 335–39; Gertrude the Great, 209; Margery Kempe, 21, 301; Mechthild of Magdeburg, 23–26

baby, 45

baptism, 62; of St. Thecla, 65